Will Eisner's
New York

The Will Eisner Library

Coming Soon from W. W. Norton & Company

Hardcover Compilations

The Contract With God *Trilogy*
Brush Strokes: My Life in Pictures

Paperbacks

A Contract With God
A Life Force
New York: The Big City
City People Notebook
Will Eisner Reader
The Dreamer
Invisible People
To the Heart of the Storm
Dropsie Avenue
Life on Another Planet
Family Matter
Minor Miracles
Name of the Game
The Building
The Plot: The Secret Story of the Protocols of the Elders of Zion

Other Books by Will Eisner

Fagin the Jew
Last Day in Vietnam
Eisner/Miller
The Spirit Archives
Eisner Sketchbook
Will Eisner's Shoptalk
Hawks of the Seas

Will Eisner's New York

Life in the Big City

Will Eisner

W. W. Norton & Company

New York • London

For information about permission to reproduce selections from this book,
write to Permissions, W. W. Norton & Company, Inc.,
500 Fifth Avenue, New York, NY 10110

Manufacturing by R. R. Donnelley, Willard Division
Production manager: Julia Druskin

Library of Congress Cataloging-in-Publication Data

Eisner, Will.
[Selections. 2006]
Will Eisner's New York : life in the big city / Will Eisner ;
introduction by Neil Gaiman.
p. cm. – (The Will Eisner library)
Four graphic novels, originally published 1987-2000 by
various publishers.
Contents: New York : the big city — The building — City people
notebook —Invisible people.
ISBN 13: 978-0-393-06106-2
ISBN 10: 0-393-06106-X
1. Graphic novels. I. Title. II. Title: New York, life in the big city.

PN6727.E4A6 2006
741.5—dc22

2006046674

W. W. Norton & Company, Inc.
500 Fifth Avenue, New York, N.Y. 10110
www.wwnorton.com

W. W. Norton & Company Ltd.
Castle House, 75/76 Wells Street, London W1T 3QT

1 2 3 4 5 6 7 8 9 0

Contents

Will Eisner's New York:
An Introduction

It is probably worth bearing in mind that when, almost two decades ago, the publisher of a magazine of comics criticism attempted to find someone to write a "hatchet-job" on a book by Will Eisner, nobody would step up to the plate (and this in an industry in which a quiet afternoon tea can resemble the night of the long knives) and the publisher was forced to write the article himself. I read it, but now find it hard to remember the substance of the attack, other than, I think, an accusation of sentimentality. So, rereading the four original graphic novels that make up this book, I was certainly prepared for sentiment, and was surprised at how brutal so many of the tales are—as brutal, as uncaring, as a city. Two garment workers and a baby die in a fire; a hydrant that is an immigrant's only source of water is sealed off; an old woman is robbed in front of witnesses who do nothing but jeer; a man's life is destroyed by a newspaper typo. There is sentiment in here, true, for sentiment is part of being human, and it would be a foolish observer of humanity who would leave it out (certainly Dickens did not), and Will Eisner was indeed a remarkable observer, but there is little sentimentality.

Eisner himself is visible in the stories of the *City People Notebook*, drawing, observing, moving through the city. You learn little about the man, his face hidden, so I shall pull a few scraps from my own mental notebook, by way of introduction.

I knew Will when he was well past the age at which most people have retired, yet there was nothing old about him: not about the way he moved (purposefully, easily), the way he thought, the way he smiled, or the way he treated others. One was only reminded that Will had been in comics since Genesis when discussing some new wrinkle with him, some idea that could change the way the world of comics would operate forevermore. "When we tried that in 1942 . . ." he'd say, and tell us whether or not it had worked back then, and why it had fallen out of use.

The working life of Will Eisner could be a three-act play. In the first act, as chronicled by Will's semiautobiographical roman à clef *The Dreamer*, he was a man who believed in comics as a medium, a man who wrote and drew excellent comics—particularly *The Spirit*, perhaps the finest and most consistently ambitious creation of its kind—a man who created business models in which he kept the ownership of his work and his creations. In the second act Will Eisner left comics at a time when the future for comics looked bleak: *The Spirit* newspaper supplement was in the decline, and comics for adults were seen as an impossibility. But Will brought his knowledge of comics to the U.S. Army and created *PS Magazine*, a maintenance magazine chiefly of educational comics for adults that he drew for the first twenty years of its existence. And the third act consisted of an entire career, begun at an age when most people are planning their retirement with the short stories that made up *A Contract With God*. Eisner's was a remarkable body of work, produced over a period of more than sixty years, clear-eyed and consistent.

Will Eisner was amiable, gentle, friendly, approachable, encouraging, yet with steel beneath. He had a practicality, an awareness of human frailty and fallibility, an enormous generosity of spirit. In the work of his third act, Eisner demonstrated himself to be an American storyteller, like Ray Bradbury, like O. Henry, unashamedly populist while creating stories for a populace who were not there to read them, not yet.

It would be easy and dishonest to view the stories in this book as valentines to the Big City, to New York. And yet, if they are, these are peculiar valentines—a concatenation of unconsummated desires, unmet loves, fates avoided and unavoidable, people damaged and bruised, hopefully or hopelessly on their way to the grave, with or without each other.

• • •

New York: The Big City is a series of vignettes, some silent, some not; some are stories and some merely moments. While Eisner was producing most of the drawings in this book, he was teaching at the School of Visual Arts in New York, and there is a teacher's eye in the way many of these stories and especially the short-shorts are told. Eisner's mastery of silent storytelling is apparent. Dialogue, when he uses it, tends to be drawn with a broad brush, a cartoon of speech with never a word wasted, but his ear for the rhythms of the ways New Yorkers talk is remarkable. On occasion, rereading these, I am reminded that Jules Feiffer was Eisner's assistant, over half a century ago: "Go to work, Charlie," repeats the wife in "Trash," who has thrown out Charlie's cap and with it all his hopes and dreams and youth. Charlie says, "I don't feel so good! I'm tired, my feet hurt . . . Maybe I shouldn't carry so many samples! That bag gets heavier every day." And he carries the heavy bag past the garbage men who are disposing of his past.

All his life, Eisner was, as I have remarked, an observer of people. The tales and fragments in *City People Notebook* are, as the title suggests, observations, notebook pages, and stories built up from notebook pages, ranging from sketches all the way to complete short stories, stories about Space and Time, neither of which are quite the same in a city.

The Building is a ghost story, although the four ghosts in it are, we learn, as much ghosts while they are alive as when they are dead. Mensh, who could not save children; Gilda Greene, who did not marry a poet; Tonatti, the street violinist who died as the building died; and Hammond the developer, a driven man. *The Building* has an optimistic ending, though, which contrasts painfully with the last three short stories, *Invisible People*. The protagonists of "Sanctum," "Mortal Combat," and "The Power" could be characters from *The Spirit*, forty years earlier, but the fundamental hospitality and (occasionally ironic) justice of the world of *The Spirit* has been replaced by a place as bleak and unwelcoming as any in Kafka. There is no justice here: there is no place for you in the world, magic will not help you, nor will love. The last three stories are cold things, as unsentimental as three stories can be.

• • •

Will died a year ago today, and I still miss him. He was modest and wise and, above all, *interested*.

"What keeps you working?" I asked him in 2001 at the Chicago Humanities Festival, where he and I and Art Spiegelman and Scott McCloud were guests—something that would have been unthinkable in the 1930s, when Will began to draw comics. I wanted to know why he kept going, why he kept making comics when his contemporaries (people like Bob Kane—*before* he did Batman) had long ago retired and stopped making art and telling stories.

He told me about a film he had seen, in which a jazz musician kept playing because he was still in search of the Note. That it was out there somewhere, and he kept going to reach it. And that was why Will kept going: in the hopes that he'd one day do something that satisfied him. He was still looking for the Note. . . .

Neil Gaiman
January 2006

Editor's Note

Will Eisner's New York is comprised of four distinct graphic novels that the author created between 1981 and 1992. The stories in W. W. Norton's earlier Eisner volume, *The* Contract With God *Trilogy*, all took place in the mythical Dropsie Avenue neighborhood of The Bronx. Most of the denizens of this volume stray from that particular block, but not far, into the borough of Manhattan.

It's not at all surprising that Will Eisner, a quintessential New Yorker, nearly always set his graphic novels in America's largest metropolis. Born in Brooklyn in 1917, the young Eisner hawked newspapers on Wall Street during the early years of the Great Depression to help his immigrant Jewish family. He attended DeWitt Clinton High School while it was still in Manhattan, and took classes at the Art Students League. In 1936, while still a teenager, he started his first business, Eisner & Iger Studio, a "packager" of editorial material for other publishers at the virtual birth of the comic book industry. He and his partner worked in a tiny ten-foot square "office" in a building at 43rd and Madison.

In 1940 Eisner began writing and drawing his classic *Spirit* weekly newspaper insert, with assistants, out of a three-room studio at 5 Tudor City. (His seminal character's adventures took place in "Central" City, but everyone knew it was New York City.) Following his service in World War II Eisner rented space at 37 Wall Street, ironically the same building he had staked territory in front of as a newsboy. When I first visited Will in 1971, his American Visuals Corporation office was at 461 Park Avenue South. By 1983 he succumbed to his wife Ann's urging that they leave their Westchester

County residence for the year-round sunshine of Florida, but even then Eisner for several more years commuted by air weekly to New York to teach at the School of Visual Arts and to conduct side business. He and Ann continued to return to New York City at least twice annually till the end of his life.

• • •

The Building and *Invisible People*, the two more conventional graphic novels in this work, are fictional stories with certain roots in reality. The haunted structure in *The Building* was clearly modeled after New York's landmark Flatiron Building, and Eisner's three accounts of people achieving "invisible" status were inspired by the real life story of Carolyn Lamboly. A *New York Times* report of her 1990 suicide and the governmental lapses leading to her despair sparked the creation of *Invisible People*. There are also subtle connections to the "reality" established in Eisner's earliest graphic novel. In the "Sanctum" chapter of *Invisible People*, the ill-fated protagonist, Pincus Pleatnik, lives in an apartment at 55 Dropsie Avenue, the very same building that Eisner used as the centerpiece of three other graphic novels (collected as *The* Contract With God *Trilogy: Life on Dropsie Avenue*). Interconnecting further, two also ill-fated characters from *A Contract With God*—the surly Superintendent and his guard dog, along with the Super's porn-lined basement apartment—make cameo appearances as Pincus desperately tries to hold his life together. Mr. Scruggs also makes a fateful cameo in "Mortal Combat."

The other components of this volume, *New York: The Big City* and *City People Notebook* are not graphic novels *per se*, or even graphic short stories. Rather they consist primarily of brief, incisive vignettes based on Eisner's observations from real life or small fictions he built around the ordinary stage settings—hydrants, stoops, sewer grates—of city streets. The elements that add up to *New York: The Big City* were originally serialized from 1981 to 1983 in *The Spirit Magazine* (Kitchen Sink Press). *City People Notebook*, which followed, was initially based on what Eisner called "out-takes" from "an accumulation of sketches, notes and 'thumbnail' outlines intended for graphic novels [and] part of the research [he] did for *Big City*." Superficially the vignettes in these two books are similar in nature. But there are distinctions, including differing drawing techniques. In the earlier work he drew with ink and "wash" (diluted India ink), resulting in softer line work and varying shades of gray. Titles were added with mechanical lettering. In the follow-up book he still drew in pen and brush but added the gray tones separately via overlays, resulting in sharper black line art and uniform gray tones, and the titles are hand lettered. Another nice touch distinguishes the newer material: Eisner inserts himself as a recurring character in *City People Notebook*, opening and ending sections with sketchpad in hand, accompanied by a short street person for comical effect.

The term out-take is normally associated with movies (scenes snipped from the final edit). It is not typically used in the comics industry. Occasionally a film director will include selected out-takes (usually comical) during end credits. Since Eisner himself uses the term in the context of his creation of *City People Notebook*, it seemed fitting to include out-takes at the end of this book. Three previously unpublished pages show examples of work that Eisner excised or replaced for varying reasons from three of the books forming this collection. They provide the reader with a rare glimpse of what lands on the cutting-room floor of a master cartoonist.

Denis Kitchen
Amherst, Massachusetts
January 2006

List of New Illustrations

The following seven new illustrations were penciled by Will Eisner prior to his death in January 2005 and inked by Peter Poplaski:

Out-Takes:

Will Eisner's
New York

Introduction to
New York: The Big City

I have, here, undertaken a series of vignettes built around nine elements which, taken together, are my portrayal of a big city . . . any city.

Seen from afar, major cities are an accumulation of big buildings, big population and big acreage. For me it is not "real." The big city as it is seen by its inhabitants is the real thing. The true picture is in the crevices on its floors and around the smaller pieces of its architecture, where daily life swirls.

Portraiture is a very personal thing, so in the end this effort reflects my own perspective. Because I grew up in New York City, its internal architecture and street objects are inescapably reflected. But I also know many other big cities, and what I show is meant to be common to them all.

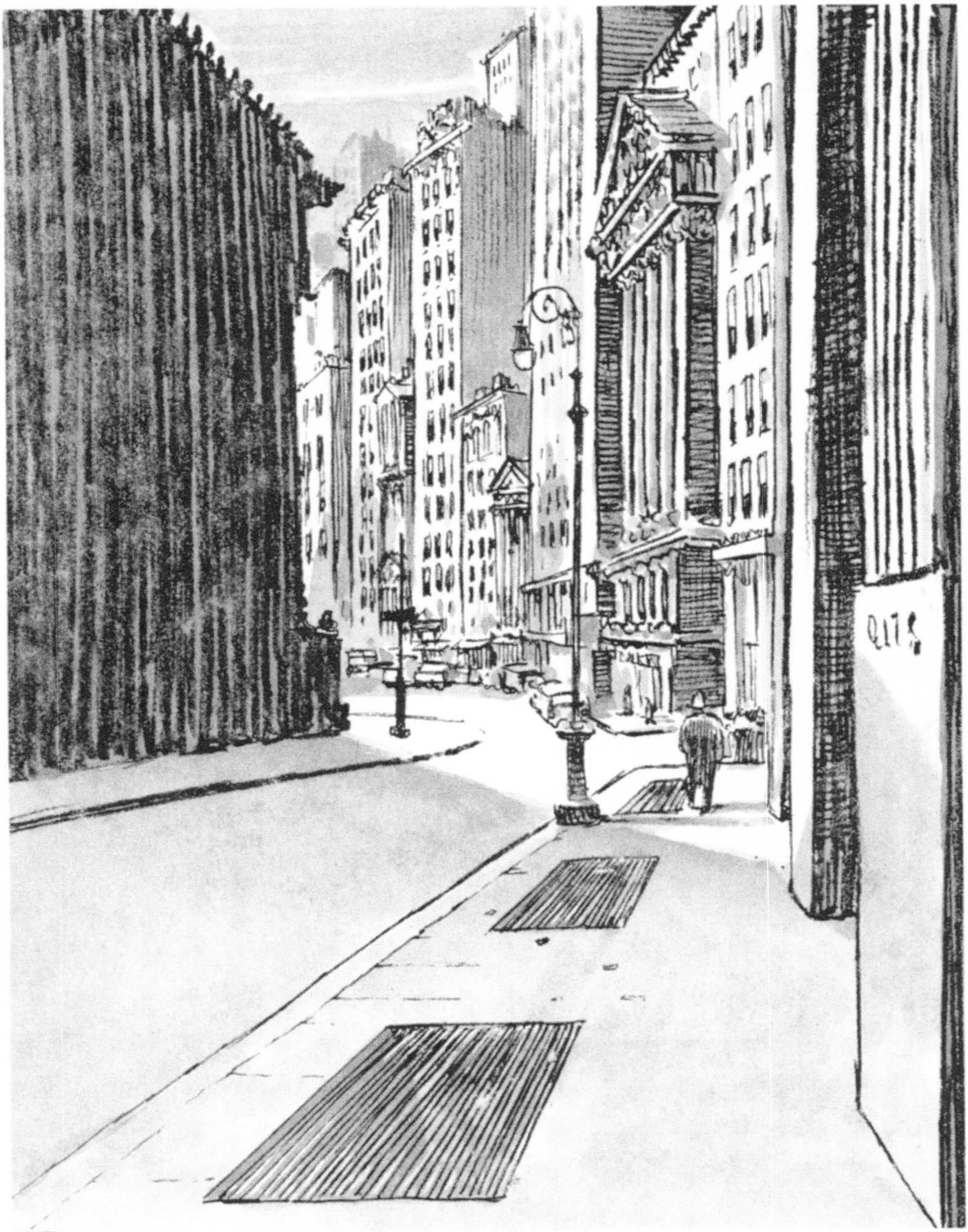

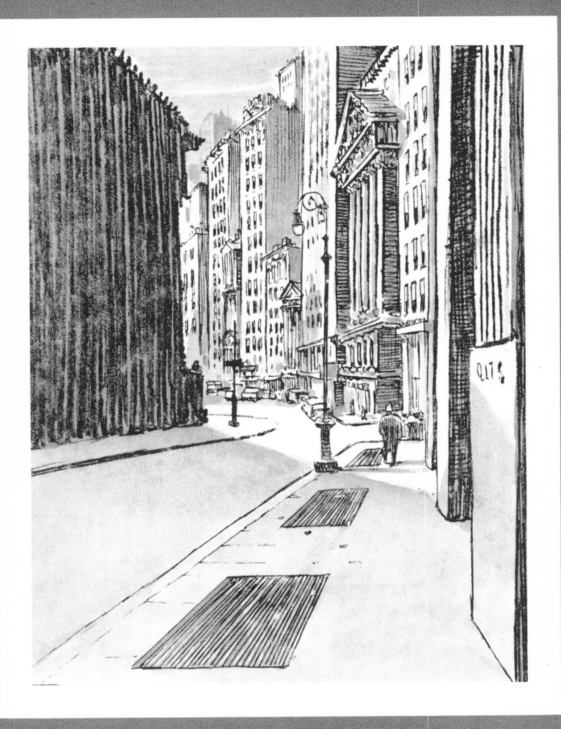

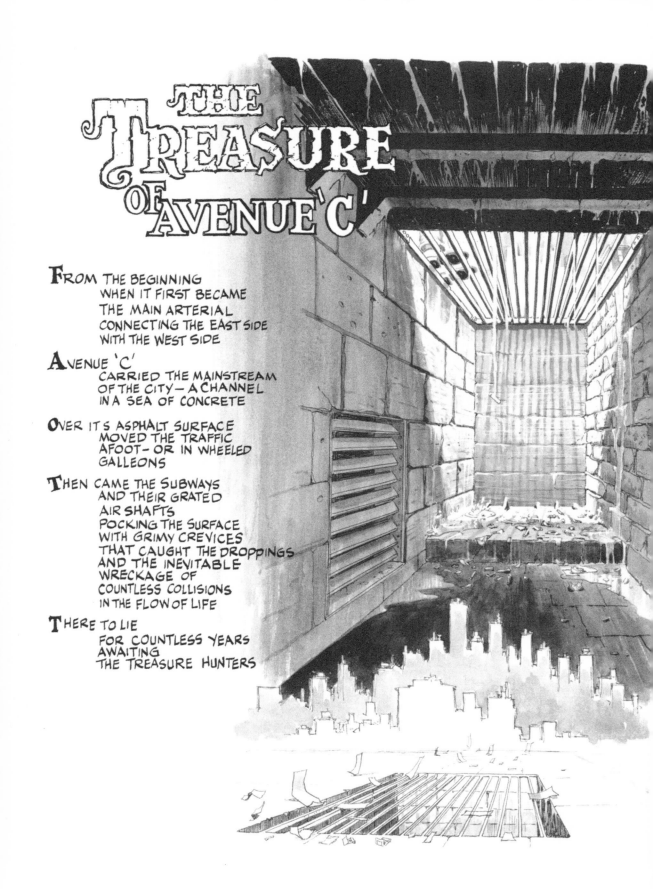

THE TREASURE OF AVENUE 'C'

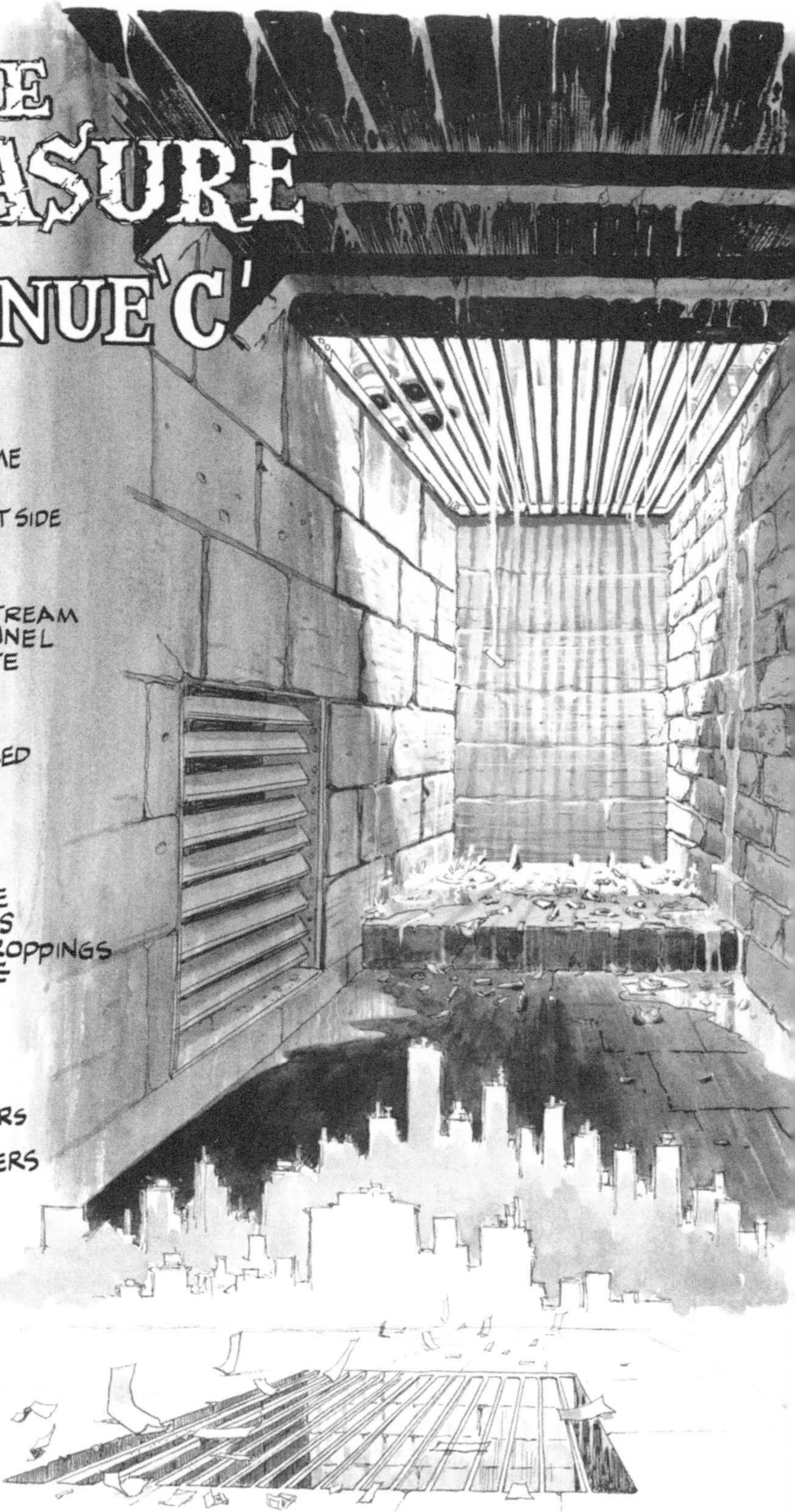

FROM THE BEGINNING
WHEN IT FIRST BECAME
THE MAIN ARTERIAL
CONNECTING THE EAST SIDE
WITH THE WEST SIDE

AVENUE 'C'
CARRIED THE MAINSTREAM
OF THE CITY — A CHANNEL
IN A SEA OF CONCRETE

OVER IT'S ASPHALT SURFACE
MOVED THE TRAFFIC
AFOOT — OR IN WHEELED
GALLEONS

THEN CAME THE SUBWAYS
AND THEIR GRATED
AIR SHAFTS
POCKING THE SURFACE
WITH GRIMY CREVICES
THAT CAUGHT THE DROPPINGS
AND THE INEVITABLE
WRECKAGE OF
COUNTLESS COLLISIONS
IN THE FLOW OF LIFE

THERE TO LIE
FOR COUNTLESS YEARS
AWAITING
THE TREASURE HUNTERS

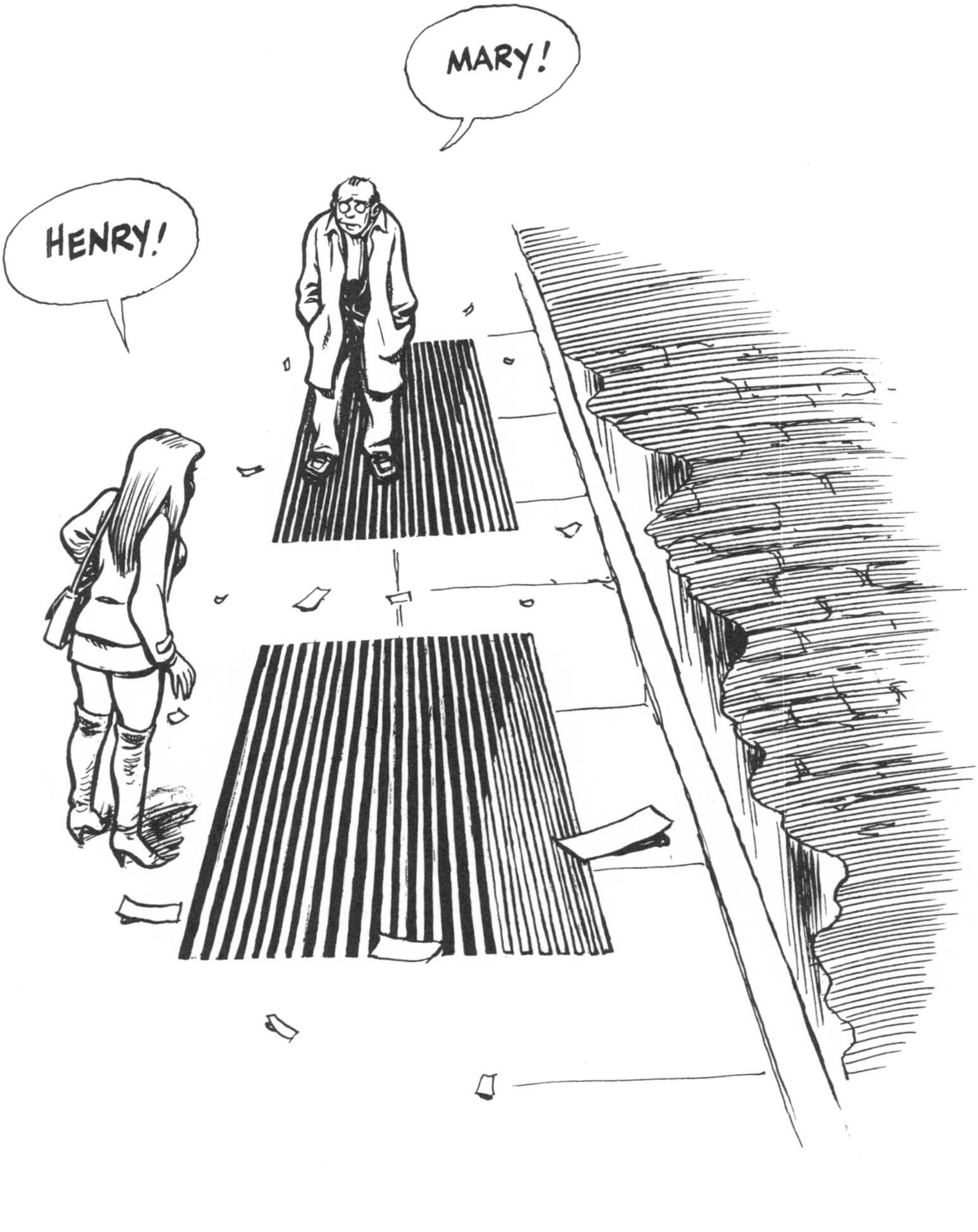
HENRY!
MARY!

THE RING

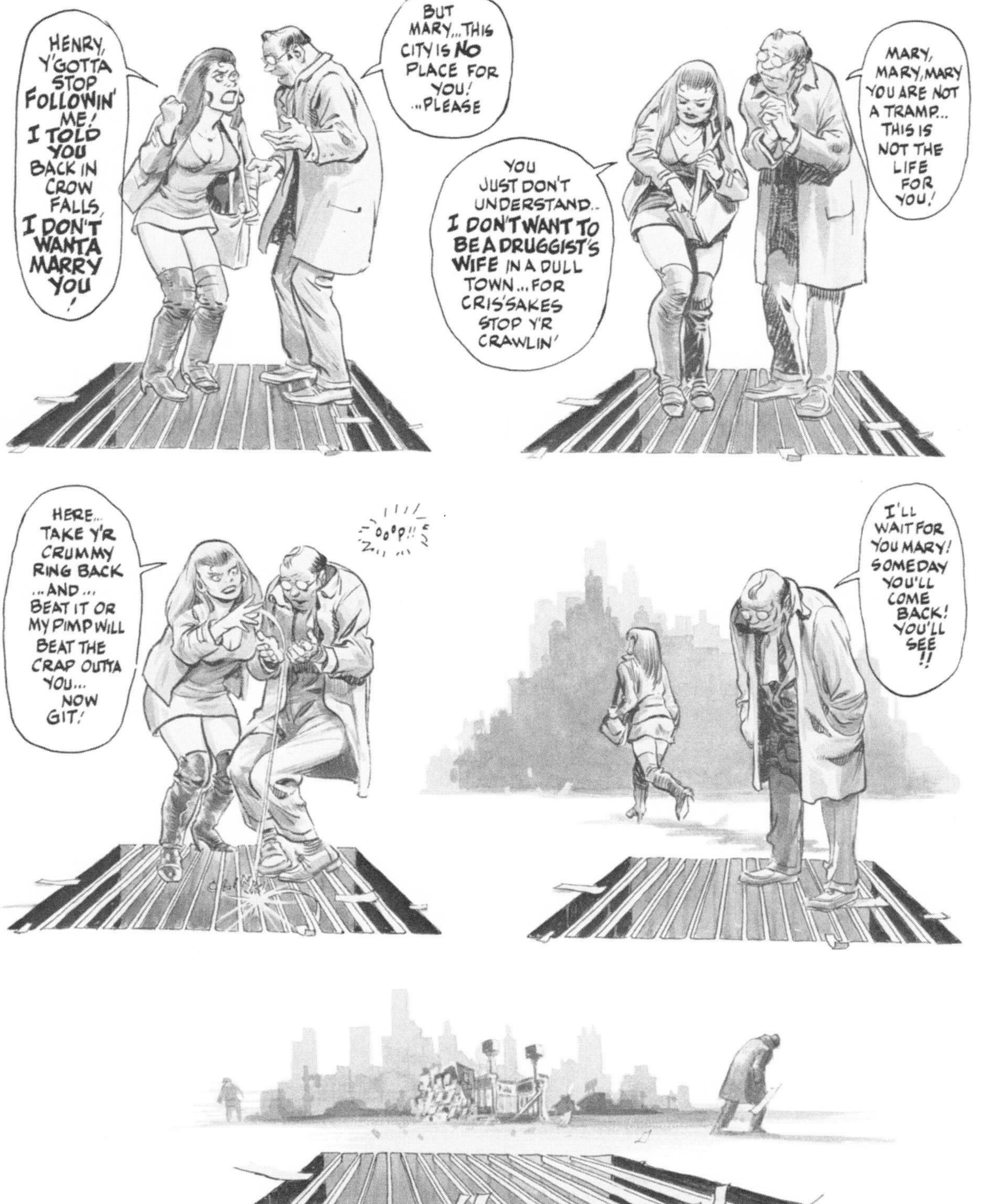
HENRY, Y'GOTTA STOP FOLLOWIN' ME! I TOLD YOU BACK IN CROW FALLS, I DON'T WANTA MARRY YOU!
BUT MARY... THIS CITY IS NO PLACE FOR YOU! ...PLEASE
MARY, MARY, MARY YOU ARE NOT A TRAMP... THIS IS NOT THE LIFE FOR YOU!
YOU JUST DON'T UNDERSTAND.. I DON'T WANT TO BE A DRUGGIST'S WIFE IN A DULL TOWN... FOR CRIS'SAKES STOP Y'R CRAWLIN'
HERE... TAKE Y'R CRUMMY RING BACK ...AND... BEAT IT OR MY PIMP WILL BEAT THE CRAP OUTTA YOU... NOW GIT!
OOOP!!
I'LL WAIT FOR YOU MARY! SOMEDAY YOU'LL COME BACK! YOU'LL SEE!!

THE MONEY

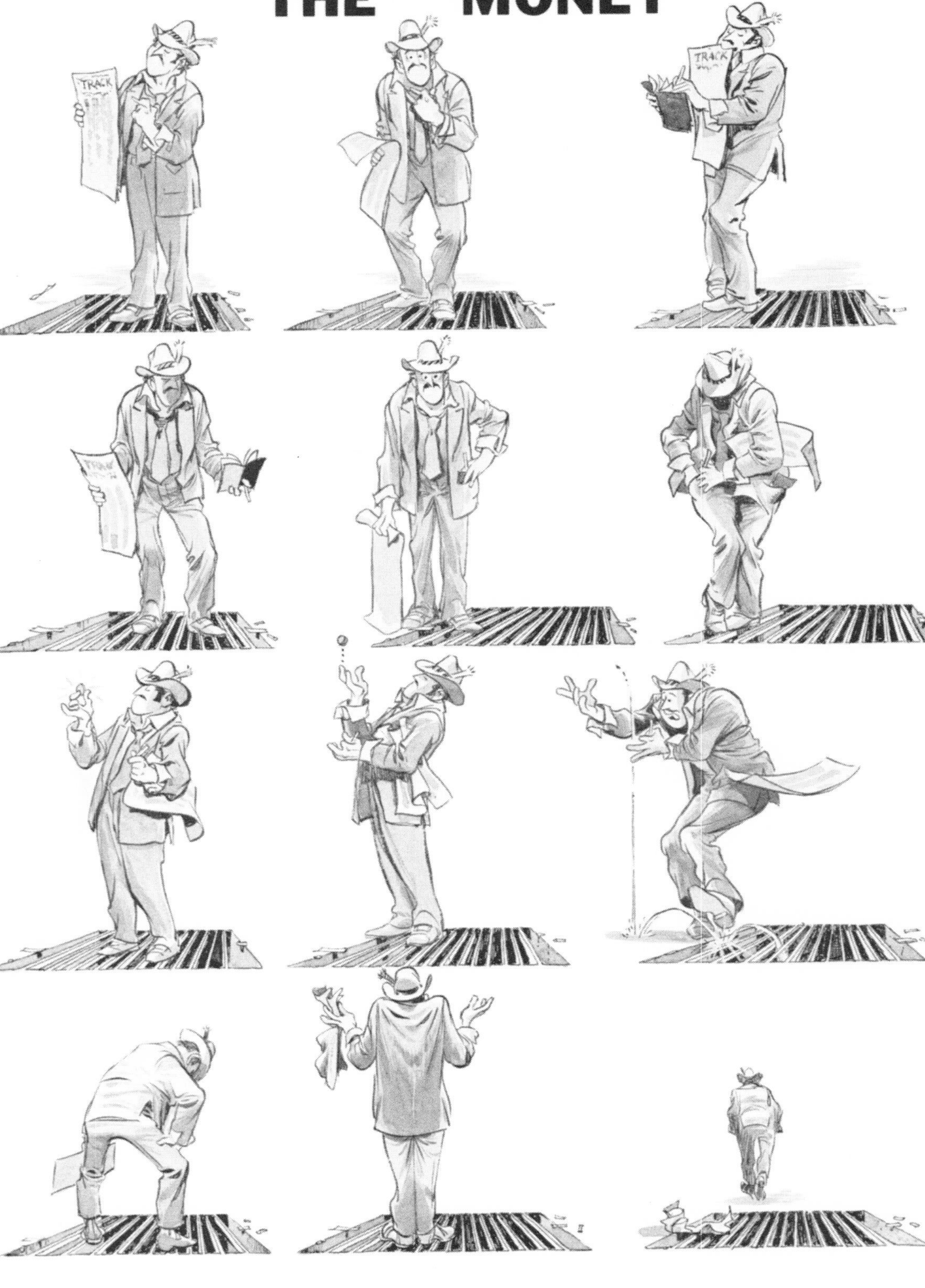
TRACK
TRACK

THE WEAPON

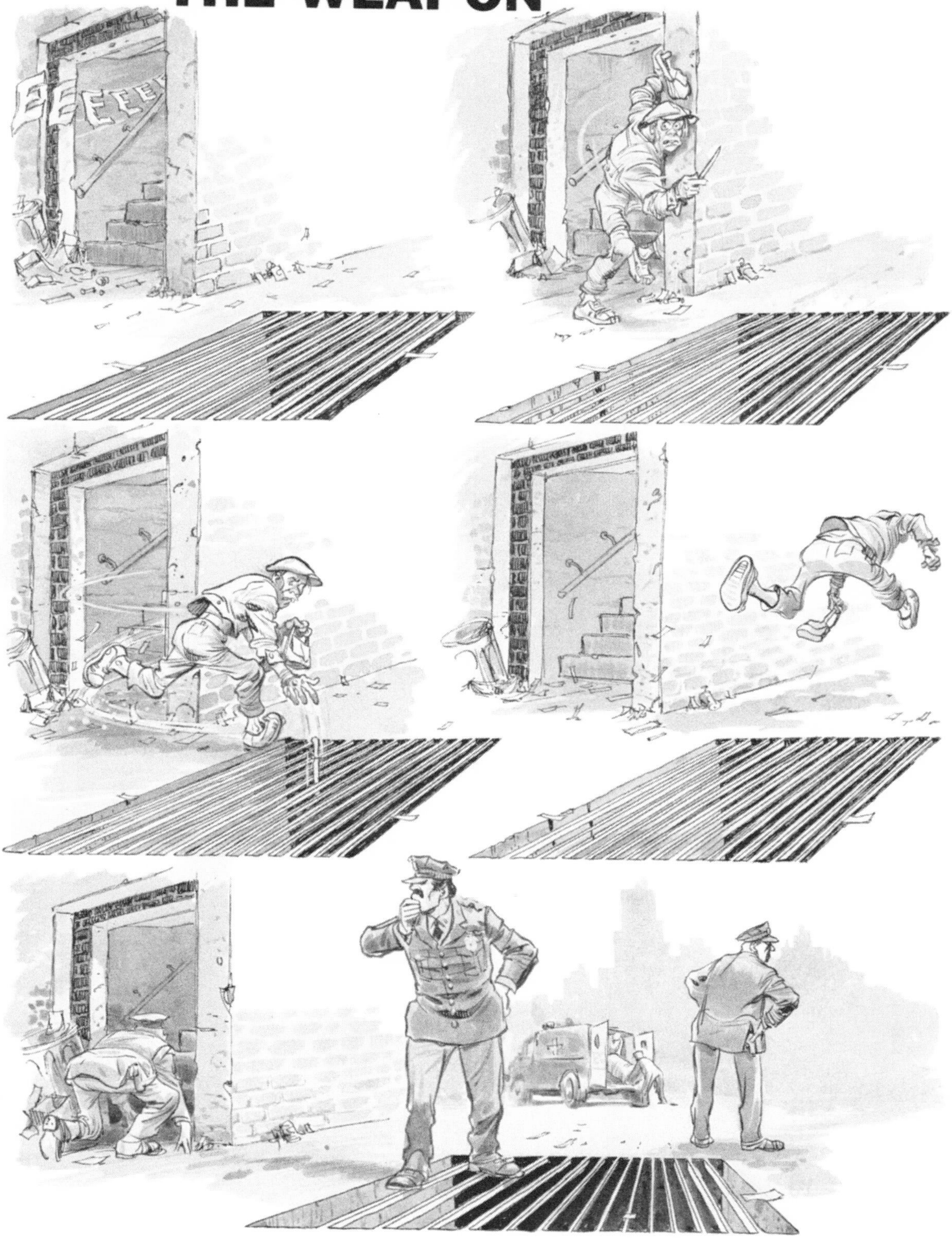
EEEEE

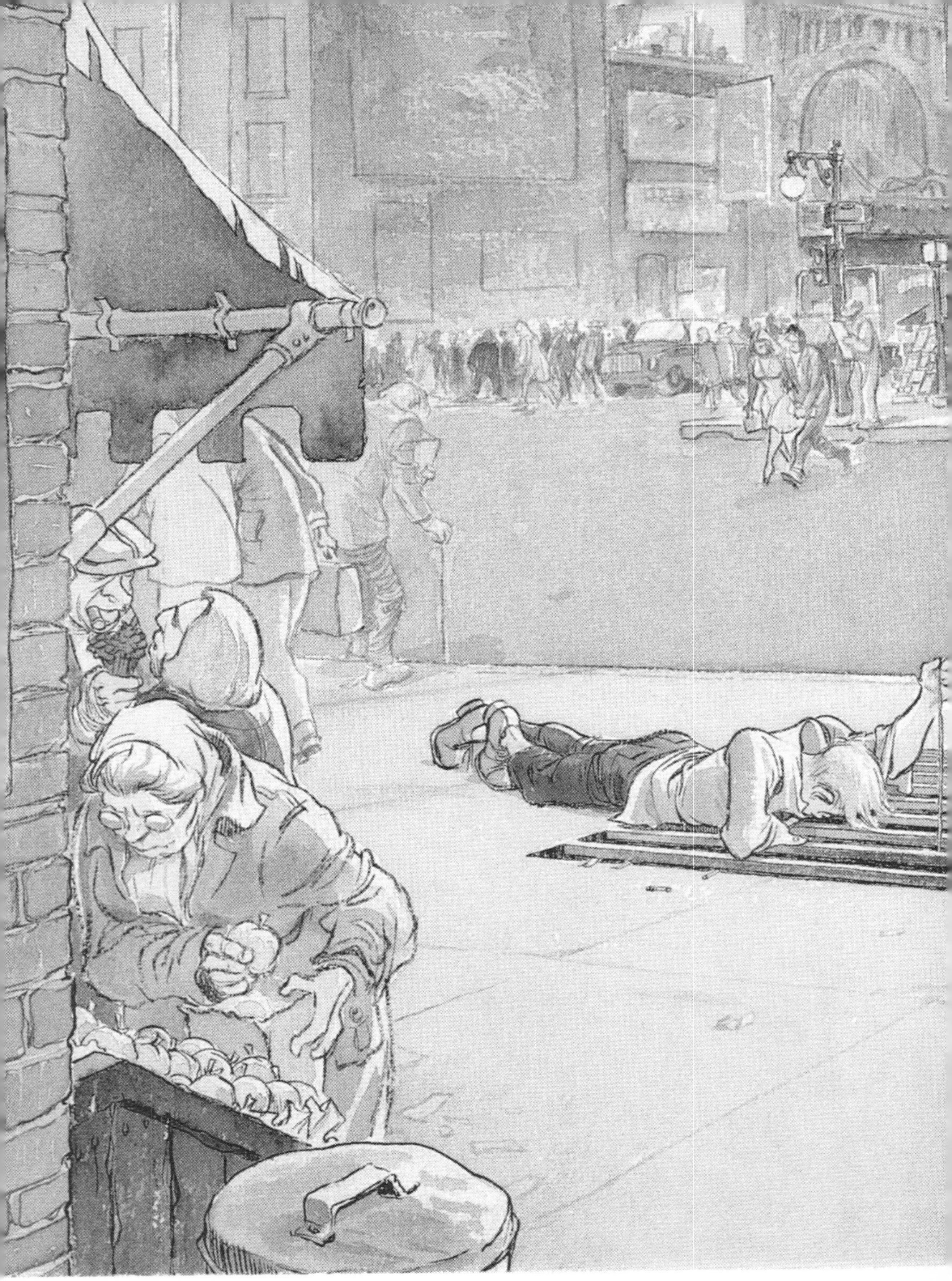

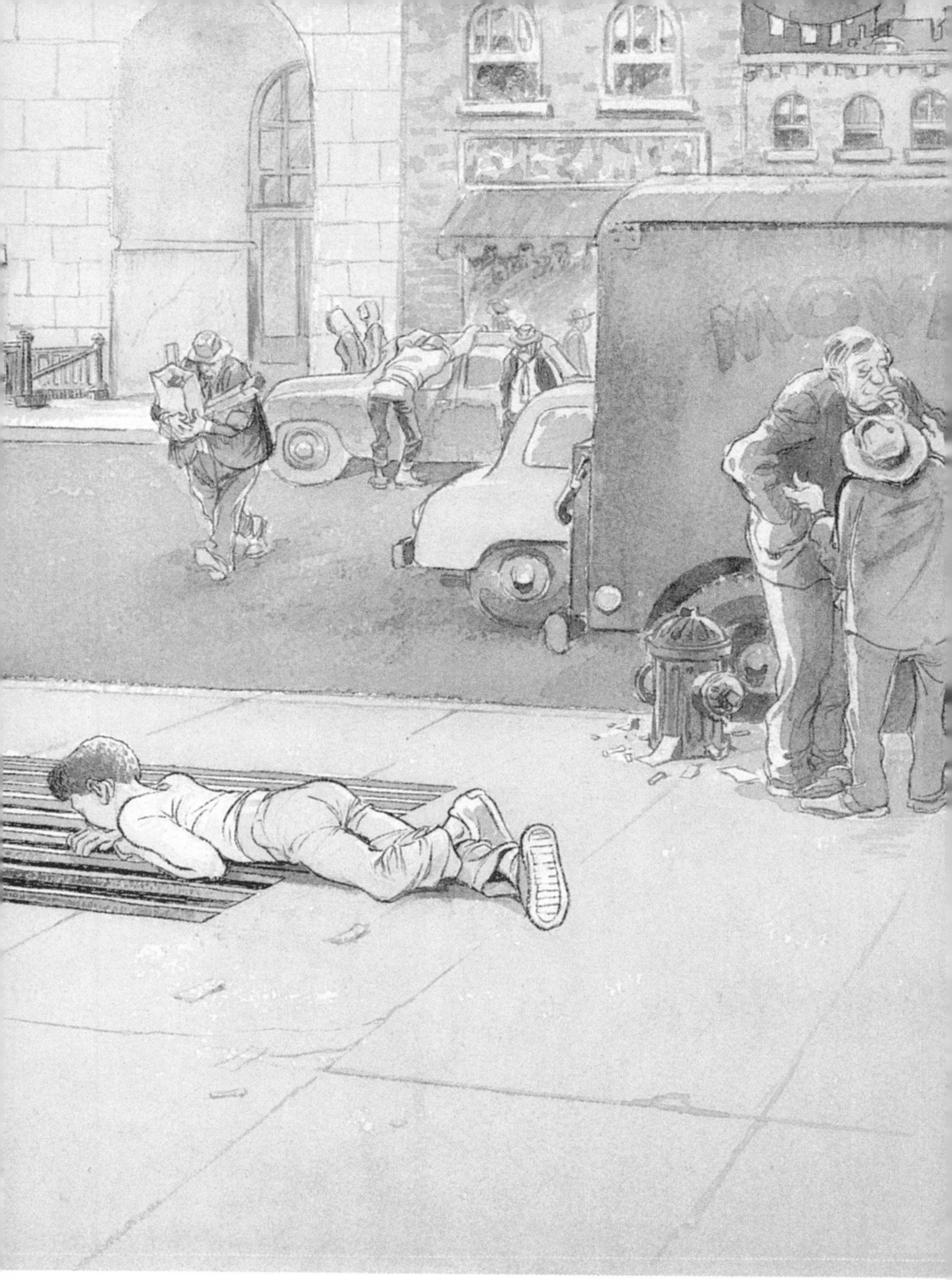

THE KEY

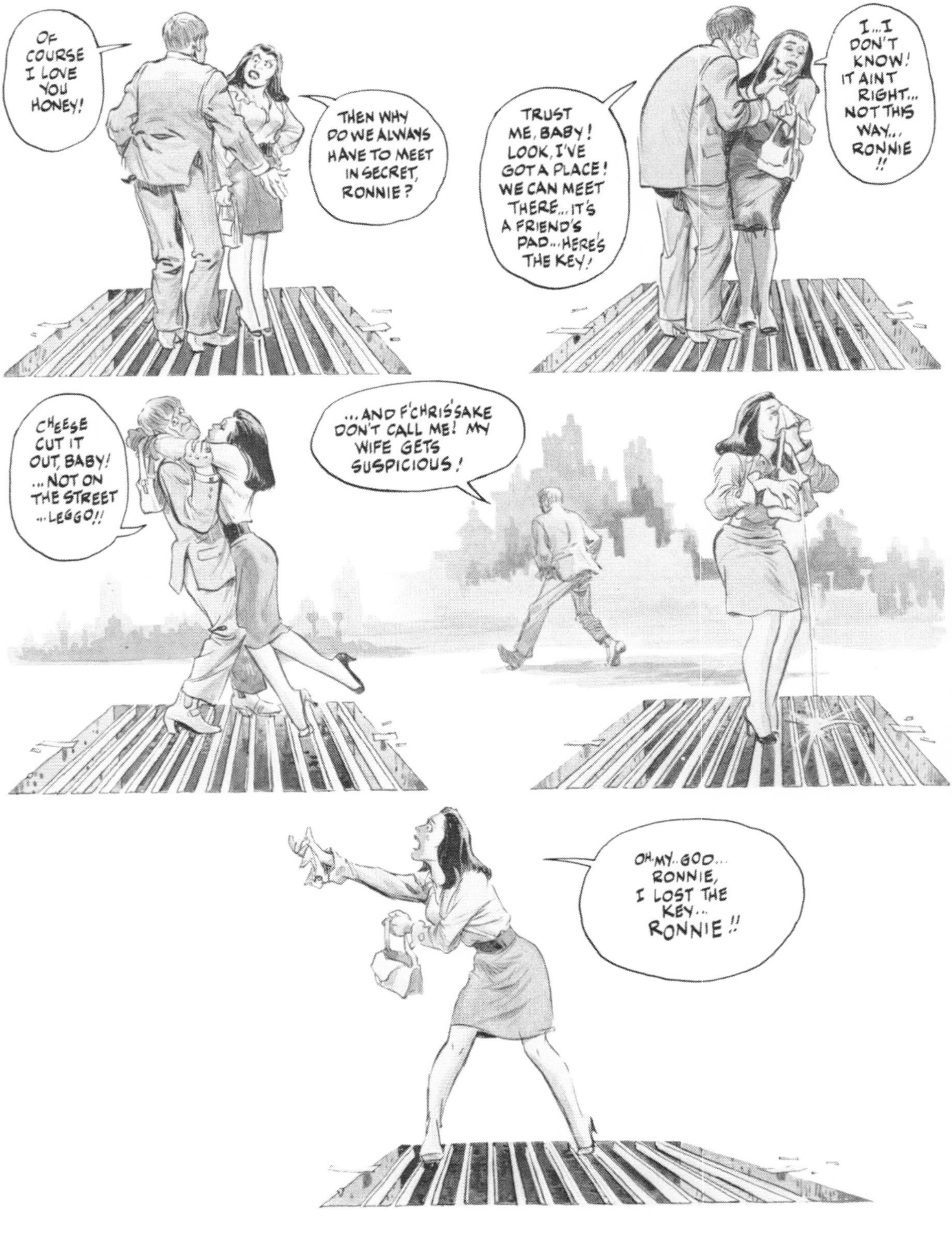
OF COURSE I LOVE YOU HONEY!
THEN WHY DO WE ALWAYS HAVE TO MEET IN SECRET, RONNIE?
TRUST ME, BABY! LOOK, I'VE GOT A PLACE! WE CAN MEET THERE... IT'S A FRIEND'S PAD... HERE'S THE KEY!
I...I DON'T KNOW! IT AINT RIGHT... NOT THIS WAY... RONNIE!!
CHEESE CUT IT OUT, BABY! ...NOT ON THE STREET ...LEGGO!!
...AND F'CHRIS'SAKE DON'T CALL ME! MY WIFE GETS SUSPICIOUS!
OH.MY..GOD... RONNIE, I LOST THE KEY... RONNIE!!

THE TREASURE

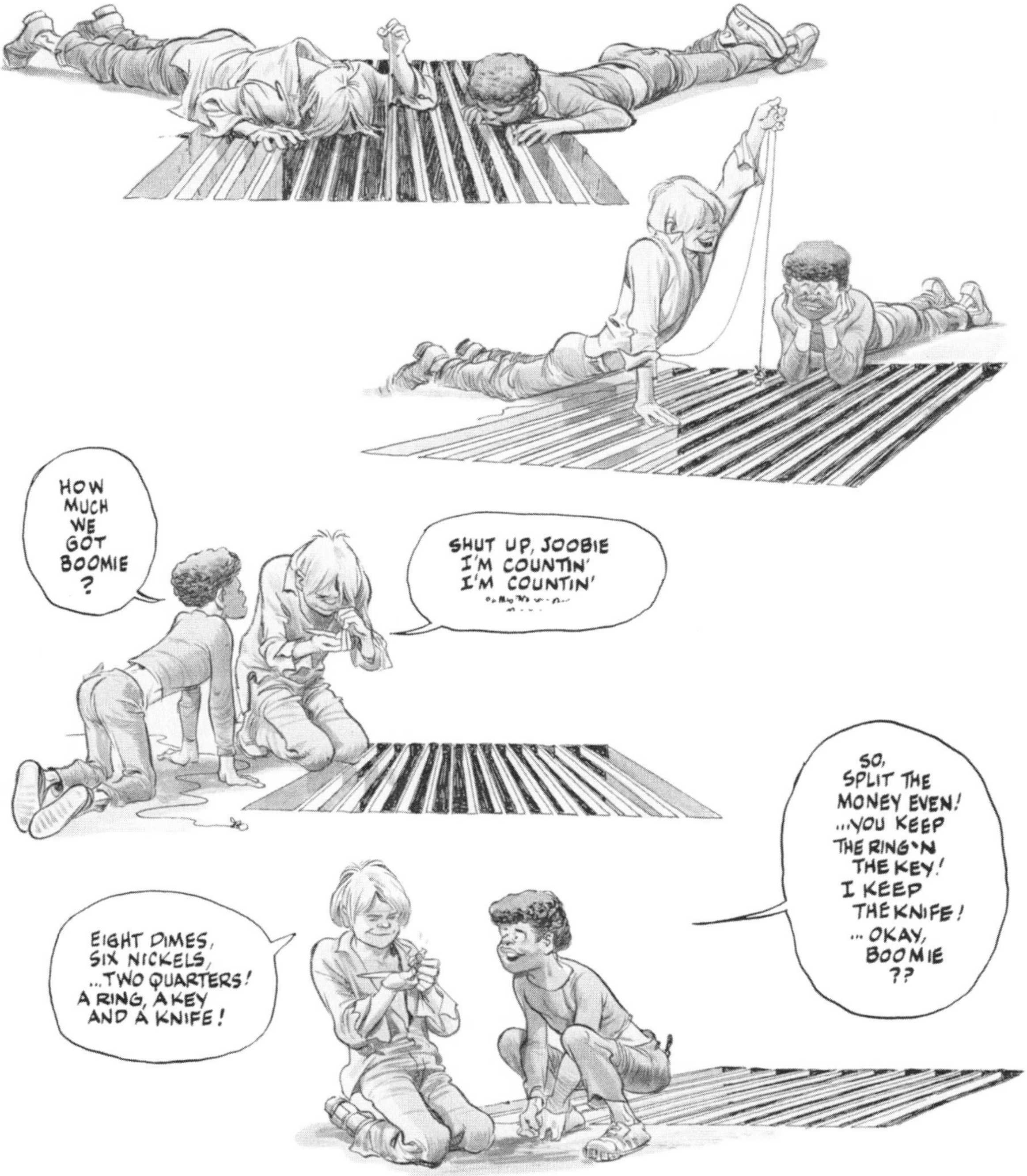
HOW MUCH WE GOT BOOMIE ?
SHUT UP, JOOBIE I'M COUNTIN' I'M COUNTIN'
EIGHT DIMES, SIX NICKELS, ...TWO QUARTERS! A RING, A KEY AND A KNIFE!
SO, SPLIT THE MONEY EVEN! ...YOU KEEP THE RING 'N THE KEY! I KEEP THE KNIFE! ... OKAY, BOOMIE ??

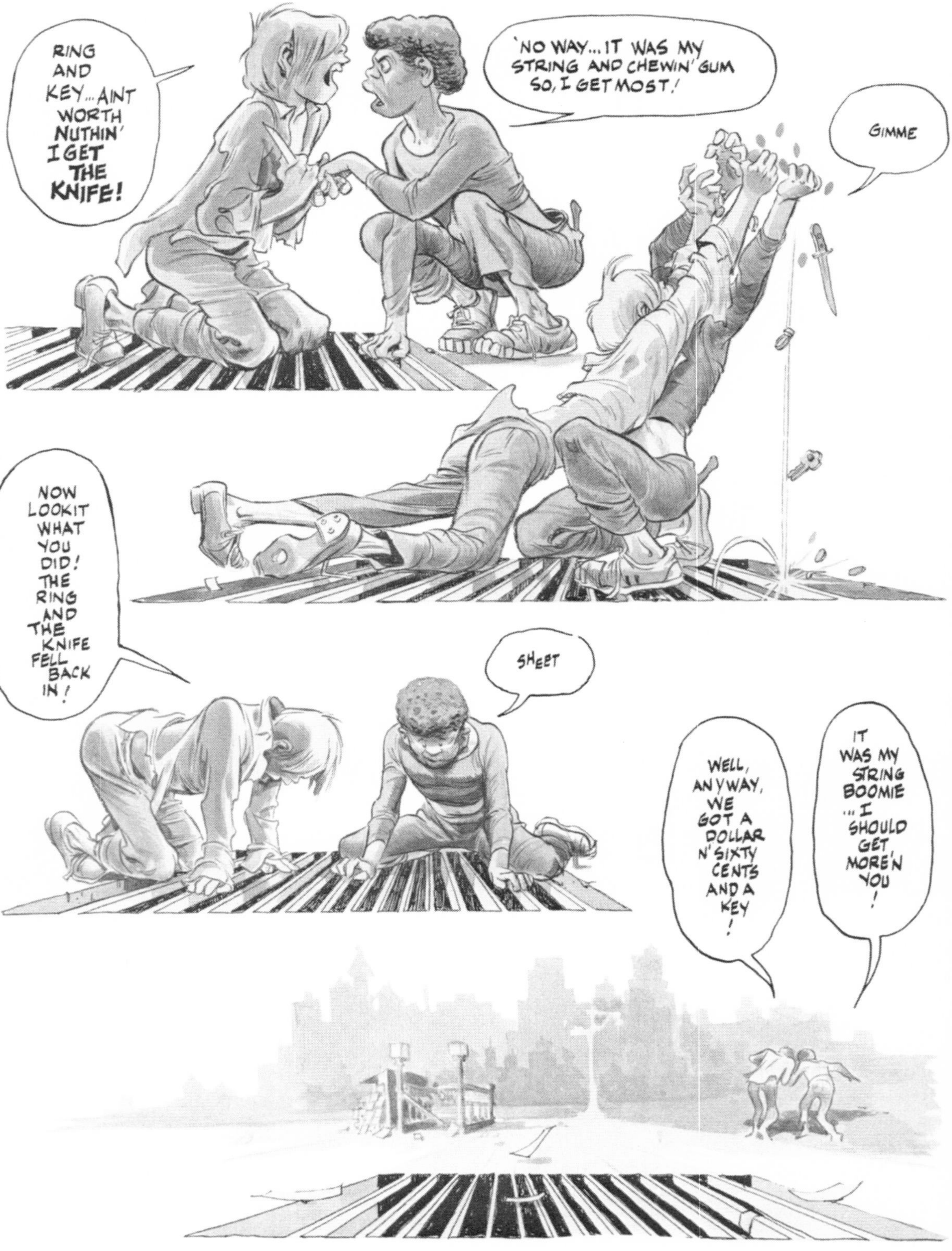
RING AND KEY...AINT WORTH NUTHIN' I GET THE KNIFE!
'NO WAY...IT WAS MY STRING AND CHEWIN' GUM SO, I GET MOST!
GIMME
NOW LOOKIT WHAT YOU DID! THE RING AND THE KNIFE FELL BACK IN!
SHEET
WELL, ANYWAY, WE GOT A DOLLAR N' SIXTY CENTS AND A KEY!
IT WAS MY STRING BOOMIE ...I SHOULD GET MORE'N YOU!

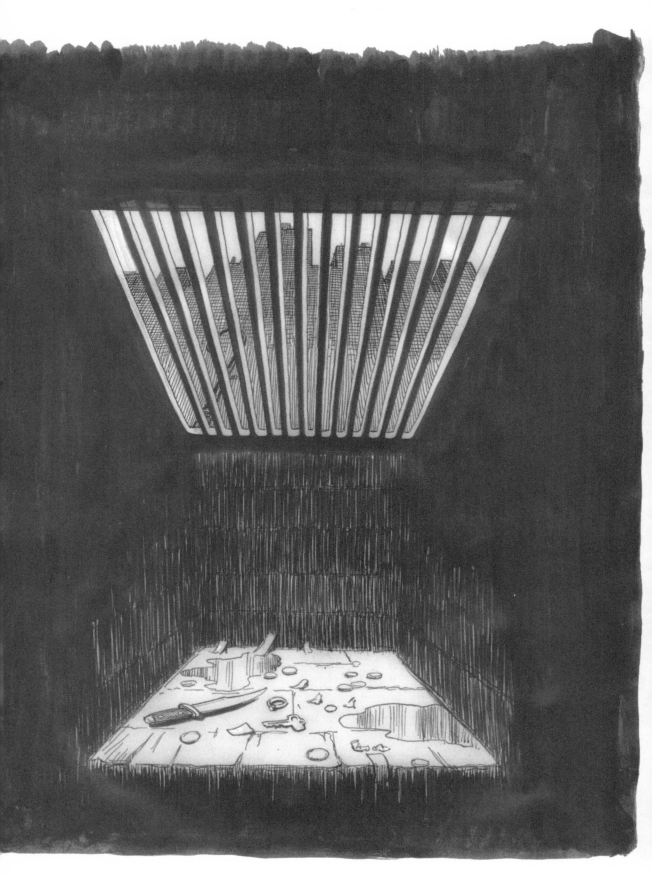

STOOPS

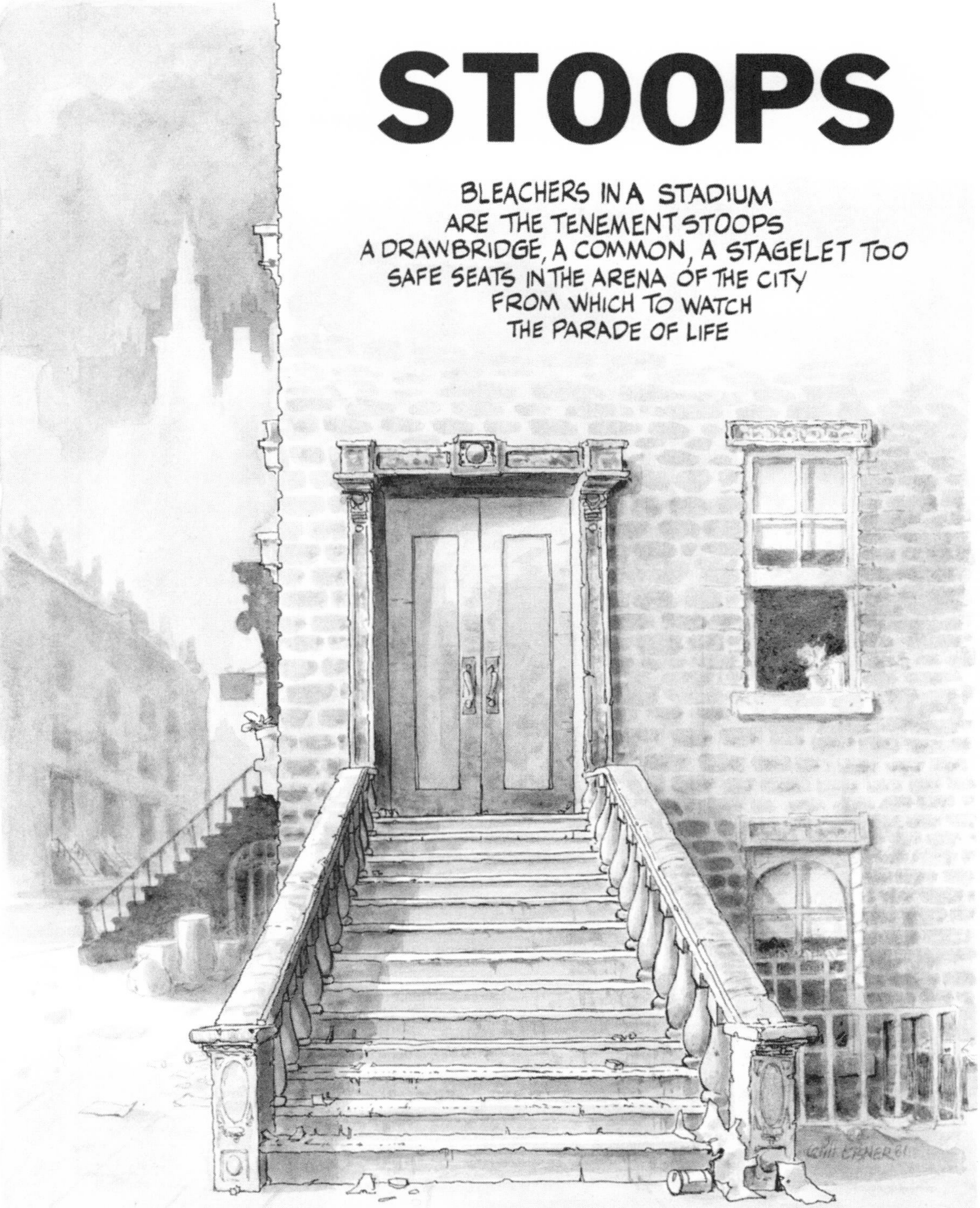
BLEACHERS IN A STADIUM
ARE THE TENEMENT STOOPS
A DRAWBRIDGE, A COMMON, A STAGELET TOO
SAFE SEATS IN THE ARENA OF THE CITY
FROM WHICH TO WATCH
THE PARADE OF LIFE

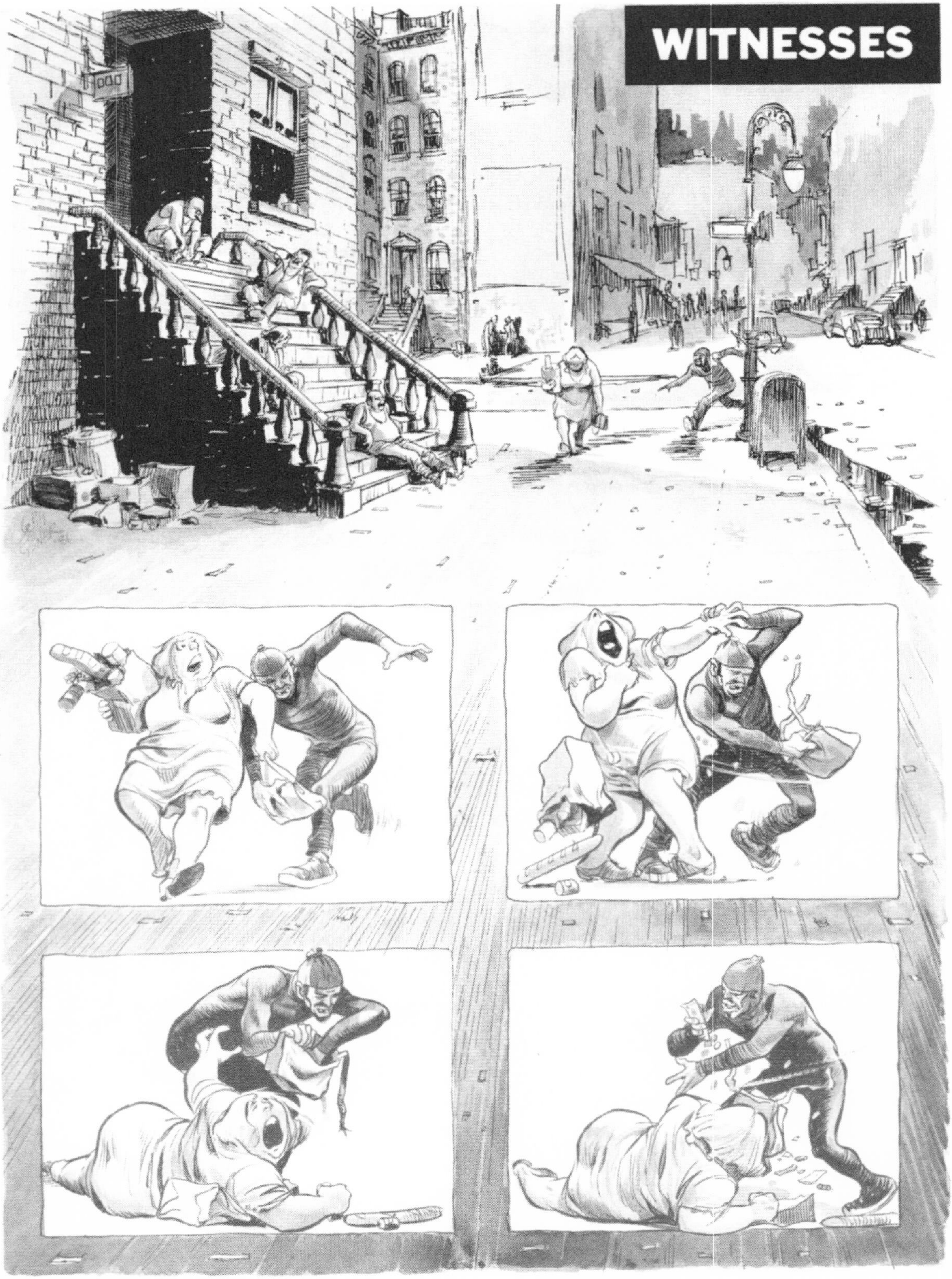
WITNESSES

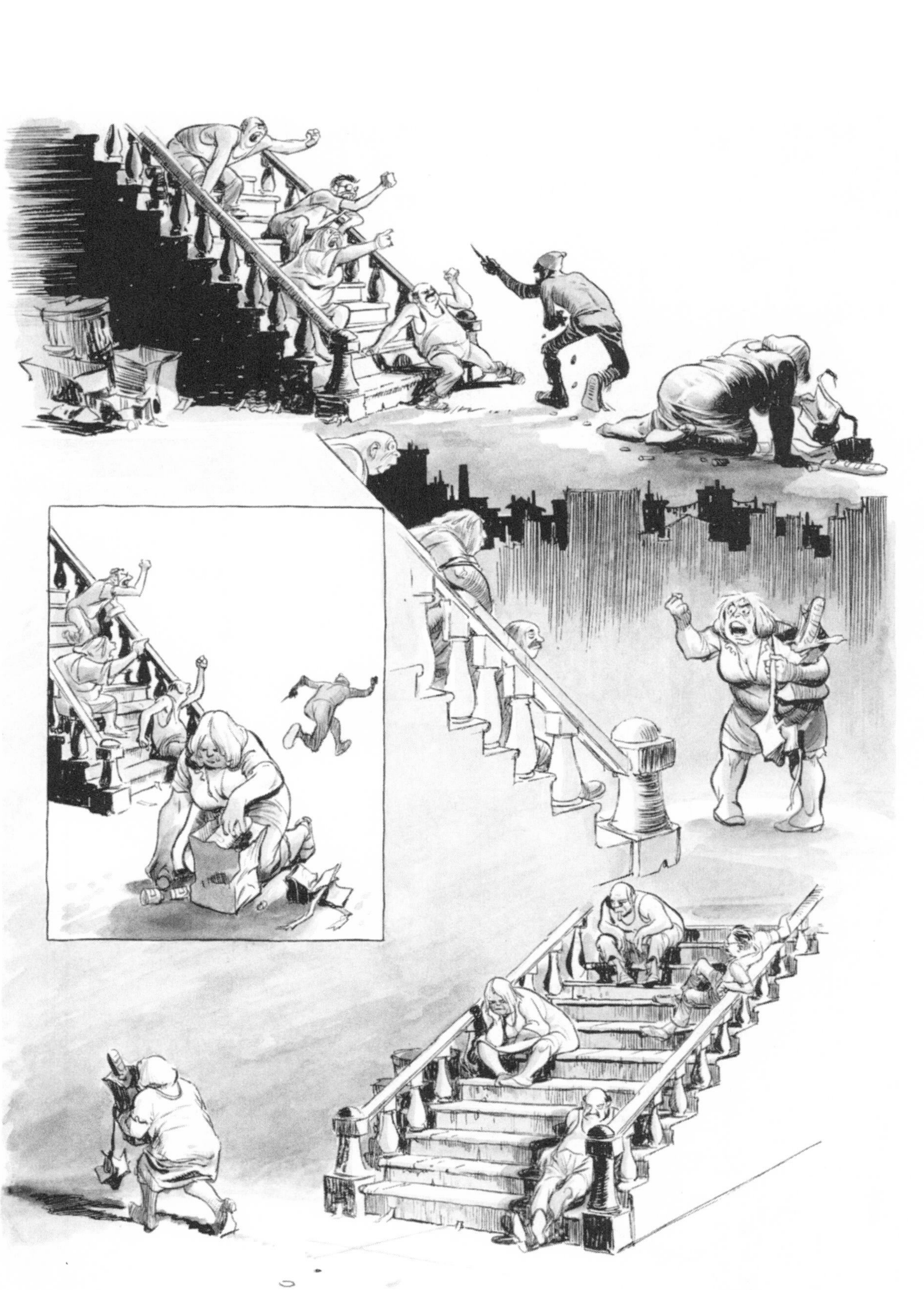

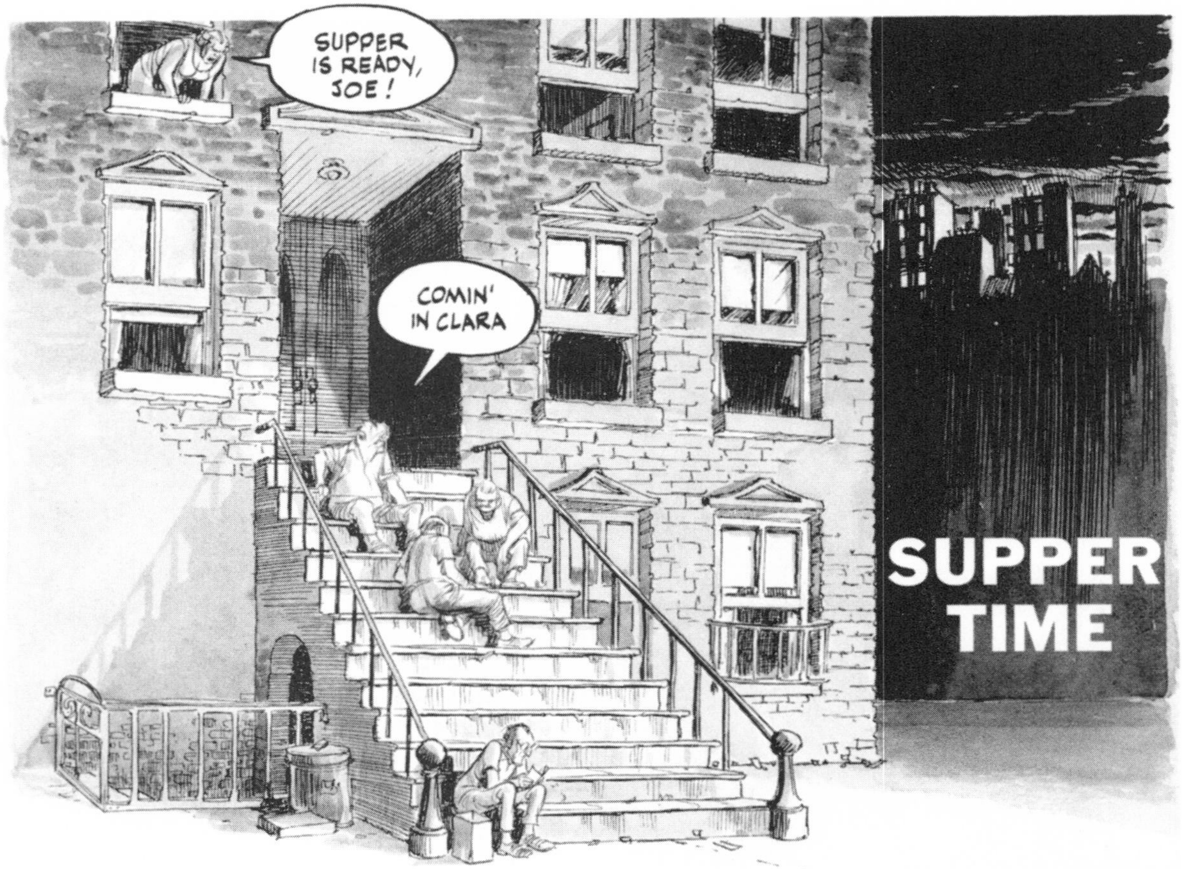
SUPPER IS READY, JOE!
COMIN' IN CLARA
SUPPER TIME

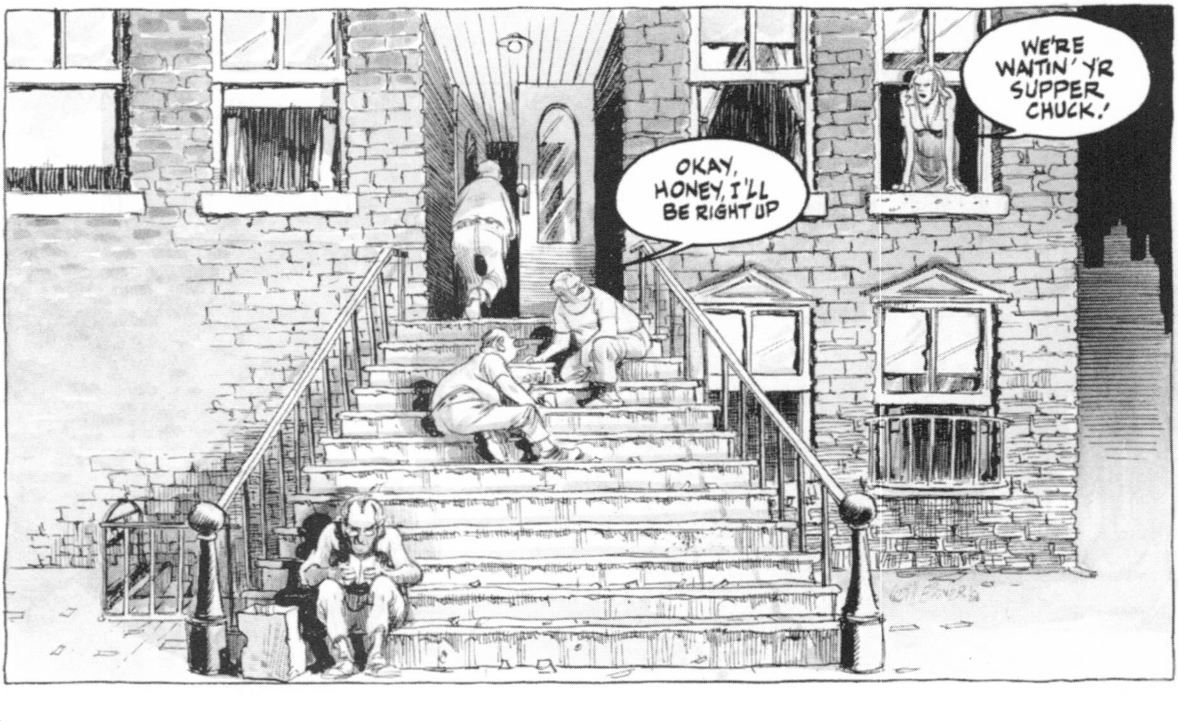
WE'RE WAITIN' Y'R SUPPER CHUCK.!
OKAY, HONEY, I'LL BE RIGHT UP

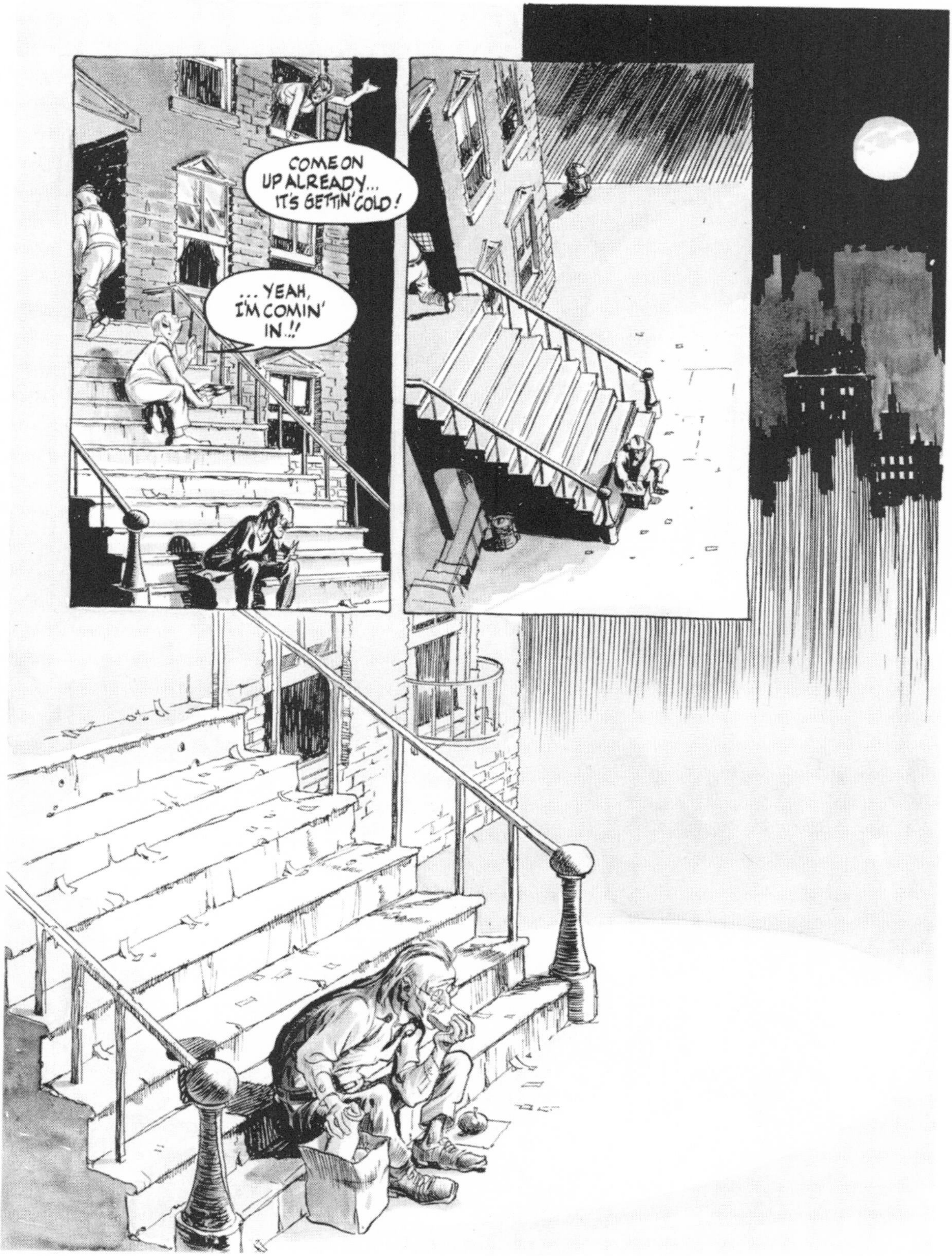
COME ON UP ALREADY... IT'S GETTIN' COLD!
... YEAH, I'M COMIN' IN.!!

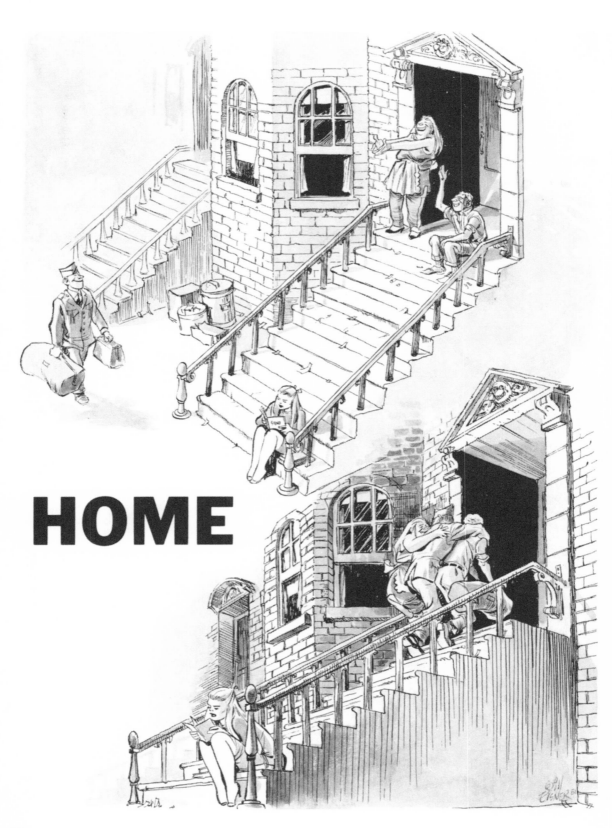

HOME

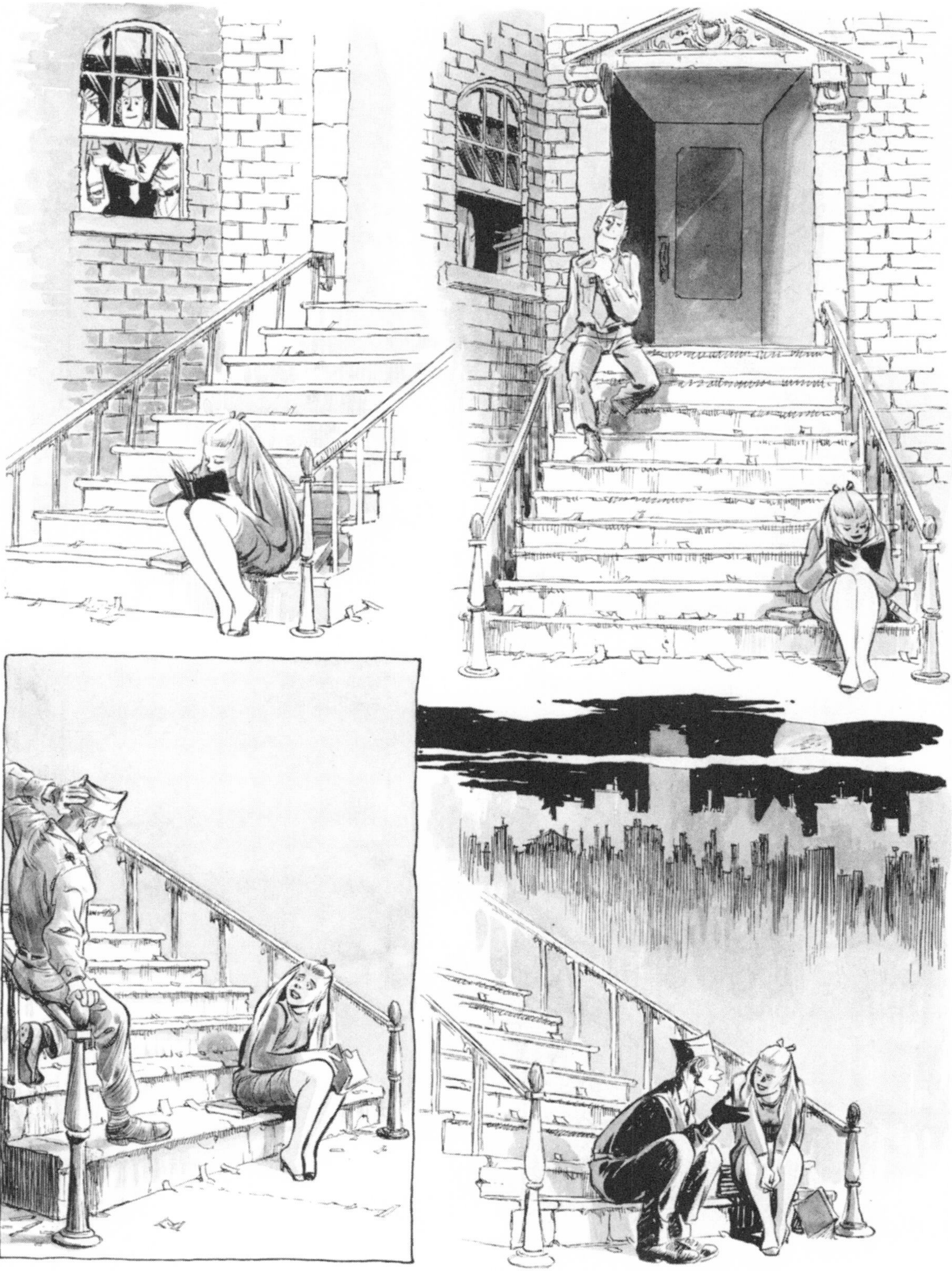

STOOPBALL

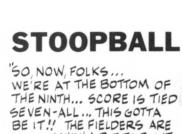

"SO, NOW, FOLKS... WE'RE AT THE BOTTOM OF THE NINTH... SCORE IS TIED SEVEN-ALL... THIS GOTTA BE IT!! THE FIELDERS ARE INCHIN' A BIT TO RIGHT FIELD...A TWO-BAGGER CAN DO IT WITH A RUNNER ON FIRST..."

"THE PITCHER IS CASIN' THE OUTFIELD! IT'S ALL RIDING ON THIS... HE'S COOL

" THERE'S THE WINDUP, THE RIGHT FIELD IS IN MOTION, THEY'RE READIN' HIM...

HE BURNS IT IN!!"

" IT'S AWAY YEE HOO

" IT'S A HIT IT'S A HIT...

" A TWO-BASE HIT...A-AAND IT'S STILL GOIN'...

"...GOIN', GOIN',...GONE RIGHT OUTTA THE PARK...AAAAND THAT'S IT..."

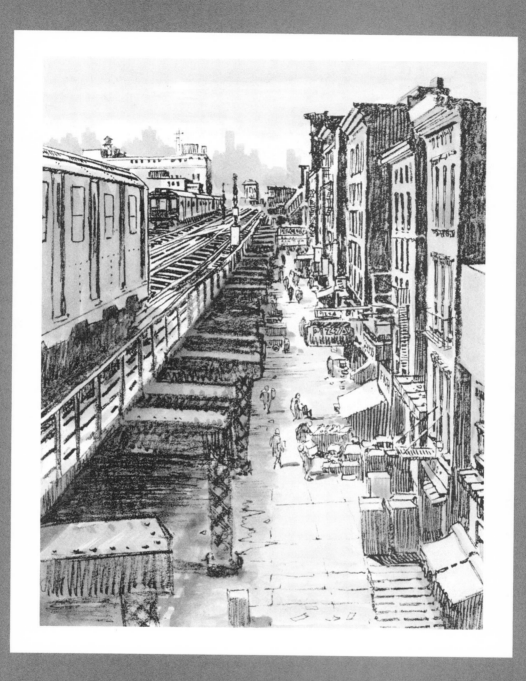

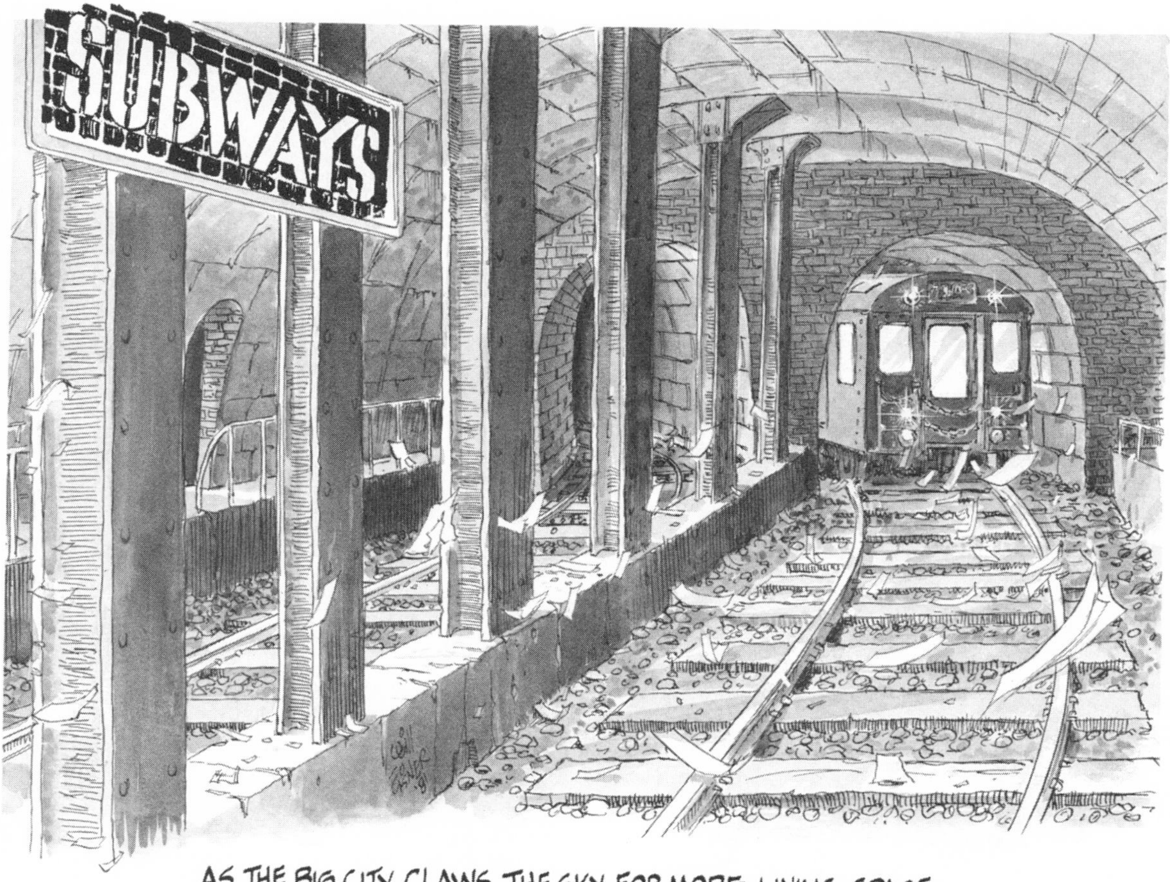
SUBWAYS

AS THE BIG CITY CLAWS THE SKY FOR MORE LIVING SPACE
SO IT BURROWS INTO THE EARTH FOR COMMUTATION
CATACOMBING ITSELF WITH CAPILLARIES
THROUGH WHICH SHUTTLE THE TRAINS.
MARSHALLED AT NIGHT IN NAKED YARDS ON ITS OUTSKIRTS
THEY REST UNTIL DAWN...THEN AN UNSEEN INTELLIGENCE
DISPERSES THEM INTO THE TIDAL FLOW OF CITY LIFE.
HUMORLESS IRON REPTILES, CLACKING STUPIDLY
ON A WEBBING OF GRACEFUL STEEL RAILS,
THEY SNAKE THROUGH THE MAZE OF BUILDINGS
UNTIL FINALLY, FINDING A TUNNEL MOUTH,
THEY PLUNGE INTO THE BOWELS OF THE CITY.

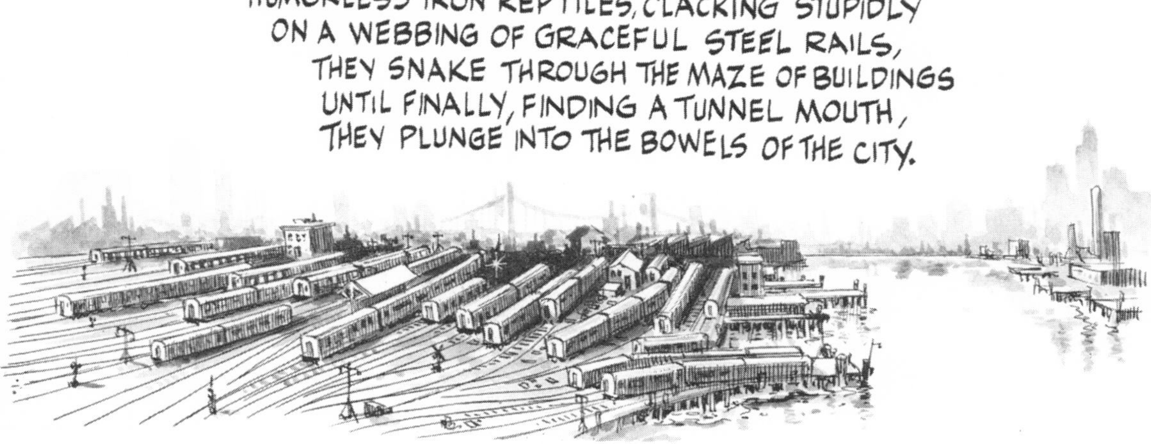

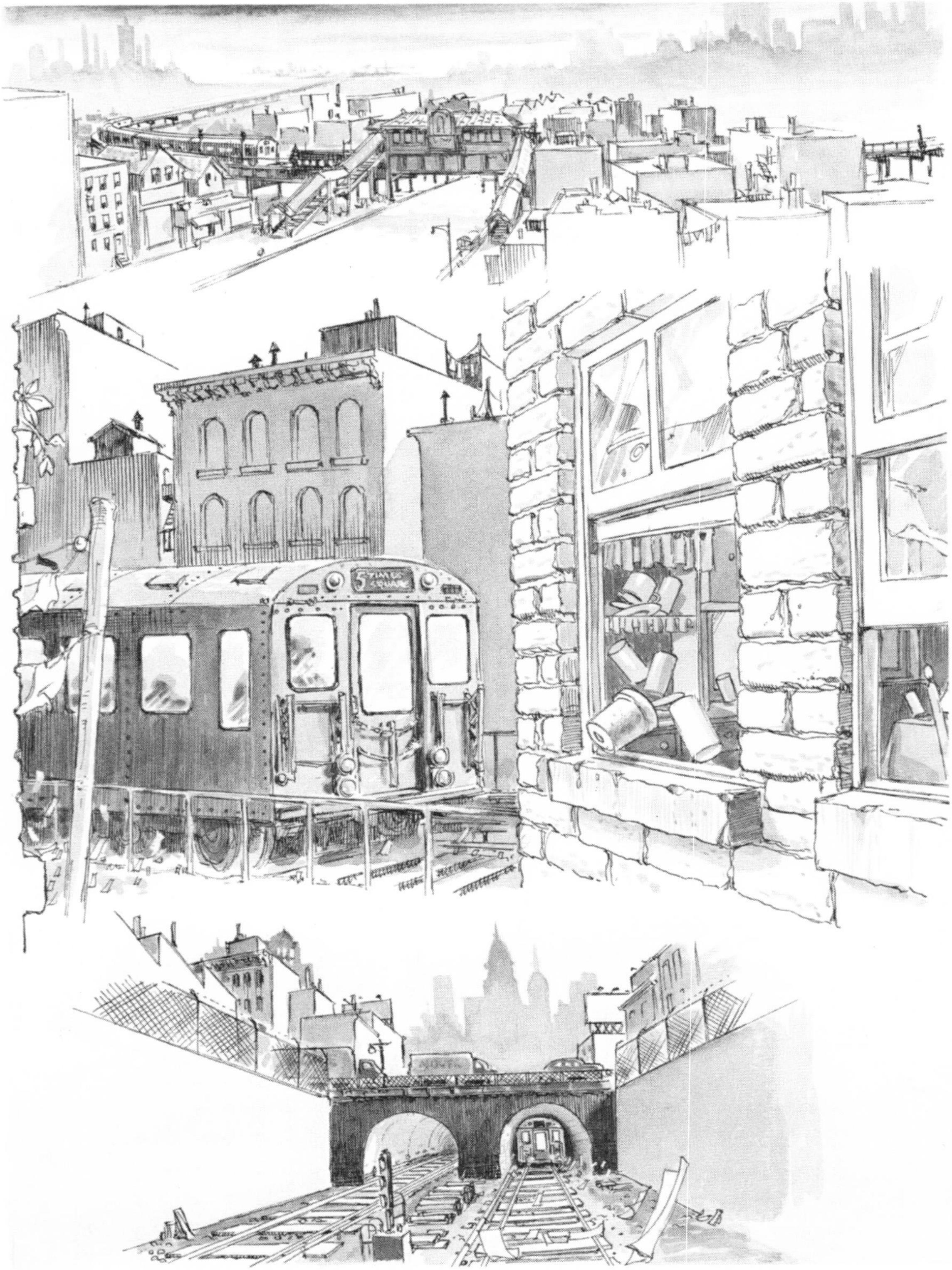
5 TIMES SQUARE

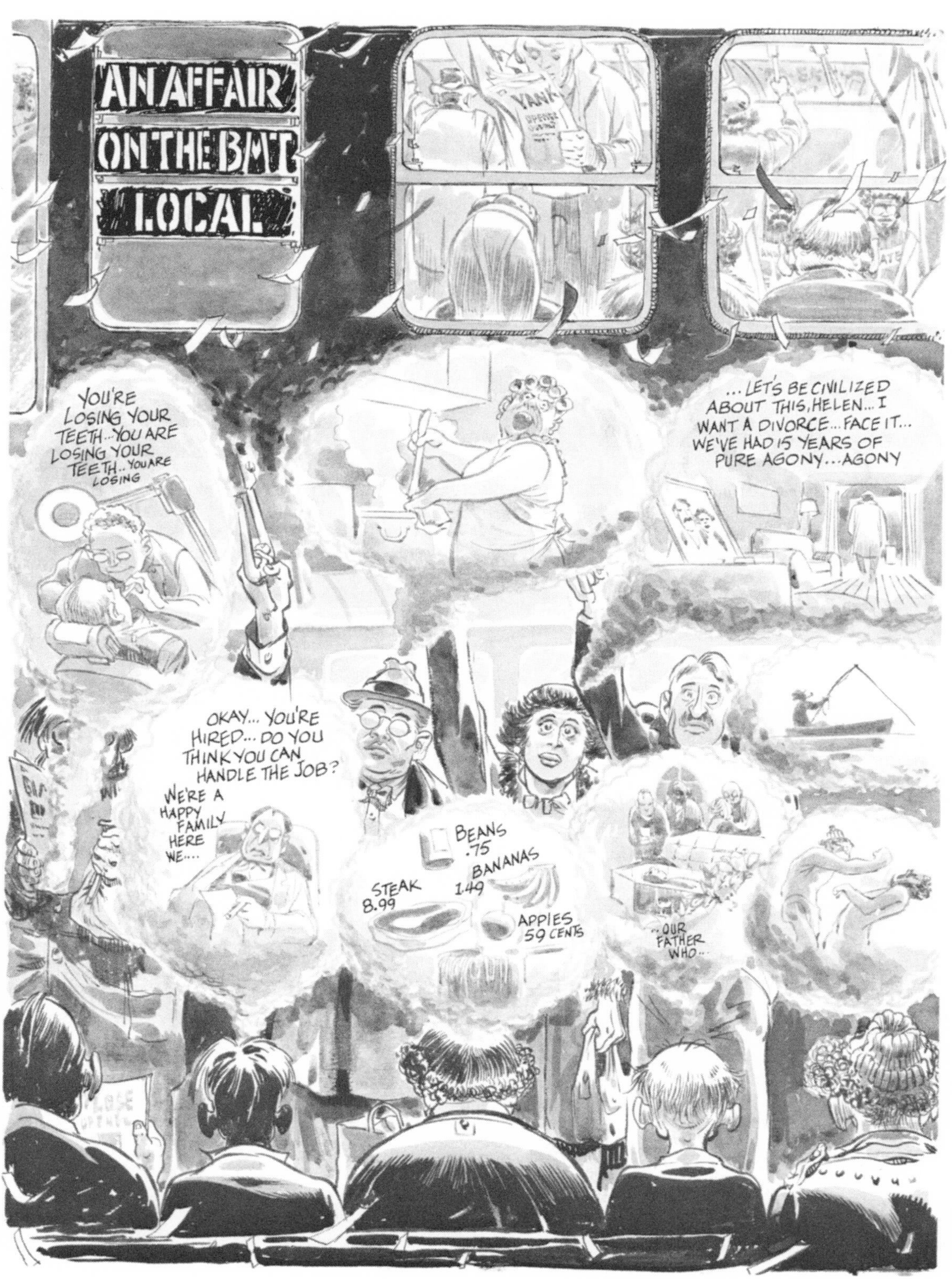
AN AFFAIR ON THE BMT LOCAL
YANK
YOU'RE LOSING YOUR TEETH... YOU ARE LOSING YOUR TEETH... YOU ARE LOSING
... LET'S BE CIVILIZED ABOUT THIS, HELEN... I WANT A DIVORCE... FACE IT... WE'VE HAD 15 YEARS OF PURE AGONY... AGONY
OKAY... YOU'RE HIRED... DO YOU THINK YOU CAN HANDLE THE JOB?
WE'RE A HAPPY FAMILY HERE WE....
BEANS .75
BANANAS 1.49
STEAK 8.99
APPLES 59 CENTS
...OUR FATHER WHO...

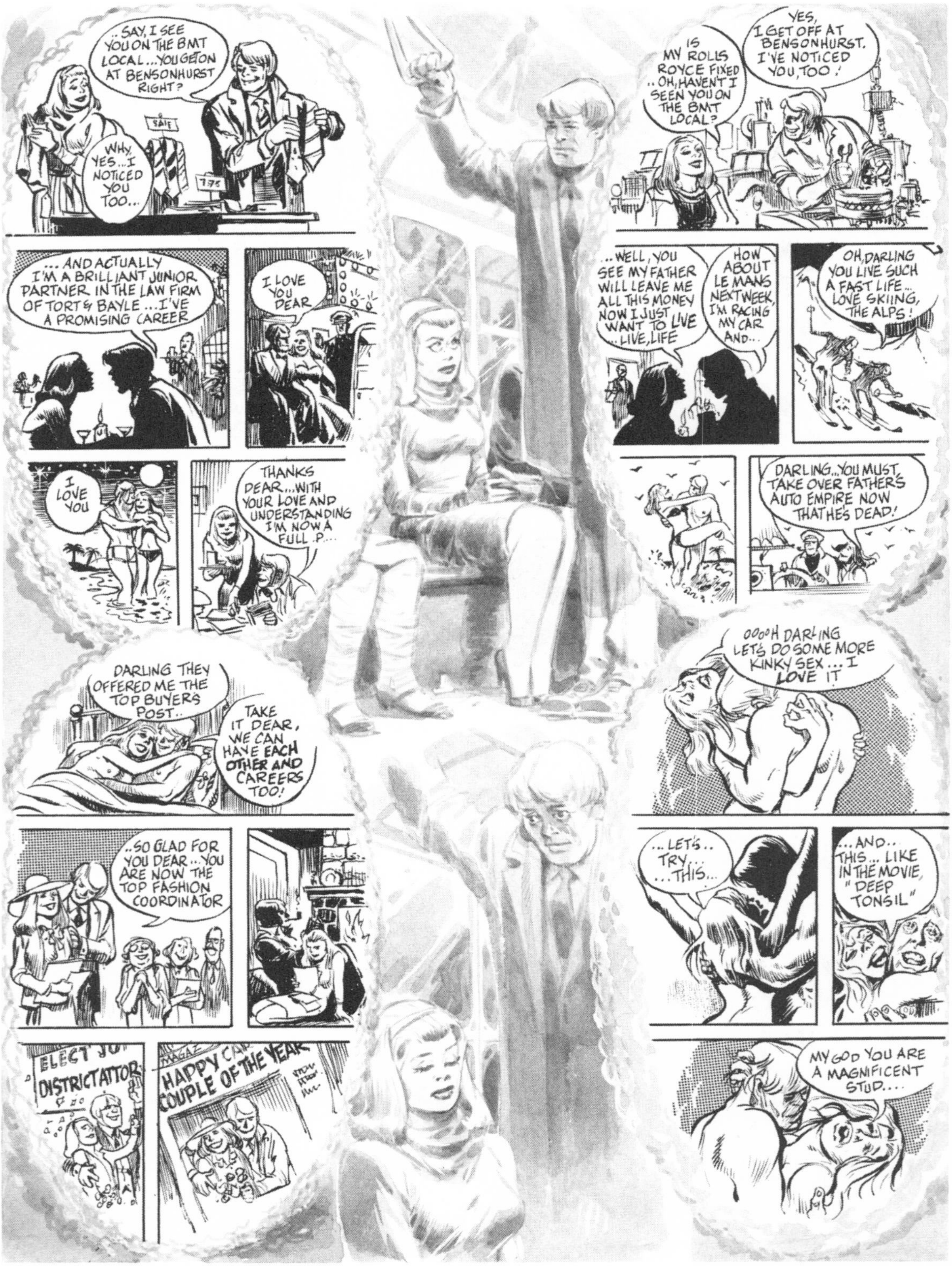

.. SAY, I SEE YOU ON THE BMT LOCAL ... YOU GET ON AT BENSONHURST RIGHT?
WHY, YES ... I NOTICED YOU TOO...
... AND ACTUALLY I'M A BRILLIANT JUNIOR PARTNER IN THE LAW FIRM OF TORT & BAYLE ... I'VE A PROMISING CAREER
I LOVE YOU DEAR
I LOVE YOU
THANKS DEAR ... WITH YOUR LOVE AND UNDERSTANDING I'M NOW A FULL .P...
DARLING THEY OFFERED ME THE TOP BUYERS POST..
TAKE IT DEAR, WE CAN HAVE EACH OTHER AND CAREERS TOO!
.. SO GLAD FOR YOU DEAR ... YOU ARE NOW THE TOP FASHION COORDINATOR
DISTRICT ATTOR
COUPLE OF THE YEAR
MY IS ROLLS ROYCE FIXED .. OH, HAVEN'T I SEEN YOU ON THE BMT LOCAL?
YES, I GET OFF AT BENSONHURST. I'VE NOTICED YOU, TOO!
... WELL, YOU SEE MY FATHER WILL LEAVE ME ALL THIS MONEY NOW I JUST WANT TO LIVE ... LIVE, LIFE
HOW ABOUT LE MANS NEXT WEEK, I'M RACING MY CAR AND...
OH, DARLING YOU LIVE SUCH A FAST LIFE ... LOVE SKIING, THE ALPS!
DARLING ... YOU MUST TAKE OVER FATHER'S AUTO EMPIRE NOW THAT HE'S DEAD!
OOOOH DARLING LET'S DO SOME MORE KINKY SEX ... I LOVE IT
... LET'S .. TRY ... ... THIS...
... AND .. THIS ... LIKE IN THE MOVIE, "DEEP TONSIL"
MY GOD YOU ARE A MAGNIFICENT STUD....

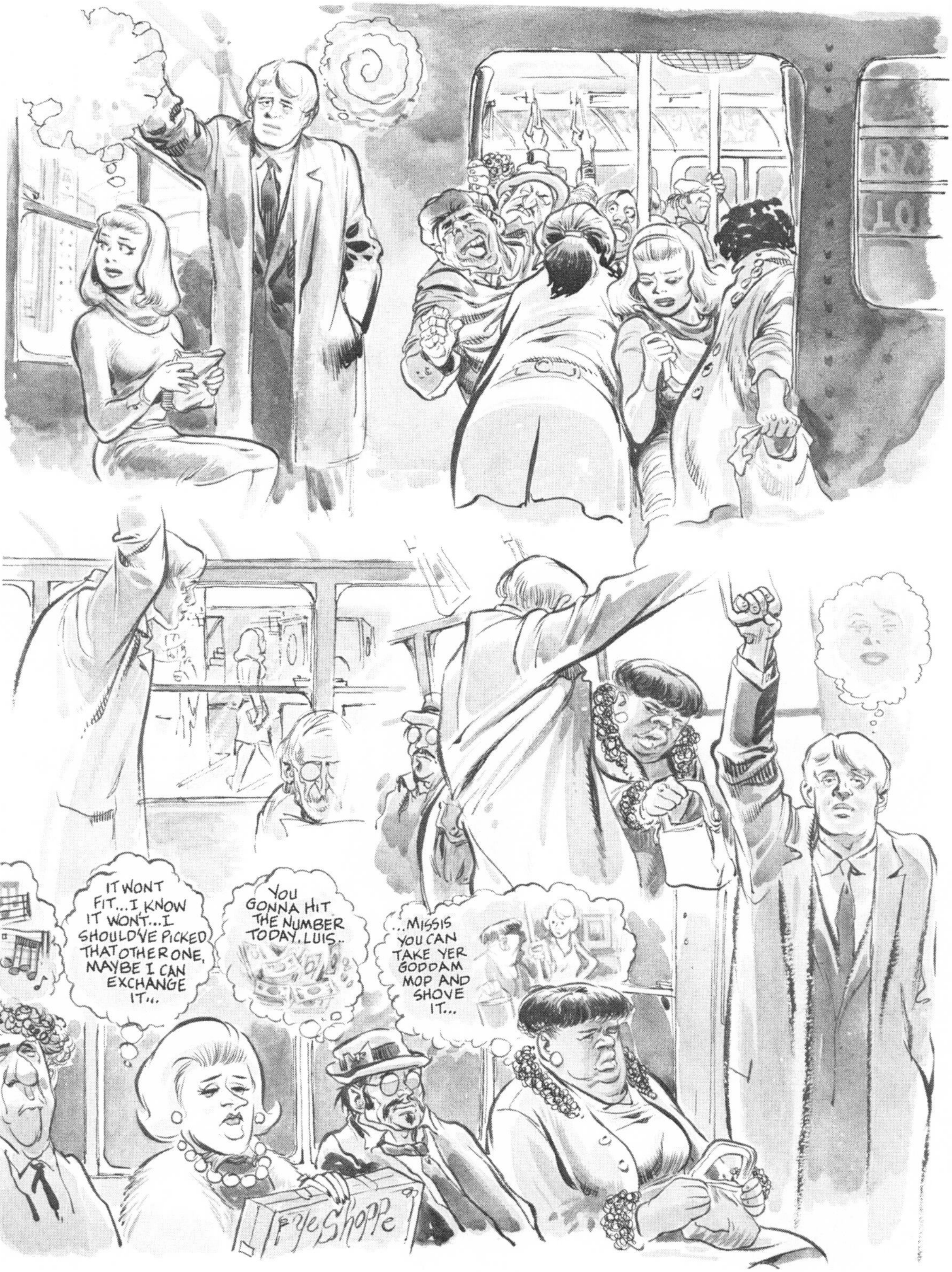
IT WONT FIT...I KNOW IT WON'T...I SHOULD'VE PICKED THAT OTHER ONE, MAYBE I CAN EXCHANGE IT...
YOU GONNA HIT THE NUMBER TODAY, LUIS..
...MISSIS YOU CAN TAKE YER GODDAM MOP AND SHOVE IT...

THEATER

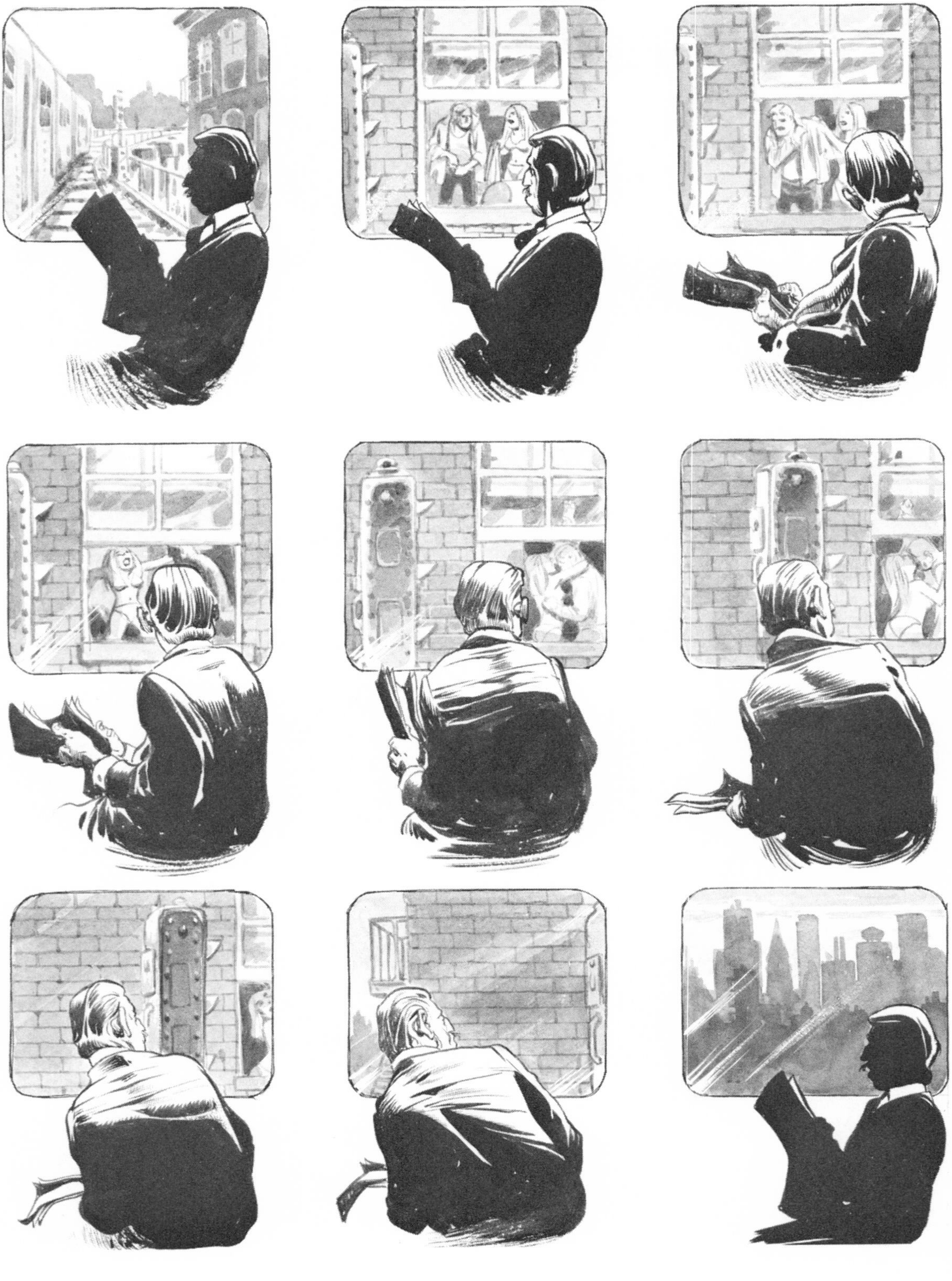

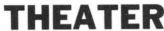

ART

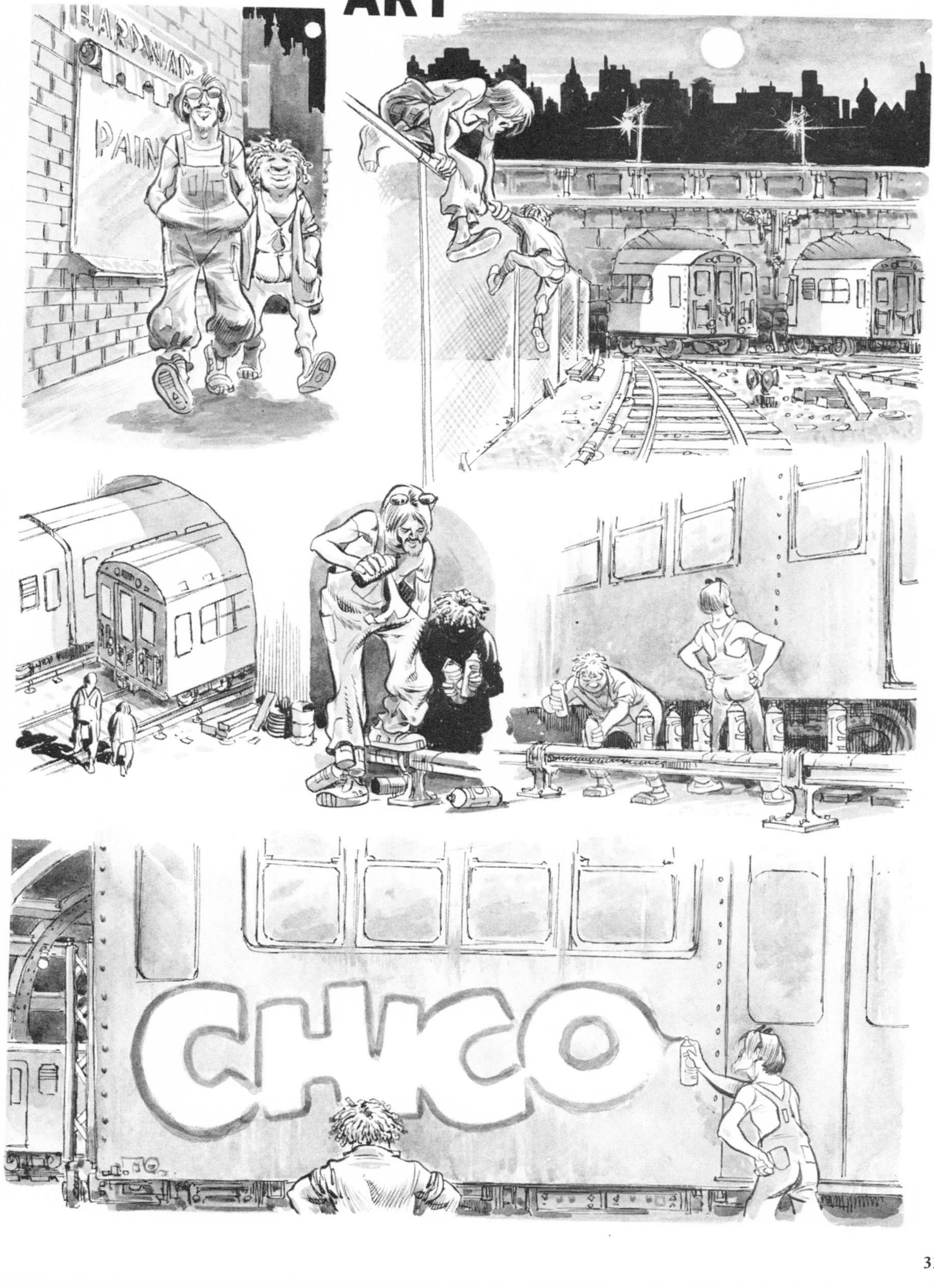
CHICO

NIGHT RIDER

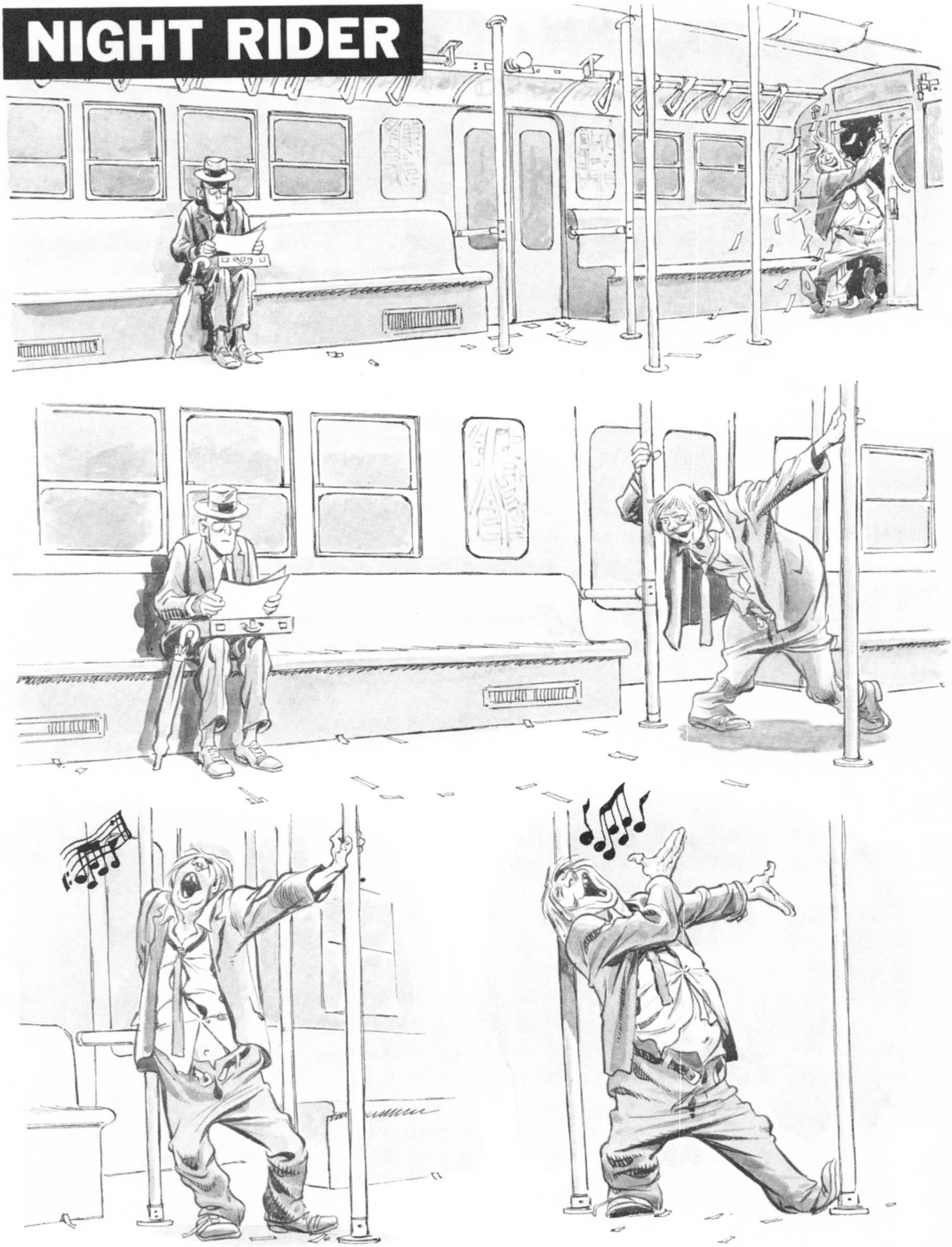

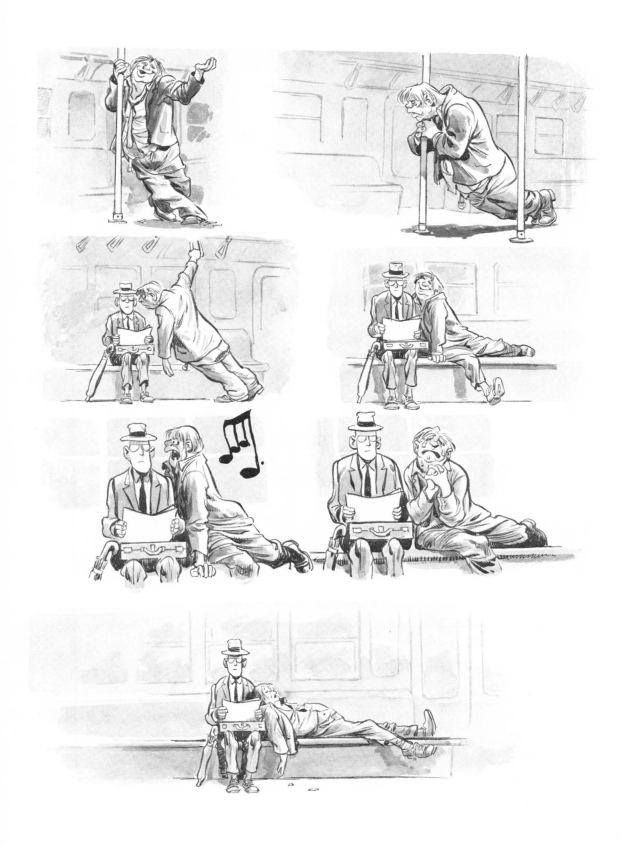

BLACKOUT

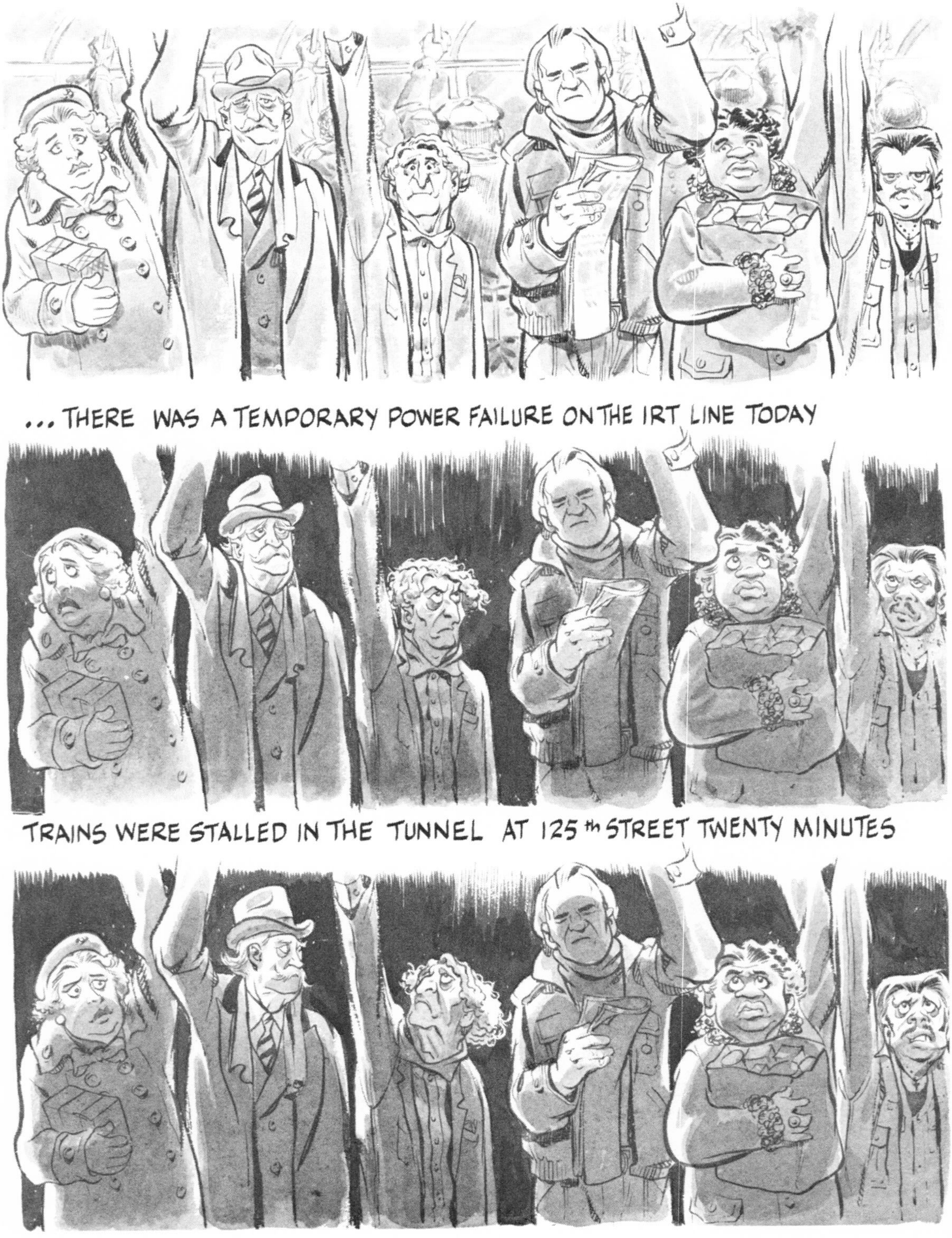

...THERE WAS A TEMPORARY POWER FAILURE ON THE IRT LINE TODAY
TRAINS WERE STALLED IN THE TUNNEL AT 125th STREET TWENTY MINUTES

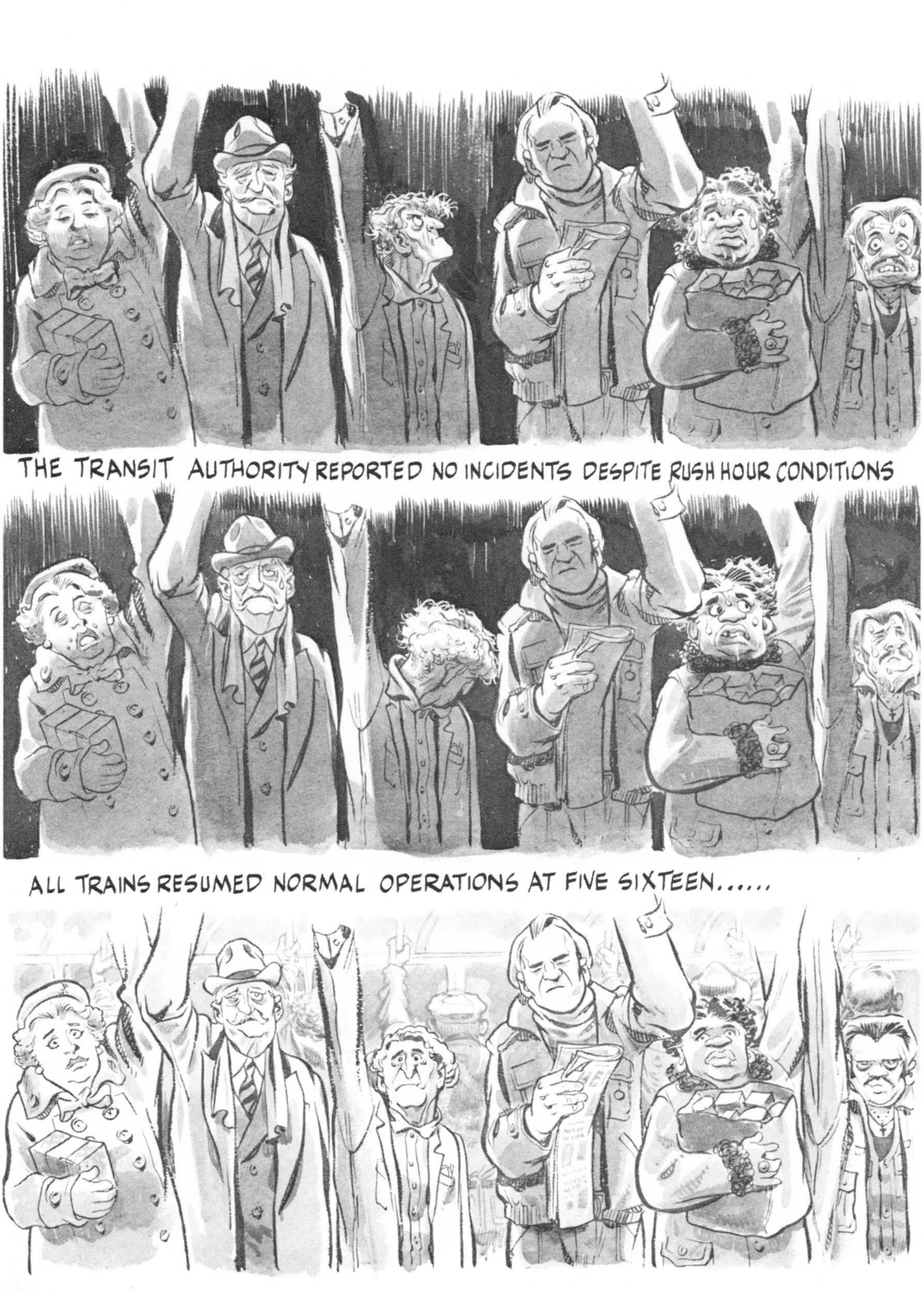
THE TRANSIT AUTHORITY REPORTED NO INCIDENTS DESPITE RUSH HOUR CONDITIONS
ALL TRAINS RESUMED NORMAL OPERATIONS AT FIVE SIXTEEN......

THE LAST MAN

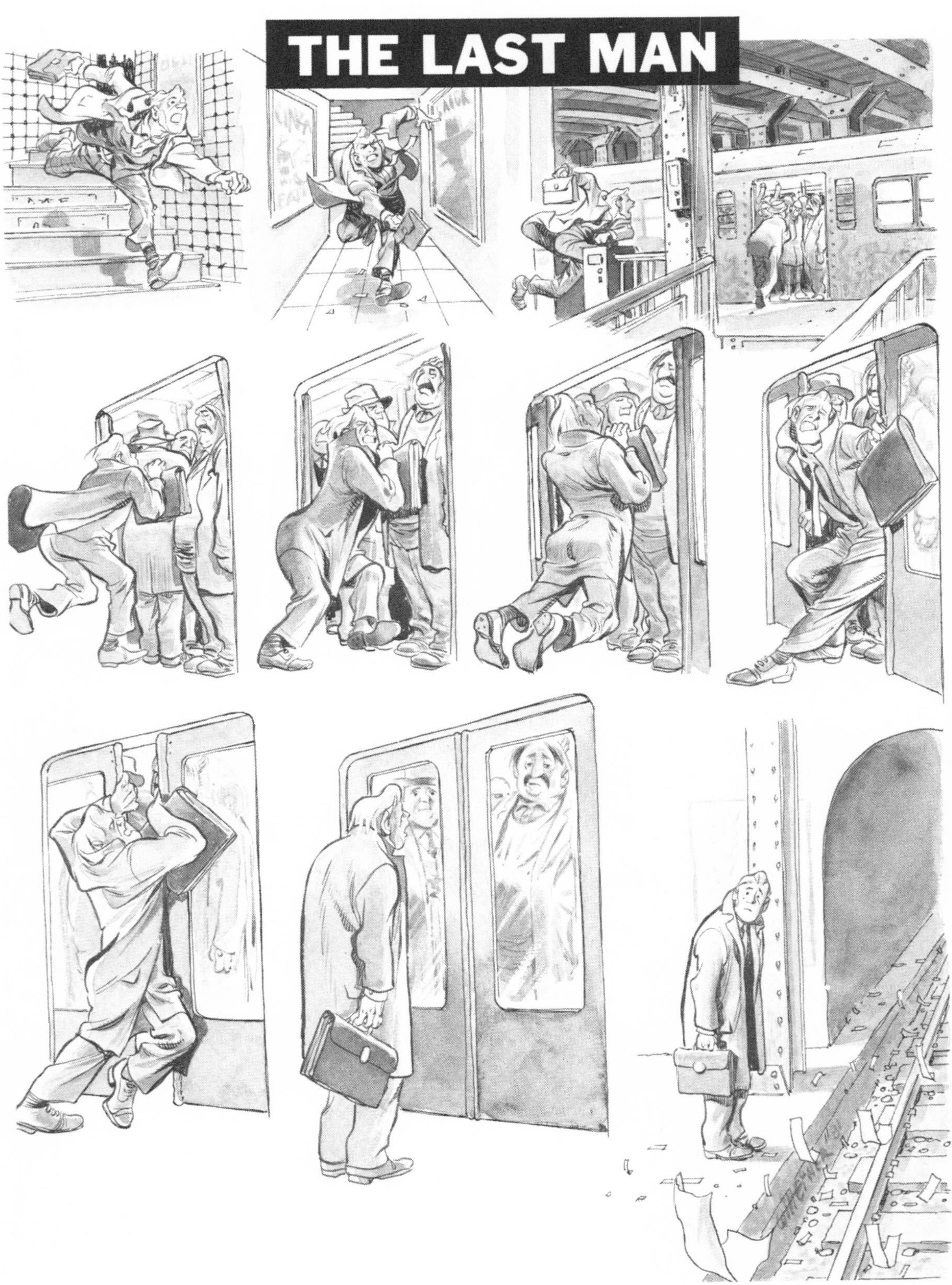

FELD'S
COATS
CLOTHING
SAM
SAMS UNDERSHIRTS
GARMENTS
FABRIC

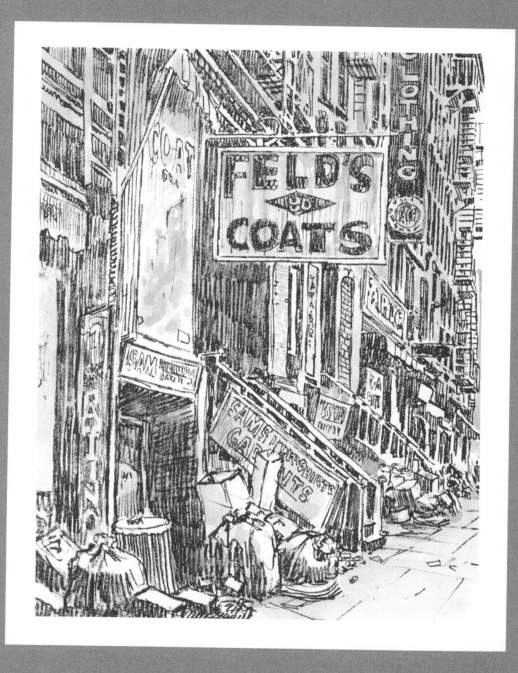

GARBAGE

THE BIG CITY
IS, AFTER ALL,
A HIVE
OF CONCRETE AND STEEL
IN WHICH LIVING THINGS
SWARM.
DEPOSITING,
IN THE COURSE
OF THEIR LIVES,
THE RESIDUE
OF THEIR EXISTENCE
IN THE COUNTLESS
GARBAGE CANS
THAT SIT DUMBLY
AMID THE SWIRL.
BATTERED URNS,
THE FINAL
REPOSITORY
OF YESTERDAY'S
STUFF.

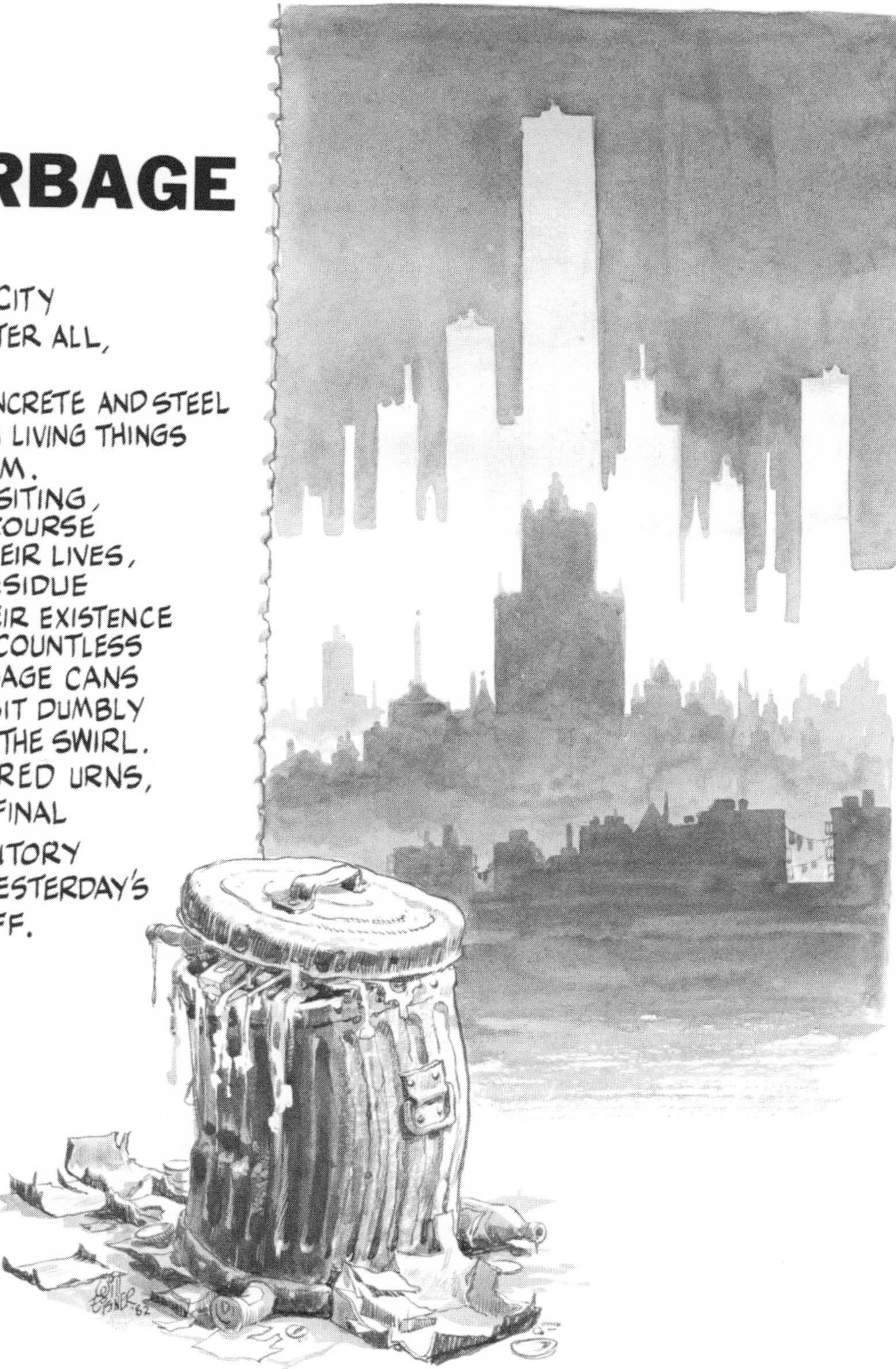

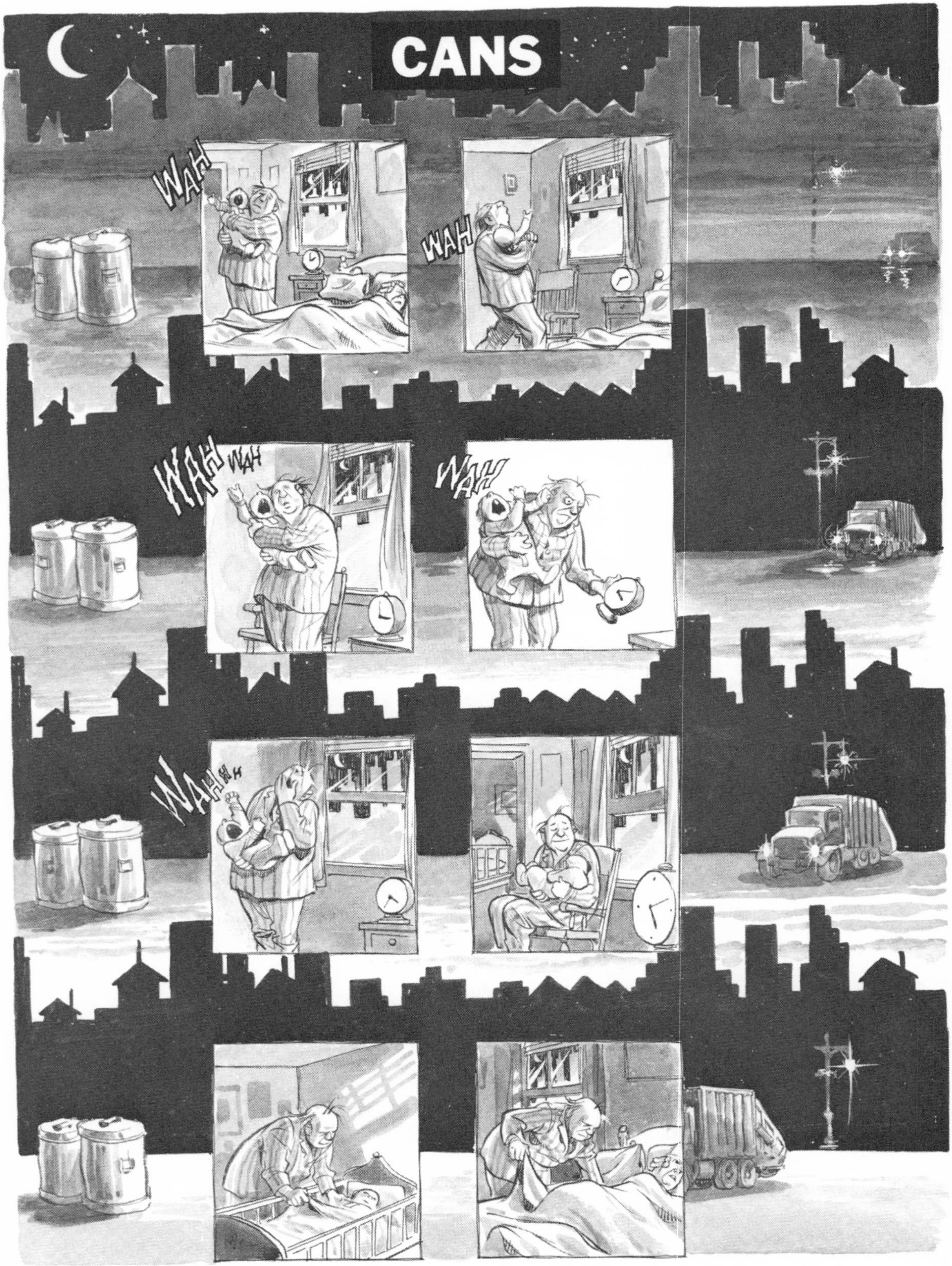
CANS
WAH
WAH
WAH
WAH
WAH

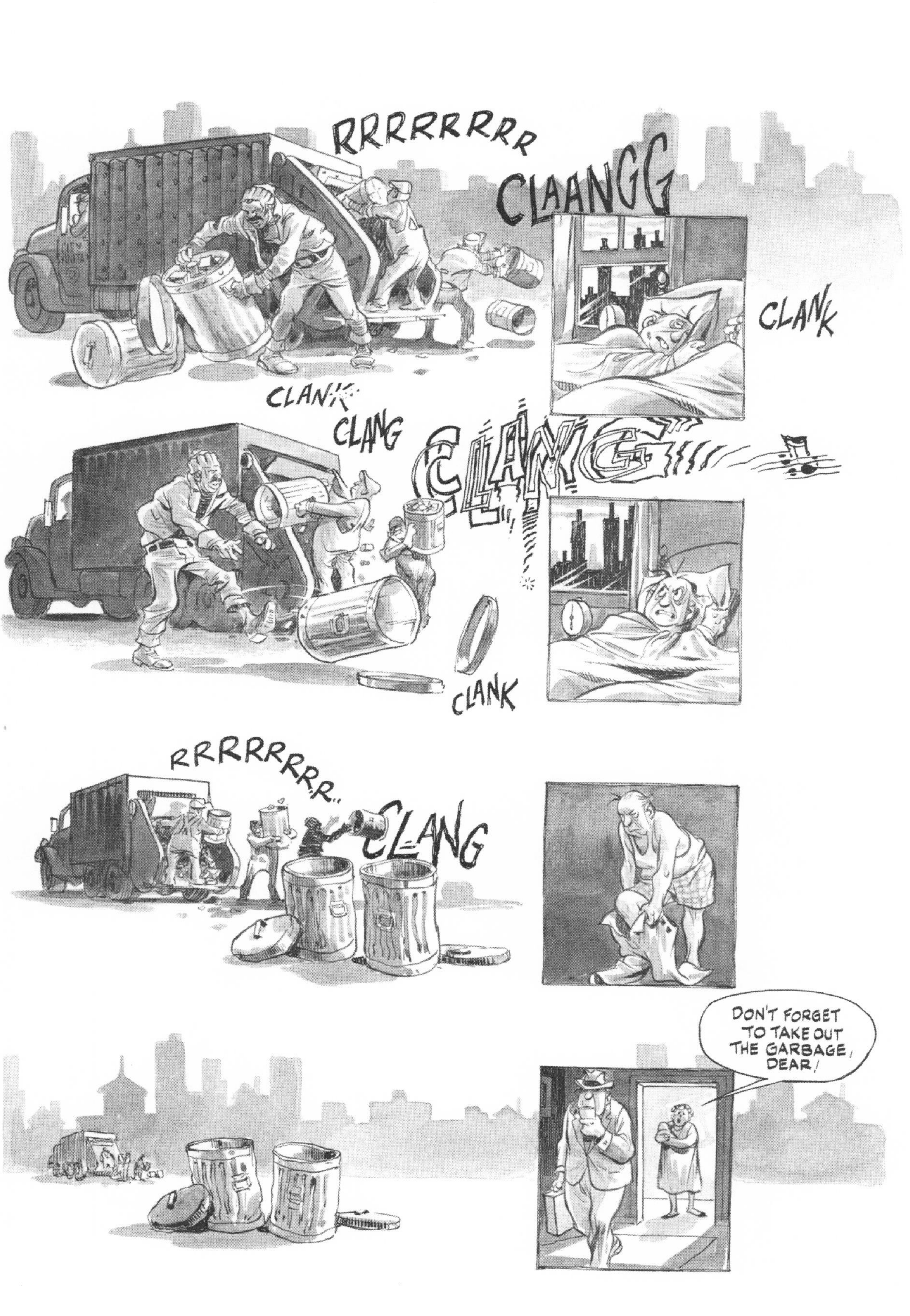
RRRRRRRRR
CLAANGG
CLANK
CLANK
CLANG
CLANG
CLANK
RRRRRRRRR..
CLANG
DON'T FORGET TO TAKE OUT THE GARBAGE, DEAR!

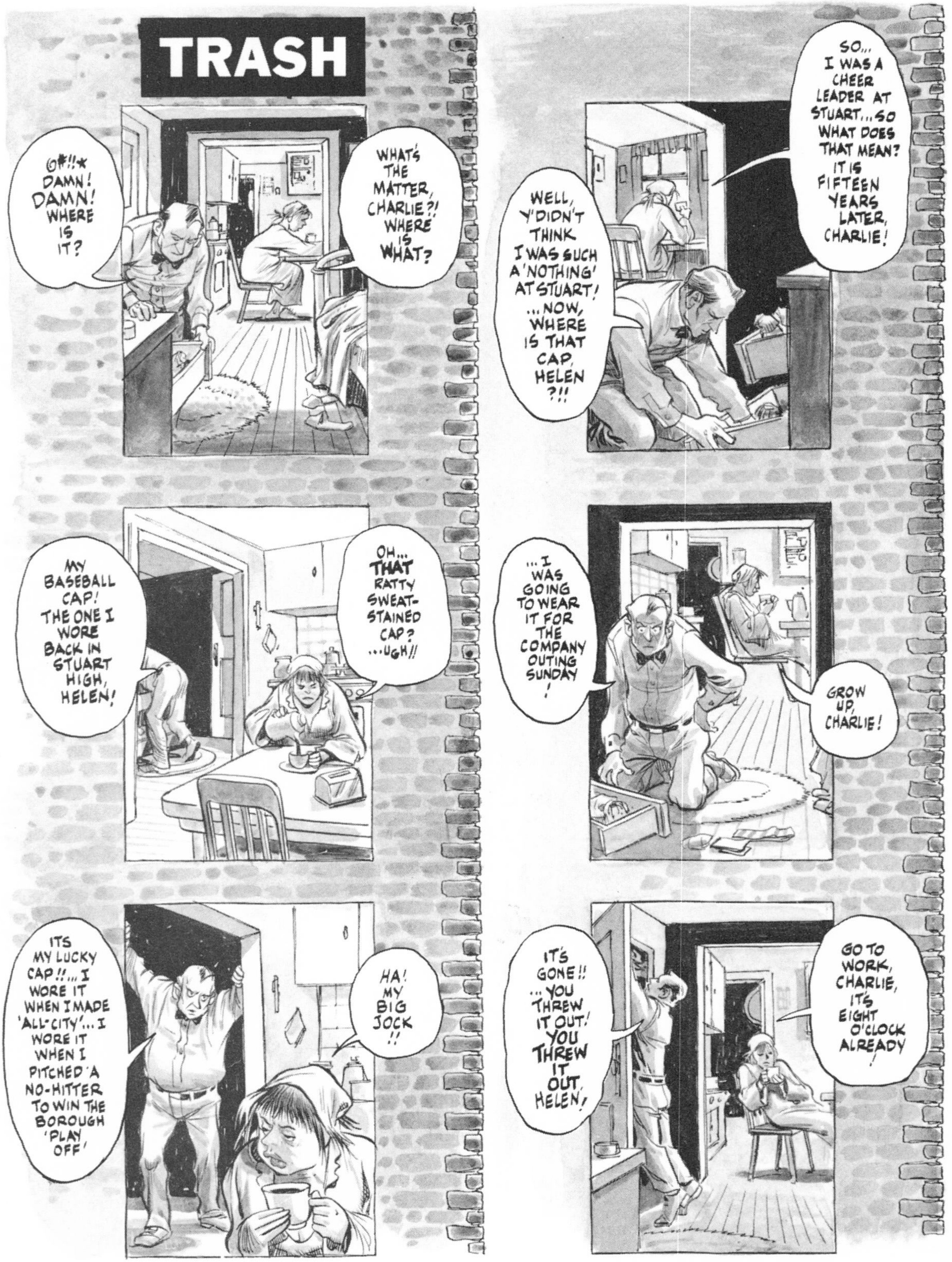
TRASH
@#!!* DAMN! DAMN! WHERE IS IT?
WHAT'S THE MATTER, CHARLIE?! WHERE IS WHAT?
MY BASEBALL CAP! THE ONE I WORE BACK IN STUART HIGH, HELEN!
OH... THAT RATTY SWEAT-STAINED CAP? ...UGH!!
ITS MY LUCKY CAP!!... I WORE IT WHEN I MADE 'ALL-CITY'... I WORE IT WHEN I PITCHED A NO-HITTER TO WIN THE BOROUGH 'PLAY OFF'
HA! MY BIG JOCK!!
WELL, Y'DIDN'T THINK I WAS SUCH A 'NOTHING' AT STUART! ...NOW, WHERE IS THAT CAP, HELEN?!!
SO... I WAS A CHEER LEADER AT STUART... SO WHAT DOES THAT MEAN? IT IS FIFTEEN YEARS LATER, CHARLIE!
...I WAS GOING TO WEAR IT FOR THE COMPANY OUTING SUNDAY!
GROW UP, CHARLIE!
IT'S GONE!! ...YOU THREW IT OUT! YOU THREW IT OUT, HELEN!
GO TO WORK, CHARLIE, IT'S EIGHT O'CLOCK ALREADY!

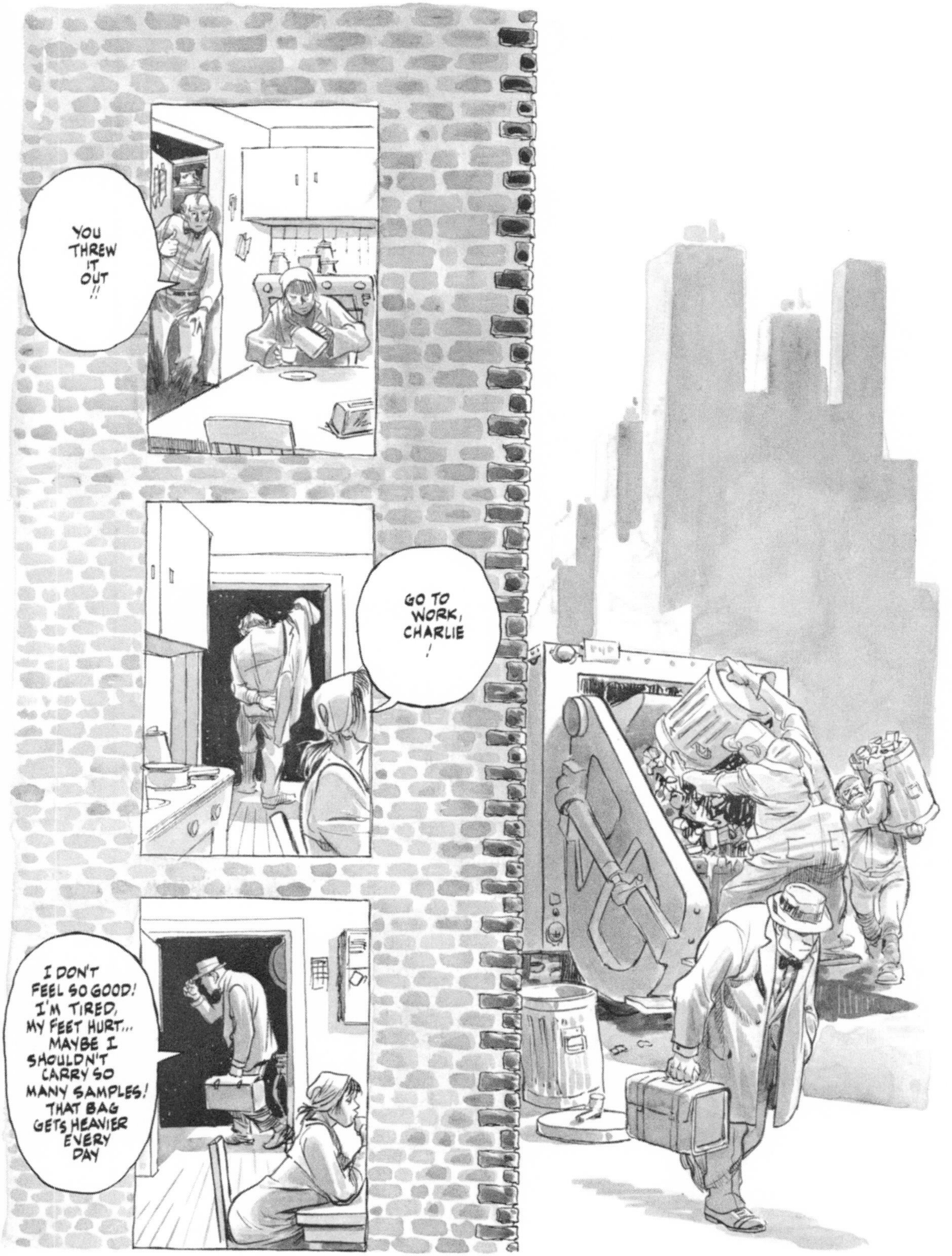
YOU THREW IT OUT !!
GO TO WORK, CHARLIE !
I DON'T FEEL SO GOOD! I'M TIRED, MY FEET HURT... MAYBE I SHOULDN'T CARRY SO MANY SAMPLES! THAT BAG GETS HEAVIER EVERY DAY

THE SOURCE

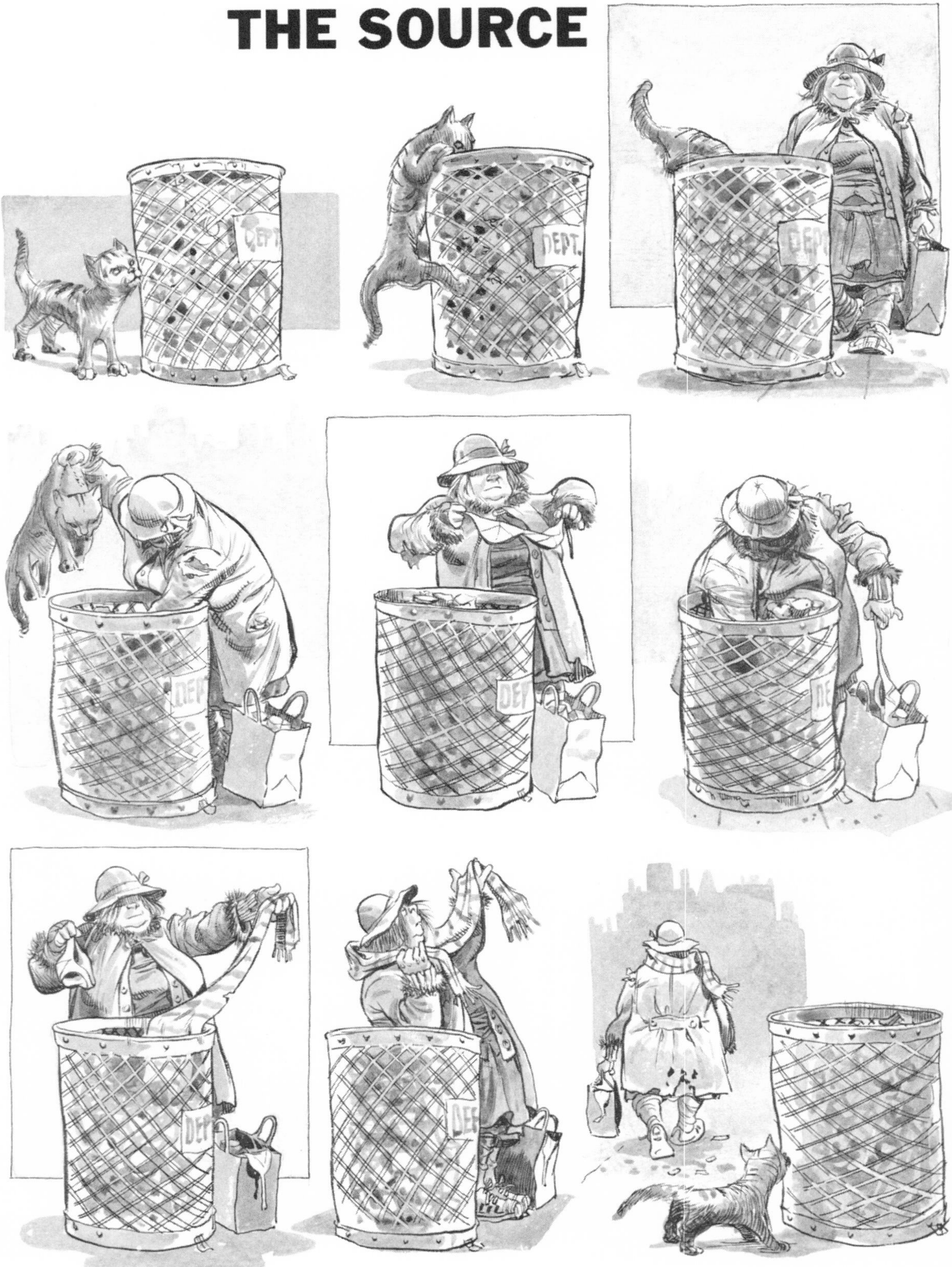
DEPT.

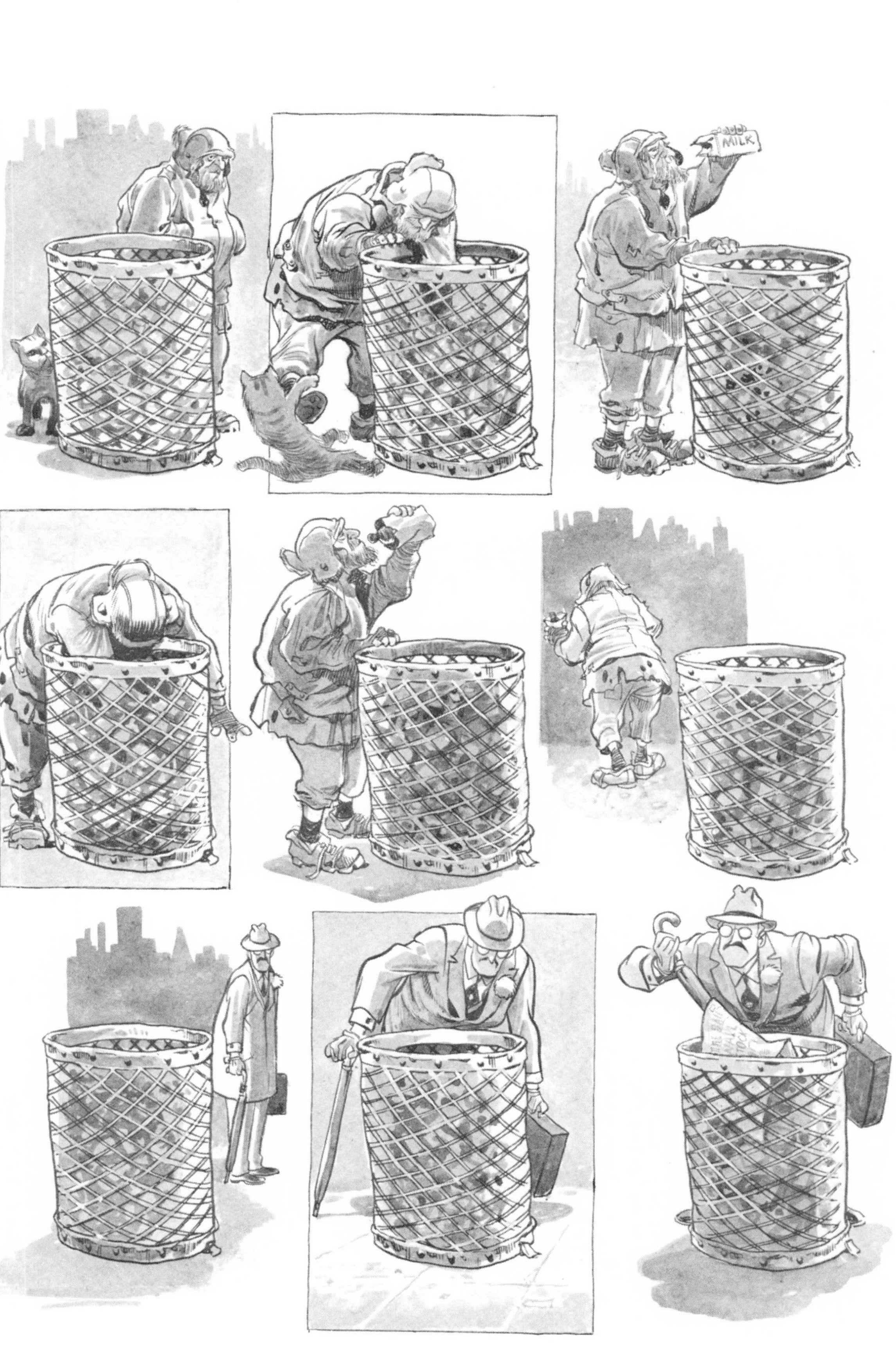
MILK

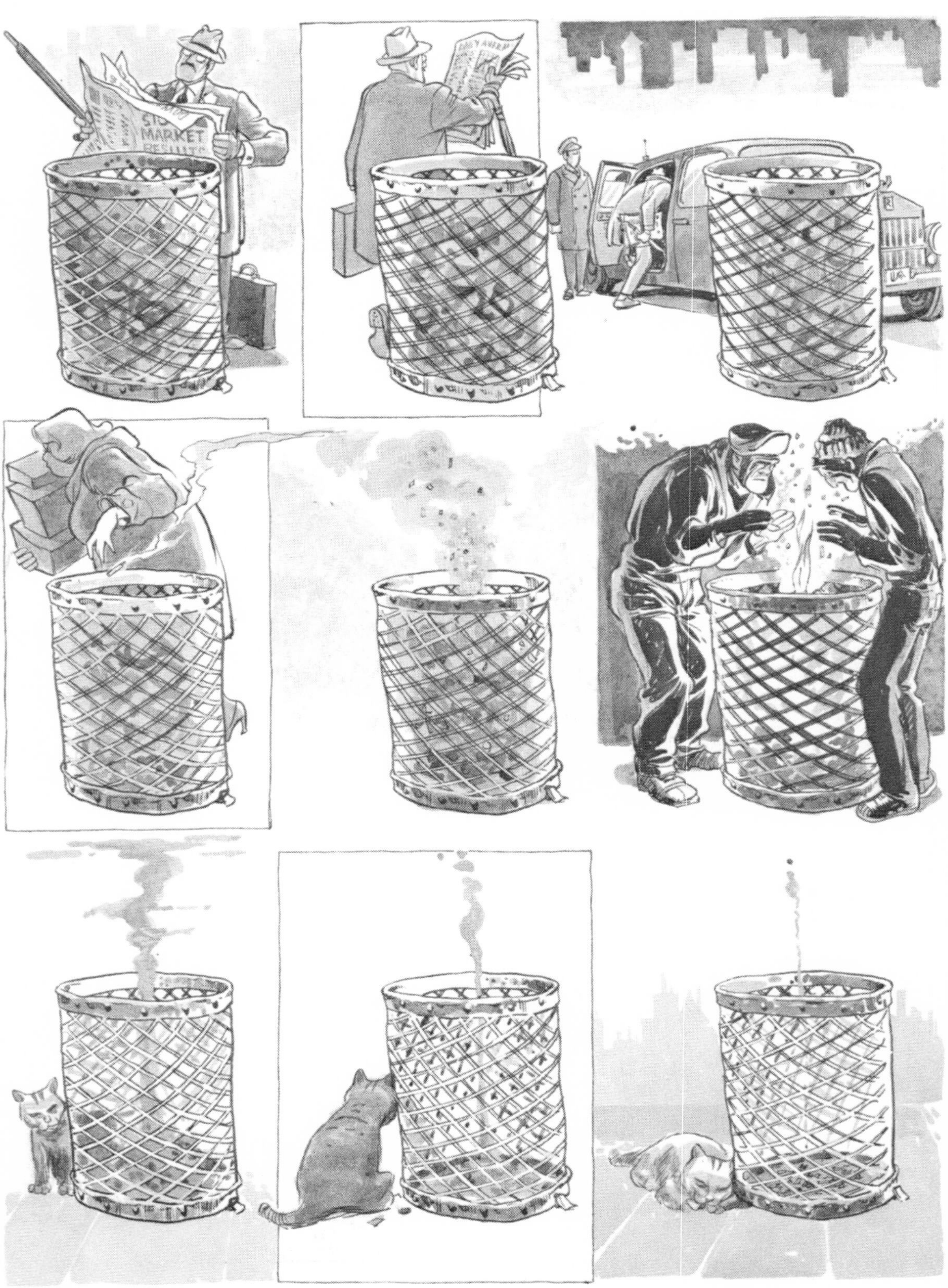
MARKET

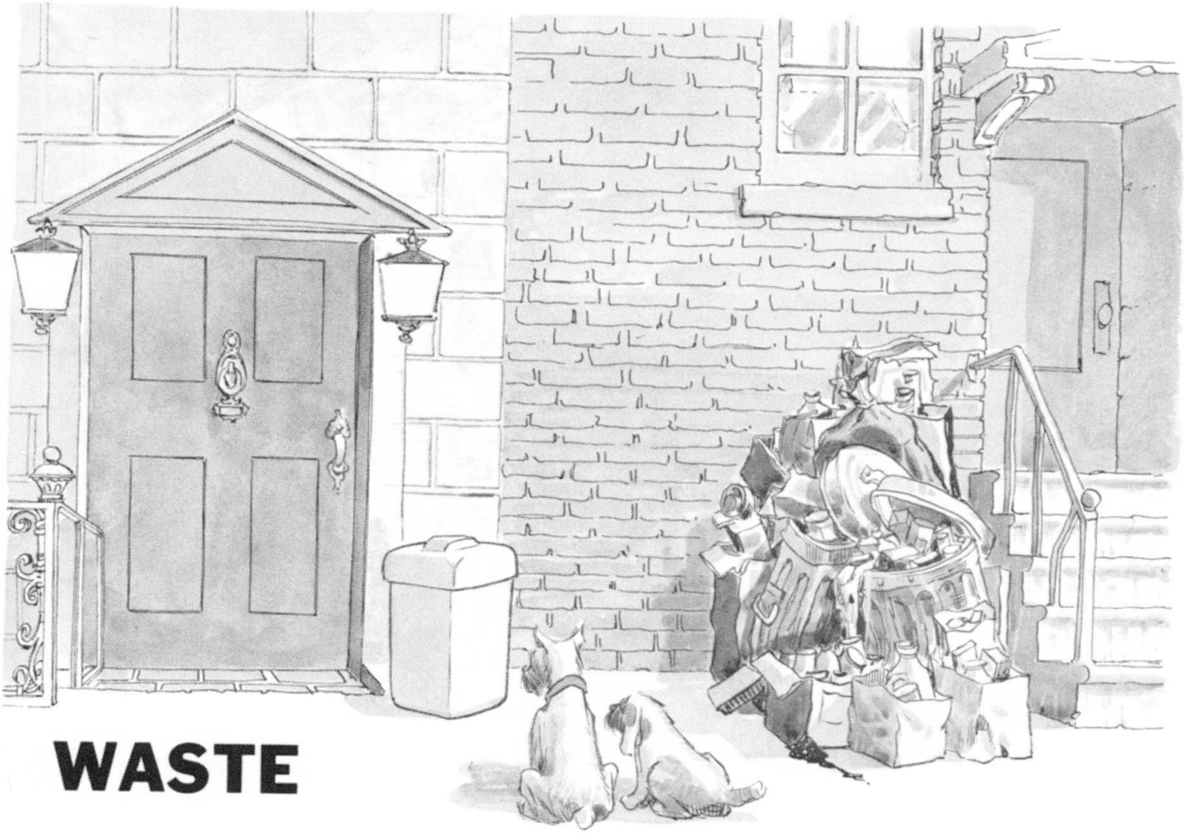

WASTE

WHY IS THE GARBAGE
OF THE RICH
ALWAYS SMALLER THAN
THE GARBAGE OF THE POOR ?

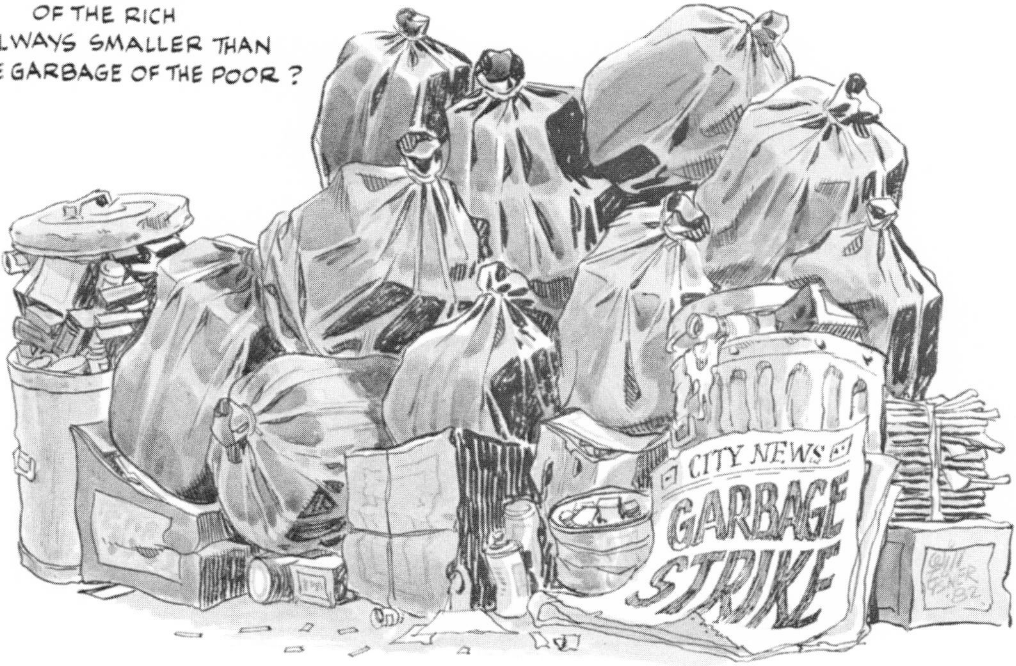
CITY NEWS
GARBAGE
STRIKE

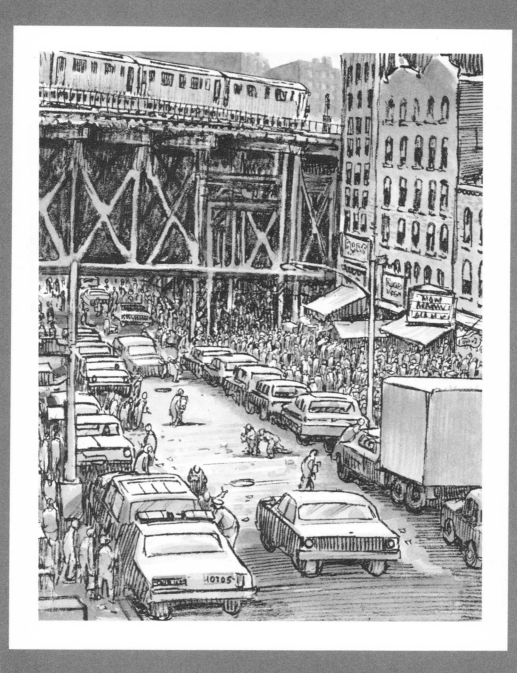

STREET MUSIC

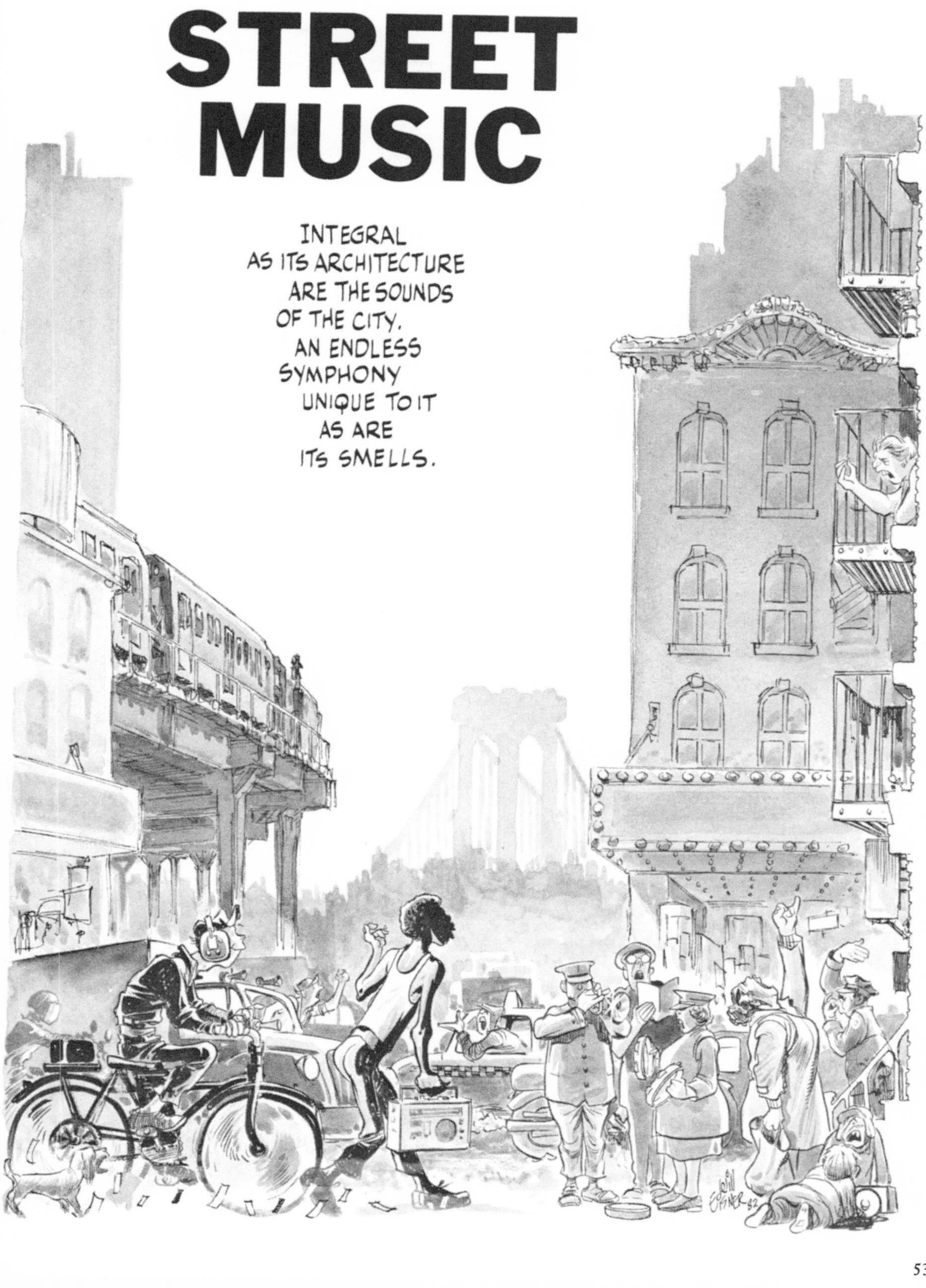
INTEGRAL
AS ITS ARCHITECTURE
ARE THE SOUNDS
OF THE CITY.
AN ENDLESS
SYMPHONY
UNIQUE TO IT
AS ARE
ITS SMELLS.

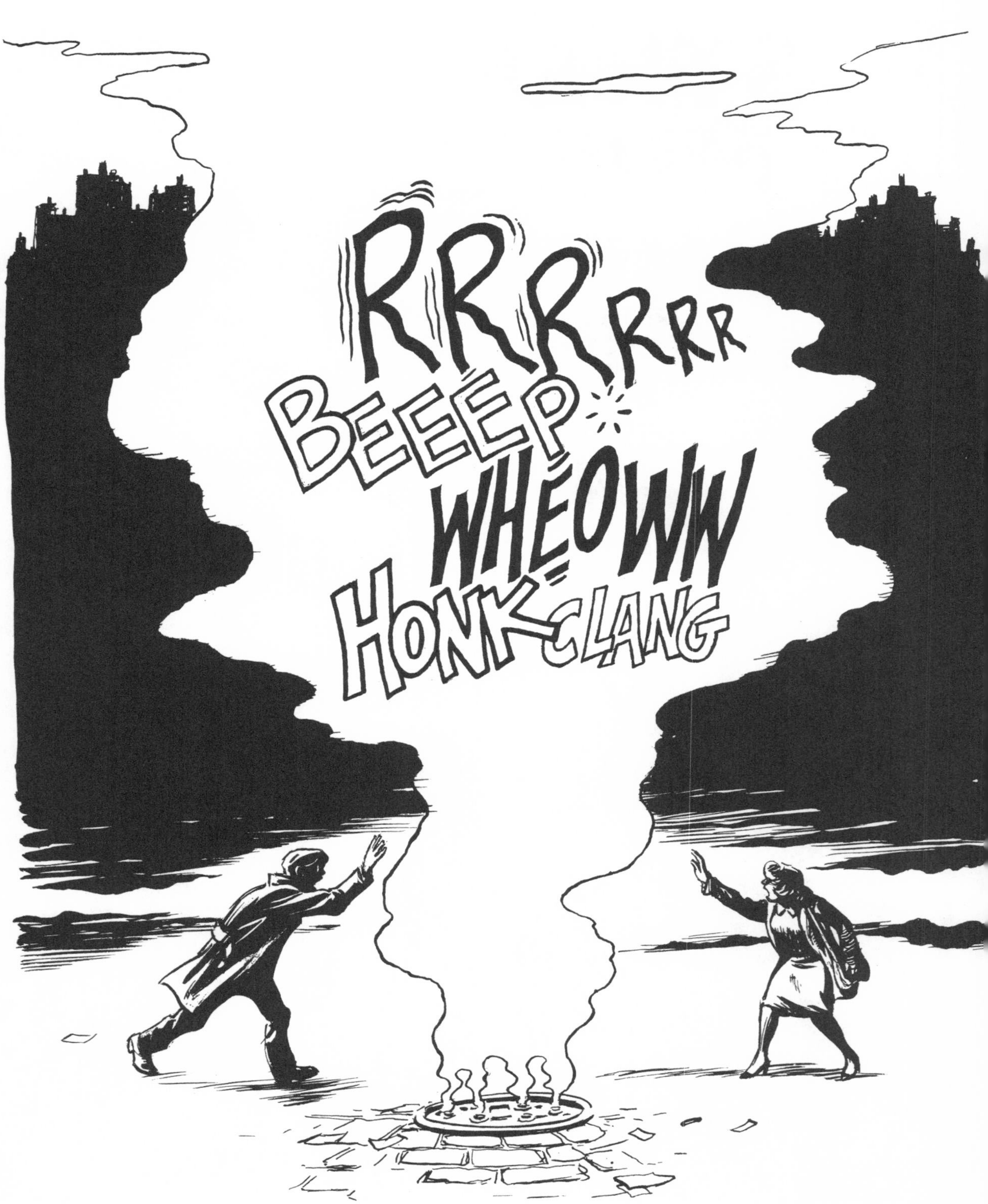
RRRRRR
BEEEP
WHEOWW
HONK
CLANG

LOVE SONG FORTISSIMO

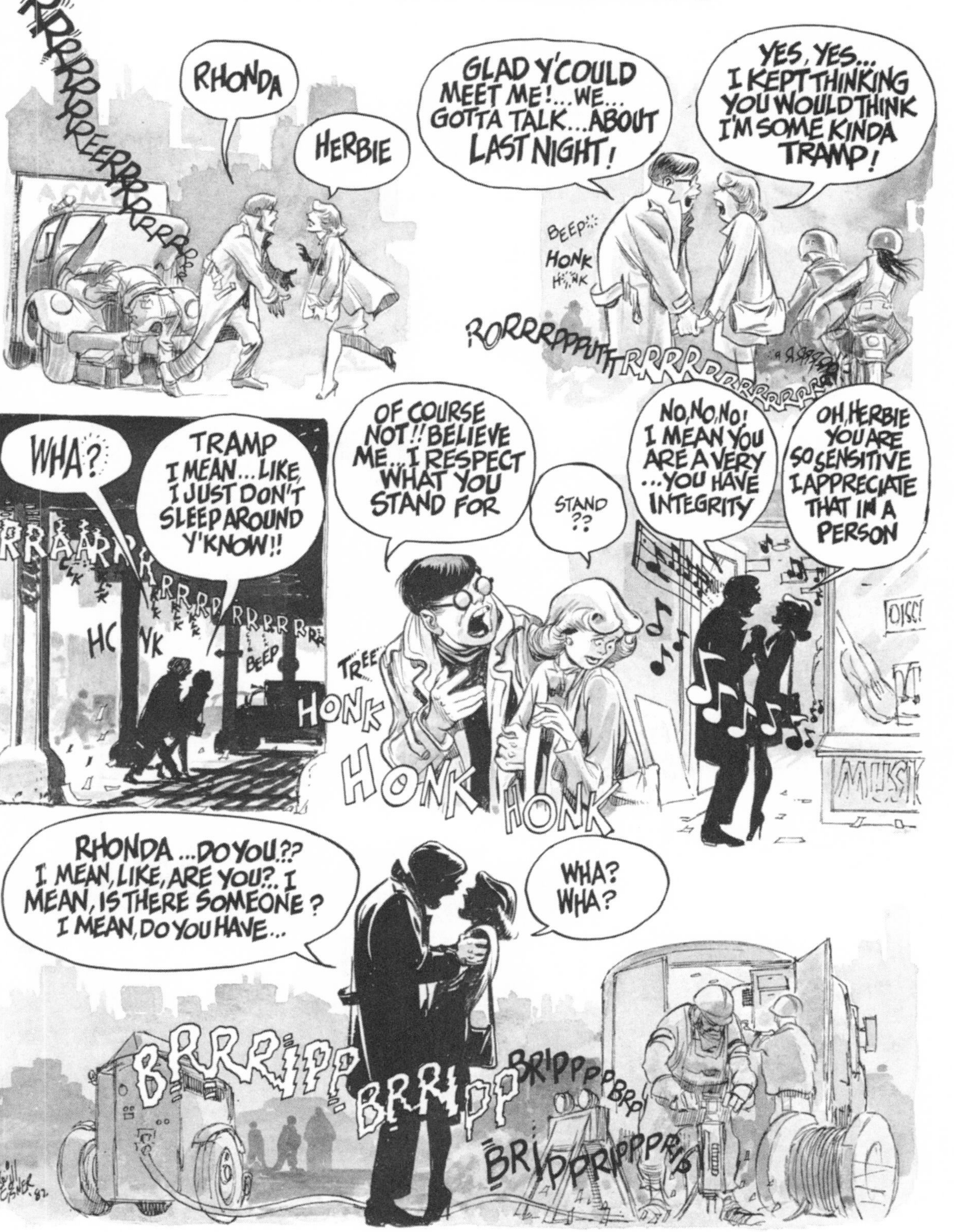
RRRRRRRREERRRRRRR
RHONDA
HERBIE
GLAD Y'COULD MEET ME!...WE... GOTTA TALK...ABOUT LAST NIGHT!
YES, YES... I KEPT THINKING YOU WOULD THINK I'M SOME KINDA TRAMP!
BEEP
HONK
HONK
RORRRPPPUTTTRRRRRRRRRRR
WHA?
TRAMP I MEAN...LIKE, I JUST DON'T SLEEP AROUND Y'KNOW!!
RRAARRRRRRRRR
HONK
BEEP
OF COURSE NOT!! BELIEVE ME...I RESPECT WHAT YOU STAND FOR
STAND ??
NO, NO, NO! I MEAN YOU ARE A VERY ...YOU HAVE INTEGRITY
OH, HERBIE YOU ARE SO SENSITIVE I APPRECIATE THAT I'M A PERSON
TREE
HONK
HONK
HONK
DISC
MUSIK
RHONDA...DO YOU.?? I MEAN, LIKE, ARE YOU?..I MEAN, IS THERE SOMEONE? I MEAN, DO YOU HAVE...
WHA? WHA?
BRRRIPP
BRRIPP
BRIPPPPBRP
BRIPPPRIPPPRIP
Will Eisner '82

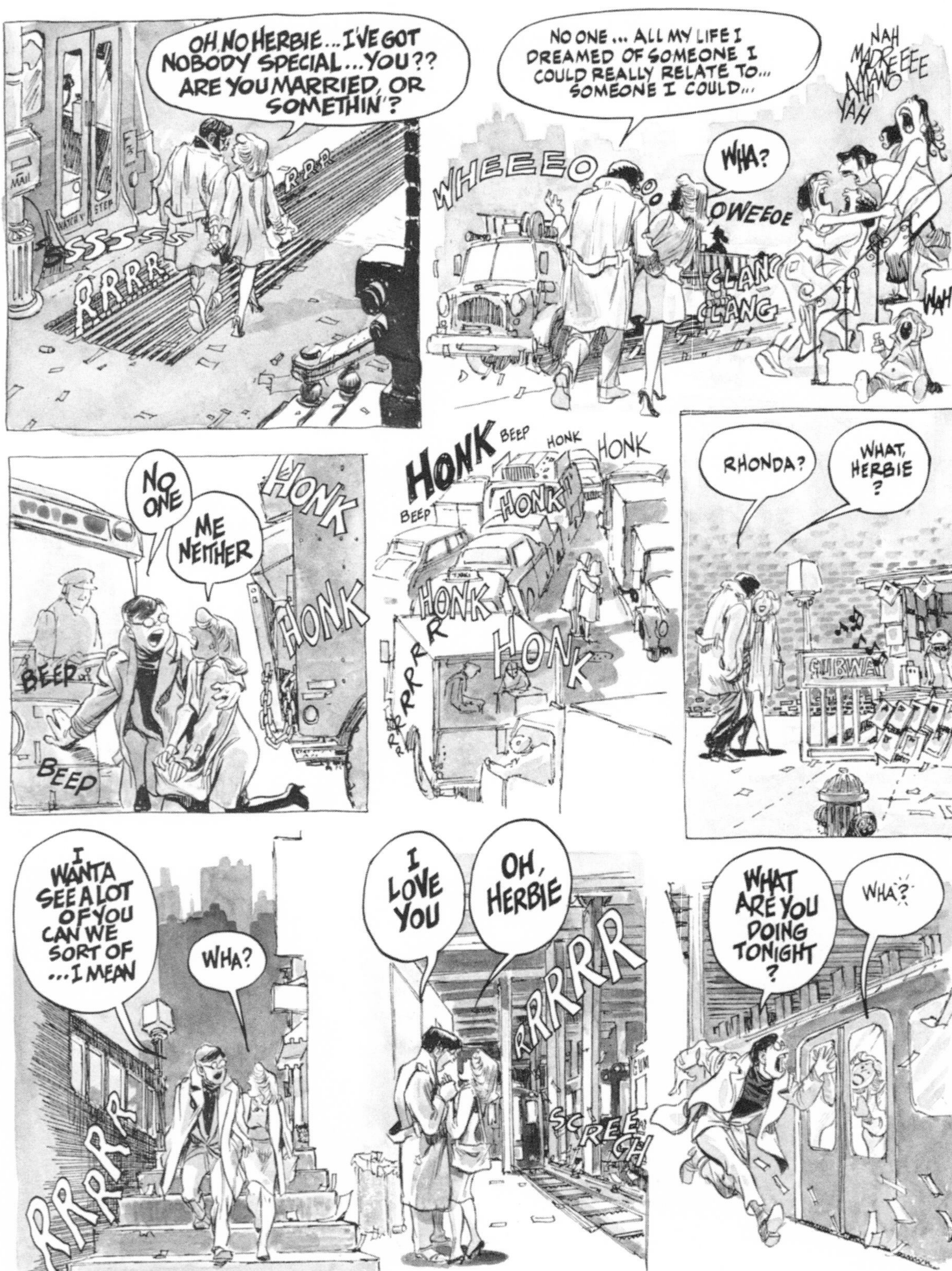
OH, NO HERBIE... I'VE GOT NOBODY SPECIAL... YOU?? ARE YOU MARRIED, OR SOMETHIN'?
RRR
SSSSSS
RRRR
NO ONE... ALL MY LIFE I DREAMED OF SOMEONE I COULD REALLY RELATE TO... SOMEONE I COULD...
WHEEEEO
WHA?
OWEEOE
CLANG
CLANG
NAH
MADRE EEEE
YAH
WAH
NO ONE
ME NEITHER
HONK
HONK
BEEP
BEEP
HONK
BEEP
HONK
HONK
BEEP
HONK
HONK
HONK
RRRRRR
RHONDA?
WHAT, HERBIE?
SUBWAY
I WANTA SEE A LOT OF YOU CAN WE SORT OF ...I MEAN
WHA?
RRRR
I LOVE YOU
OH, HERBIE
RRRRR
SCREECH
WHAT ARE YOU DOING TONIGHT?
WHA?

PIANISSIMO

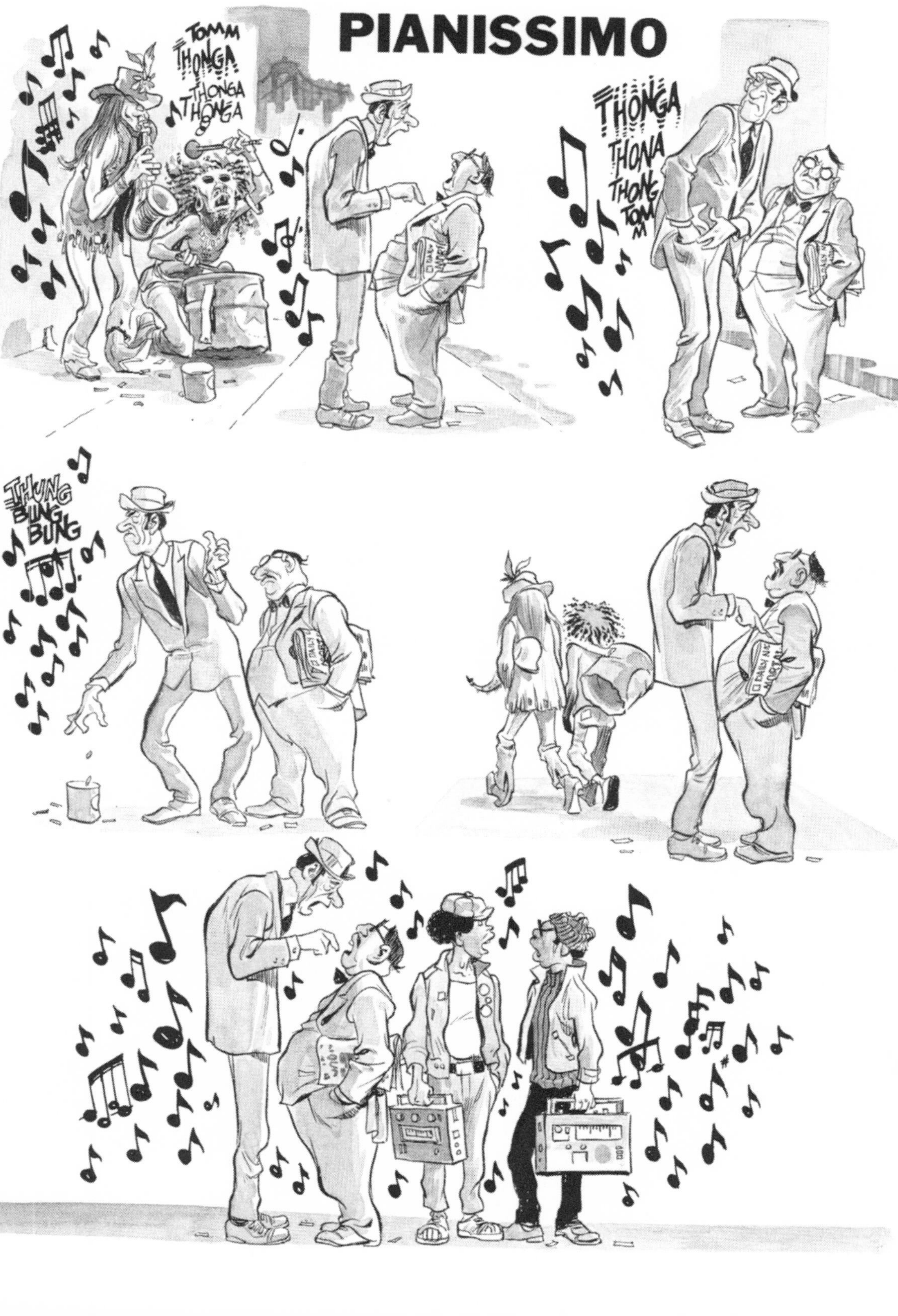
TOMM
THONGA
THONGA
THONGA
THONGA
THONA
THONG
TOM
THUNG
BUNG
BUNG

IN CONCERT

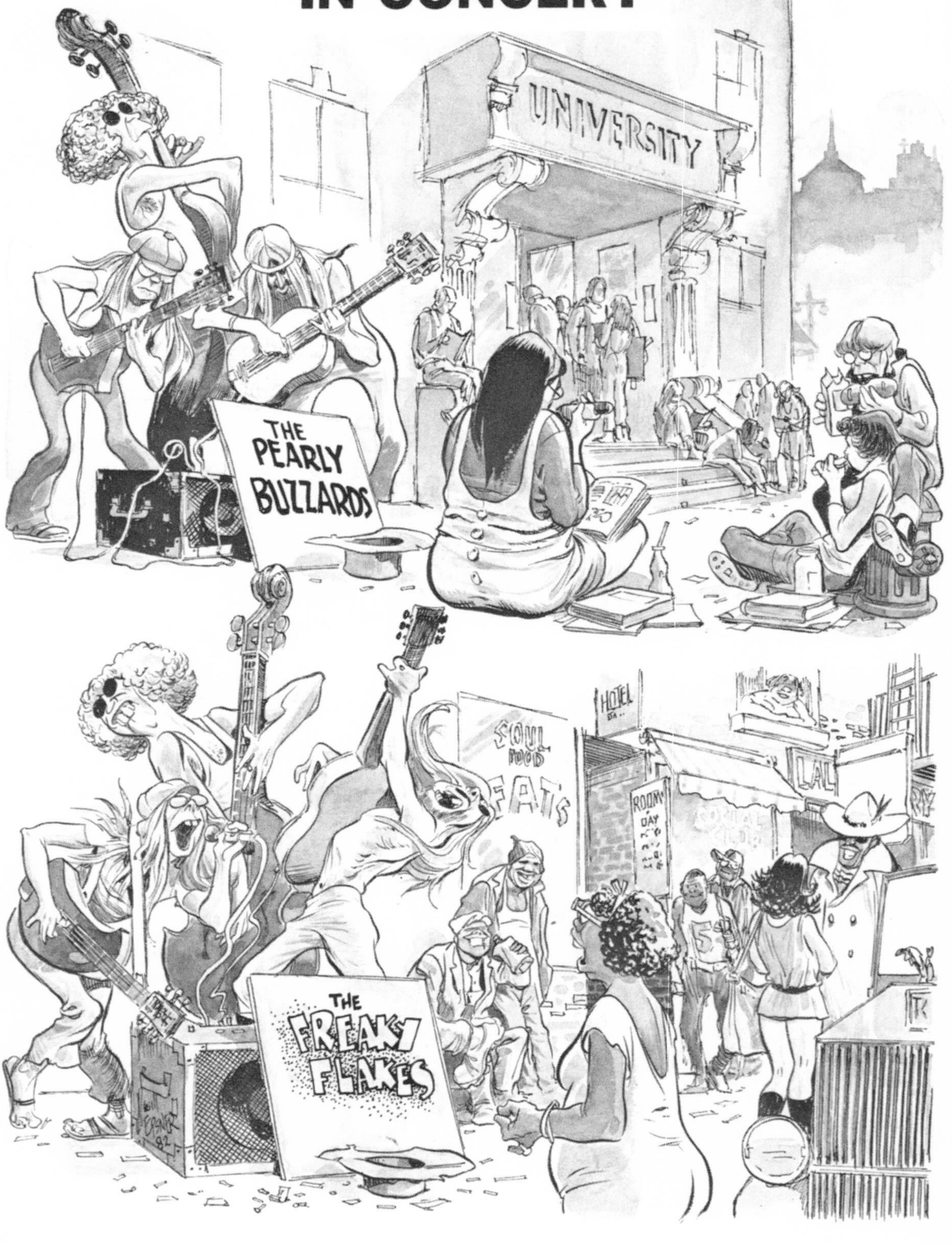
UNIVERSITY
THE PEARLY BUZZARDS
HOTEL
SOUL FOOD
FAT's
ROOMS DAY
THE FREAKY FLAKES

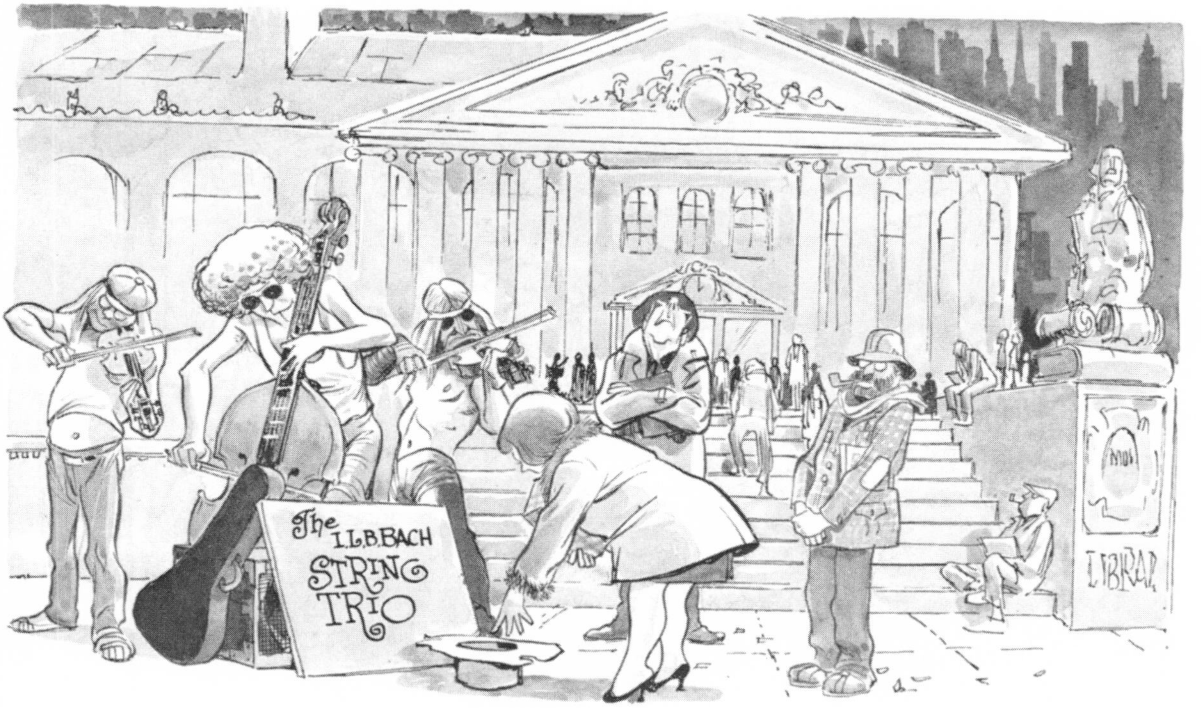
The I.L.B.BACH
STRING TRIO

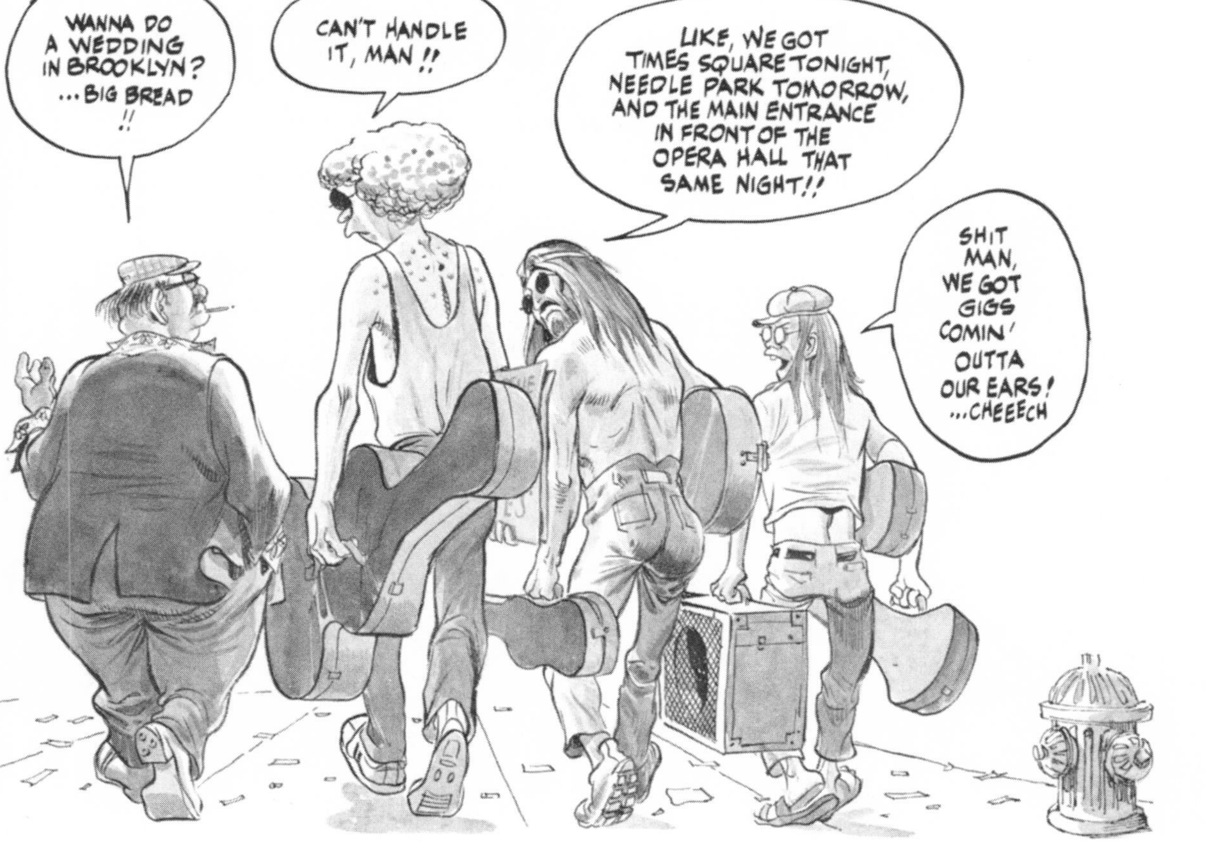
WANNA DO A WEDDING IN BROOKLYN? ...BIG BREAD !!
CAN'T HANDLE IT, MAN !!
LIKE, WE GOT TIMES SQUARE TONIGHT, NEEDLE PARK TOMORROW, AND THE MAIN ENTRANCE IN FRONT OF THE OPERA HALL THAT SAME NIGHT!!
SHIT MAN, WE GOT GIGS COMIN' OUTTA OUR EARS! ...CHEEECH

OPERA

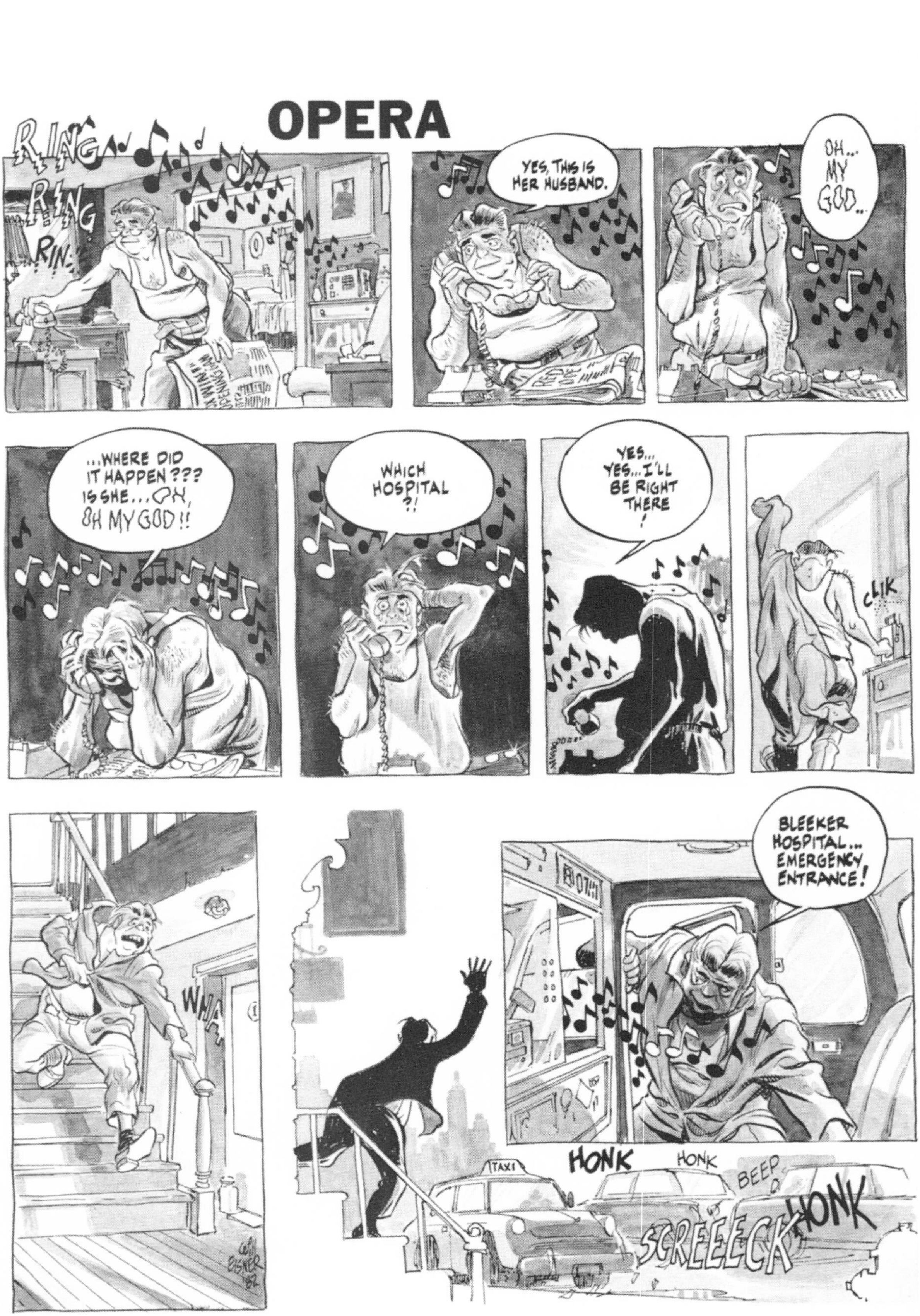
RING
RING
RIN
YES, THIS IS HER HUSBAND.
OH... MY GOD..
...WHERE DID IT HAPPEN??? IS SHE...OH, OH MY GOD!!
WHICH HOSPITAL ?!
YES... YES...I'LL BE RIGHT THERE !
CLIK
WHA
BLEEKER HOSPITAL... EMERGENCY ENTRANCE!
HONK
HONK
BEEP
SCREEECK
HONK
Will Eisner '82

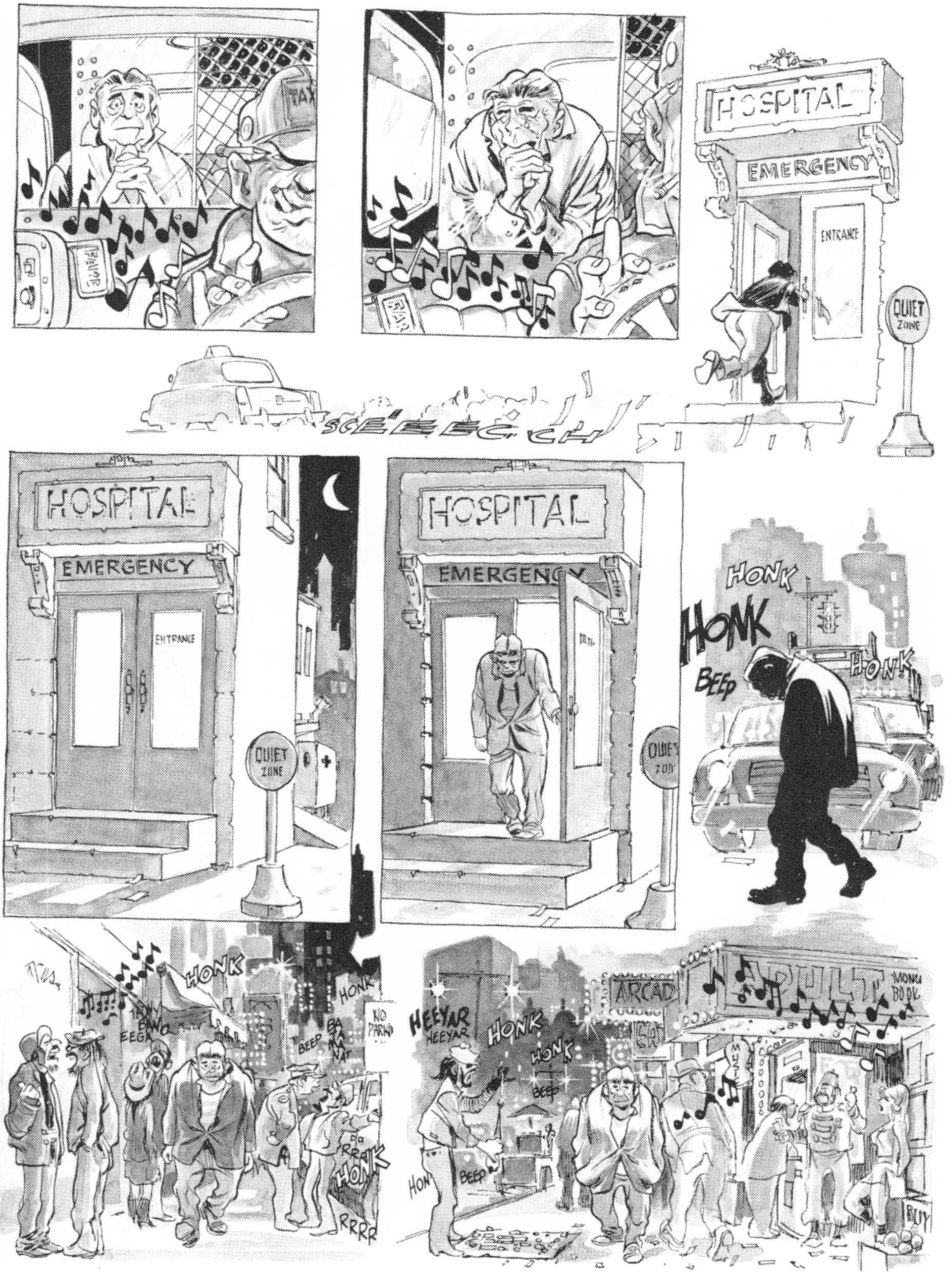
TAXI
HOSPITAL
EMERGENCY
ENTRANCE
QUIET ZONE
SCEEEECCH
HOSPITAL
EMERGENCY
ENTRANCE
QUIET ZONE
HOSPITAL
EMERGENCY
HONK
HONK
HONK
BEEP
HONK
HONK
BEEP
NO PARKING
HONK
RRRR
HEEYAR HEEYAR
HONK
HONK
BEEP
ARCADE
HON
BEEP
BUY

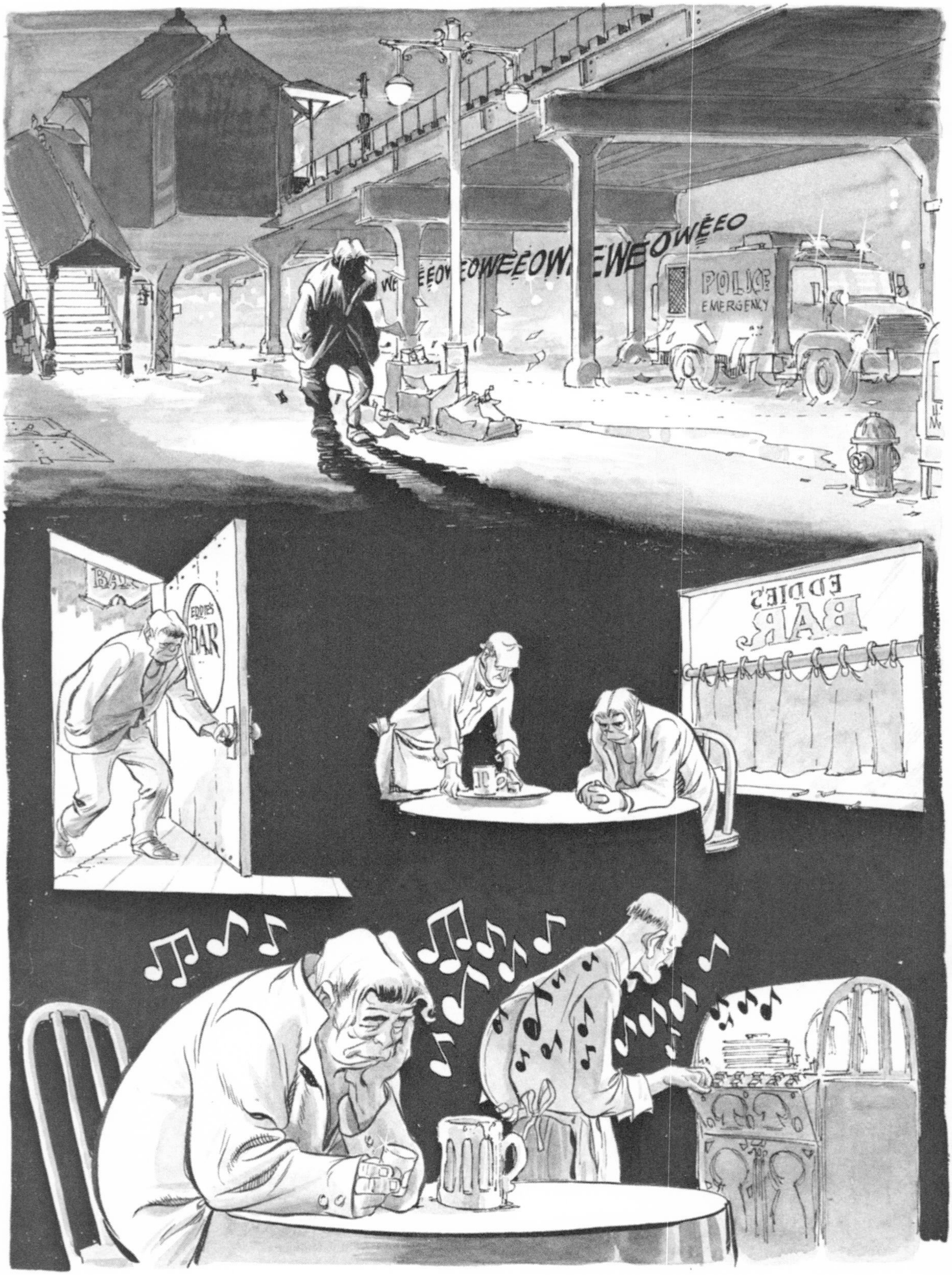
POLICE
EMERGENCY
EDDIE'S
BAR
EDDIE'S
BAR

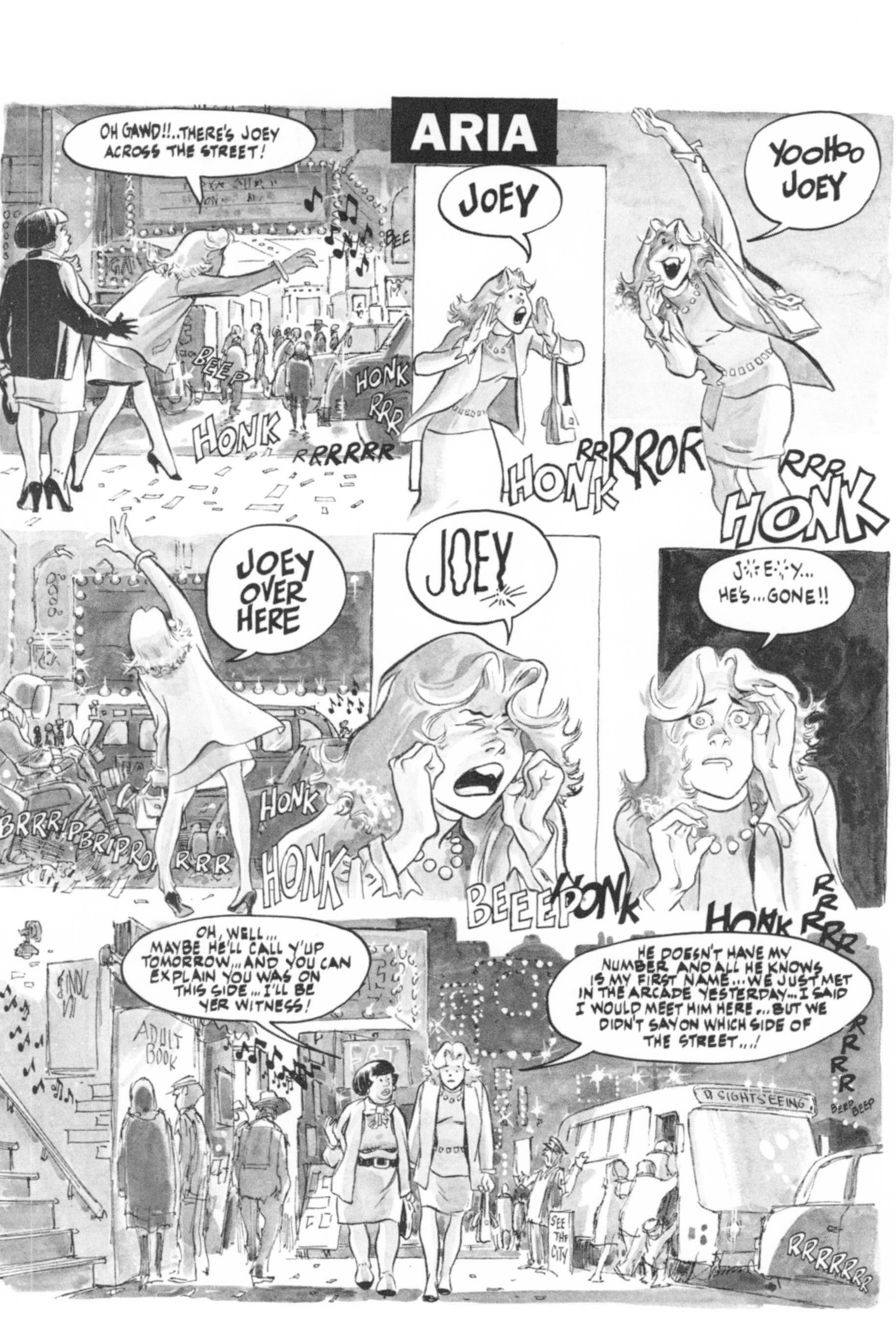
ARIA
OH GAWD!!..THERE'S JOEY ACROSS THE STREET!
BEEP
HONK
RRR
HONK
RRRRRR
JOEY
HONK
RRRROK
YOOHOO JOEY
RRR
HONK
JOEY OVER HERE
BRRRIP BRRIPROR
RRR
HONK
HONK
JOEY
J·O·E·Y... HE'S...GONE!!
BEEEP
HONK
HONK
RRRR
OH, WELL... MAYBE HE'LL CALL Y'UP TOMORROW...AND YOU CAN EXPLAIN YOU WAS ON THIS SIDE...I'LL BE YER WITNESS!
HE DOESN'T HAVE MY NUMBER AND ALL HE KNOWS IS MY FIRST NAME...WE JUST MET IN THE ARCADE YESTERDAY...I SAID I WOULD MEET HIM HERE...BUT WE DIDN'T SAY ON WHICH SIDE OF THE STREET...!
ADULT BOOK
SIGHTSEEING
SEE THE CITY
RRRR
BEEP BEEP
RRRRRRR

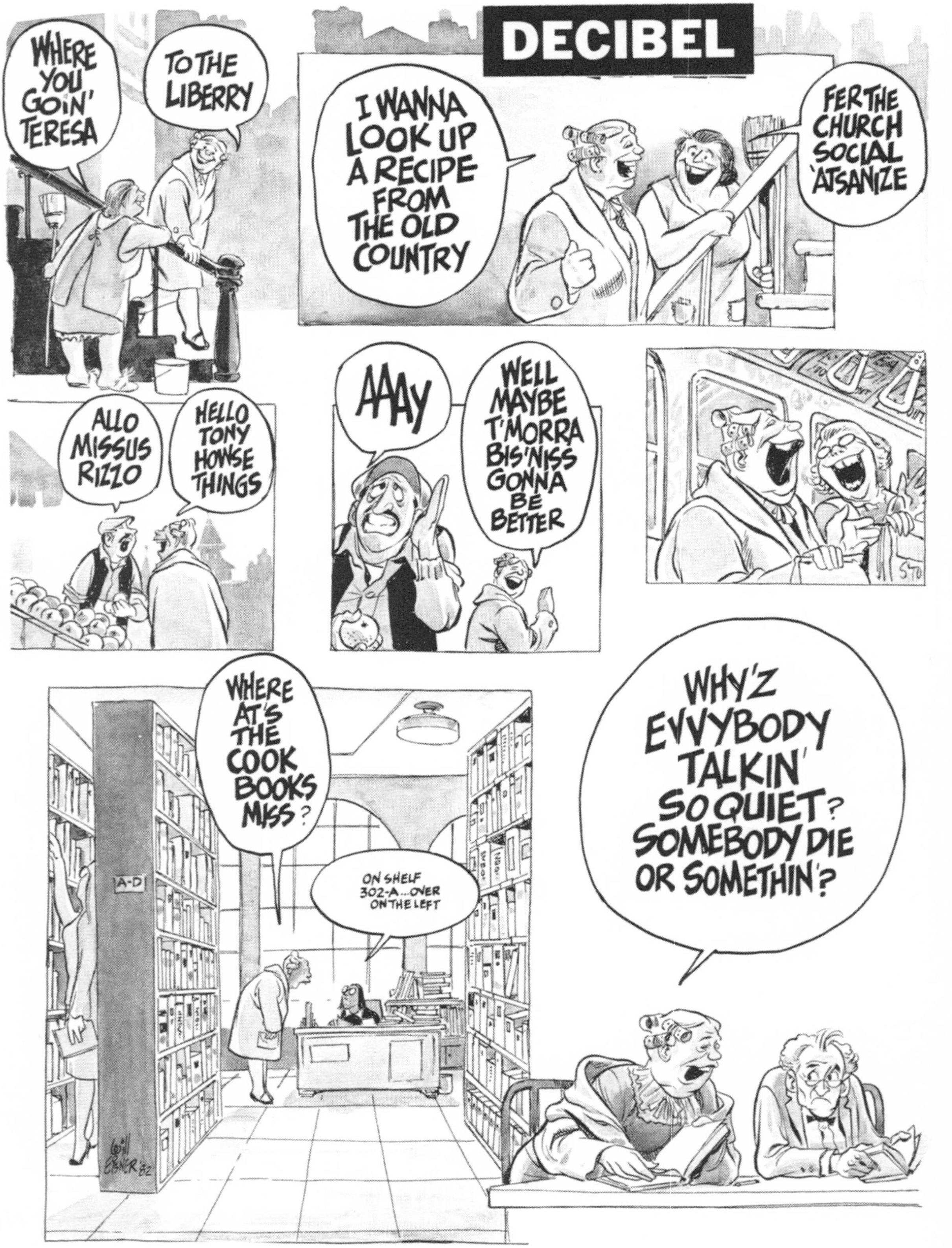
DECIBEL
WHERE YOU GOIN' TERESA
TO THE LIBERRY
I WANNA LOOK UP A RECIPE FROM THE OLD COUNTRY
FER THE CHURCH SOCIAL 'ATSANIZE
ALLO MISSUS RIZZO
HELLO TONY HOWSE THINGS
AAAY
WELL MAYBE T'MORRA BIS'NISS GONNA BE BETTER
WHERE AT'S THE COOK BOOKS MISS?
A-D
ON SHELF 302-A...OVER ON THE LEFT
WHY'Z EVVYBODY TALKIN' SO QUIET? SOMEBODY DIE OR SOMETHIN'?
Will Eisner '82

RHYTHM

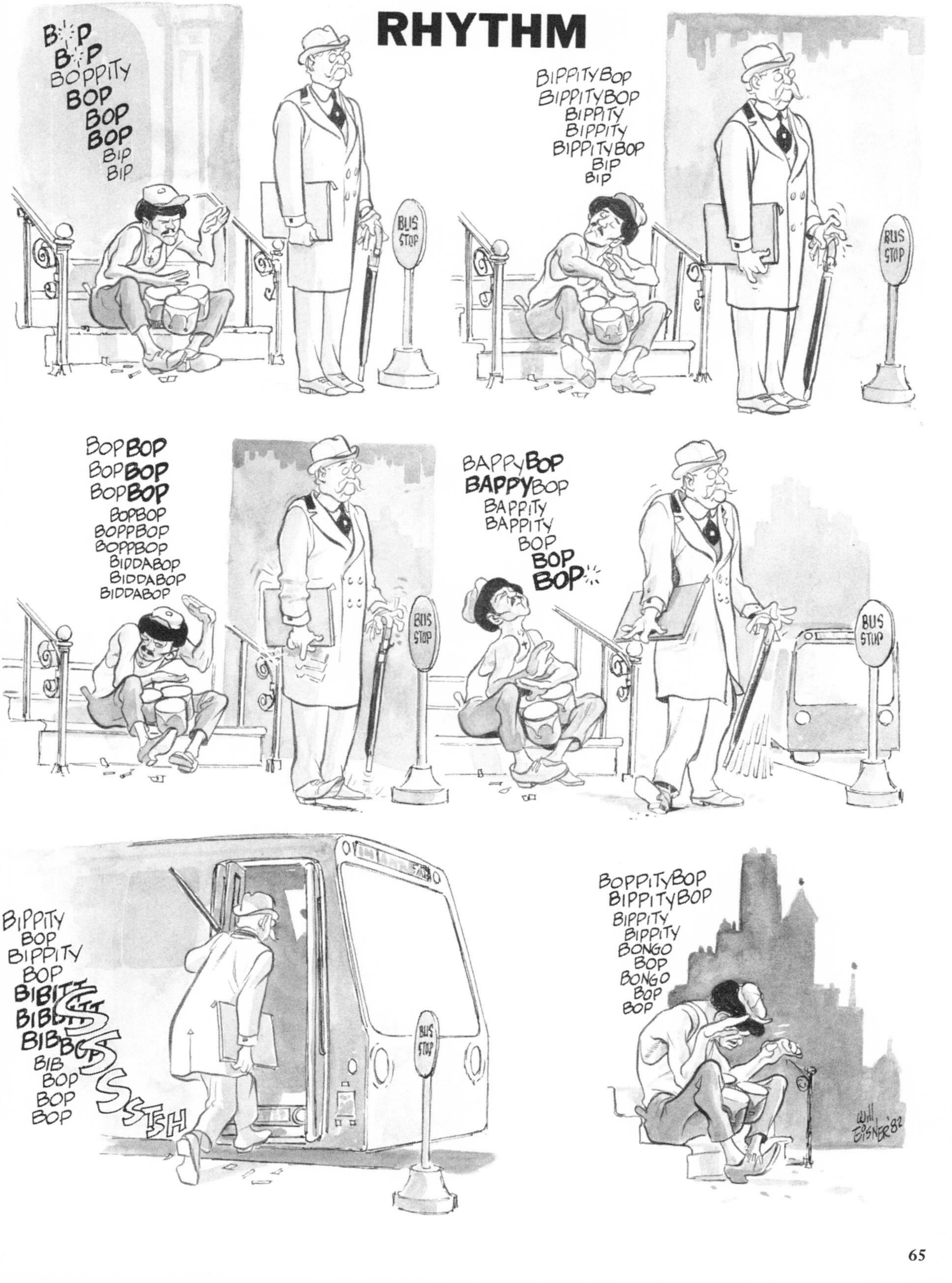

B P
B P
BOPPITY
BOP
BOP
BOP
BIP
BIP
BUS STOP
BIPPITYBOP
BIPPITYBOP
BIPPITY
BIPPITY
BIPPITYBOP
BIP
BIP
BUS STOP
BOPBOP
BOPBOP
BOPBOP
BOPBOP
BOPPBOP
BOPPBOP
BIDDABOP
BIDDABOP
BIDDABOP
BUS STOP
BAPPYBOP
BAPPYBOP
BAPPITY
BAPPITY
BOP
BOP
BOP
BUS STOP
BIPPITY
BOP
BIPPITY
BOP
BIB
BOP
BOP
BOP
SSSTSH
BUS STOP
BOPPITYBOP
BIPPITYBOP
BIPPITY
BIPPITY
BONGO
BOP
BONGO
BOP
BOP
Will Eisner '82

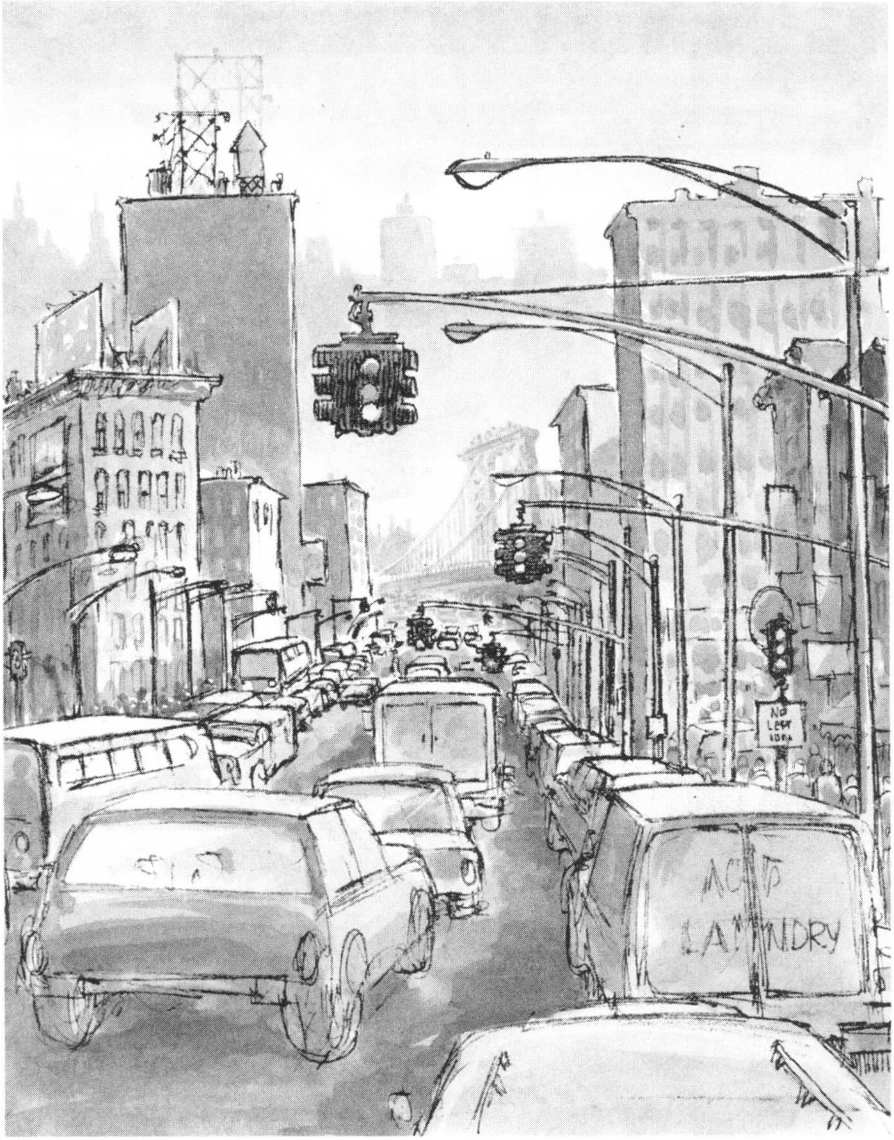
NO
LEFT

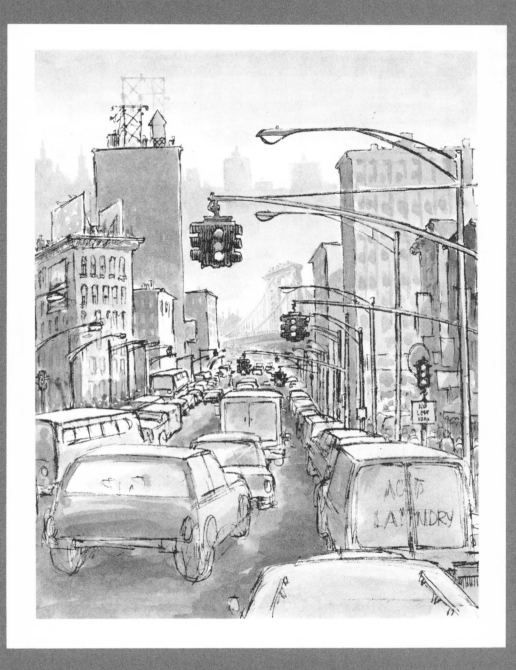

SENTINELS

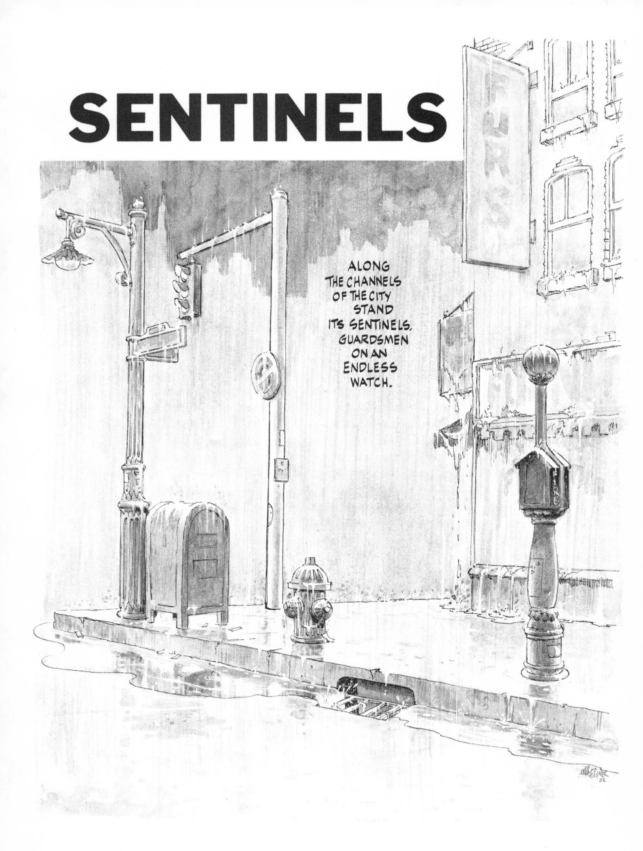

ALONG THE CHANNELS OF THE CITY STAND ITS SENTINELS, GUARDSMEN ON AN ENDLESS WATCH.

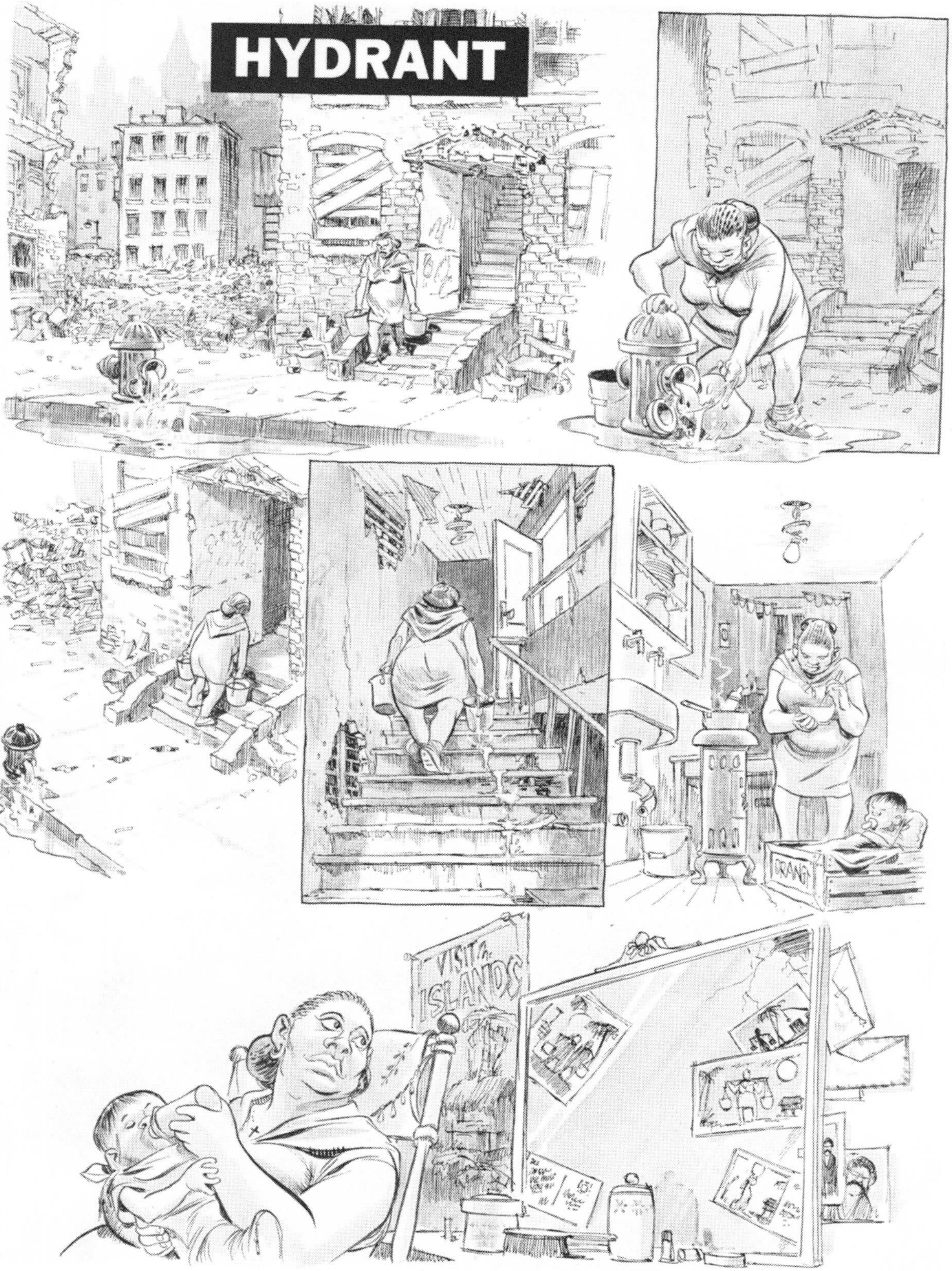
HYDRANT
VISIT
ISLANDS

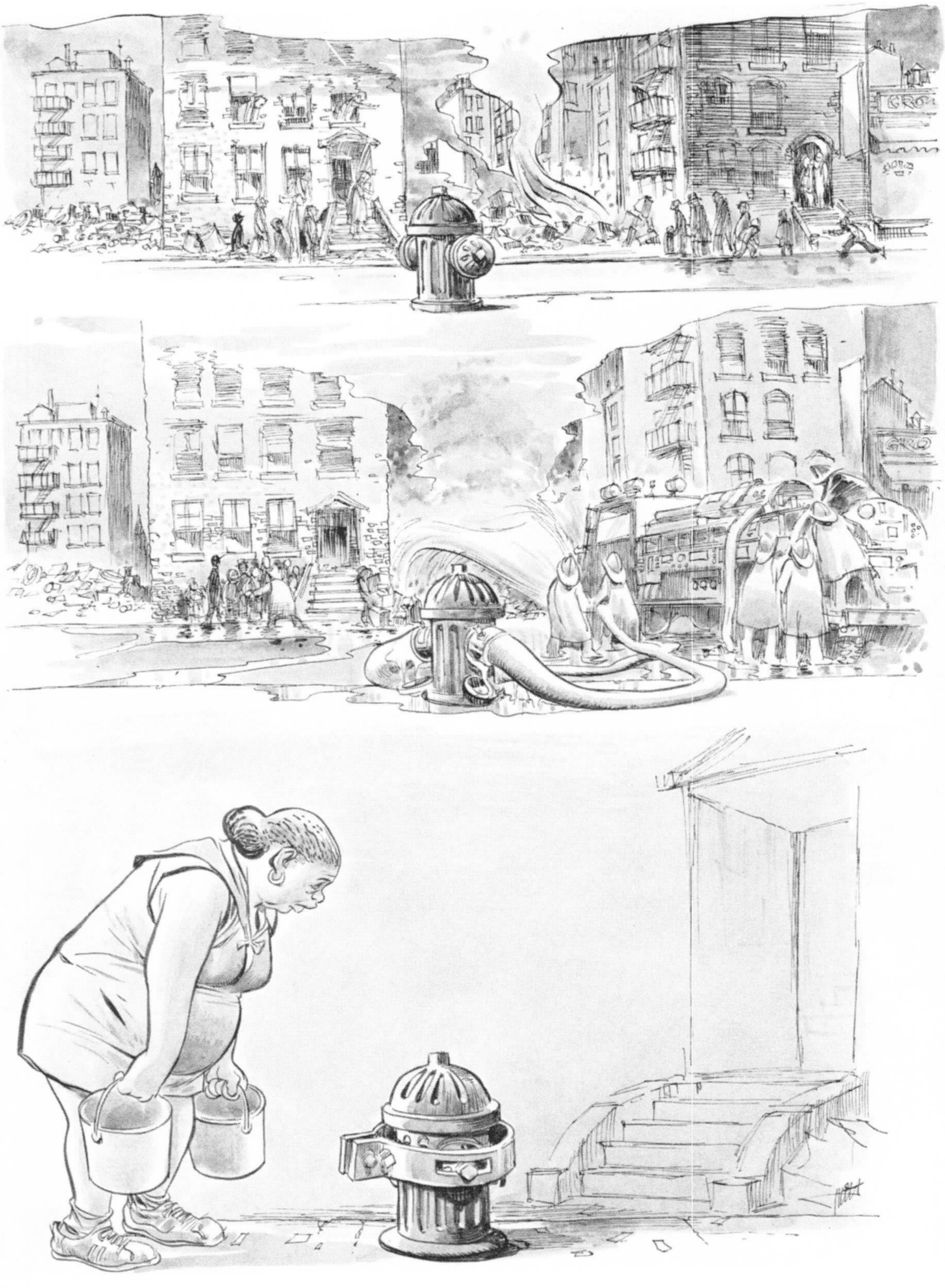

WAYSIDE

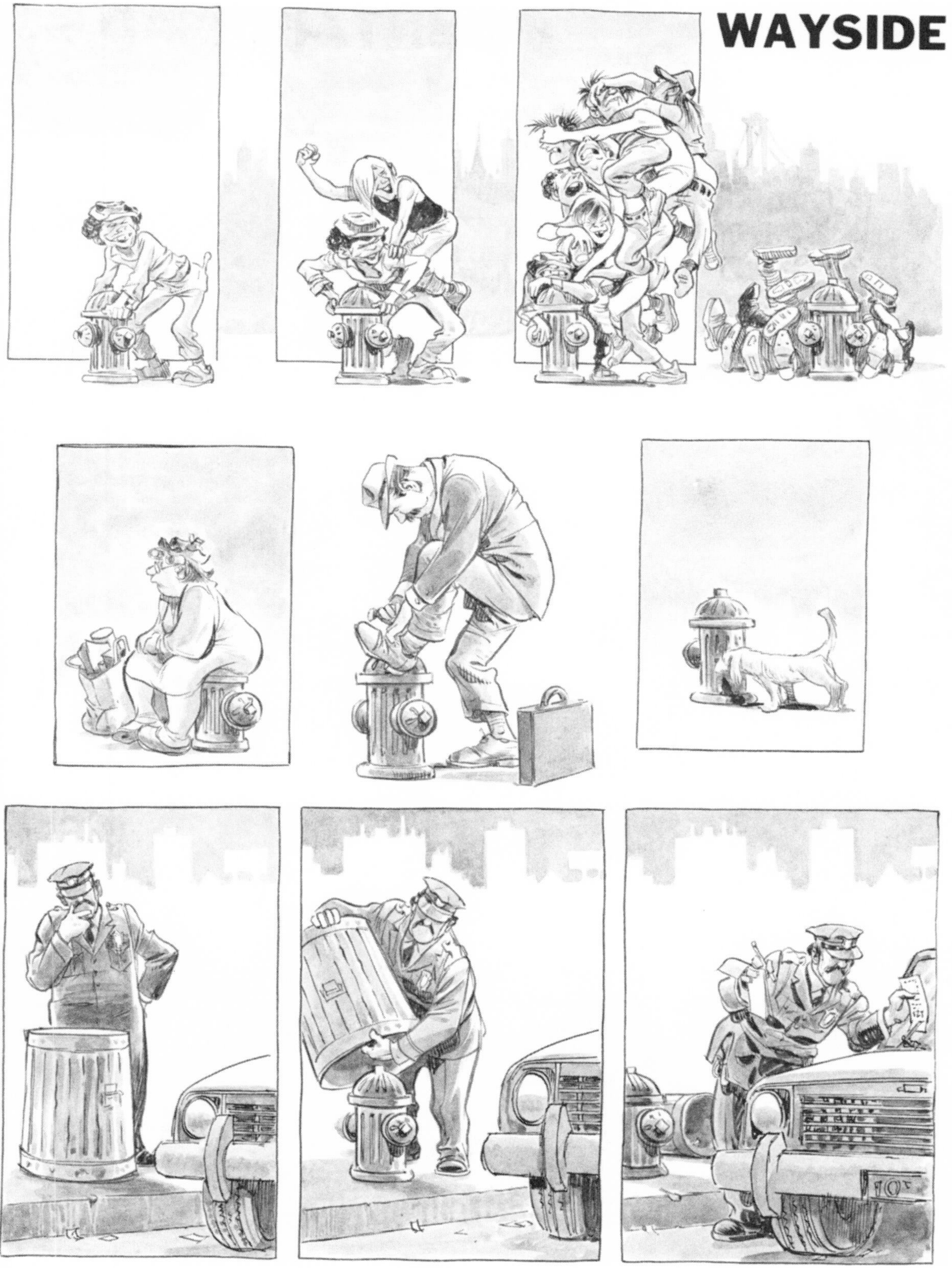

FOUNTAINHEAD

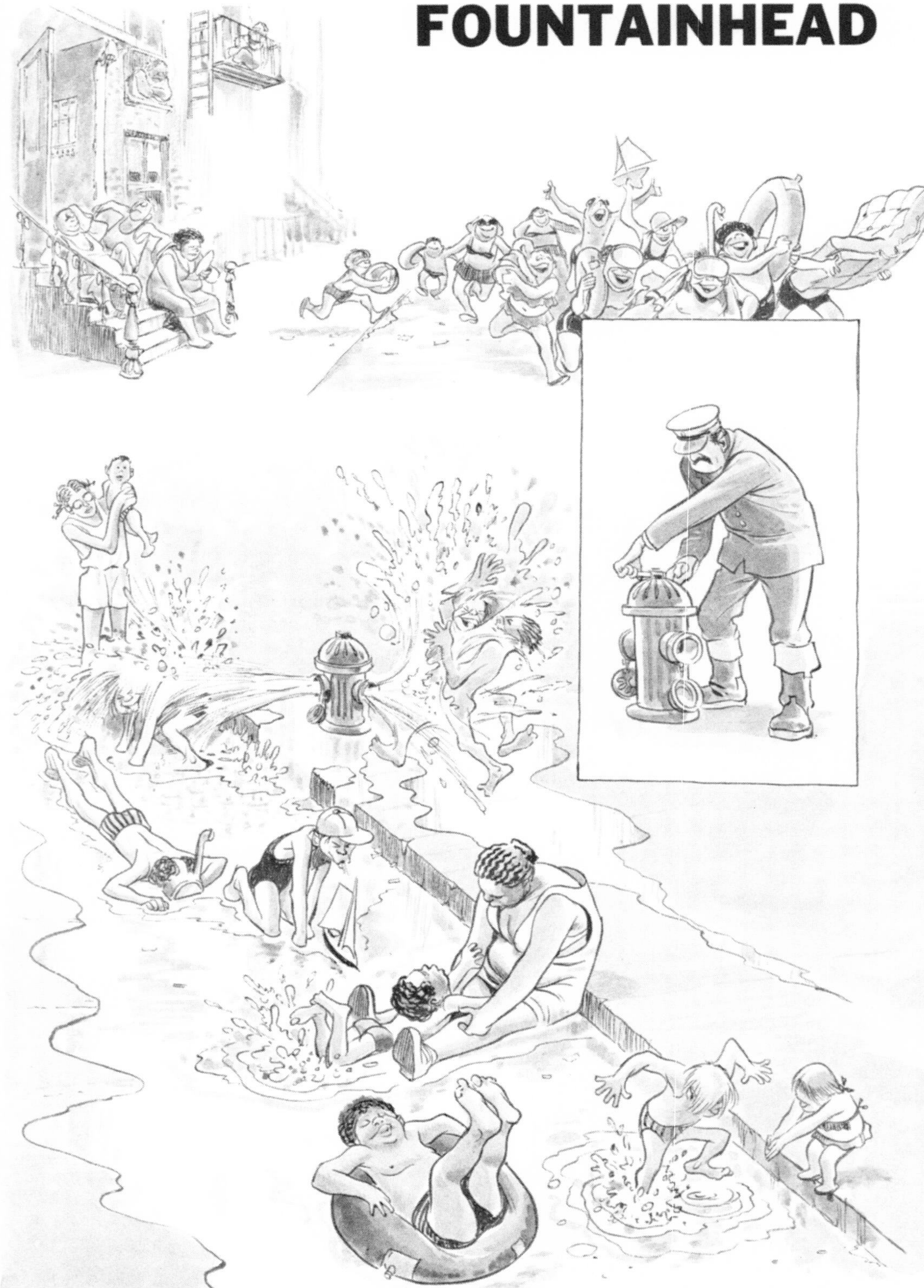

FIRE ALARM

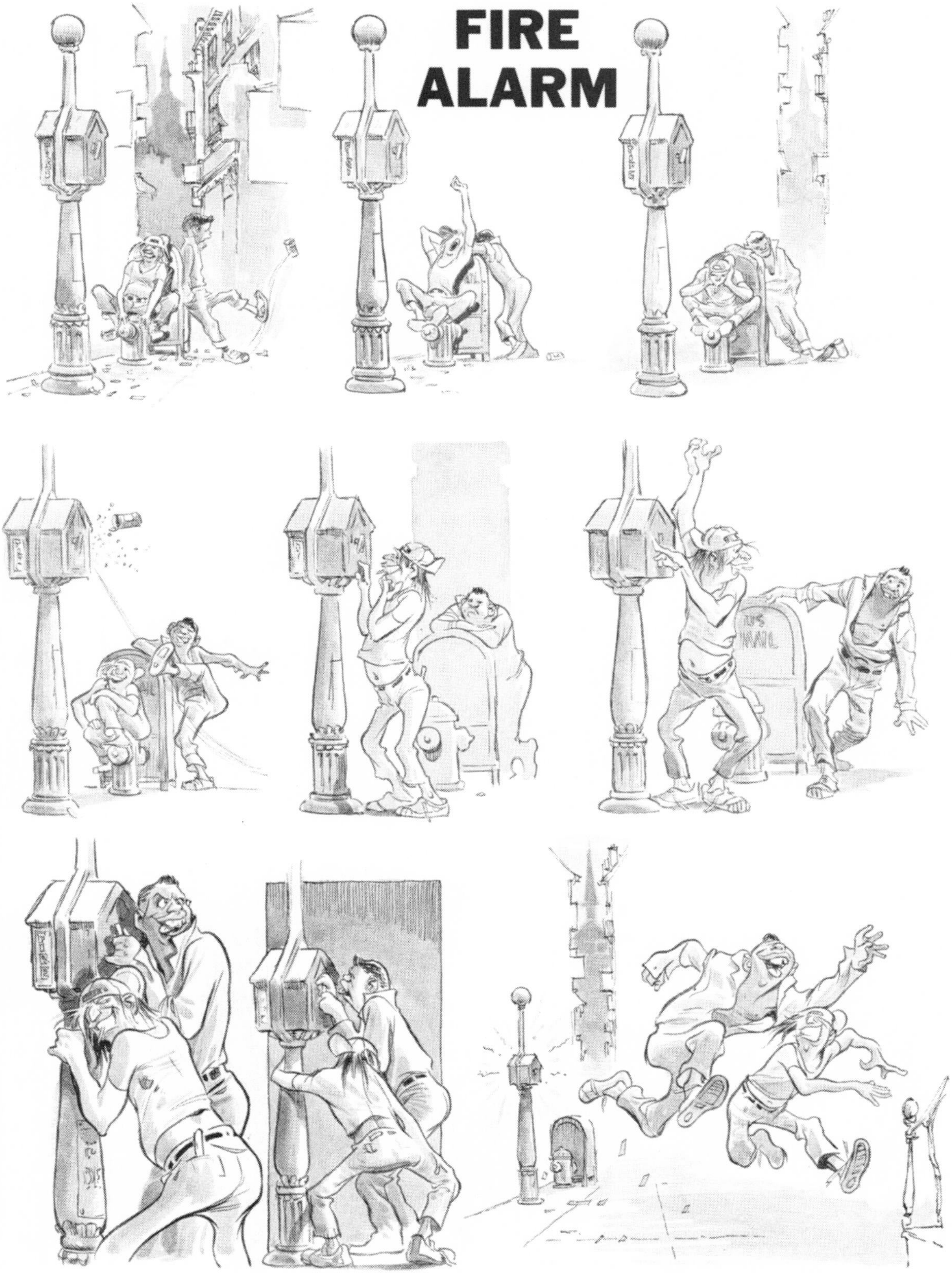
US MAIL

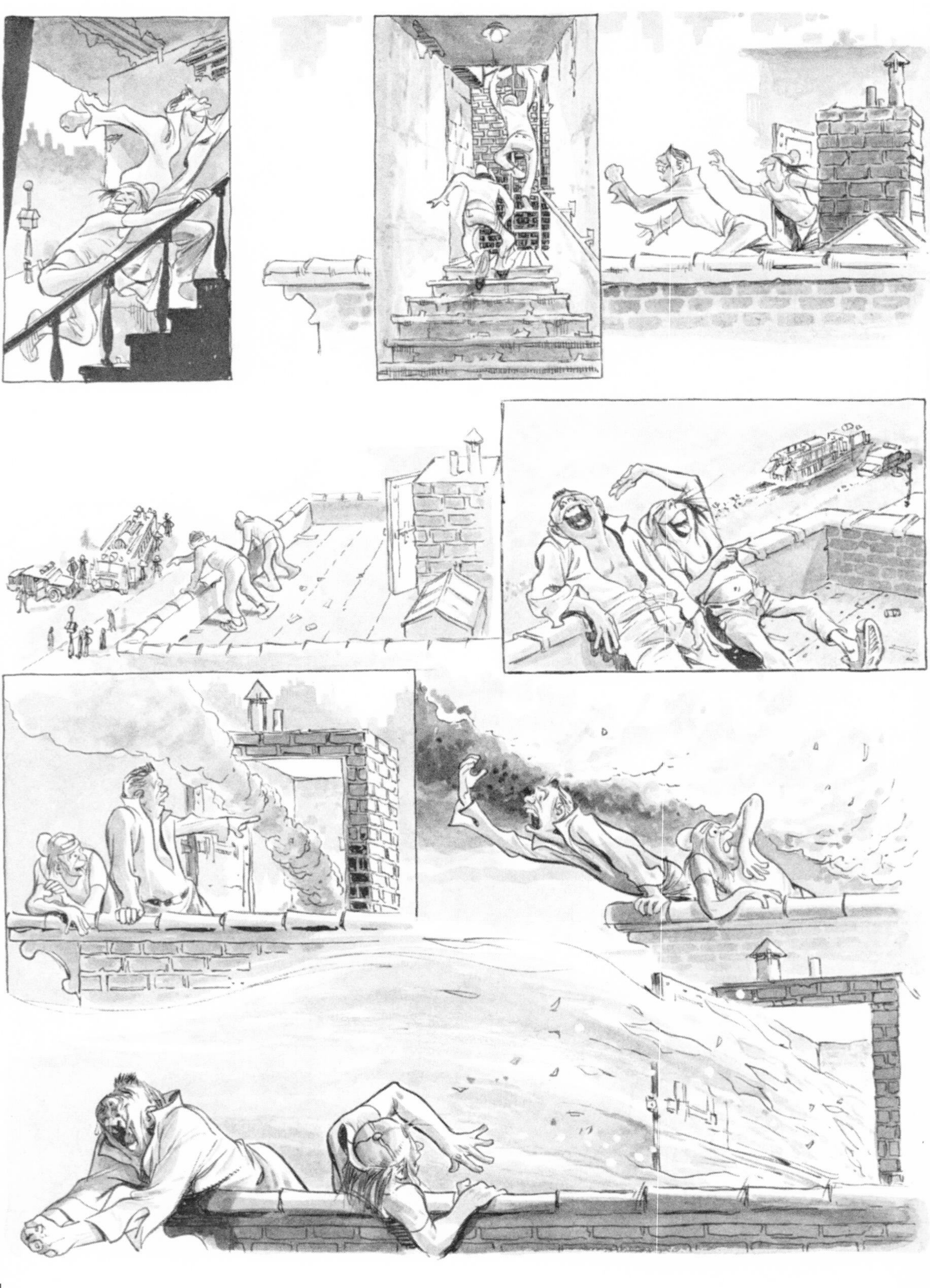

MAILBOX

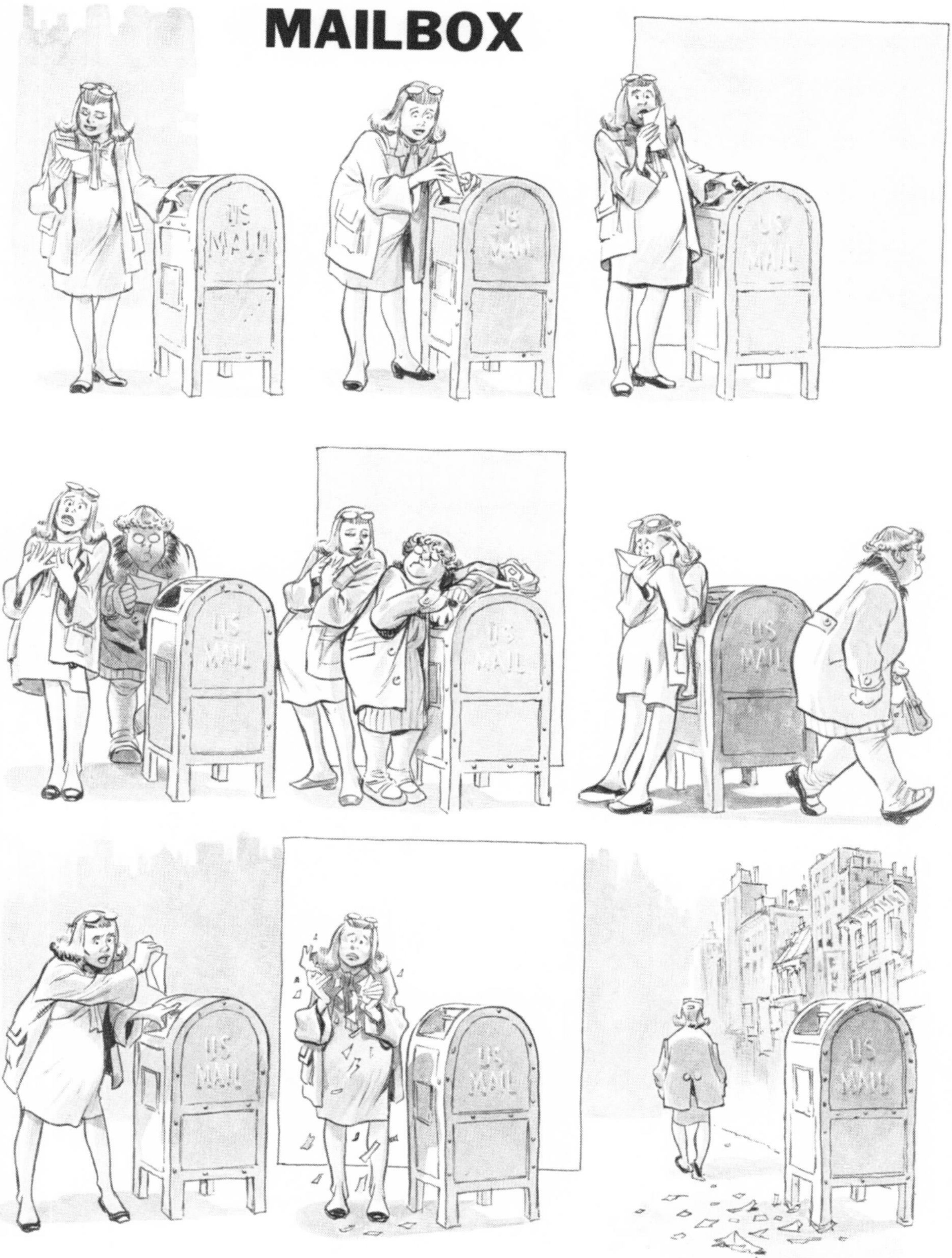
US MAIL
US MAIL
US MAIL
US MAIL
US MAIL
US MAIL
US MAIL
US MAIL
US MAIL

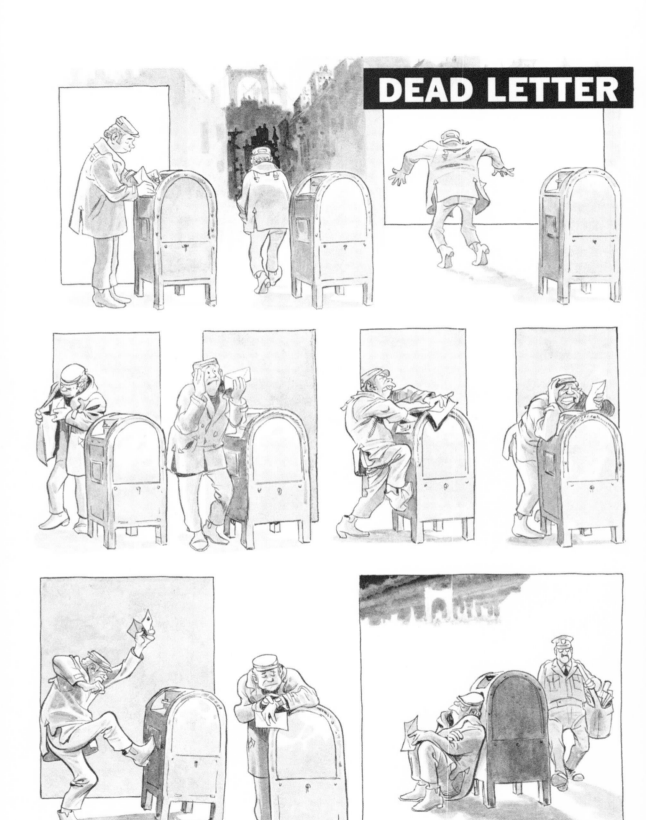

DEAD LETTER

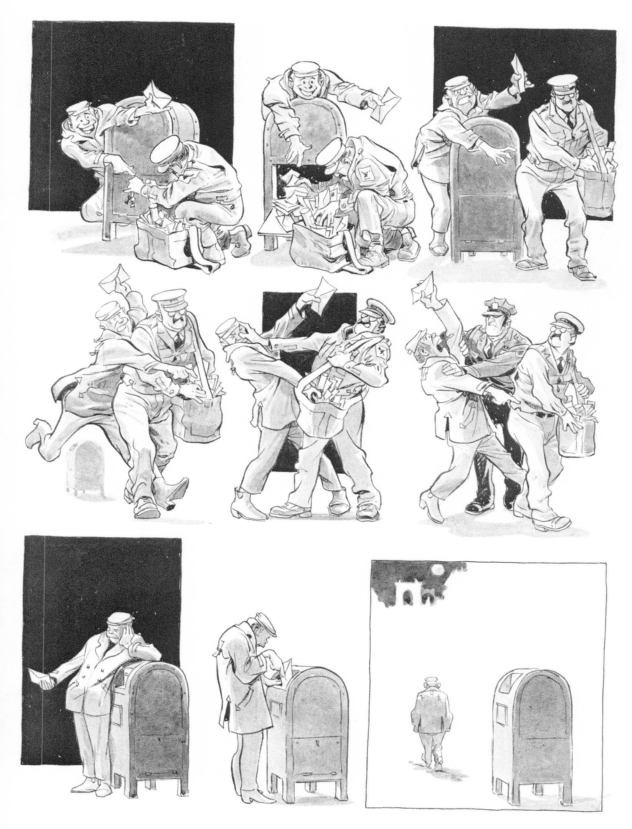

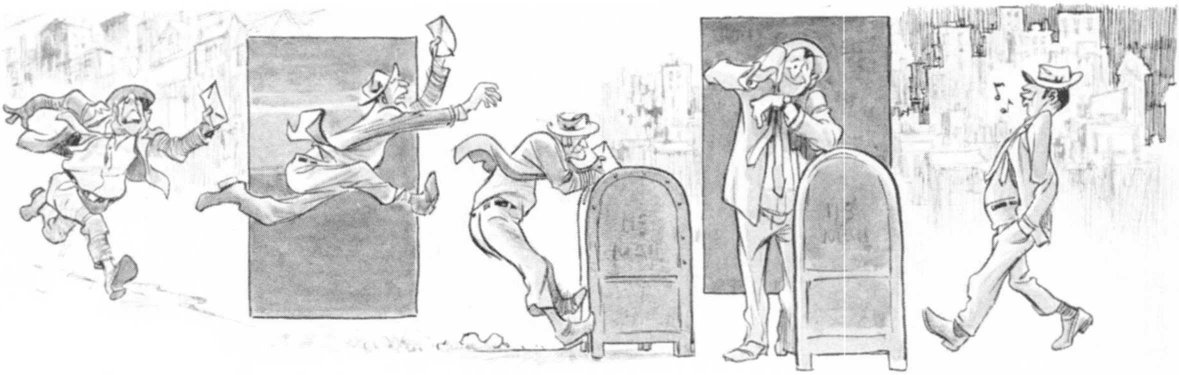

LAST MINUTE MAIL

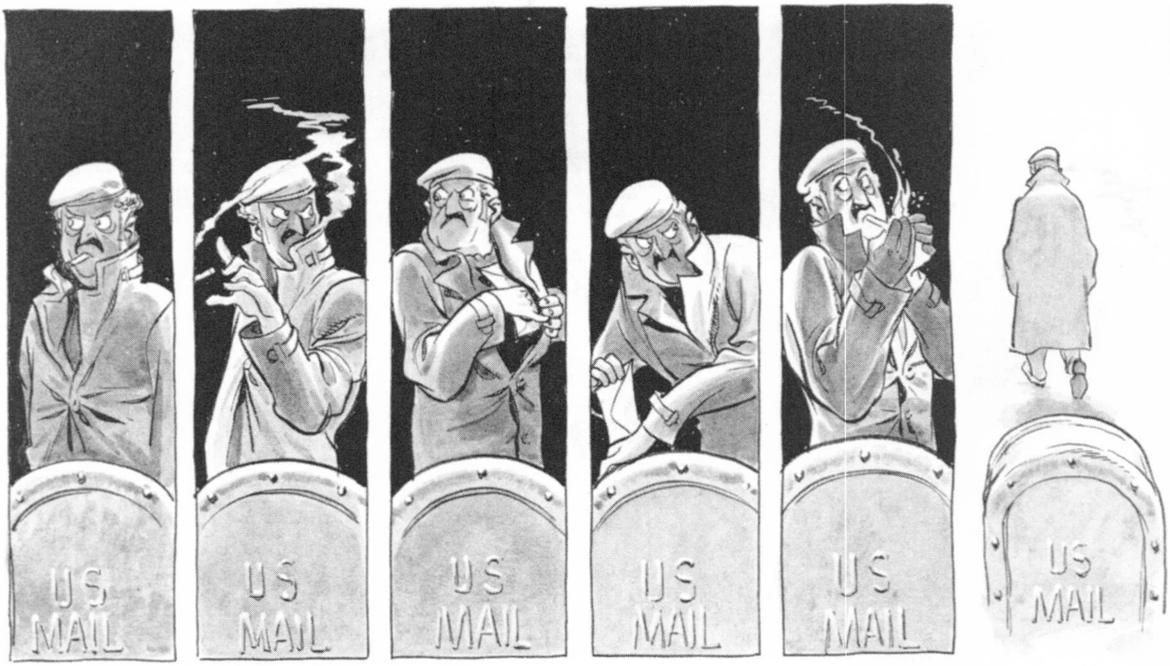
US MAIL

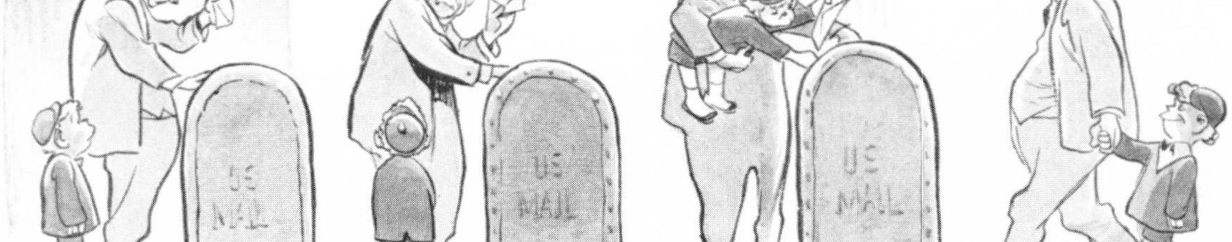

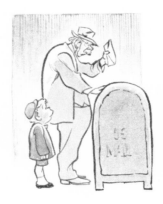

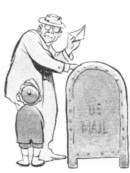

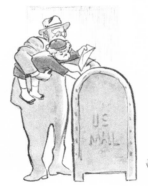

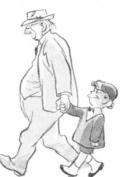

SIGNAL

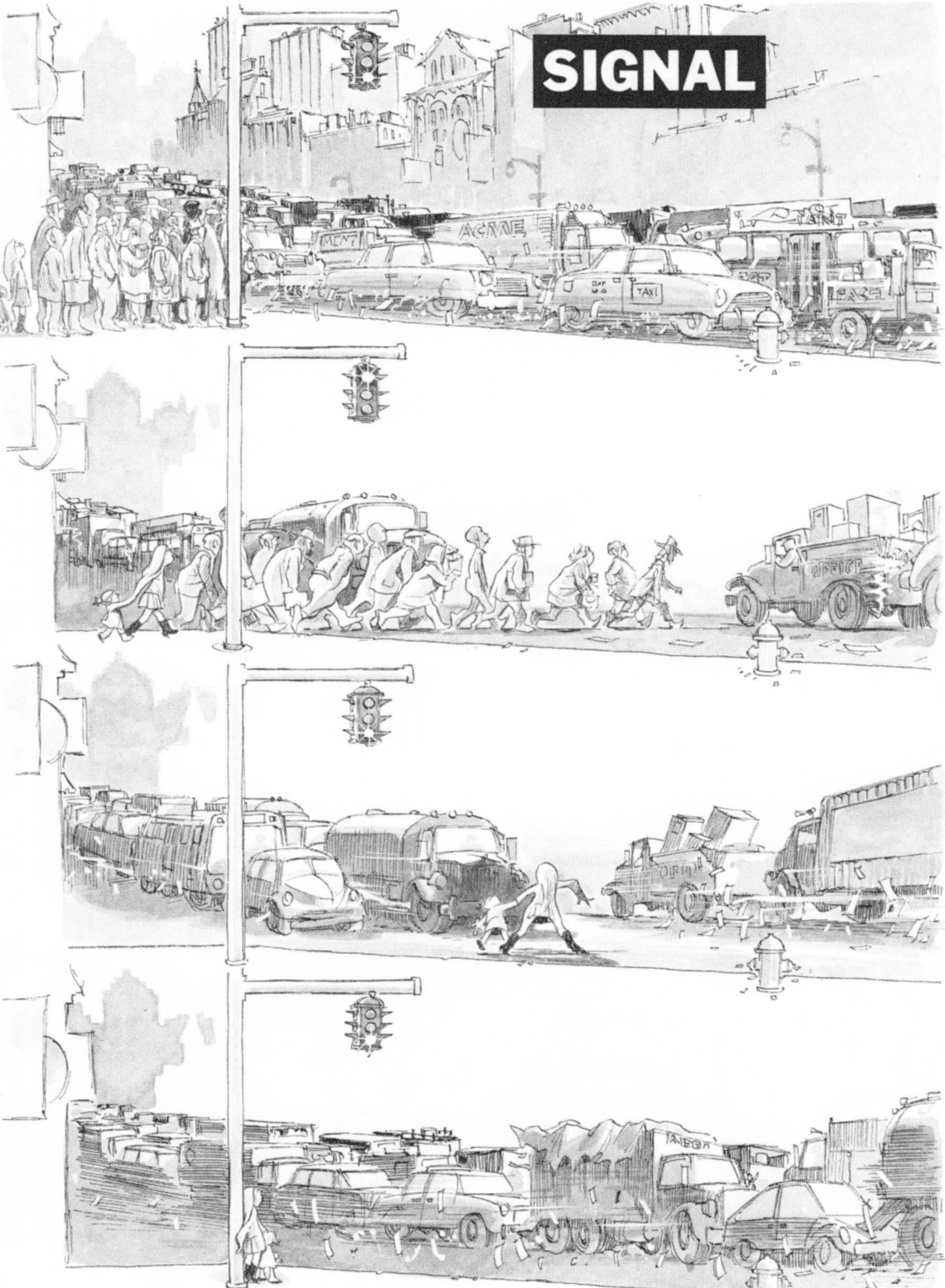
ACME
TAXI

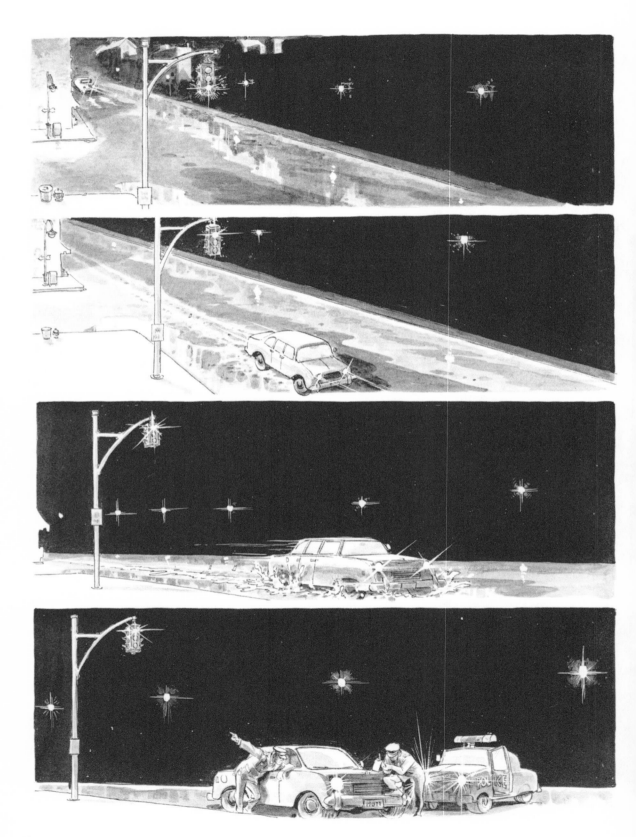

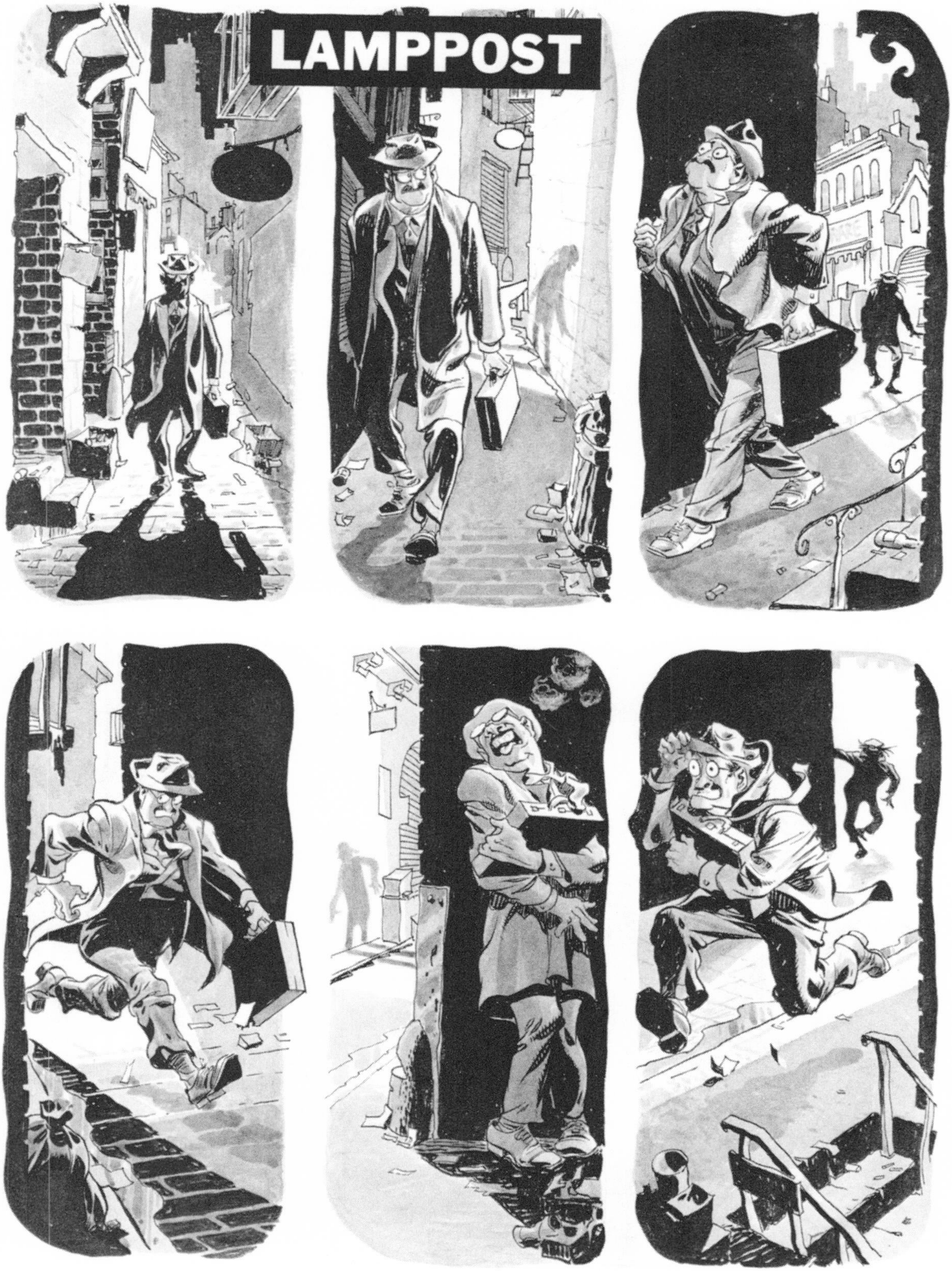
LAMPPOST

RINGALEVIO

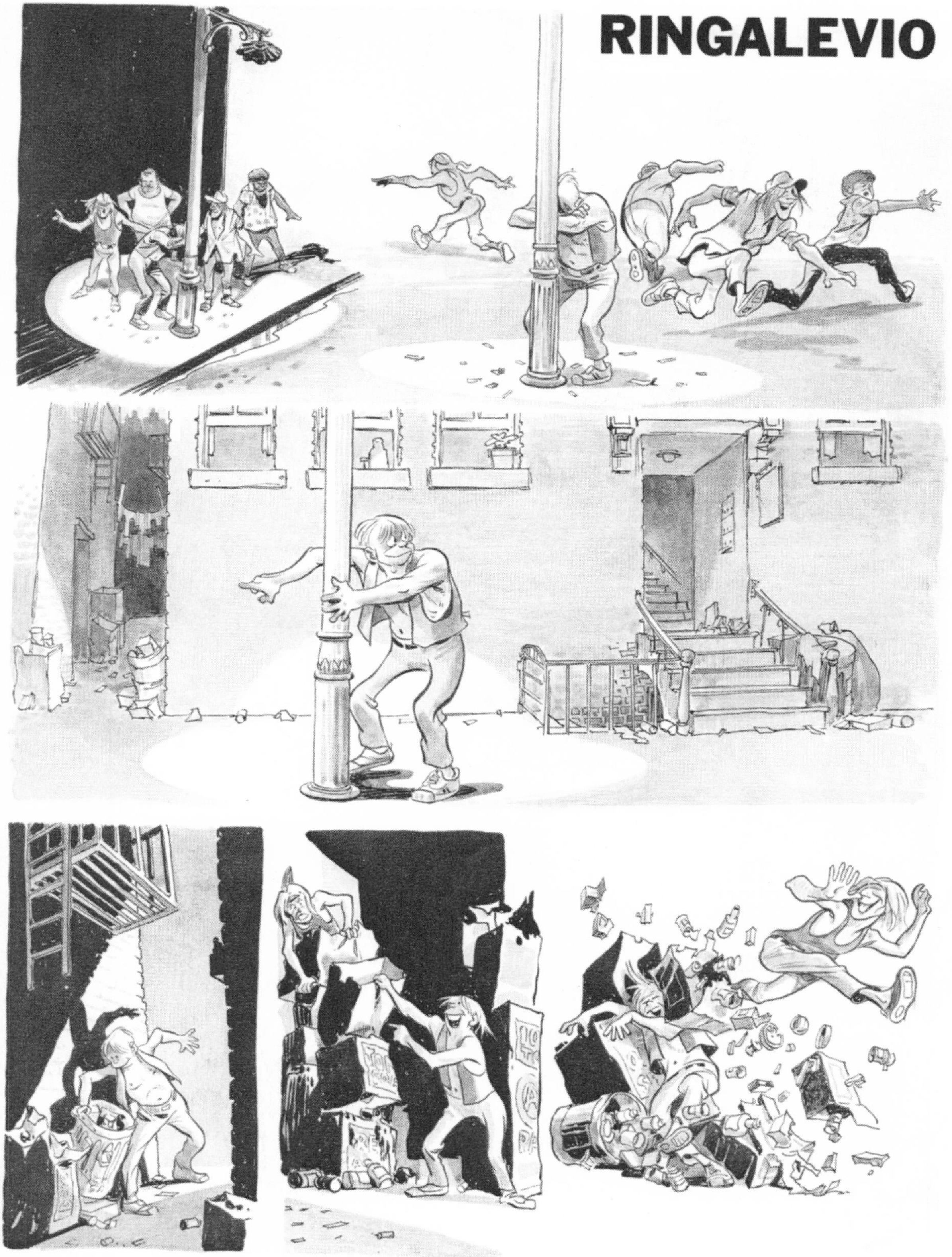

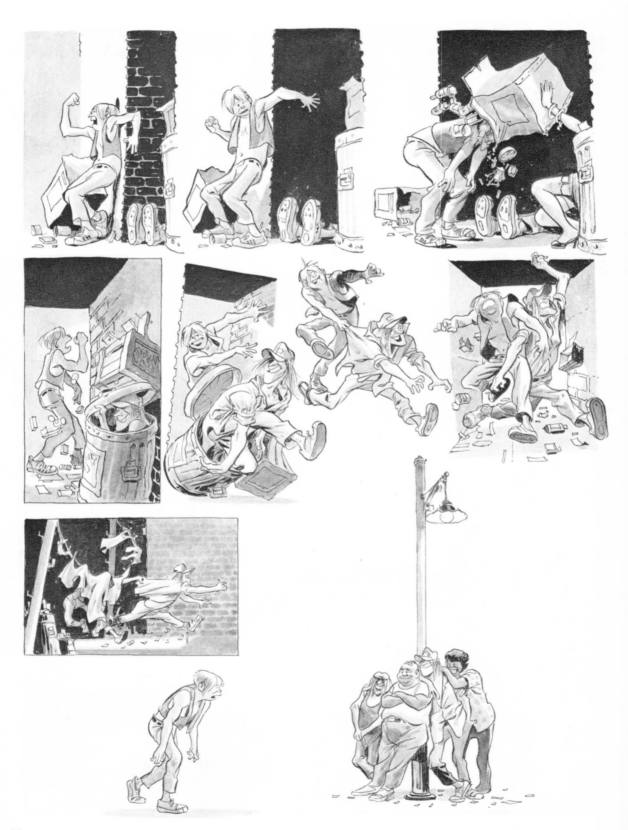

SEWERS

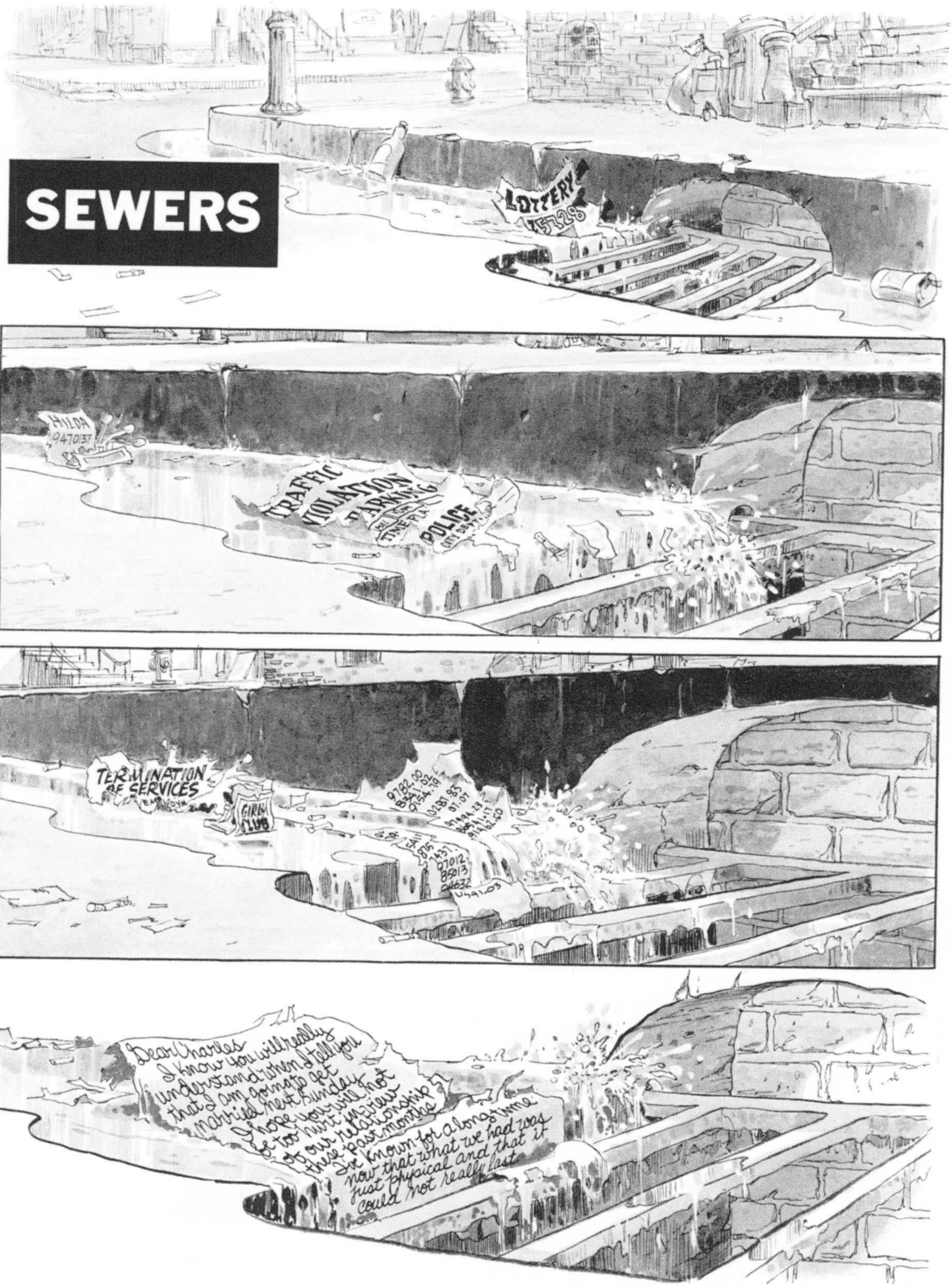
LOTTERY
HILDA
947037
TRAFFIC
VIOLATION
PARKING
POLICE
CITY DEPT.
TERMINATION OF SERVICES
GIRL CLUB
9782.00
8341.02
9154.19
0281.83
01.07
07494.23
91462.60
875
7437.
07012
85013
24632
U491.03
Dear Charles
I know you will really
understand when I tell you
that I am going to get
married next Sunday
I hope you will not
be too hurt in view
of our relationship
these past months
I've known for a long time
now that what we had was
just physical and that it
could not really last

THE RIVER

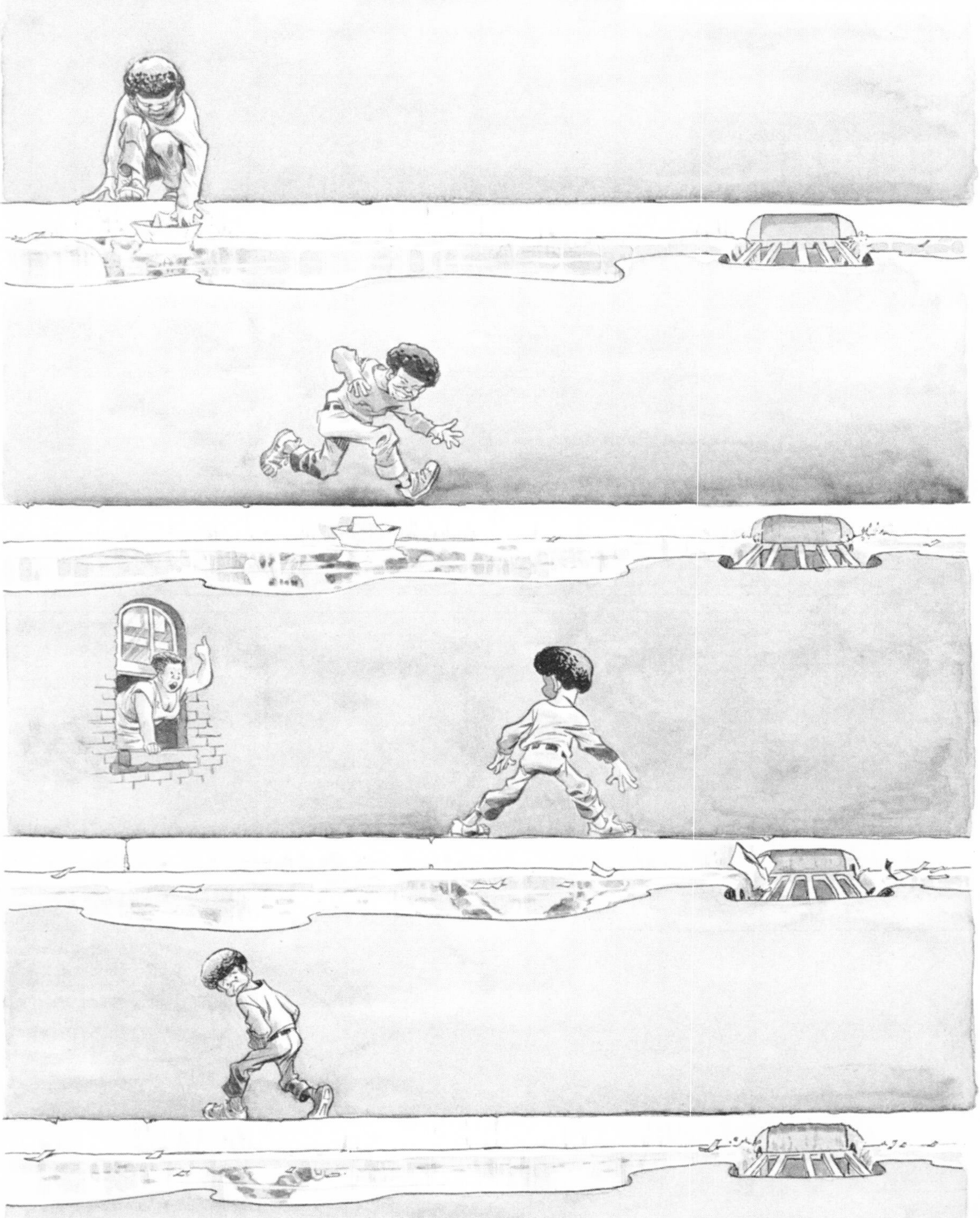

WINDOWS

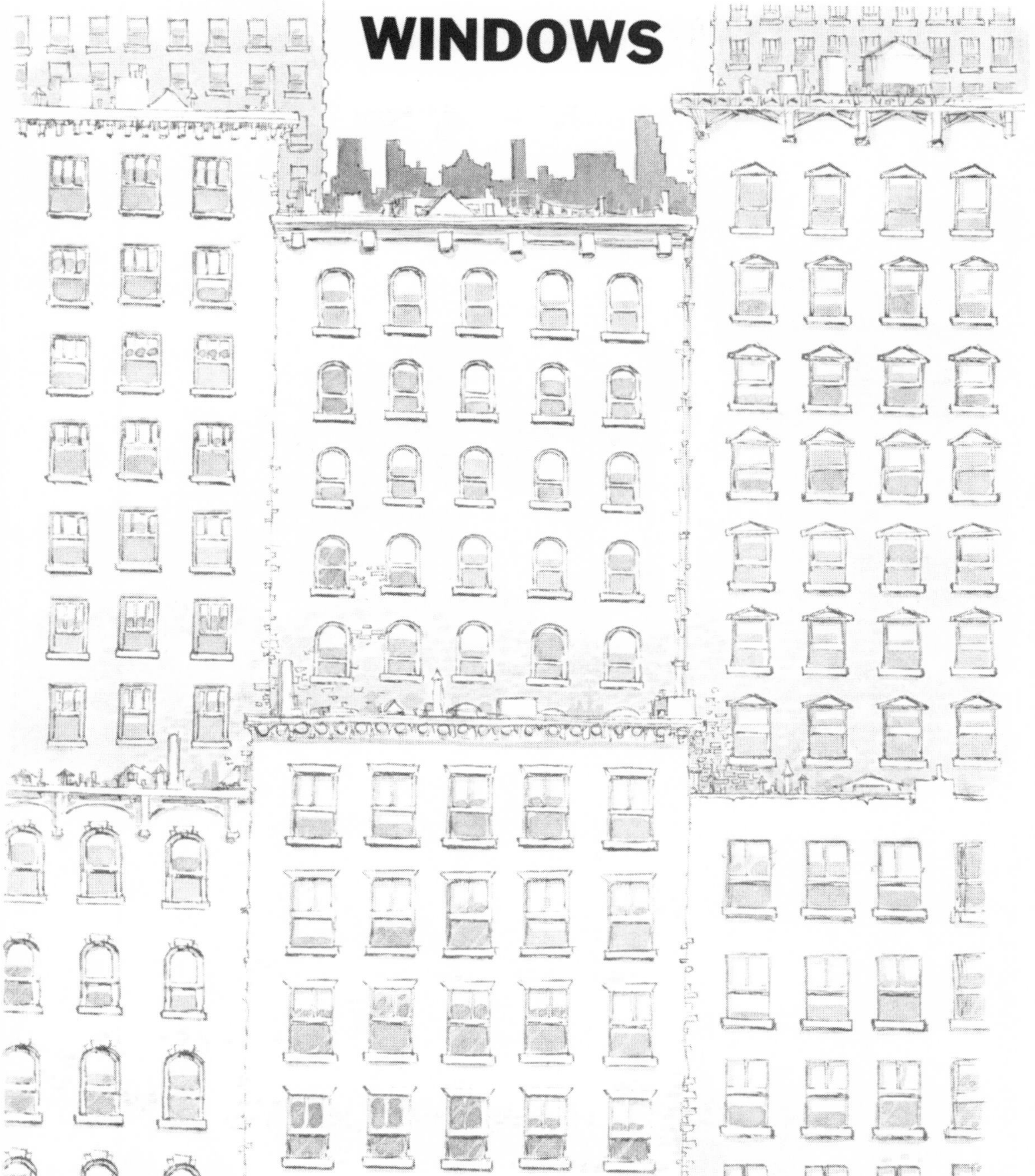

A VIEW OF LIFE

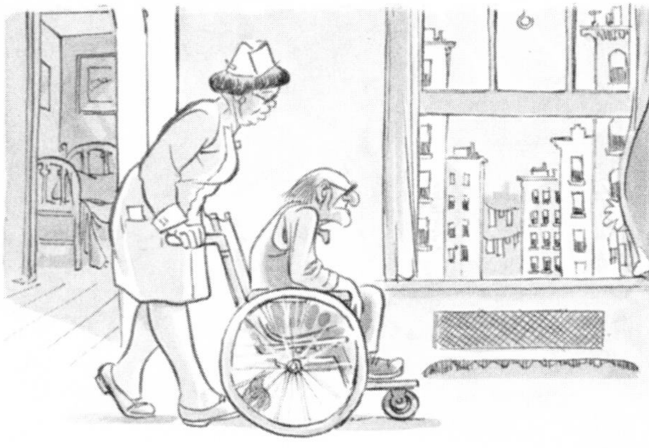

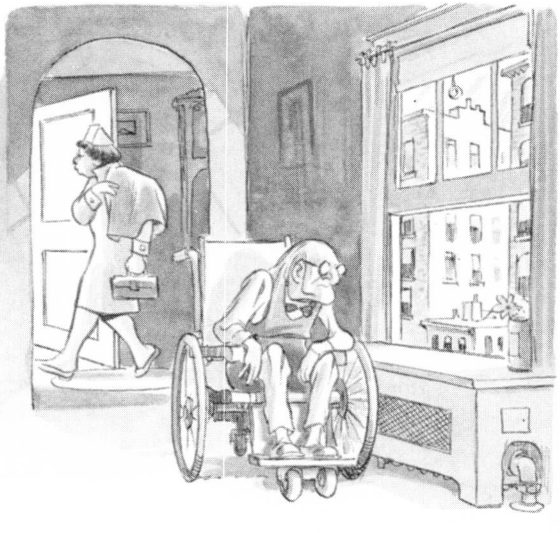

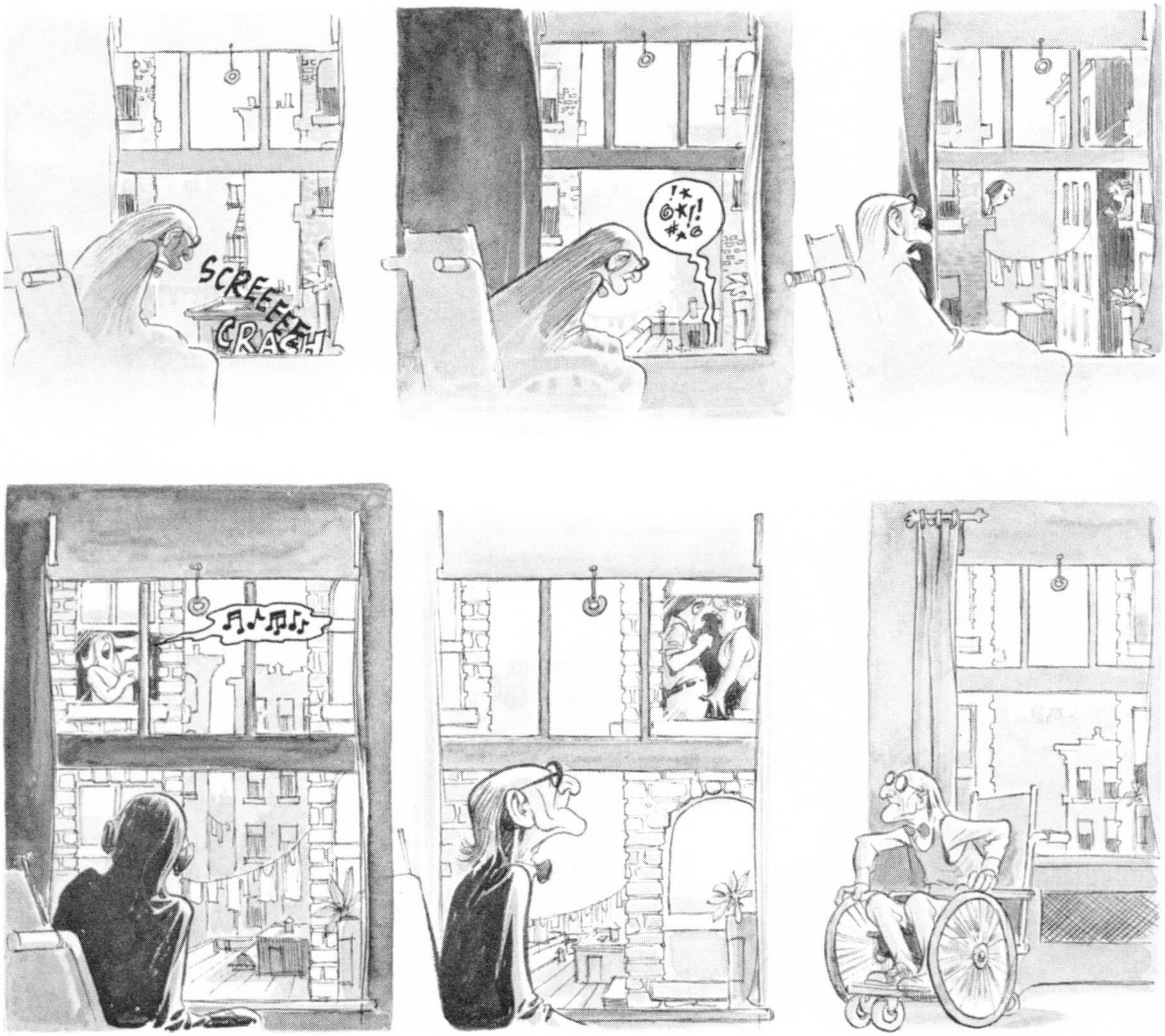
SCREEEEEEH
CRASH

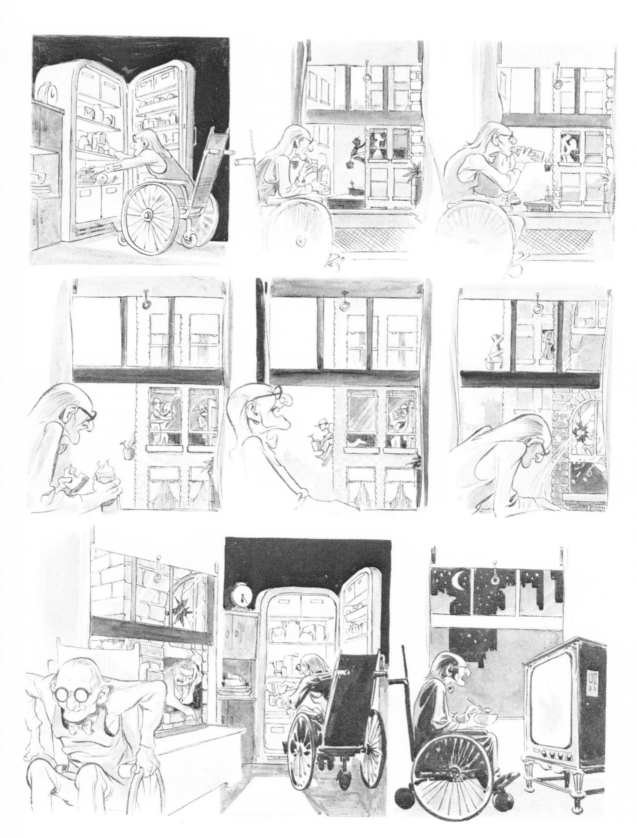

CROWS NEST

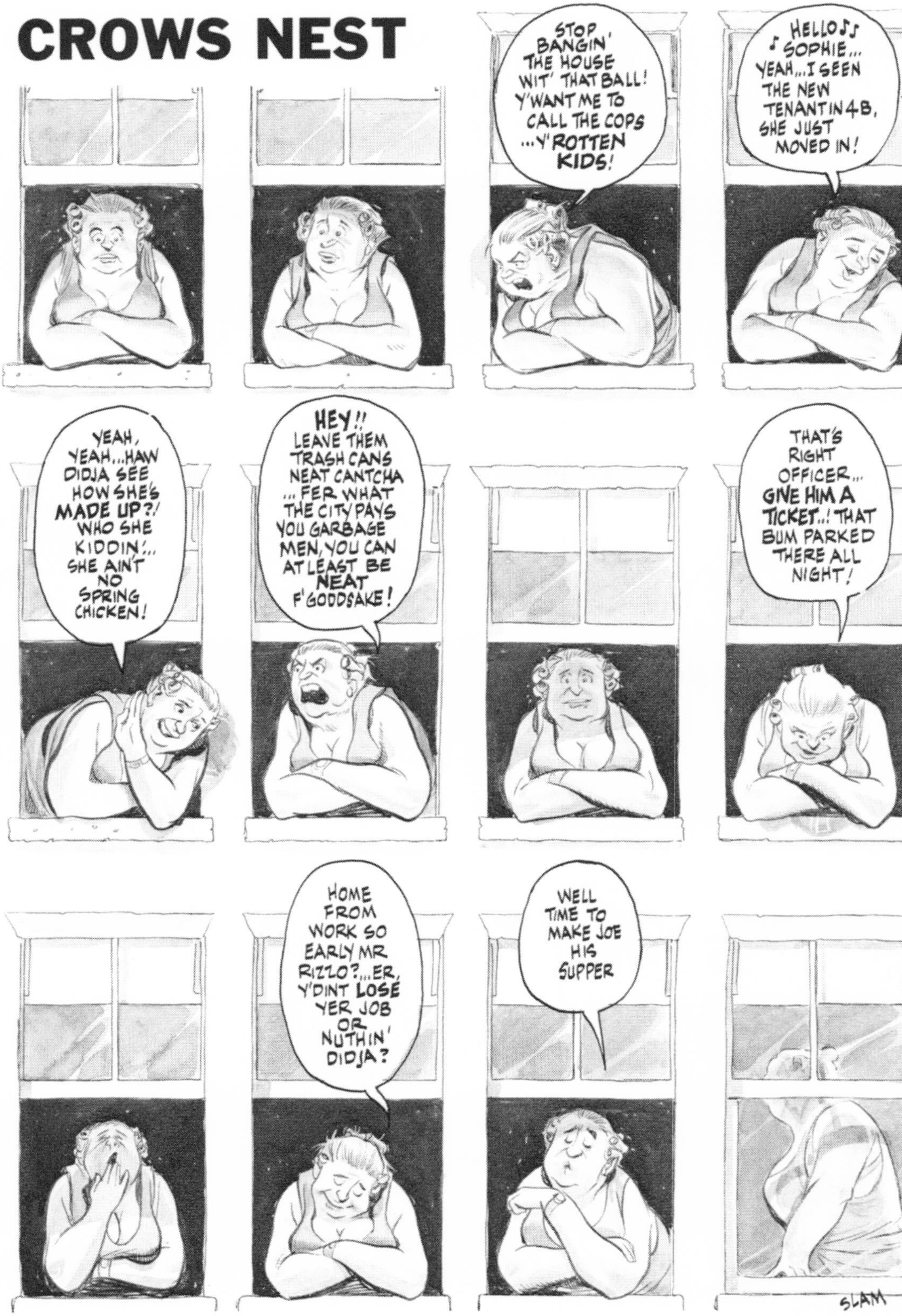
STOP BANGIN' THE HOUSE WIT' THAT BALL! Y'WANT ME TO CALL THE COPS ...Y' ROTTEN KIDS!
♪ HELLO♪♪ SOPHIE... YEAH...I SEEN THE NEW TENANT IN 4B, SHE JUST MOVED IN!
YEAH, YEAH...HAW DIDJA SEE HOW SHE'S MADE UP?! WHO SHE KIDDIN'... SHE AIN'T NO SPRING CHICKEN!
HEY!! LEAVE THEM TRASH CANS NEAT CANTCHA ... FER WHAT THE CITY PAYS YOU GARBAGE MEN, YOU CAN AT LEAST BE NEAT F'GOODSAKE!
THAT'S RIGHT OFFICER... GIVE HIM A TICKET..! THAT BUM PARKED THERE ALL NIGHT!
HOME FROM WORK SO EARLY MR RIZZO?...ER, Y'DINT LOSE YER JOB OR NUTHIN' DIDJA?
WELL TIME TO MAKE JOE HIS SUPPER
SLAM

OBSERVER

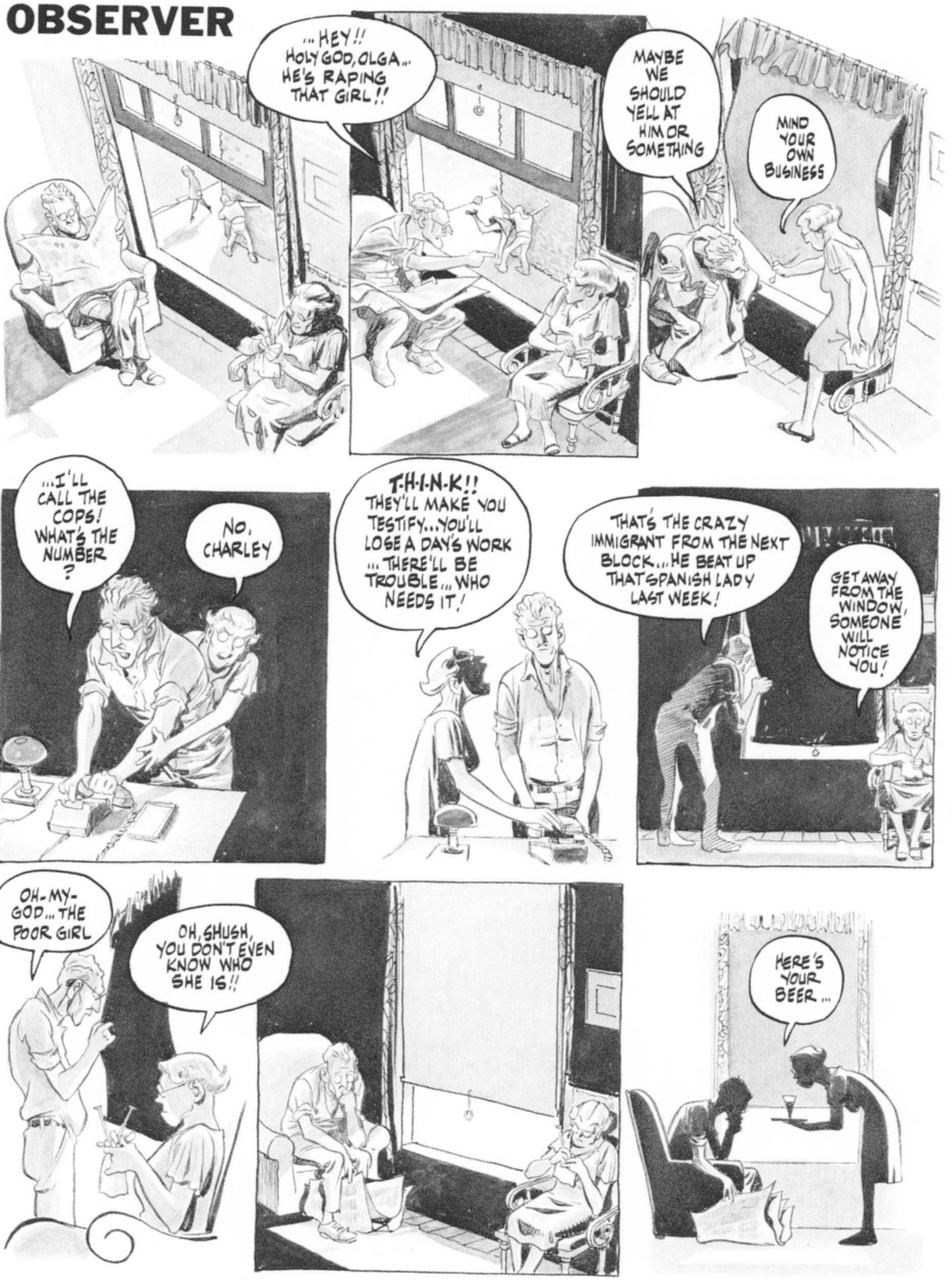
...HEY!! HOLY GOD, OLGA... HE'S RAPING THAT GIRL!!
MAYBE WE SHOULD YELL AT HIM OR SOMETHING
MIND YOUR OWN BUSINESS
...I'LL CALL THE COPS! WHAT'S THE NUMBER?
NO, CHARLEY
T-H-I-N-K!! THEY'LL MAKE YOU TESTIFY...YOU'LL LOSE A DAY'S WORK ... THERE'LL BE TROUBLE... WHO NEEDS IT!
THAT'S THE CRAZY IMMIGRANT FROM THE NEXT BLOCK... HE BEAT UP THAT SPANISH LADY LAST WEEK!
GET AWAY FROM THE WINDOW, SOMEONE WILL NOTICE YOU!
OH-MY-GOD... THE POOR GIRL
OH, SHUSH, YOU DON'T EVEN KNOW WHO SHE IS!!
HERE'S YOUR BEER...

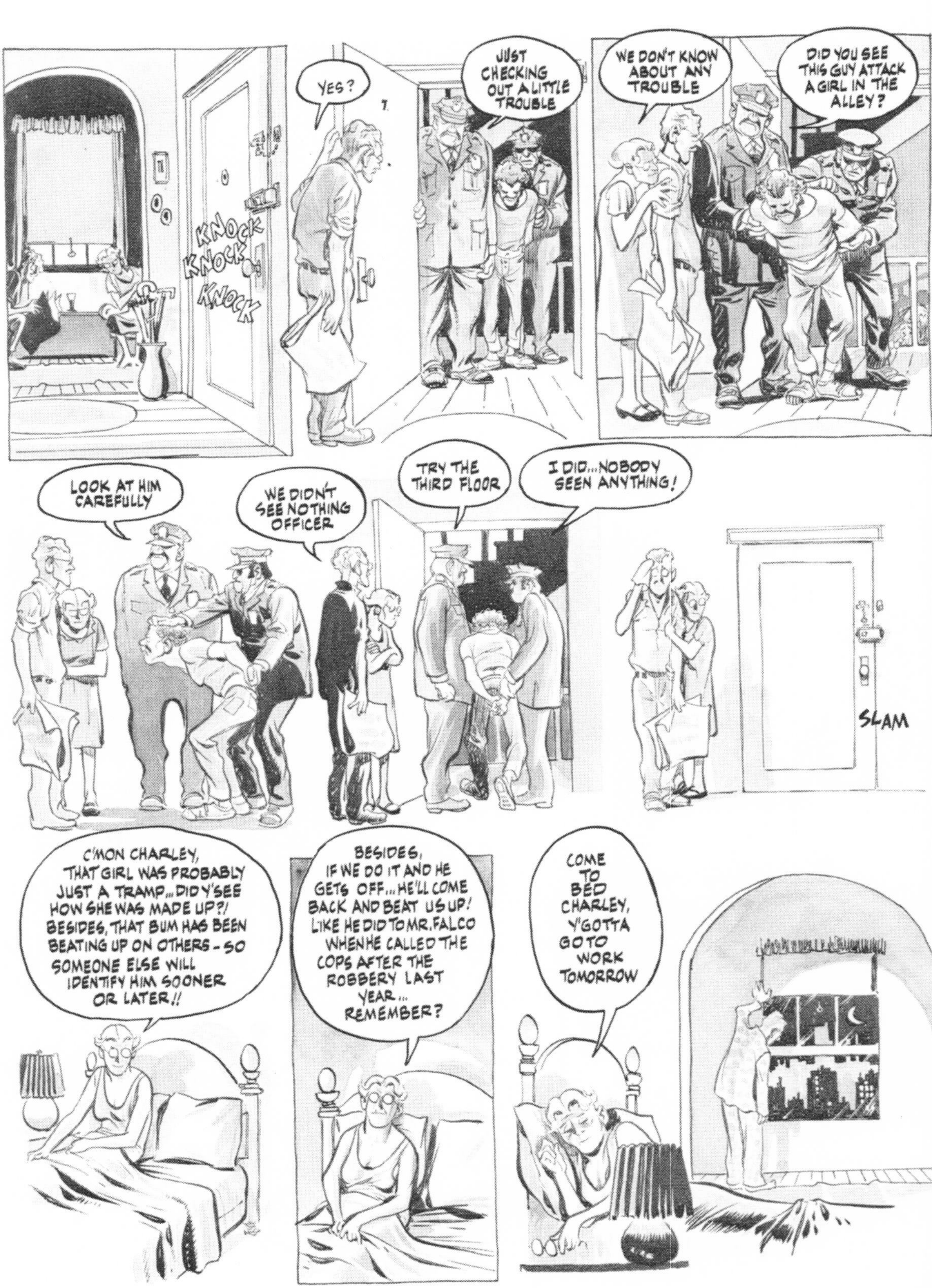
KNOCK
KNOCK
KNOCK
YES?
JUST CHECKING OUT A LITTLE TROUBLE
WE DON'T KNOW ABOUT ANY TROUBLE
DID YOU SEE THIS GUY ATTACK A GIRL IN THE ALLEY?
LOOK AT HIM CAREFULLY
WE DIDN'T SEE NOTHING OFFICER
TRY THE THIRD FLOOR
I DID...NOBODY SEEN ANYTHING!
SLAM
C'MON CHARLEY, THAT GIRL WAS PROBABLY JUST A TRAMP...DID Y'SEE HOW SHE WAS MADE UP?! BESIDES, THAT BUM HAS BEEN BEATING UP ON OTHERS - SO SOMEONE ELSE WILL IDENTIFY HIM SOONER OR LATER!!
BESIDES, IF WE DO IT AND HE GETS OFF...HE'LL COME BACK AND BEAT US UP! LIKE HE DID TO MR. FALCO WHEN HE CALLED THE COPS AFTER THE ROBBERY LAST YEAR... REMEMBER?
COME TO BED CHARLEY, Y'GOTTA GO TO WORK TOMORROW

FIRE EXIT

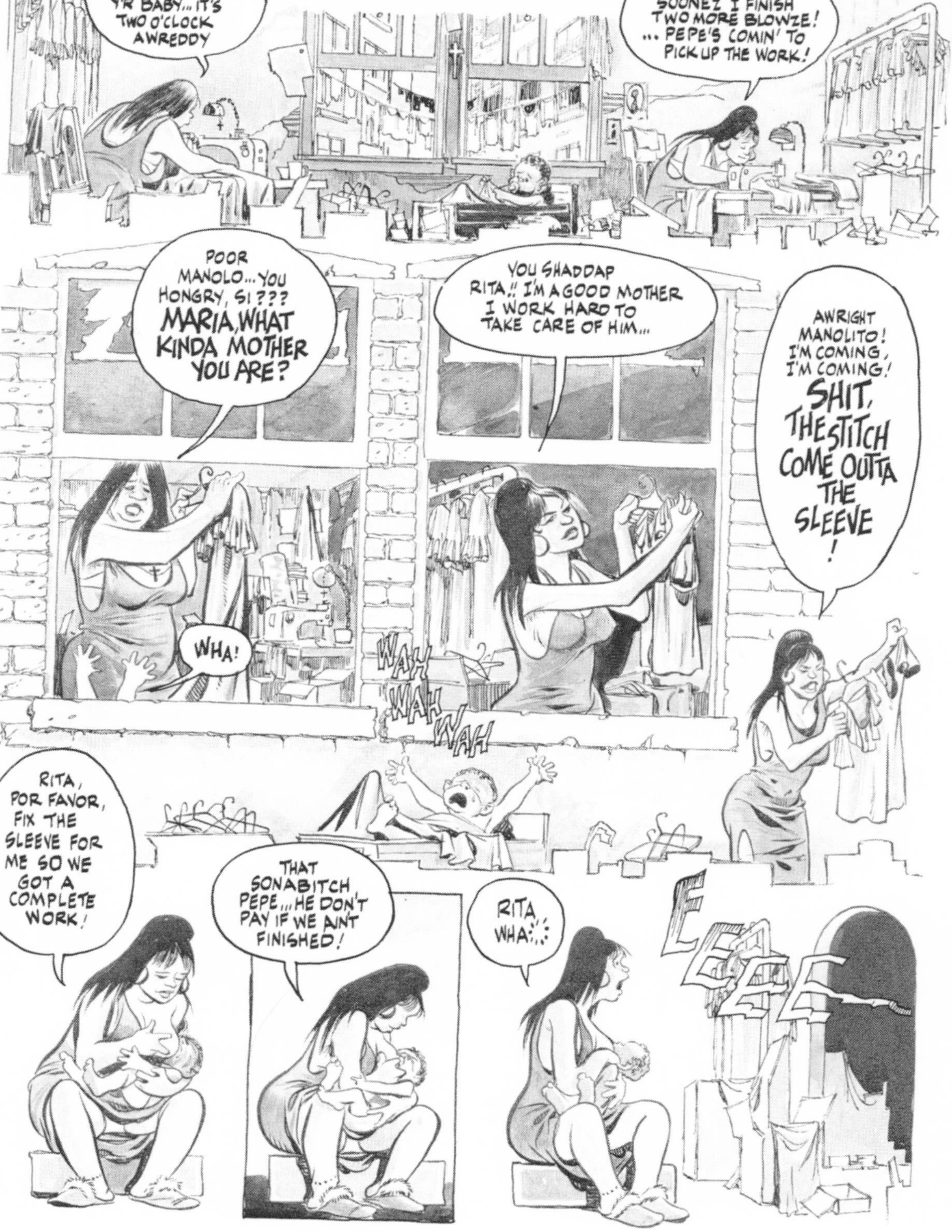
MARIA !!...WHEN YOU GONNA FEED Y'R BABY... IT'S TWO O'CLOCK AWREDDY
SOON, RITA! SOONEZ I FINISH TWO MORE BLOWZE! ... PEPE'S COMIN' TO PICK UP THE WORK!
POOR MANOLO... YOU HONGRY, SI??? MARIA, WHAT KINDA MOTHER YOU ARE?
YOU SHADDAP RITA!! I'M A GOOD MOTHER I WORK HARD TO TAKE CARE OF HIM...
AWRIGHT MANOLITO! I'M COMING, I'M COMING! SHIT, THE STITCH COME OUTTA THE SLEEVE!
WHA!
WAH WAH WAH
RITA, POR FAVOR, FIX THE SLEEVE FOR ME SO WE GOT A COMPLETE WORK!
THAT SONABITCH PEPE... HE DON'T PAY IF WE AIN'T FINISHED!
RITA WHA...

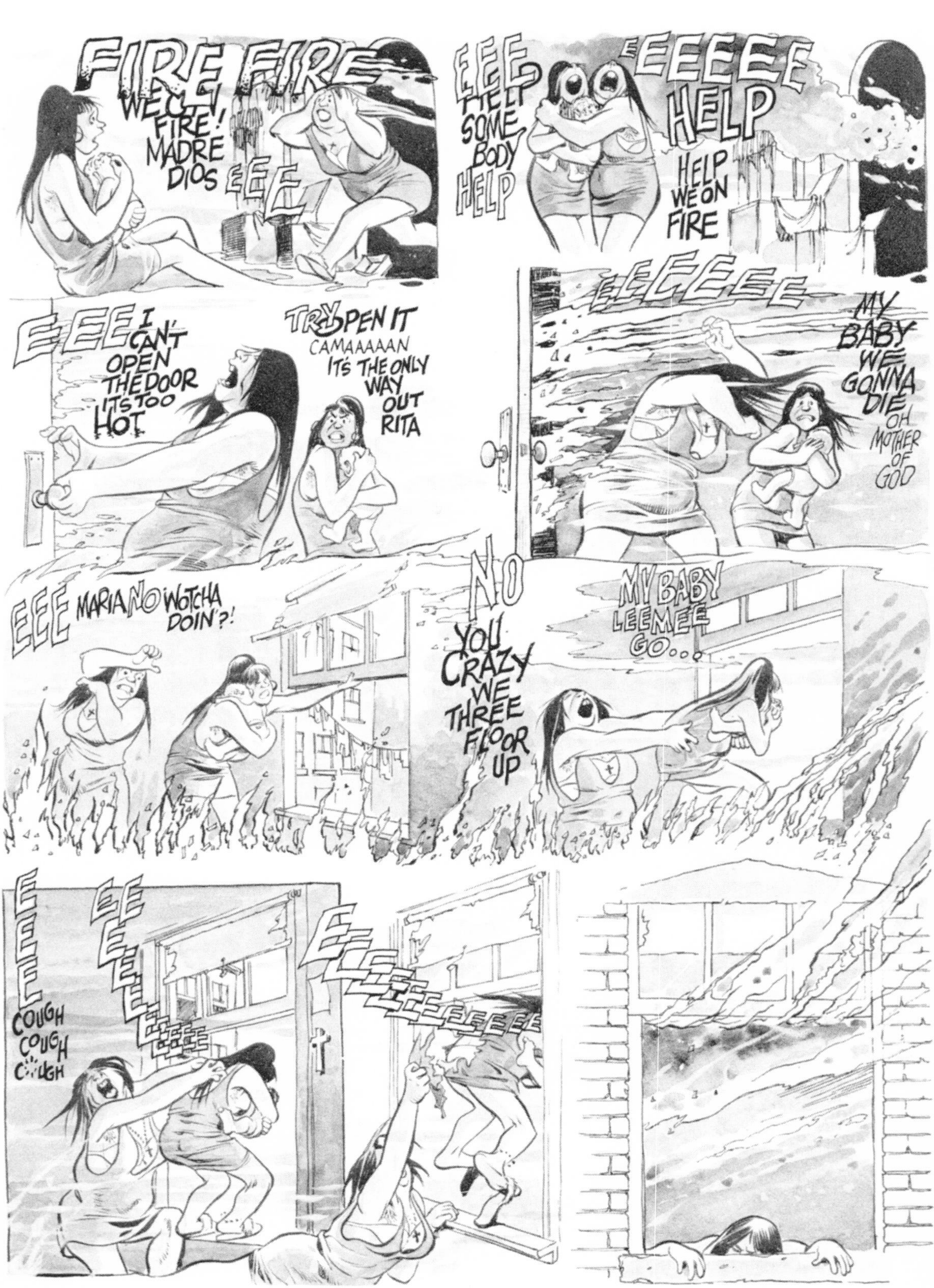
FIRE FIRE
FIRE! MADRE DIOS
EEE
EEE
SOME BODY HELP
EEEEEEE
HELP
HELP WE ON FIRE
EEE
I CAN'T OPEN THE DOOR ITS TOO HOT
TRY OPEN IT
CAMAAAAAAN
IT'S THE ONLY WAY OUT RITA
EEEEEEE
MY BABY WE GONNA DIE
OH MOTHER OF GOD
EEE
MARIA NO
WOTCHA DOIN'?!
NO
YOU CRAZY WE THREE FLOOR UP
MY BABY LEEMEE GO...
EEEEL
COUGH COUGH COUGH
EEEEEEEEE
EEEEEEEEEEEE

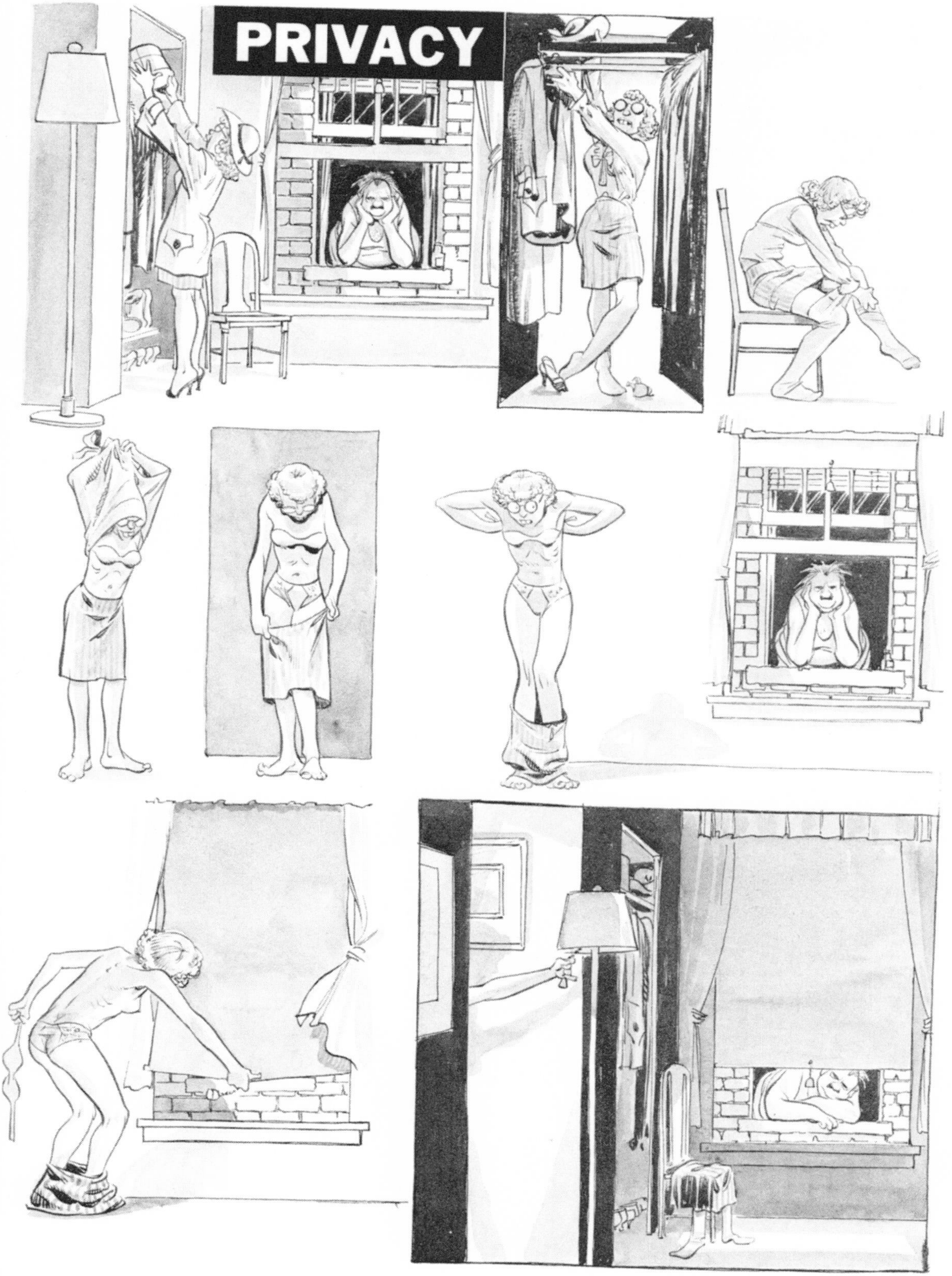
PRIVACY

DISPOSAL

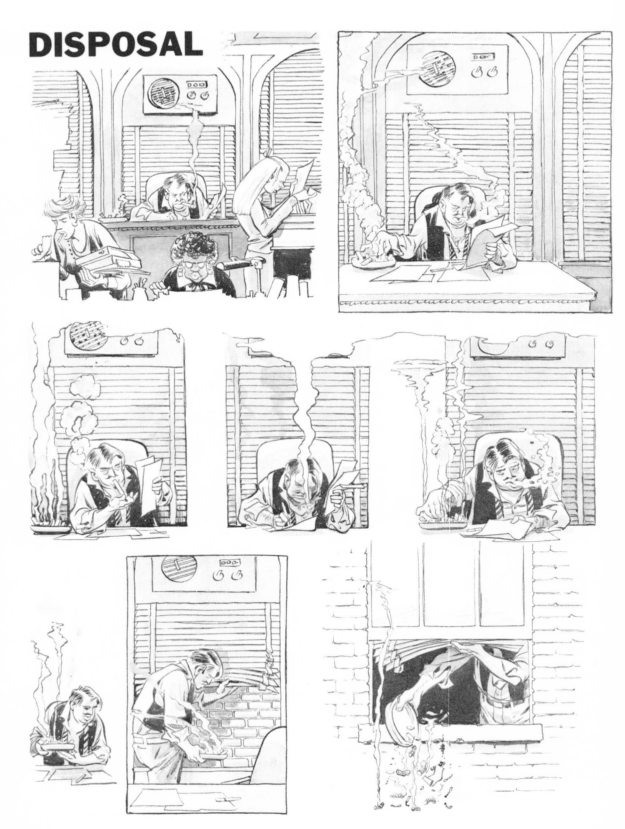

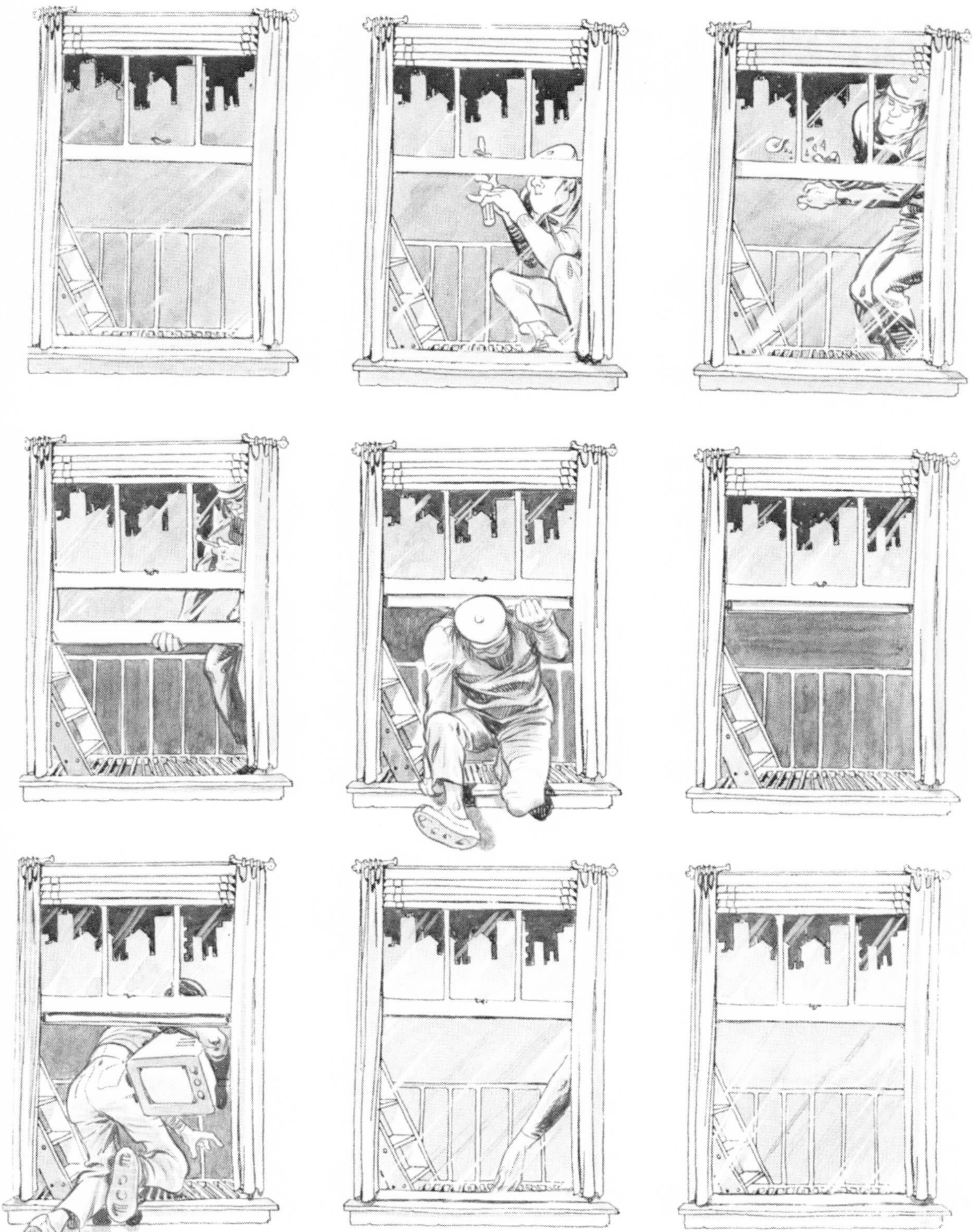

PEEPER

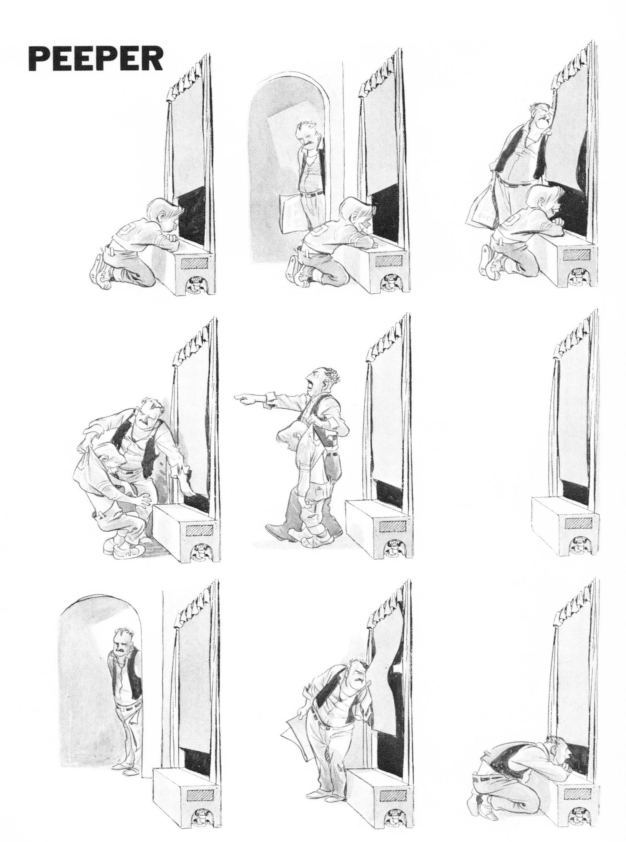

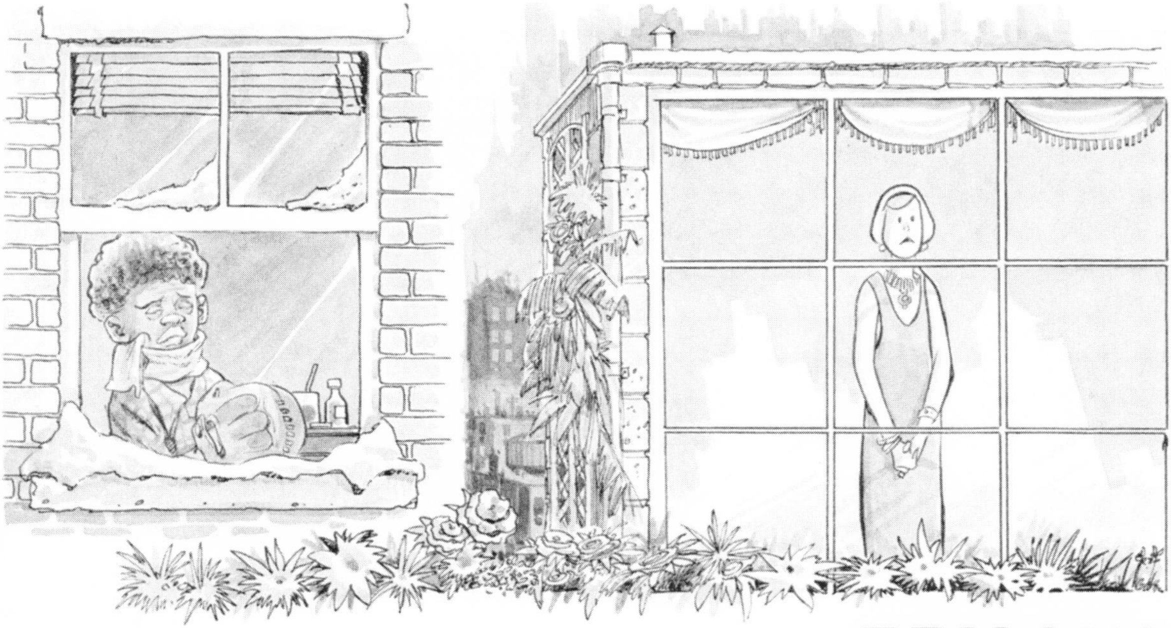

PRISONS

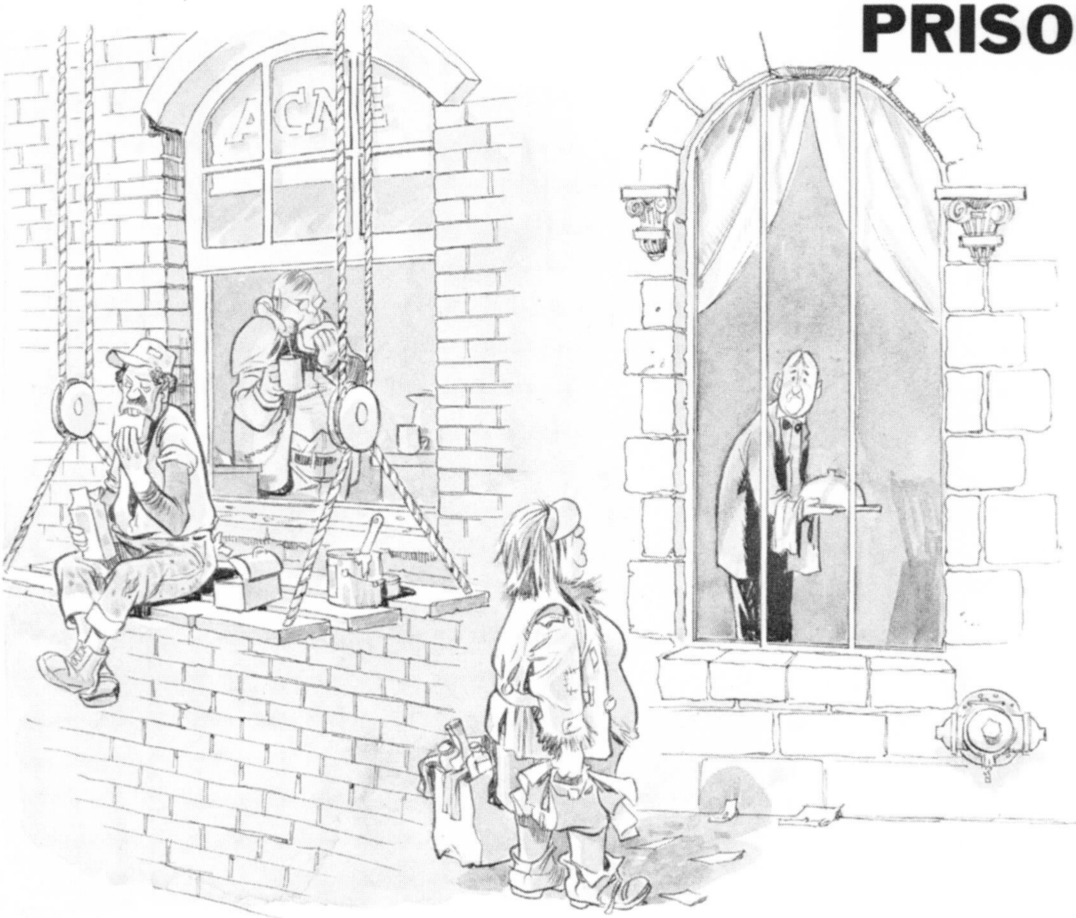
ACME

WORM'S EYE VIEW

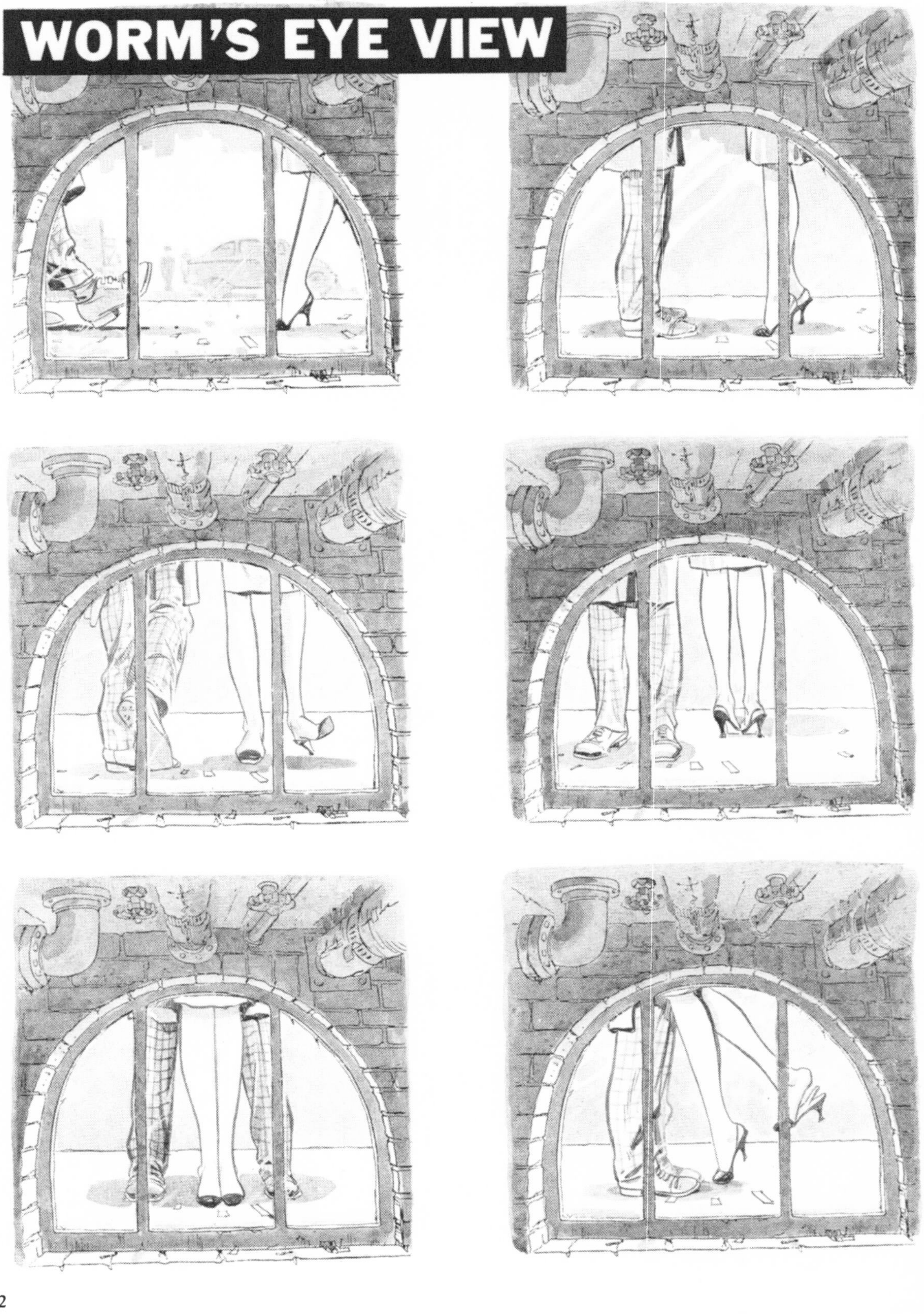

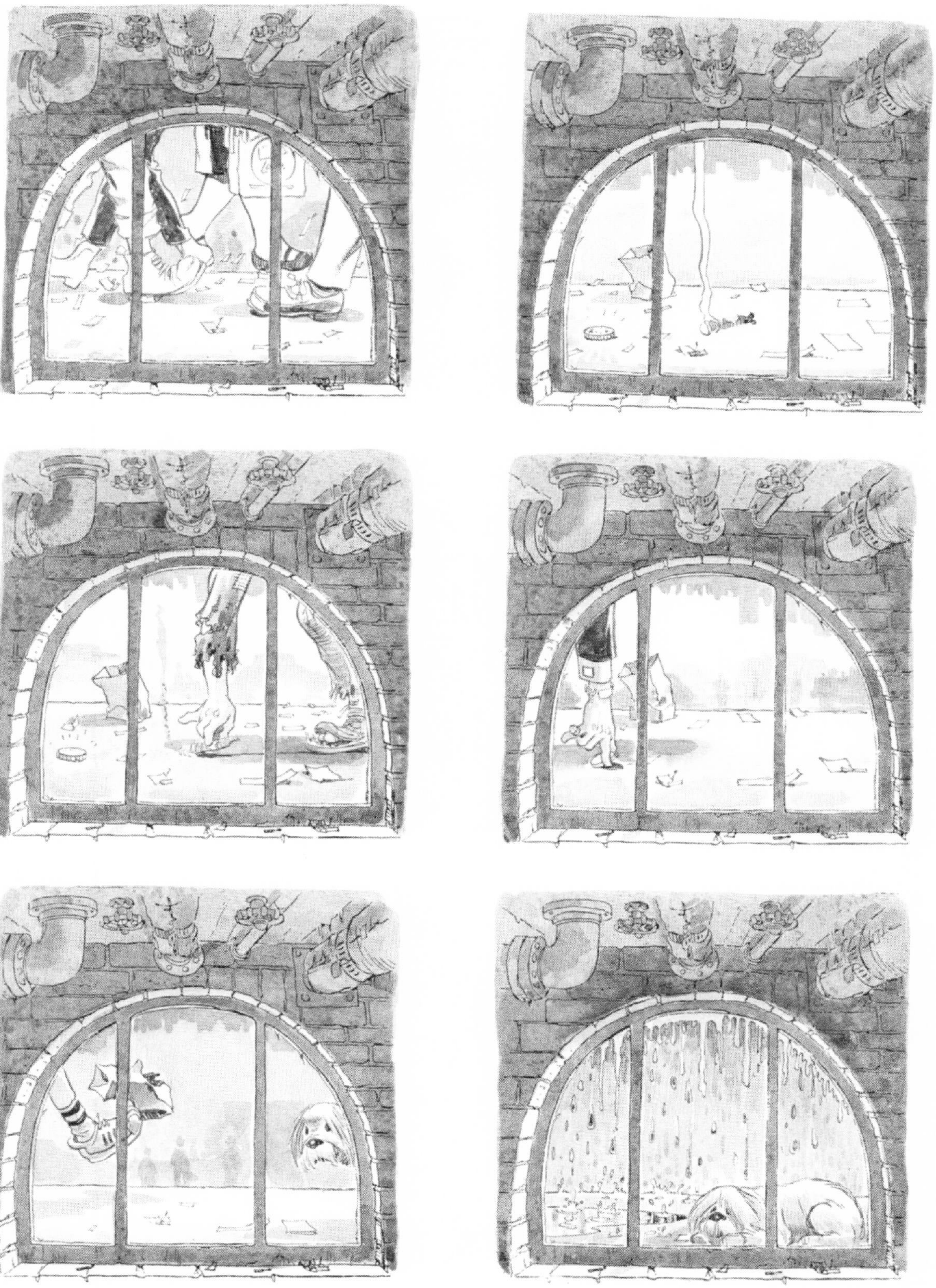

SERMONETTE

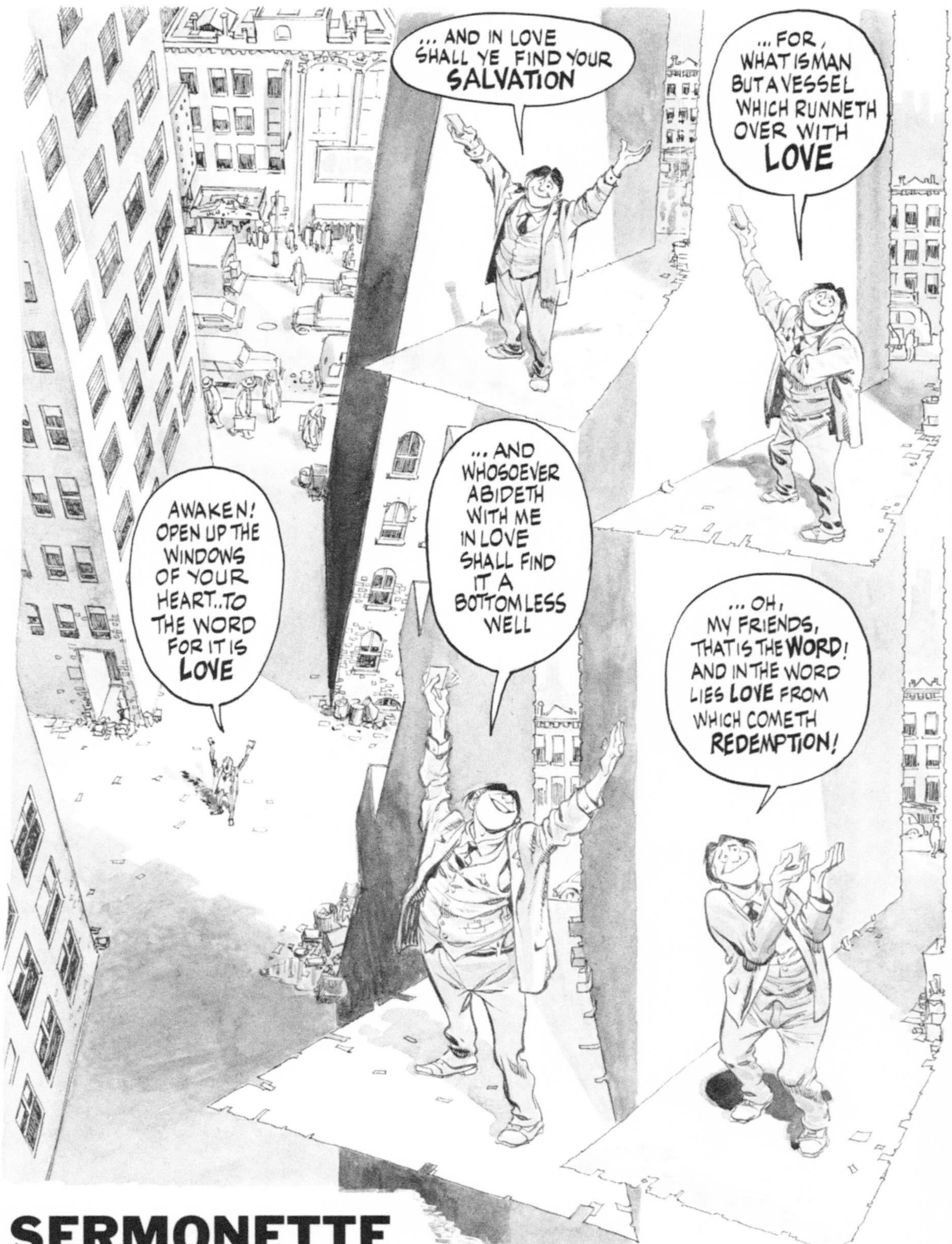
... AND IN LOVE SHALL YE FIND YOUR SALVATION
... FOR, WHAT IS MAN BUT A VESSEL WHICH RUNNETH OVER WITH LOVE
AWAKEN! OPEN UP THE WINDOWS OF YOUR HEART..TO THE WORD FOR IT IS LOVE
... AND WHOSOEVER ABIDETH WITH ME IN LOVE SHALL FIND IT A BOTTOMLESS WELL
... OH, MY FRIENDS, THAT IS THE WORD! AND IN THE WORD LIES LOVE FROM WHICH COMETH REDEMPTION!

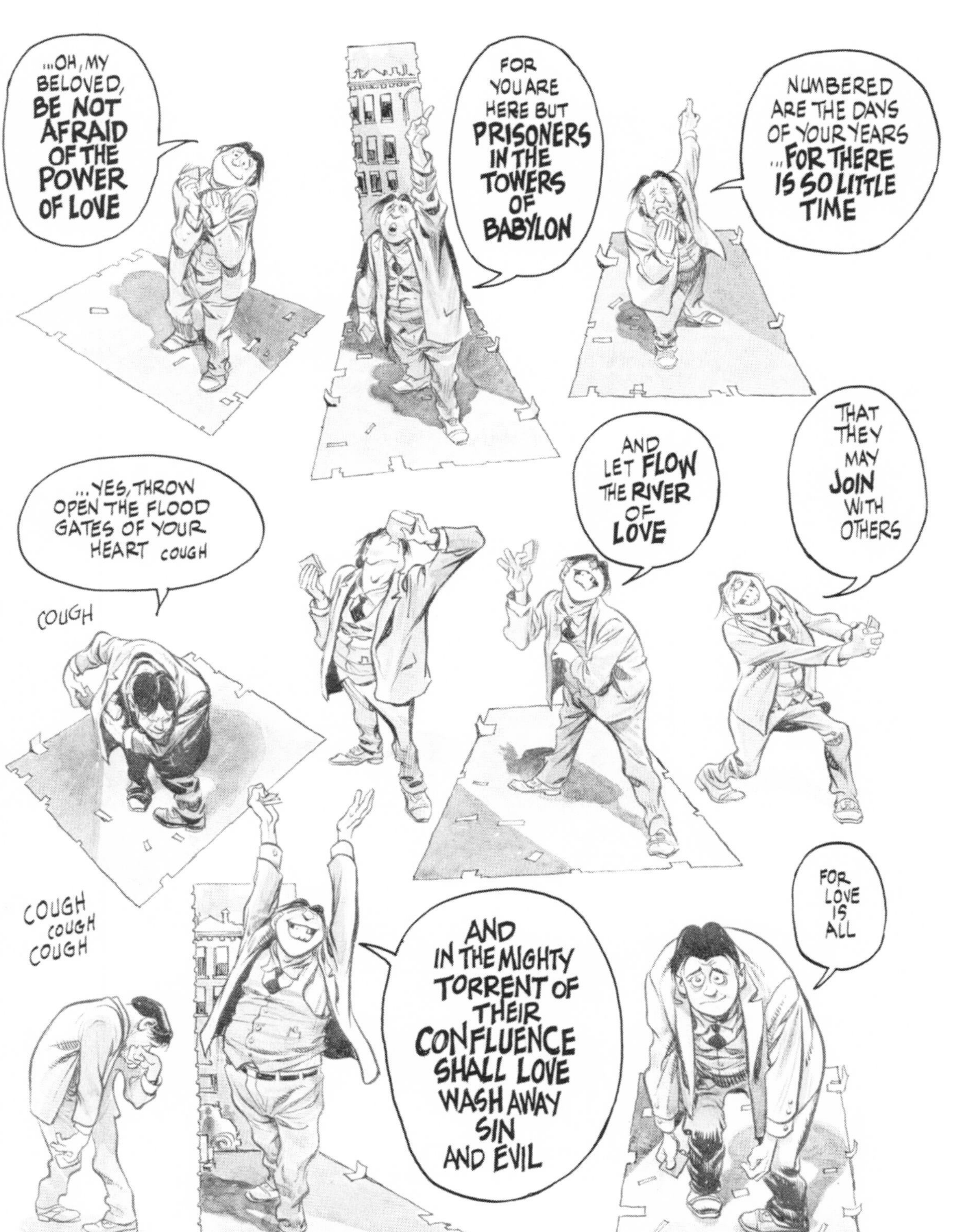
...OH, MY BELOVED, BE NOT AFRAID OF THE POWER OF LOVE
FOR YOU ARE HERE BUT PRISONERS IN THE TOWERS OF BABYLON
NUMBERED ARE THE DAYS OF YOUR YEARS ...FOR THERE IS SO LITTLE TIME
...YES, THROW OPEN THE FLOOD GATES OF YOUR HEART COUGH
COUGH
AND LET FLOW THE RIVER OF LOVE
THAT THEY MAY JOIN WITH OTHERS
COUGH COUGH COUGH
AND IN THE MIGHTY TORRENT OF THEIR CONFLUENCE SHALL LOVE WASH AWAY SIN AND EVIL
FOR LOVE IS ALL

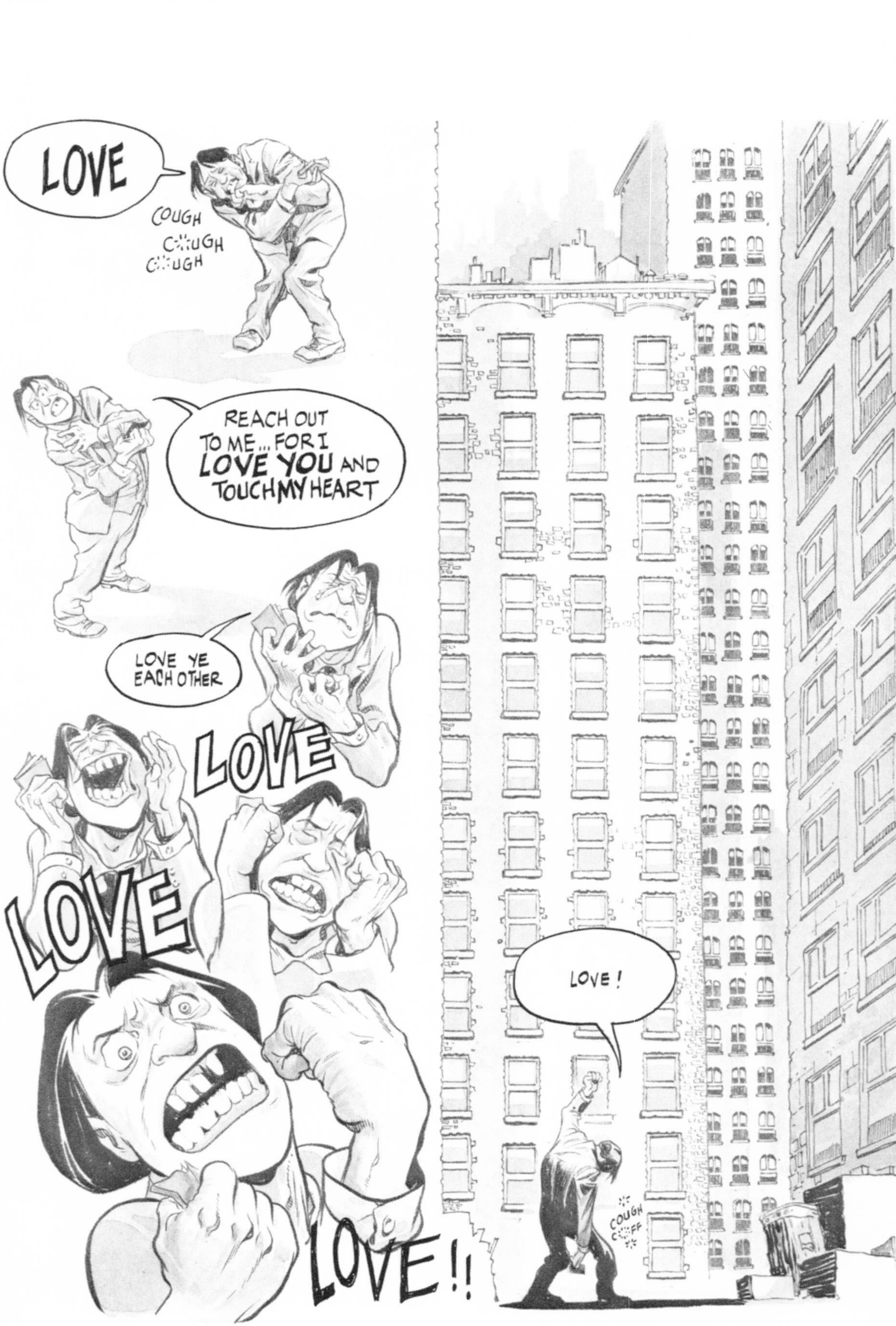
LOVE
COUGH
C::UGH
C::UGH
REACH OUT TO ME... FOR I LOVE YOU AND TOUCH MY HEART
LOVE YE EACH OTHER
LOVE
LOVE
LOVE!!
LOVE!
COUGH
C::FF

WALLS

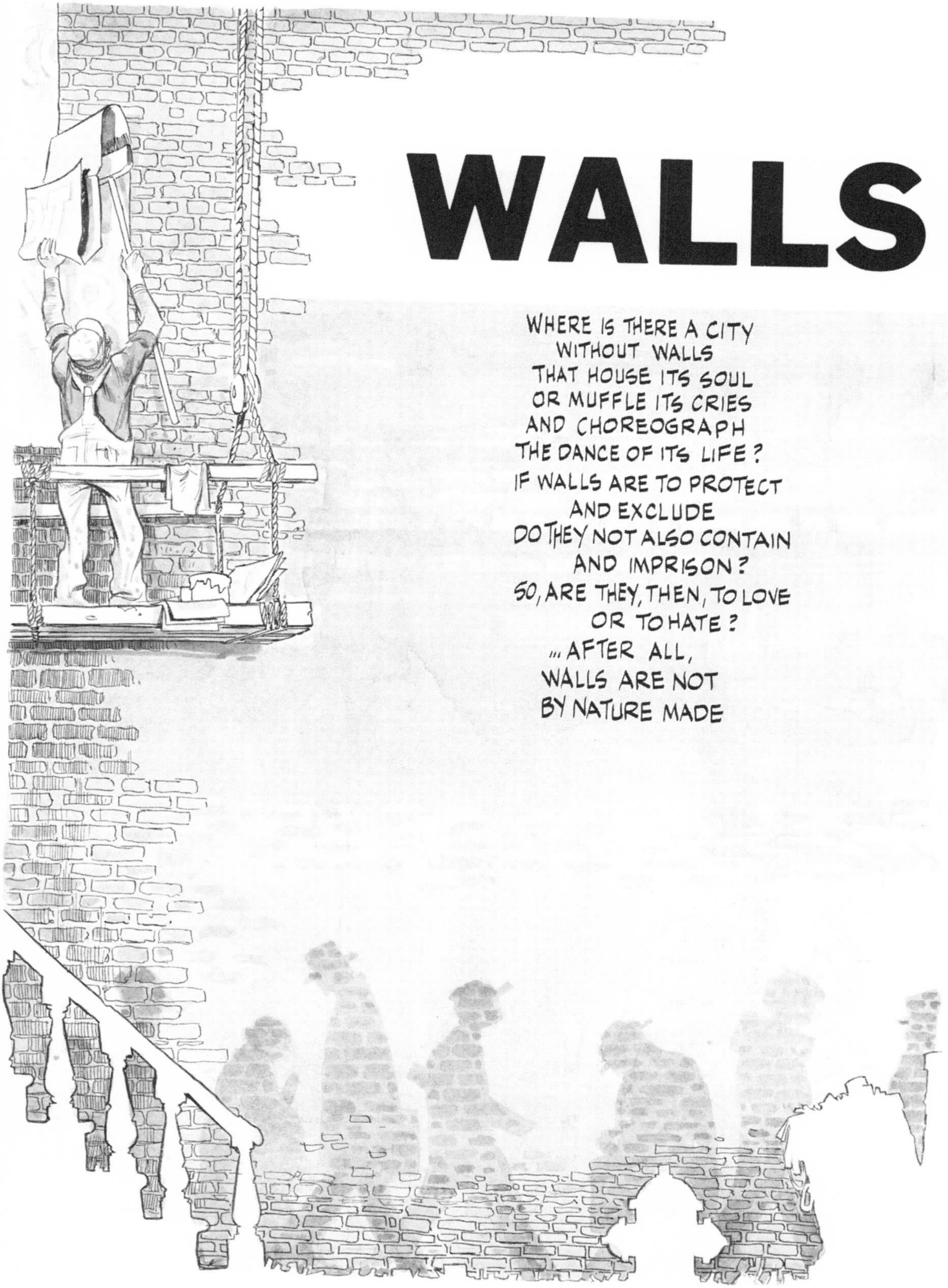

WHERE IS THERE A CITY
WITHOUT WALLS
THAT HOUSE ITS SOUL
OR MUFFLE ITS CRIES
AND CHOREOGRAPH
THE DANCE OF ITS LIFE?
IF WALLS ARE TO PROTECT
AND EXCLUDE
DO THEY NOT ALSO CONTAIN
AND IMPRISON?
SO, ARE THEY, THEN, TO LOVE
OR TO HATE?
... AFTER ALL,
WALLS ARE NOT
BY NATURE MADE

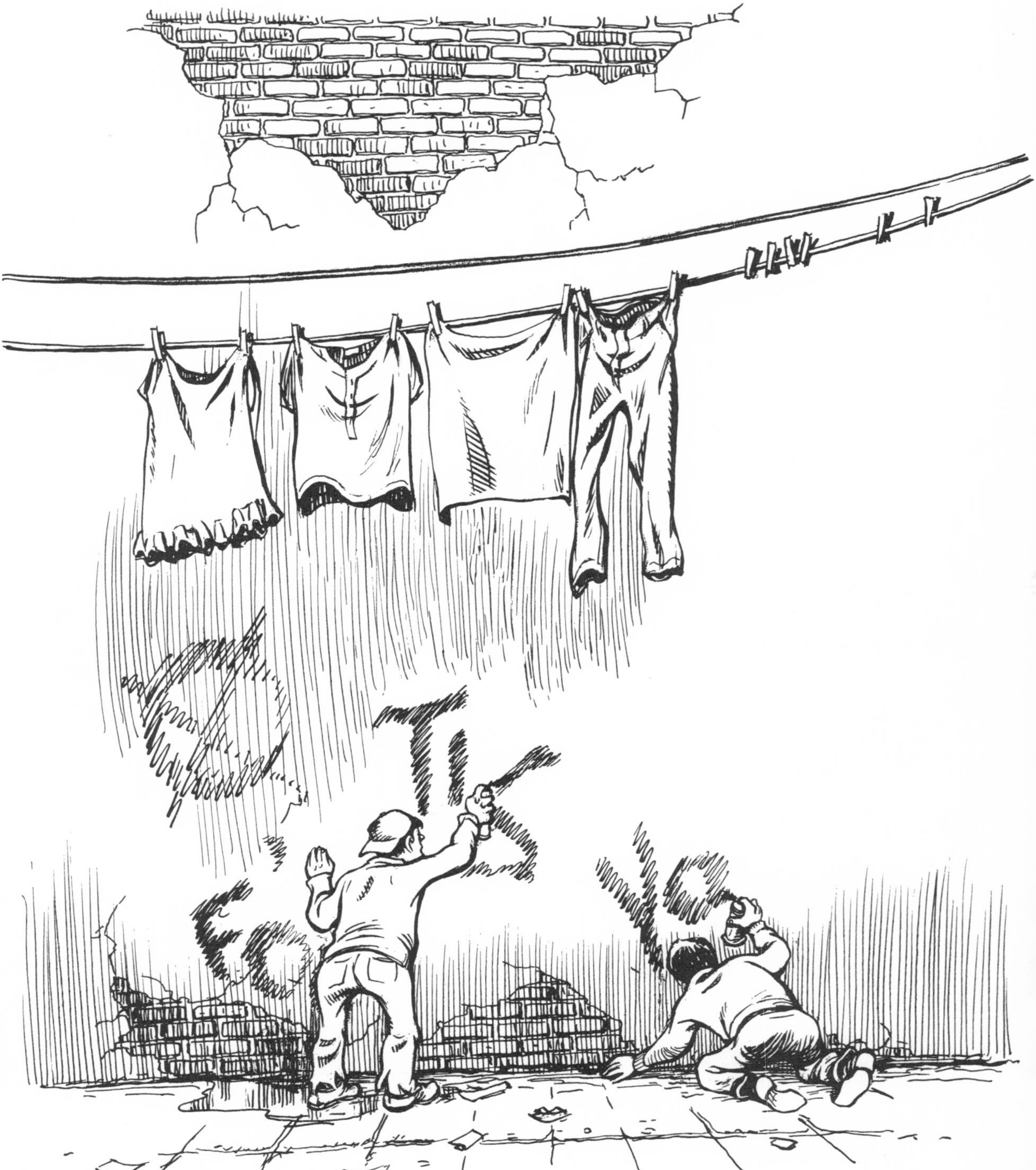

SPACE

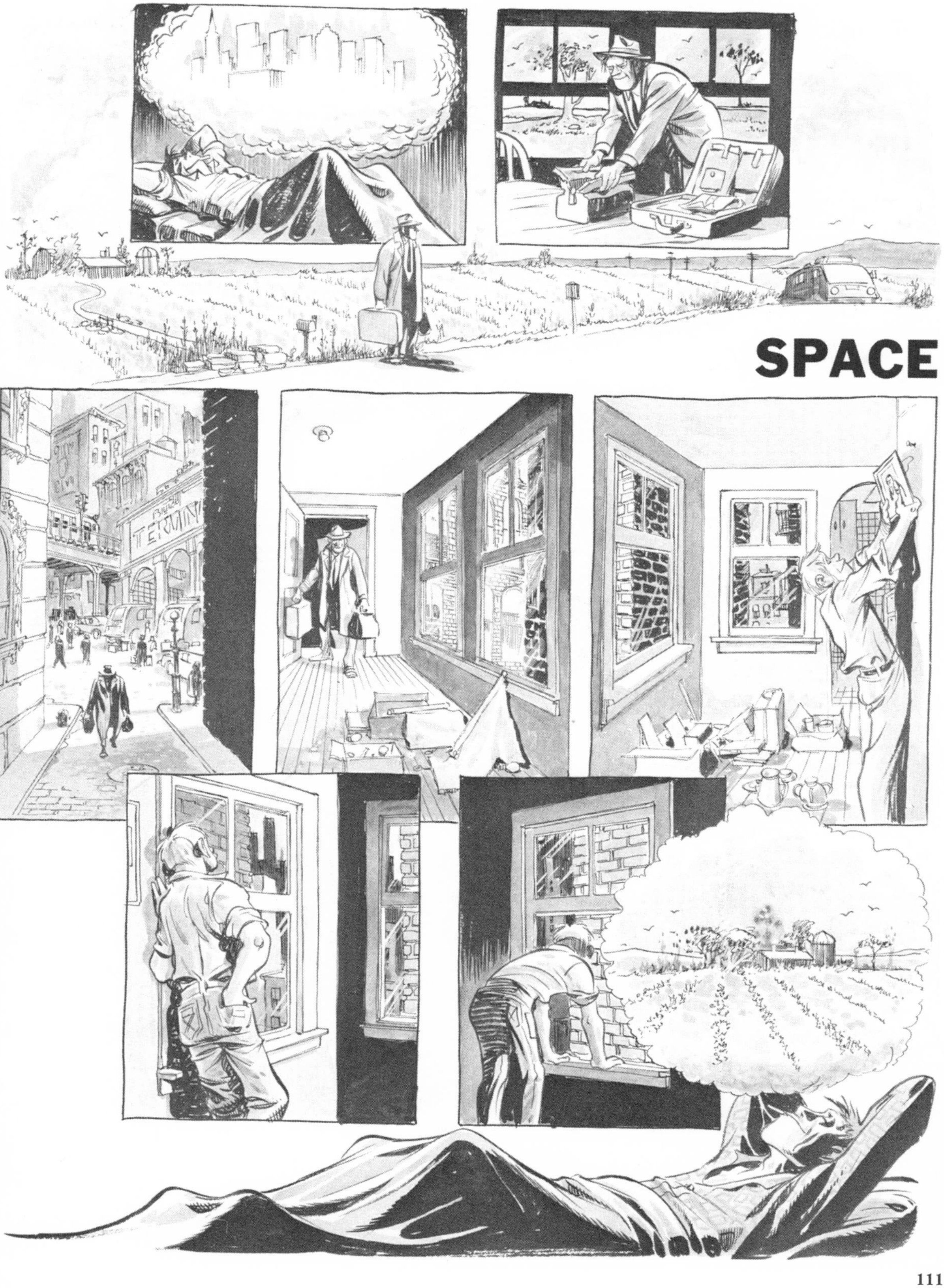
TERMINAL

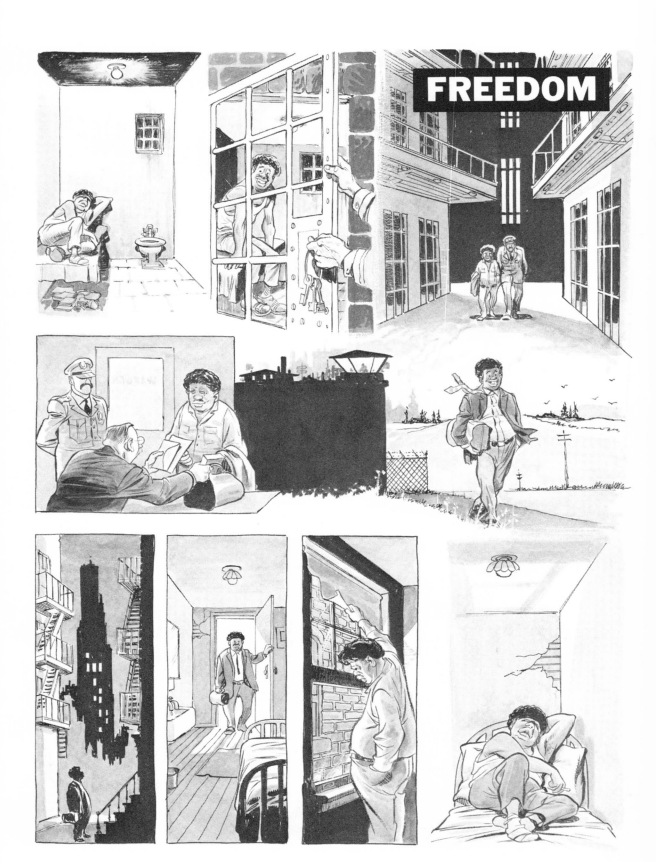

FREEDOM

MAZE

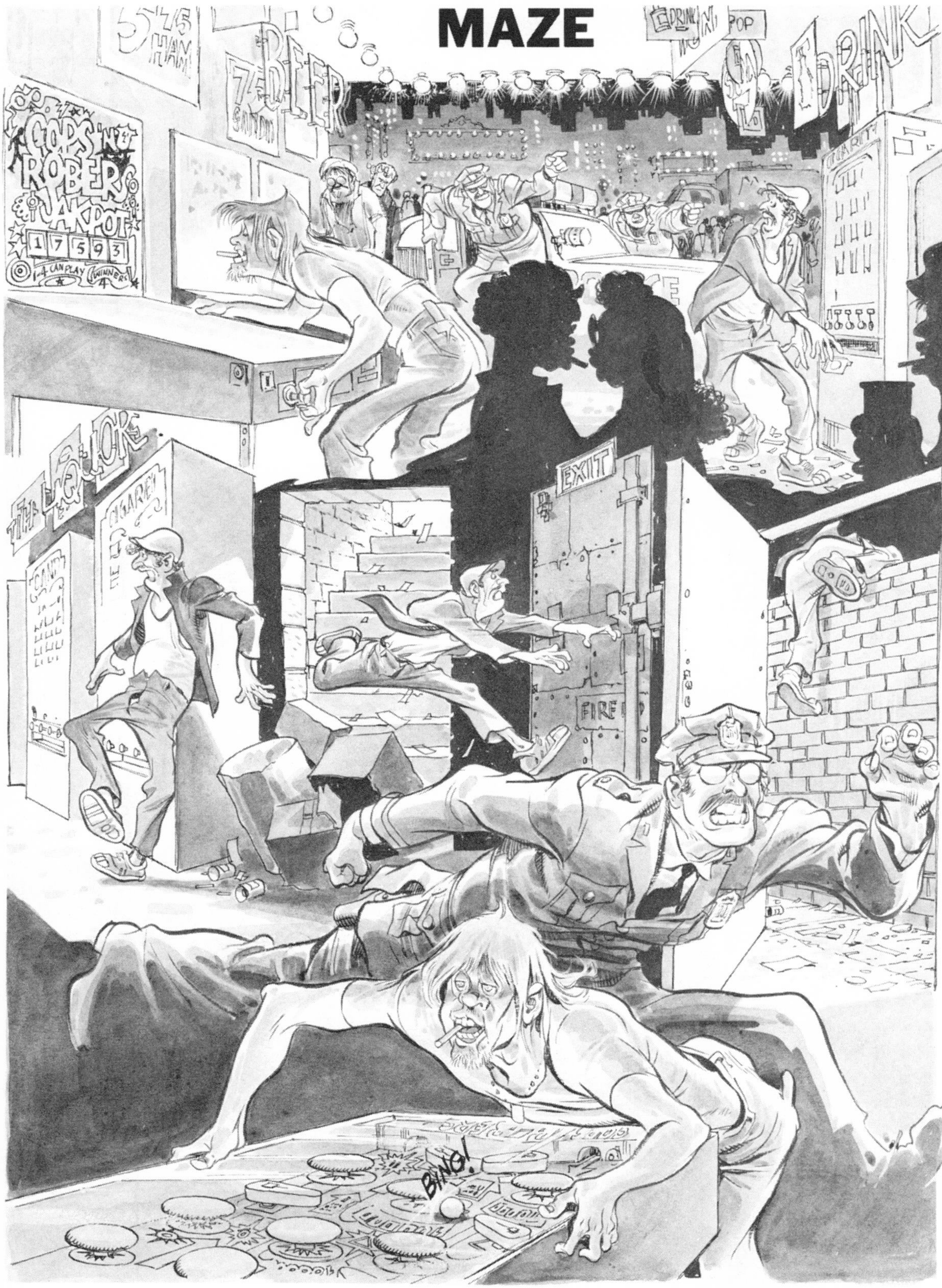
HAM
BEER
POP
DRINK
17593
EXIT
FIRE
BING!

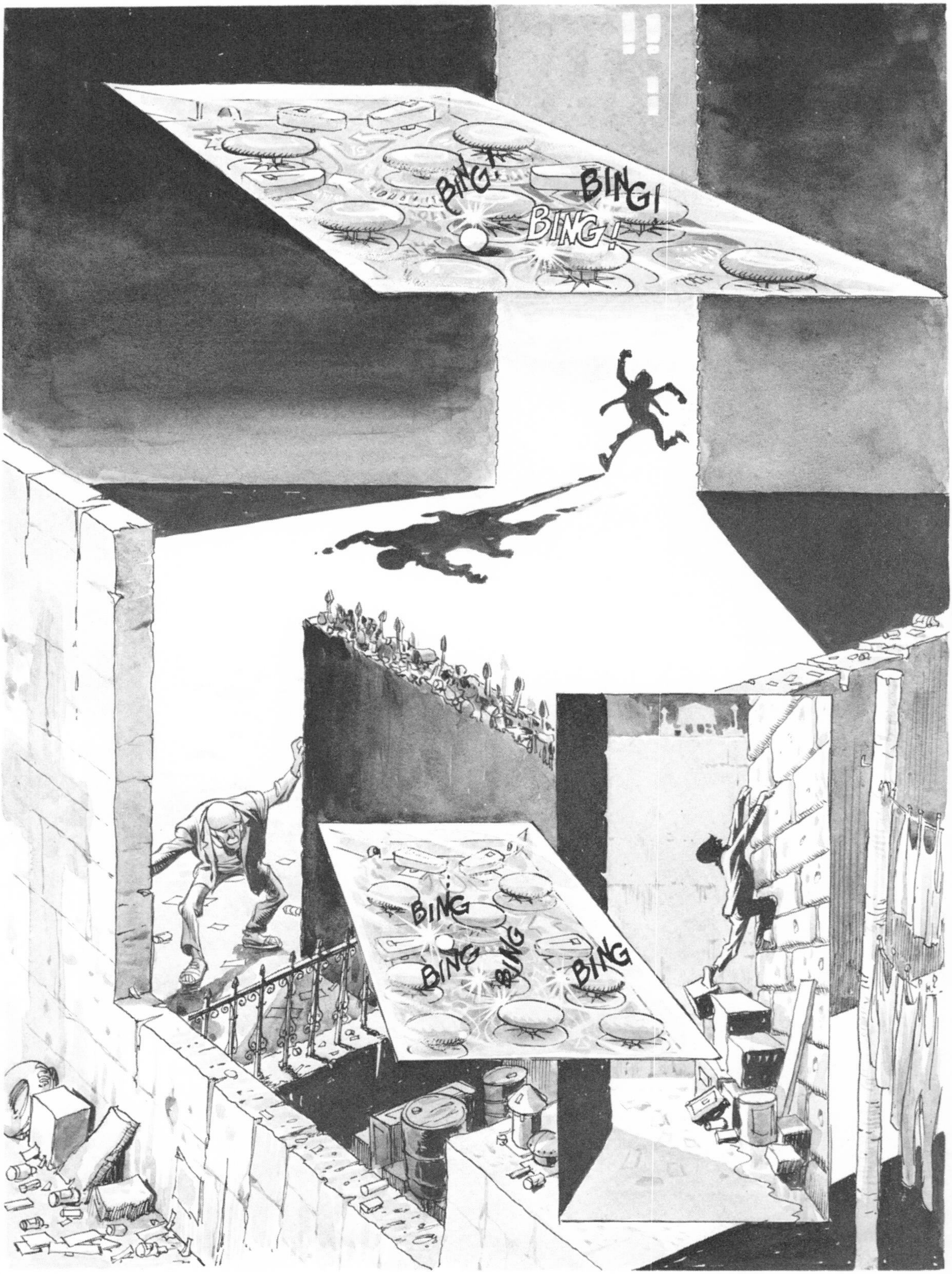
BING!
BING!
BING!
BING
BING
BING
BING

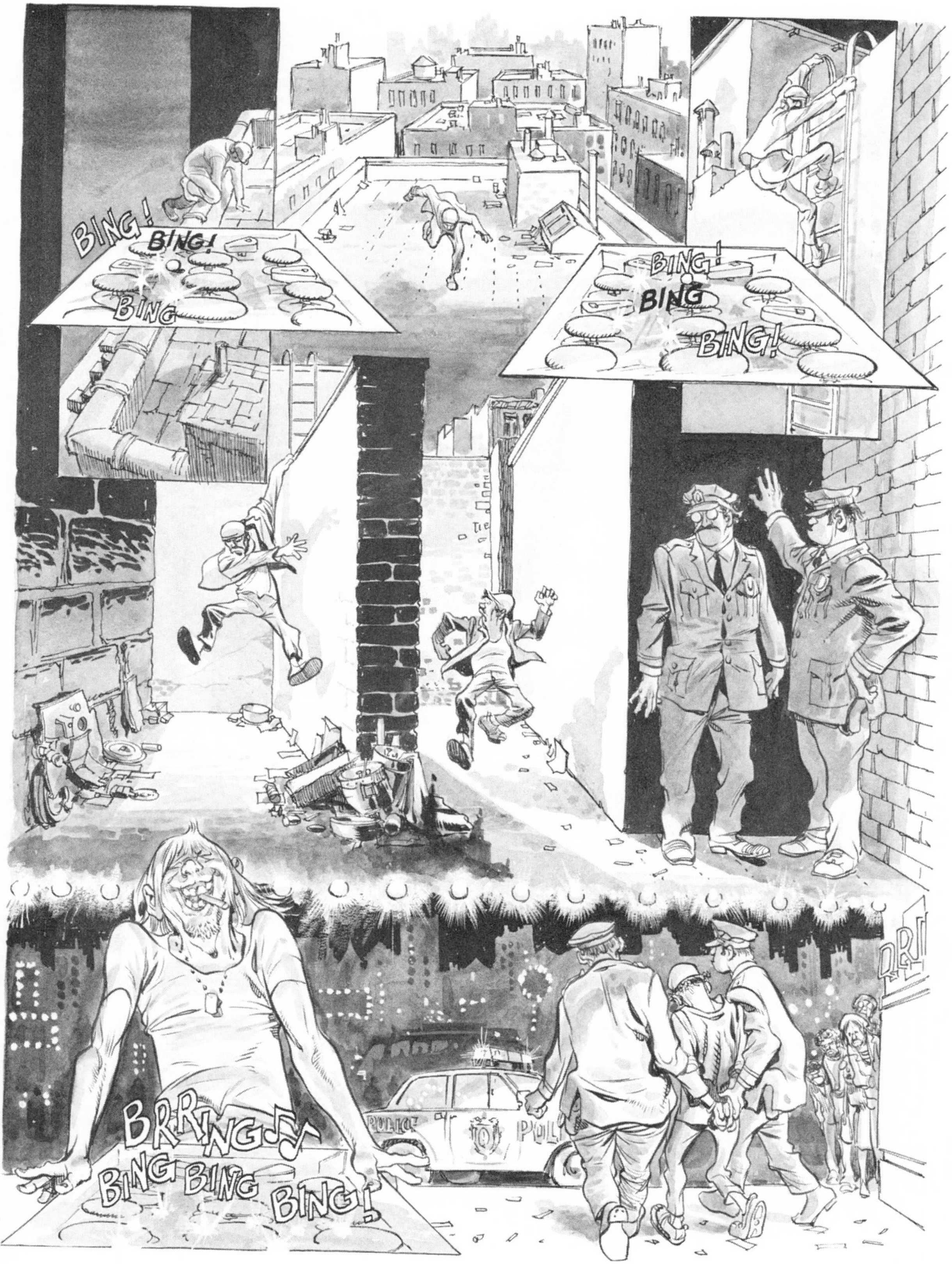
BING!
BING!
BING
BING!
BING
BING!
BRRRING
BING BING BING!
POLICE
POLI

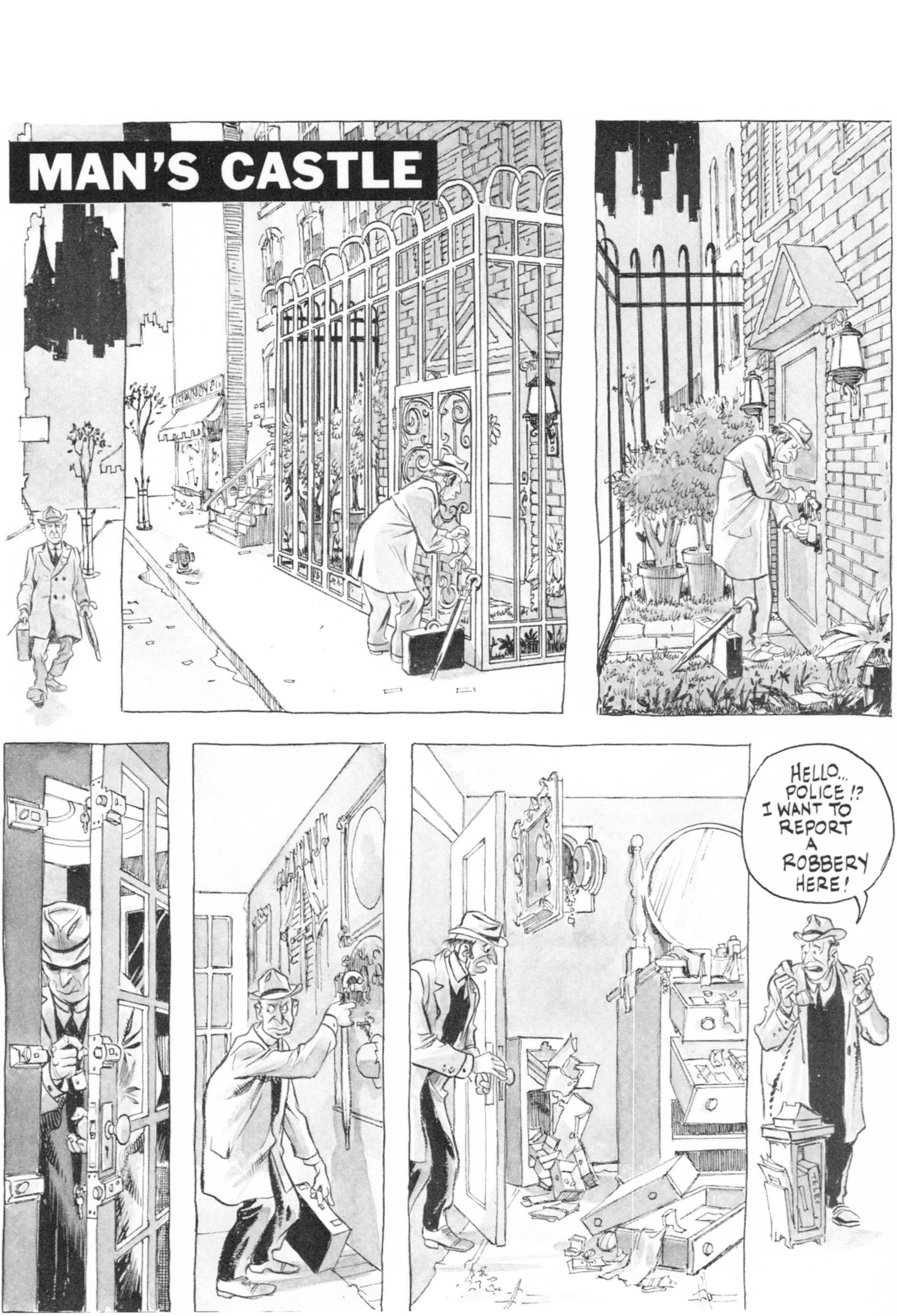
MAN'S CASTLE
HELLO... POLICE !? I WANT TO REPORT A ROBBERY HERE!

BULLETIN BOARD

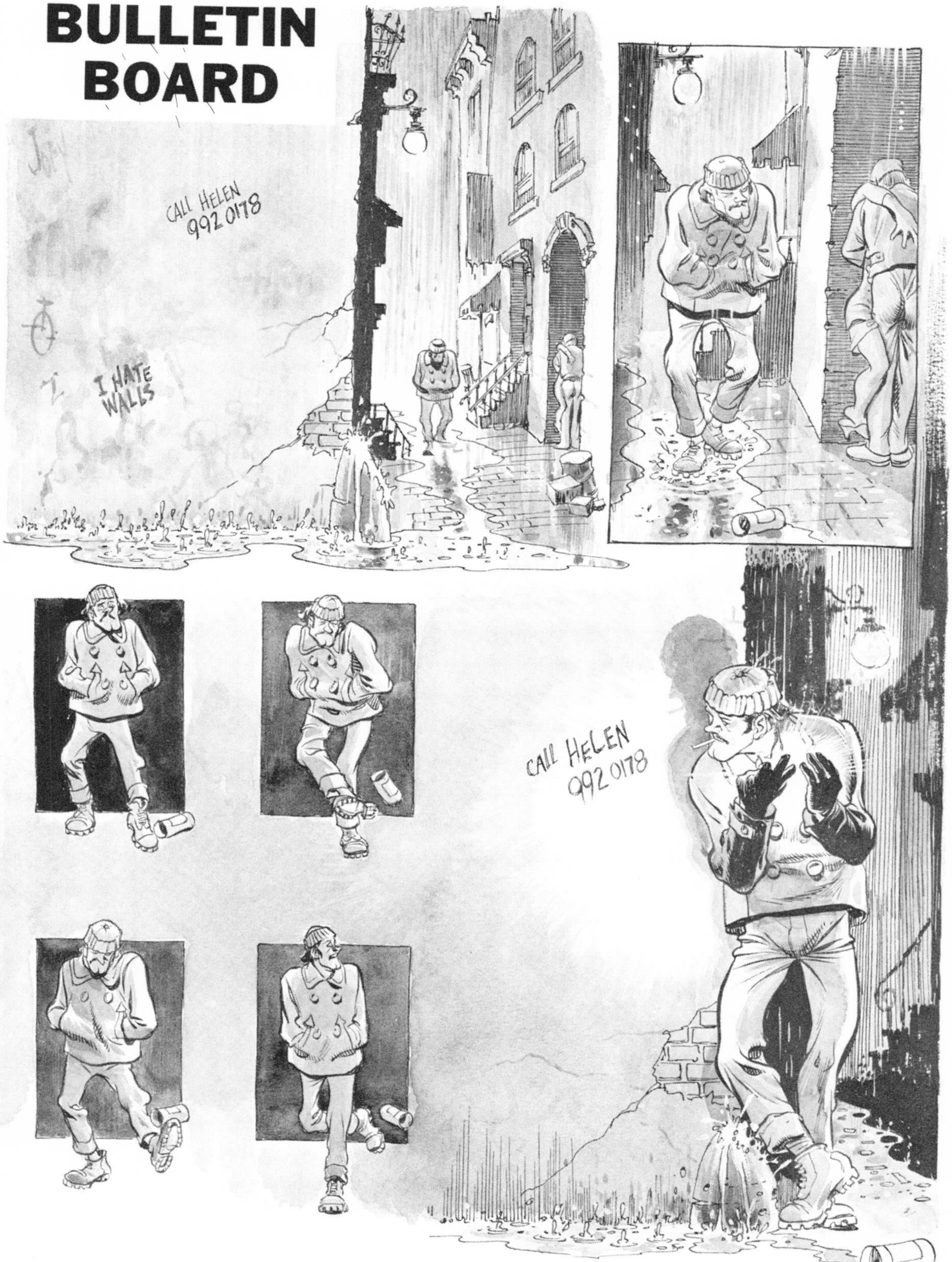
CALL HELEN
992 0178
I HATE WALLS
CALL HELEN
992 0178

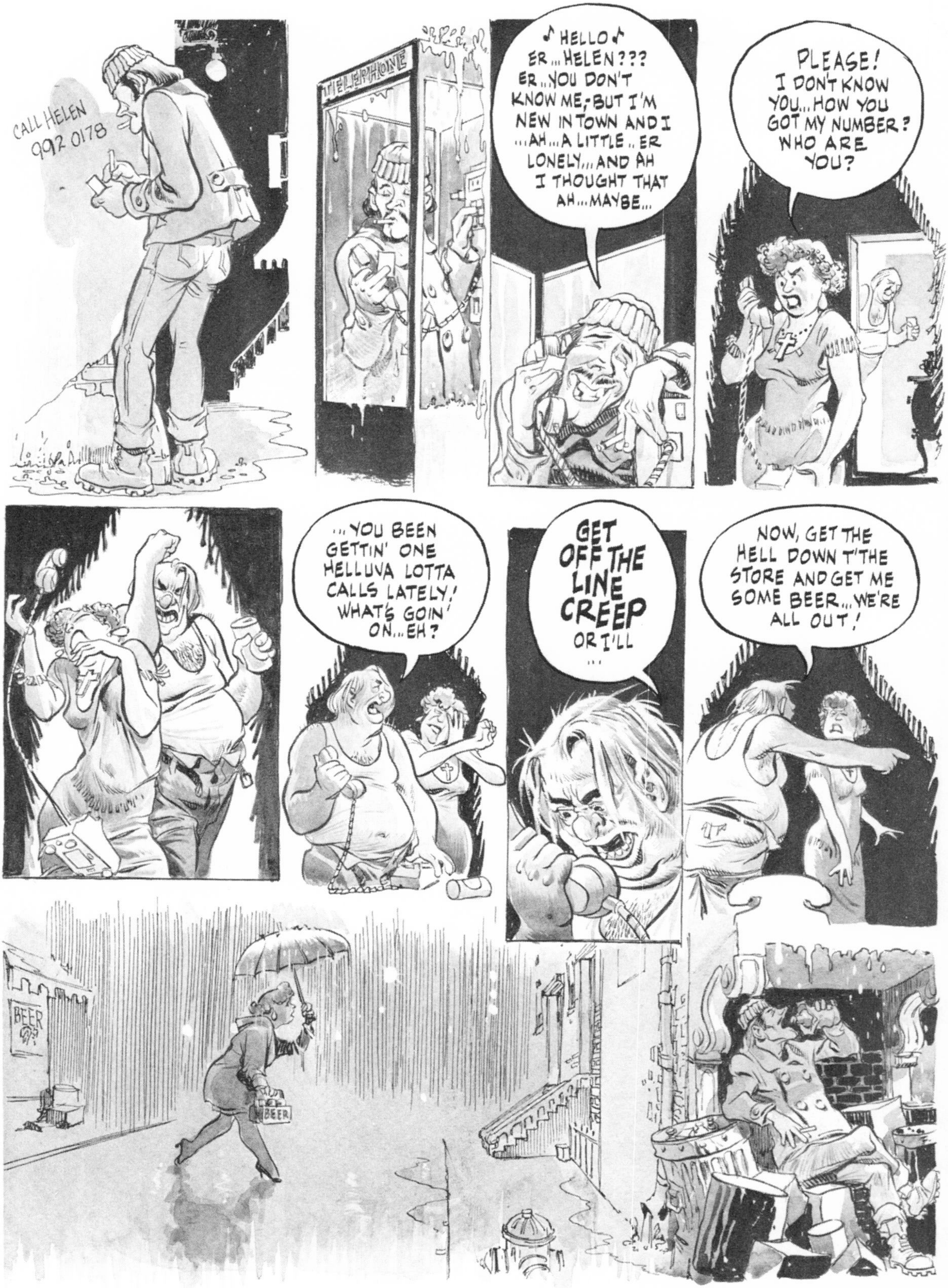

CALL HELEN 992 0178
TELEPHONE
♪ HELLO ♪ ER... HELEN??? ER...YOU DON'T KNOW ME,-BUT I'M NEW IN TOWN AND I ...AH...A LITTLE..ER LONELY,...AND AH I THOUGHT THAT AH...MAYBE...
PLEASE! I DON'T KNOW YOU...HOW YOU GOT MY NUMBER? WHO ARE YOU?
...YOU BEEN GETTIN' ONE HELLUVA LOTTA CALLS LATELY! WHAT'S GOIN' ON...EH?
GET OFF THE LINE CREEP OR I'LL ...
NOW, GET THE HELL DOWN T'THE STORE AND GET ME SOME BEER...WE'RE ALL OUT!
BEER
BEER

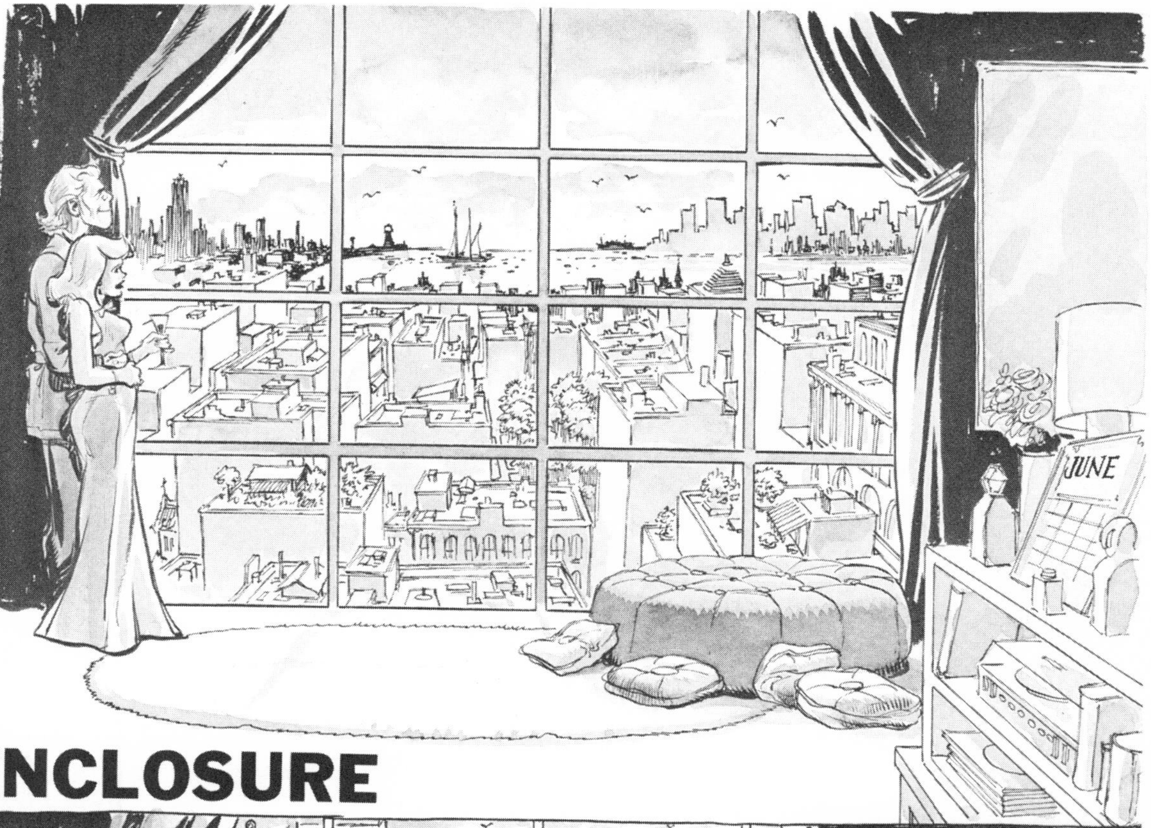
JUNE

ENCLOSURE

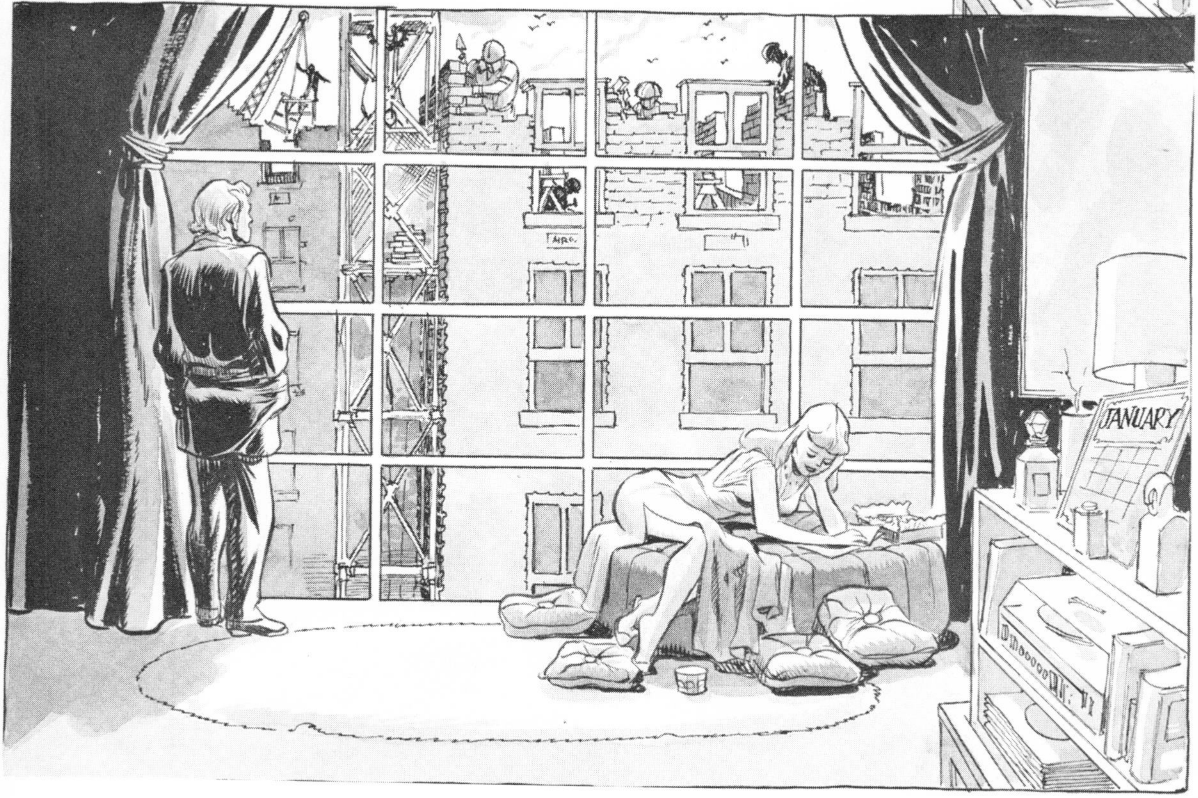
JANUARY

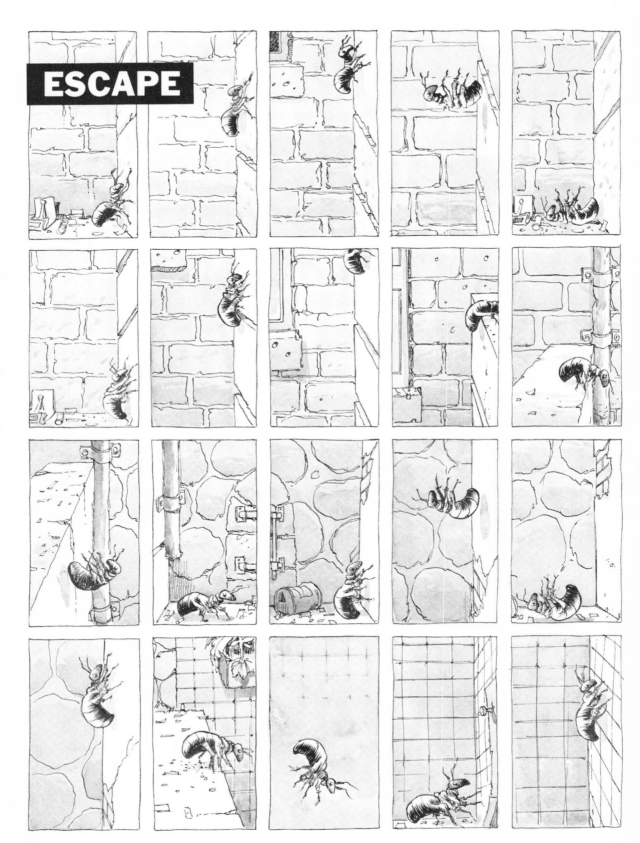

ESCAPE

WALLS HAVE EARS

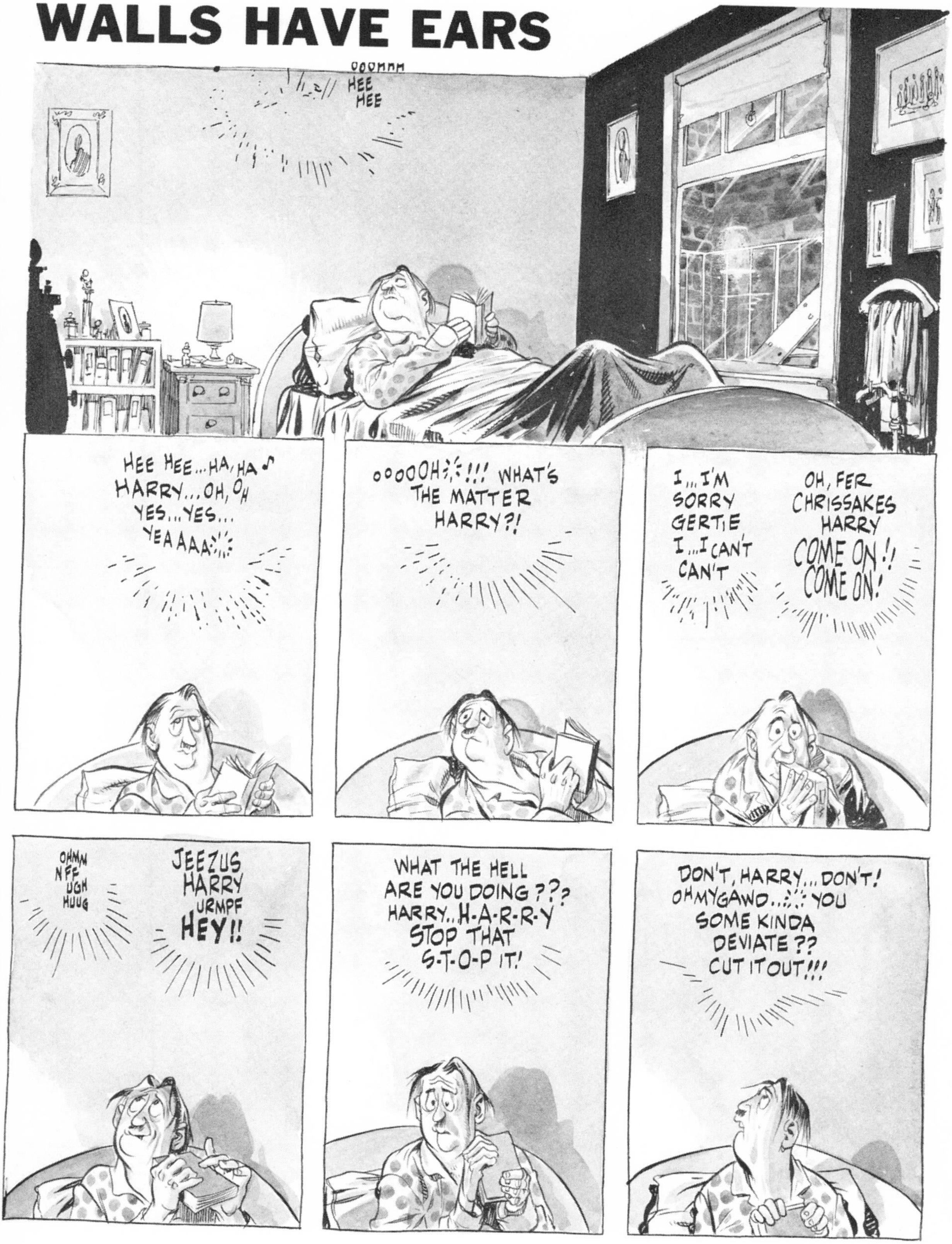
OOOMMM
HEE HEE
HEE HEE...HA, HA
HARRY...OH, OH YES...YES... YEAAAA
OOOOOH!!! WHAT'S THE MATTER HARRY?!
I...I'M SORRY GERTIE I...I CAN'T CAN'T
OH, FER CHRISSAKES HARRY COME ON!! COME ON!
OHMM NFF UGH HUUG
JEEZUS HARRY URMPF HEY!!
WHAT THE HELL ARE YOU DOING??? HARRY..H-A-R-R-Y STOP THAT S-T-O-P IT!
DON'T, HARRY... DON'T! OHMYGAWD... YOU SOME KINDA DEVIATE?? CUT IT OUT!!!

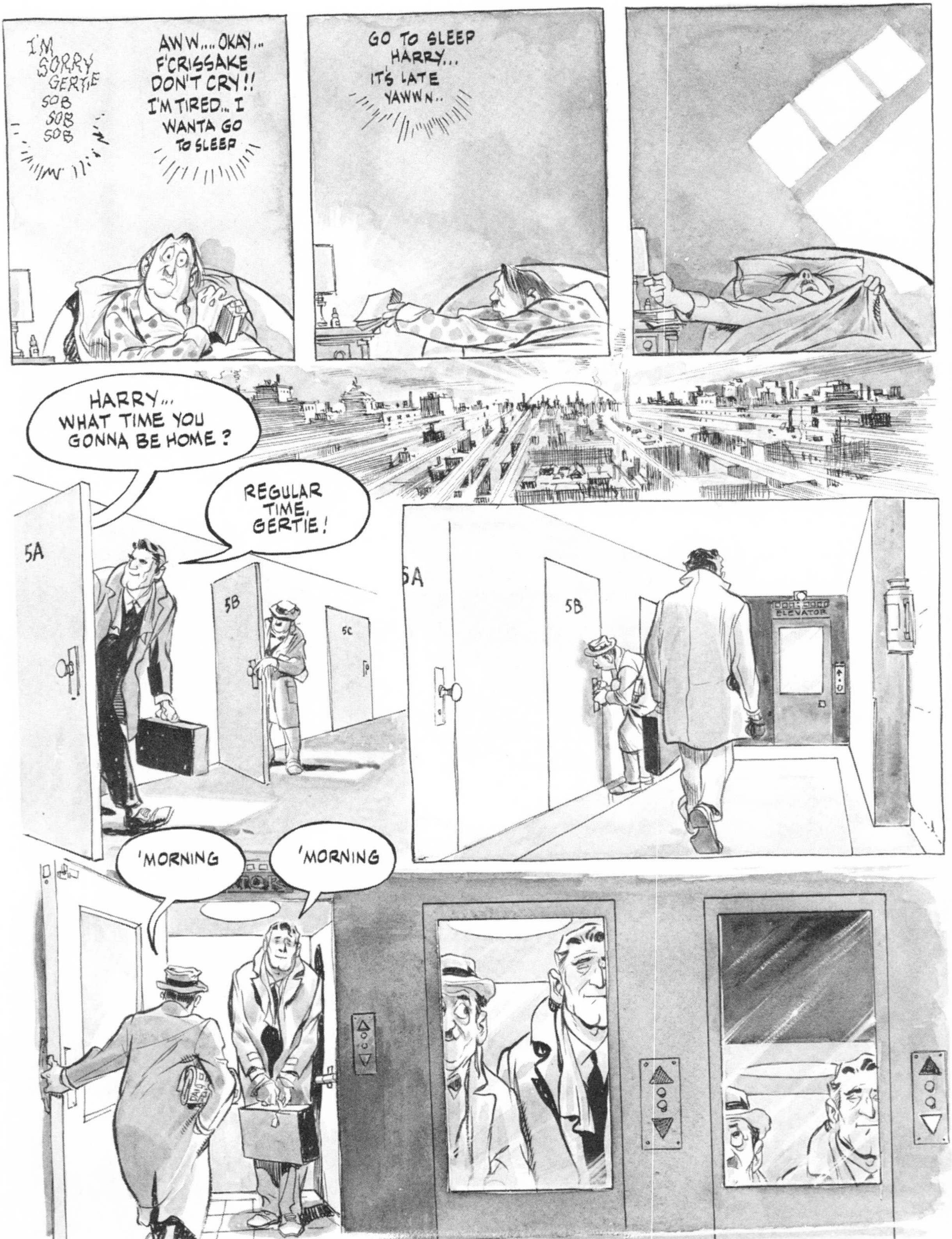
I'M SORRY GERTIE
SOB SOB SOB
AWW.... OKAY... F'CRISSAKE DON'T CRY!! I'M TIRED.. I WANTA GO TO SLEEP
GO TO SLEEP HARRY... IT'S LATE
YAWWN..
HARRY... WHAT TIME YOU GONNA BE HOME?
REGULAR TIME, GERTIE!
5A
5B
5C
5A
5B
ELEVATOR
'MORNING
'MORNING

PRIVACY

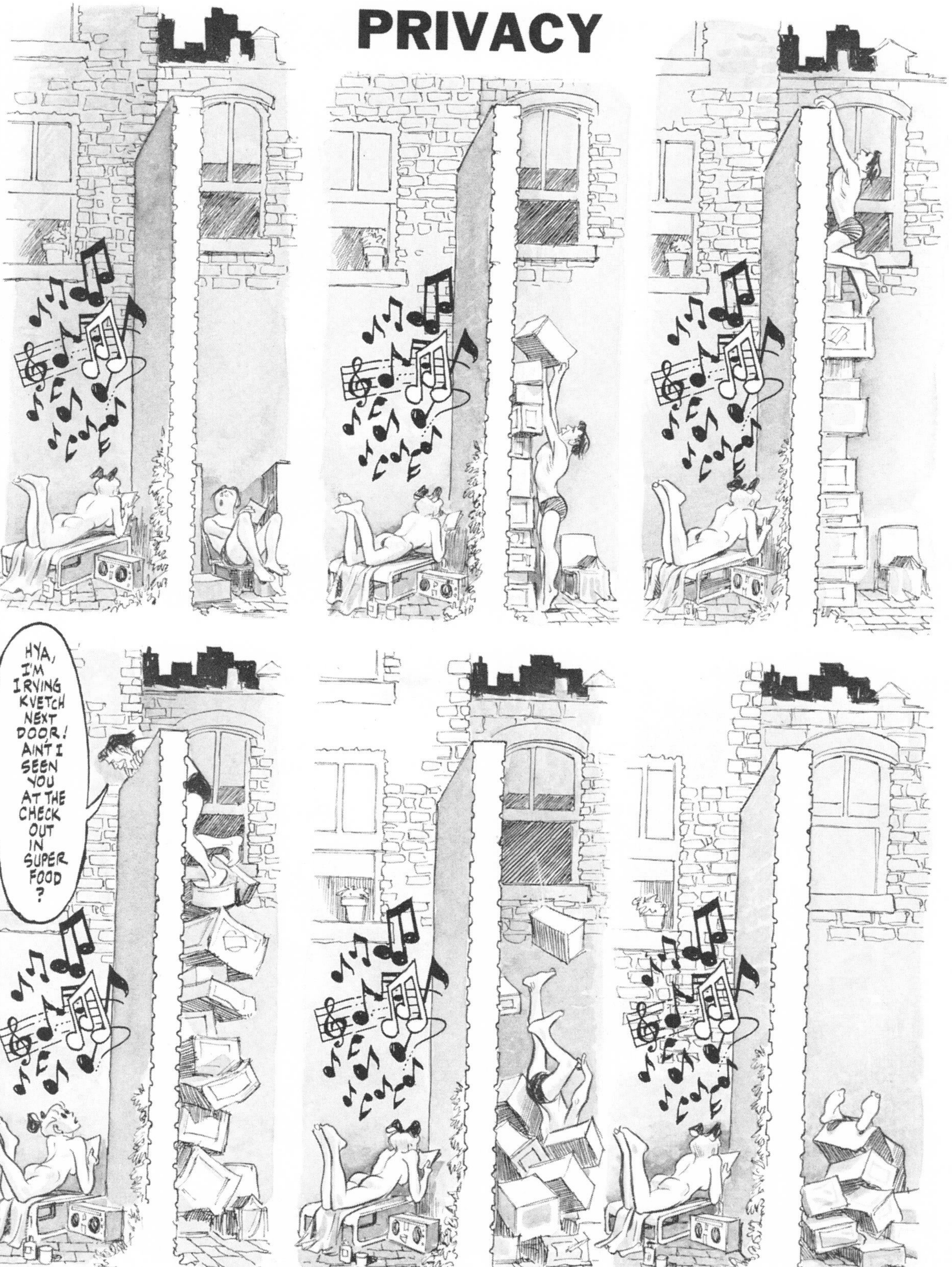
HYA, I'M IRVING KVETCH NEXT DOOR! AIN'T I SEEN YOU AT THE CHECK OUT IN SUPER FOOD ?

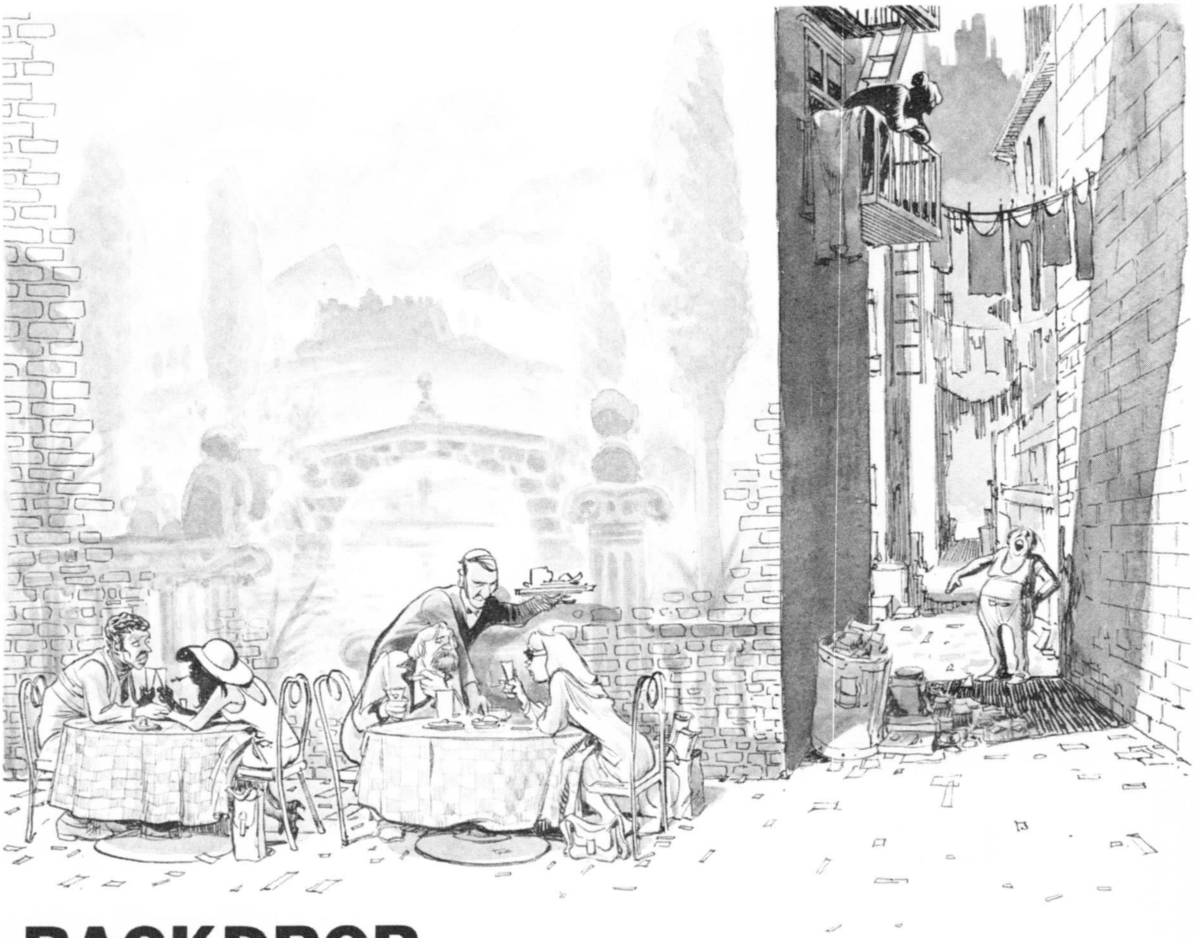

BACKDROP

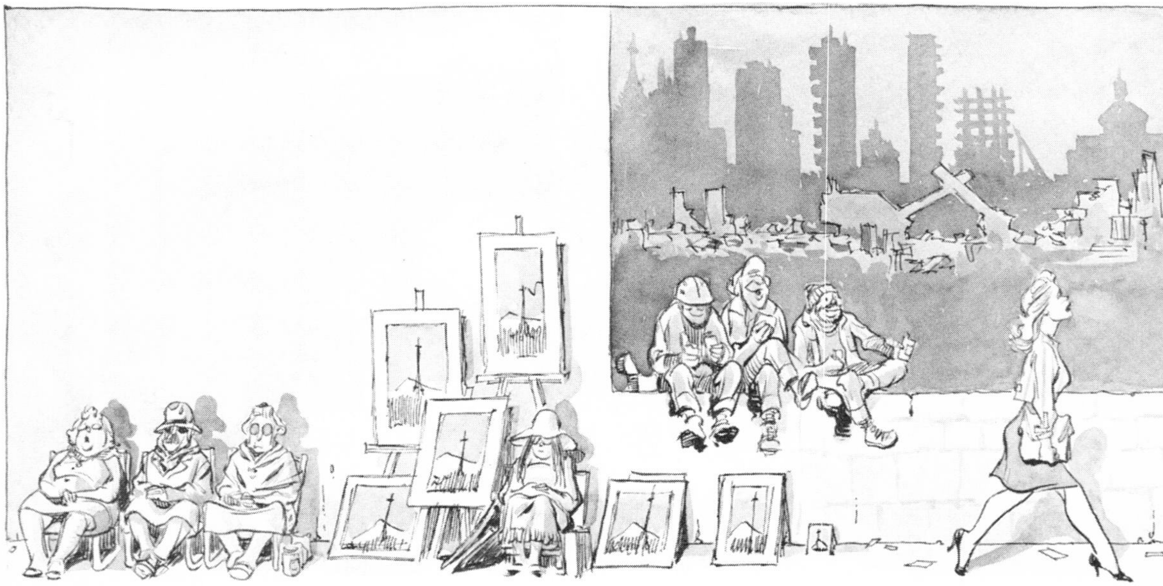

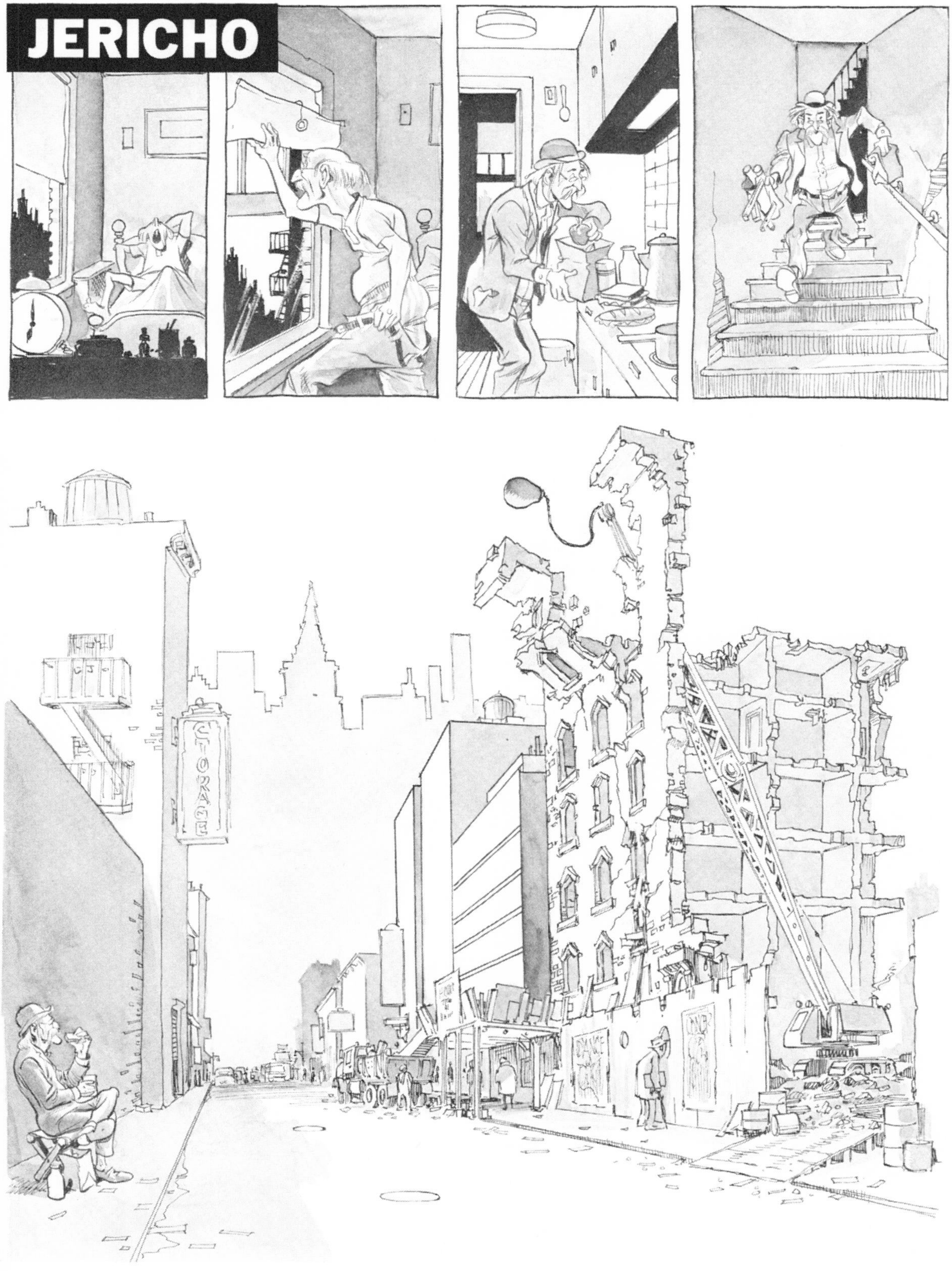
JERICHO
STORAGE

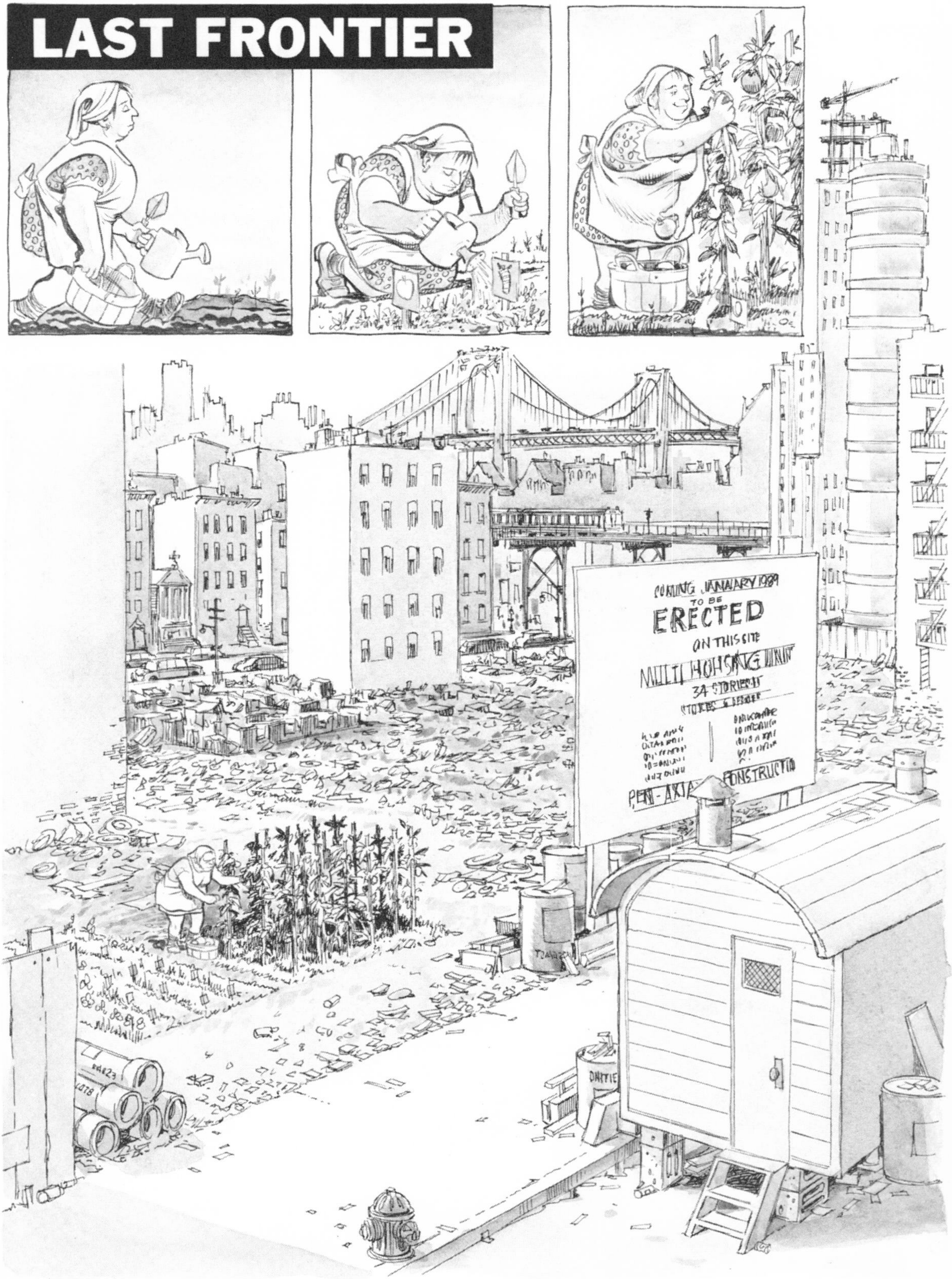
LAST FRONTIER
COMING JANUARY 1989
TO BE
ERECTED
ON THIS SITE
34 STORIES
CONSTRUCTION

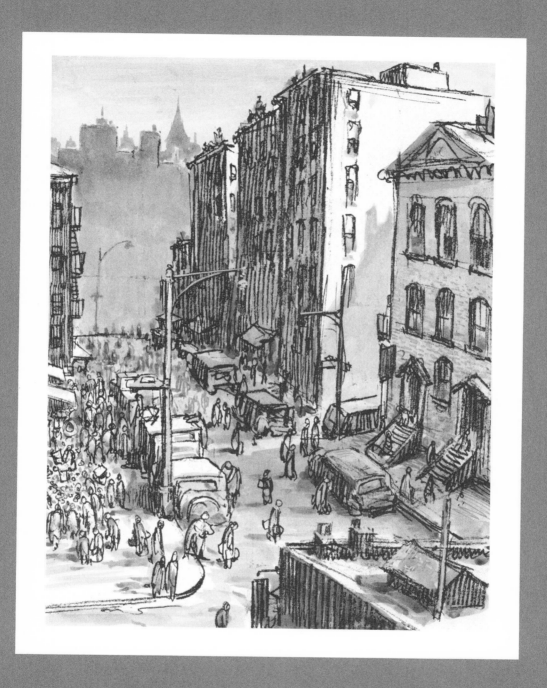

THE BLOCK

IN THE BIG CITY,
A VALLEY
FORMED BY THE BISECTION
OF STEEL AND CONCRETE
CLIFF DWELLINGS,
IS CALLED A BLOCK.
TO ITS INHABITANTS
IT IS THE WHOLE WORLD!

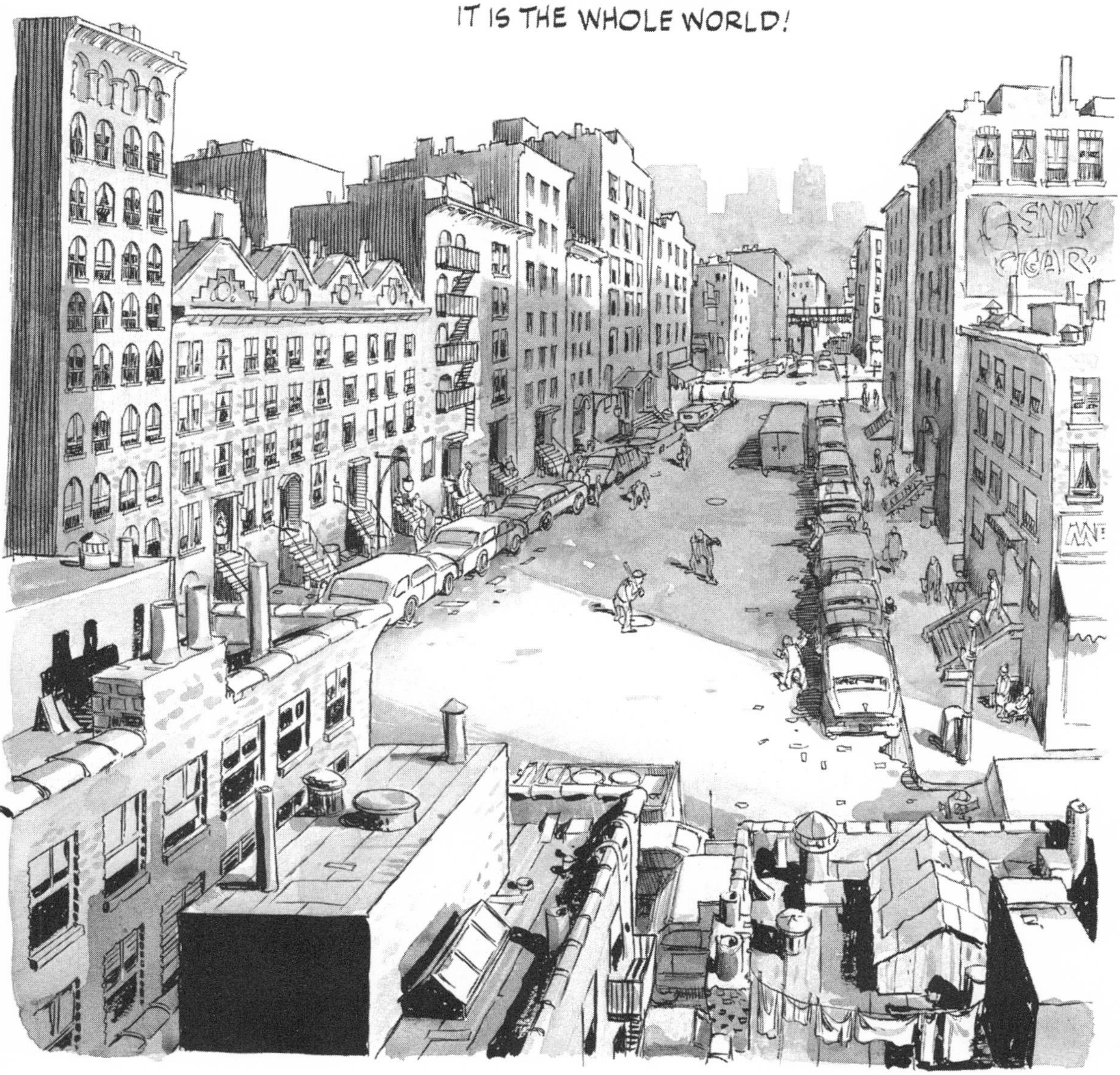

THE OLD NEIGHBORHOOD

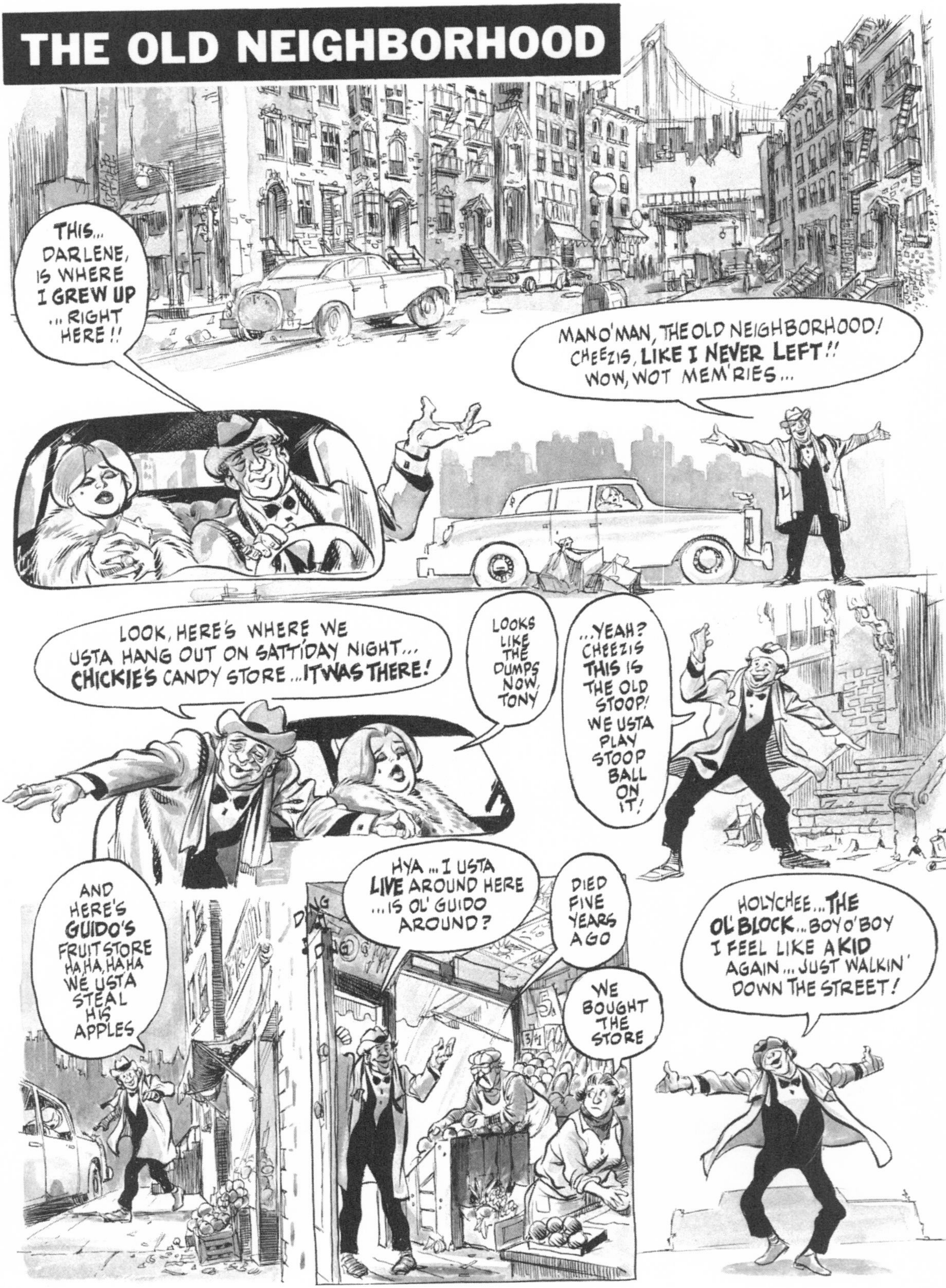
THIS... DARLENE, IS WHERE I GREW UP ...RIGHT HERE!!
MAN O'MAN, THE OLD NEIGHBORHOOD! CHEEZIS, LIKE I NEVER LEFT!! WOW, WOT MEM'RIES...
LOOK, HERE'S WHERE WE USTA HANG OUT ON SATTIDAY NIGHT... CHICKIE'S CANDY STORE ...IT WAS THERE!
LOOKS LIKE THE DUMPS NOW, TONY
...YEAH? CHEEZIS THIS IS THE OLD STOOP! WE USTA PLAY STOOP BALL ON IT!
AND HERE'S GUIDO'S FRUIT STORE HA HA, HA HA WE USTA STEAL HIS APPLES
HYA ... I USTA LIVE AROUND HERE ...IS OL' GUIDO AROUND?
DIED FIVE YEARS AGO
WE BOUGHT THE STORE
HOLYCHEE... THE OL' BLOCK... BOY O' BOY I FEEL LIKE A KID AGAIN ... JUST WALKIN' DOWN THE STREET!

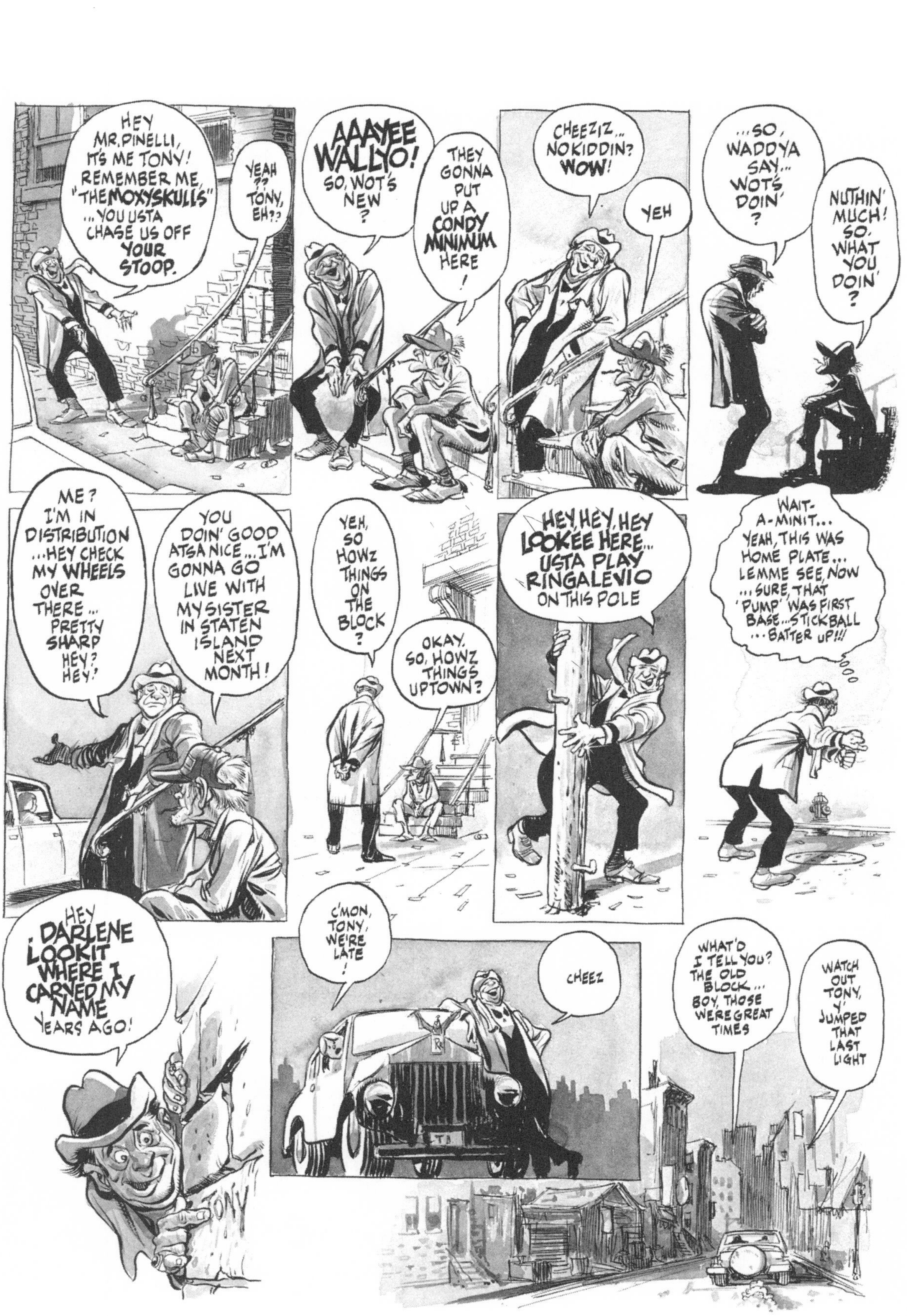
HEY MR. PINELLI, IT'S ME TONY! REMEMBER ME, "THE MOXYSKULLS" ... YOU USTA CHASE US OFF YOUR STOOP.
YEAH ?? TONY, EH??
AAAYEE WALLYO! SO, WOT'S NEW ?
THEY GONNA PUT UP A CONDY MINIMUM HERE !
CHEEZIZ... NOKIDDIN? WOW!
YEH
...SO, WADDYA SAY... WOT'S DOIN' ?
NUTHIN' MUCH! SO, WHAT YOU DOIN' ?
ME? I'M IN DISTRIBUTION ...HEY CHECK MY WHEELS OVER THERE... PRETTY SHARP HEY? HEY!
YOU DOIN' GOOD ATSA NICE... I'M GONNA GO LIVE WITH MY SISTER IN STATEN ISLAND NEXT MONTH!
YEH, SO HOWZ THINGS ON THE BLOCK ?
OKAY. SO, HOWZ THINGS UPTOWN?
HEY, HEY, HEY LOOKEE HERE... USTA PLAY RINGALEVIO ON THIS POLE
WAIT-A-MINIT... YEAH, THIS WAS HOME PLATE... LEMME SEE, NOW ...SURE, THAT 'PUMP' WAS FIRST BASE... STICKBALL ...BATTER UP!!!
HEY DARLENE LOOKIT WHERE I CARVED MY NAME YEARS AGO!
TONY
C'MON, TONY, WE'RE LATE !
CHEEZ
WHAT'D I TELL YOU? THE OLD BLOCK... BOY, THOSE WERE GREAT TIMES
WATCH OUT TONY, Y' JUMPED THAT LAST LIGHT

NEIGHBORHOOD GIRL

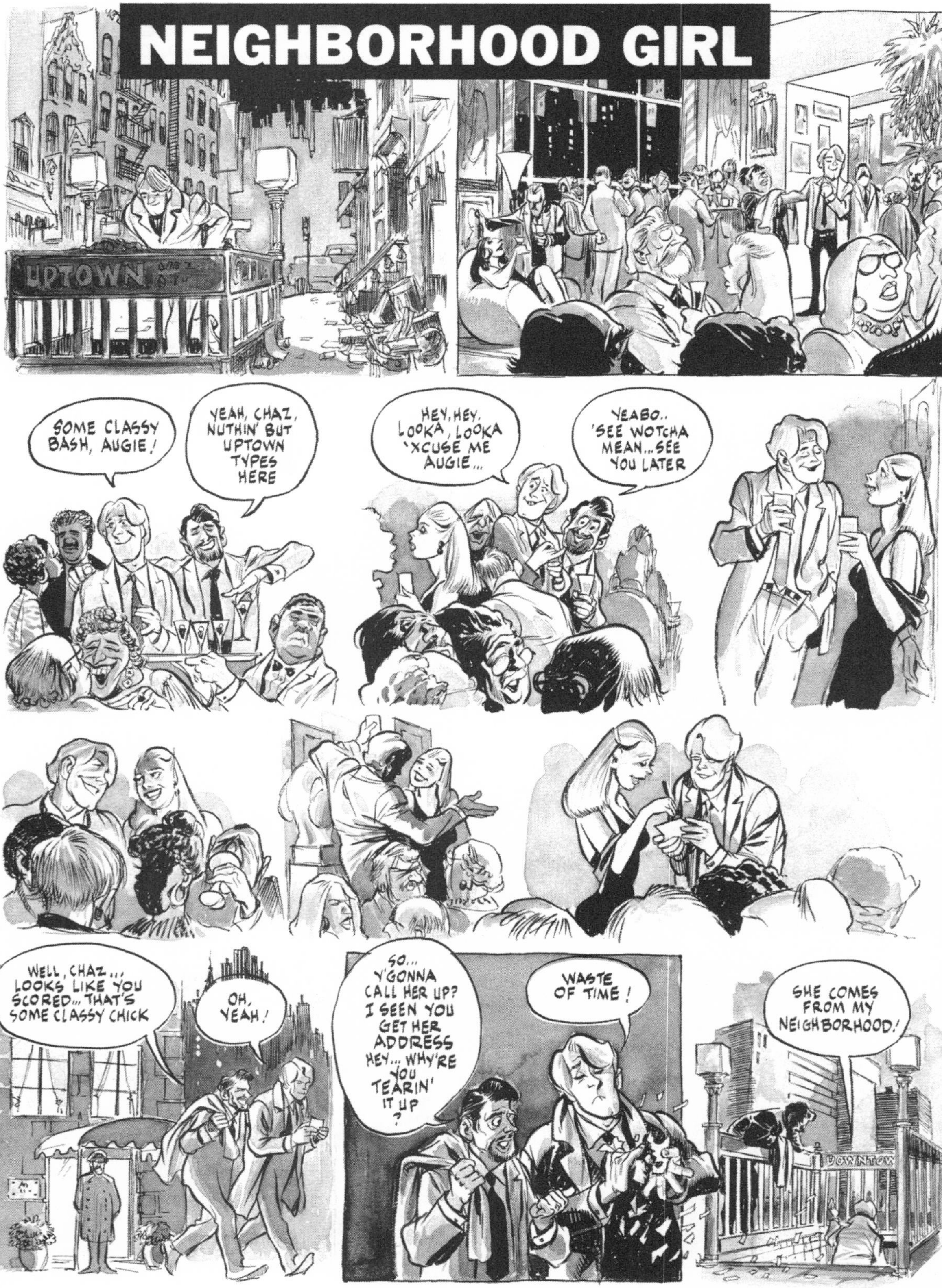
UPTOWN
SOME CLASSY BASH, AUGIE!
YEAH, CHAZ, NUTHIN' BUT UPTOWN TYPES HERE
HEY, HEY. LOOKA, LOOKA 'XCUSE ME AUGIE...
YEABO.. 'SEE WOTCHA MEAN...SEE YOU LATER
WELL, CHAZ... LOOKS LIKE YOU SCORED... THAT'S SOME CLASSY CHICK
OH, YEAH!
SO... Y'GONNA CALL HER UP? I SEEN YOU GET HER ADDRESS HEY... WHY'RE YOU TEARIN' IT UP ?
WASTE OF TIME!
SHE COMES FROM MY NEIGHBORHOOD!

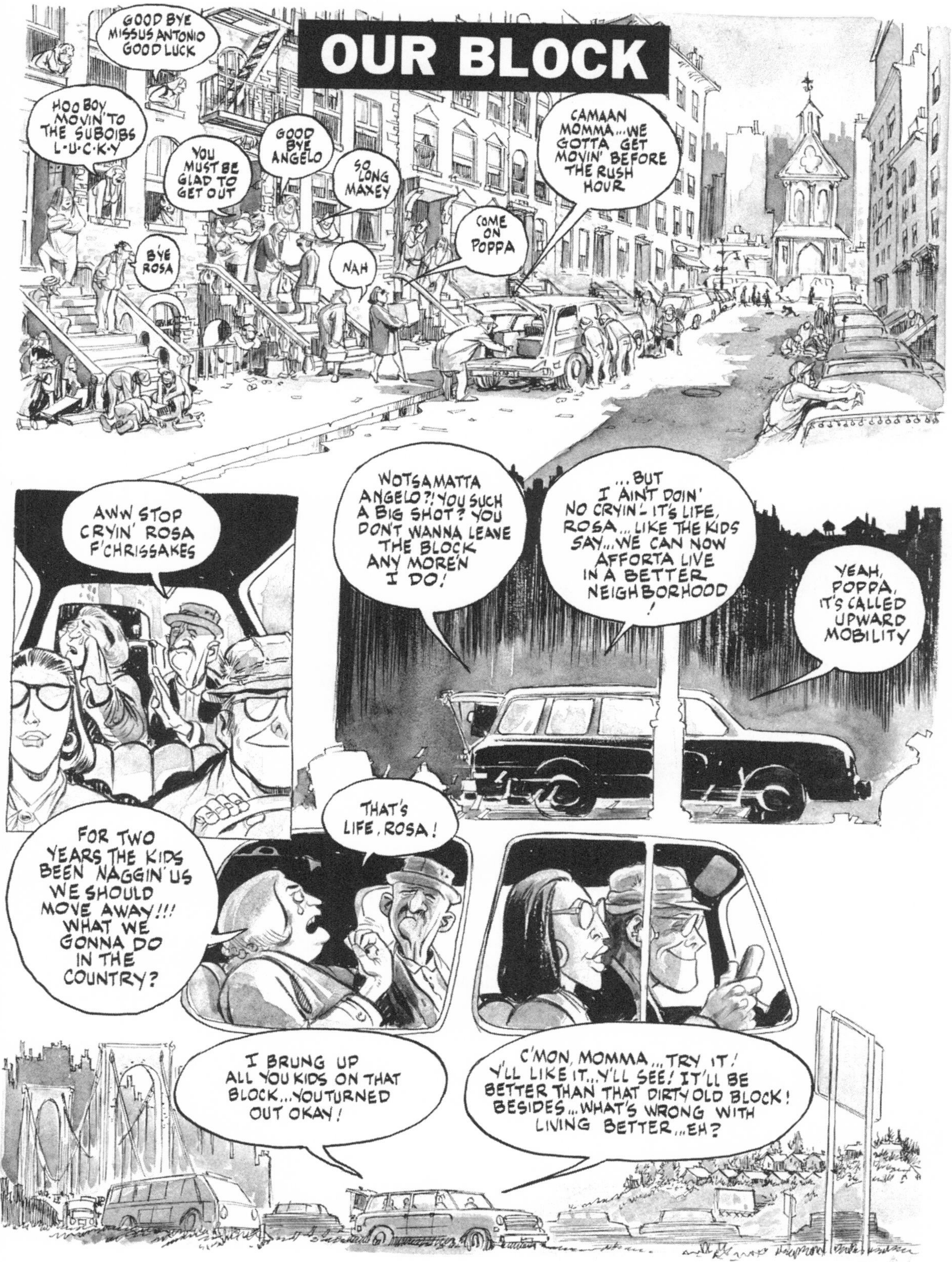
OUR BLOCK
GOOD BYE MISSUS ANTONIO GOOD LUCK
HOO BOY MOVIN' TO THE SUBOIBS L-U-C-K-Y
YOU MUST BE GLAD TO GET OUT
GOOD BYE ANGELO
SO LONG MAXEY
CAMAAN MOMMA... WE GOTTA GET MOVIN' BEFORE THE RUSH HOUR
COME ON POPPA
B'YE ROSA
NAH
AWW STOP CRYIN' ROSA F'CHRISSAKES
WOTSAMATTA ANGELO?! YOU SUCH A BIG SHOT? YOU DON'T WANNA LEAVE THE BLOCK ANY MORE'N I DO!
...BUT I AIN'T DOIN' NO CRYIN'- IT'S LIFE, ROSA... LIKE THE KIDS SAY... WE CAN NOW AFFORTA LIVE IN A BETTER NEIGHBORHOOD!
YEAH, POPPA, IT'S CALLED UPWARD MOBILITY
FOR TWO YEARS THE KIDS BEEN NAGGIN' US WE SHOULD MOVE AWAY!!! WHAT WE GONNA DO IN THE COUNTRY?
THAT'S LIFE, ROSA!
I BRUNG UP ALL YOU KIDS ON THAT BLOCK... YOU TURNED OUT OKAY!
C'MON, MOMMA... TRY IT! Y'LL LIKE IT... Y'LL SEE! IT'LL BE BETTER THAN THAT DIRTY OLD BLOCK! BESIDES... WHAT'S WRONG WITH LIVING BETTER... EH?

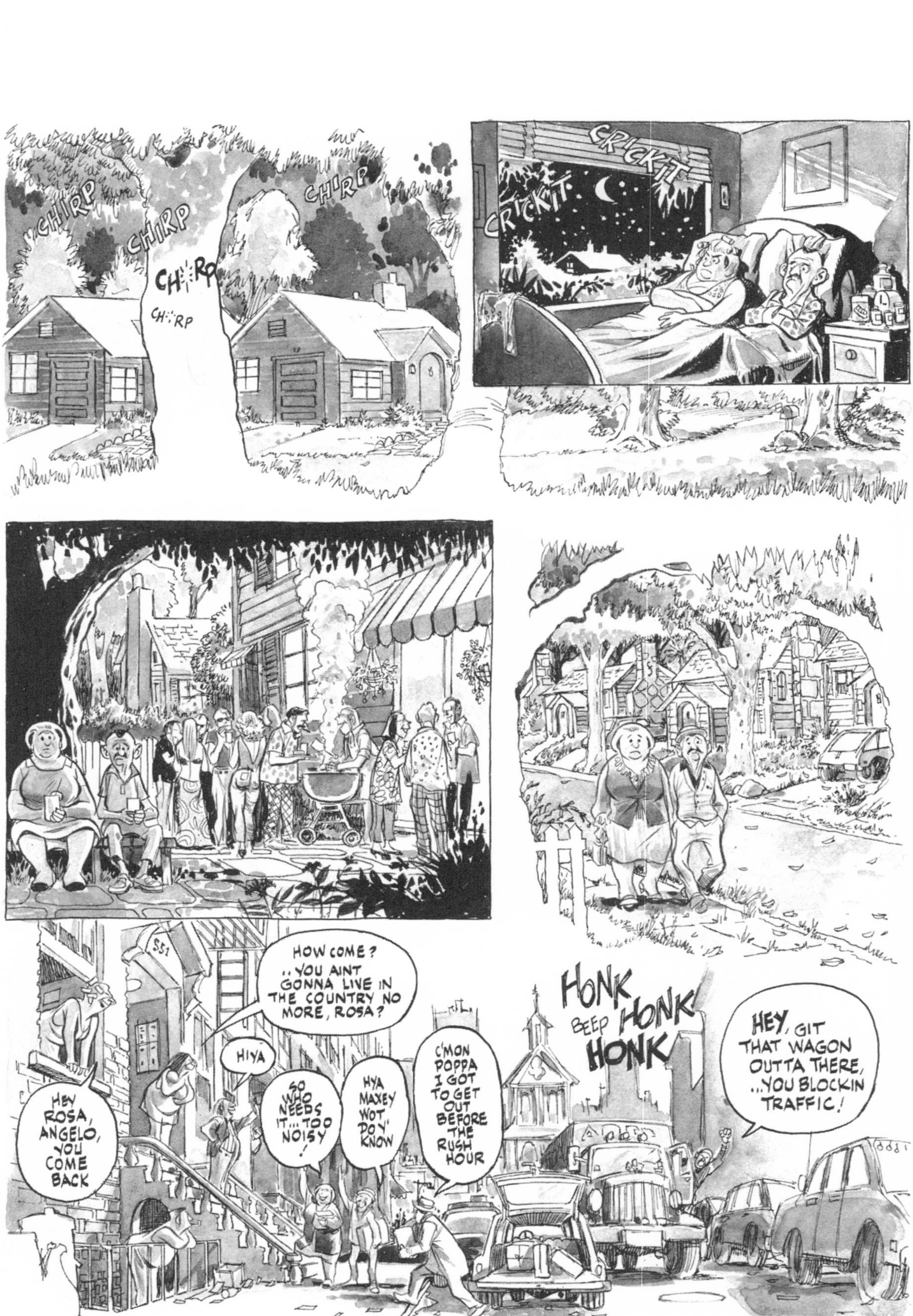
CHIRP
CHIRP
CHIRP
CHIRP
CHIRP
CRICKIT
CRICKIT
HEY ROSA, ANGELO, YOU COME BACK
HIYA
HOW COME? ..YOU AINT GONNA LIVE IN THE COUNTRY NO MORE, ROSA?
SO WHO NEEDS IT... TOO NOISY!
HYA MAXEY WOT DO Y' KNOW
C'MON POPPA I GOT TO GET OUT BEFORE THE RUSH HOUR
HONK
BEEP
HONK
HONK
HEY, GIT THAT WAGON OUTTA THERE, ..YOU BLOCKIN TRAFFIC!

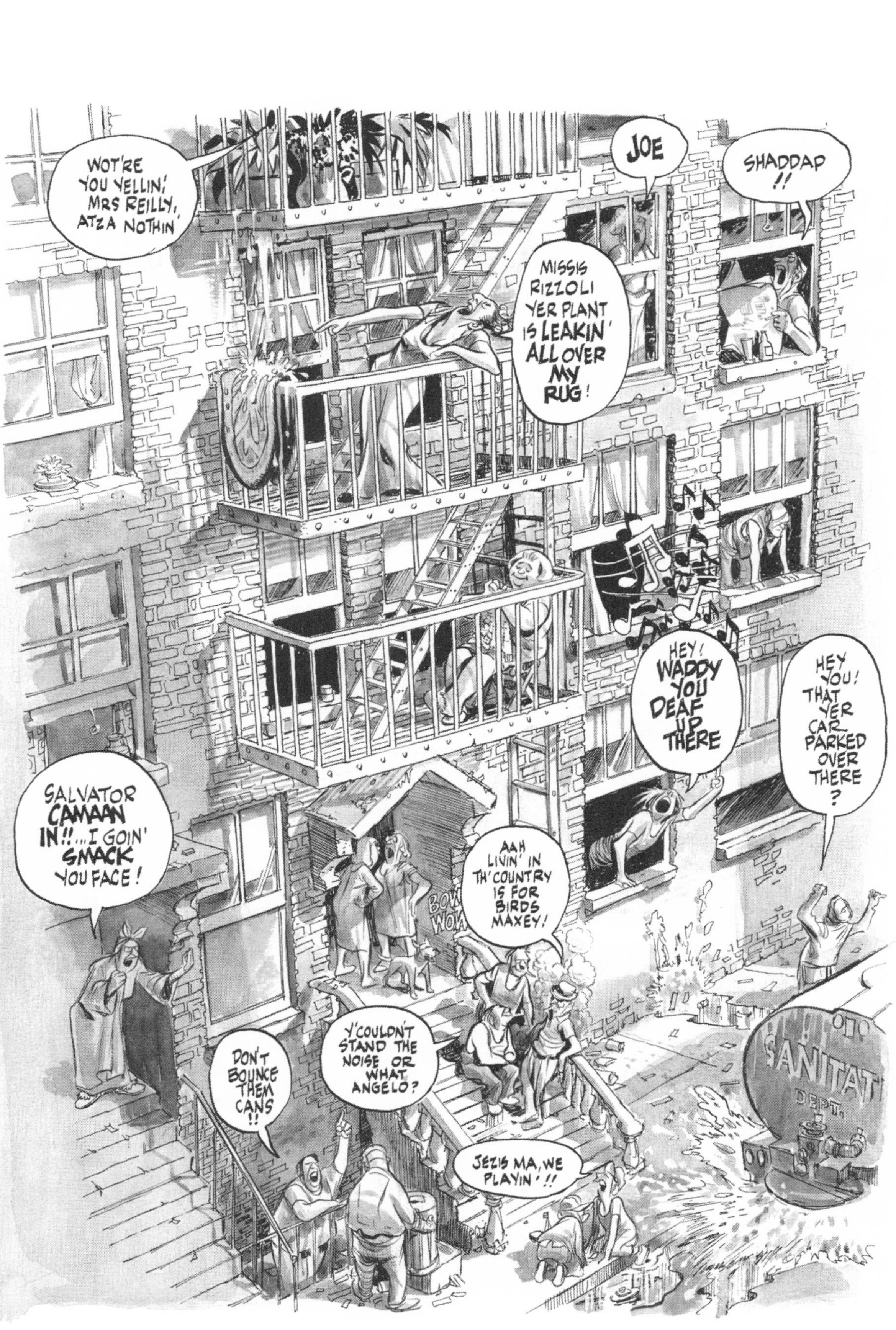
WOT'RE YOU YELLIN' MRS REILLY, ATZA NOTHIN'
JOE
SHADDAP !!
MISSIS RIZZOLI YER PLANT IS LEAKIN' ALL OVER MY RUG!
HEY! WADDY YOU DEAF UP THERE
HEY YOU! THAT YER CAR PARKED OVER THERE ?
SALVATOR CAMAAN IN!!...I GOIN' SMACK YOU FACE!
AAH LIVIN' IN TH' COUNTRY IS FOR BIRDS MAXEY!
DON'T BOUNCE THEM CANS !!
Y'COULDN'T STAND THE NOISE OR WHAT ANGELO?
JEZIS MA, WE PLAYIN' !!

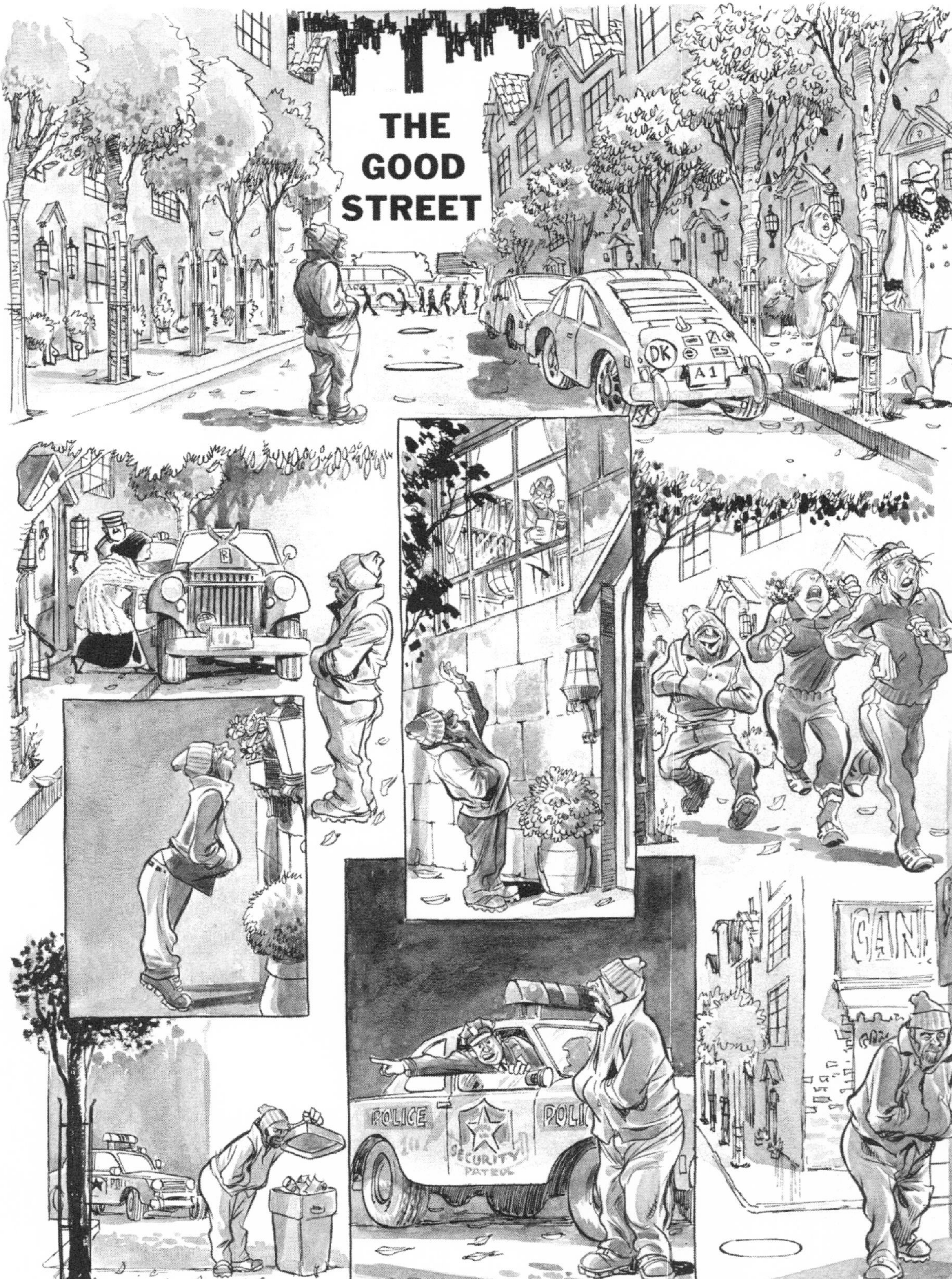
THE GOOD STREET
DK
A1
POLICE
SECURITY
POLI
CAN

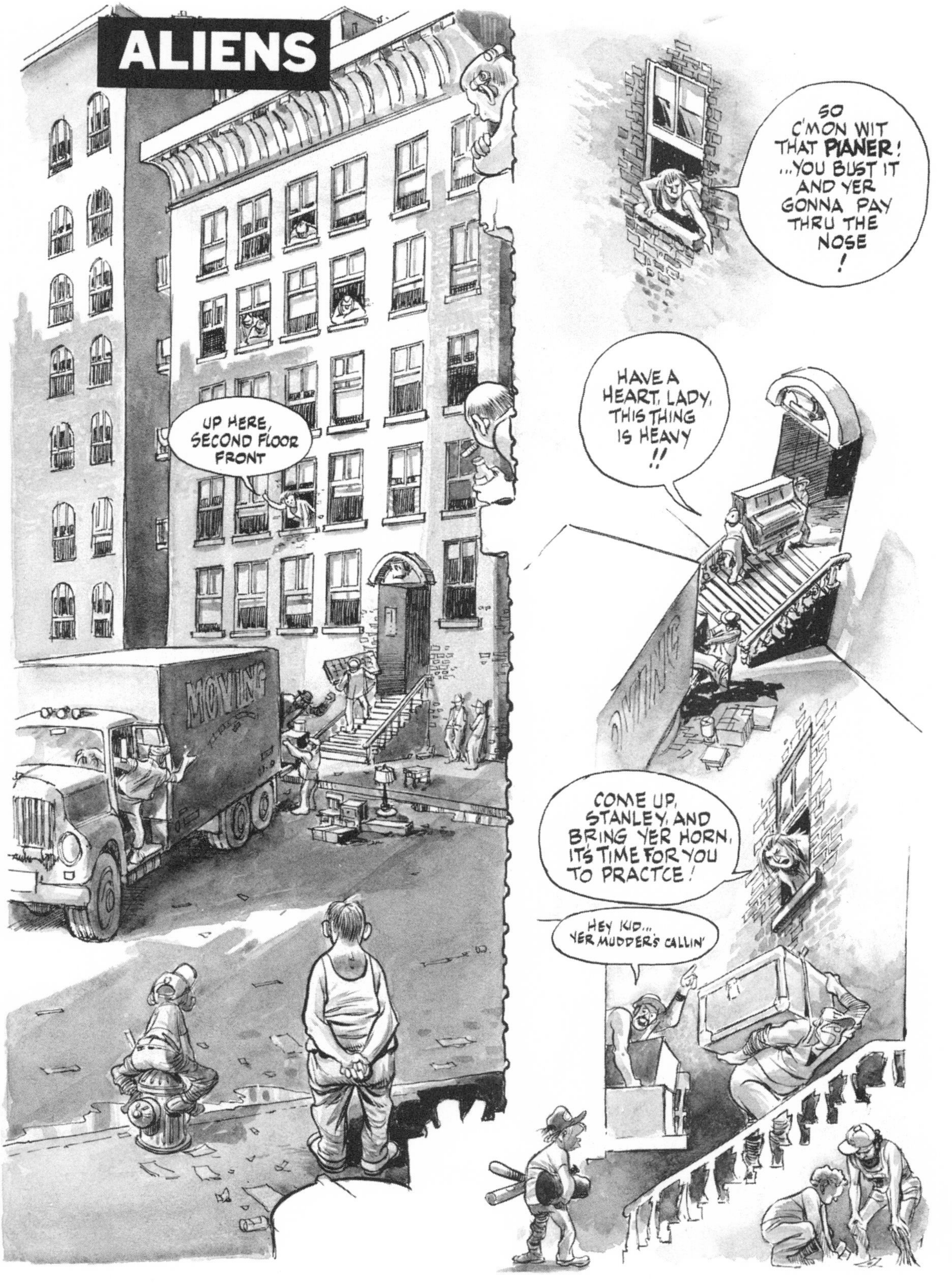
ALIENS
UP HERE, SECOND FLOOR FRONT
MOVING
SO C'MON WIT THAT PIANER! ...YOU BUST IT AND YER GONNA PAY THRU THE NOSE!
HAVE A HEART, LADY, THIS THING IS HEAVY!!
COME UP, STANLEY, AND BRING YER HORN, IT'S TIME FOR YOU TO PRACTCE!
HEY KID... YER MUDDER'S CALLIN'

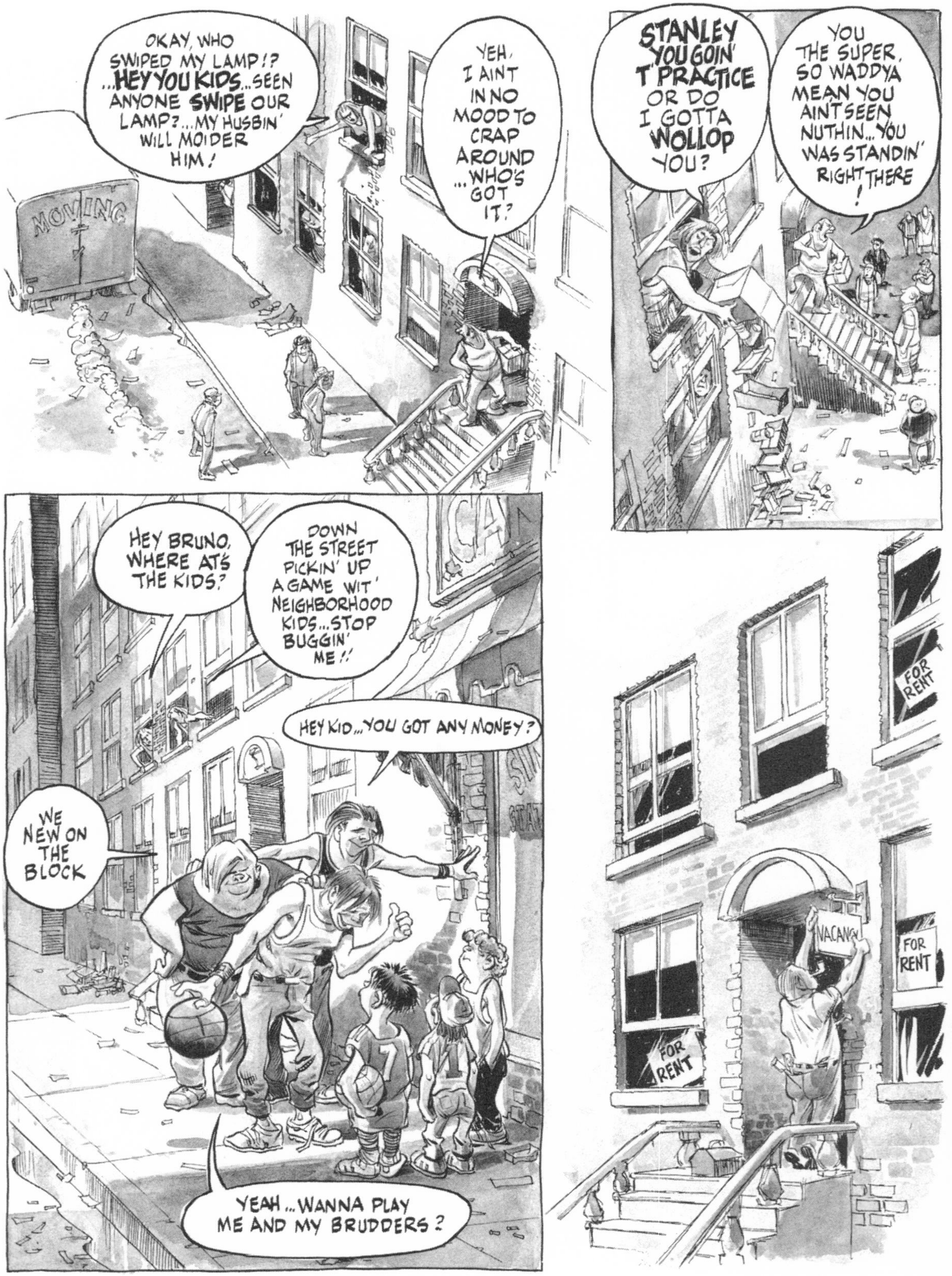

MOVING
OKAY, WHO SWIPED MY LAMP!? ...HEY YOU KIDS... SEEN ANYONE SWIPE OUR LAMP?... MY HUSBIN' WILL MOIDER HIM!
YEH, I AINT IN NO MOOD TO CRAP AROUND ...WHO'S GOT IT?
STANLEY YOU GOIN' T' PRACTICE OR DO I GOTTA WOLLOP YOU?
YOU THE SUPER, SO WADDYA MEAN YOU AINT SEEN NUTHIN... YOU WAS STANDIN' RIGHT THERE!
HEY BRUNO, WHERE AT'S THE KIDS?
DOWN THE STREET PICKIN' UP A GAME WIT' NEIGHBORHOOD KIDS... STOP BUGGIN' ME!!
HEY KID... YOU GOT ANY MONEY?
WE NEW ON THE BLOCK
YEAH... WANNA PLAY ME AND MY BRUDDERS?
FOR RENT
FOR RENT
FOR RENT

HIGH RENT DISTRICT

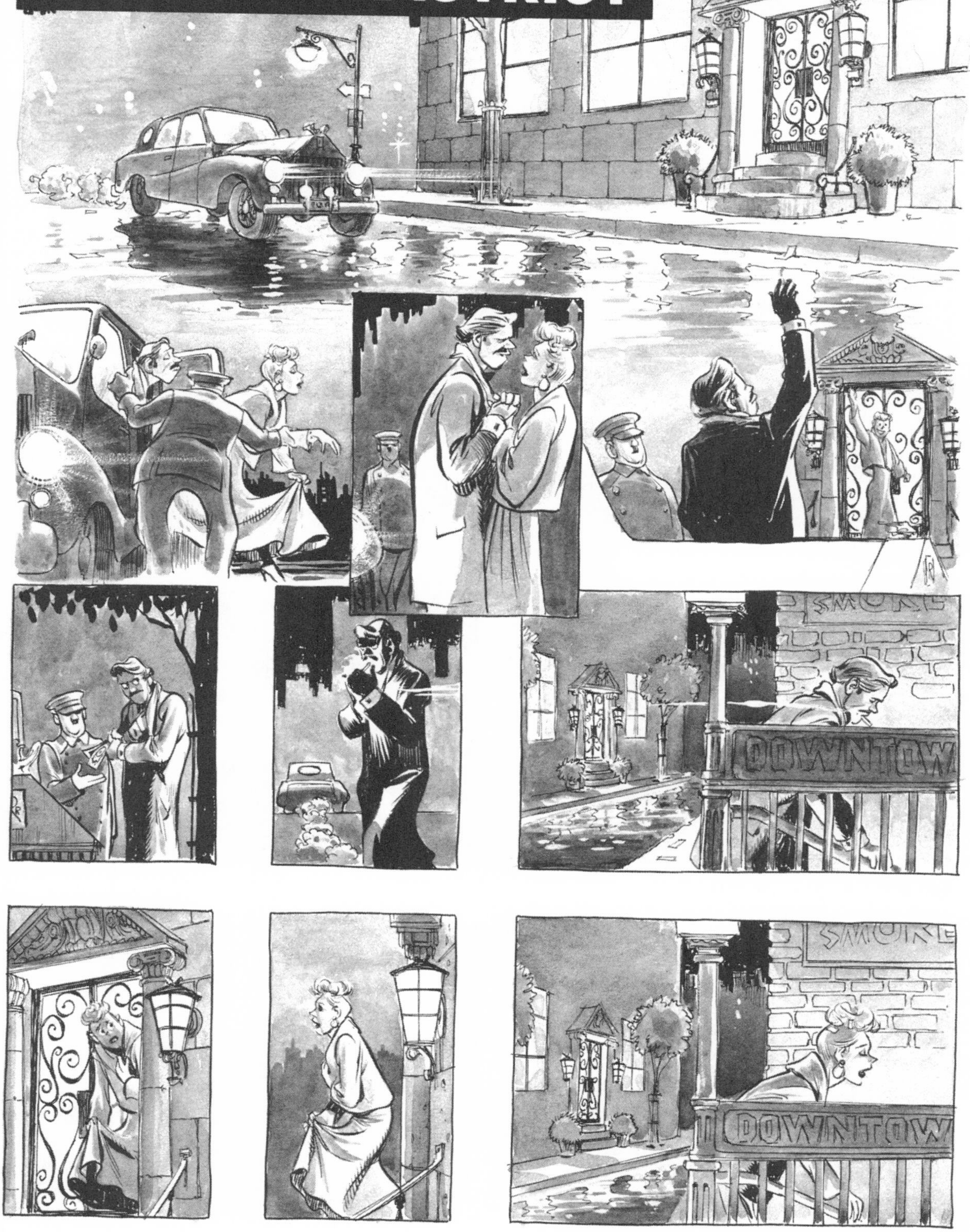
DOWNTOW
SMOKE
DOWNTOW

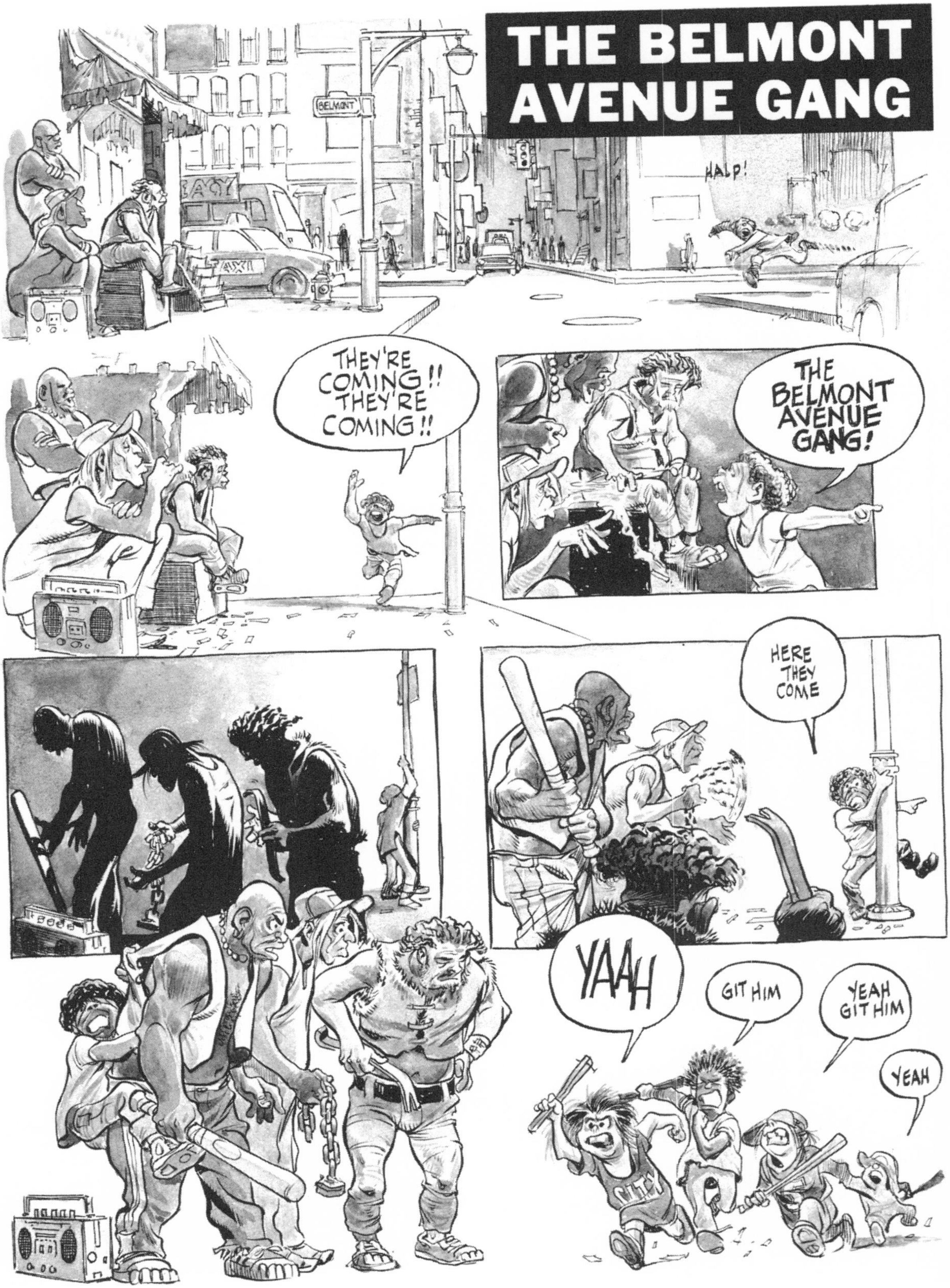
THE BELMONT AVENUE GANG
BELMONT
HALP!
THEY'RE COMING!! THEY'RE COMING!!
THE BELMONT AVENUE GANG!
HERE THEY COME
YAAH
GIT HIM
YEAH GIT HIM
YEAH

GENTRIFICATION

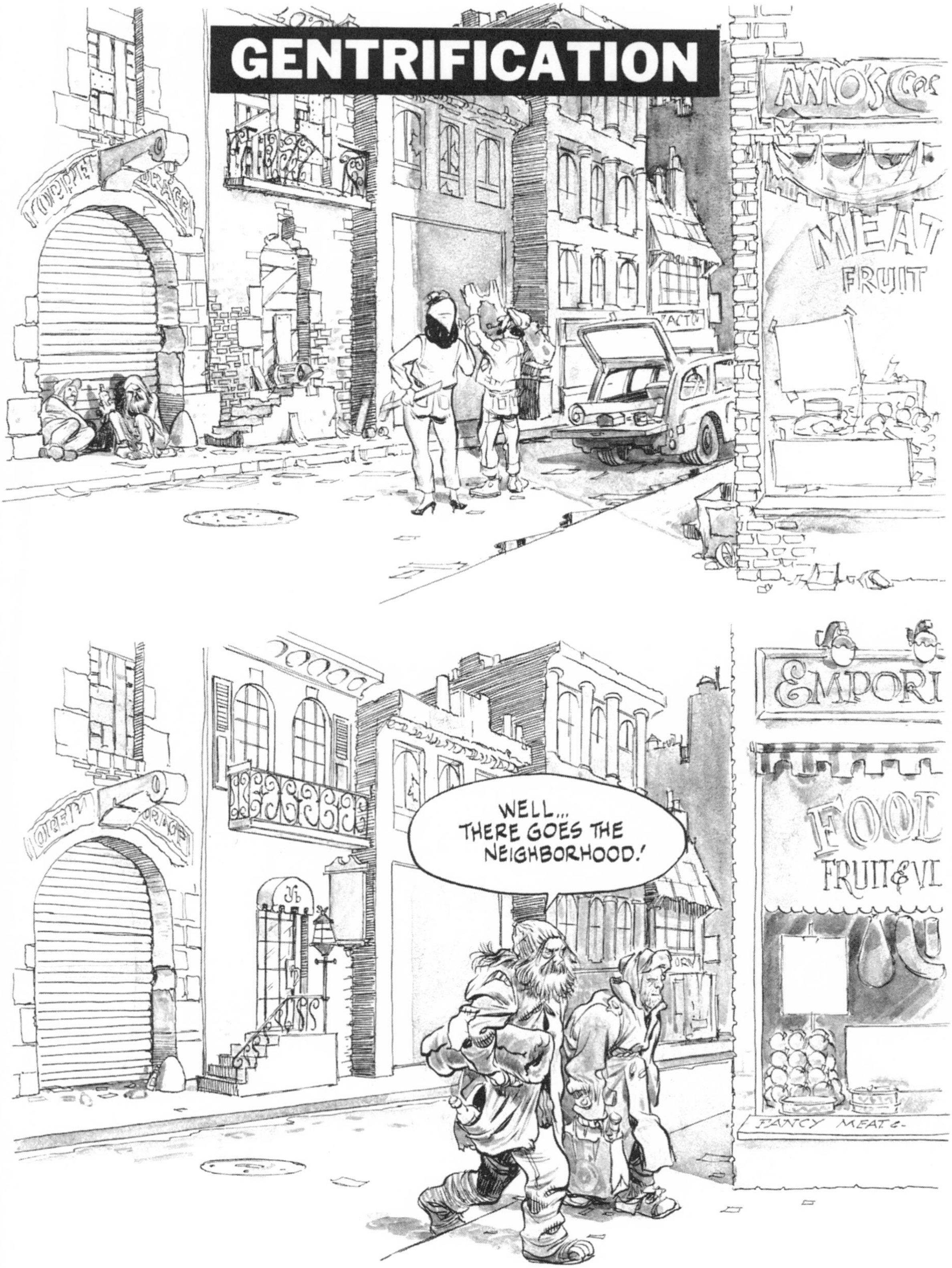
AMO'S
MEAT
FRUIT
EMPORI
FOOD
FRUIT&VE
WELL... THERE GOES THE NEIGHBORHOOD!
FANCY MEAT

Introduction to
The Building

After many years of living in a big city,
one gradually develops a sense of wonder, because
so much that happens there is unexplained
and seems magical.

When I was growing up in the turbulence
of city life, it required only a surface alertness
in order to deal with the welter of changes and
experiences that sped by. There was little
time to reflect on the rapid replacement
of people and buildings.
I took these things for granted.

As I grew older and accumulated memories,
I came to feel more keenly about the
disappearances of people and landmarks.
Especially troubling to me was the callous removal
of buildings. I felt that, somehow, they had
a kind of soul.

I know now that these structures, barnacled with
laughter and stained by tears, are more than lifeless
edifices. It cannot be that having been part
of life, they did not somehow absorb the radiation
from human interaction.

And I wonder what is left behind when a
building is torn down.

THE BUILDING

For over
80 years
the building
stood
astride the
intersection
of two major
avenues.
It was
a landmark
whose walls
weathered
the rain
of tears
and the
pelting
of laughter.

In time,
an invisible
accumulation
of dramas
ringed
its base.

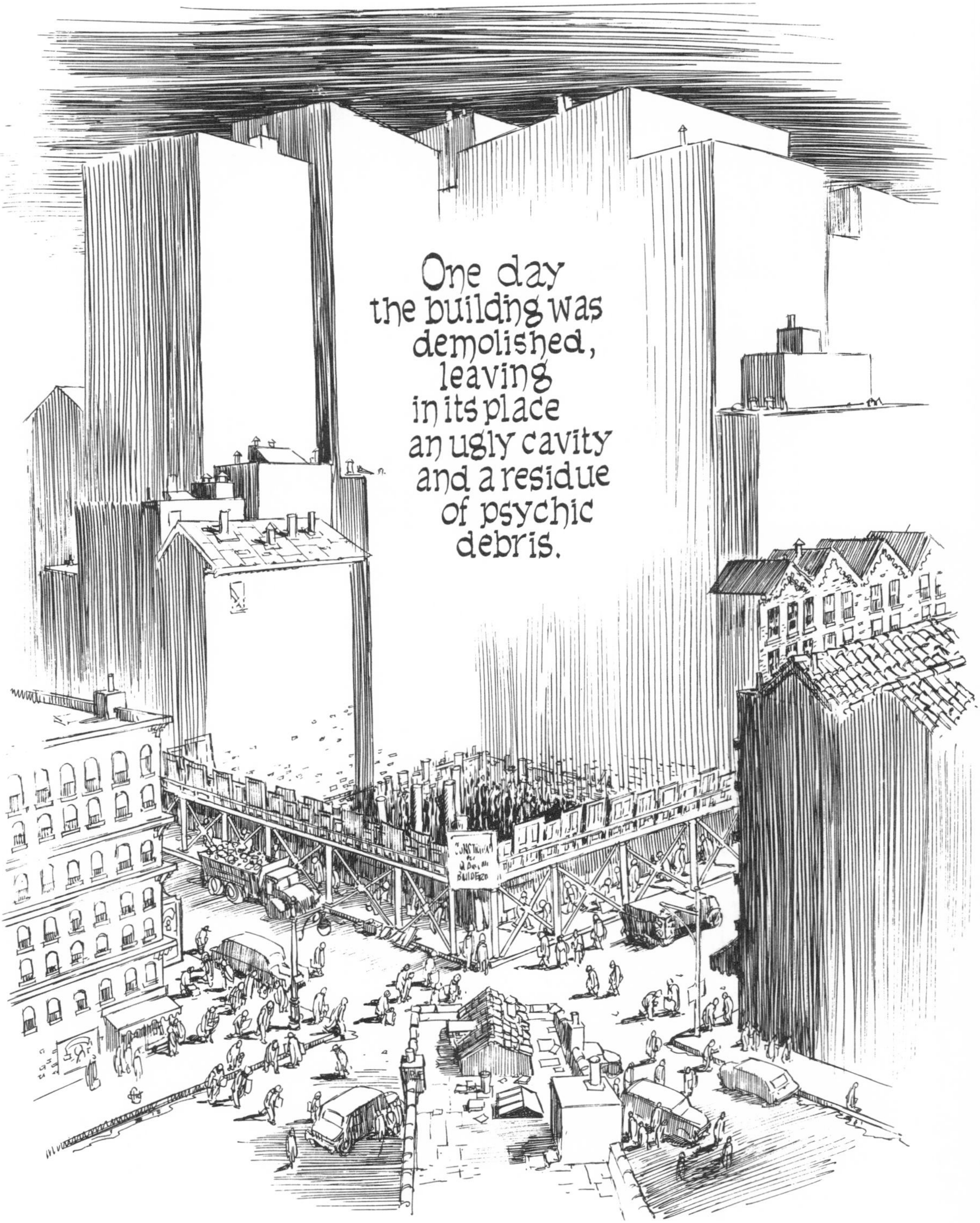
One day
the building was
demolished,
leaving
in its place
an ugly cavity
and a residue
of psychic
debris.

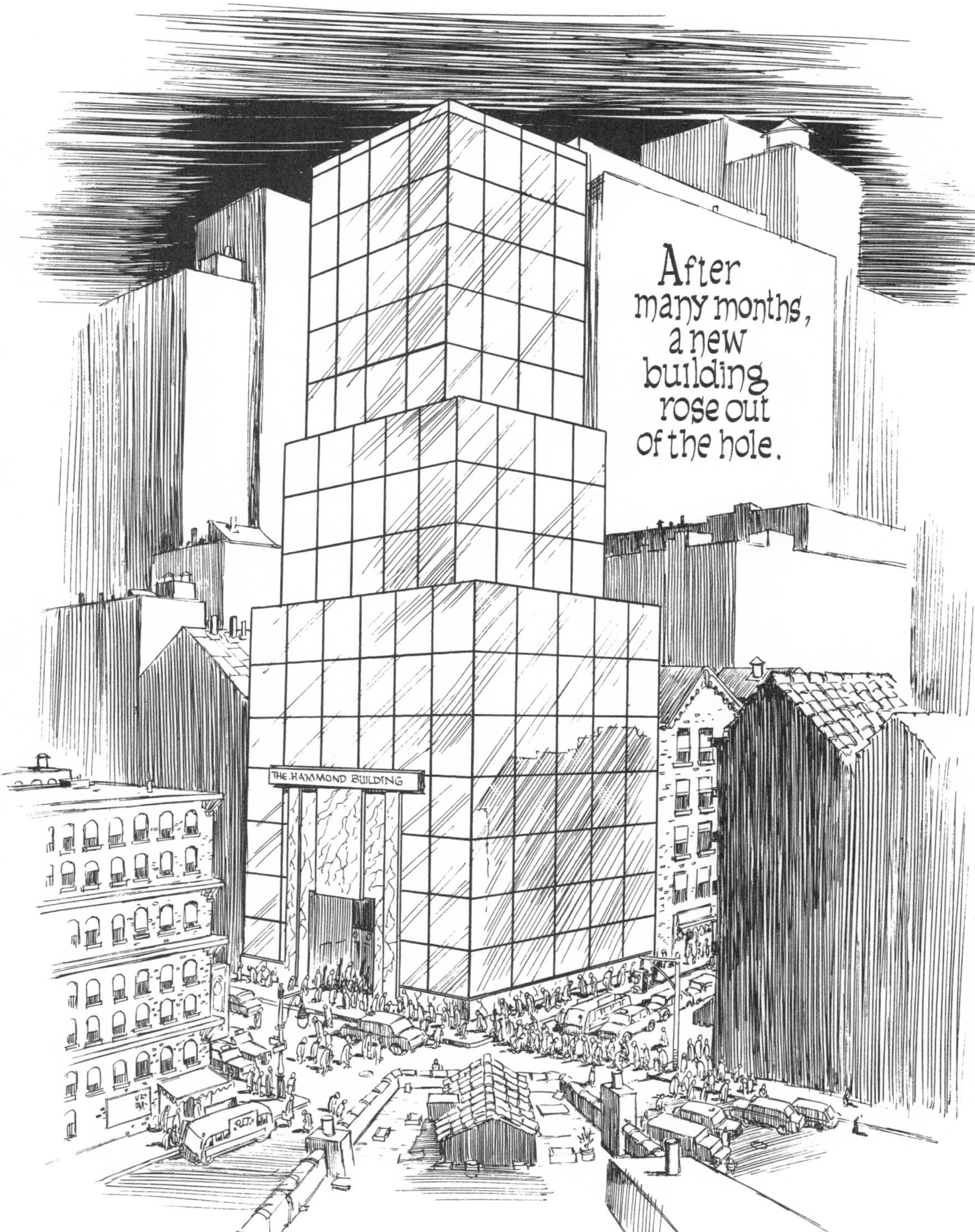
After many months, a new building rose out of the hole.
THE HAMMOND BUILDING

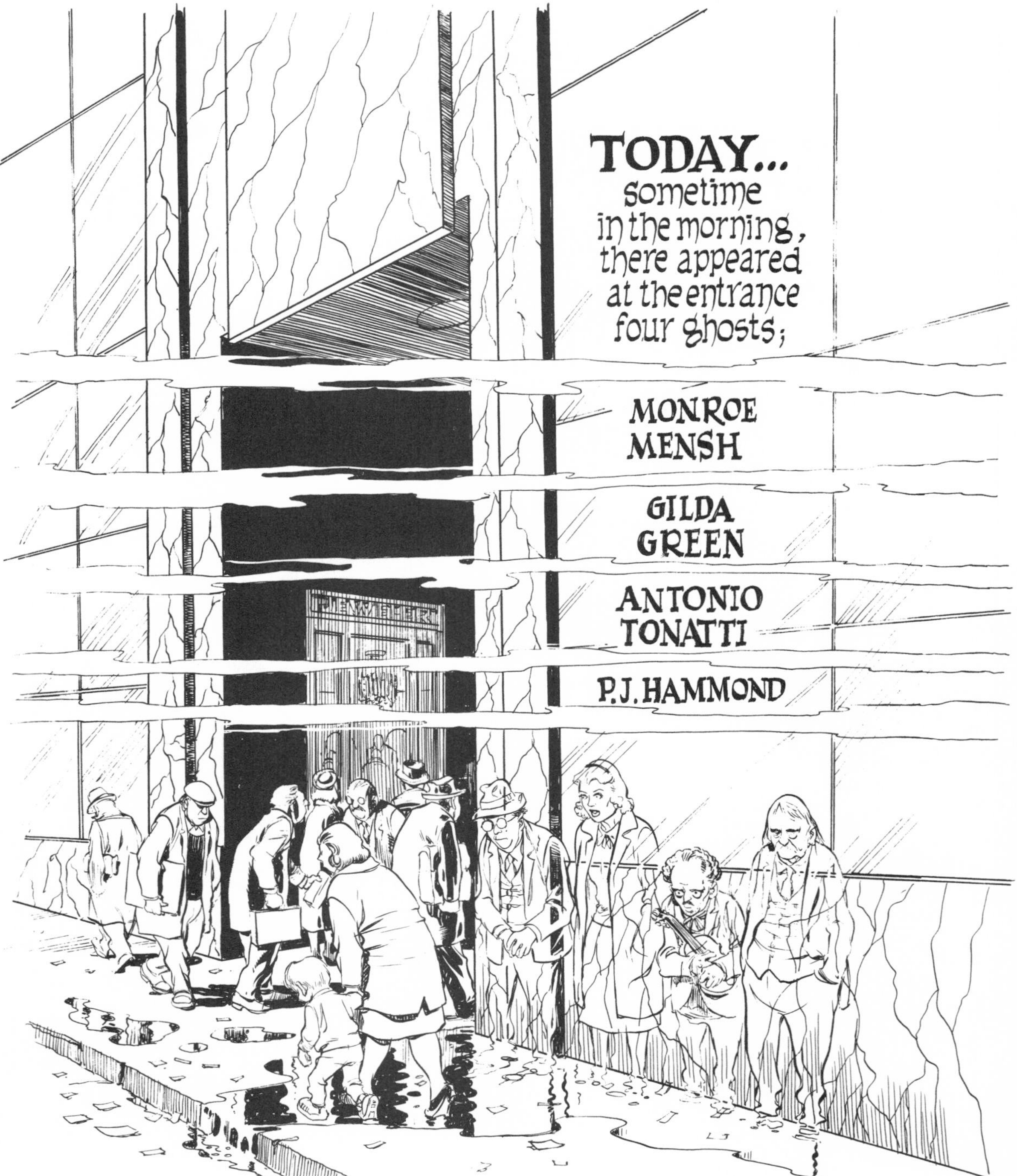
TODAY...
sometime
in the morning,
there appeared
at the entrance
four ghosts;
MONROE
MENSH
GILDA
GREEN
ANTONIO
TONATTI
P.J. HAMMOND

MONROE MENSH

Monroe was
a child of the city

and he grew up
anonymously,
skilled in the art
of city living.

Unmarried,
he pursued
a routine
existence.

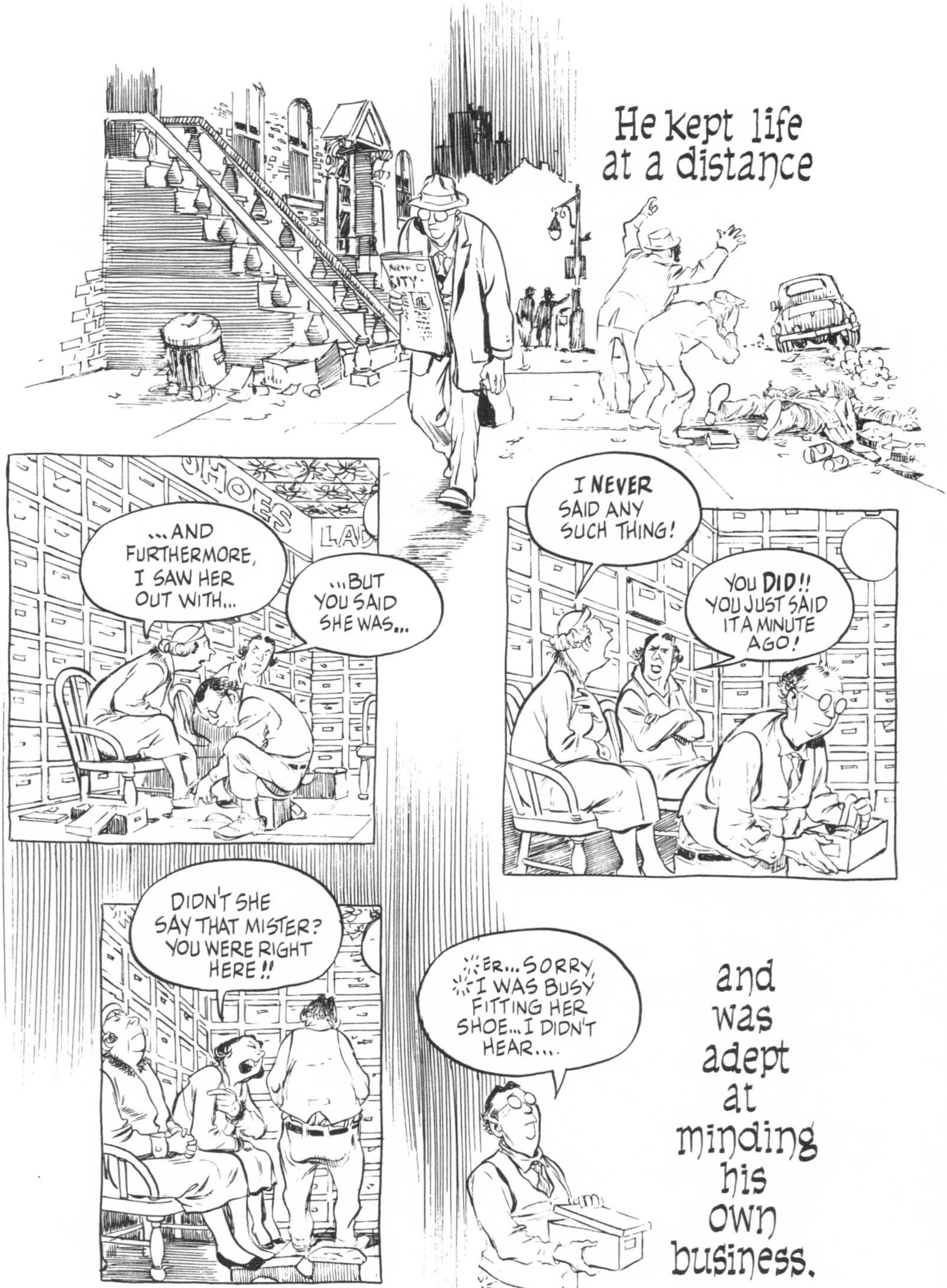
He kept life at a distance
...AND FURTHERMORE, I SAW HER OUT WITH...
...BUT YOU SAID SHE WAS...
I NEVER SAID ANY SUCH THING!
YOU DID!! YOU JUST SAID IT A MINUTE AGO!
DIDN'T SHE SAY THAT MISTER? YOU WERE RIGHT HERE!!
ER...SORRY, I WAS BUSY FITTING HER SHOE...I DIDN'T HEAR....
and was adept at minding his own business.

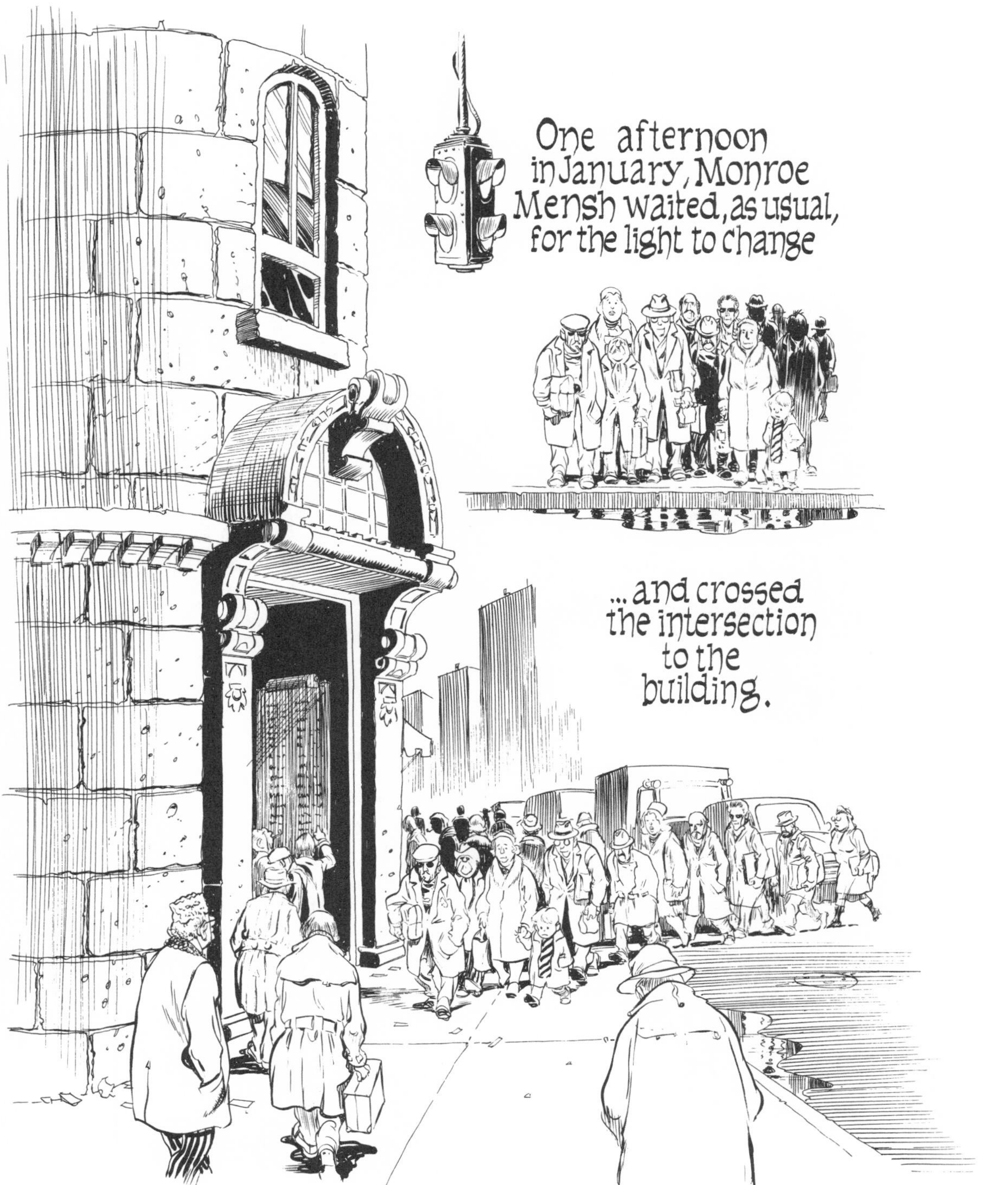
One afternoon in January, Monroe Mensh waited, as usual, for the light to change
...and crossed the intersection to the building.

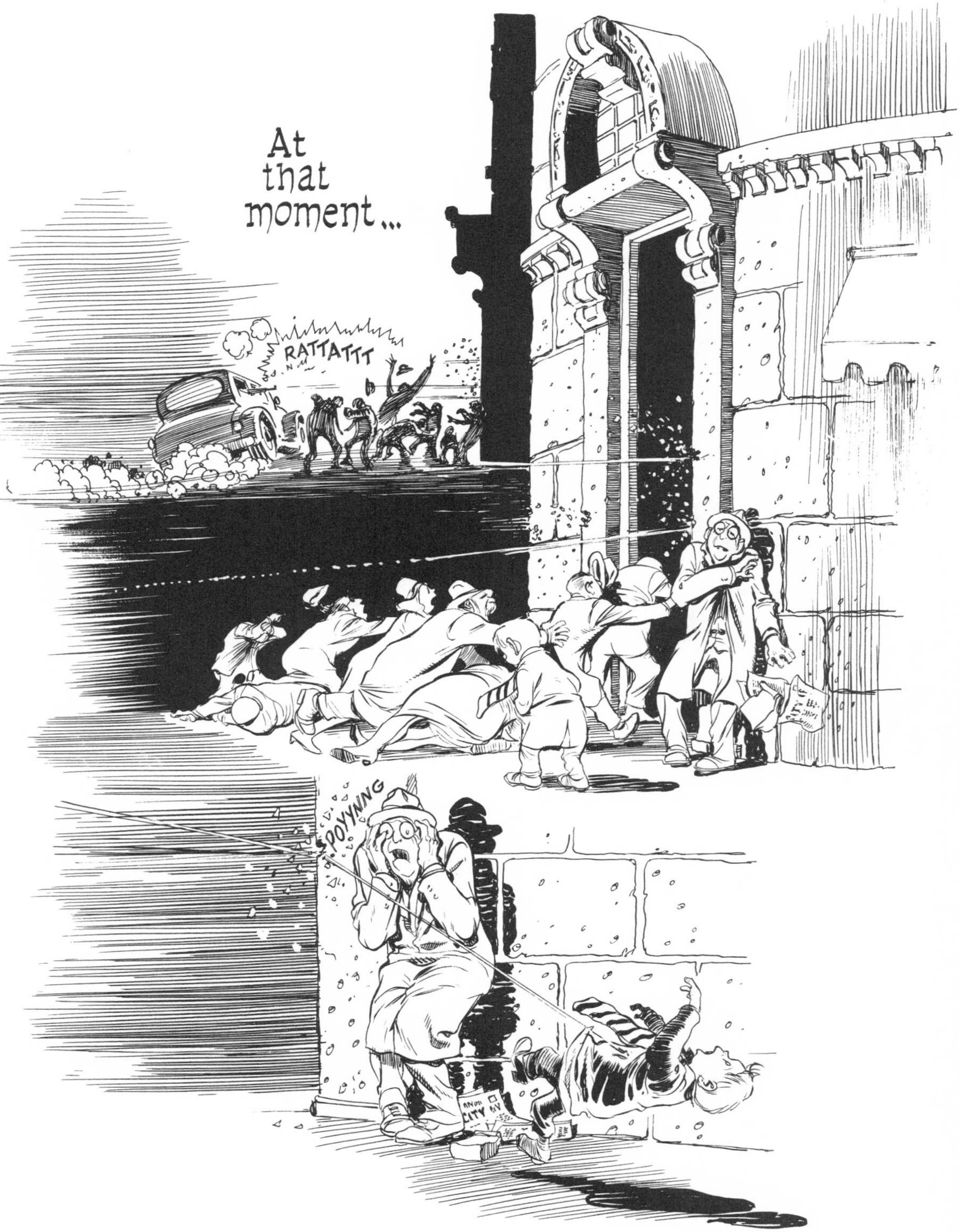
At that moment...
RATTATTT
SPOYYNNG

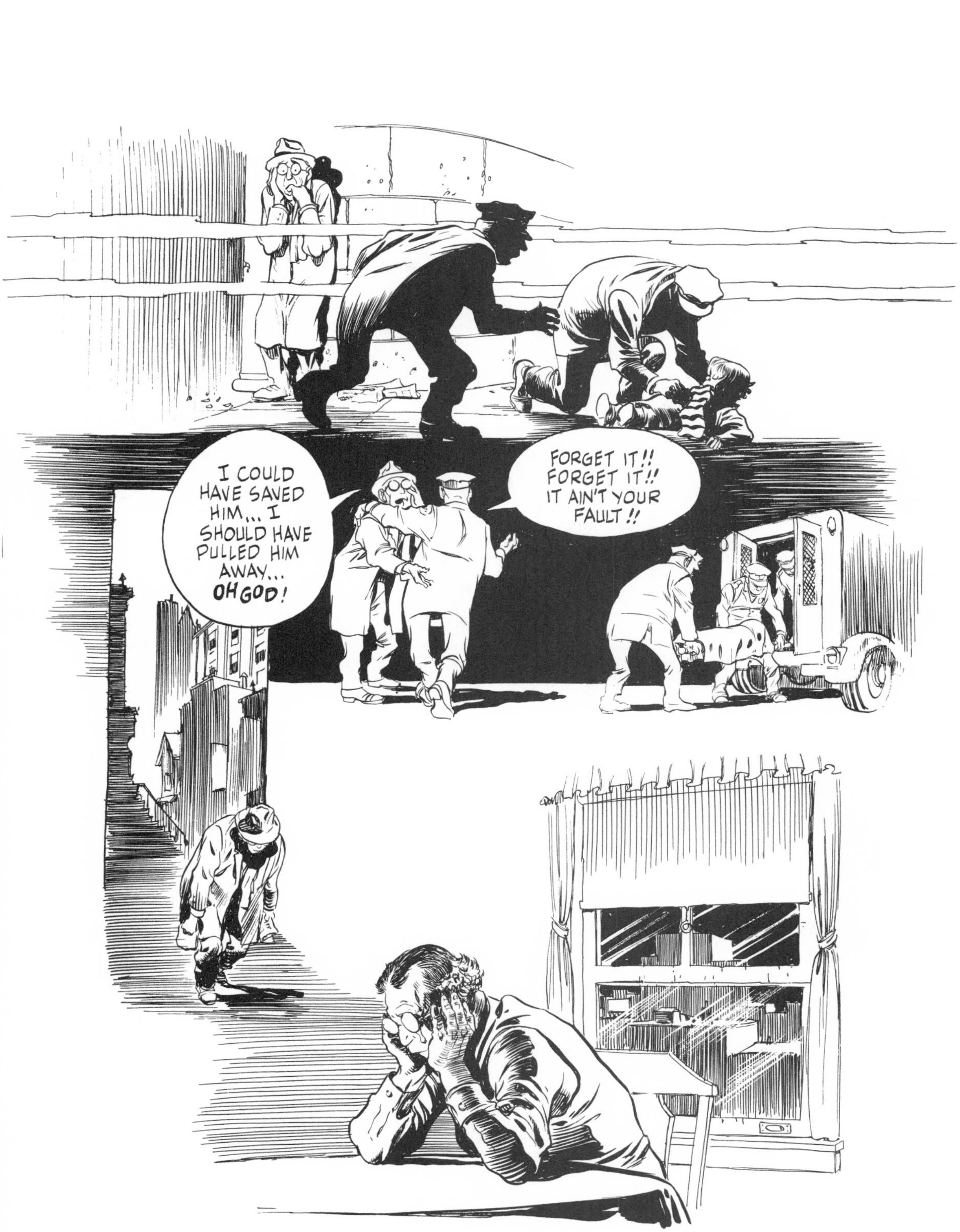
I COULD HAVE SAVED HIM... I SHOULD HAVE PULLED HIM AWAY... OH GOD!
FORGET IT!! FORGET IT!! IT AIN'T YOUR FAULT!!

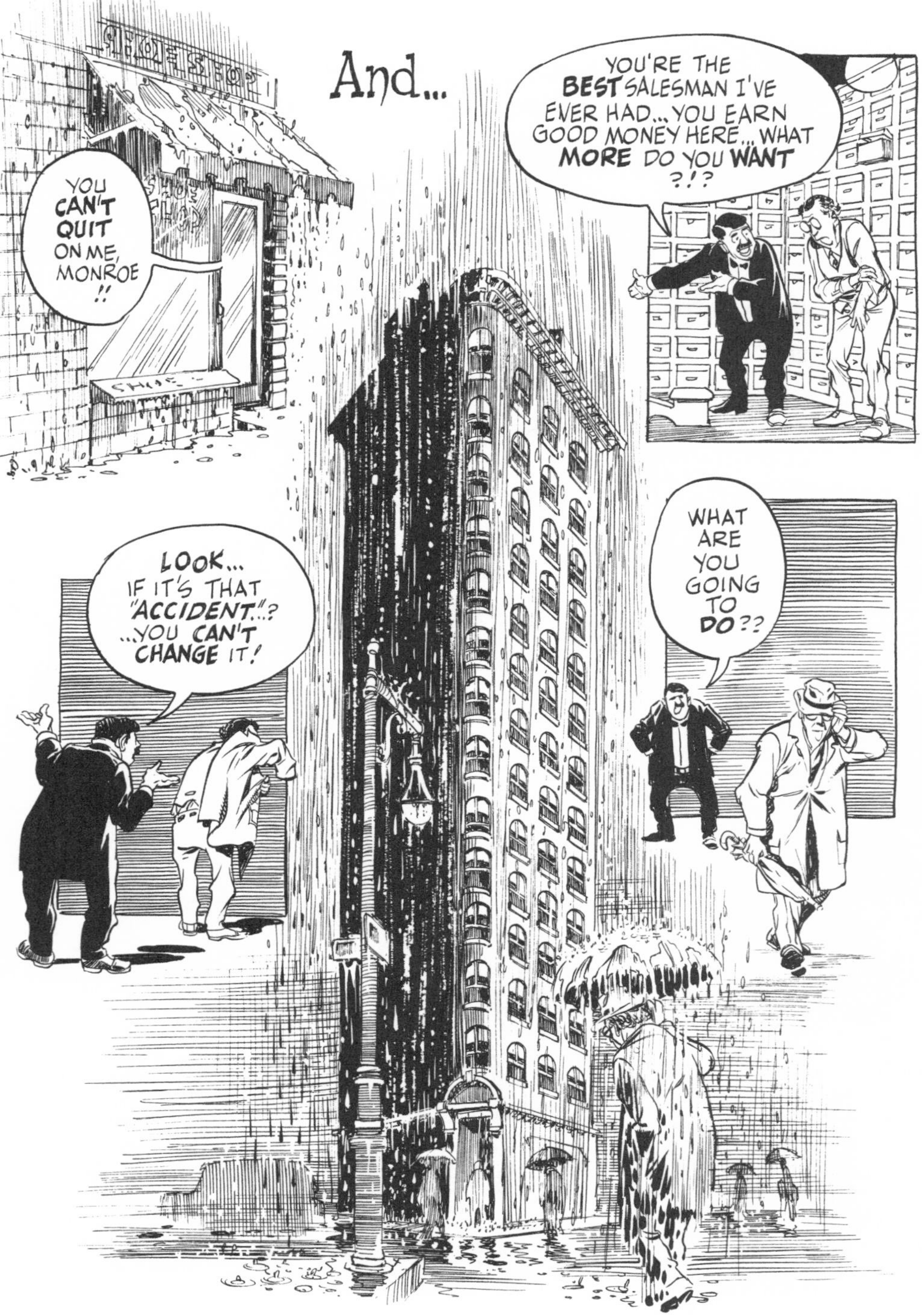
And...
YOU CAN'T QUIT ON ME, MONROE !!
YOU'RE THE BEST SALESMAN I'VE EVER HAD... YOU EARN GOOD MONEY HERE... WHAT MORE DO YOU WANT ?!?
LOOK... IF IT'S THAT "ACCIDENT"..? ...YOU CAN'T CHANGE IT!
WHAT ARE YOU GOING TO DO??

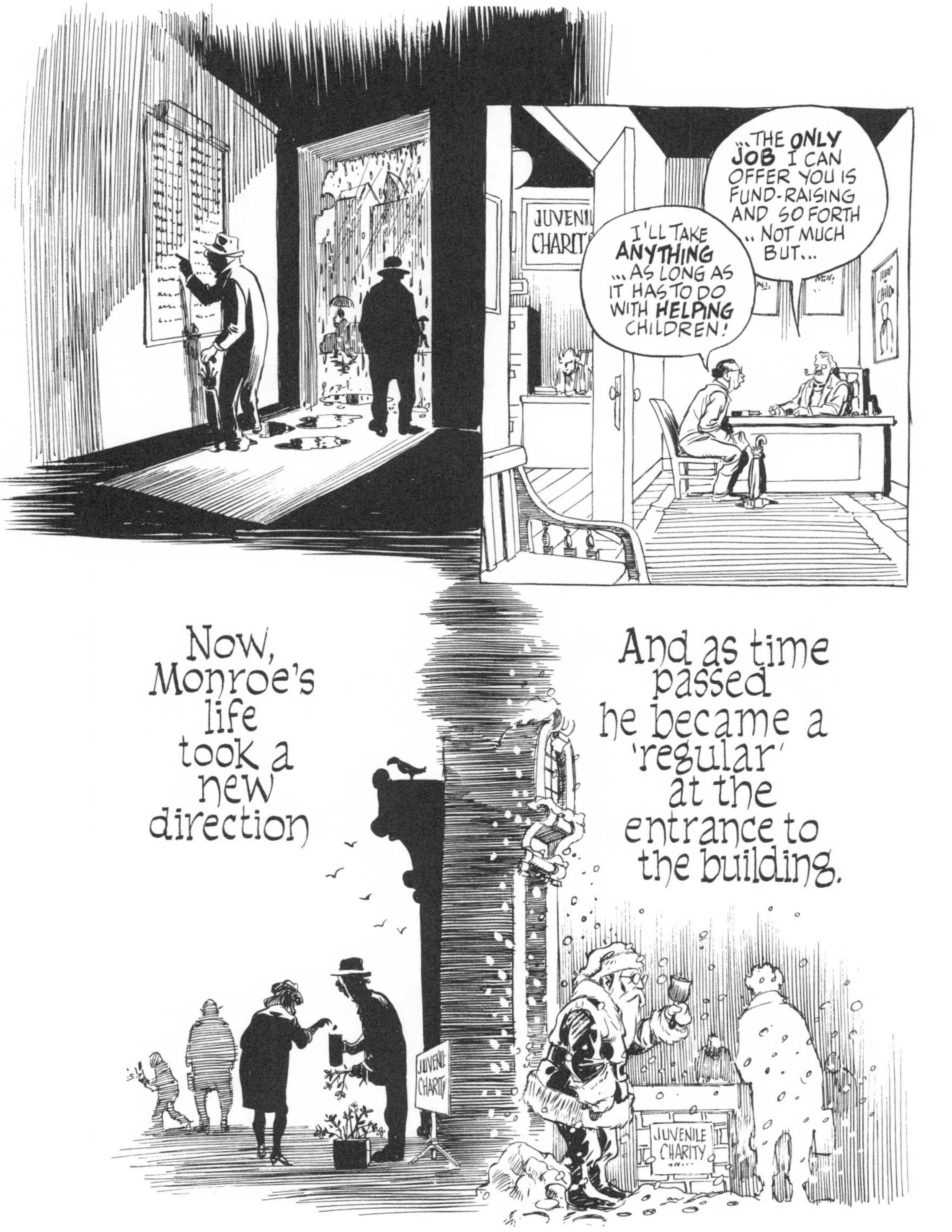
JUVENIL CHARIT
...THE ONLY JOB I CAN OFFER YOU IS FUND-RAISING AND SO FORTH .. NOT MUCH BUT...
I'LL TAKE ANYTHING ...AS LONG AS IT HAS TO DO WITH HELPING CHILDREN!
Now, Monroe's life took a new direction
And as time passed he became a 'regular' at the entrance to the building.
JUVENILE CHARITY
JUVENILE CHARITY

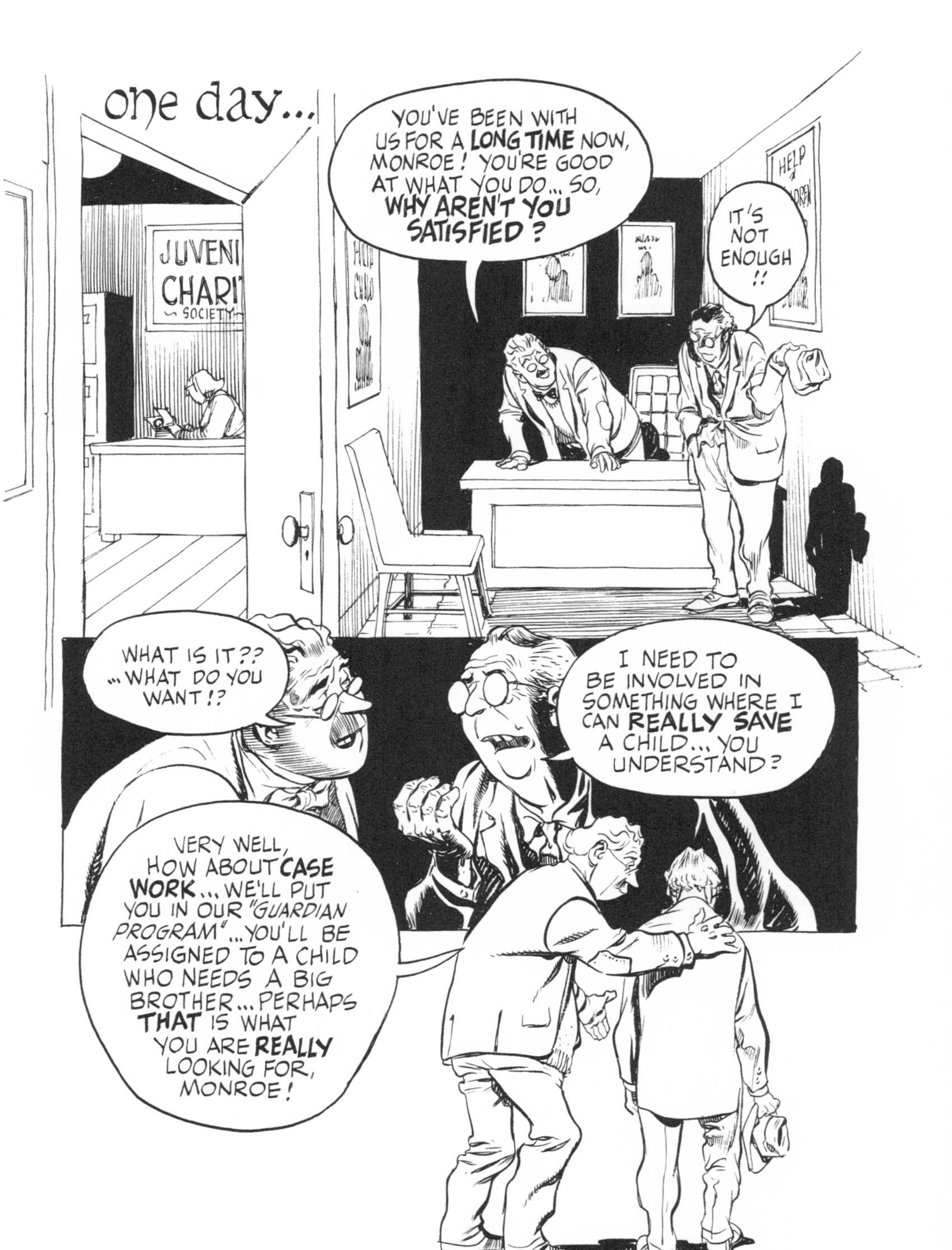
one day...
JUVENI
CHARIT
SOCIETY
YOU'VE BEEN WITH US FOR A LONG TIME NOW, MONROE! YOU'RE GOOD AT WHAT YOU DO... SO, WHY AREN'T YOU SATISFIED?
HELP
IT'S NOT ENOUGH!!
WHAT IS IT?? ...WHAT DO YOU WANT!?
I NEED TO BE INVOLVED IN SOMETHING WHERE I CAN REALLY SAVE A CHILD... YOU UNDERSTAND?
VERY WELL, HOW ABOUT CASE WORK... WE'LL PUT YOU IN OUR "GUARDIAN PROGRAM"...YOU'LL BE ASSIGNED TO A CHILD WHO NEEDS A BIG BROTHER...PERHAPS THAT IS WHAT YOU ARE REALLY LOOKING FOR, MONROE!

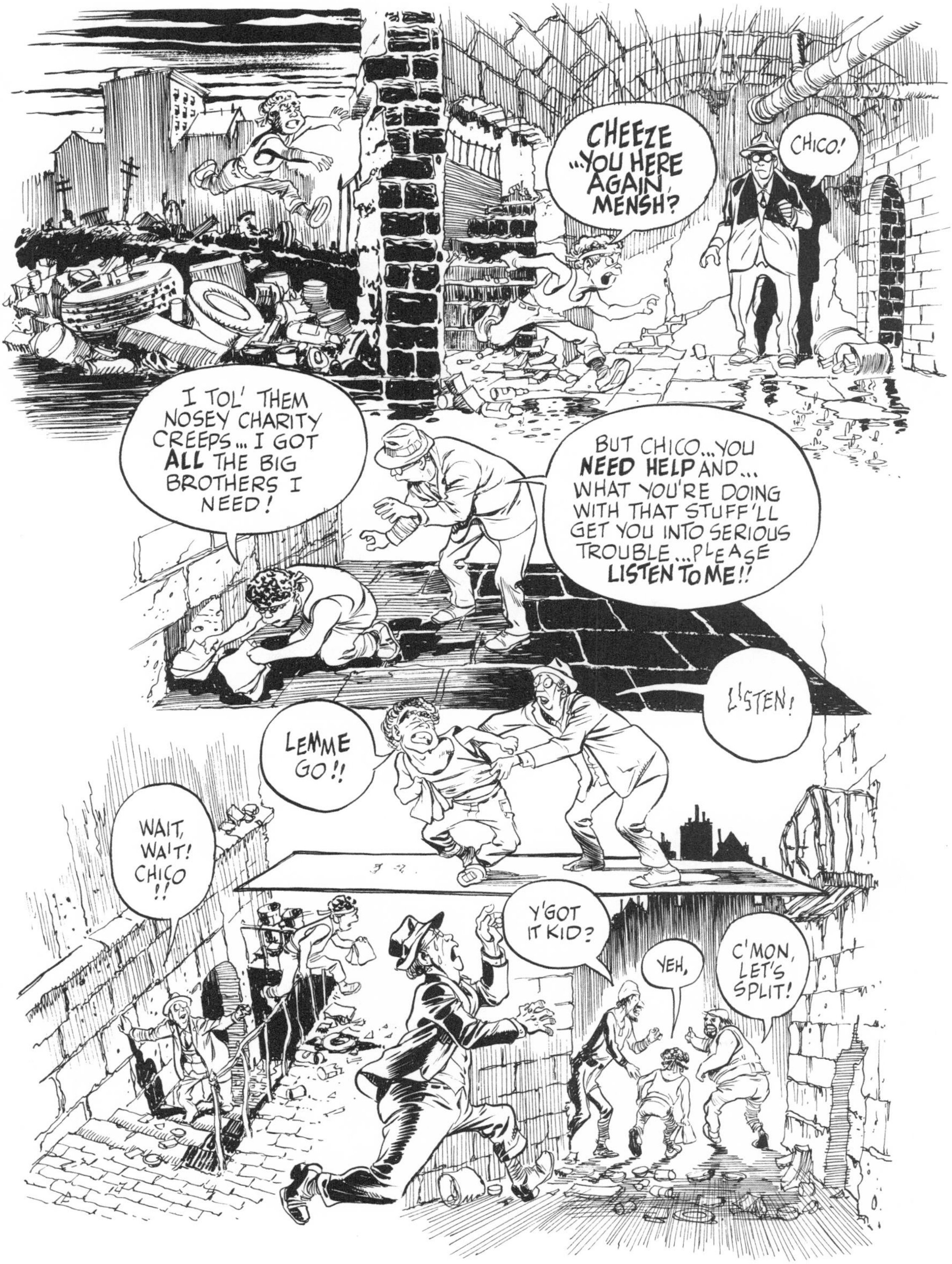
CHEEZE ...YOU HERE AGAIN, MENSH?
CHICO!
I TOL' THEM NOSEY CHARITY CREEPS... I GOT **ALL** THE BIG BROTHERS I NEED!
BUT CHICO... YOU **NEED HELP** AND... WHAT YOU'RE DOING WITH THAT STUFF'LL GET YOU INTO SERIOUS TROUBLE... PLEASE **LISTEN TO ME!!**
LISTEN!
LEMME GO!!
WAIT, WAIT! CHICO!!
Y'GOT IT KID?
YEH,
C'MON, LET'S SPLIT!

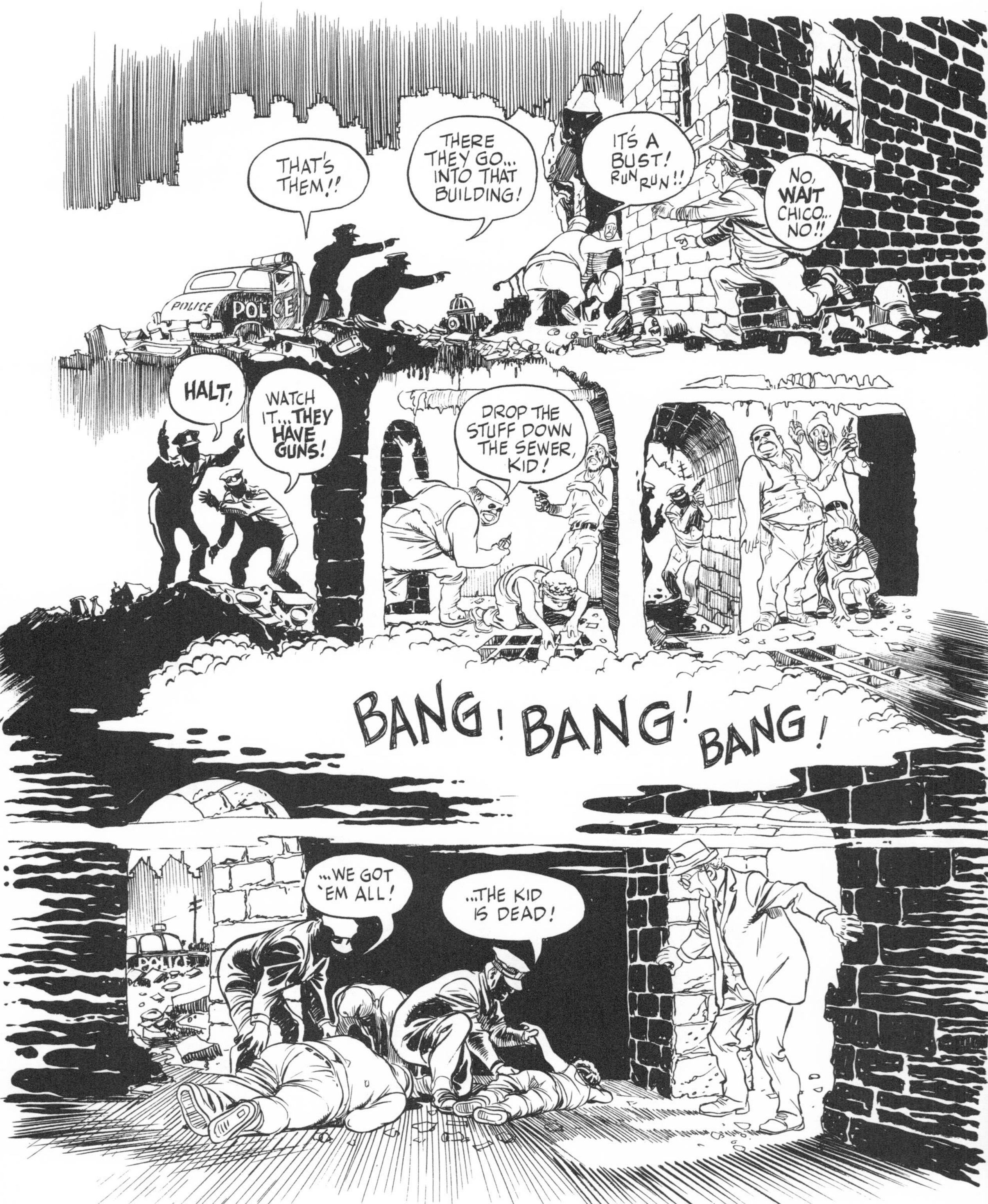
THAT'S THEM!!
THERE THEY GO... INTO THAT BUILDING!
IT'S A BUST! RUN RUN!!
NO, WAIT CHICO... NO!!
POLICE
POLICE
HALT!
WATCH IT... THEY HAVE GUNS!
DROP THE STUFF DOWN THE SEWER, KID!
BANG! BANG! BANG!
...WE GOT 'EM ALL!
...THE KID IS DEAD!
POLICE

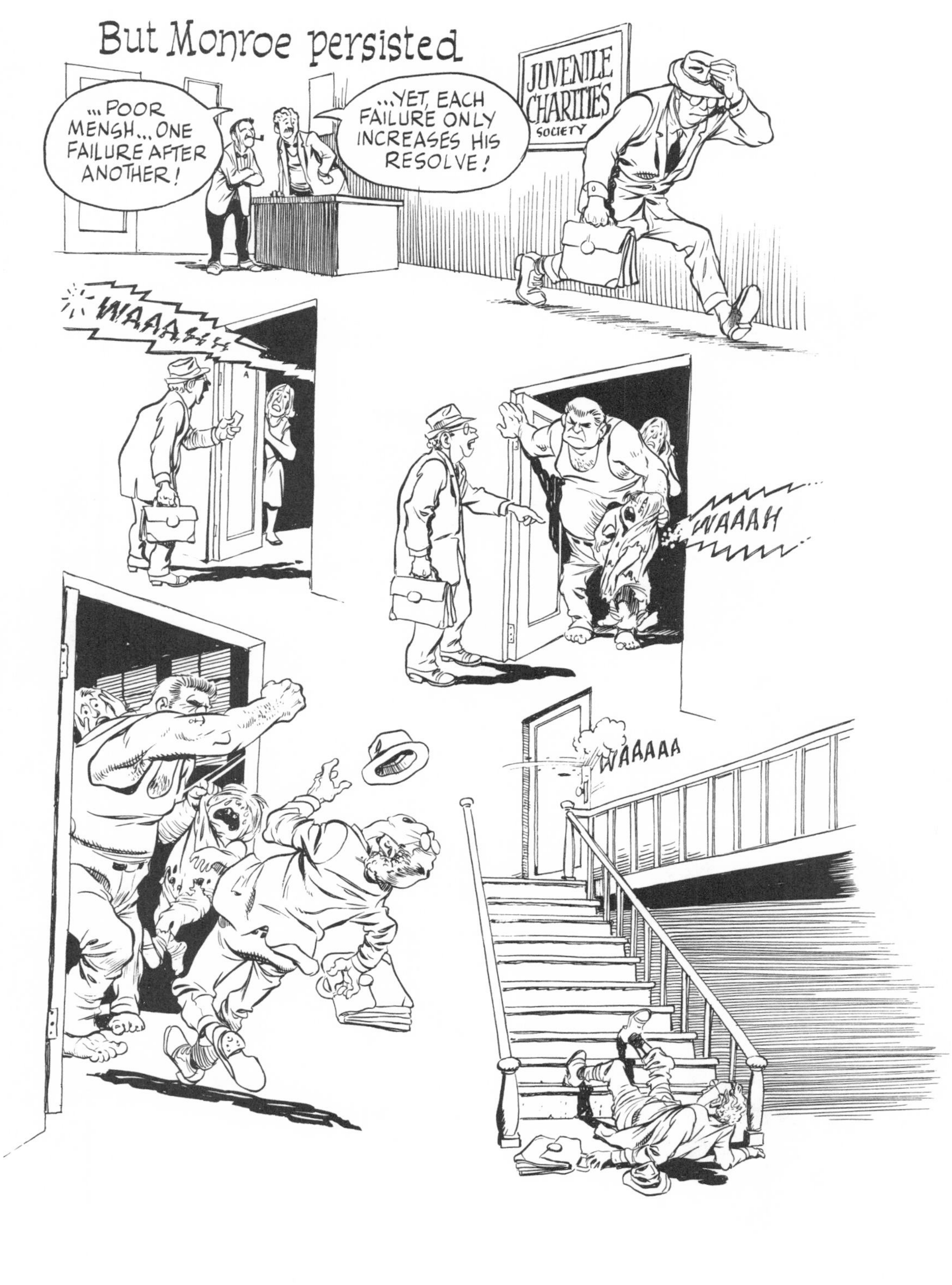
But Monroe persisted
...POOR MENGH...ONE FAILURE AFTER ANOTHER!
...YET, EACH FAILURE ONLY INCREASES HIS RESOLVE!
JUVENILE CHARITIES SOCIETY
WAAAAHH
WAAAH
WAAAAA

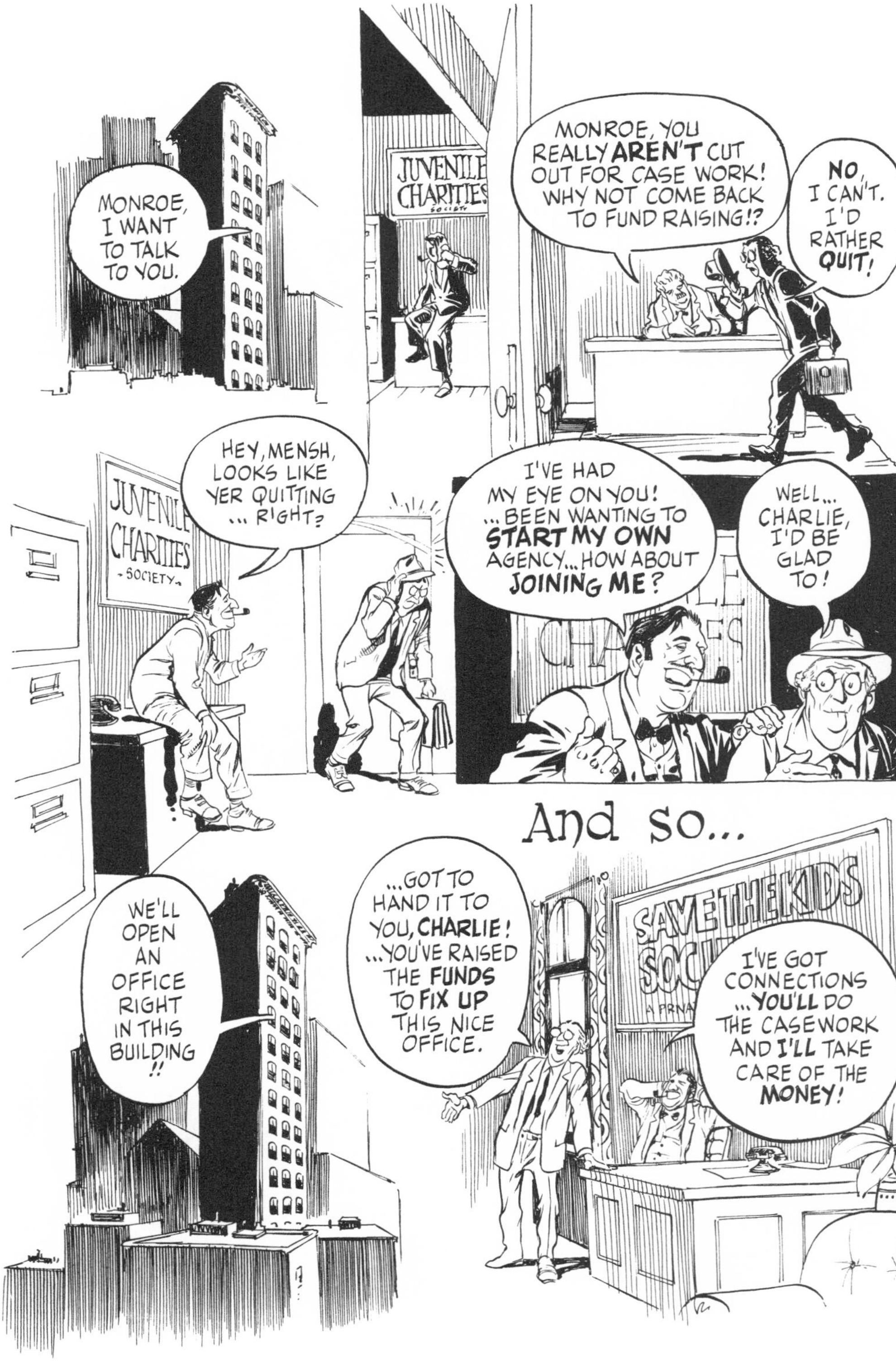
MONROE, I WANT TO TALK TO YOU.
JUVENILE CHARITIES SOCIETY
MONROE, YOU REALLY AREN'T CUT OUT FOR CASE WORK! WHY NOT COME BACK TO FUND RAISING!?
NO, I CAN'T. I'D RATHER QUIT!
JUVENILE CHARITIES SOCIETY
HEY, MENSH, LOOKS LIKE YER QUITTING ... RIGHT?
I'VE HAD MY EYE ON YOU! ... BEEN WANTING TO START MY OWN AGENCY... HOW ABOUT JOINING ME?
WELL... CHARLIE, I'D BE GLAD TO!
And so...
WE'LL OPEN AN OFFICE RIGHT IN THIS BUILDING!!
...GOT TO HAND IT TO YOU, CHARLIE! ...YOU'VE RAISED THE FUNDS TO FIX UP THIS NICE OFFICE.
SAVE THE KIDS
I'VE GOT CONNECTIONS ...YOU'LL DO THE CASEWORK AND I'LL TAKE CARE OF THE MONEY!

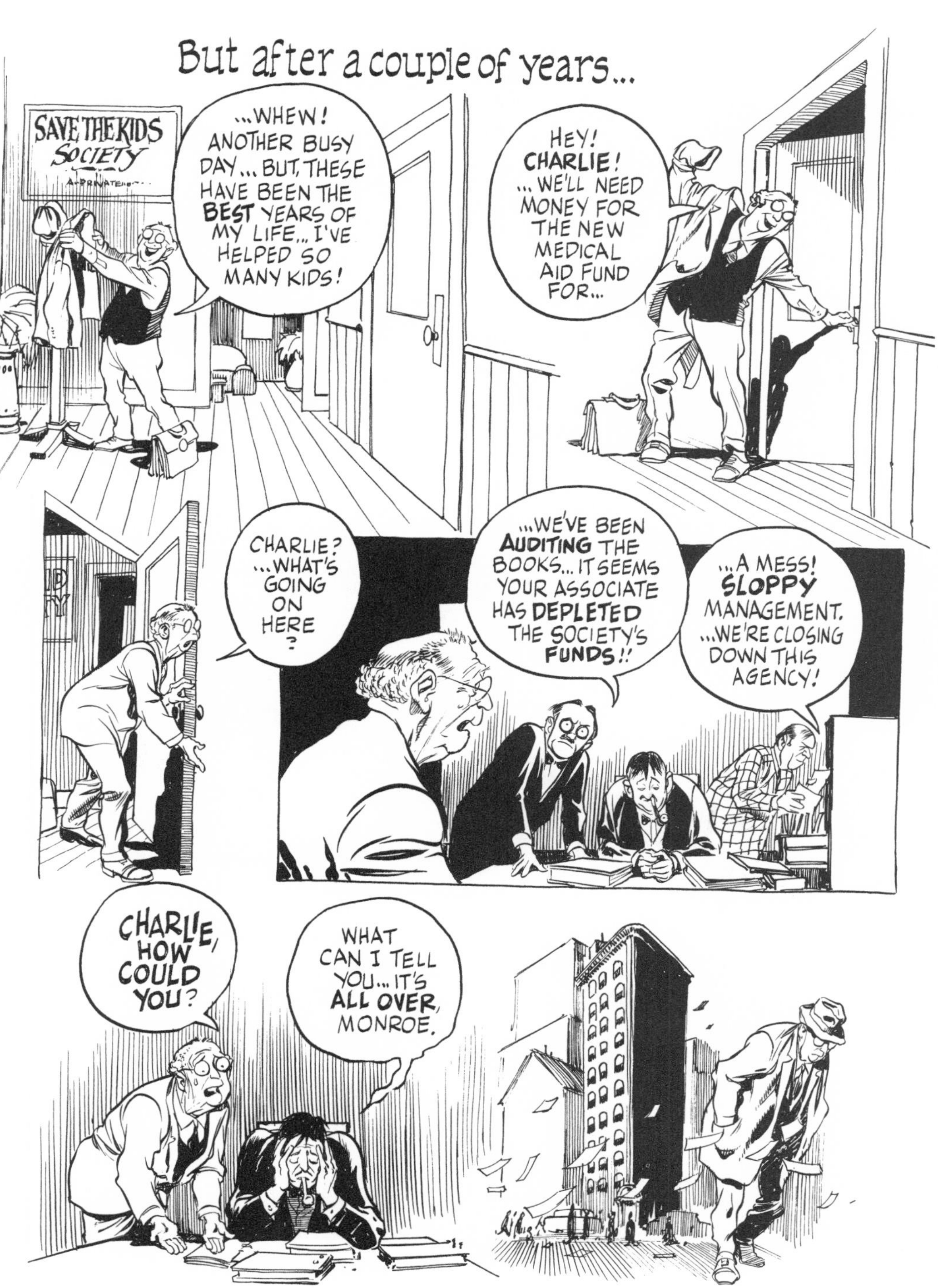

But after a couple of years...
SAVE THE KIDS SOCIETY
...WHEW! ANOTHER BUSY DAY... BUT, THESE HAVE BEEN THE BEST YEARS OF MY LIFE... I'VE HELPED SO MANY KIDS!
HEY! CHARLIE! ...WE'LL NEED MONEY FOR THE NEW MEDICAL AID FUND FOR...
CHARLIE? ...WHAT'S GOING ON HERE?
...WE'VE BEEN AUDITING THE BOOKS... IT SEEMS YOUR ASSOCIATE HAS DEPLETED THE SOCIETY'S FUNDS!!
...A MESS! SLOPPY MANAGEMENT. ...WE'RE CLOSING DOWN THIS AGENCY!
CHARLIE, HOW COULD YOU?
WHAT CAN I TELL YOU... IT'S ALL OVER, MONROE.

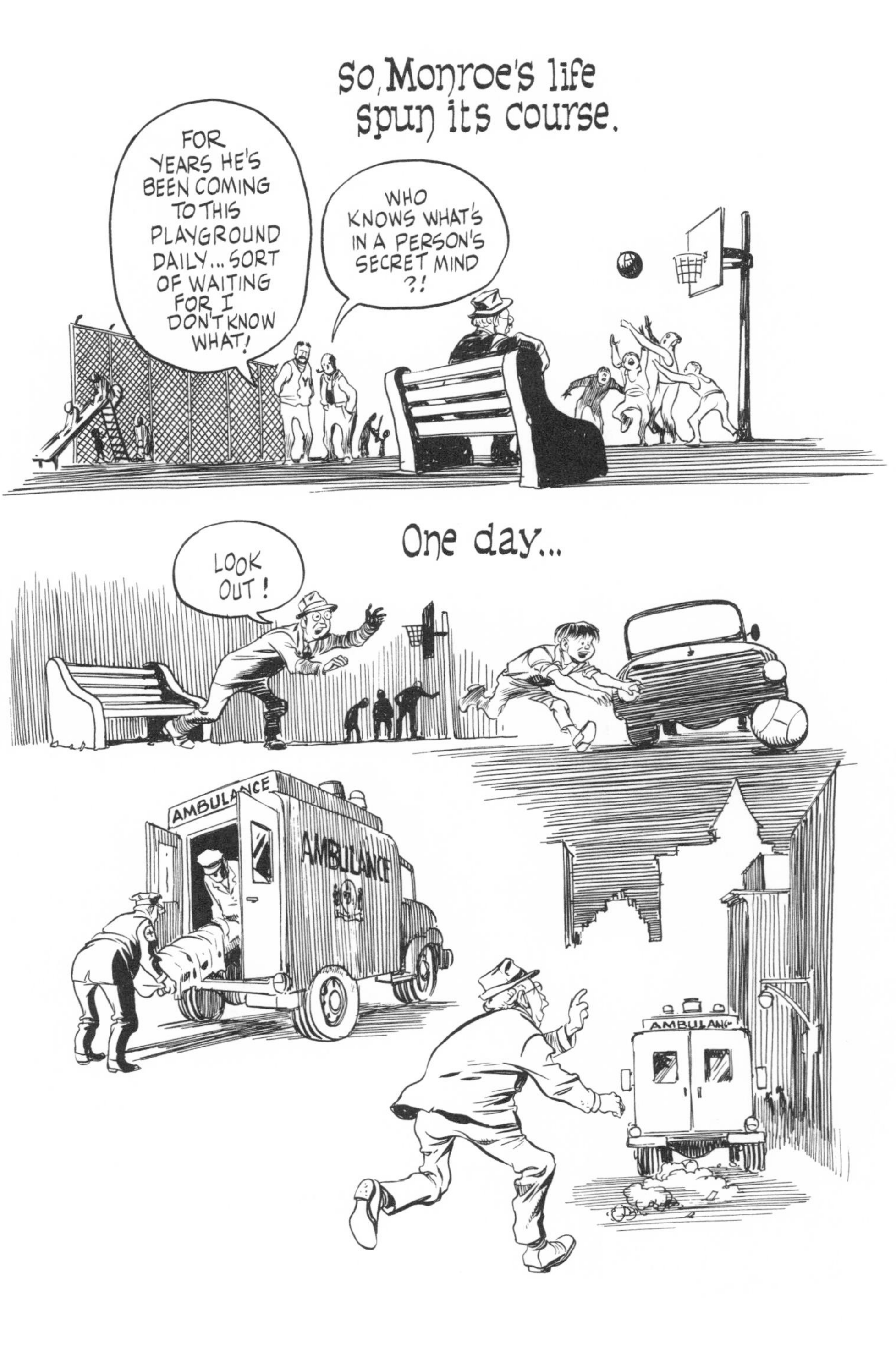
So, Monroe's life spun its course.
FOR YEARS HE'S BEEN COMING TO THIS PLAYGROUND DAILY... SORT OF WAITING FOR I DON'T KNOW WHAT!
WHO KNOWS WHAT'S IN A PERSON'S SECRET MIND ?!
One day...
LOOK OUT!
AMBULANCE
AMBULANCE
AMBULANCE

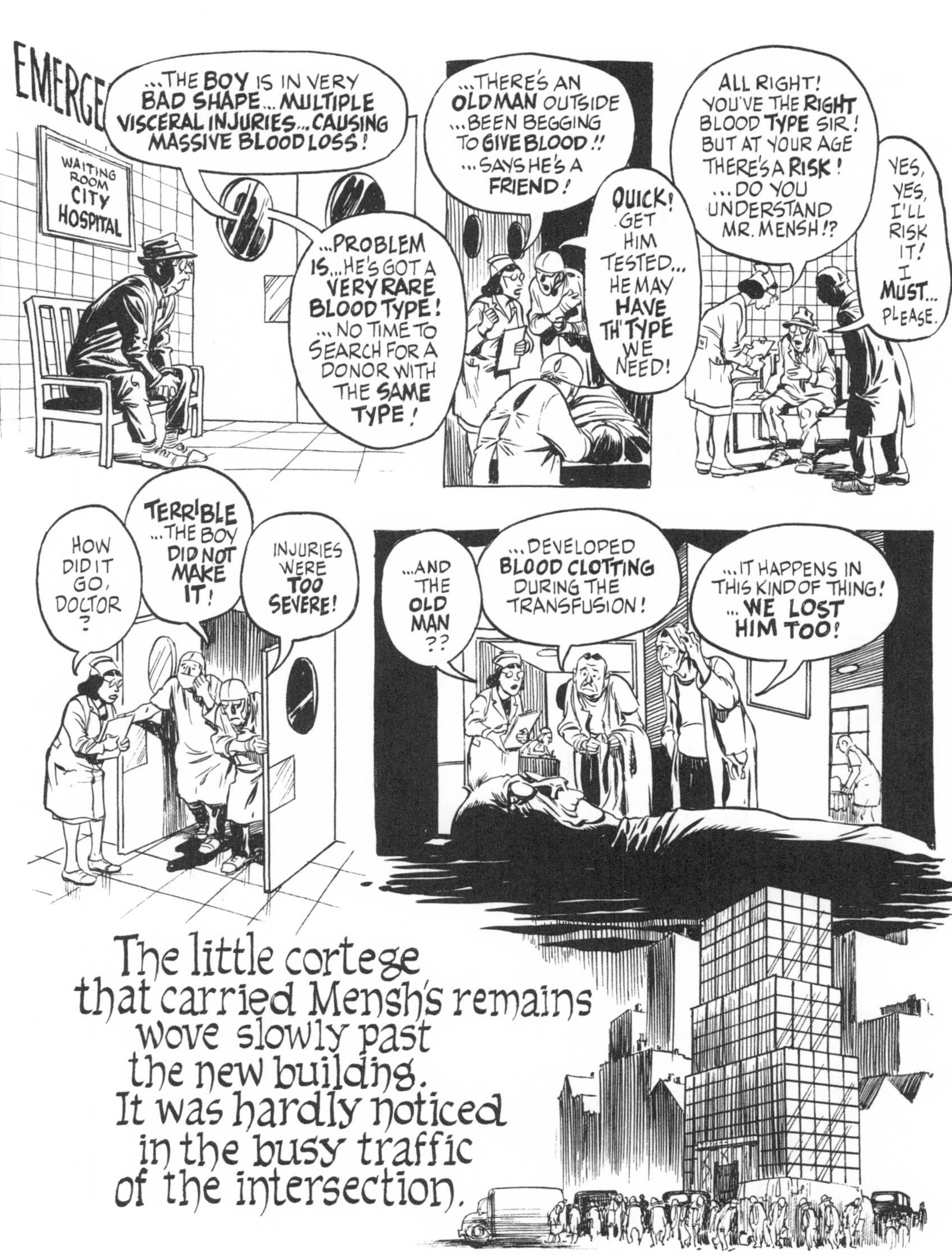
EMERGE
WAITING ROOM CITY HOSPITAL
...THE BOY IS IN VERY BAD SHAPE... MULTIPLE VISCERAL INJURIES... CAUSING MASSIVE BLOOD LOSS!
...PROBLEM IS...HE'S GOT A VERY RARE BLOOD TYPE! ...NO TIME TO SEARCH FOR A DONOR WITH THE SAME TYPE!
...THERE'S AN OLD MAN OUTSIDE ...BEEN BEGGING TO GIVE BLOOD!! ...SAYS HE'S A FRIEND!
QUICK! GET HIM TESTED... HE MAY HAVE TH' TYPE WE NEED!
ALL RIGHT! YOU'VE THE RIGHT BLOOD TYPE SIR! BUT AT YOUR AGE THERE'S A RISK! ...DO YOU UNDERSTAND MR. MENSH!?
YES, YES, I'LL RISK IT! I MUST... PLEASE.
HOW DID IT GO, DOCTOR?
TERRIBLE ...THE BOY DID NOT MAKE IT!
INJURIES WERE TOO SEVERE!
...AND THE OLD MAN??
...DEVELOPED BLOOD CLOTTING DURING THE TRANSFUSION!
...IT HAPPENS IN THIS KIND OF THING! ...WE LOST HIM TOO!
The little cortege that carried Mensh's remains wove slowly past the new building. It was hardly noticed in the busy traffic of the intersection.

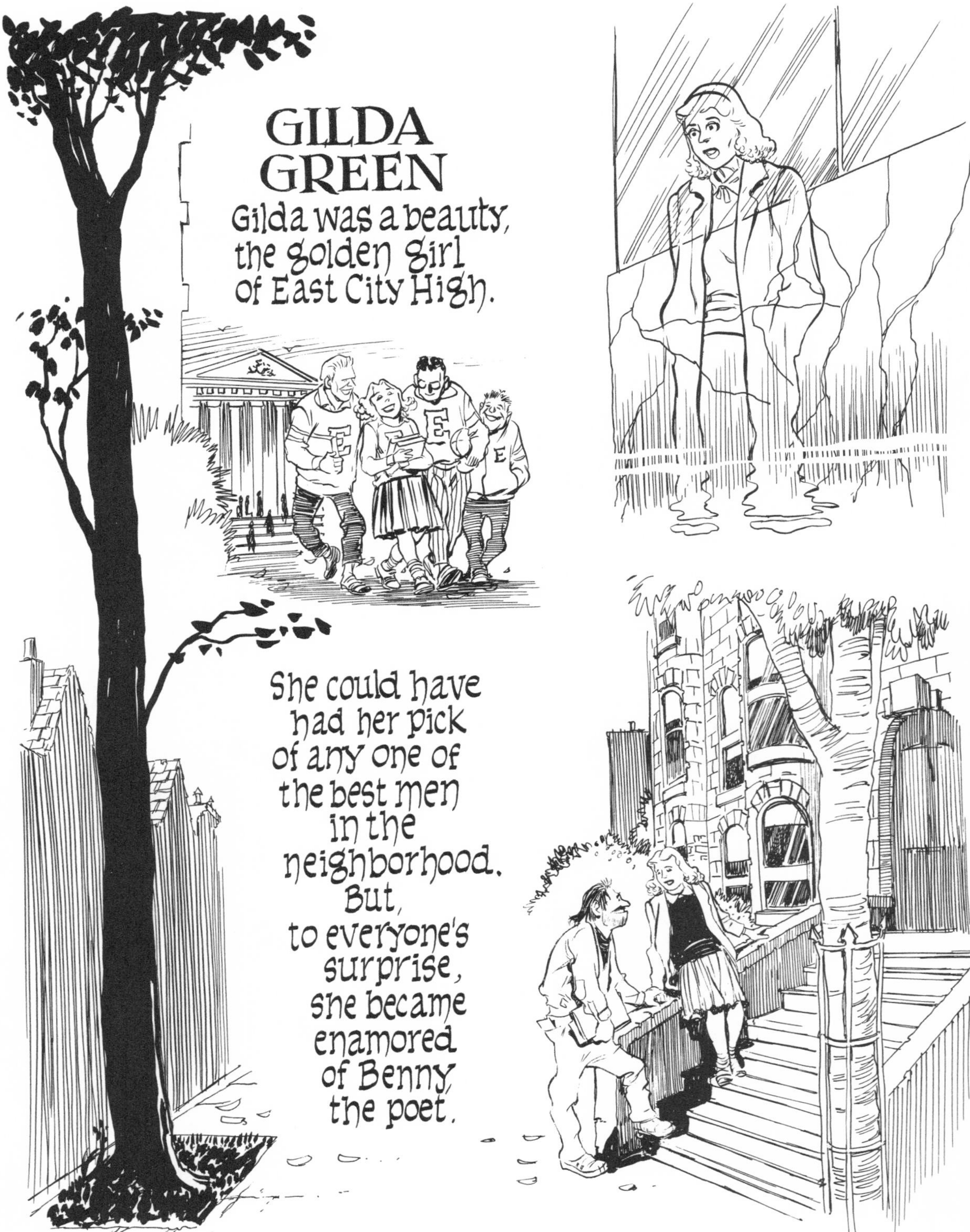
GILDA
GREEN
Gilda was a beauty,
the golden girl
of East City High.
She could have
had her pick
of any one of
the best men
in the
neighborhood.
But,
to everyone's
surprise,
she became
enamored
of Benny,
the poet.

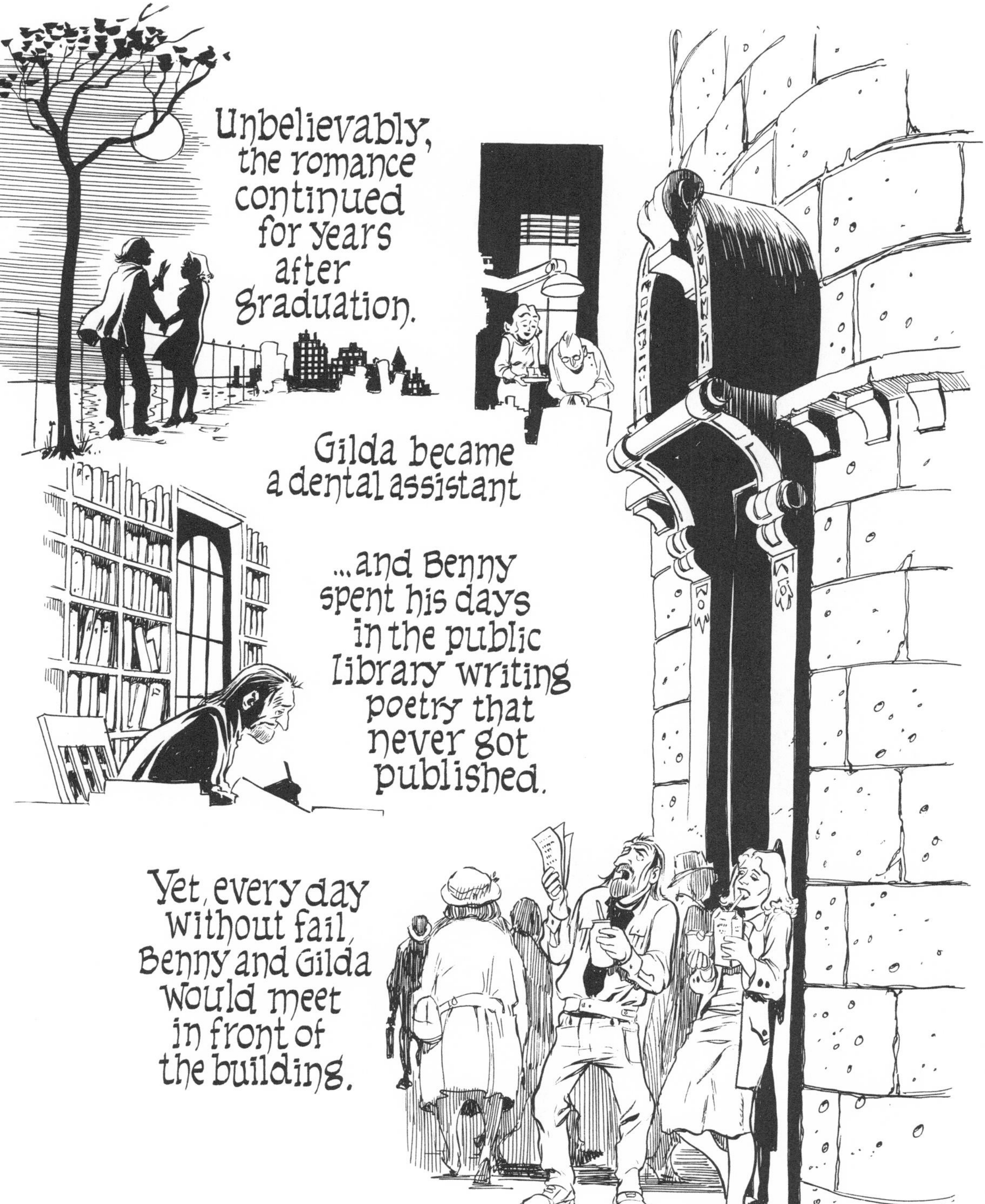

Unbelievably, the romance continued for years after graduation.
Gilda became a dental assistant
...and Benny spent his days in the public library writing poetry that never got published.
Yet, every day without fail, Benny and Gilda would meet in front of the building.

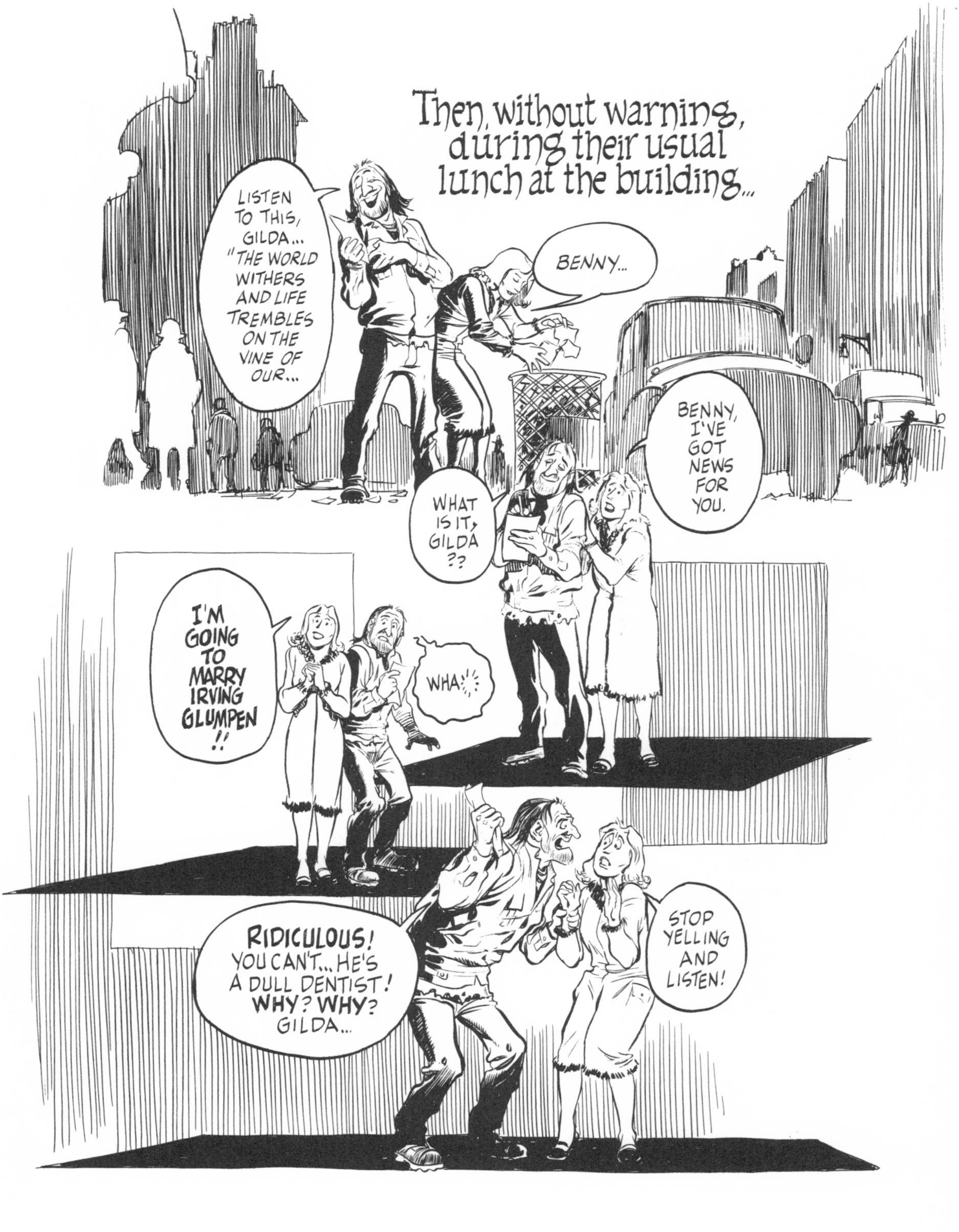

Then, without warning, during their usual lunch at the building...
LISTEN TO THIS, GILDA... "THE WORLD WITHERS AND LIFE TREMBLES ON THE VINE OF OUR...
BENNY...
BENNY, I'VE GOT NEWS FOR YOU.
WHAT IS IT, GILDA ??
I'M GOING TO MARRY IRVING GLUMPEN !!
WHA!
RIDICULOUS! YOU CAN'T... HE'S A DULL DENTIST! WHY? WHY? GILDA...
STOP YELLING AND LISTEN!

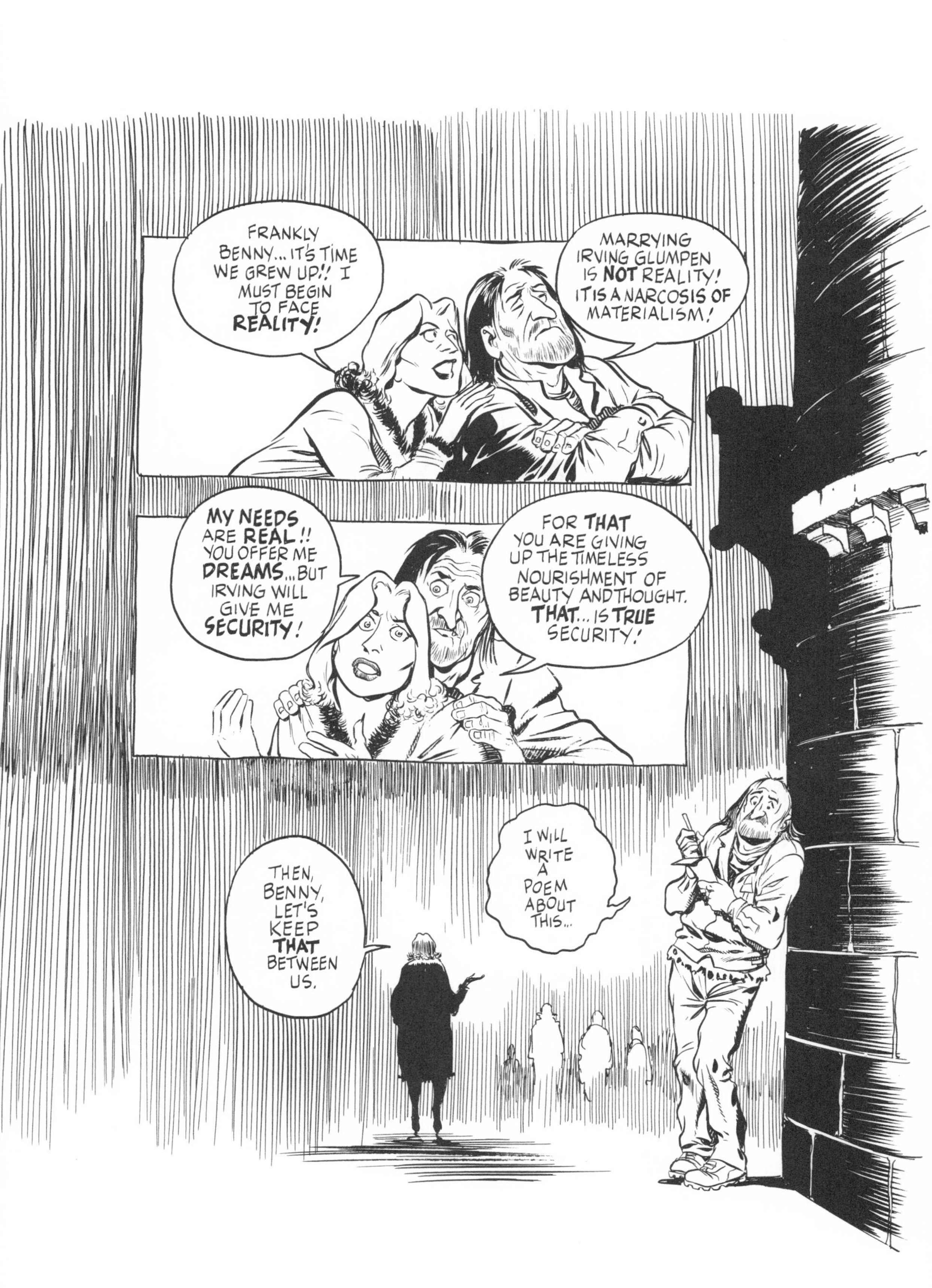
FRANKLY BENNY... IT'S TIME WE GREW UP!! I MUST BEGIN TO FACE REALITY!
MARRYING IRVING GLUMPEN IS NOT REALITY! IT IS A NARCOSIS OF MATERIALISM!
MY NEEDS ARE REAL!! YOU OFFER ME DREAMS...BUT IRVING WILL GIVE ME SECURITY!
FOR THAT YOU ARE GIVING UP THE TIMELESS NOURISHMENT OF BEAUTY AND THOUGHT. THAT... IS TRUE SECURITY!
I WILL WRITE A POEM ABOUT THIS...
THEN, BENNY, LET'S KEEP THAT BETWEEN US.

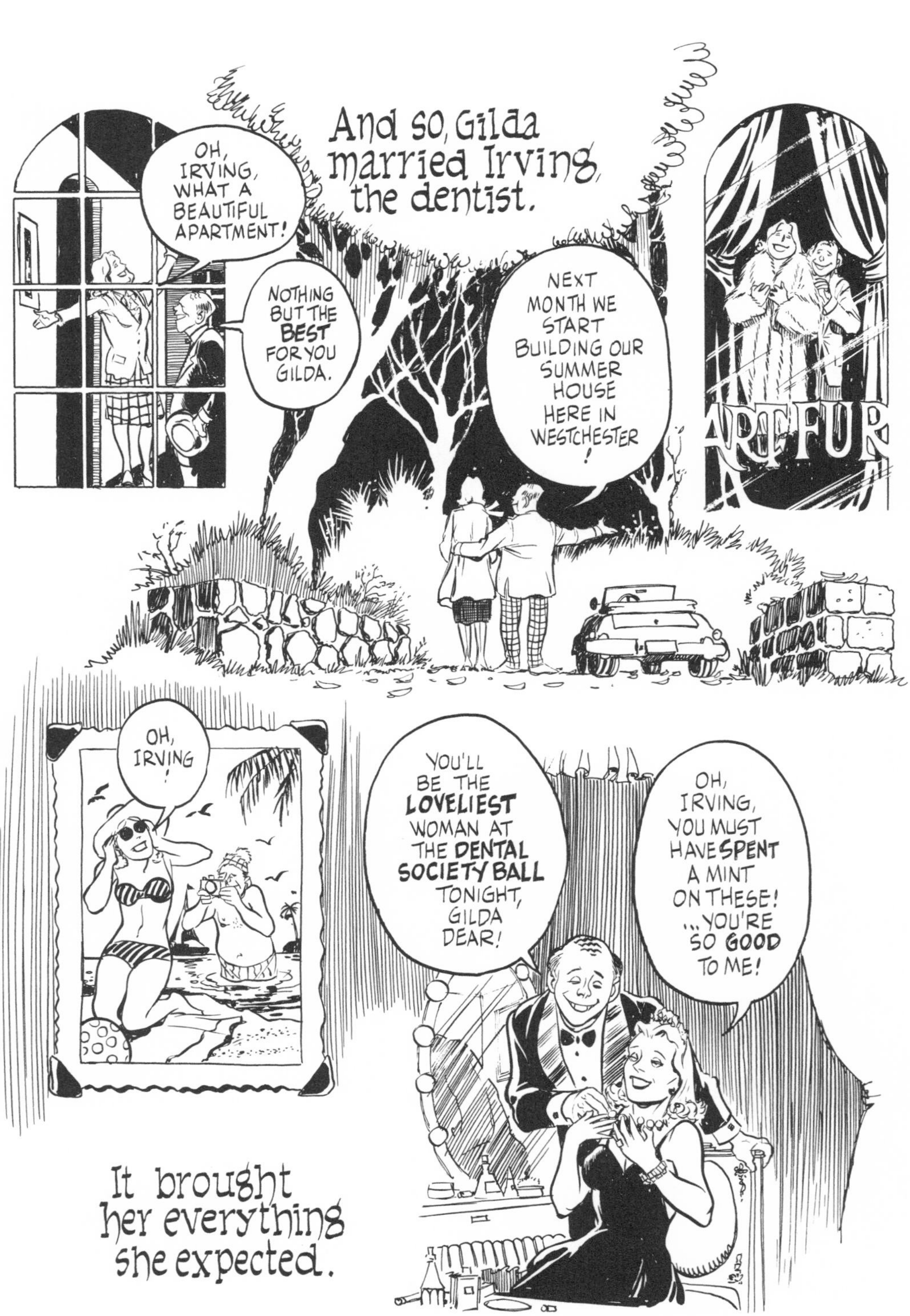
And so, Gilda married Irving, the dentist.
OH, IRVING, WHAT A BEAUTIFUL APARTMENT!
NOTHING BUT THE BEST FOR YOU GILDA.
NEXT MONTH WE START BUILDING OUR SUMMER HOUSE HERE IN WESTCHESTER!
ART FUR
OH, IRVING!
YOU'LL BE THE LOVELIEST WOMAN AT THE DENTAL SOCIETY BALL TONIGHT, GILDA DEAR!
OH, IRVING, YOU MUST HAVE SPENT A MINT ON THESE! ...YOU'RE SO GOOD TO ME!
It brought her everything she expected.

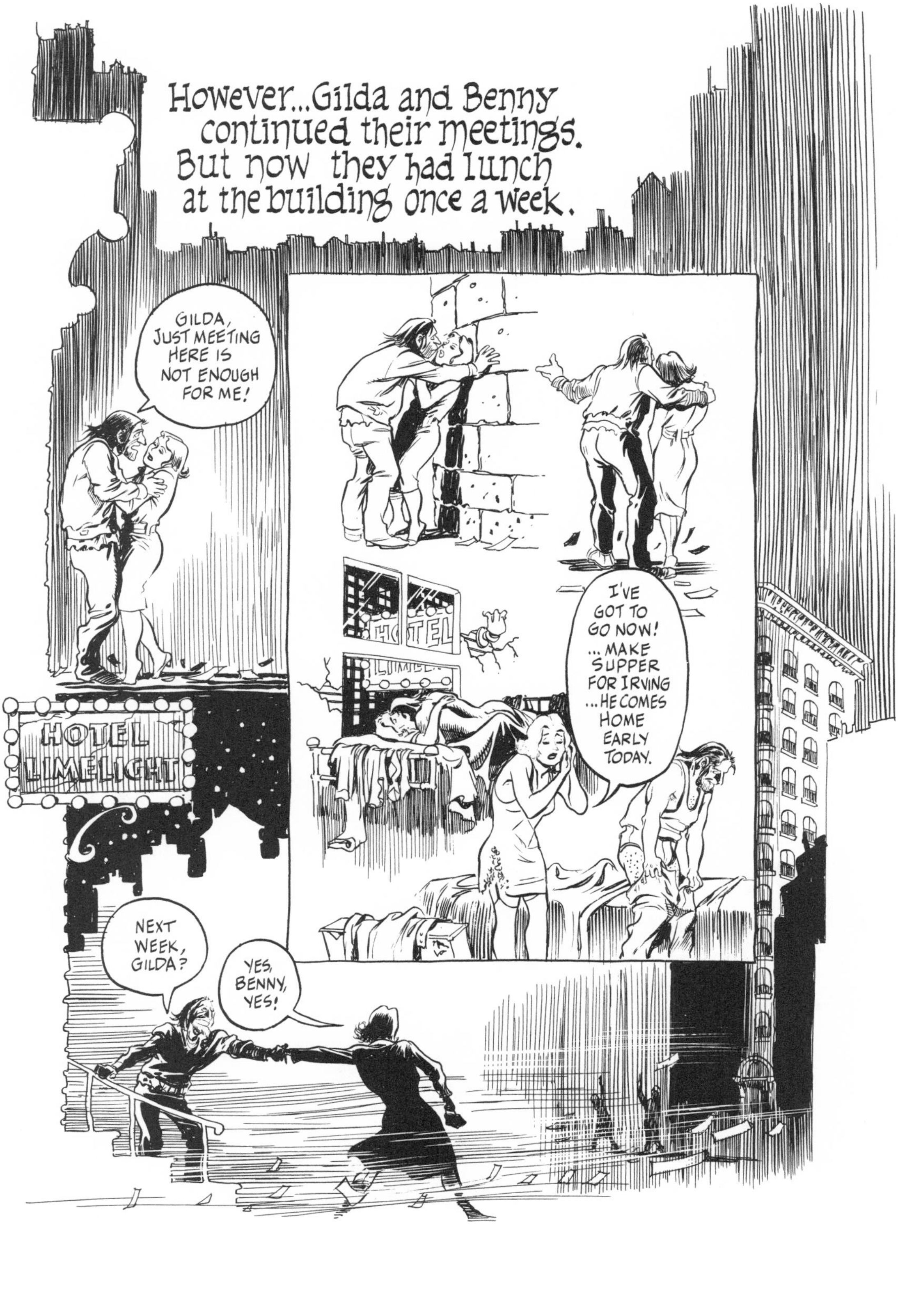
However...Gilda and Benny continued their meetings. But now they had lunch at the building once a week.
GILDA, JUST MEETING HERE IS NOT ENOUGH FOR ME!
HOTEL LIMELIGHT
HOTEL
I'VE GOT TO GO NOW! ...MAKE SUPPER FOR IRVING ...HE COMES HOME EARLY TODAY.
NEXT WEEK, GILDA?
YES, BENNY, YES!

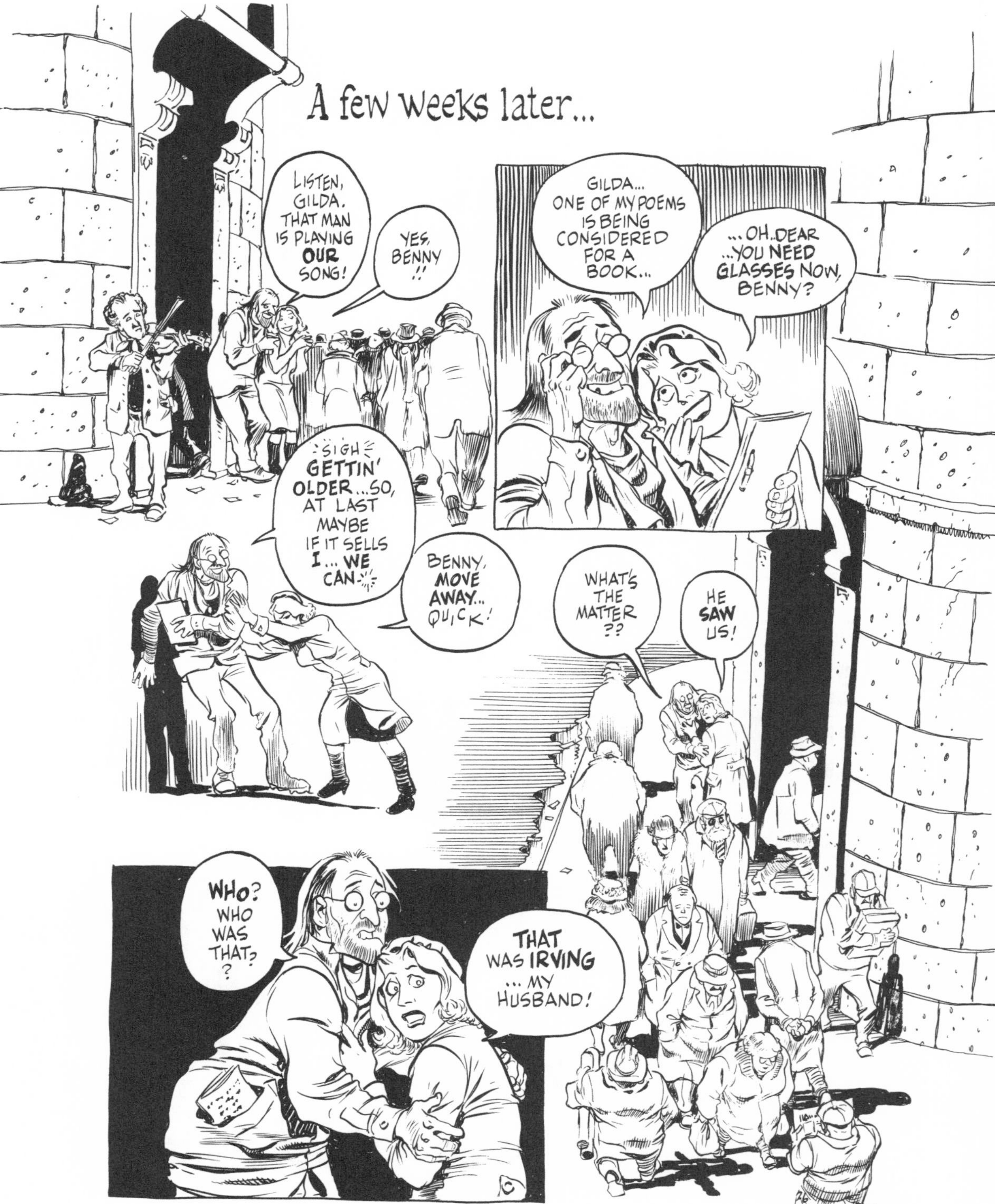

A few weeks later...
LISTEN, GILDA. THAT MAN IS PLAYING OUR SONG!
YES, BENNY !!
GILDA... ONE OF MY POEMS IS BEING CONSIDERED FOR A BOOK...
...OH..DEAR ...YOU NEED GLASSES NOW, BENNY?
SIGH GETTIN' OLDER...SO, AT LAST MAYBE IF IT SELLS I... WE CAN...
BENNY, MOVE AWAY... QUICK!
WHAT'S THE MATTER ??
HE SAW US!
WHO? WHO WAS THAT? ?
THAT WAS IRVING ... MY HUSBAND!

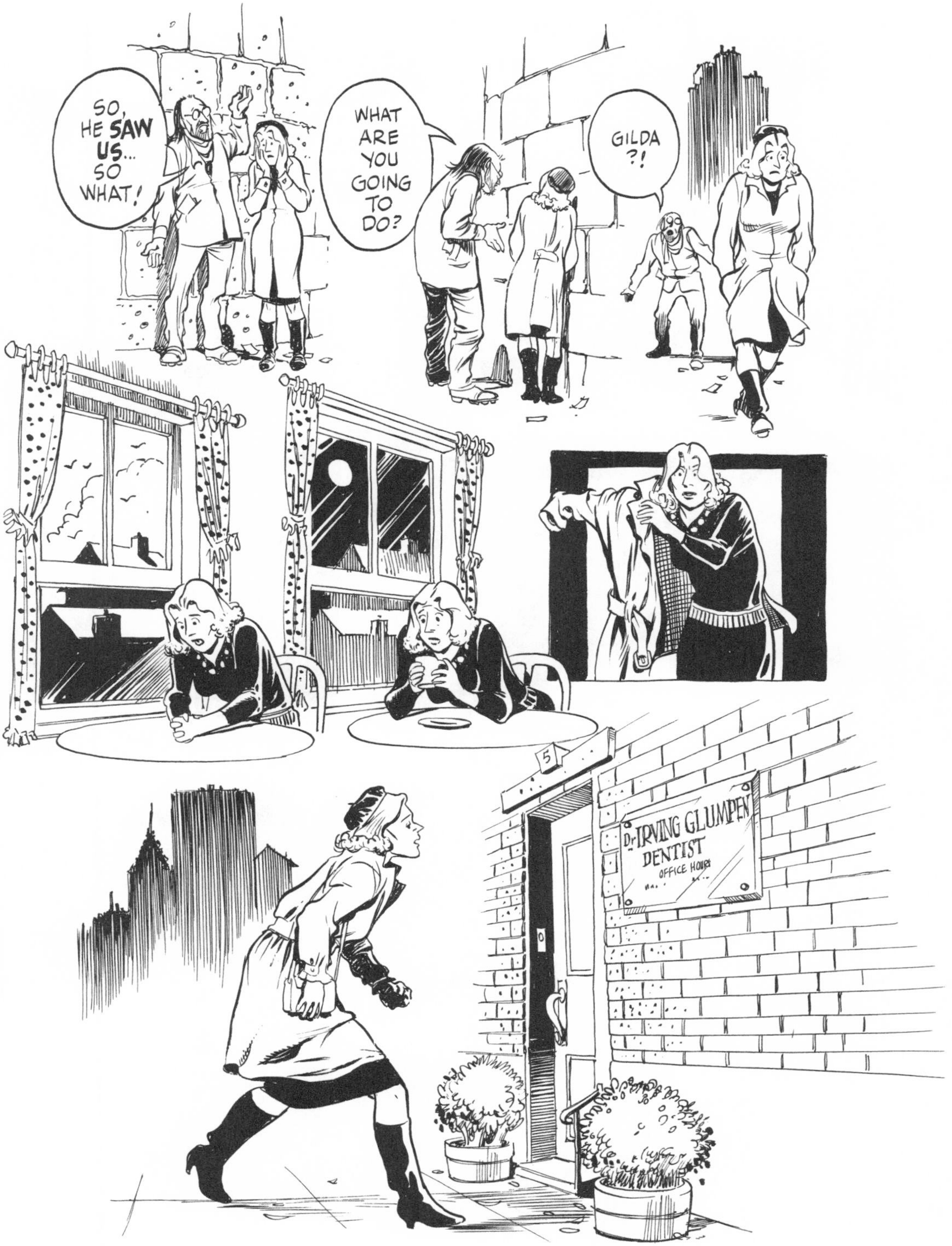
SO, HE SAW US... SO WHAT!
WHAT ARE YOU GOING TO DO?
GILDA ?!
5
Dr IRVING GLUMPEN
DENTIST
OFFICE HOURS

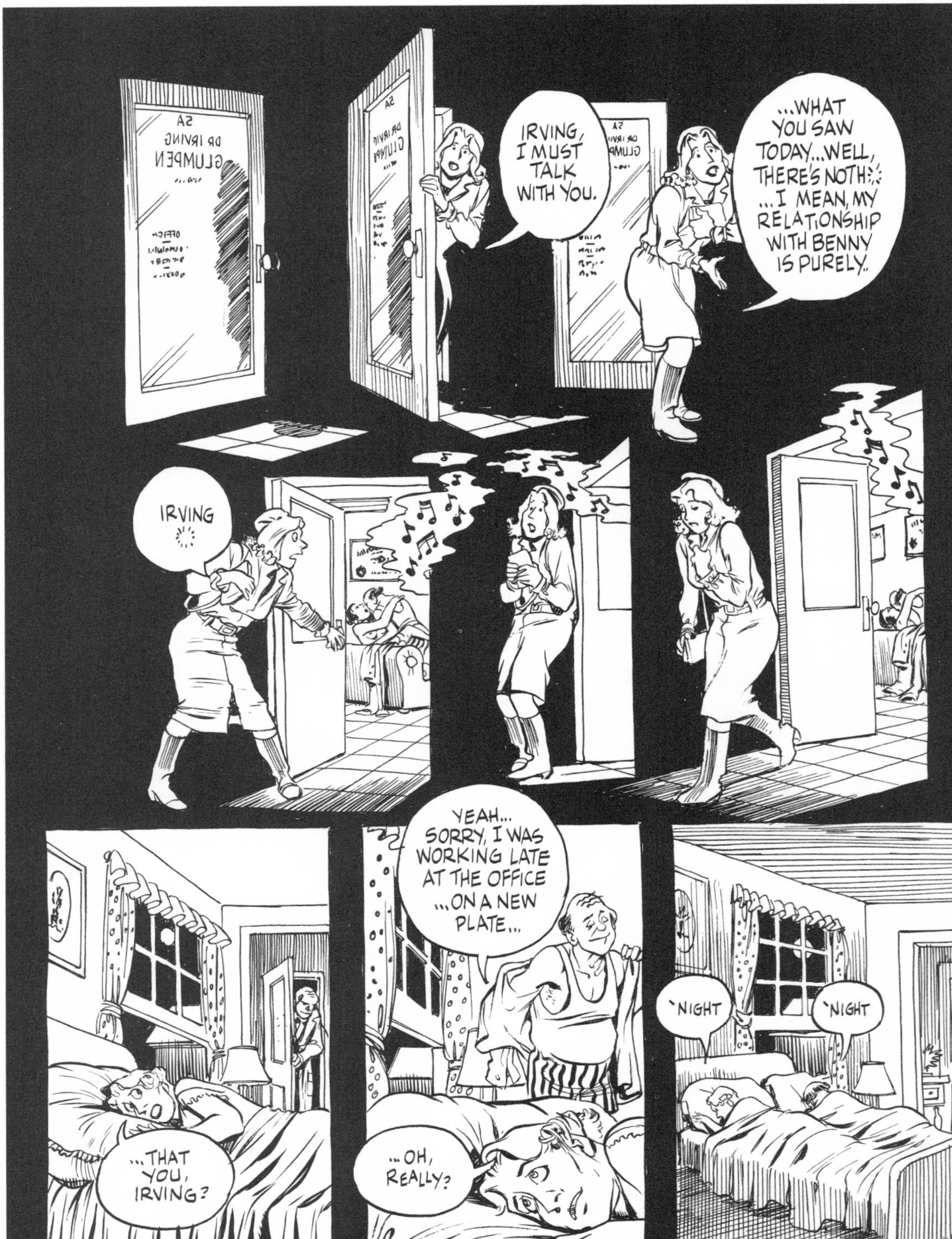
IRVING, I MUST TALK WITH YOU.
...WHAT YOU SAW TODAY...WELL, THERE'S NOTH ...I MEAN, MY RELATIONSHIP WITH BENNY IS PURELY...
IRVING
...THAT YOU, IRVING?
YEAH... SORRY, I WAS WORKING LATE AT THE OFFICE ...ON A NEW PLATE...
...OH, REALLY?
`NIGHT
`NIGHT

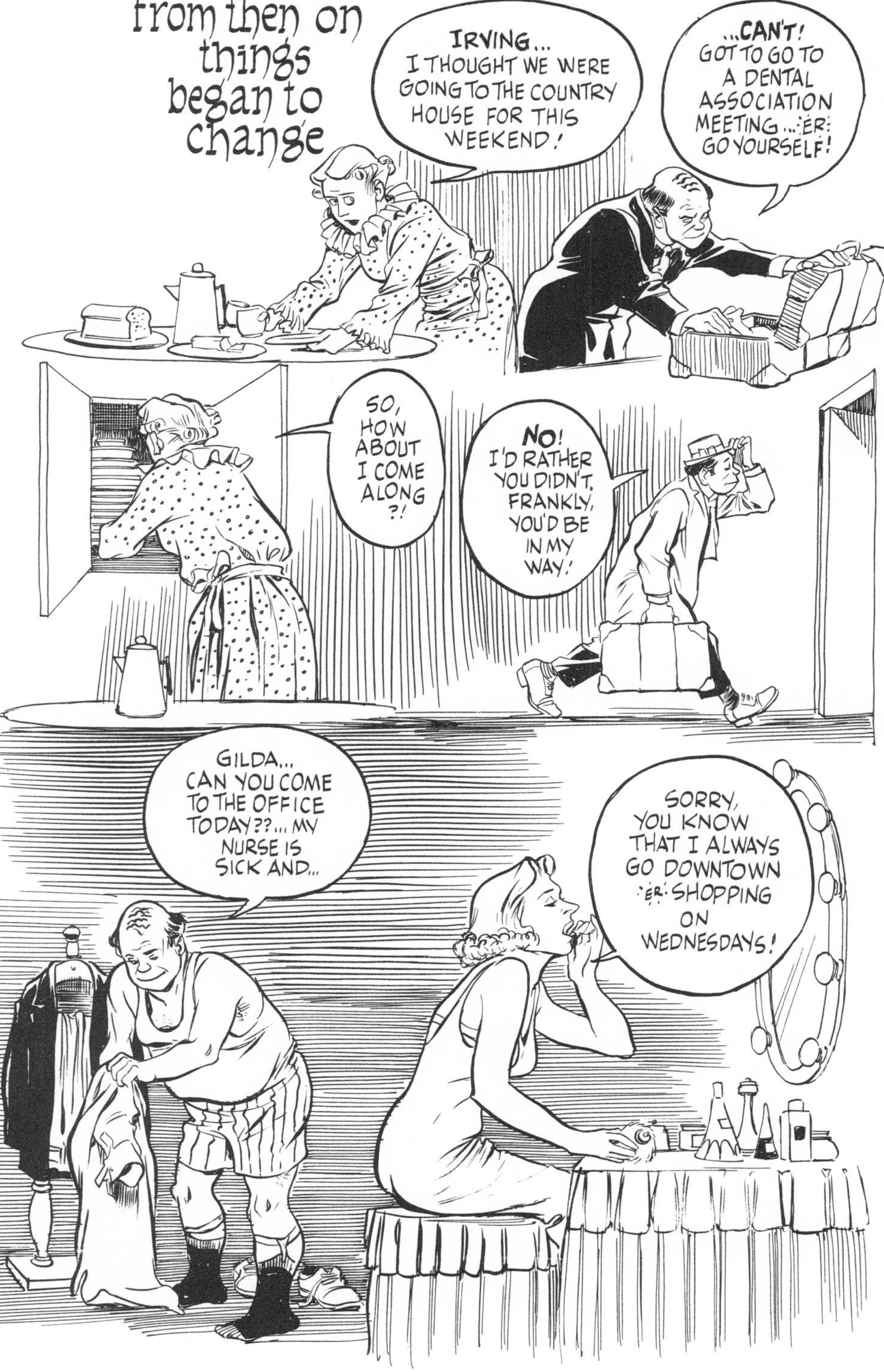
From then on things began to change
IRVING... I THOUGHT WE WERE GOING TO THE COUNTRY HOUSE FOR THIS WEEKEND!
...CAN'T! GOT TO GO TO A DENTAL ASSOCIATION MEETING... ER: GO YOURSELF!
SO, HOW ABOUT I COME ALONG ?!
NO! I'D RATHER YOU DIDN'T, FRANKLY, YOU'D BE IN MY WAY!
GILDA... CAN YOU COME TO THE OFFICE TODAY??... MY NURSE IS SICK AND...
SORRY, YOU KNOW THAT I ALWAYS GO DOWNTOWN ER: SHOPPING ON WEDNESDAYS!

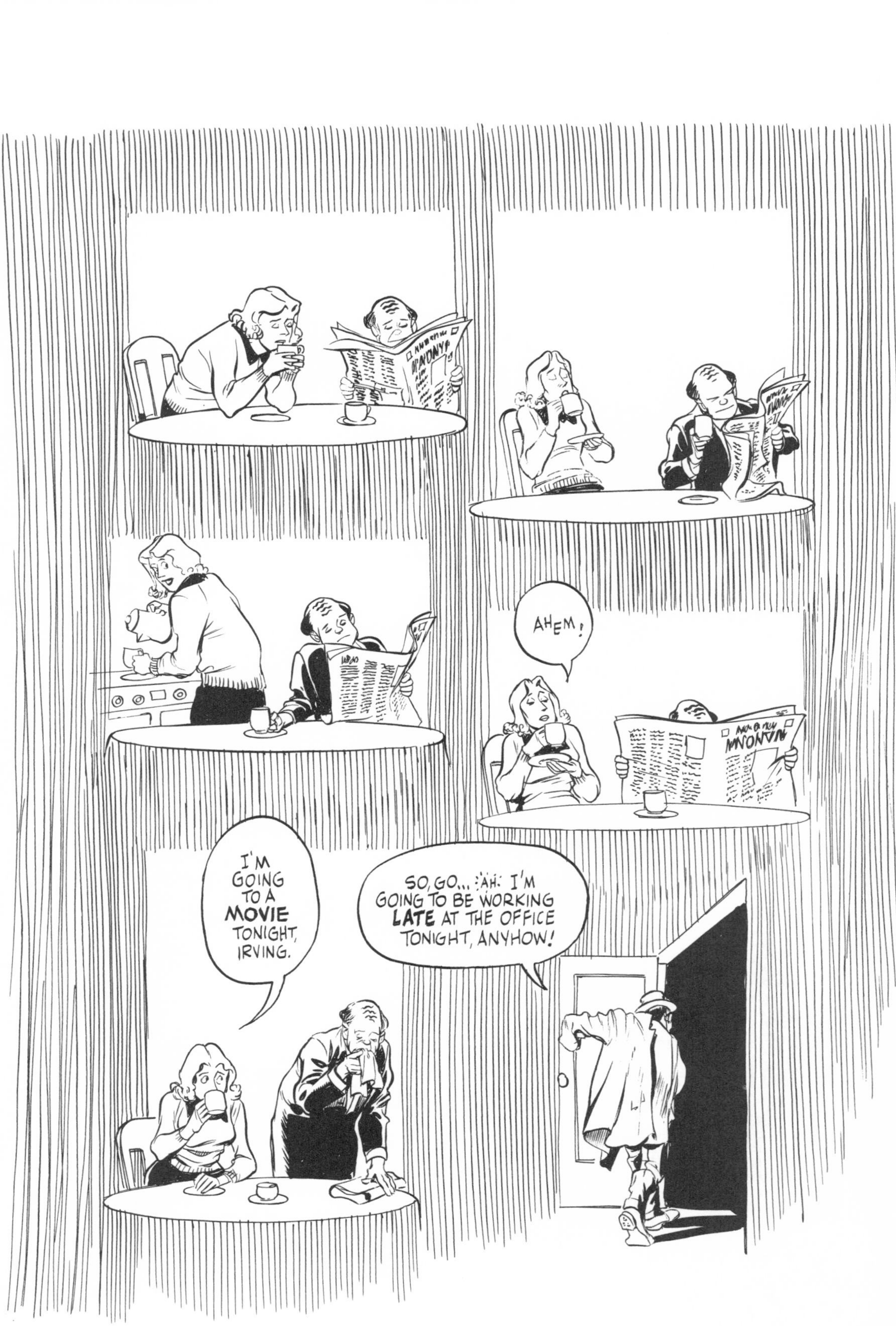
AHEM!
I'M GOING TO A MOVIE TONIGHT, IRVING.
SO, GO... AH... I'M GOING TO BE WORKING LATE AT THE OFFICE TONIGHT, ANYHOW!

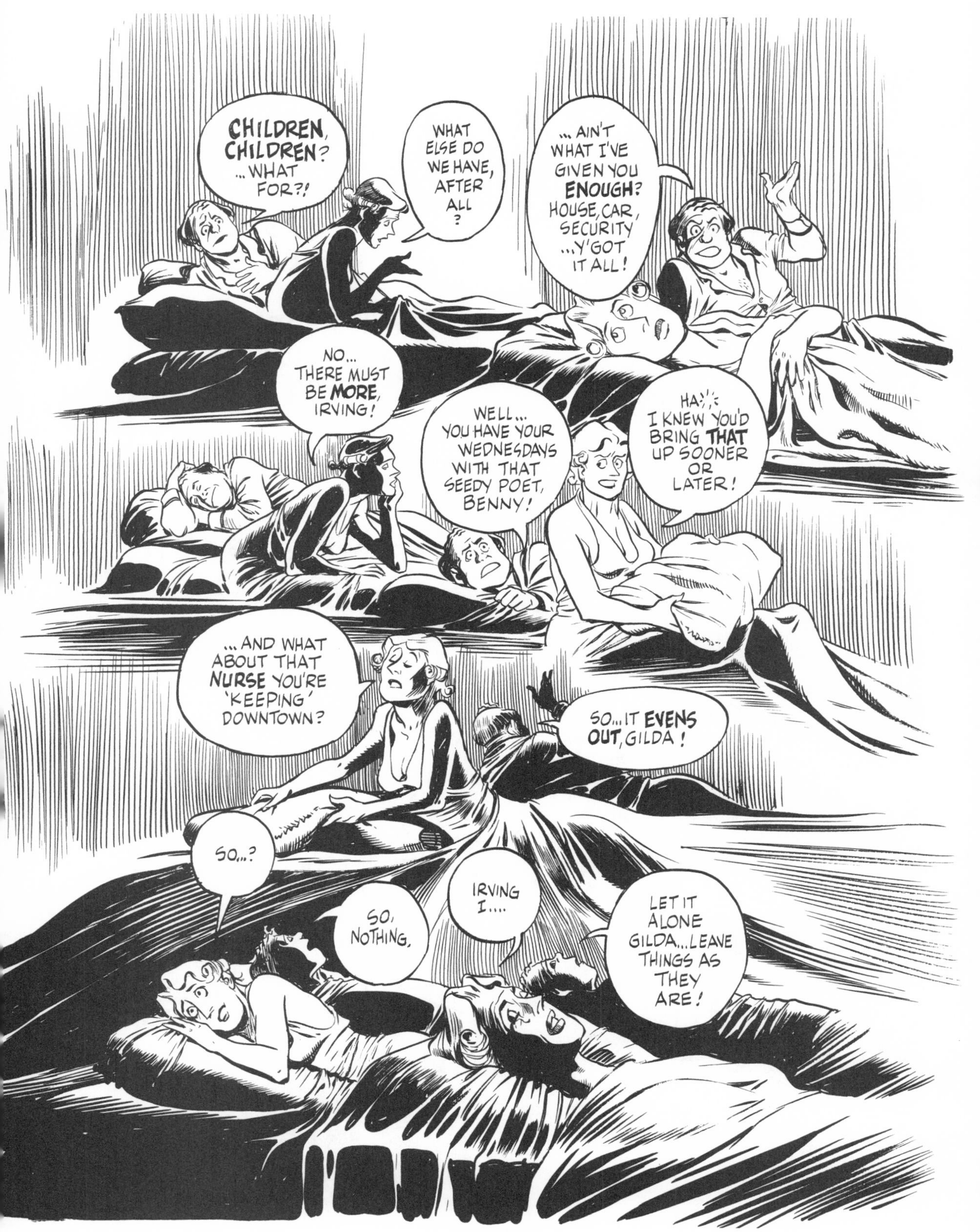

CHILDREN, CHILDREN? ...WHAT FOR?!
WHAT ELSE DO WE HAVE, AFTER ALL?
...AIN'T WHAT I'VE GIVEN YOU ENOUGH? HOUSE, CAR, SECURITY ...Y'GOT IT ALL!
NO... THERE MUST BE MORE, IRVING!
WELL... YOU HAVE YOUR WEDNESDAYS WITH THAT SEEDY POET, BENNY!
HA! I KNEW YOU'D BRING THAT UP SOONER OR LATER!
...AND WHAT ABOUT THAT NURSE YOU'RE 'KEEPING' DOWNTOWN?
SO... IT EVENS OUT, GILDA!
SO...?
SO, NOTHING.
IRVING I....
LET IT ALONE GILDA... LEAVE THINGS AS THEY ARE!

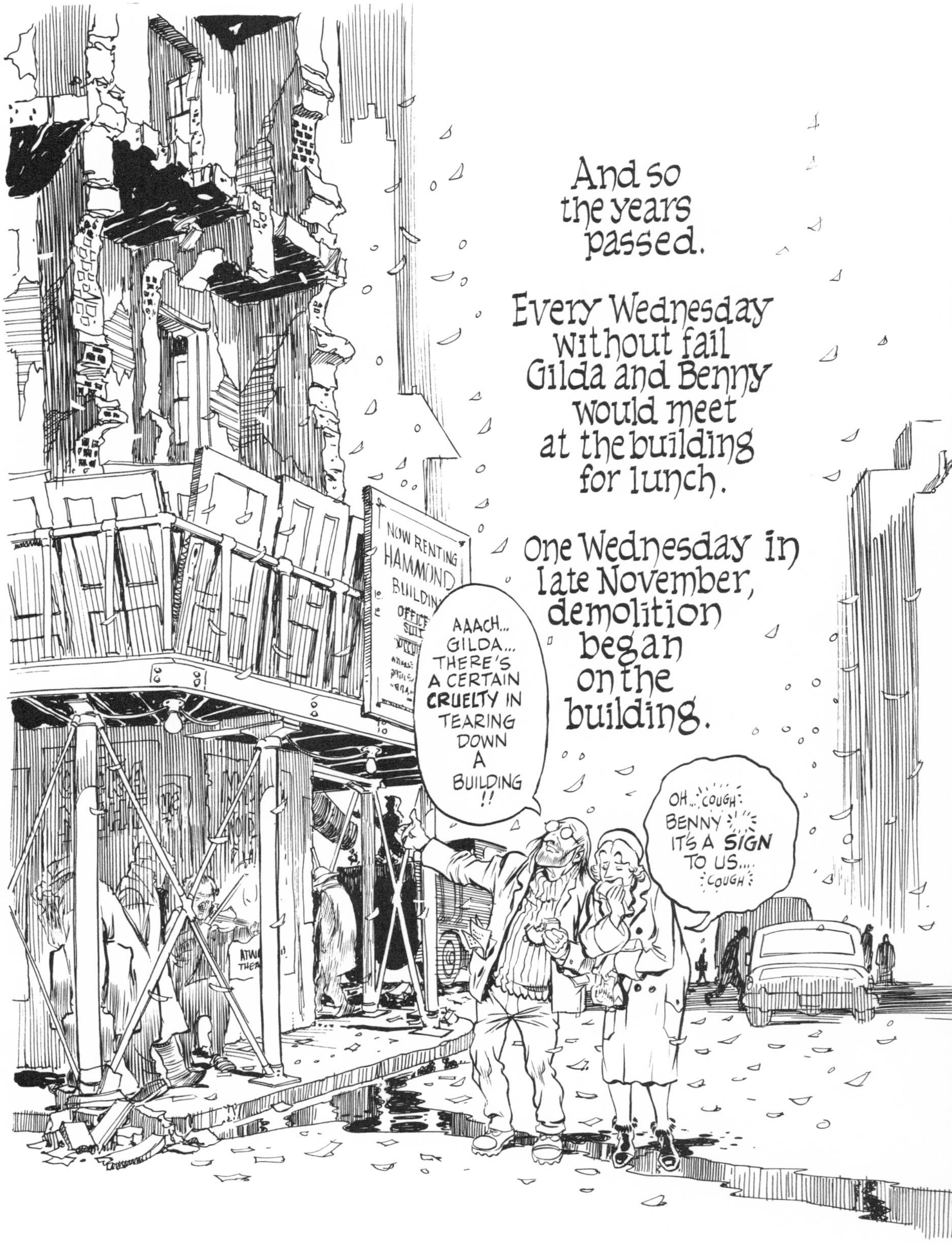
And so the years passed.
Every Wednesday without fail Gilda and Benny would meet at the building for lunch.
One Wednesday in late November, demolition began on the building.
NOW RENTING
HAMMOND
AAACH... GILDA... THERE'S A CERTAIN **CRUELTY** IN TEARING DOWN A BUILDING !!
OH... COUGH BENNY IT'S A **SIGN** TO US.... COUGH

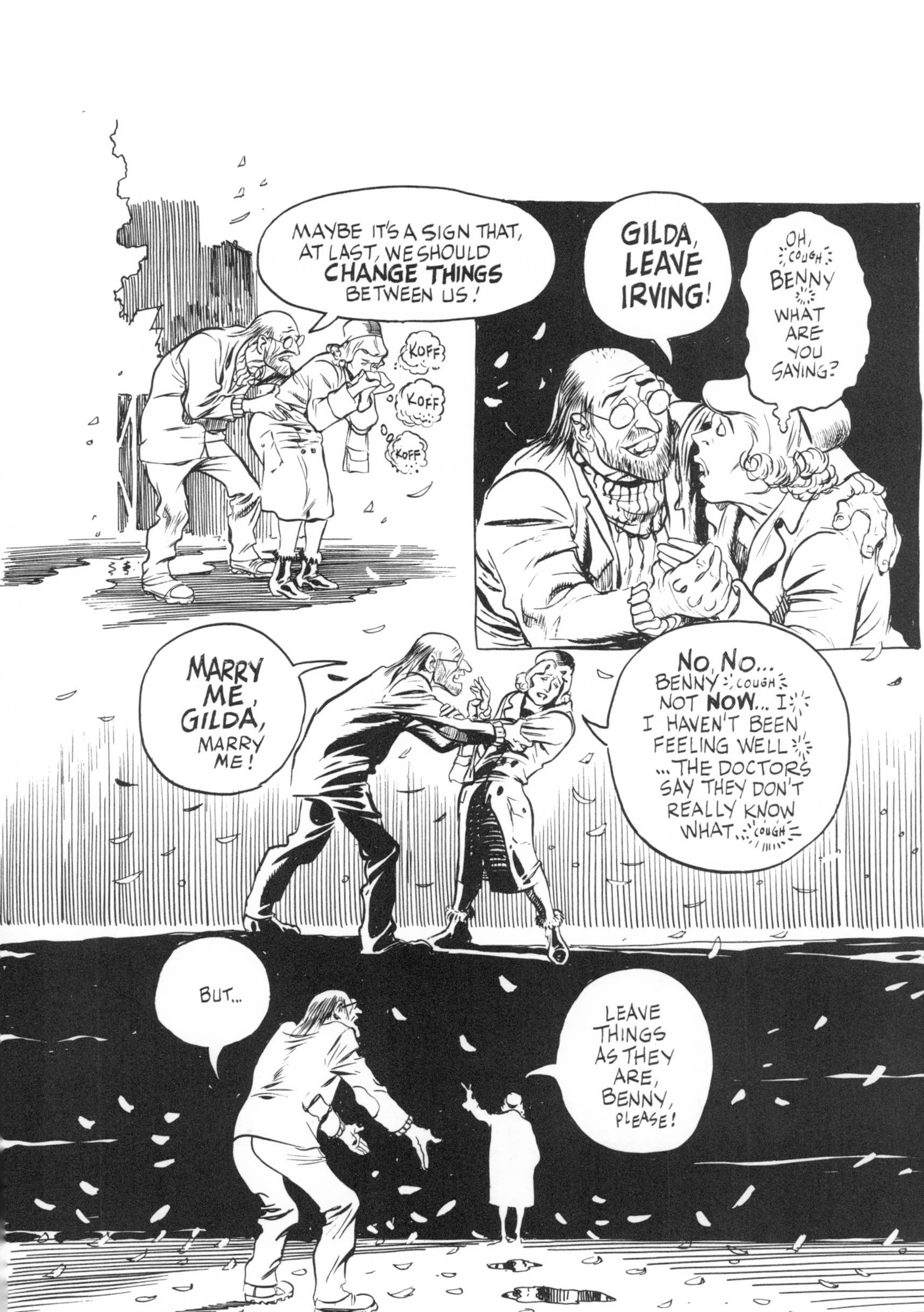
MAYBE IT'S A SIGN THAT, AT LAST, WE SHOULD **CHANGE THINGS** BETWEEN US!
KOFF
KOFF
KOFF
GILDA, LEAVE IRVING!
OH, COUGH BENNY WHAT ARE YOU SAYING?
MARRY ME, GILDA, MARRY ME!
NO, NO... BENNY COUGH NOT **NOW**... I I HAVEN'T BEEN FEELING WELL ...THE DOCTORS SAY THEY DON'T REALLY KNOW WHAT... COUGH
BUT...
LEAVE THINGS AS THEY ARE, BENNY, PLEASE!

All that winter Benny and Gilda continued to meet as always.

GILDA, YOU'RE **LOOKING WORSE!** ...WHAT'S WRONG WITH YOU?

OH! OLD AGE I GUESS, BENNY

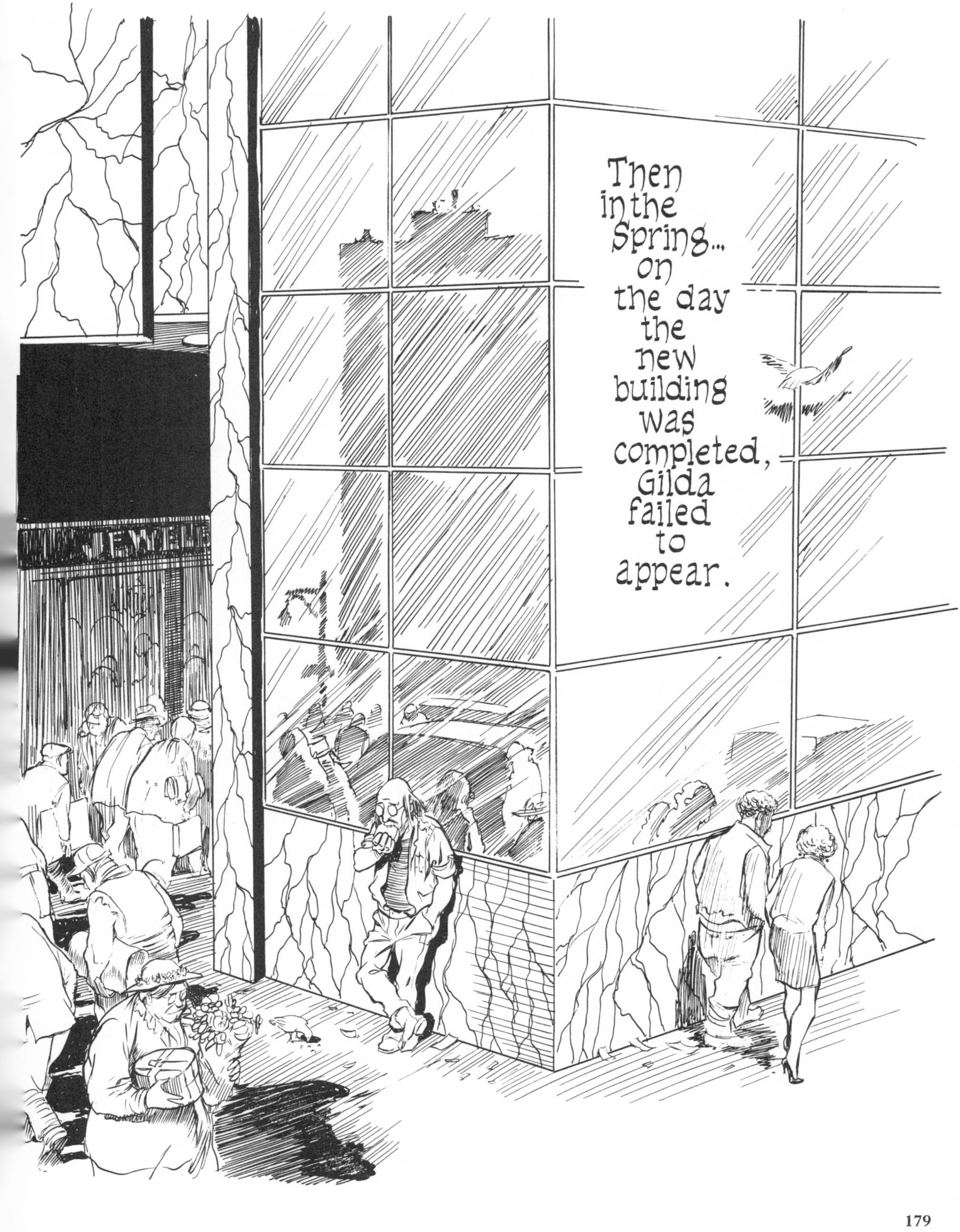
Then in the Spring... on the day the new building was completed, Gilda failed to appear.

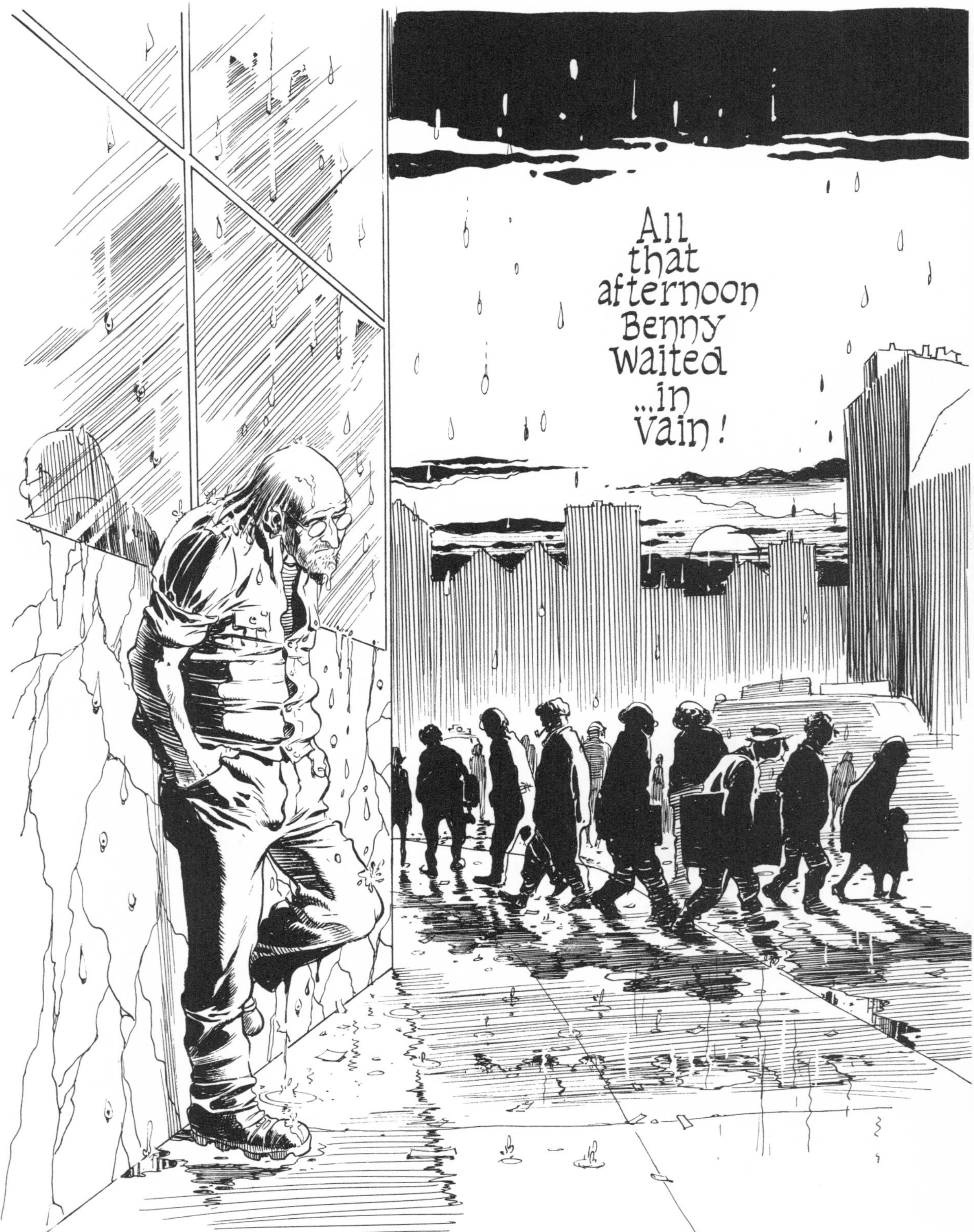
All that afternoon Benny waited ...in vain!

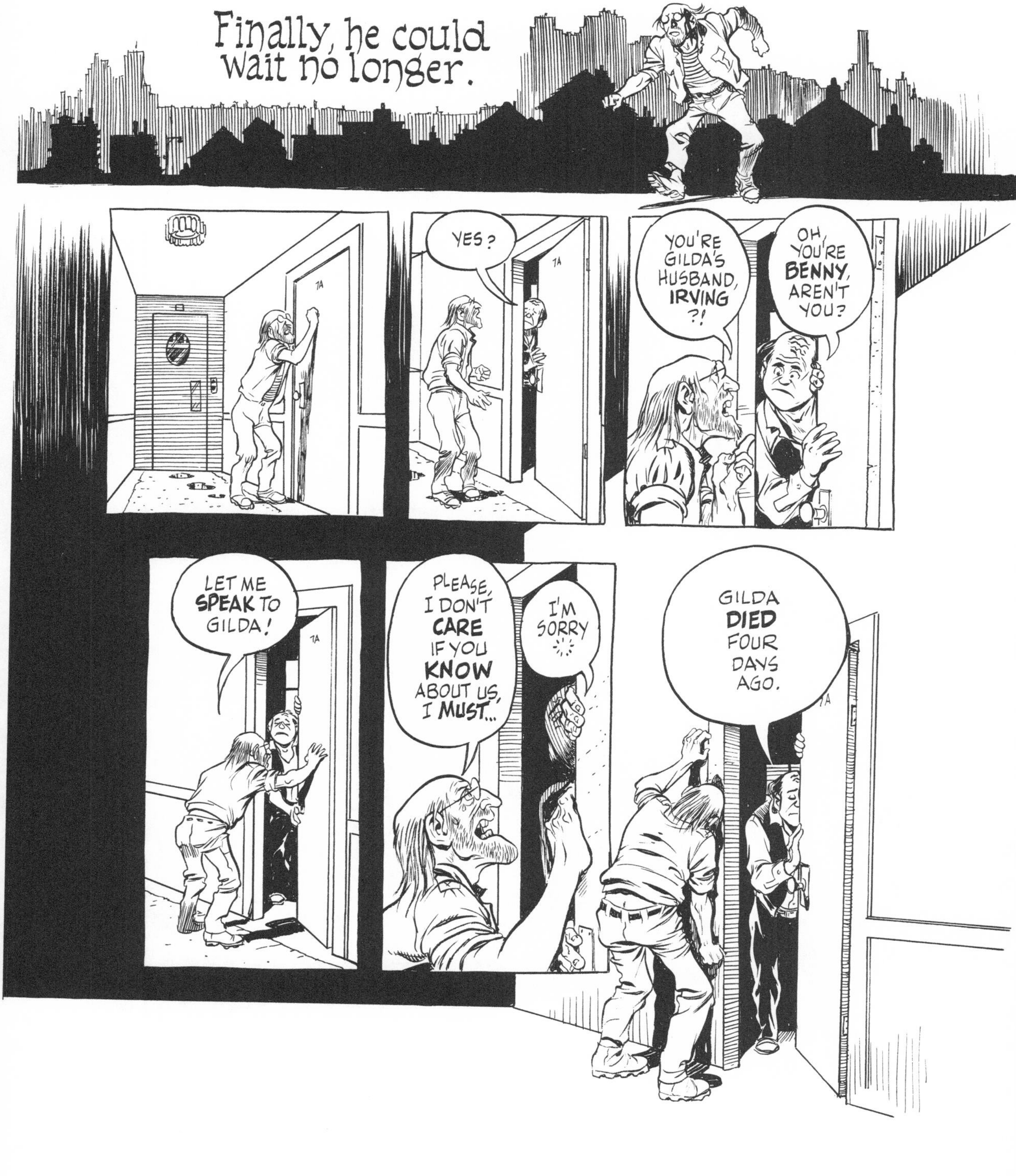
Finally, he could wait no longer.
YES?
YOU'RE GILDA'S HUSBAND, IRVING ?!
OH, YOU'RE BENNY, AREN'T YOU?
LET ME SPEAK TO GILDA!
PLEASE, I DON'T CARE IF YOU KNOW ABOUT US, I MUST...
I'M SORRY
GILDA DIED FOUR DAYS AGO.

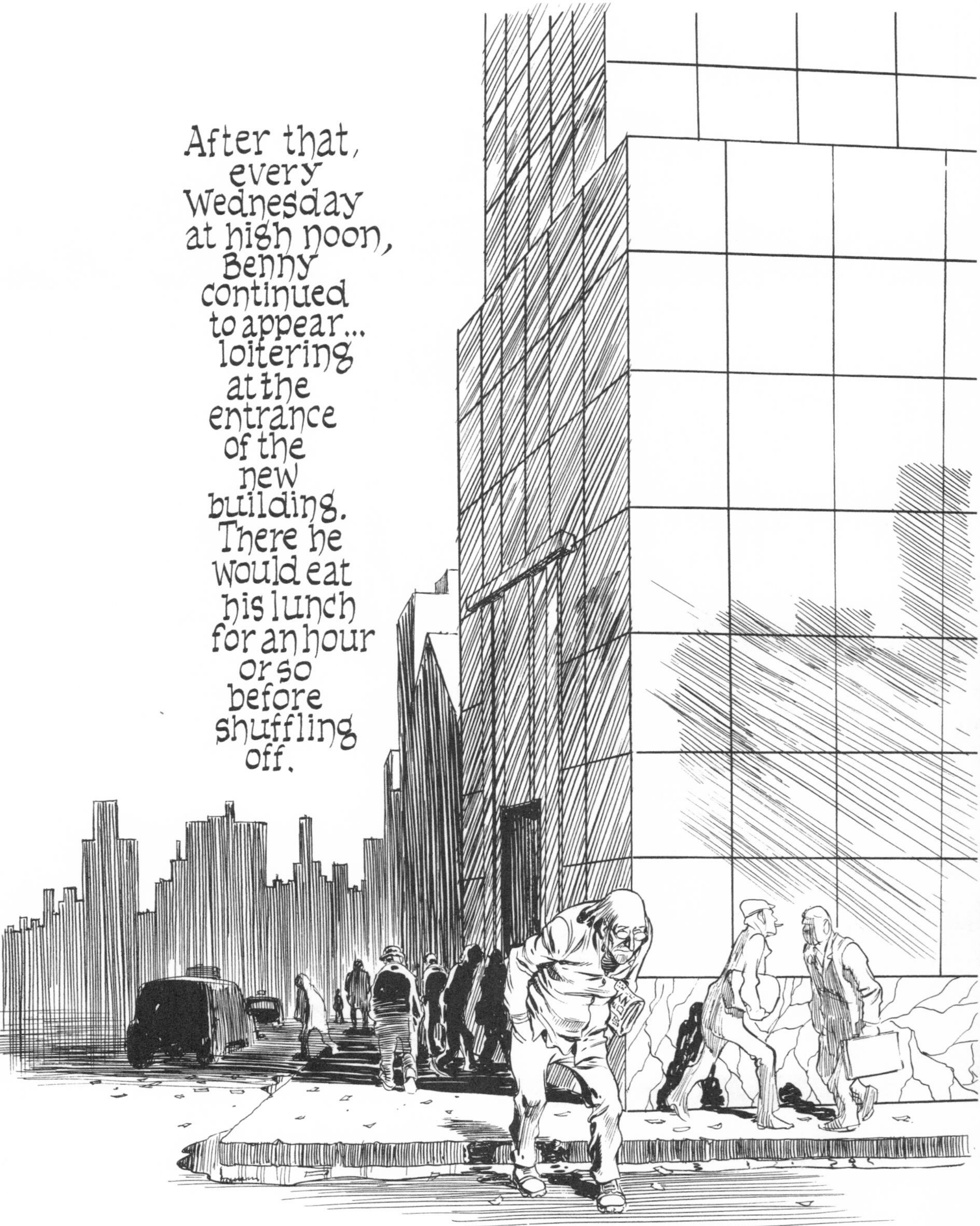
After that, every Wednesday at high noon, Benny continued to appear... loitering at the entrance of the new building. There he would eat his lunch for an hour or so before shuffling off.

ANTONIO TONATTI

From early childhood, Antonio showed a talent for music which he displayed in the more affluent homes of friends and relatives.

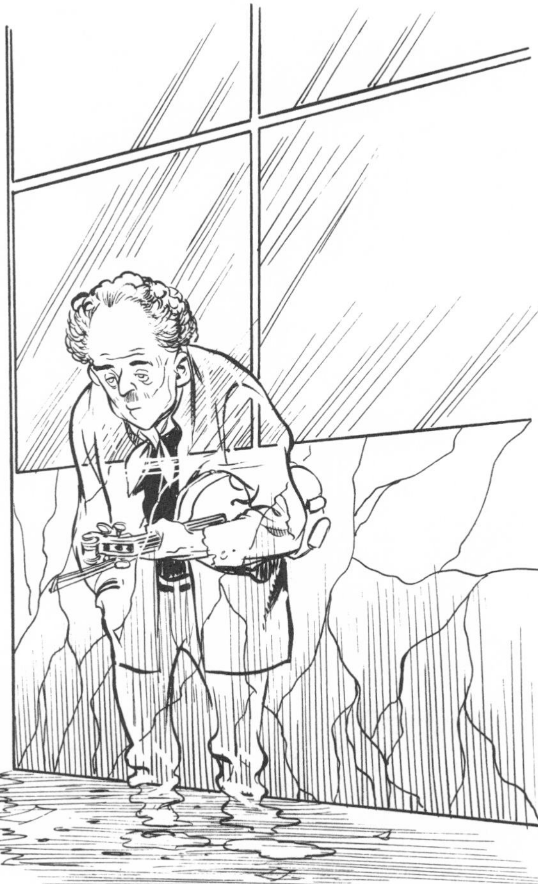

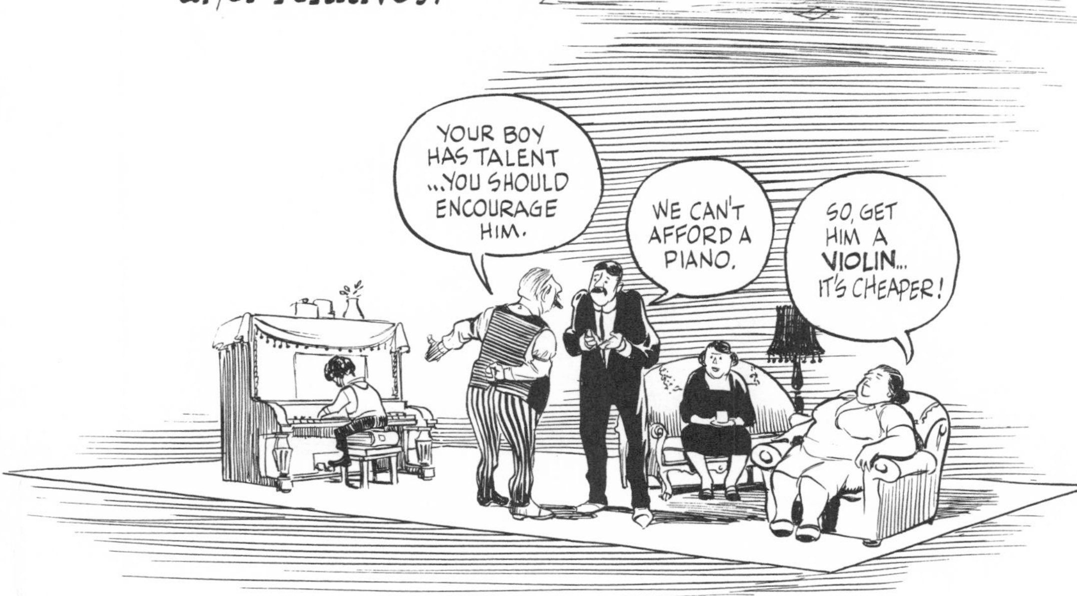
YOUR BOY HAS TALENT ...YOU SHOULD ENCOURAGE HIM.
WE CAN'T AFFORD A PIANO.
SO, GET HIM A VIOLIN... IT'S CHEAPER!

His parents were supportive, and out of their meager savings they bought him a violin.

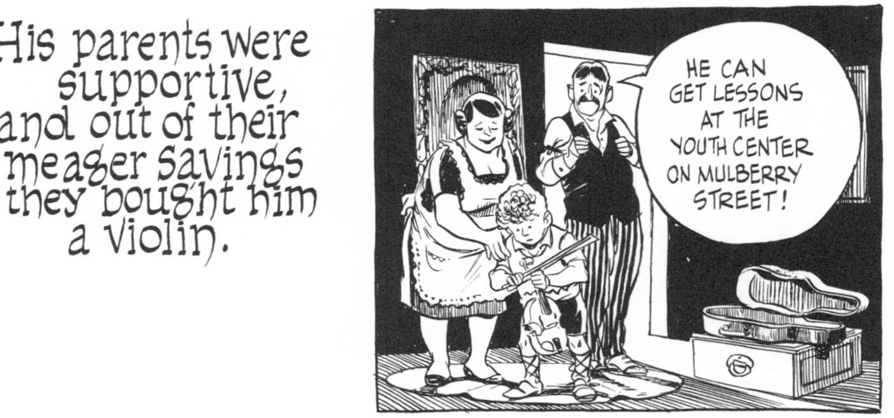
HE CAN GET LESSONS AT THE YOUTH CENTER ON MULBERRY STREET!

The years of his youth passed quickly and Antonio gave to music what he could.

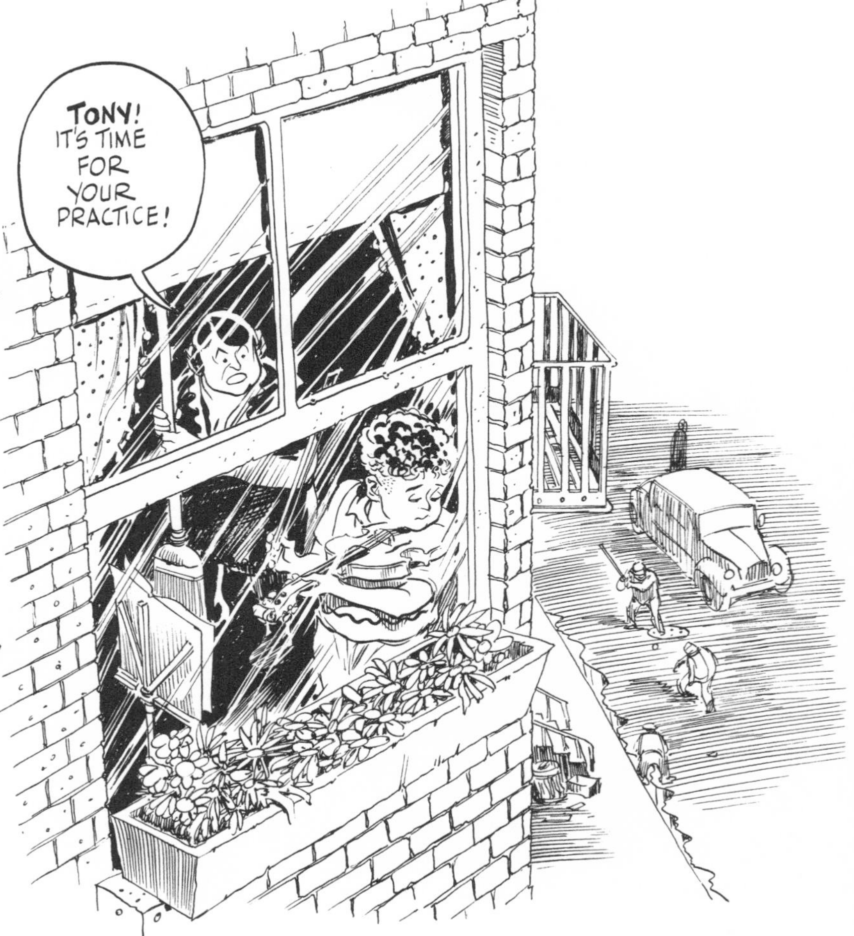
TONY! IT'S TIME FOR YOUR PRACTICE!

But...

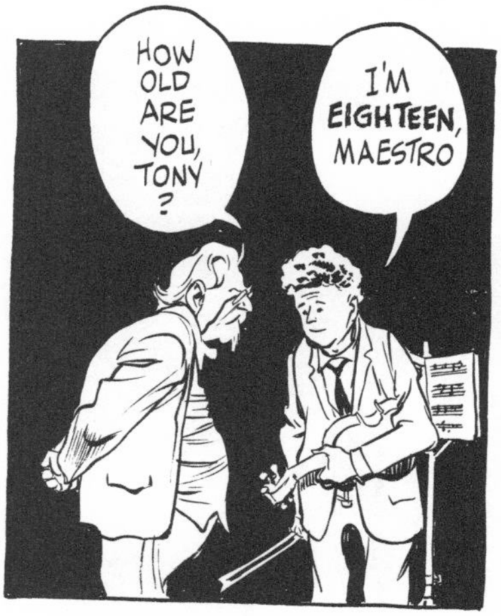
HOW OLD ARE YOU, TONY ?
I'M **EIGHTEEN**, MAESTRO

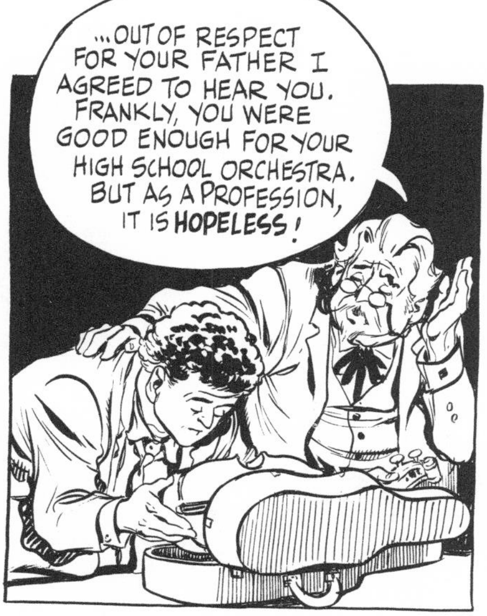
...OUT OF RESPECT FOR YOUR FATHER I AGREED TO HEAR YOU. FRANKLY, YOU WERE GOOD ENOUGH FOR YOUR HIGH SCHOOL ORCHESTRA. BUT AS A PROFESSION, IT IS **HOPELESS** !

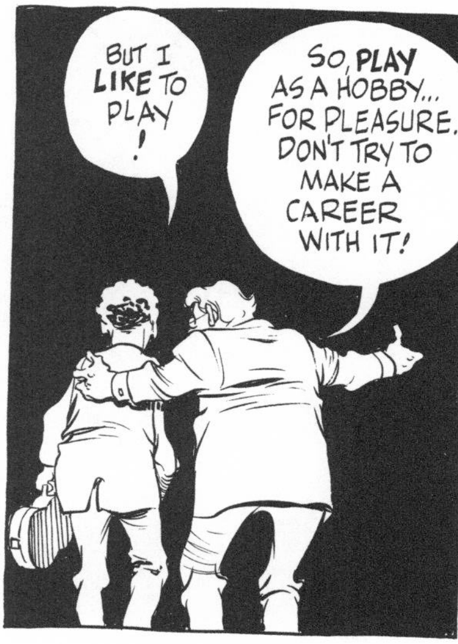
BUT I **LIKE** TO PLAY !
SO, **PLAY** AS A HOBBY... FOR PLEASURE. DON'T TRY TO MAKE A CAREER WITH IT!

So, once in a while, when friends asked him, Antonio would play at weddings or family parties.

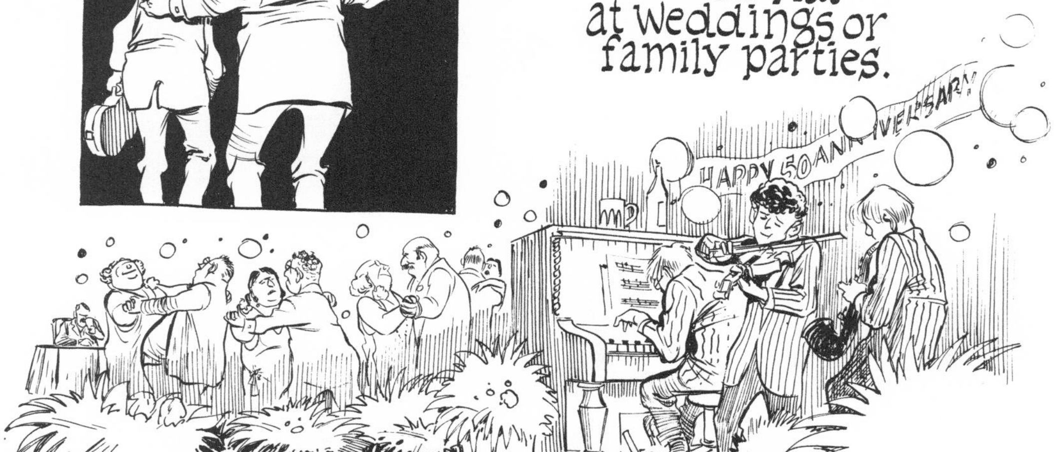
HAPPY 50 ANNIVERSARY

Antonio went to work in the family construction business.

In time, the work toughened his hands and calloused his fingers.

Oh, yes, he still played the violin... but only for special occasions like... when his wife died he played at her wake with a scratchy beauty that left everyone in tears.

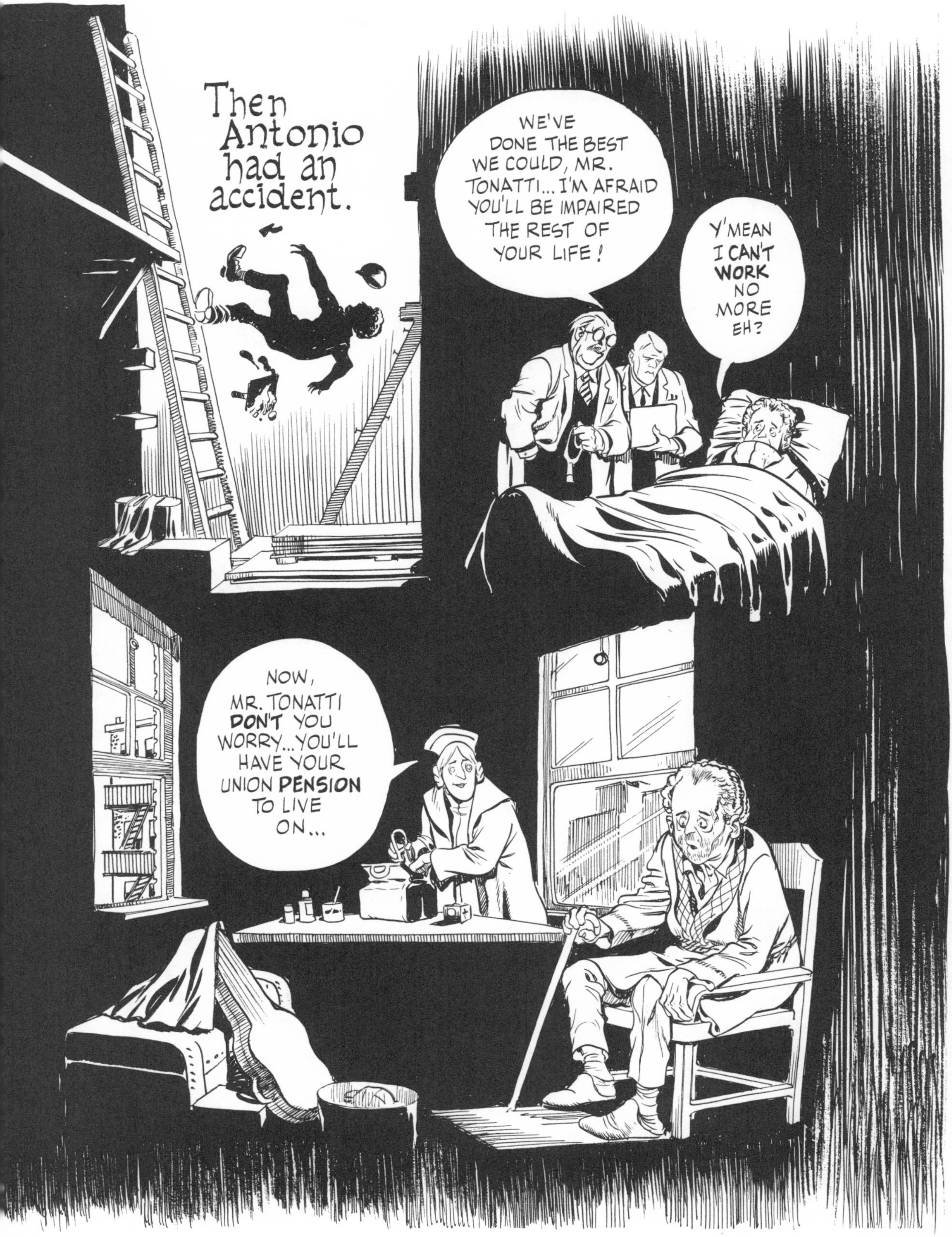
Then Antonio had an accident.
WE'VE DONE THE BEST WE COULD, MR. TONATTI... I'M AFRAID YOU'LL BE IMPAIRED THE REST OF YOUR LIFE!
Y'MEAN I CAN'T WORK NO MORE EH?
NOW, MR. TONATTI DON'T YOU WORRY...YOU'LL HAVE YOUR UNION PENSION TO LIVE ON...

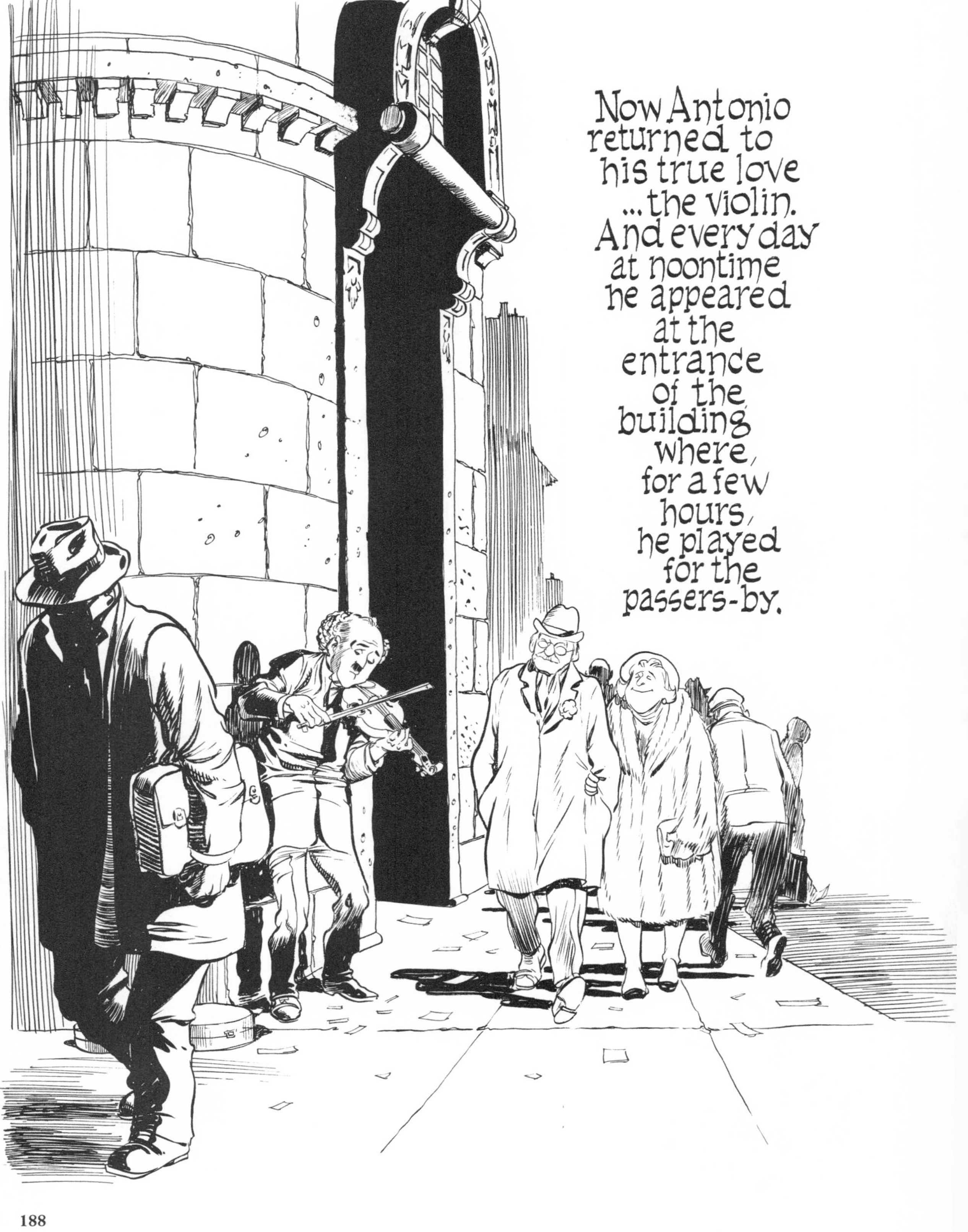
Now Antonio returned to his true love ...the violin. And every day at noontime he appeared at the entrance of the building where, for a few hours, he played for the passers-by.

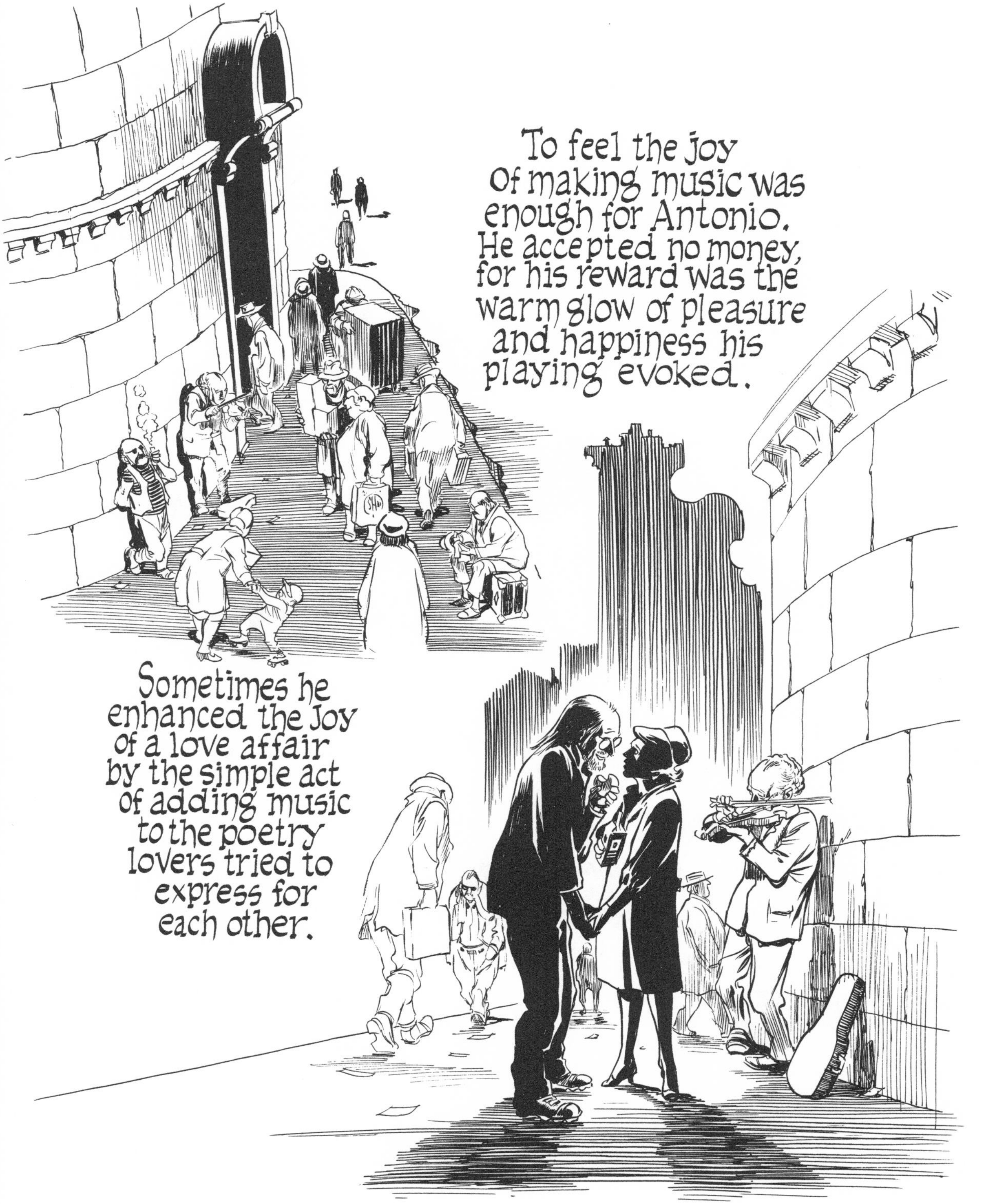
To feel the joy of making music was enough for Antonio. He accepted no money, for his reward was the warm glow of pleasure and happiness his playing evoked.
SHM
Sometimes he enhanced the Joy of a love affair by the simple act of adding music to the poetry lovers tried to express for each other.

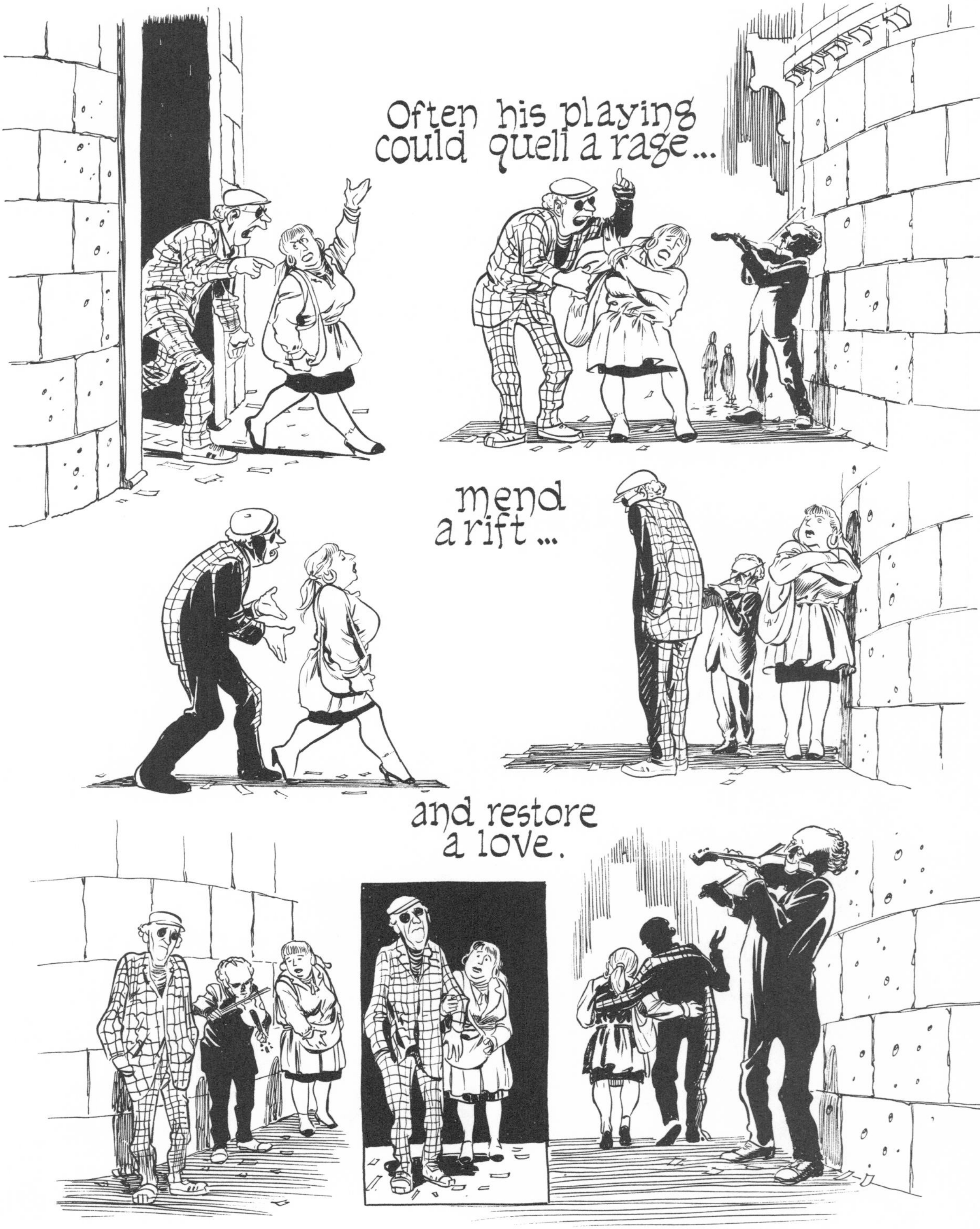
Often his playing could quell a rage...
mend a rift...
and restore a love.

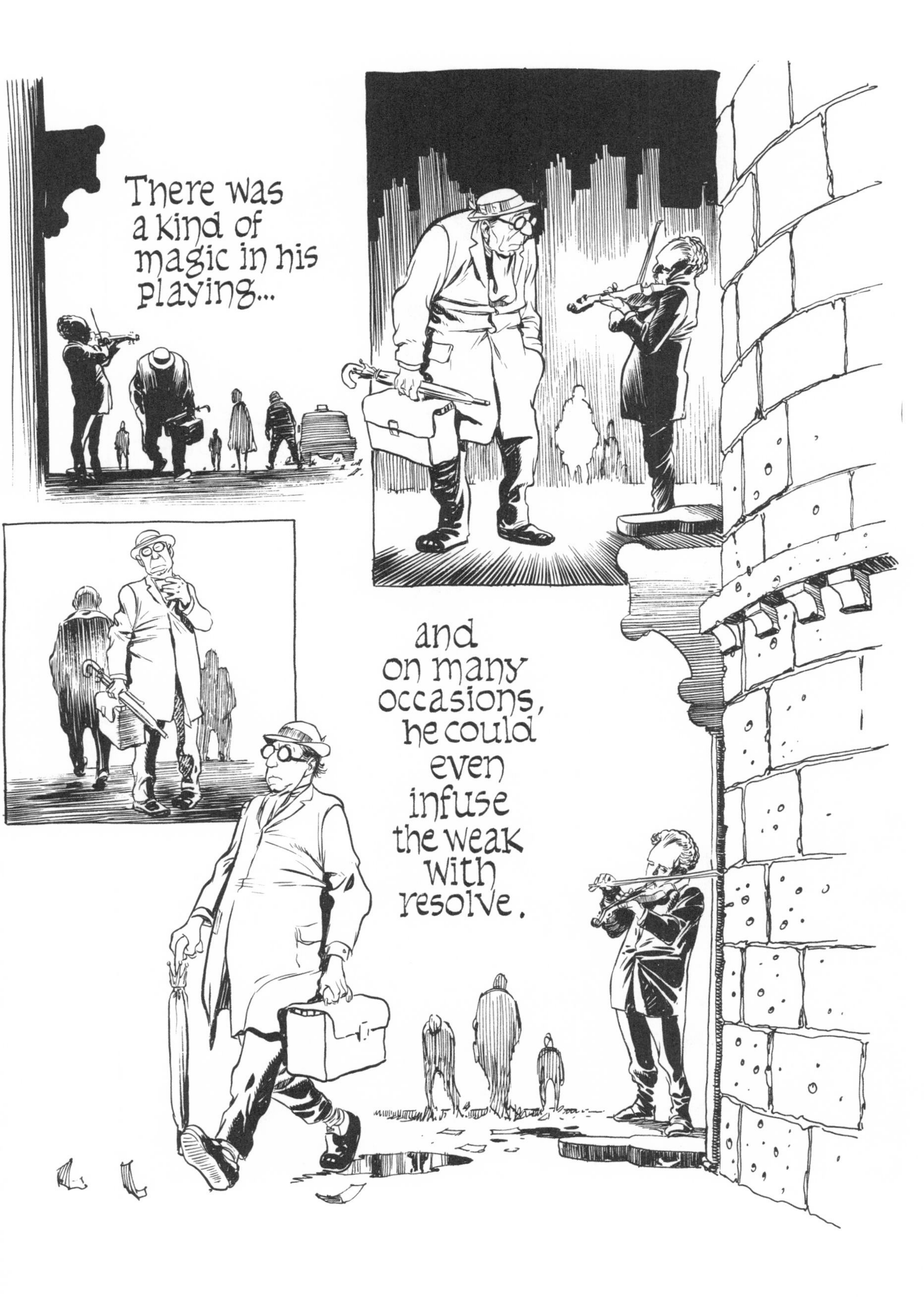
There was a kind of magic in his playing...
and on many occasions, he could even infuse the weak with resolve.

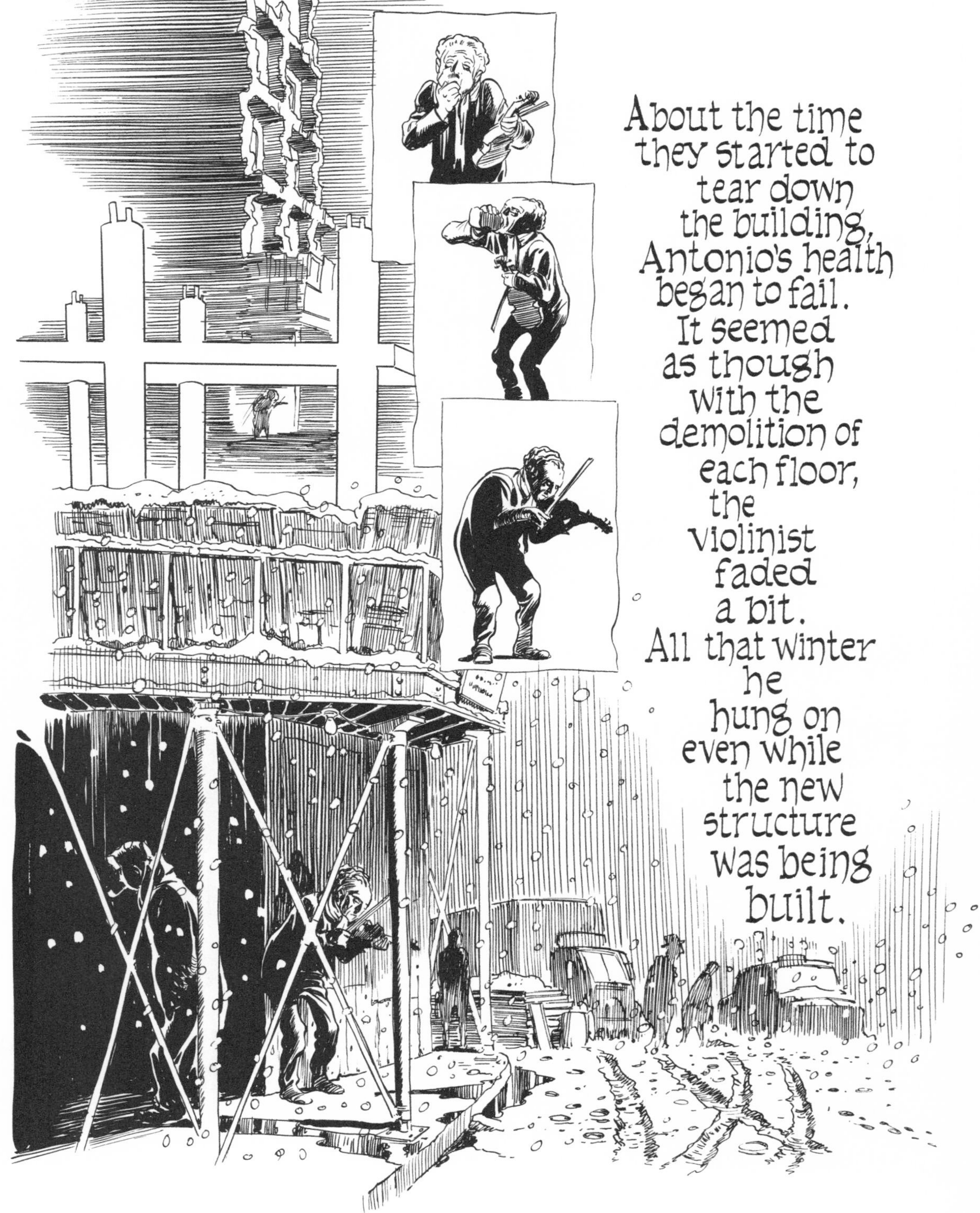
About the time they started to tear down the building, Antonio's health began to fail. It seemed as though with the demolition of each floor, the violinist faded a bit. All that winter he hung on even while the new structure was being built.

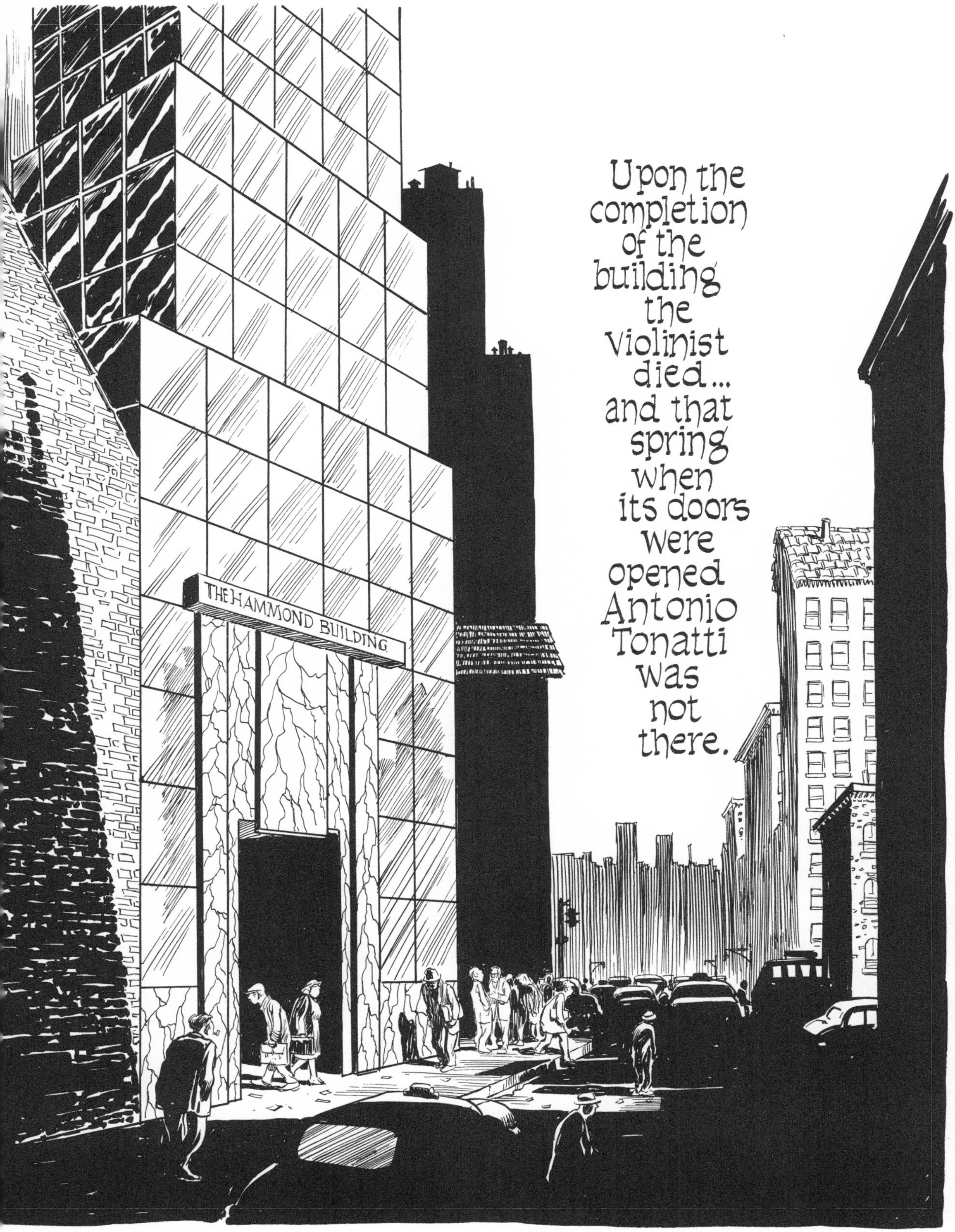
THE HAMMOND BUILDING
Upon the completion of the building the violinist died... and that spring when its doors were opened Antonio Tonatti was not there.

P. J. HAMMOND

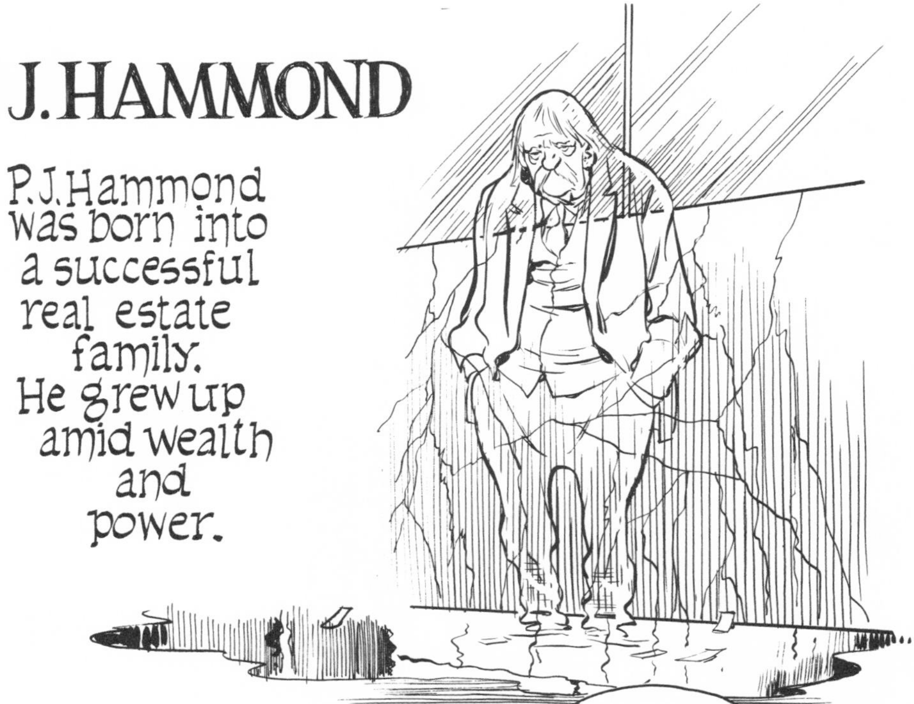
P.J.Hammond was born into a successful real estate family. He grew up amid wealth and power.

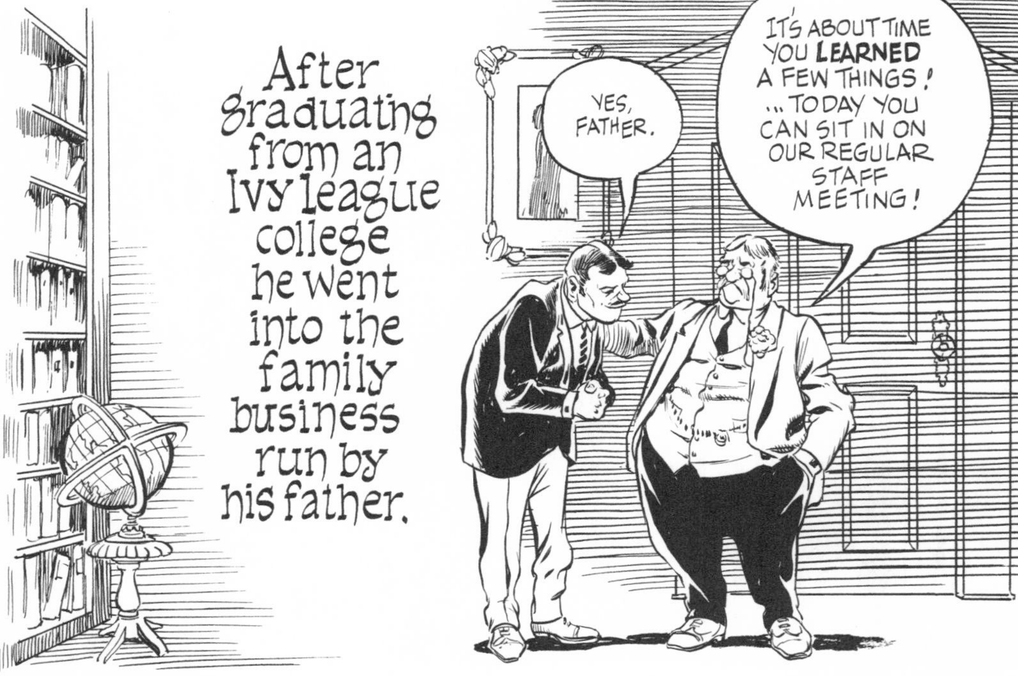
After graduating from an Ivy League college he went into the family business run by his father.
IT'S ABOUT TIME YOU **LEARNED** A FEW THINGS! ... TODAY YOU CAN SIT IN ON OUR REGULAR STAFF MEETING!
YES, FATHER.

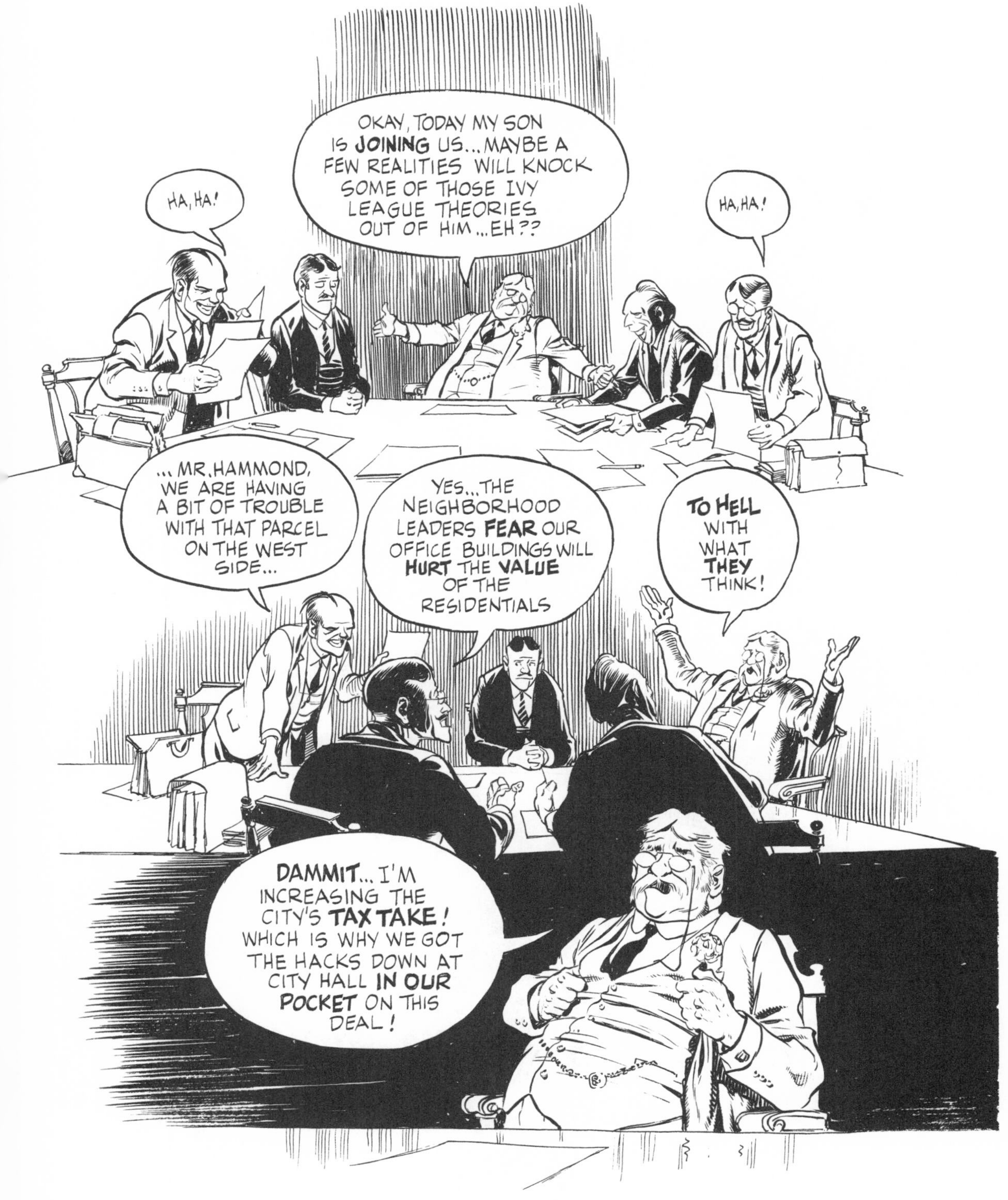
OKAY, TODAY MY SON IS JOINING US... MAYBE A FEW REALITIES WILL KNOCK SOME OF THOSE IVY LEAGUE THEORIES OUT OF HIM...EH??
HA, HA!
HA, HA!
...MR. HAMMOND, WE ARE HAVING A BIT OF TROUBLE WITH THAT PARCEL ON THE WEST SIDE...
YES...THE NEIGHBORHOOD LEADERS FEAR OUR OFFICE BUILDINGS WILL HURT THE VALUE OF THE RESIDENTIALS
TO HELL WITH WHAT THEY THINK!
DAMMIT... I'M INCREASING THE CITY'S TAX TAKE! WHICH IS WHY WE GOT THE HACKS DOWN AT CITY HALL IN OUR POCKET ON THIS DEAL!

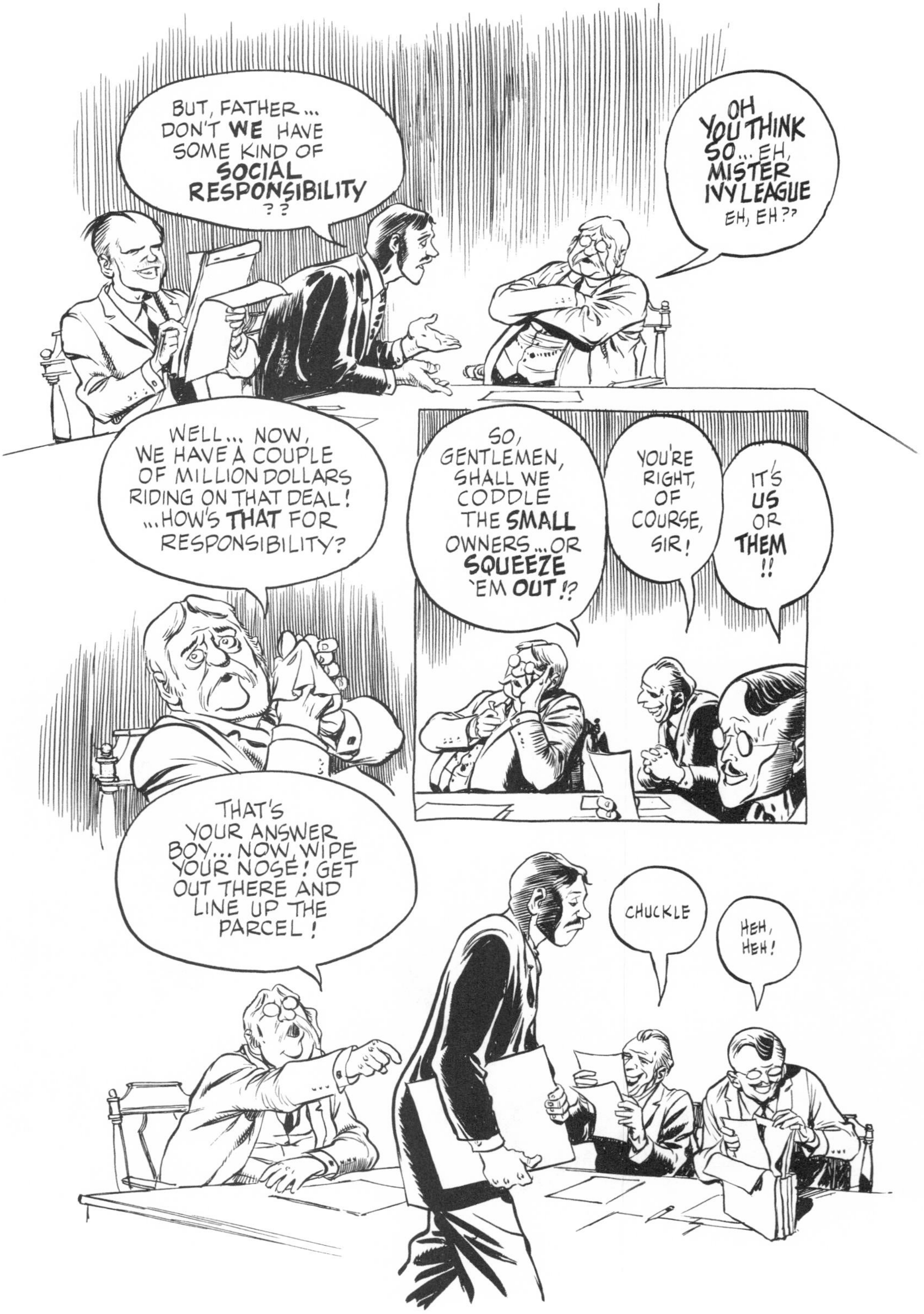
BUT, FATHER... DON'T WE HAVE SOME KIND OF SOCIAL RESPONSIBILITY ??
OH YOU THINK SO... EH, MISTER IVY LEAGUE EH, EH??
WELL... NOW, WE HAVE A COUPLE OF MILLION DOLLARS RIDING ON THAT DEAL! ...HOW'S THAT FOR RESPONSIBILITY?
SO, GENTLEMEN, SHALL WE CODDLE THE SMALL OWNERS... OR SQUEEZE 'EM OUT !?
YOU'RE RIGHT, OF COURSE, SIR!
IT'S US OR THEM !!
THAT'S YOUR ANSWER BOY... NOW, WIPE YOUR NOSE! GET OUT THERE AND LINE UP THE PARCEL!
CHUCKLE
HEH, HEH!

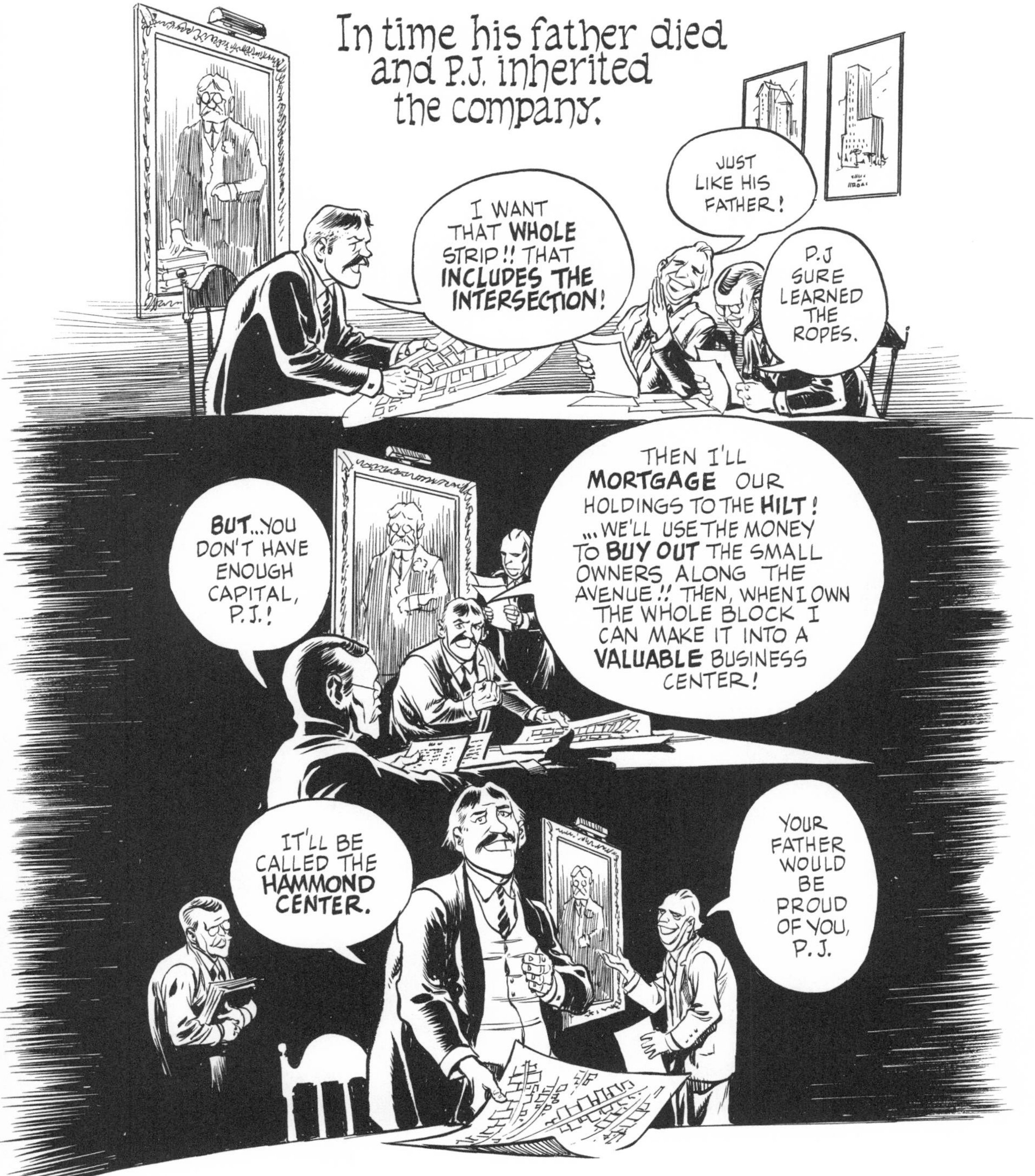
In time his father died and P.J. inherited the company.
I WANT THAT WHOLE STRIP!! THAT INCLUDES THE INTERSECTION!
JUST LIKE HIS FATHER!
P.J SURE LEARNED THE ROPES.
BUT...YOU DON'T HAVE ENOUGH CAPITAL, P.J.!
THEN I'LL MORTGAGE OUR HOLDINGS TO THE HILT! ...WE'LL USE THE MONEY TO BUY OUT THE SMALL OWNERS ALONG THE AVENUE!! THEN, WHEN I OWN THE WHOLE BLOCK I CAN MAKE IT INTO A VALUABLE BUSINESS CENTER!
IT'LL BE CALLED THE HAMMOND CENTER.
YOUR FATHER WOULD BE PROUD OF YOU, P. J.

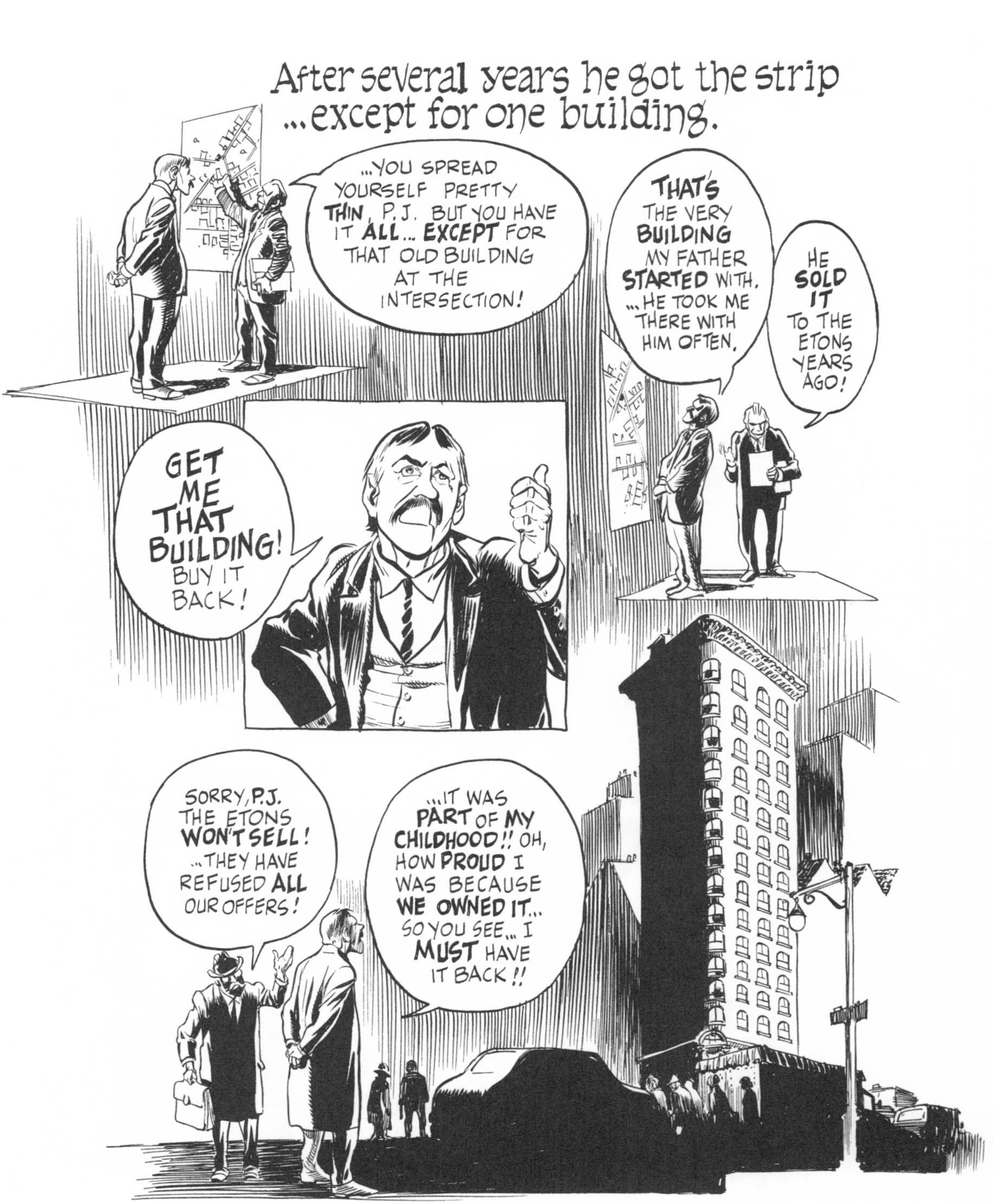
After several years he got the strip ...except for one building.
...YOU SPREAD YOURSELF PRETTY THIN, P.J. BUT YOU HAVE IT ALL... EXCEPT FOR THAT OLD BUILDING AT THE INTERSECTION!
THAT'S THE VERY BUILDING MY FATHER STARTED WITH. ...HE TOOK ME THERE WITH HIM OFTEN.
HE SOLD IT TO THE ETONS YEARS AGO!
GET ME THAT BUILDING! BUY IT BACK!
SORRY, P.J. THE ETONS WON'T SELL! ...THEY HAVE REFUSED ALL OUR OFFERS!
...IT WAS PART OF MY CHILDHOOD!! OH, HOW PROUD I WAS BECAUSE WE OWNED IT... SO YOU SEE... I MUST HAVE IT BACK!!

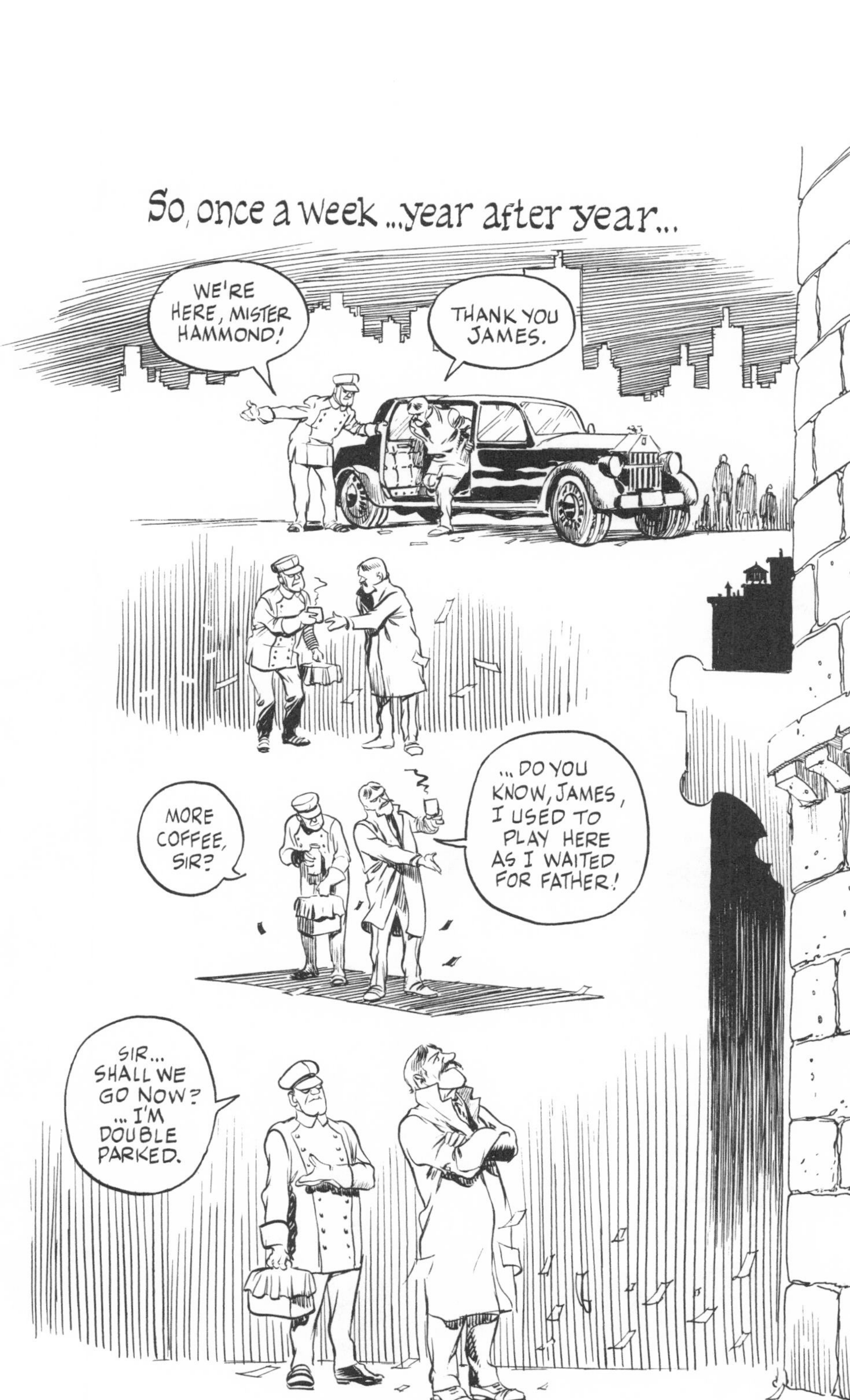
So, once a week ...year after year...
WE'RE HERE, MISTER HAMMOND!
THANK YOU JAMES.
MORE COFFEE, SIR?
... DO YOU KNOW, JAMES, I USED TO PLAY HERE AS I WAITED FOR FATHER!
SIR... SHALL WE GO NOW? ... I'M DOUBLE PARKED.

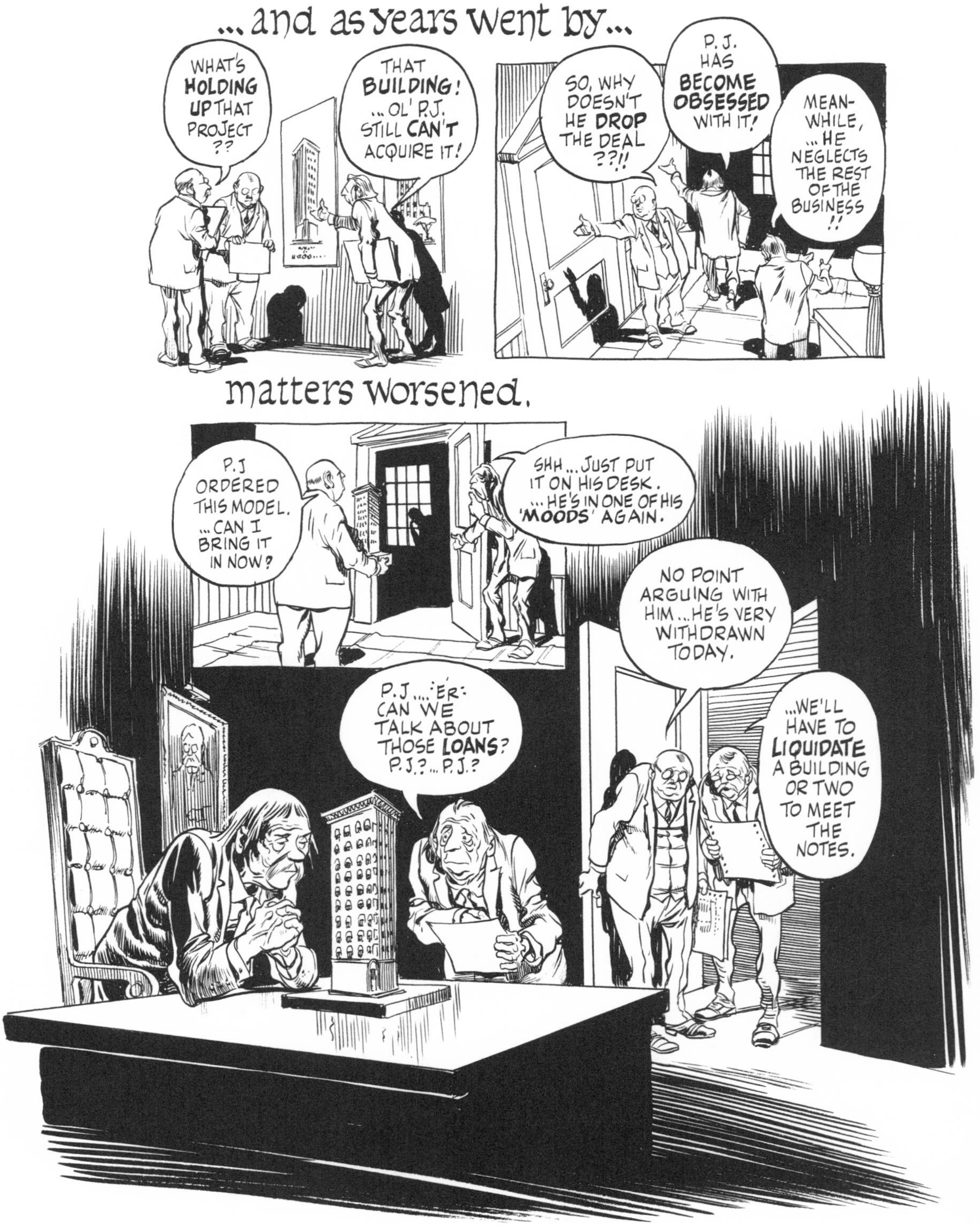
...and as years went by...
WHAT'S HOLDING UP THAT PROJECT ??
THAT BUILDING! ...OL' P.J. STILL CAN'T ACQUIRE IT!
SO, WHY DOESN'T HE DROP THE DEAL ??!!
P. J. HAS BECOME OBSESSED WITH IT!
MEAN-WHILE, ...HE NEGLECTS THE REST OF THE BUSINESS !!
matters worsened.
P.J ORDERED THIS MODEL. ...CAN I BRING IT IN NOW?
SHH ...JUST PUT IT ON HIS DESK. ...HE'S IN ONE OF HIS 'MOODS' AGAIN.
P.J ... ER: CAN WE TALK ABOUT THOSE LOANS? P.J.? ... P.J.?
NO POINT ARGUING WITH HIM ...HE'S VERY WITHDRAWN TODAY.
...WE'LL HAVE TO LIQUIDATE A BUILDING OR TWO TO MEET THE NOTES.

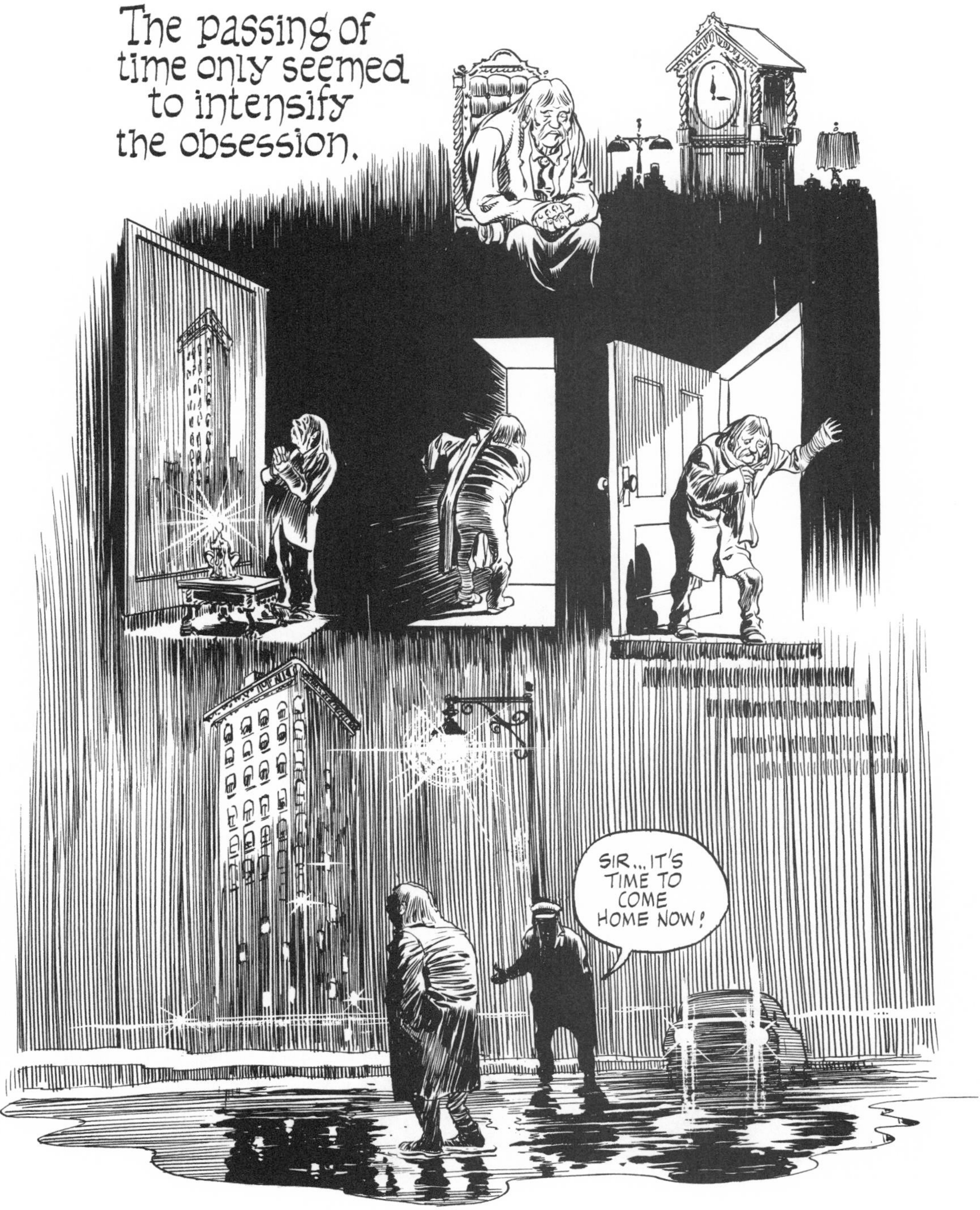
The passing of
time only seemed
to intensify
the obsession.
SIR... IT'S TIME TO COME HOME NOW!

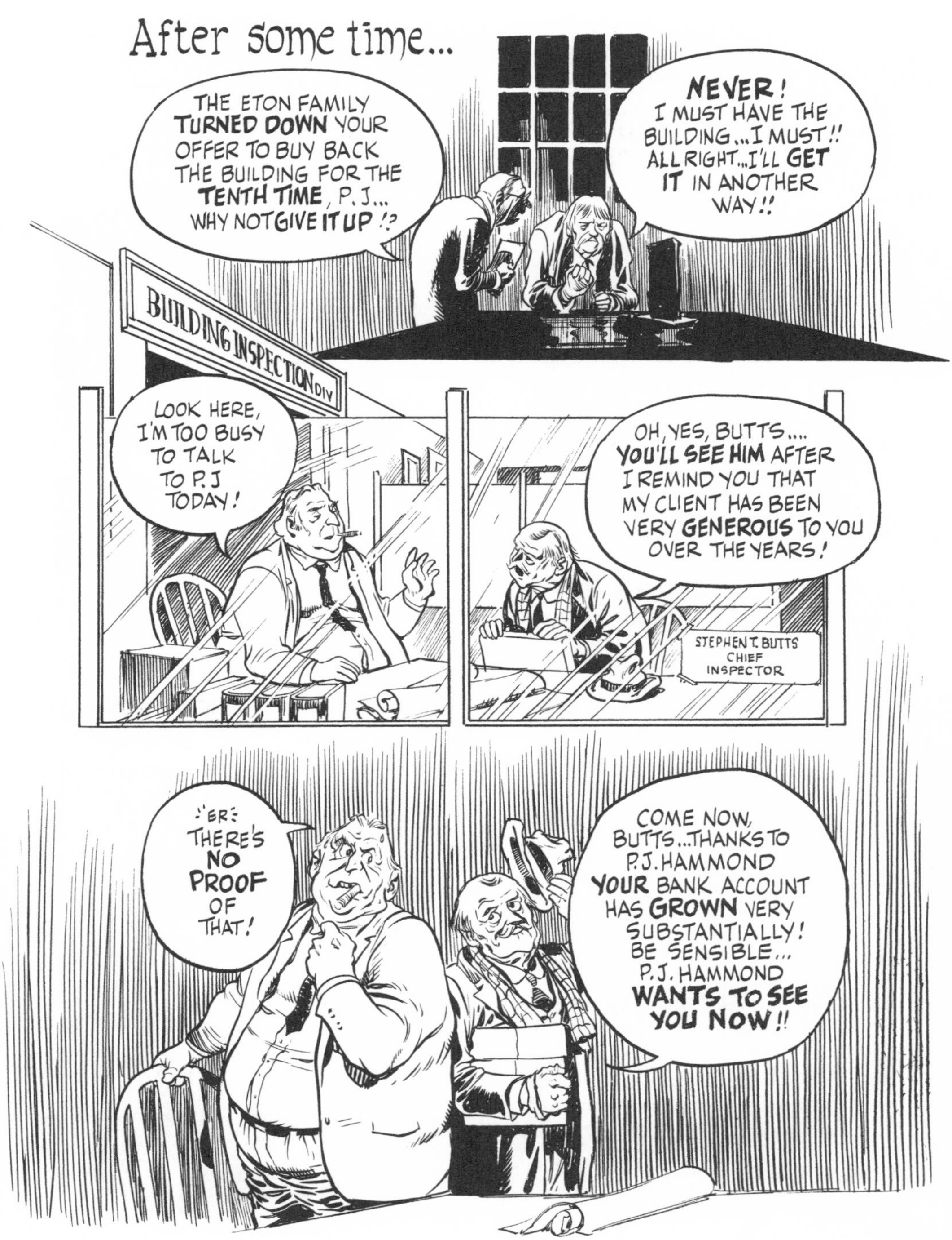
After some time...
THE ETON FAMILY TURNED DOWN YOUR OFFER TO BUY BACK THE BUILDING FOR THE TENTH TIME, P.J... WHY NOT GIVE IT UP !?
NEVER! I MUST HAVE THE BUILDING...I MUST!! ALL RIGHT...I'LL GET IT IN ANOTHER WAY!!
BUILDING INSPECTION DIV
LOOK HERE, I'M TOO BUSY TO TALK TO P.J TODAY!
OH, YES, BUTTS.... YOU'LL SEE HIM AFTER I REMIND YOU THAT MY CLIENT HAS BEEN VERY GENEROUS TO YOU OVER THE YEARS!
STEPHEN T. BUTTS CHIEF INSPECTOR
ER THERE'S NO PROOF OF THAT!
COME NOW, BUTTS...THANKS TO P.J. HAMMOND YOUR BANK ACCOUNT HAS GROWN VERY SUBSTANTIALLY! BE SENSIBLE... P.J. HAMMOND WANTS TO SEE YOU NOW!!

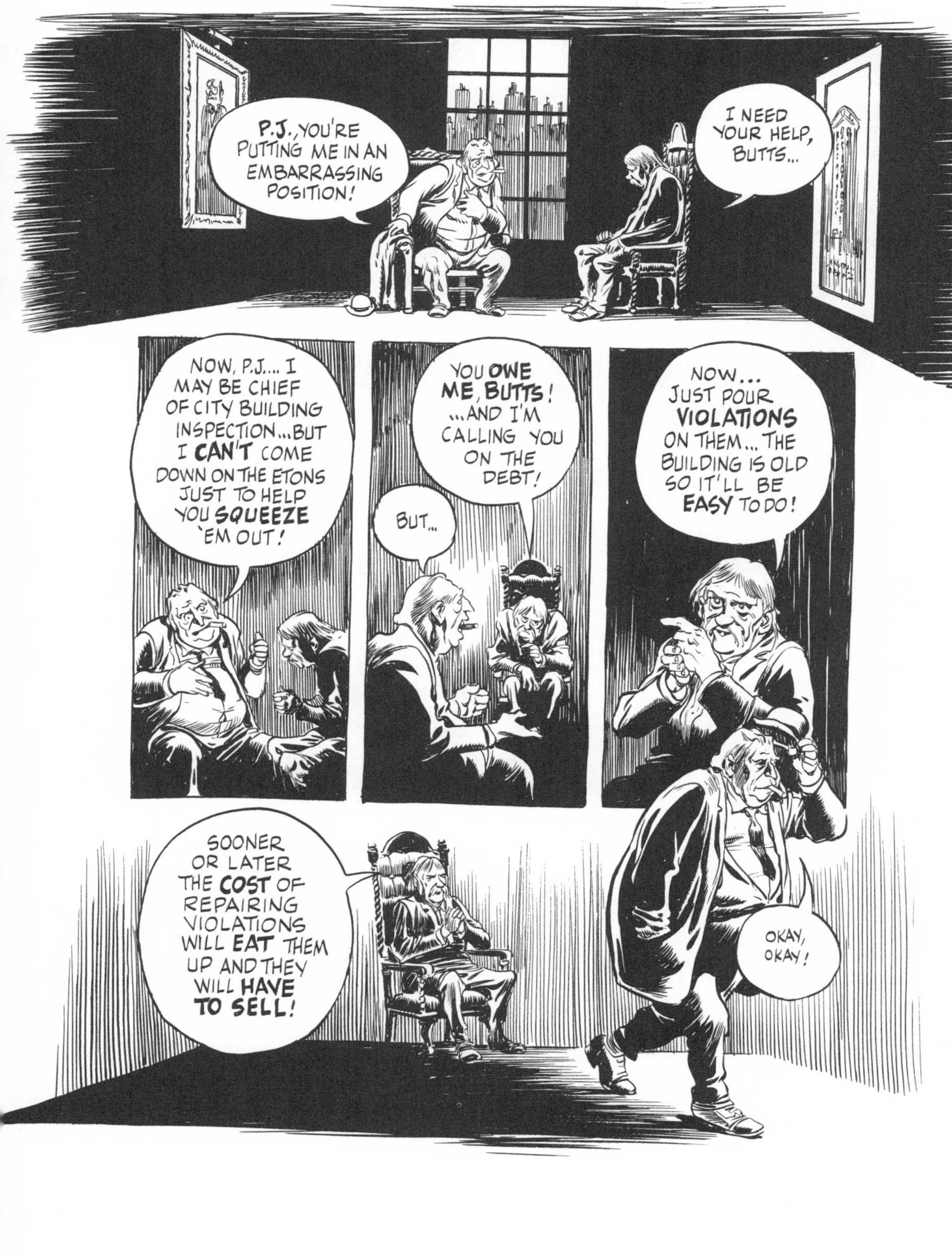
P.J., YOU'RE PUTTING ME IN AN EMBARRASSING POSITION!
I NEED YOUR HELP, BUTTS...
NOW, P.J.... I MAY BE CHIEF OF CITY BUILDING INSPECTION...BUT I CAN'T COME DOWN ON THE ETONS JUST TO HELP YOU SQUEEZE 'EM OUT!
BUT...
YOU OWE ME, BUTTS! ...AND I'M CALLING YOU ON THE DEBT!
NOW... JUST POUR VIOLATIONS ON THEM... THE BUILDING IS OLD SO IT'LL BE EASY TO DO!
SOONER OR LATER THE COST OF REPAIRING VIOLATIONS WILL EAT THEM UP AND THEY WILL HAVE TO SELL!
OKAY, OKAY!

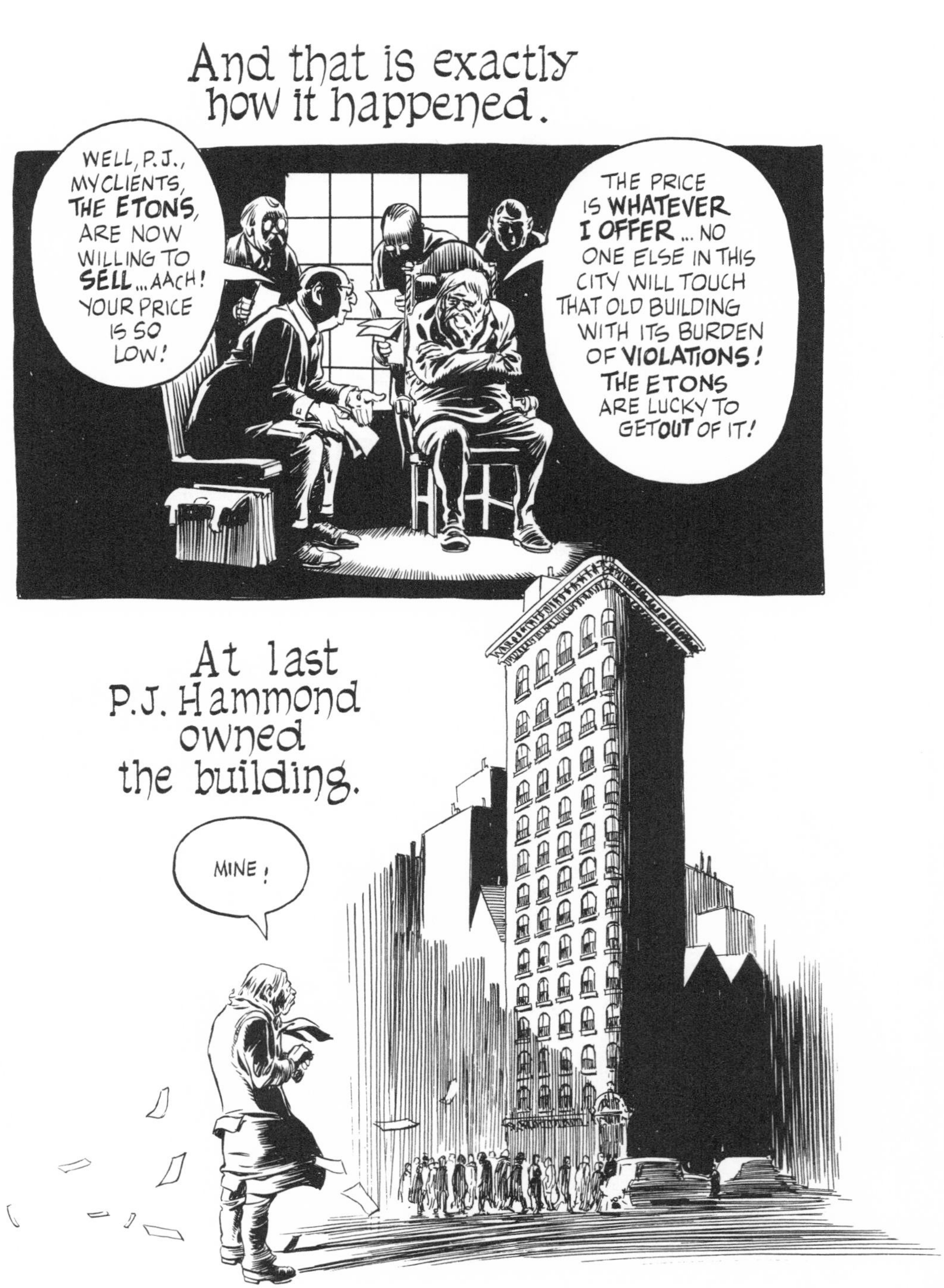
And that is exactly how it happened.
WELL, P.J., MY CLIENTS, THE ETONS, ARE NOW WILLING TO SELL... AACH! YOUR PRICE IS SO LOW!
THE PRICE IS WHATEVER I OFFER... NO ONE ELSE IN THIS CITY WILL TOUCH THAT OLD BUILDING WITH ITS BURDEN OF VIOLATIONS! THE ETONS ARE LUCKY TO GET OUT OF IT!
At last P.J. Hammond owned the building.
MINE!

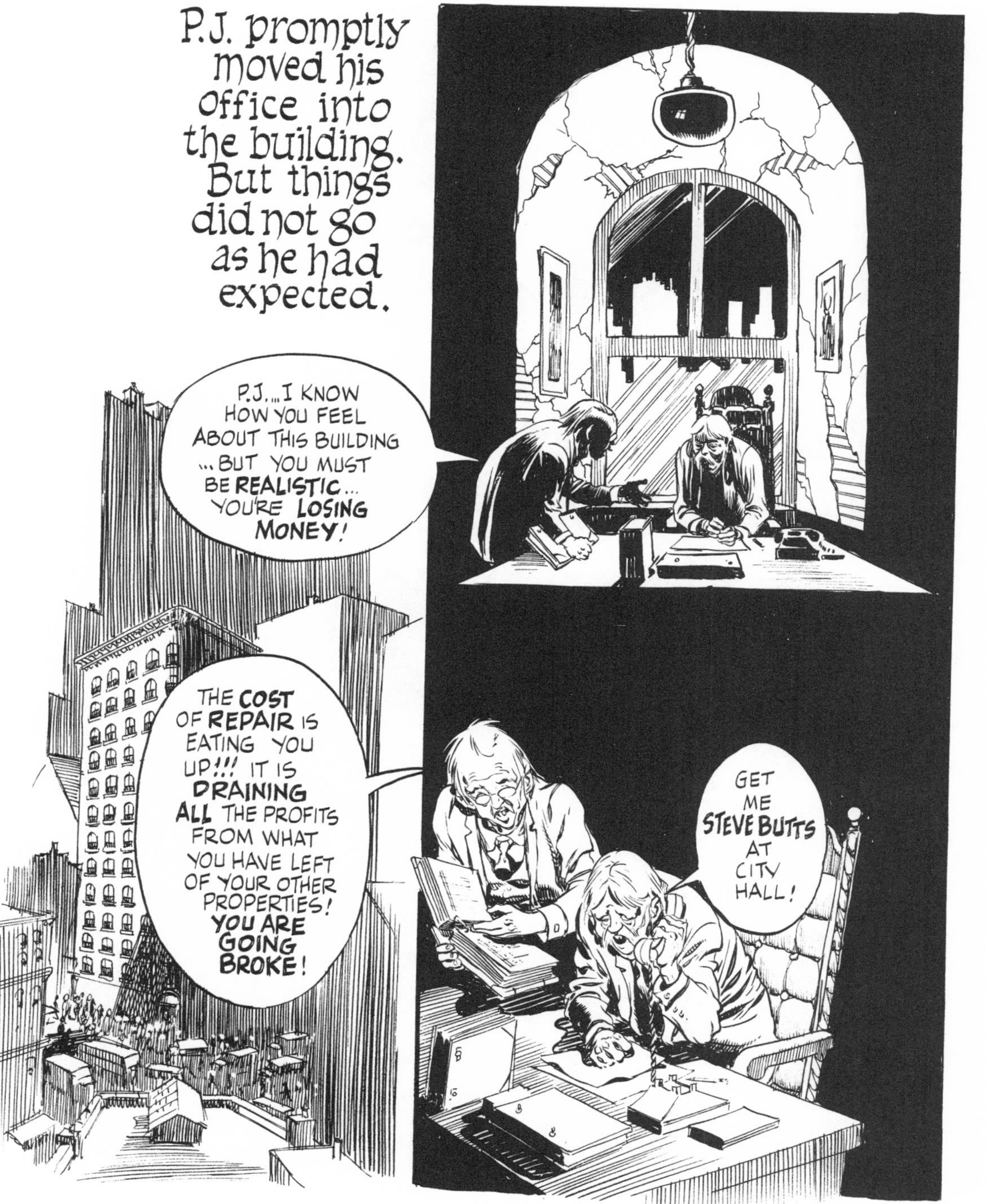
P.J. promptly moved his office into the building. But things did not go as he had expected.
P.J.... I KNOW HOW YOU FEEL ABOUT THIS BUILDING ... BUT YOU MUST BE REALISTIC... YOU'RE LOSING MONEY!
THE COST OF REPAIR IS EATING YOU UP!!! IT IS DRAINING ALL THE PROFITS FROM WHAT YOU HAVE LEFT OF YOUR OTHER PROPERTIES! YOU ARE GOING BROKE!
GET ME STEVE BUTTS AT CITY HALL!

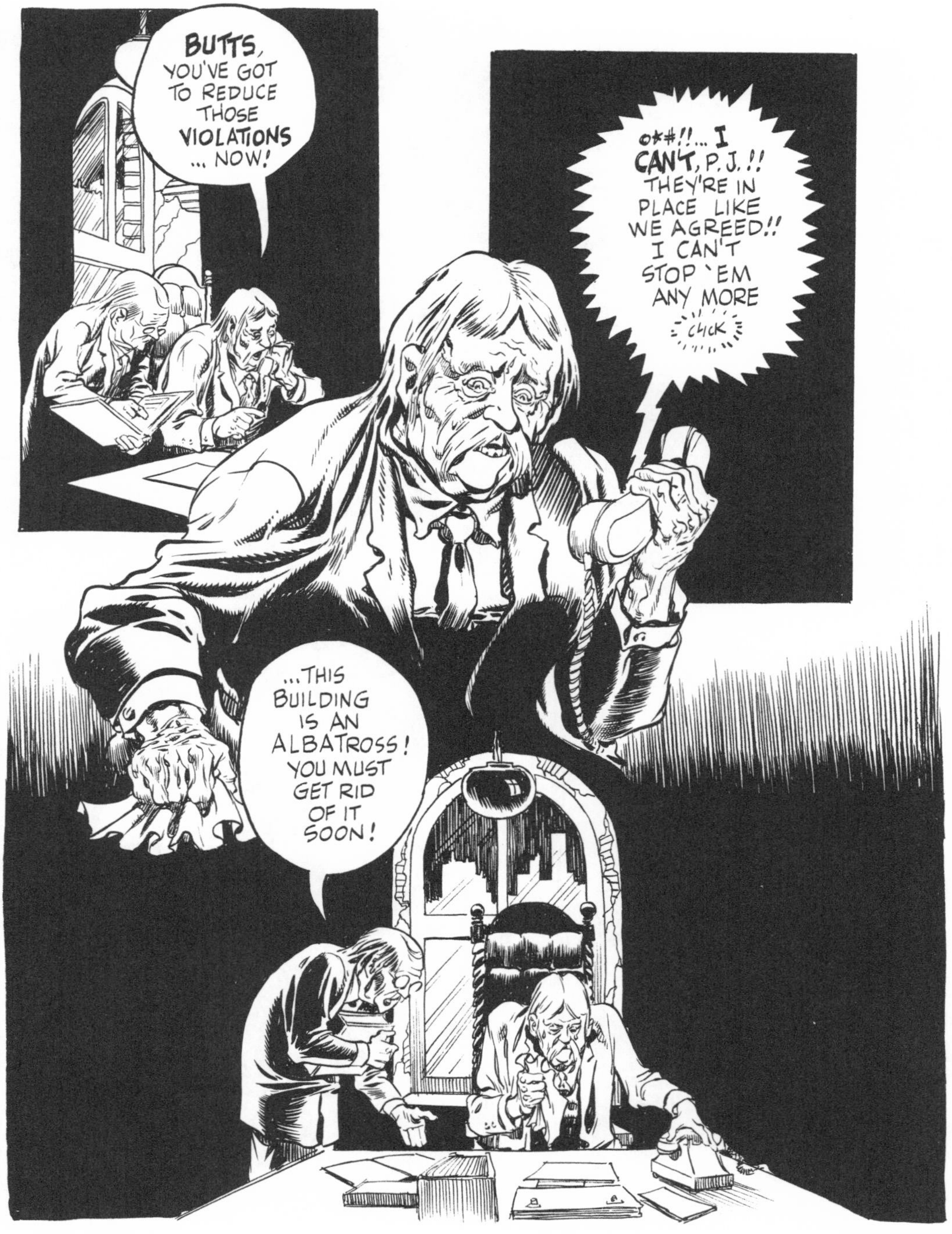
BUTTS, YOU'VE GOT TO REDUCE THOSE VIOLATIONS ... NOW!
o*#!!... I CAN'T, P.J.!! THEY'RE IN PLACE LIKE WE AGREED!! I CAN'T STOP `EM ANY MORE
CLICK
...THIS BUILDING IS AN ALBATROSS! YOU MUST GET RID OF IT SOON!

So another year went by...
NO!! YOU CAN'T SEE P.J.... HE DOESN'T WANT TO DISCUSS THE BUSINESS.
THE WAY THINGS ARE GOING THERE'LL BE NO BUSINESS SOON!
WAIT!
P.J., YOU MUST LISTEN TO US!!
THIS HAS BEEN AN AWFUL YEAR, P.J.! ...YOU HAVE POURED A FORTUNE INTO THIS DUMP!
DON'T CALL IT A DUMP!
OKAY!... I'LL PUT IT TO YOU STRAIGHT... WE'VE SOLD OFF ALL THAT'S LEFT OF YOUR PROPERTIES TO COVER YOUR LOSSES!! NOW, YOU MUST SELL THIS BUILDING OR ELSE...
WE'VE GOT A DEVELOPER WHO WILL TEAR IT DOWN AND PUT UP A NEW ONE!

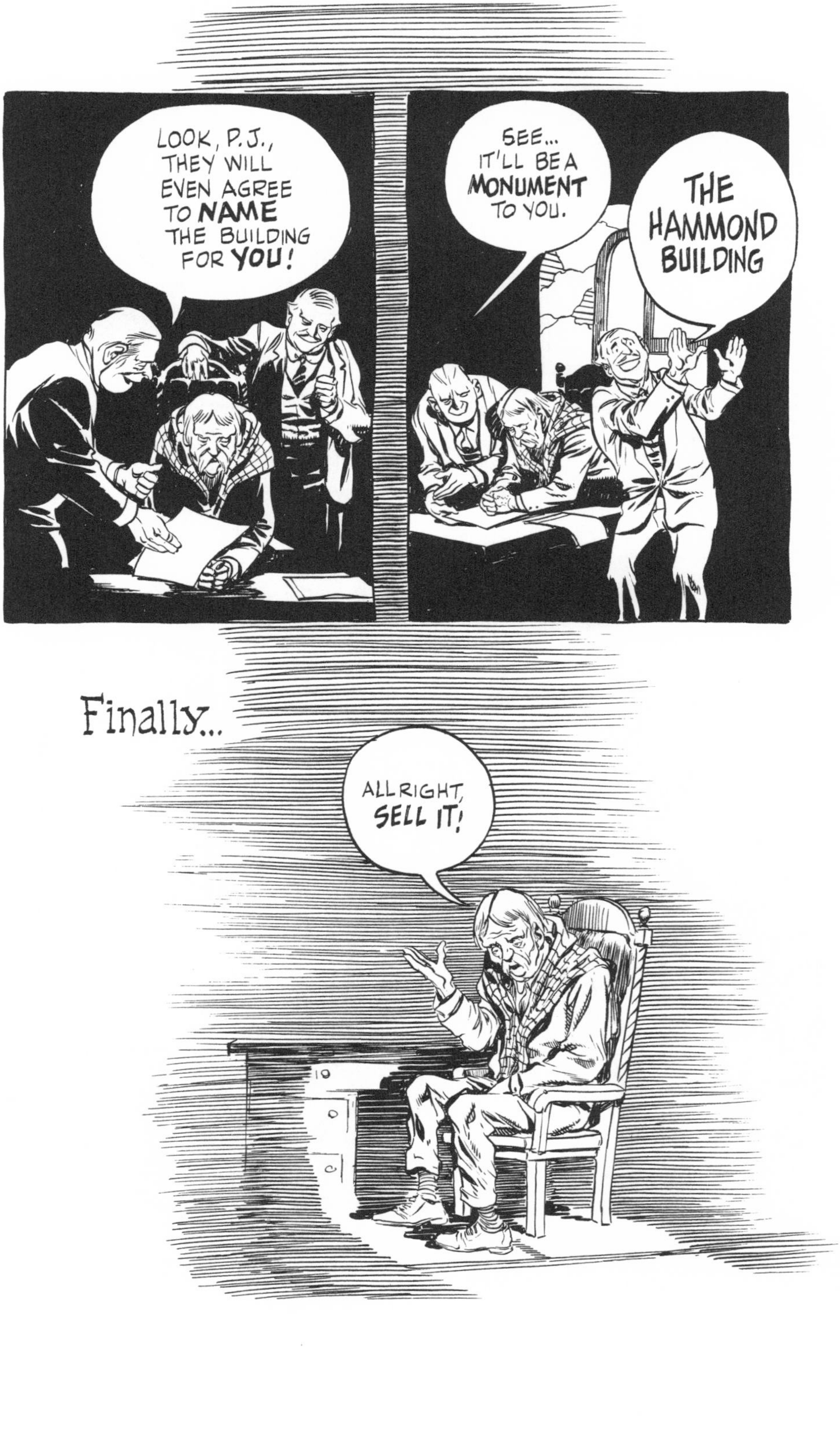
LOOK, P.J., THEY WILL EVEN AGREE TO NAME THE BUILDING FOR YOU!
SEE... IT'LL BE A MONUMENT TO YOU.
THE HAMMOND BUILDING
Finally...
ALLRIGHT, SELL IT!

Thereafter, P.J. Hammond withdrew even deeper into himself...

Then...

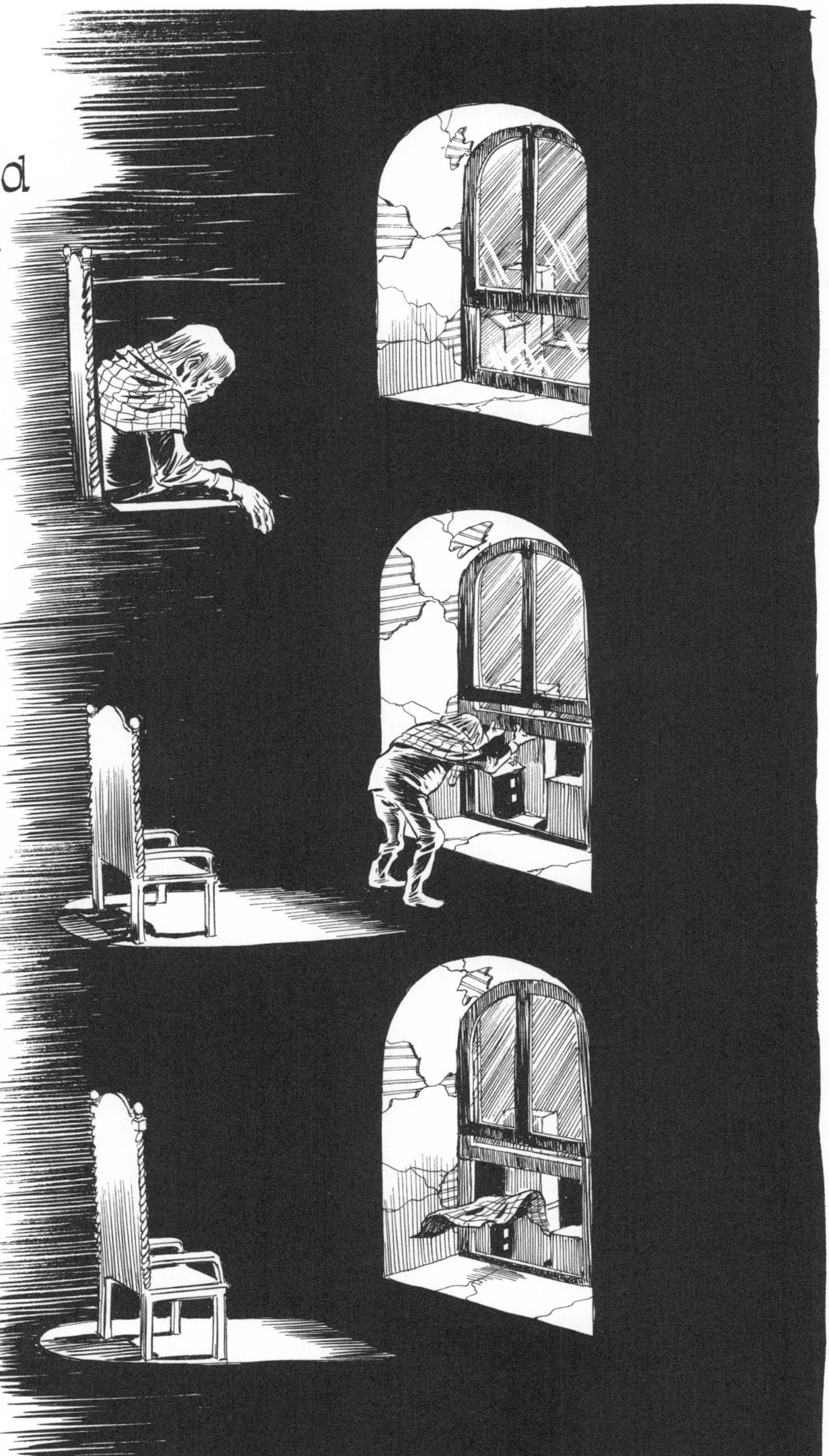

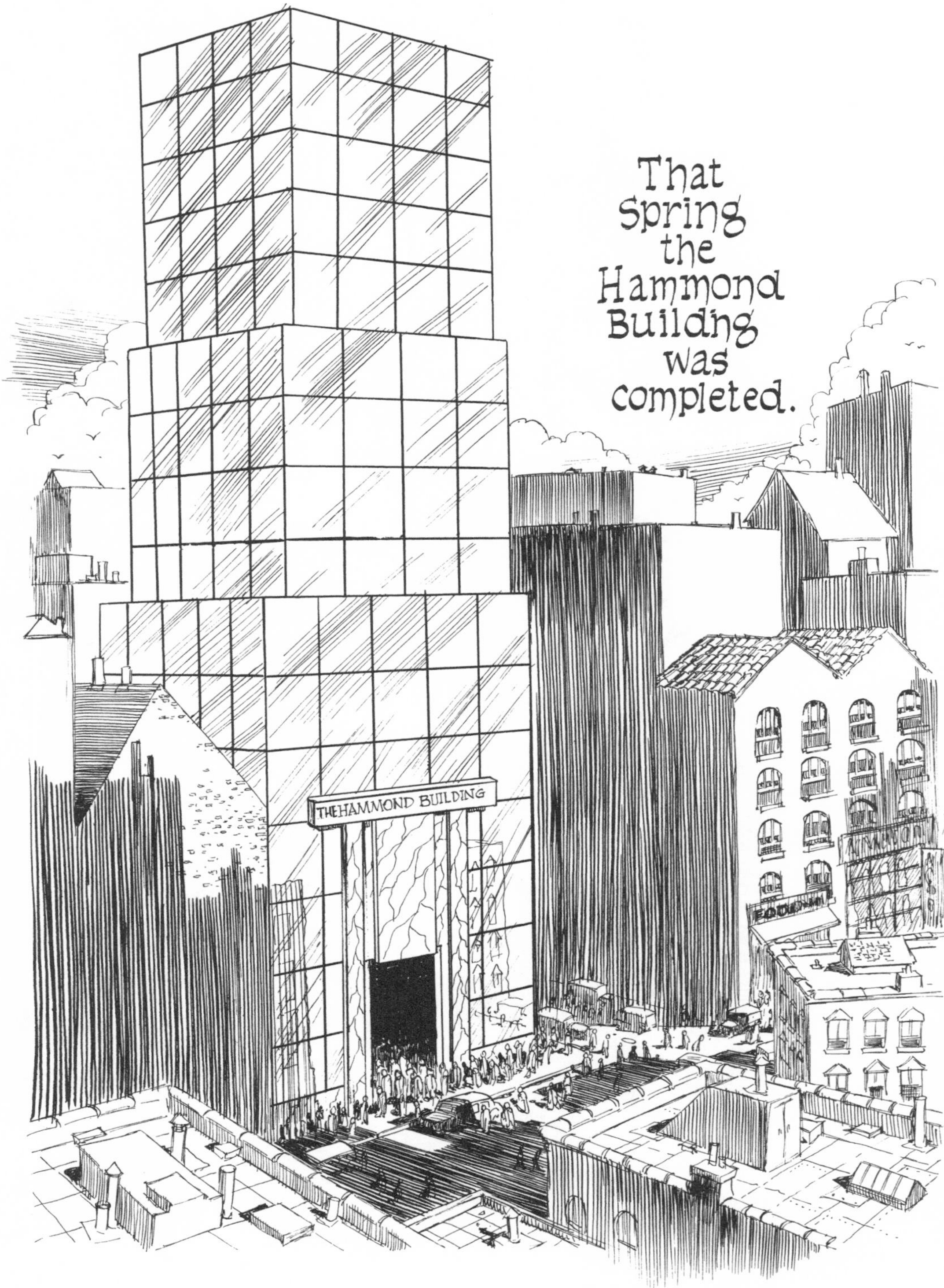
That Spring the Hammond Building was completed.
THE HAMMOND BUILDING

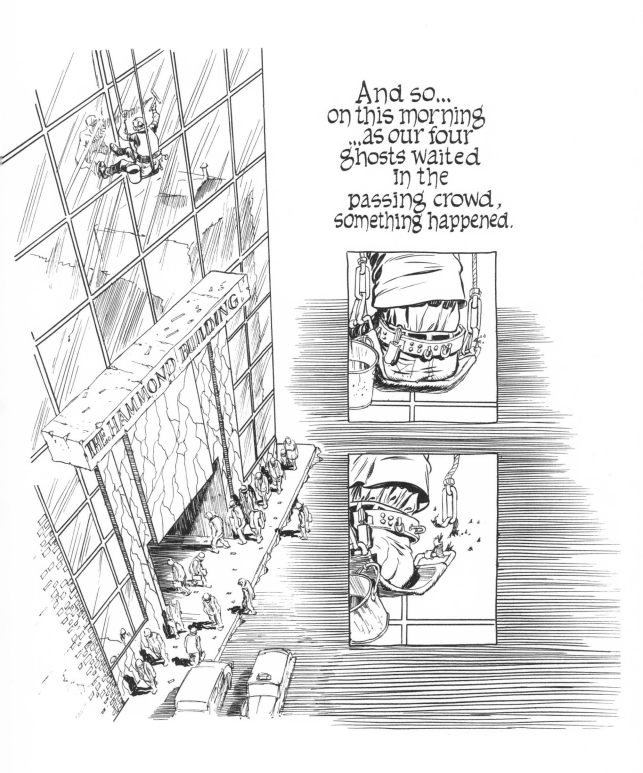

And so...
on this morning
...as our four
ghosts waited
in the
passing crowd,
something happened.

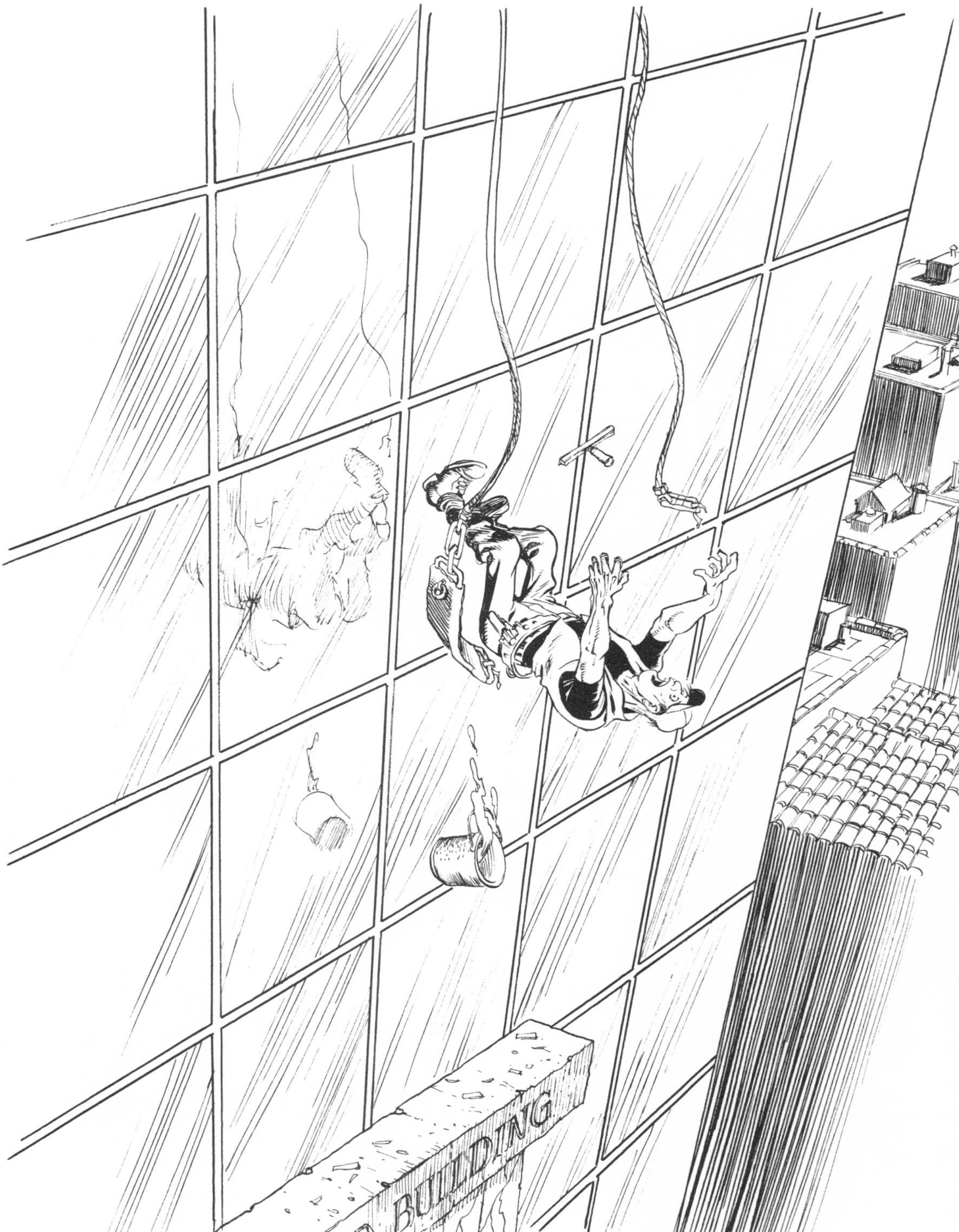
BUILDING

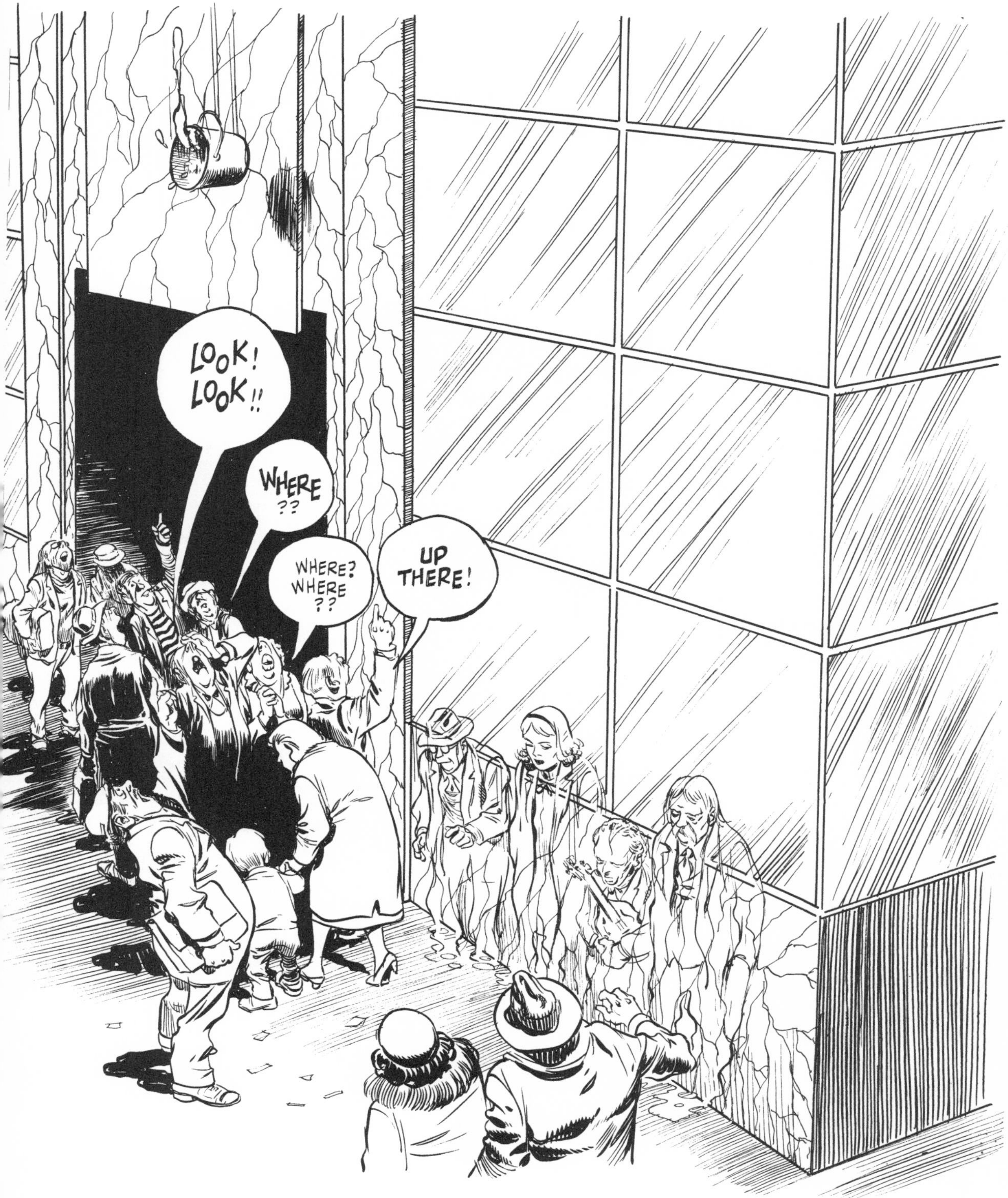
LOOK! LOOK!!
WHERE ??
WHERE? WHERE ??
UP THERE!

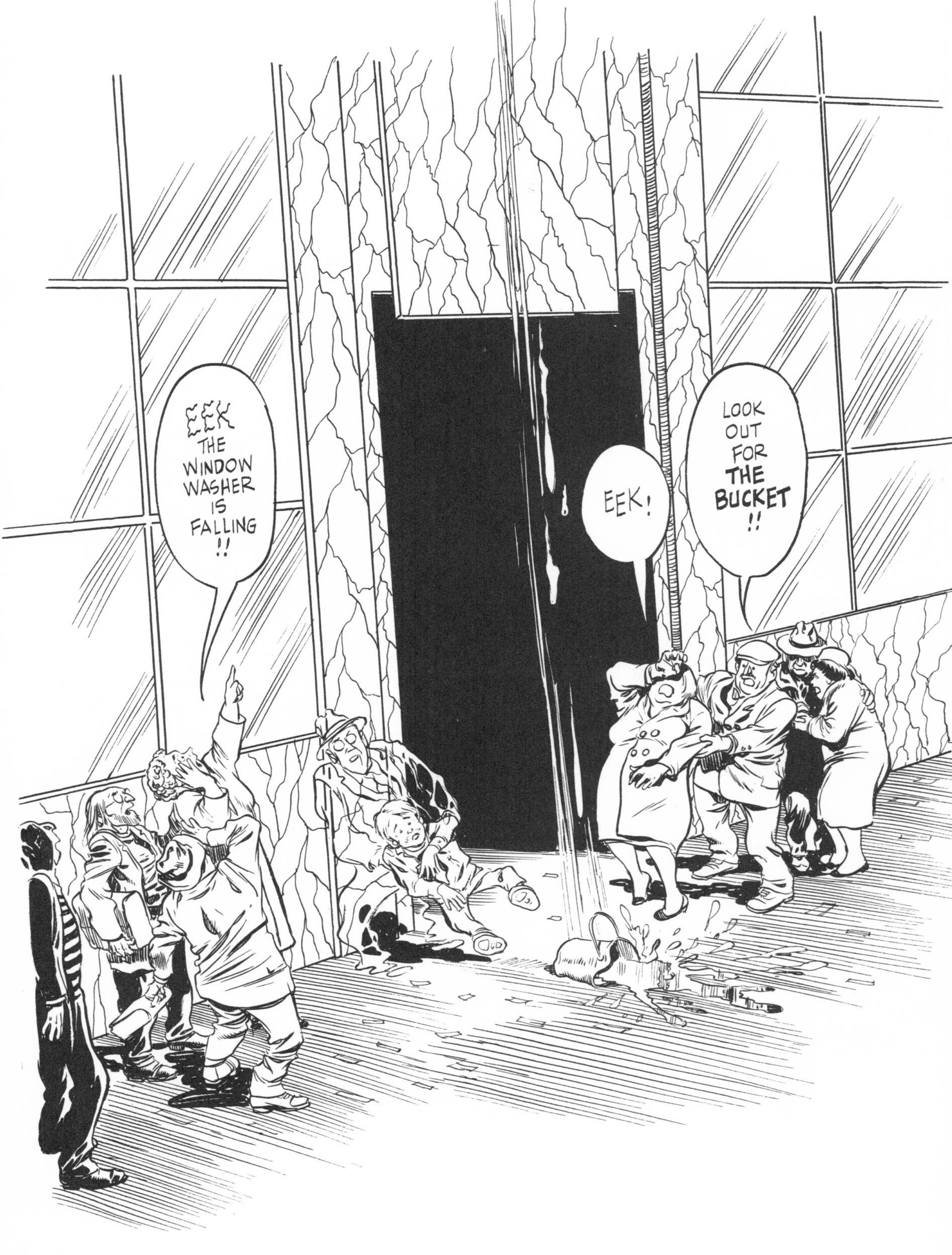
EEK THE WINDOW WASHER IS FALLING !!
EEK!
LOOK OUT FOR THE BUCKET !!

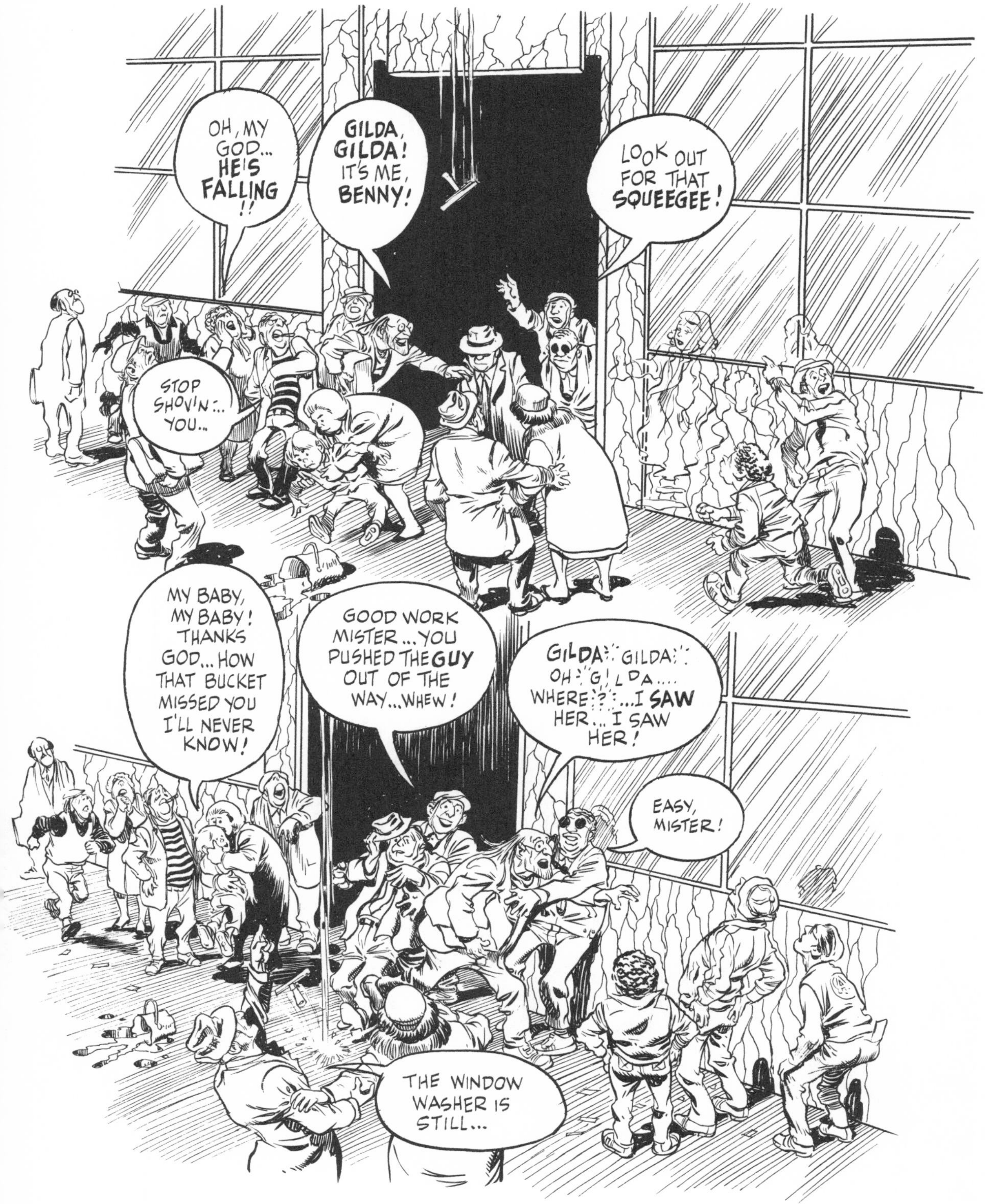
OH, MY GOD... HE'S FALLING!!
GILDA, GILDA! IT'S ME, BENNY!
LOOK OUT FOR THAT SQUEEGEE!
STOP SHOVIN'... YOU...
MY BABY, MY BABY! THANKS GOD... HOW THAT BUCKET MISSED YOU I'LL NEVER KNOW!
GOOD WORK MISTER... YOU PUSHED THE GUY OUT OF THE WAY... WHEW!
GILDA! GILDA! OH GILDA.... WHERE?...I SAW HER... I SAW HER!
EASY, MISTER!
THE WINDOW WASHER IS STILL...

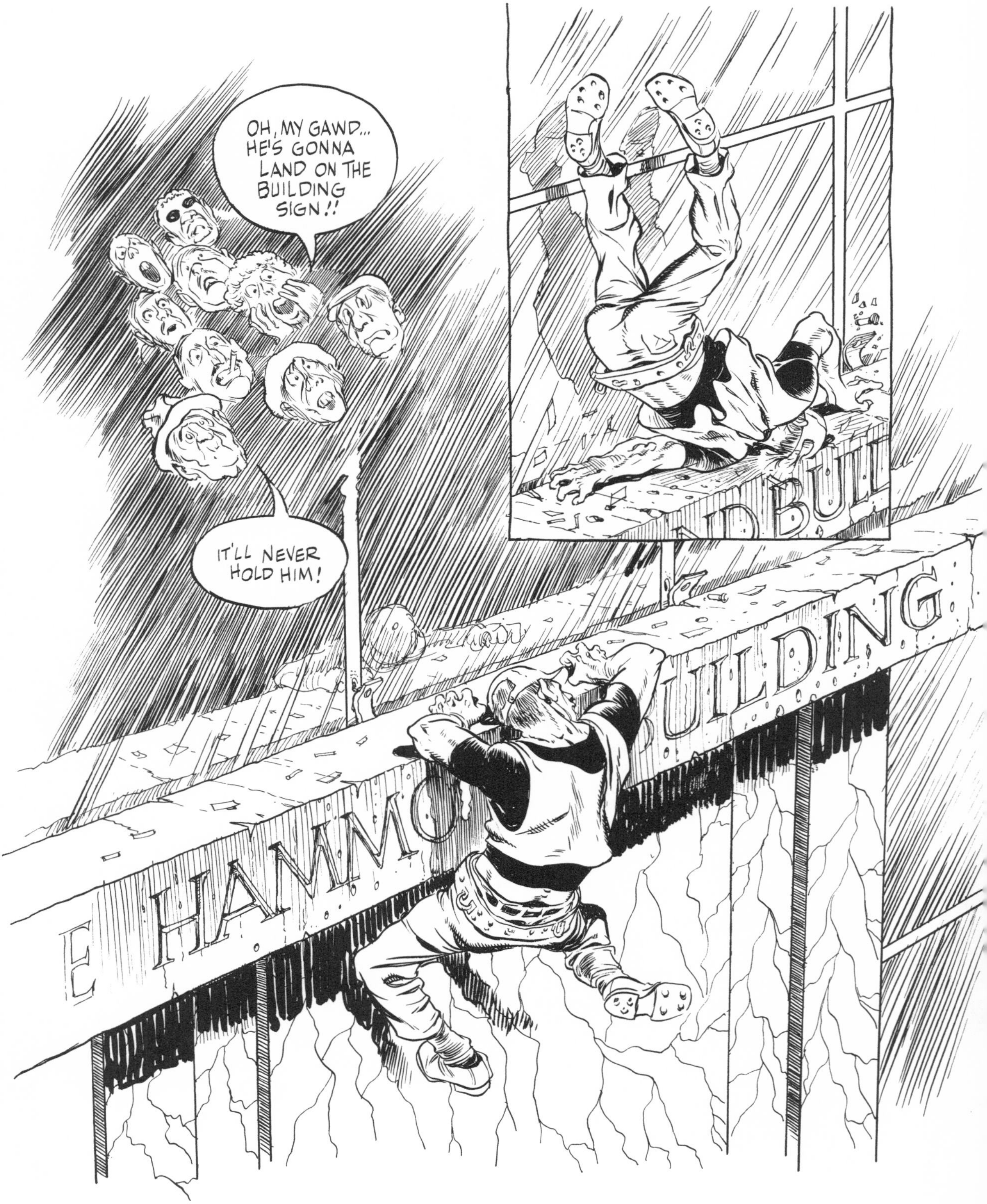
OH, MY GAWD... HE'S GONNA LAND ON THE BUILDING SIGN!!
IT'LL NEVER HOLD HIM!
E HAMMO
UILDING

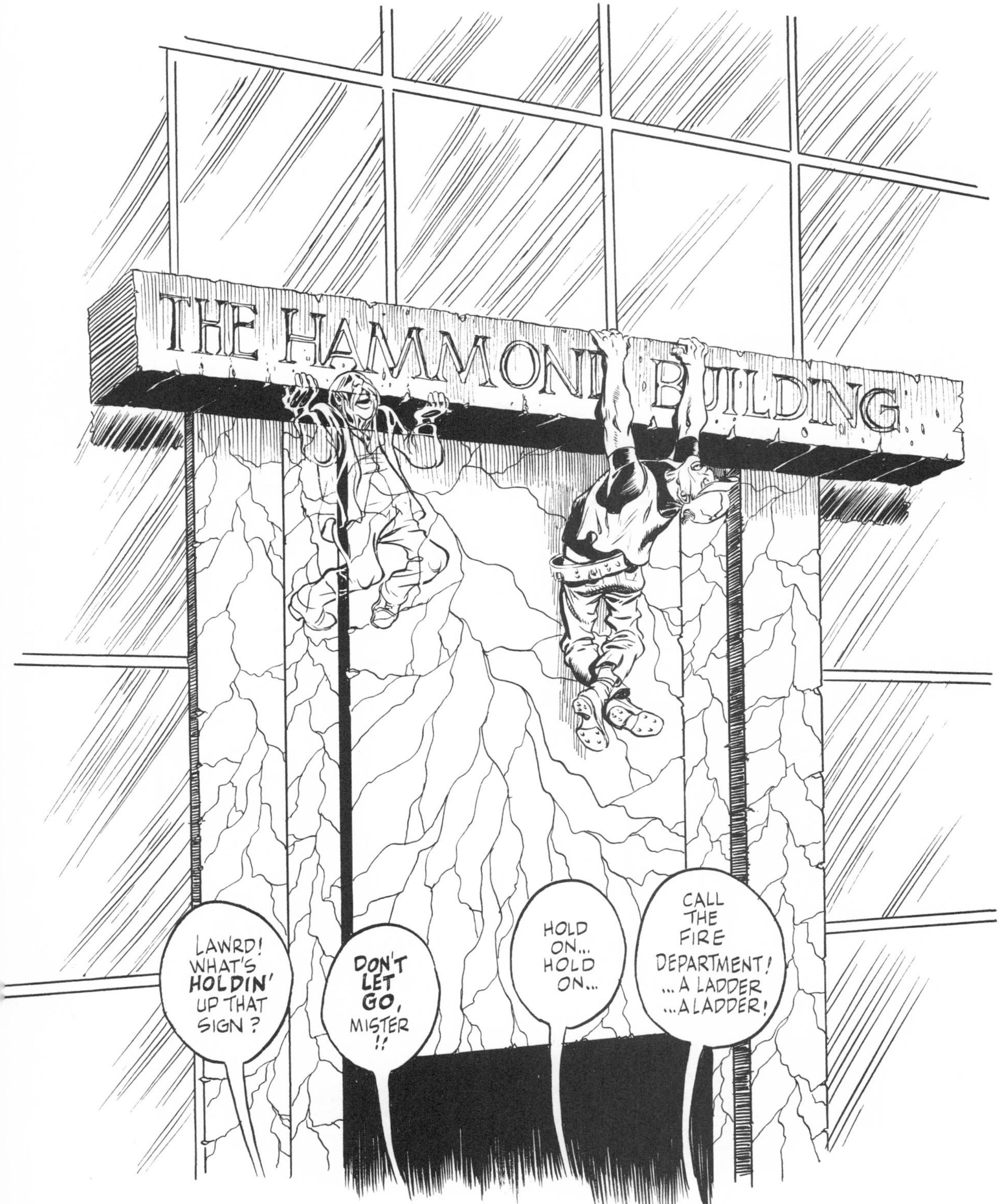
THE HAMMOND BUILDING
LAWRD! WHAT'S HOLDIN' UP THAT SIGN?
DON'T LET GO, MISTER!!
HOLD ON... HOLD ON...
CALL THE FIRE DEPARTMENT! ...A LADDER ...A LADDER!

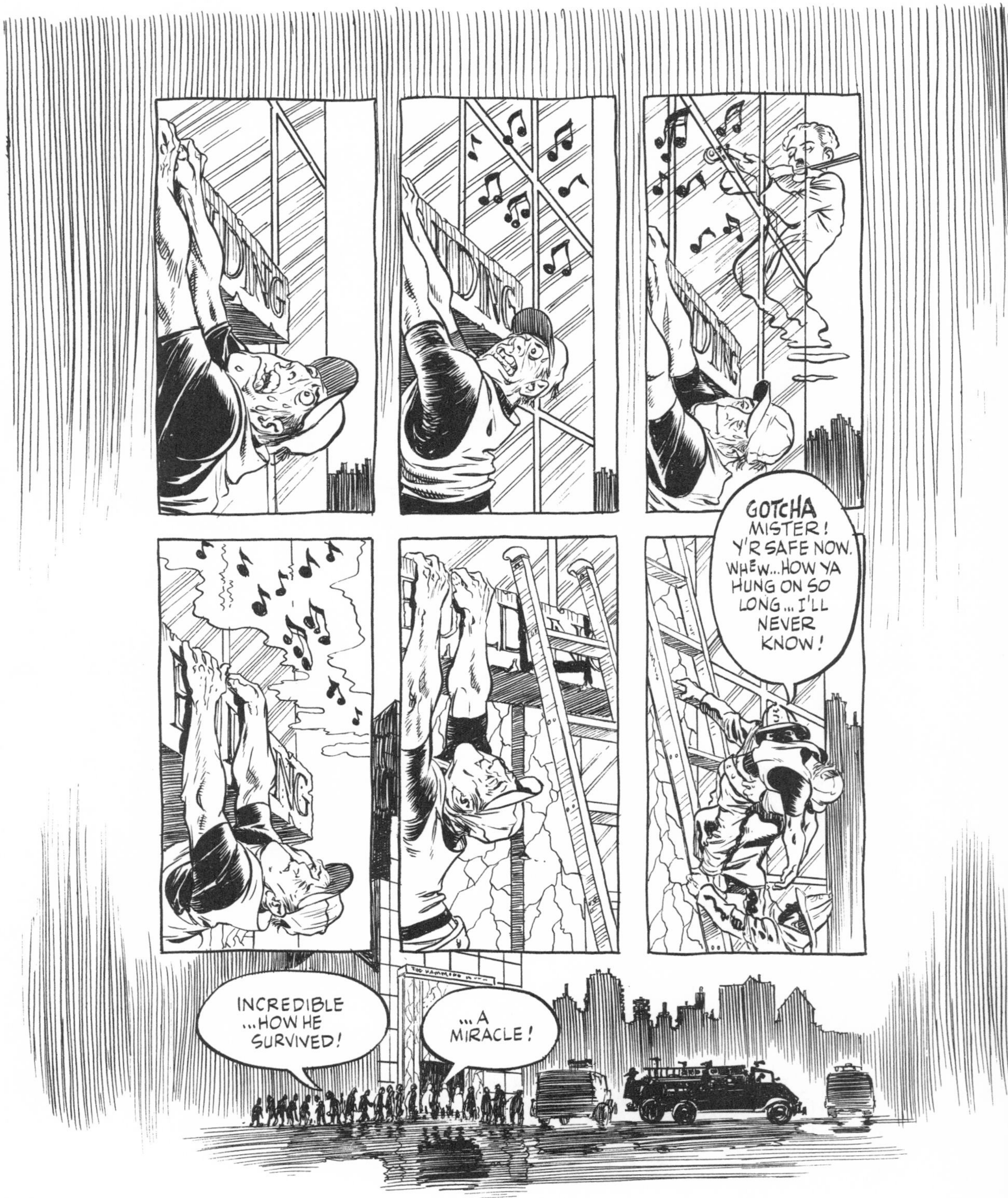

GOTCHA MISTER! Y'R SAFE NOW. WHEW...HOW YA HUNG ON SO LONG...I'LL NEVER KNOW!
INCREDIBLE ...HOW HE SURVIVED!
...A MIRACLE!

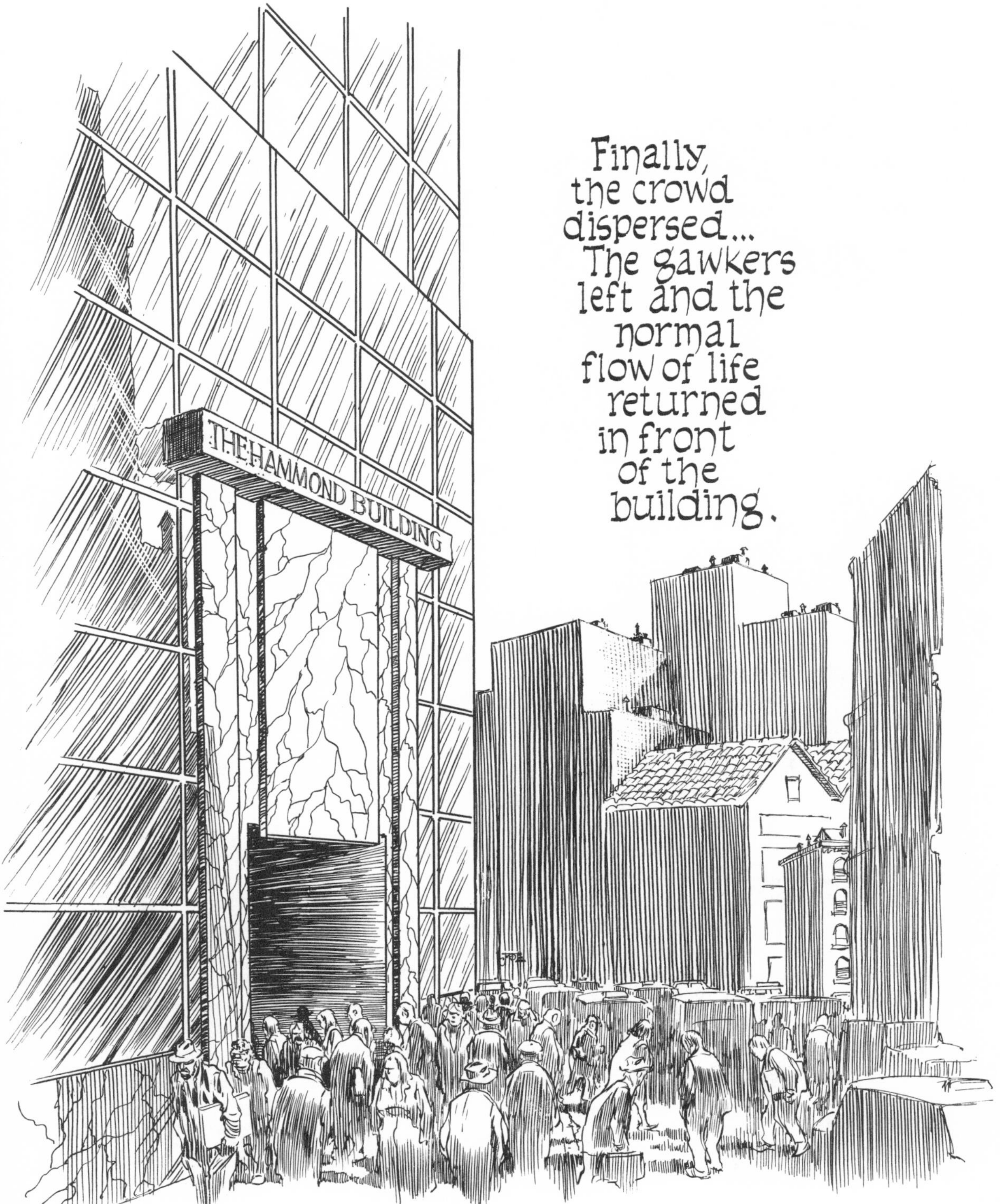
Finally, the crowd dispersed... The gawkers left and the normal flow of life returned in front of the building.
THE HAMMOND BUILDING

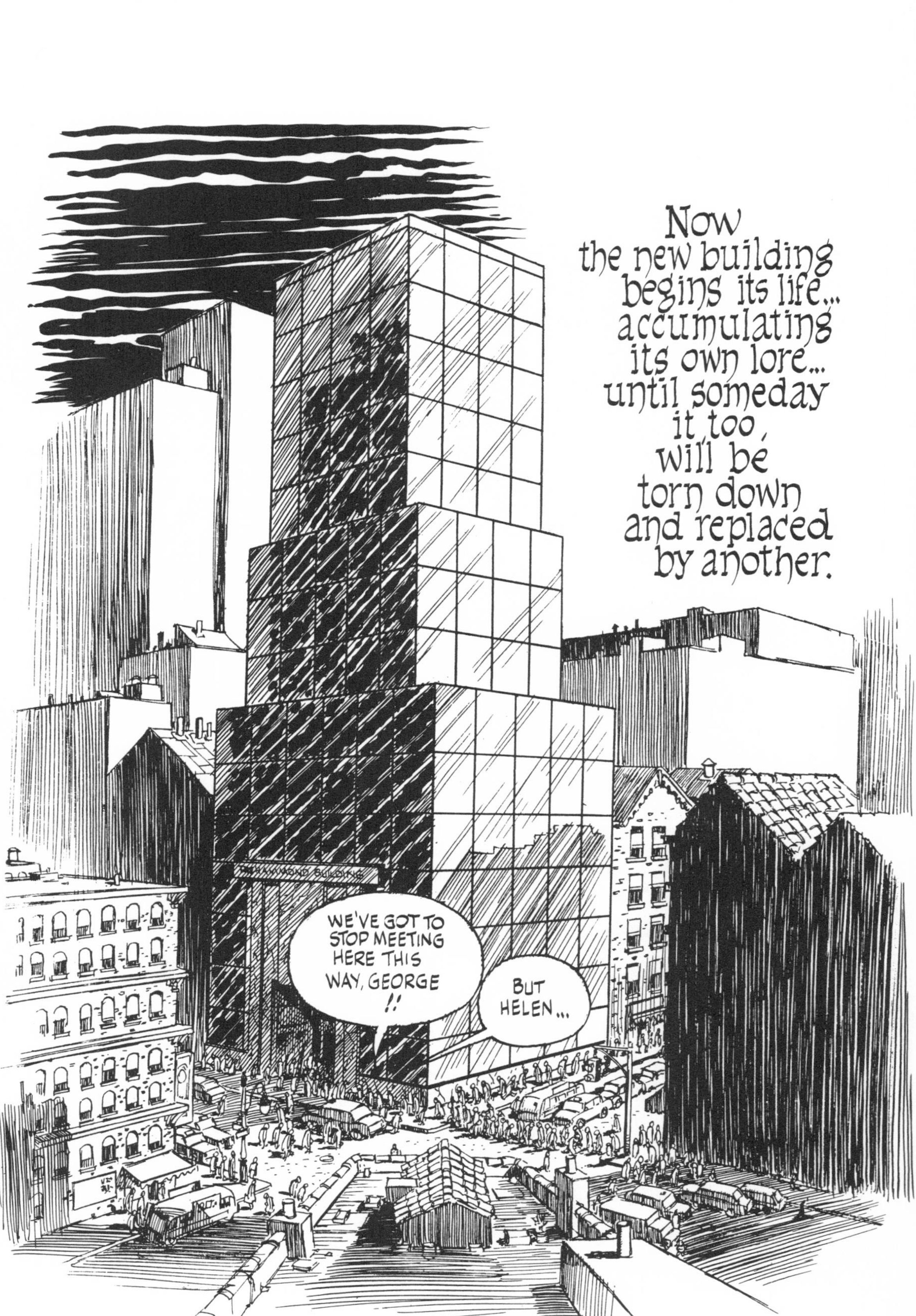
Now the new building begins its life... accumulating its own lore... until someday it too, will be torn down and replaced by another.
WE'VE GOT TO STOP MEETING HERE THIS WAY, GEORGE !!
BUT HELEN...

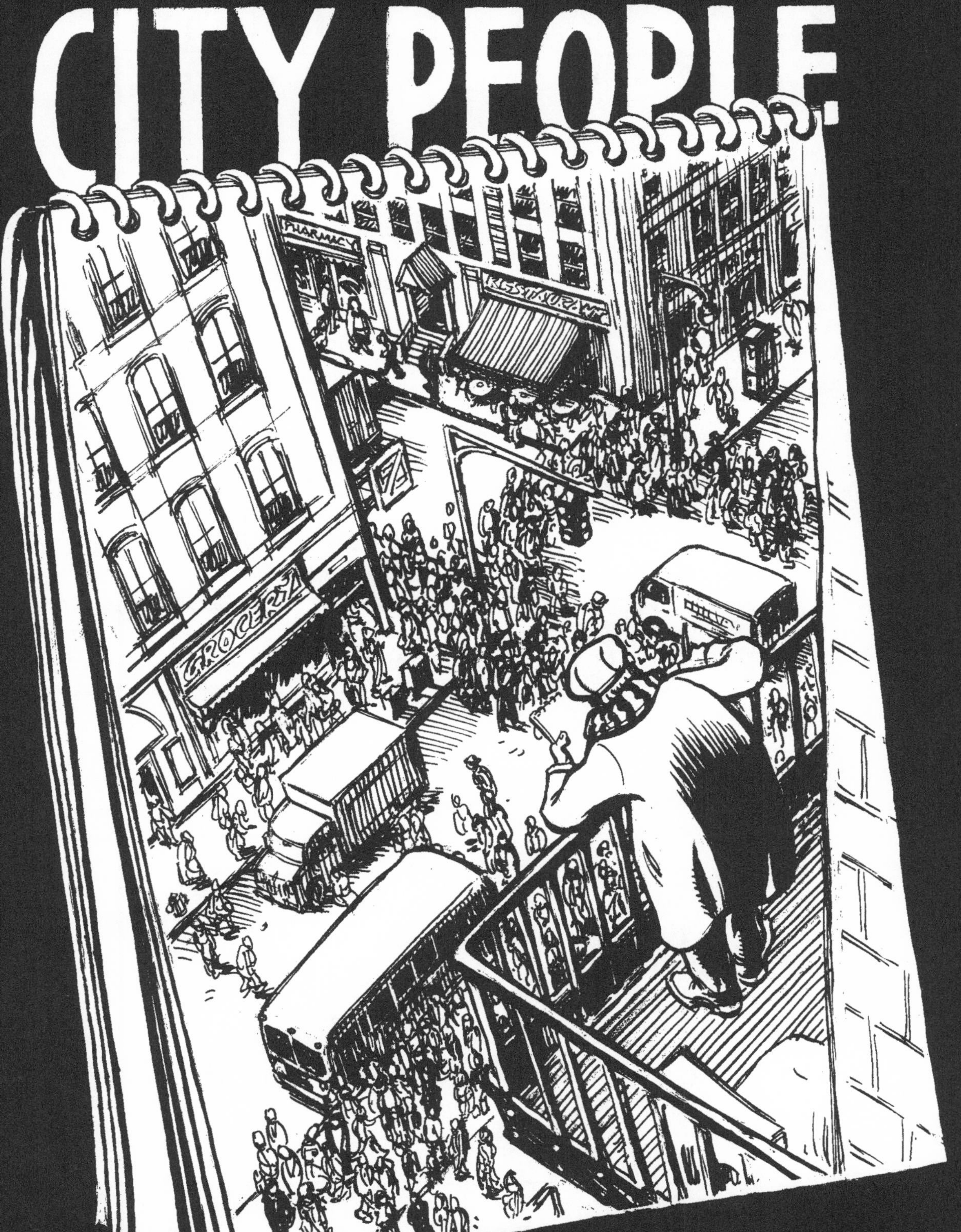
CITY PEOPLE
PHARMACY
GROCERY

New Introduction to
City People Notebook

LIVING IN A BIG CITY
CAN BE COMPARED
TO EXISTING IN A JUNGLE.
ONE BECOMES A
CREATURE OF THE
ENVIRONMENT.
THE RESPONSE TO THE
RHYTHMS AND CHOREOGRAPHY
IS VISCERAL
AND BEFORE LONG
A DWELLER'S CONDUCT IS
AS DISTINCTIVE AS
THOSE OF A
JUNGLE INHABITANT.
ARCANE SURVIVAL
SKILLS AND SUBTLE
PERSONALITY CHANGES
TAKE PLACE THAT
AFFECT BEHAVIOR.
HEREIN IS A KIND OF
ARCHAEOLOGICAL
STUDY OF CITY PEOPLE.

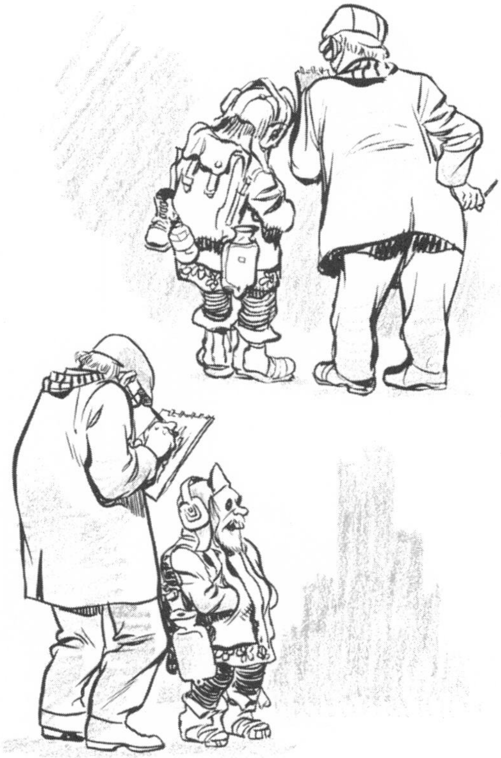

TO ME, CITY PEOPLE HAVE ALWAYS SEEMED SINGULAR IN STYLE AND SENSIBILITIES. CLEARLY, LIFE DEEP IN A BIG CITY IS VERY DIFFERENT THAN THAT OF A SMALL RURAL COMMUNITY. AS THE STREET SMARTS AND SURVIVAL SKILLS ARE ACCUMULATED, IT AFFIRMS ENVIRONMENT'S TRIUMPH OVER US ALL.

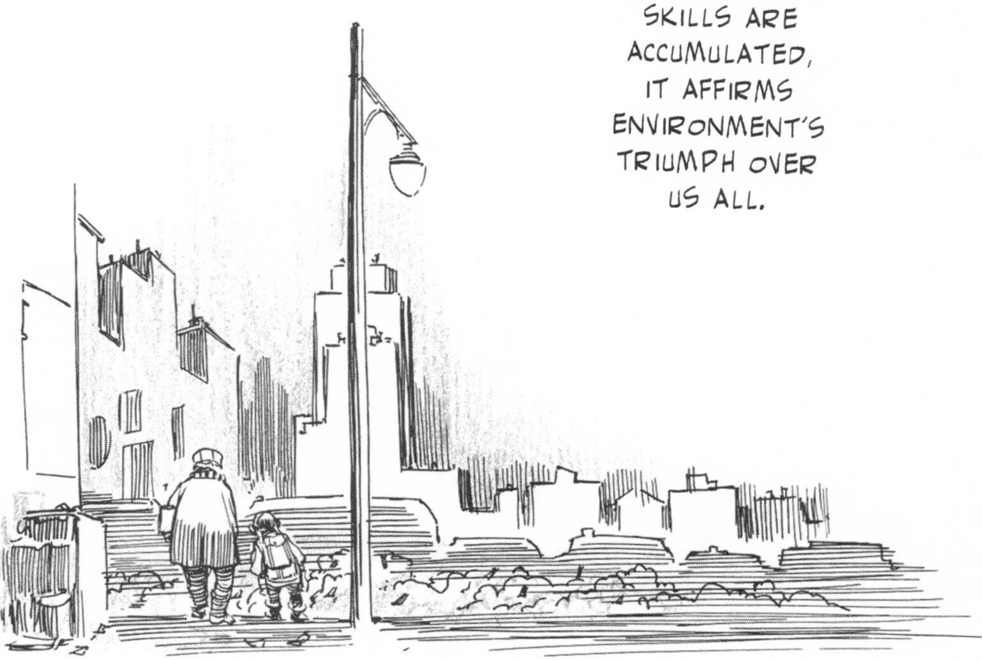

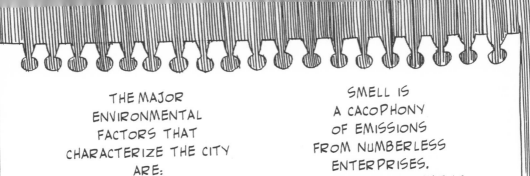

THE MAJOR
ENVIRONMENTAL
FACTORS THAT
CHARACTERIZE THE CITY
ARE:

**TIME, SMELL,
RHYTHM AND
SPACE.**

CITY TIME HAS
A SPECIAL CADENCE.
IT IS AFFECTED
BY THE BRIEF
ENDURANCE OF EVENTS.

SMELL IS
A CACOPHONY
OF EMISSIONS
FROM NUMBERLESS
ENTERPRISES.
RHYTHM IS AN ELEMENT
OF SPEED WHICH
DICTATES HOW DWELLERS
MUST NEGOTIATE MOVEMENT.
AND SPACE IS THE
LIMITED LIVING AREA
LEFT BY OBSTACLES IN
THE CONCRETE
MAZE.

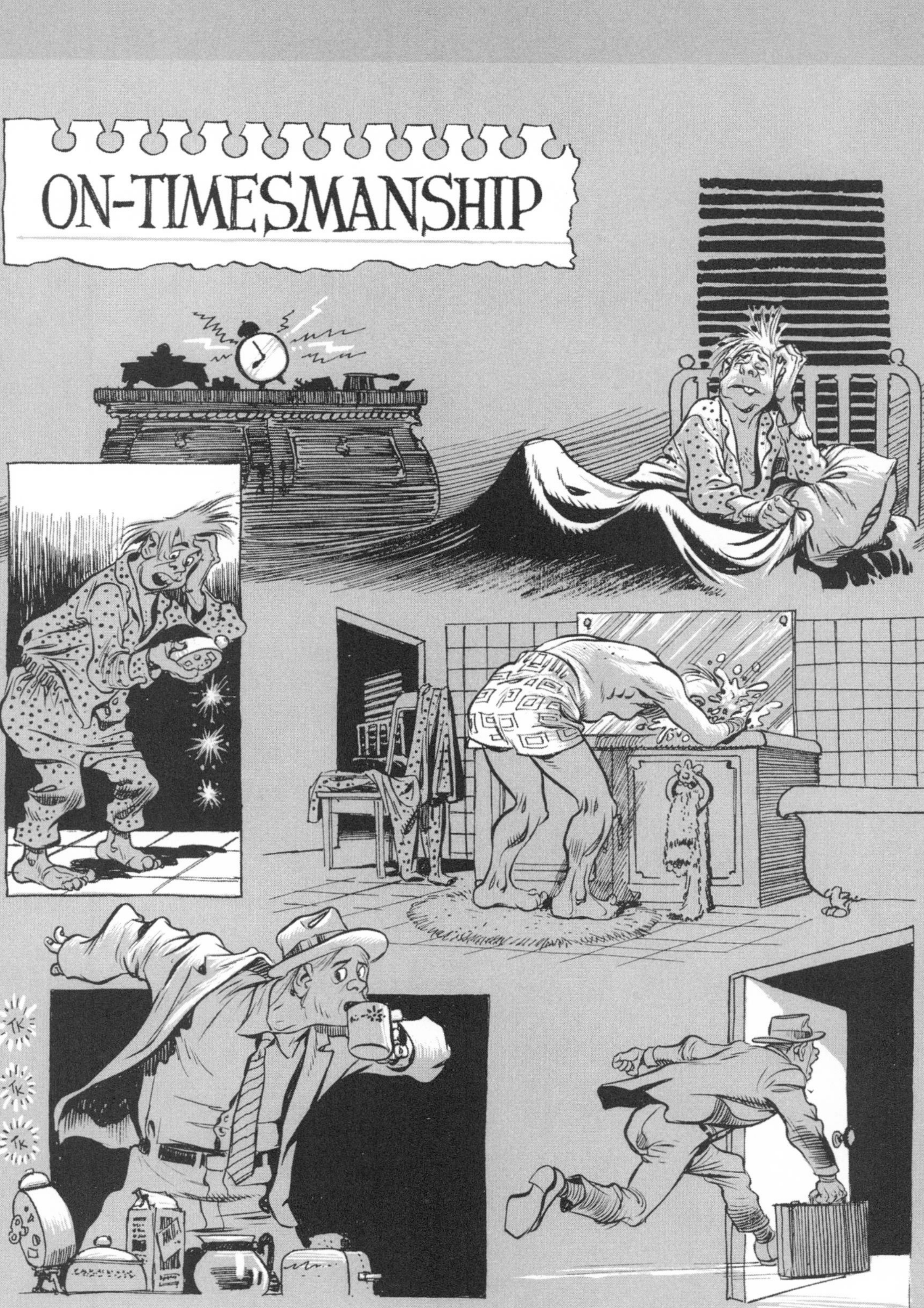
ON-TIMESMANSHIP
TK
TK
TK

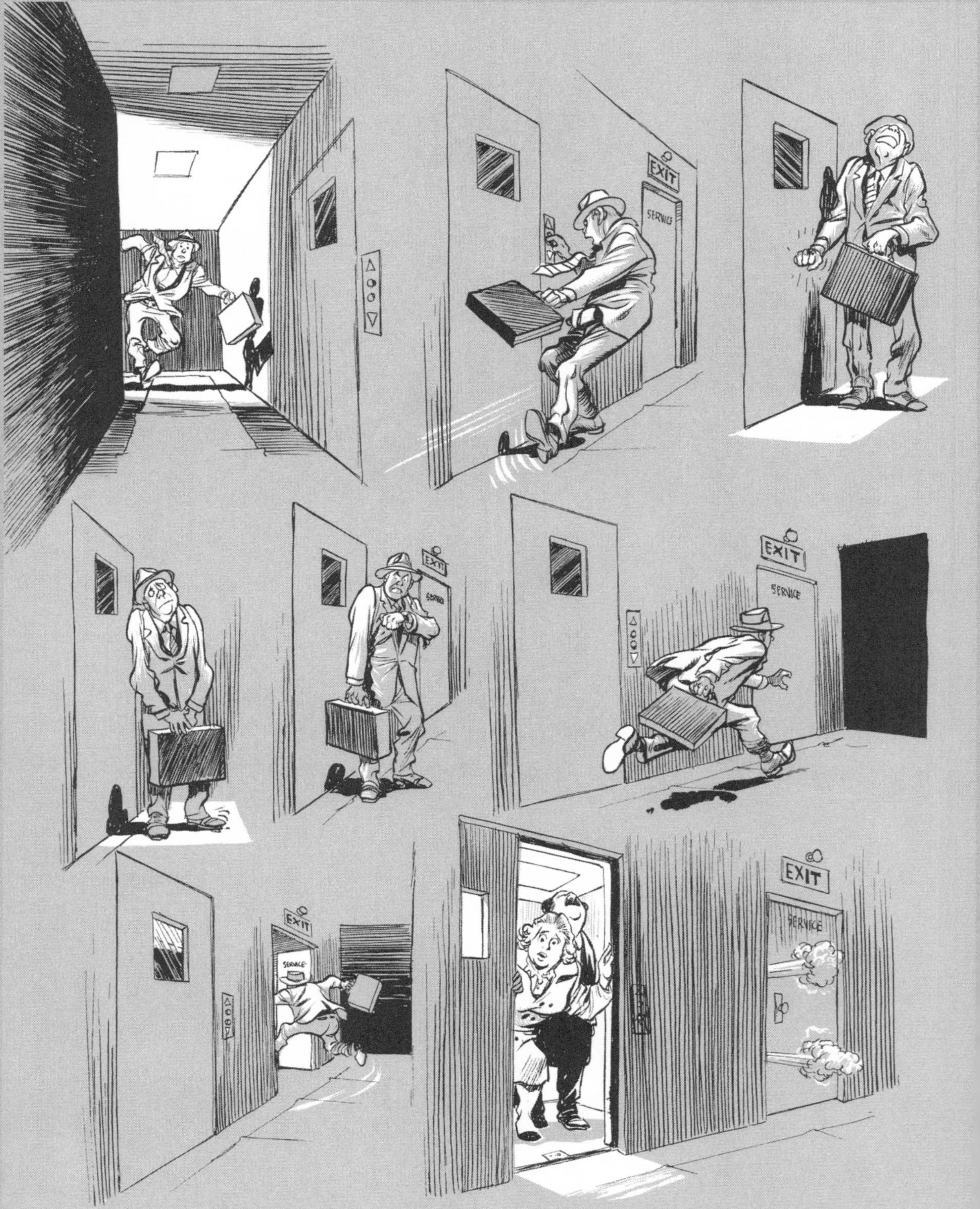
EXIT
SERVICE
EXIT
SERVICE
EXIT
SERVICE
EXIT
SERVICE

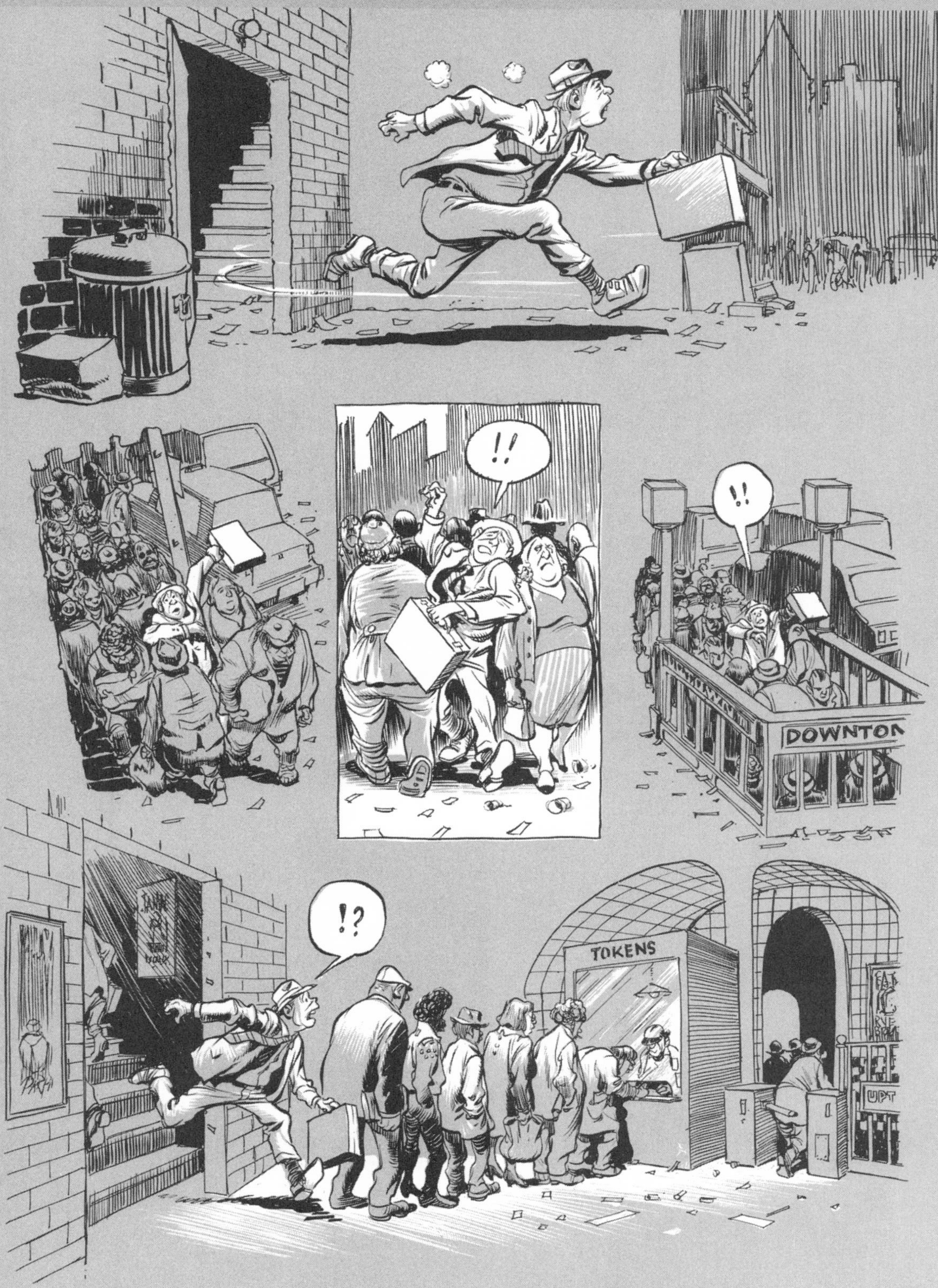
!!
!!
DOWNTO
!?
TOKENS
UPT

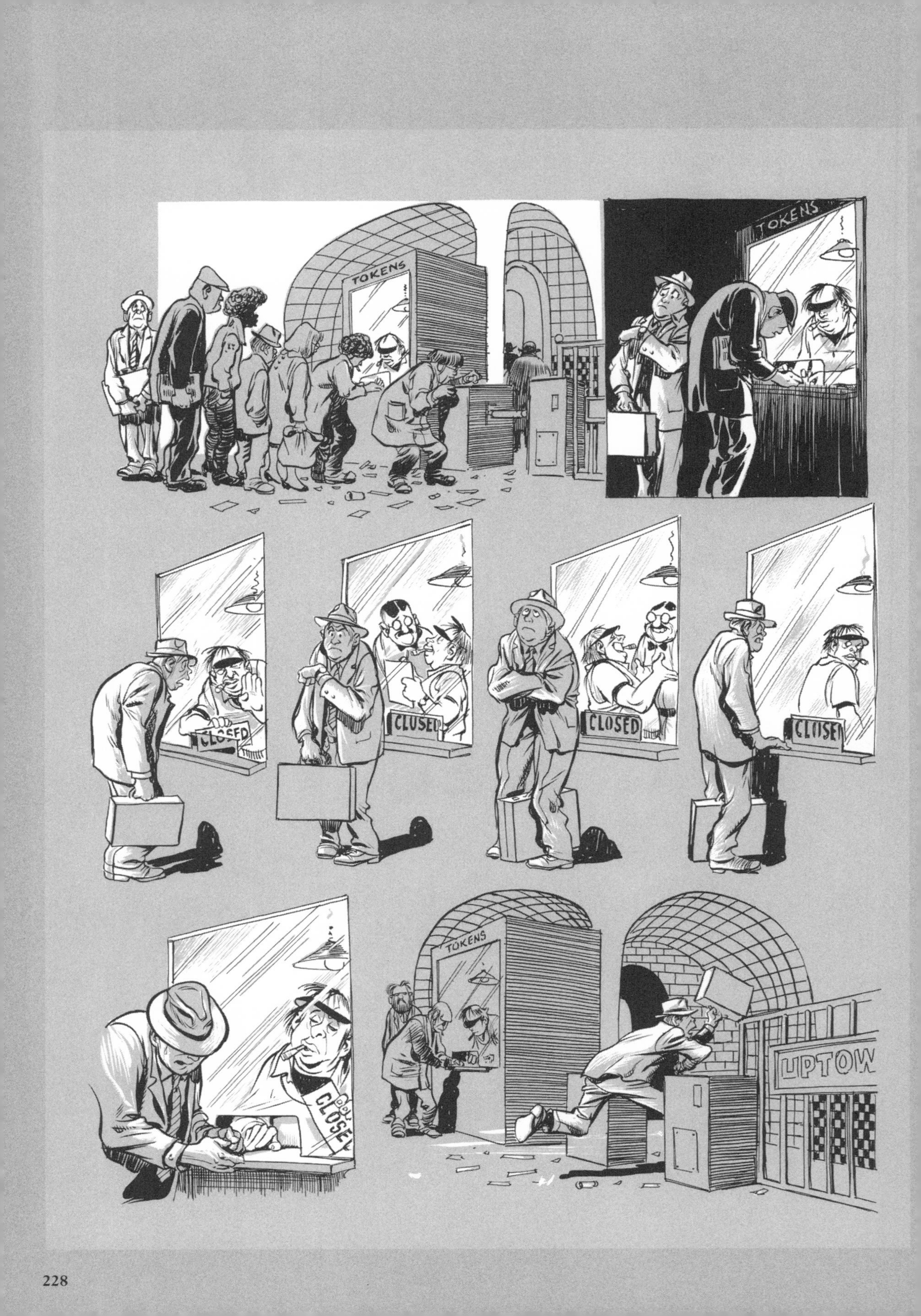
TOKENS
TOKENS
CLOSED
CLOSE
CLOSED
CLOSE
CLOSE
TOKENS
UPTOW

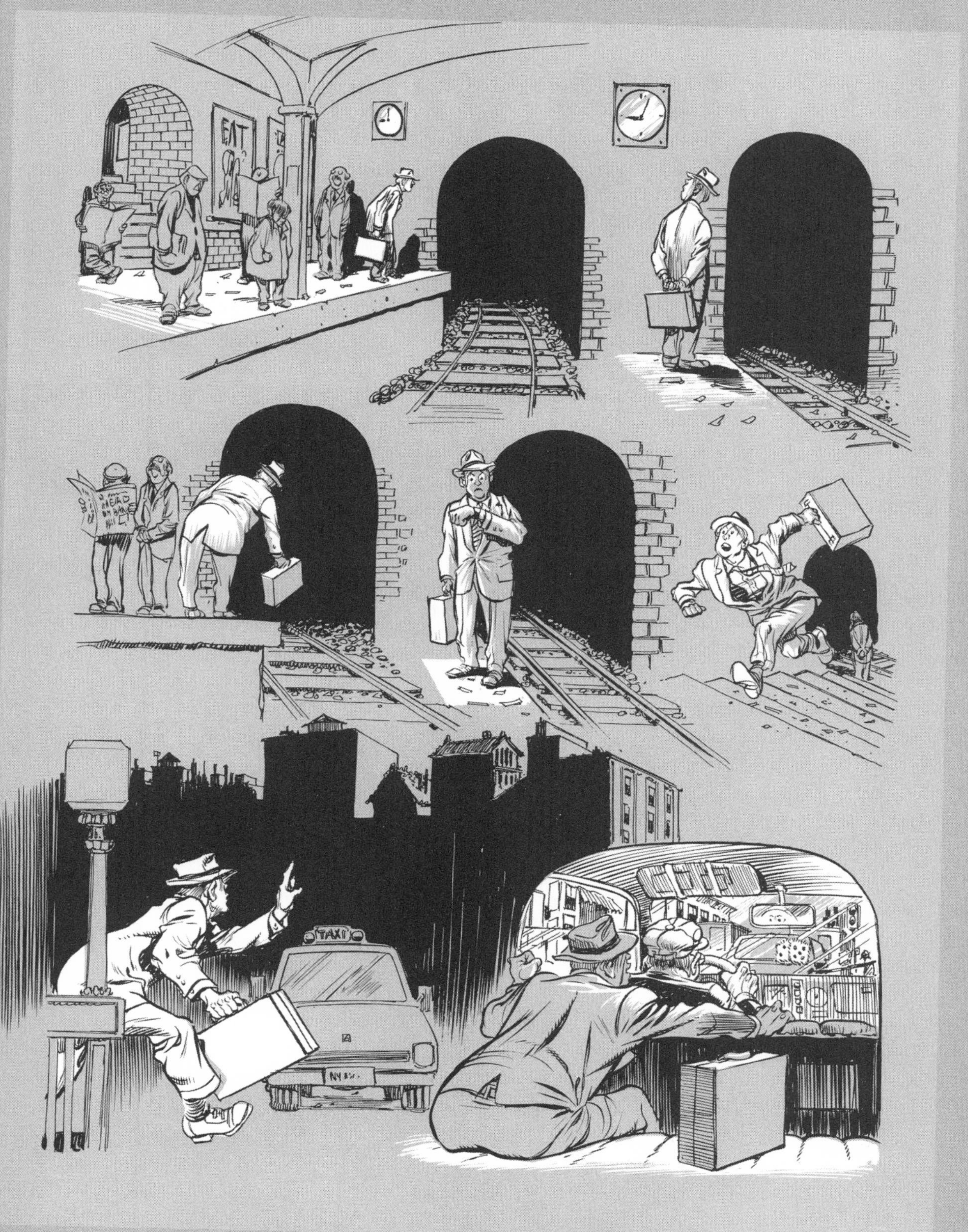
EAT
TAXI

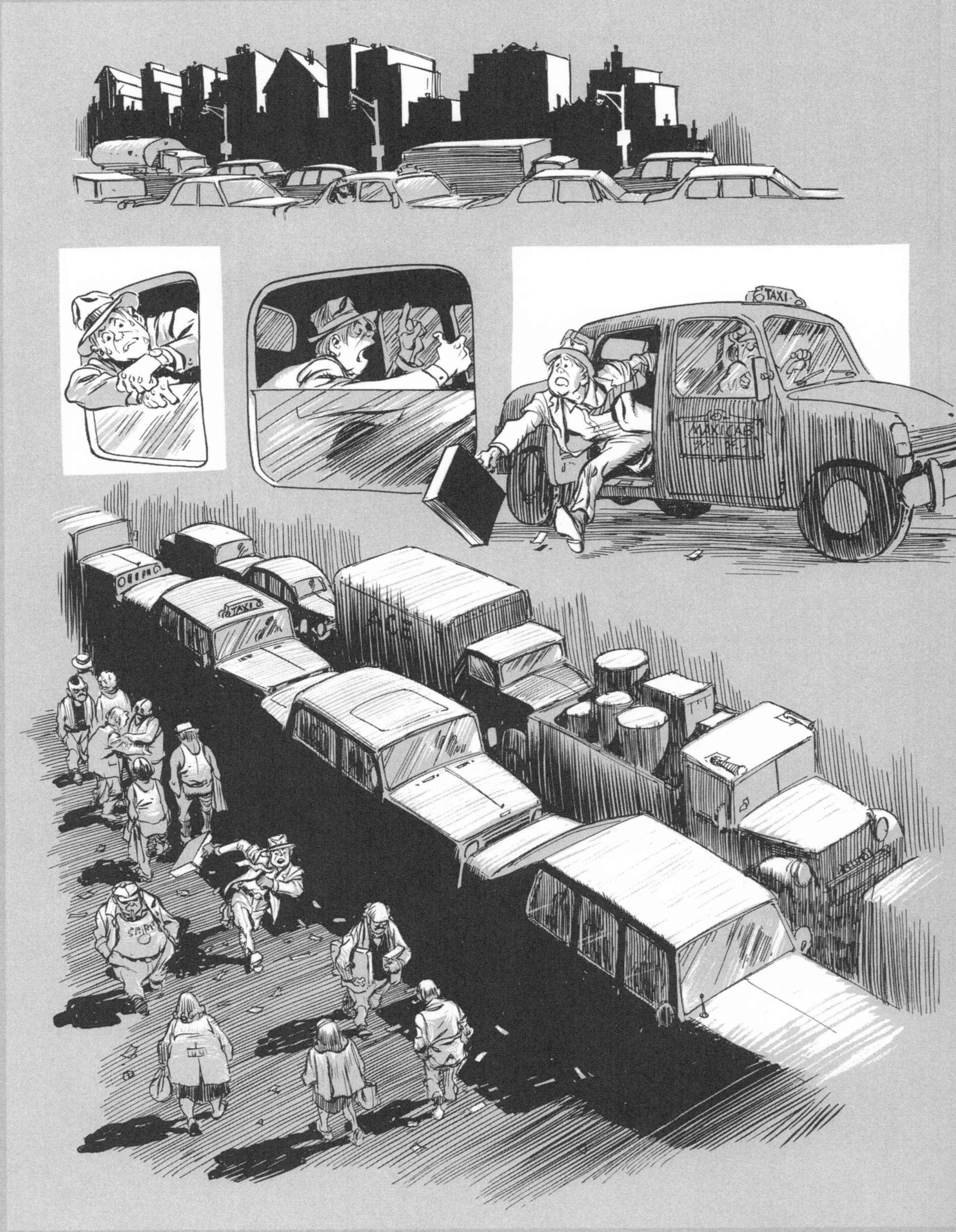
TAXI
MAXICAB
TAXI
ACE

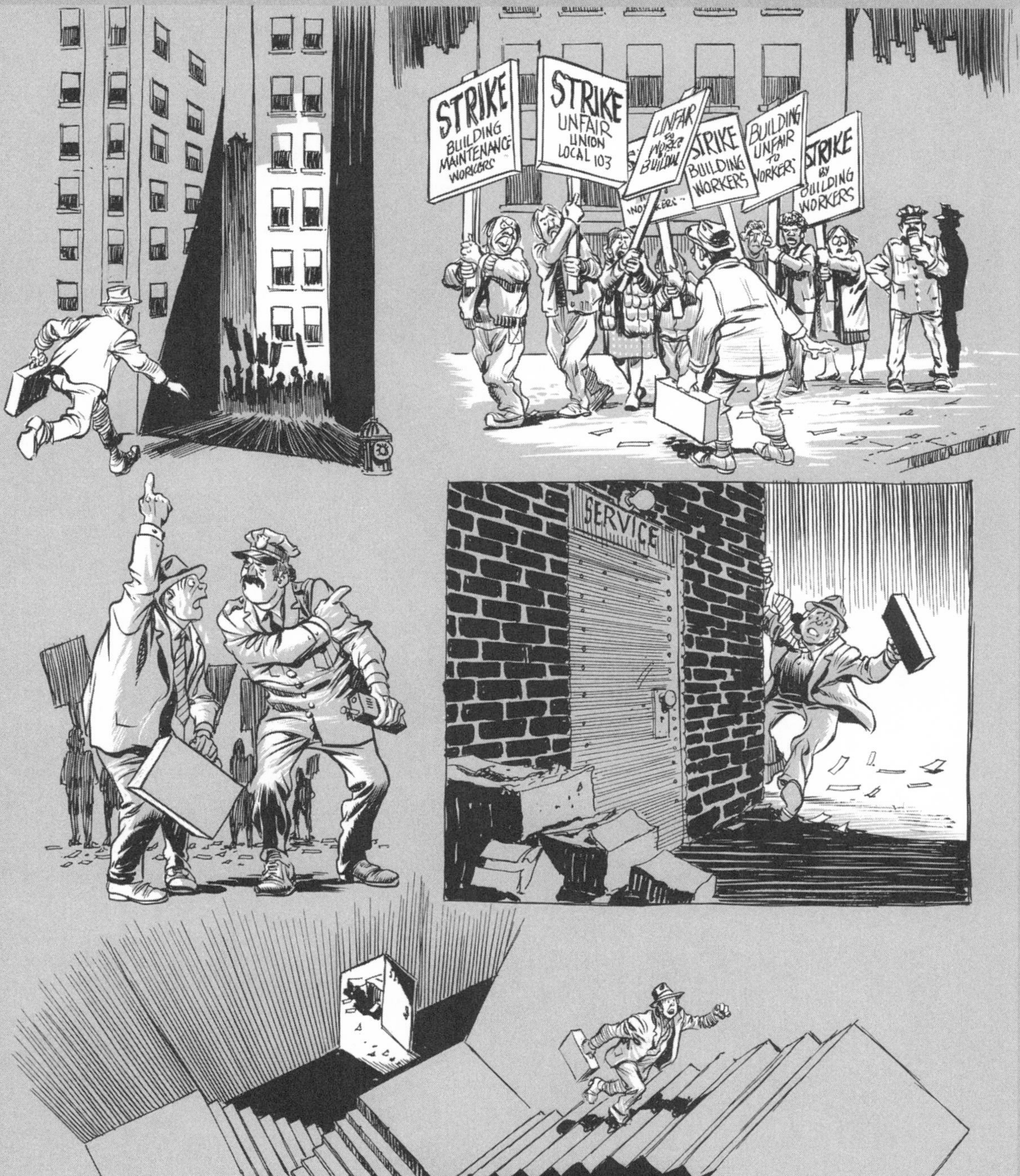
STRIKE BUILDING MAINTENANCE WORKERS
STRIKE UNFAIR UNION LOCAL 103
STRIKE BUILDING WORKERS
BUILDING UNFAIR TO WORKERS
STRIKE BY BUILDING WORKERS
SERVICE

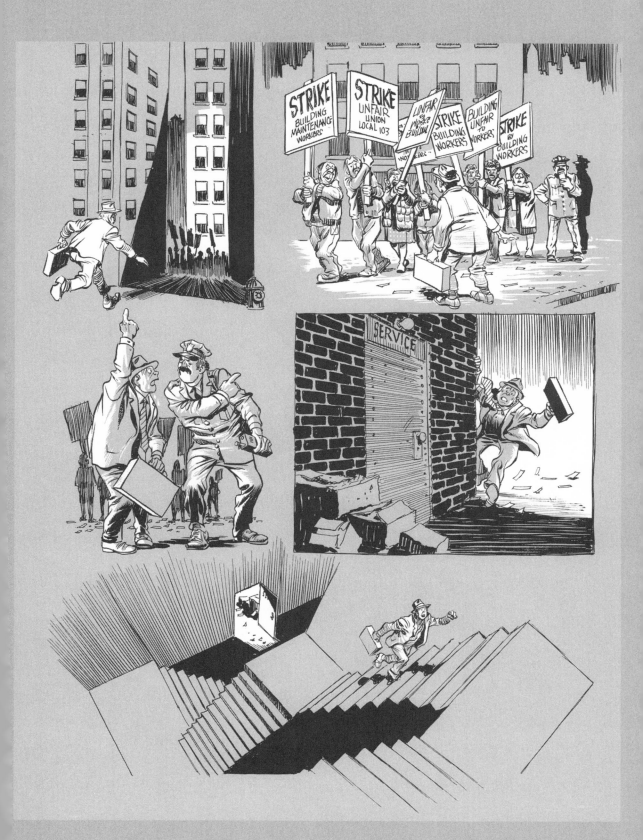

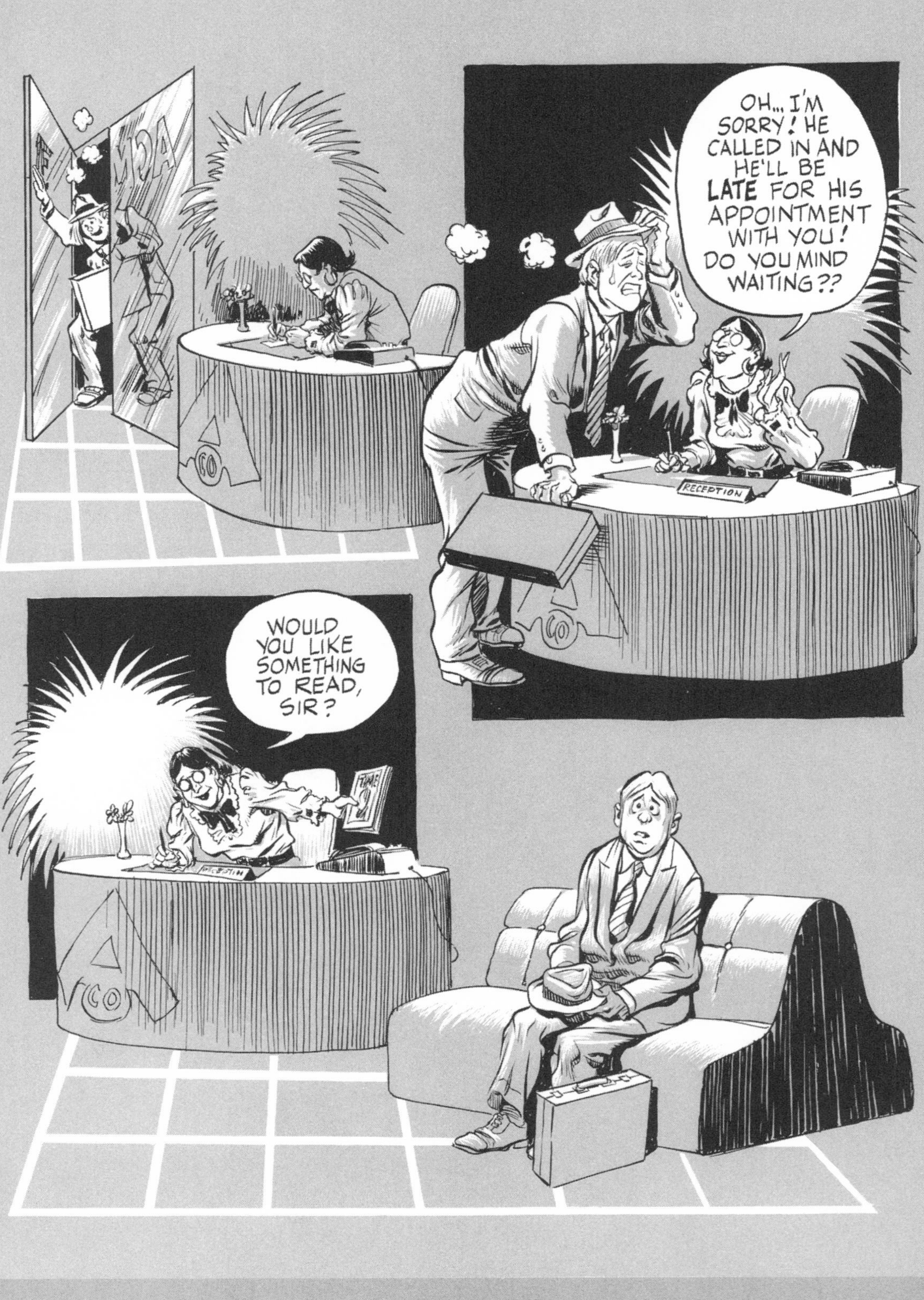
OH... I'M SORRY! HE CALLED IN AND HE'LL BE LATE FOR HIS APPOINTMENT WITH YOU! DO YOU MIND WAITING??
RECEPTION
WOULD YOU LIKE SOMETHING TO READ, SIR?
TIME

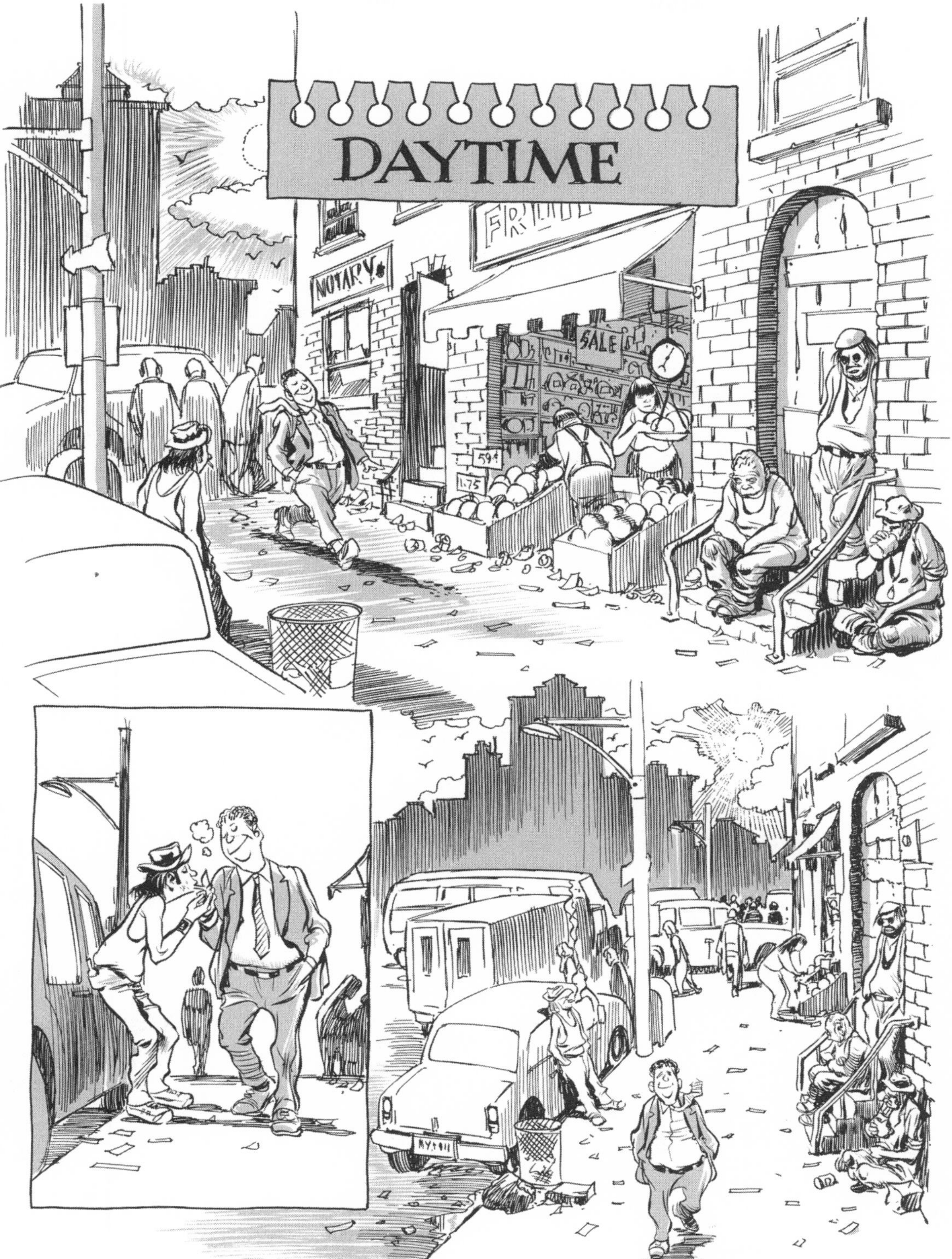

DAYTIME
NOTARY
SALE
59¢
1.75

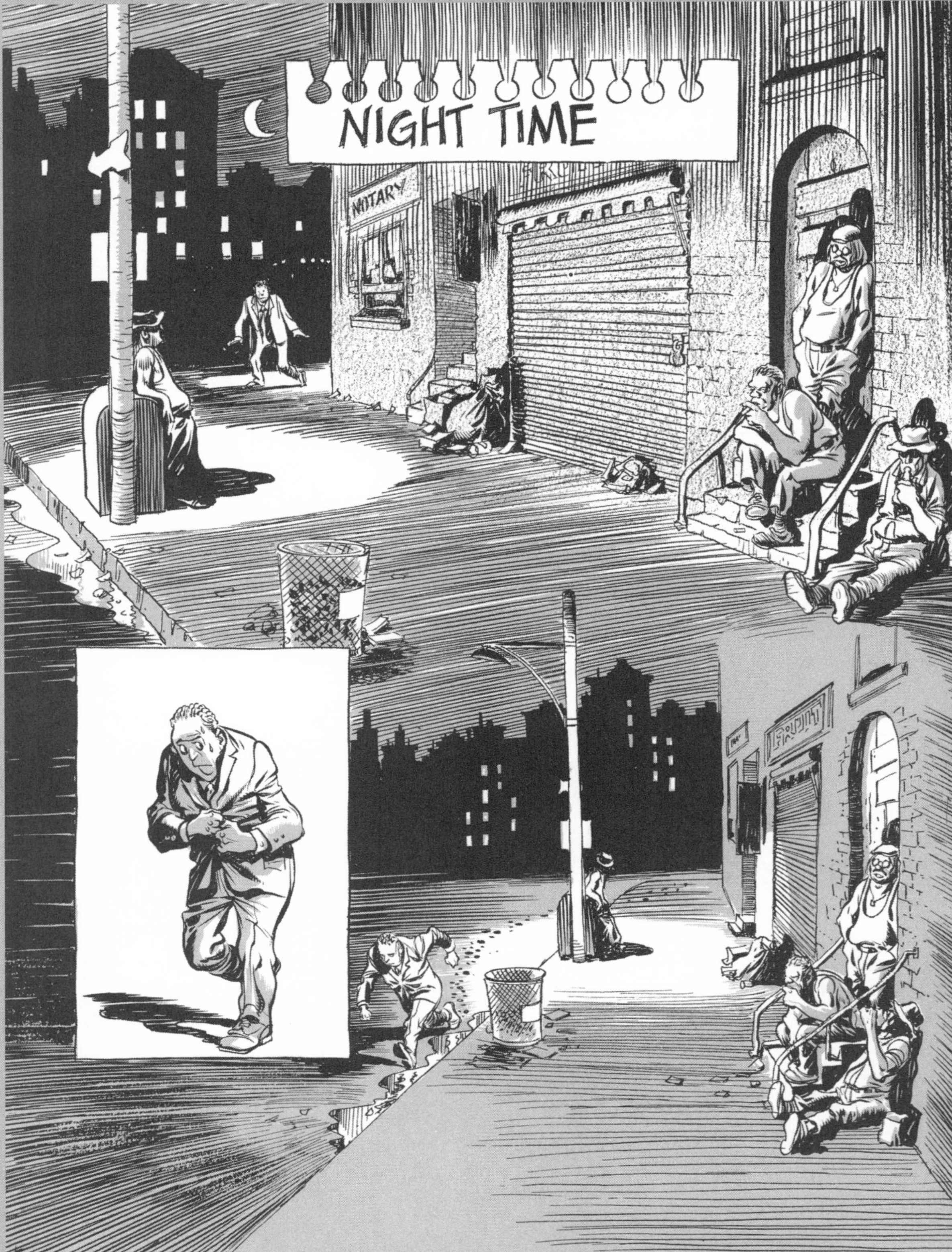
NIGHT TIME
NOTARY

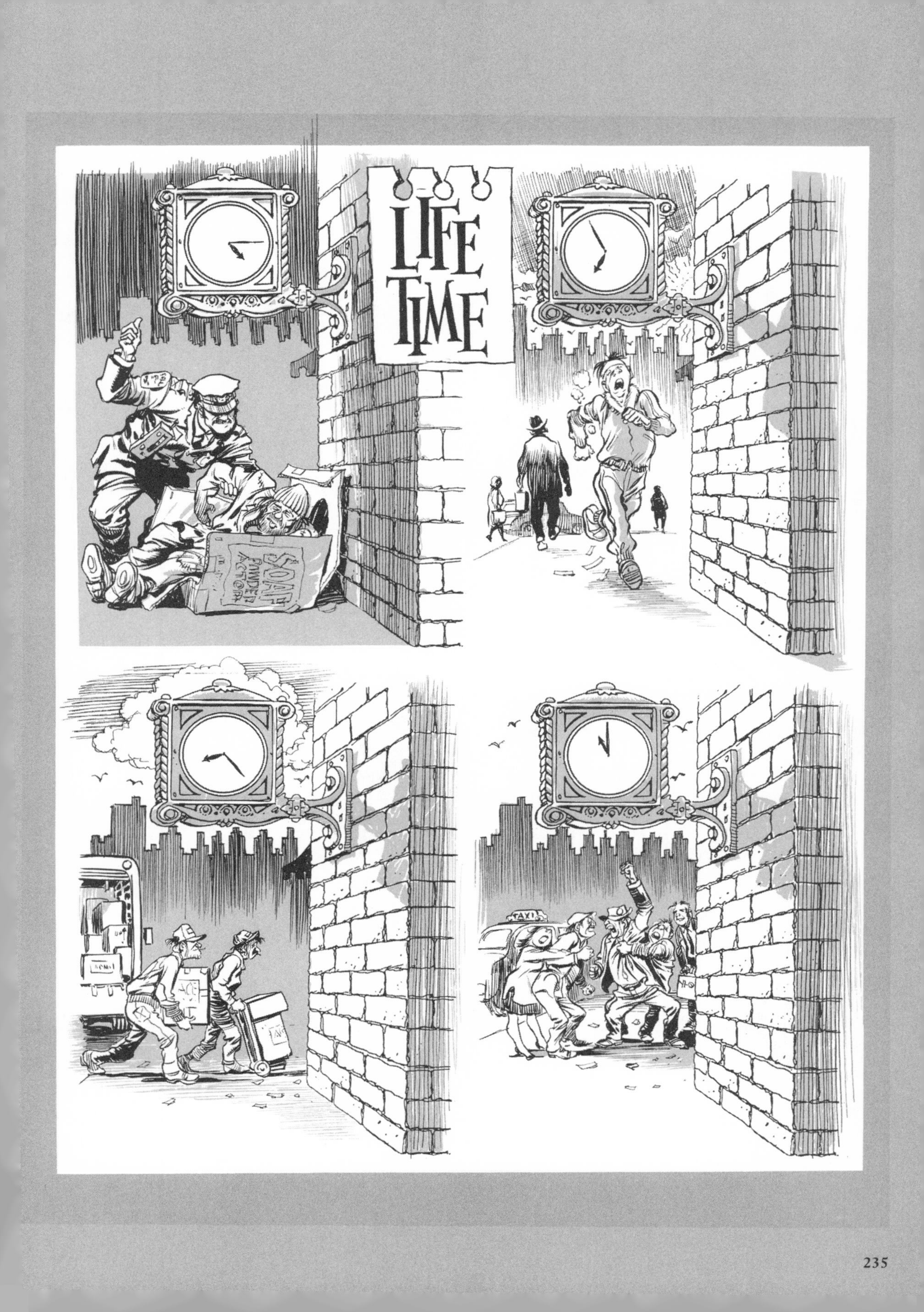
LIFE TIME
TAXI

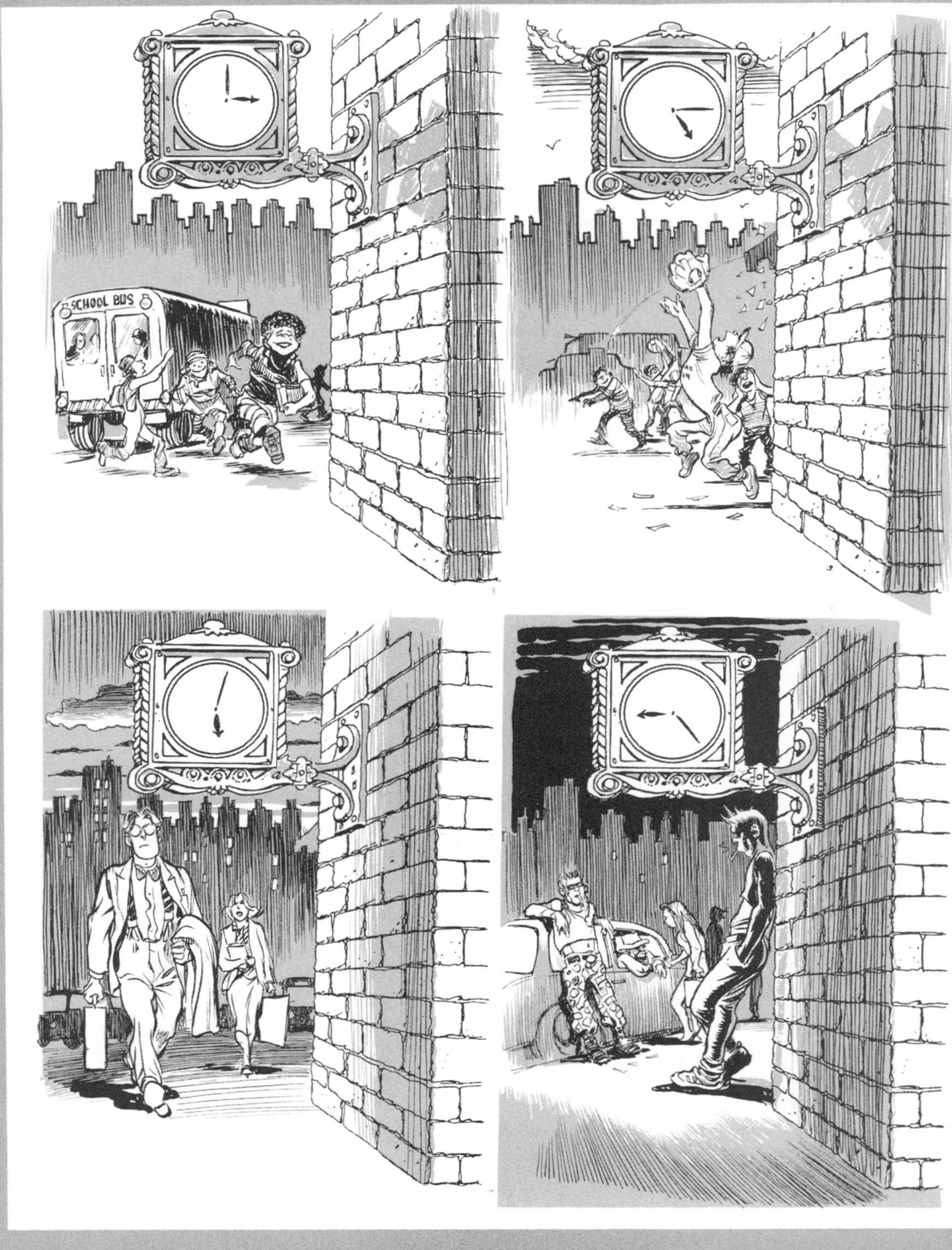
SCHOOL BUS

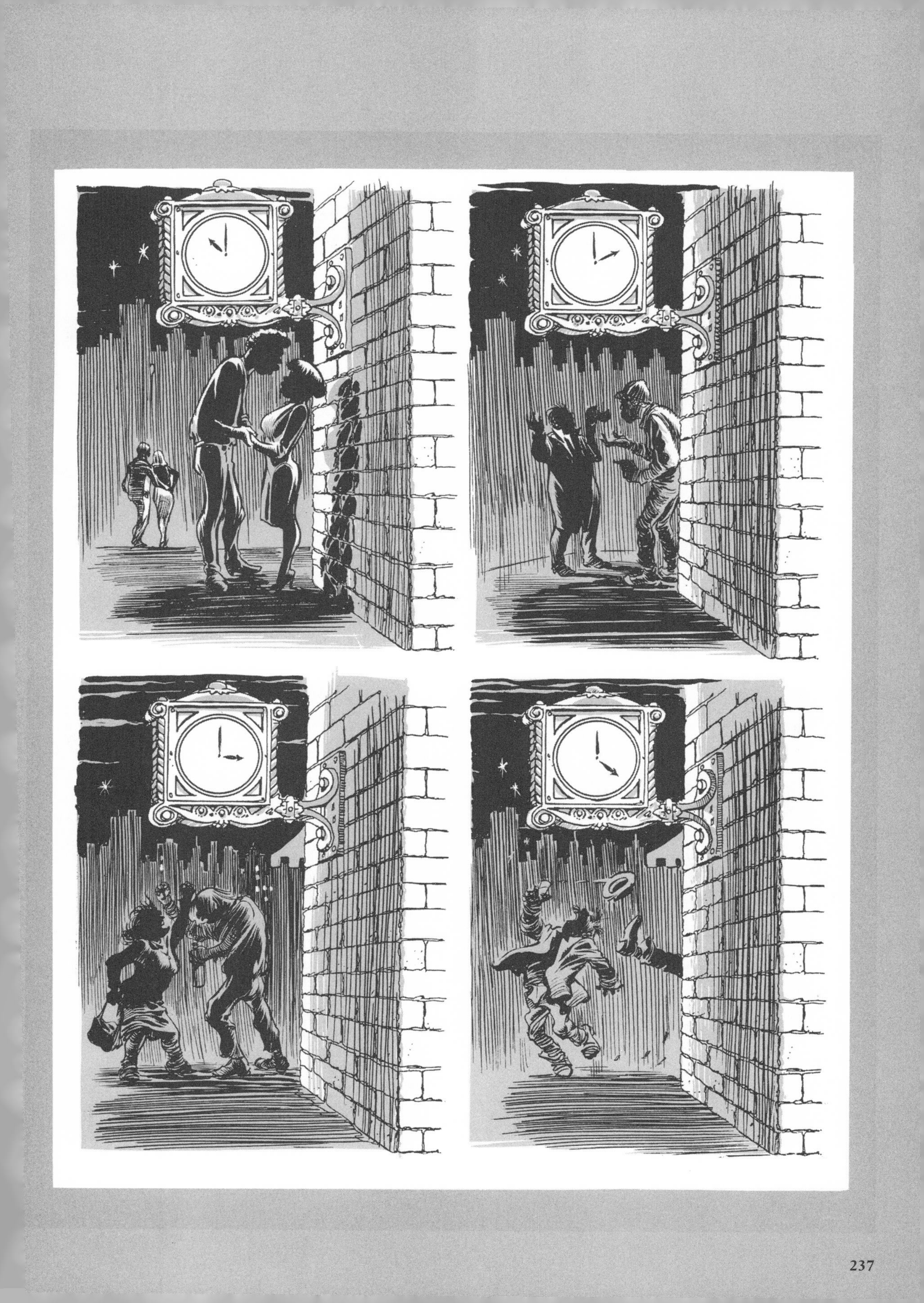

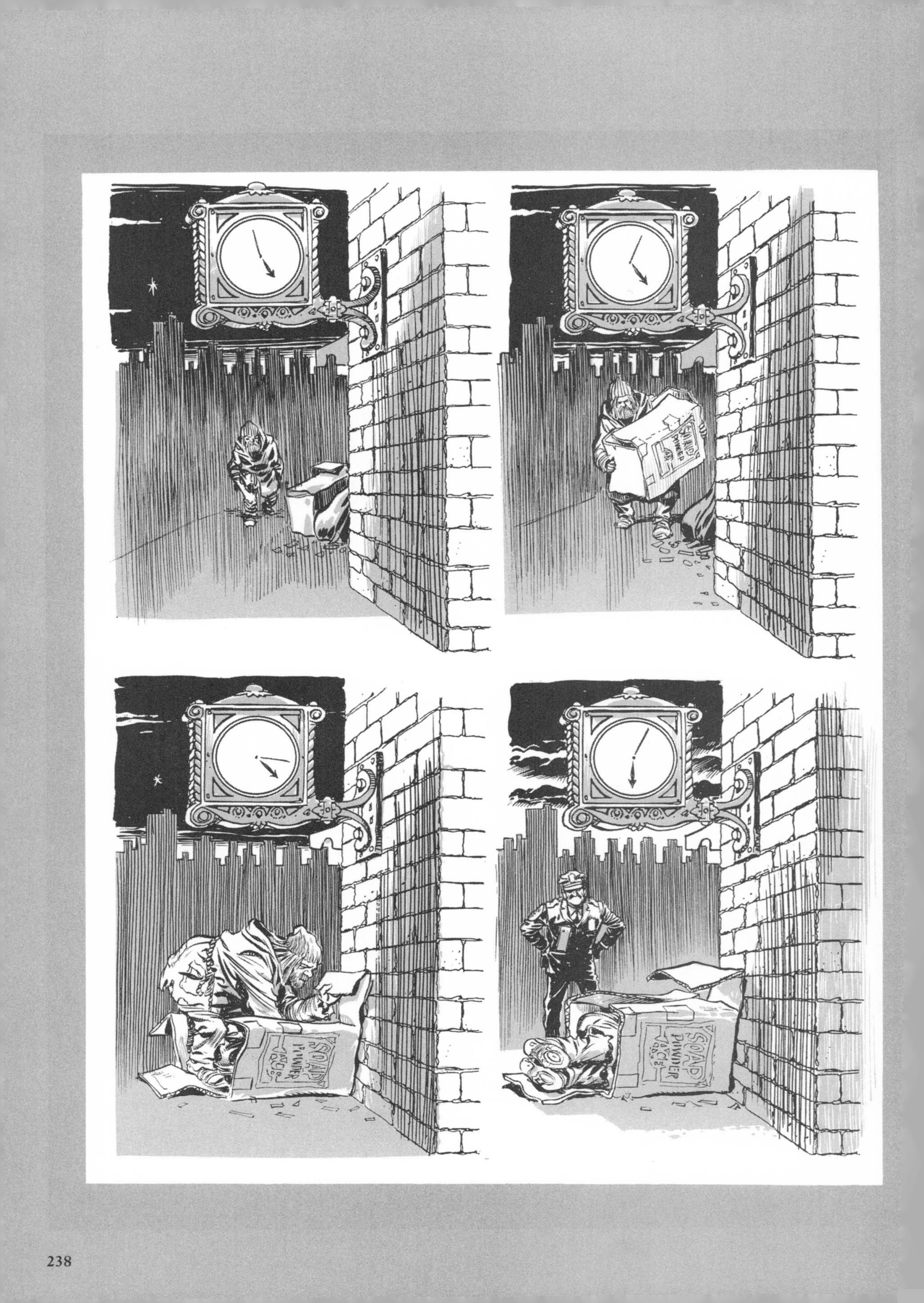
SOAP
POWDER

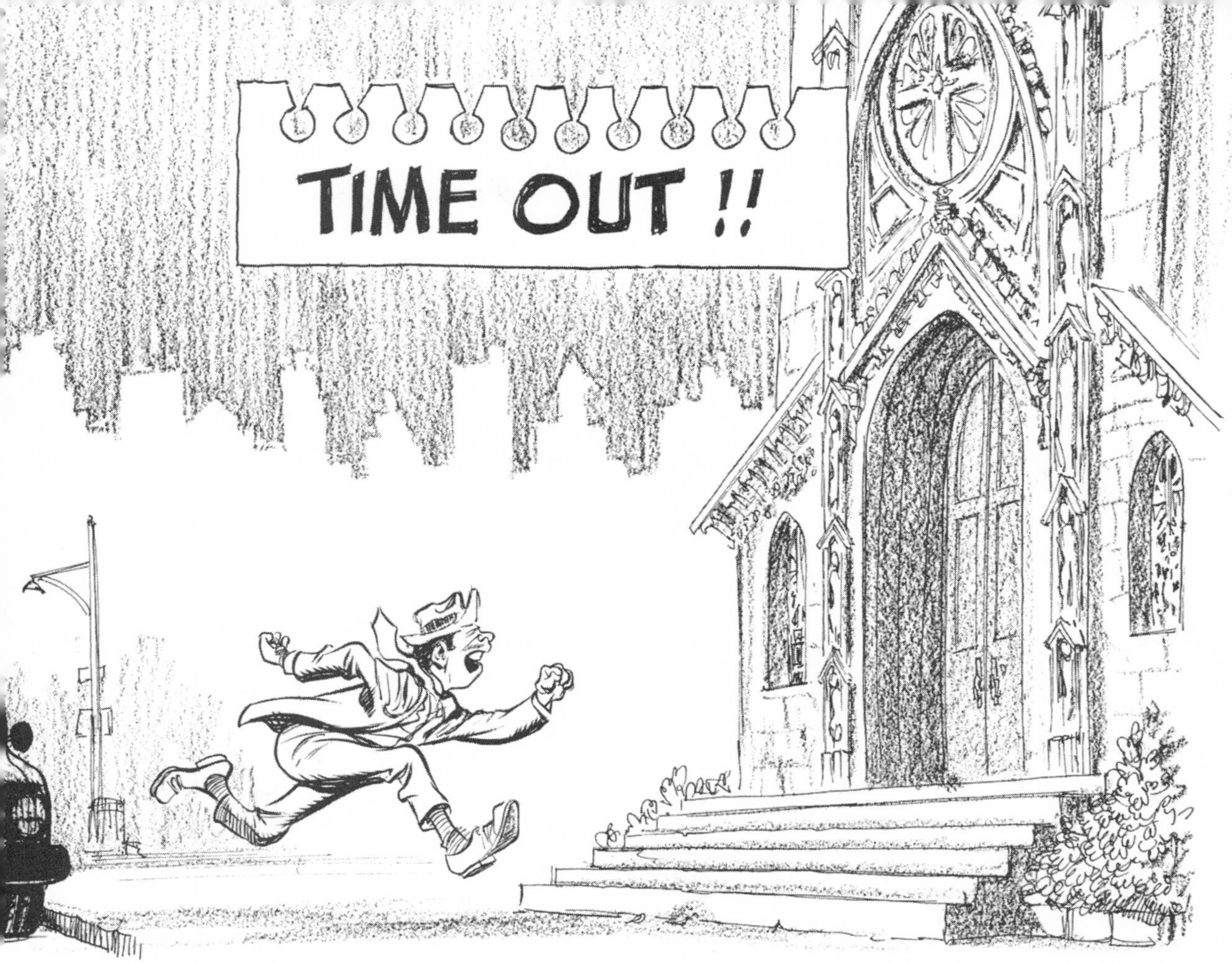
TIME OUT !!
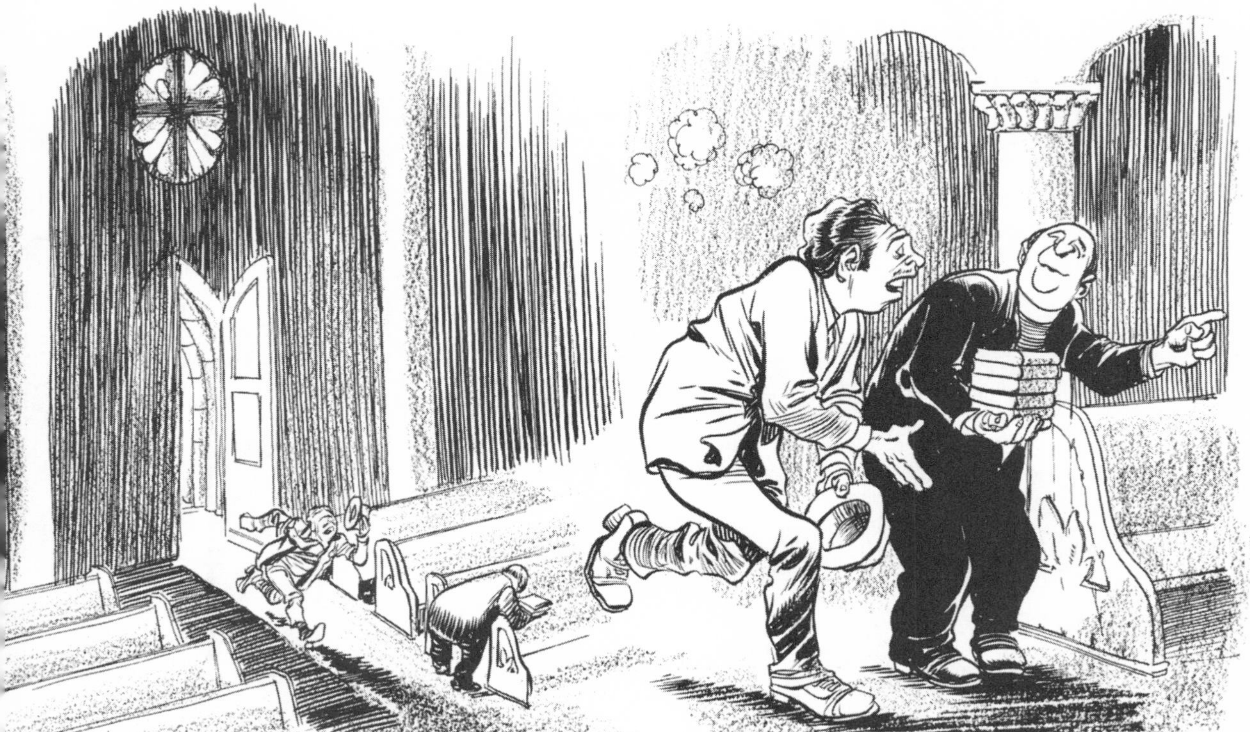

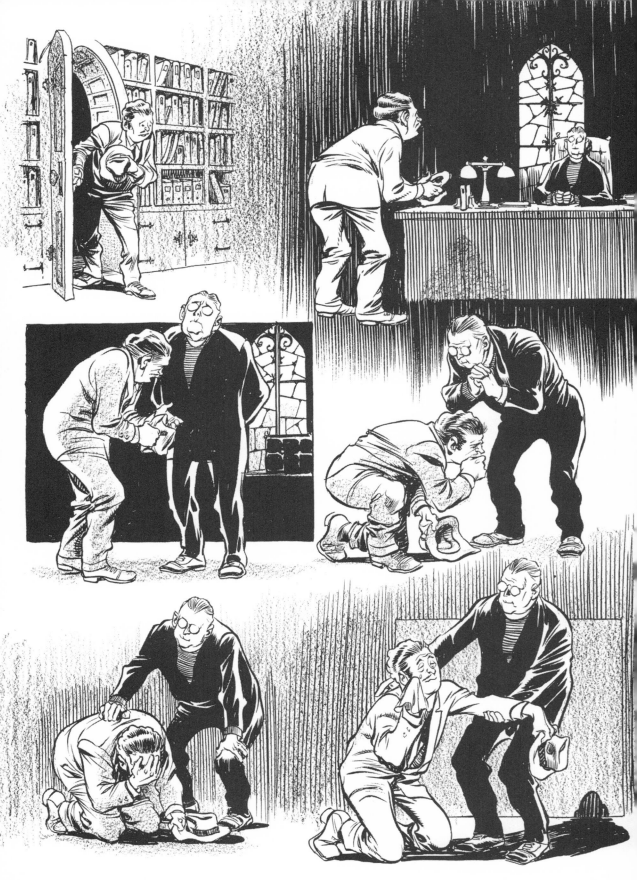

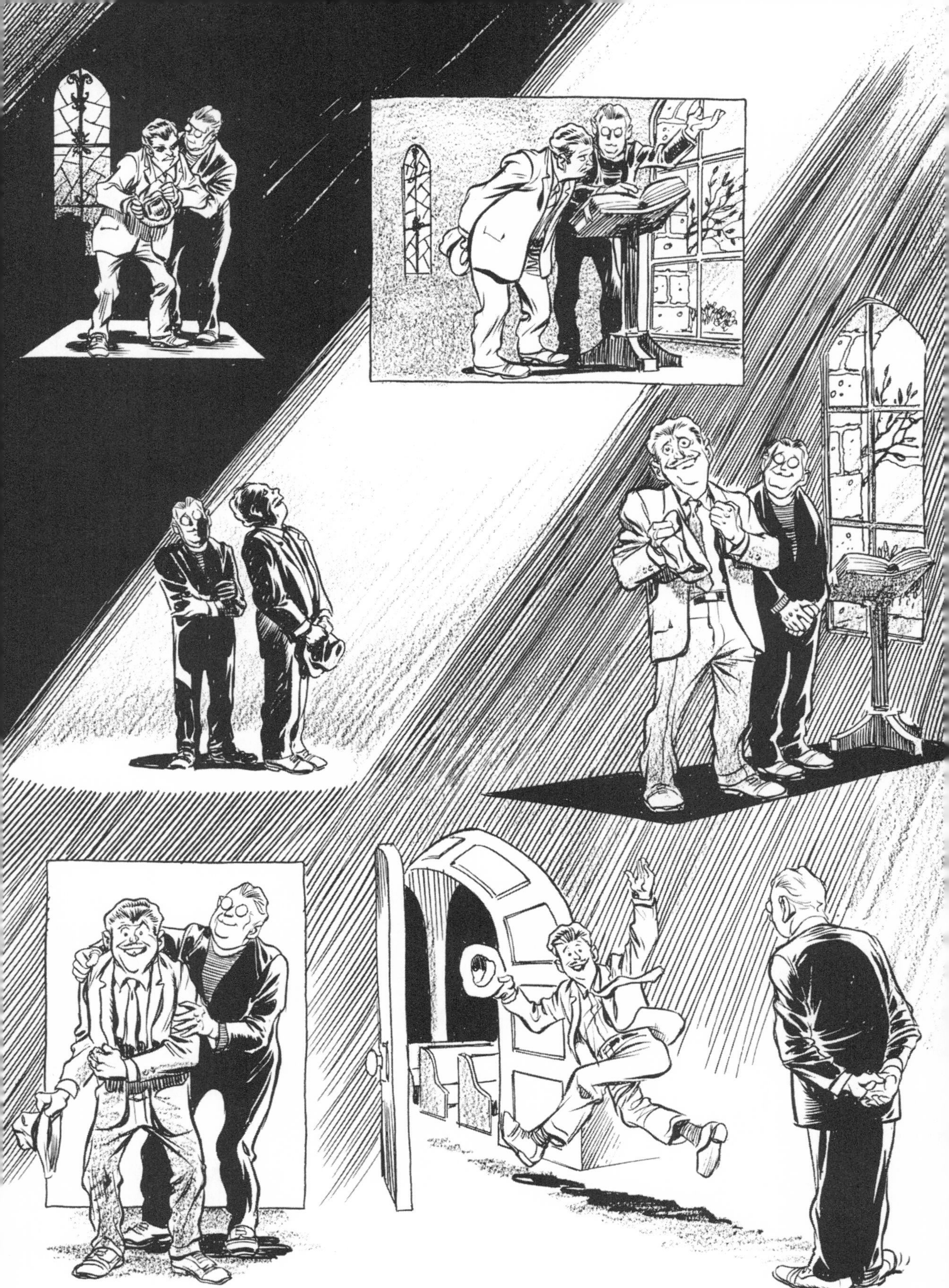

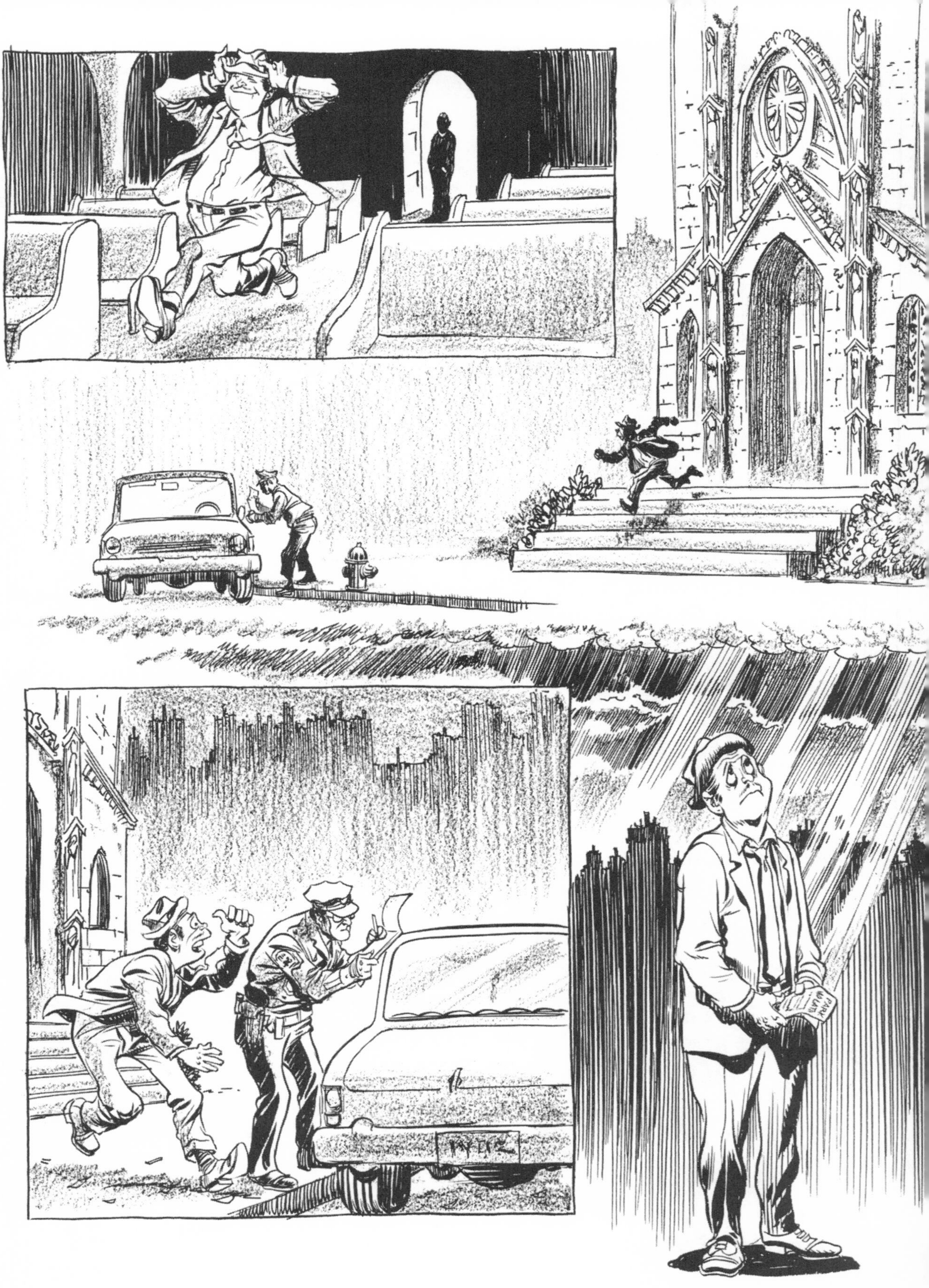
PARK

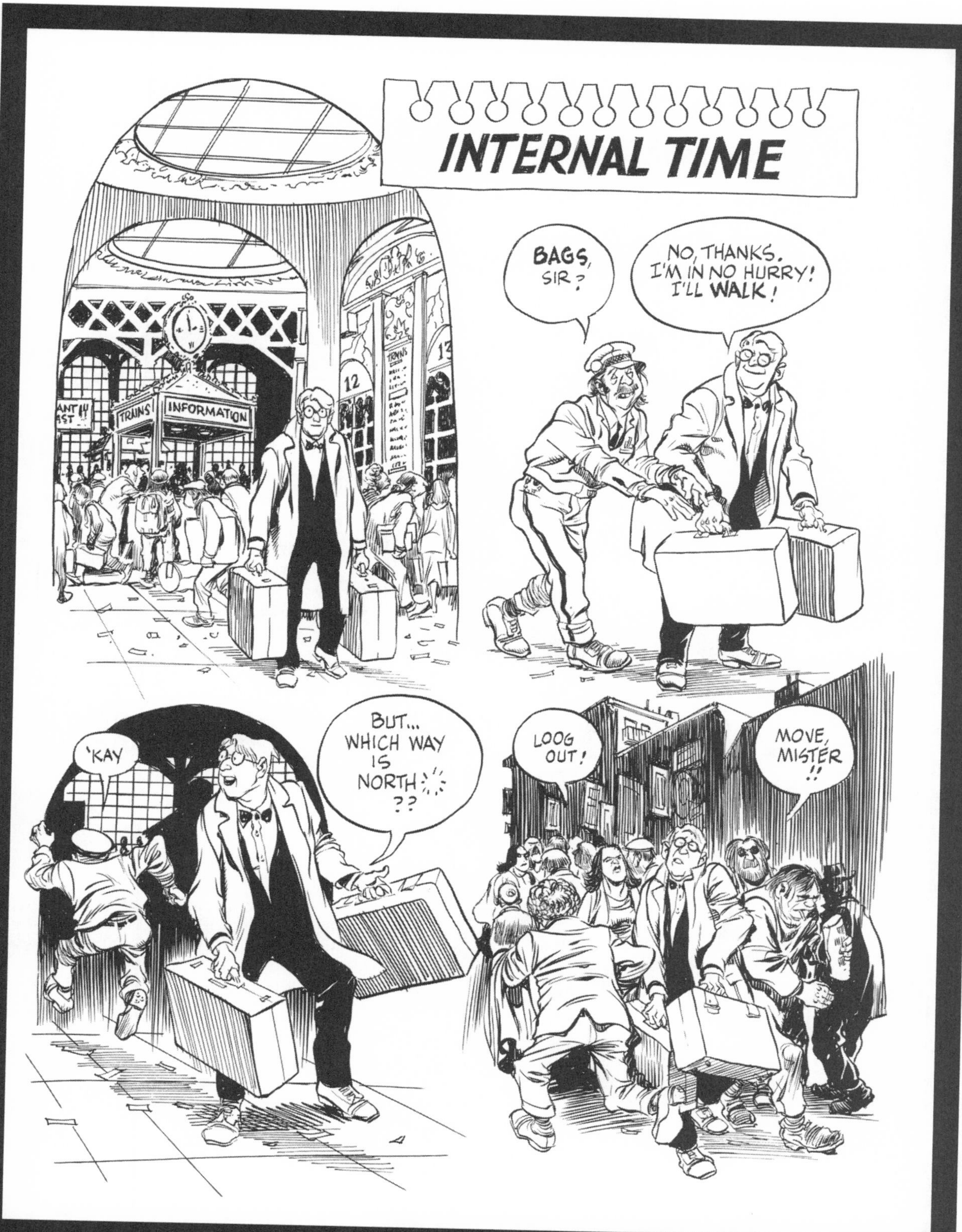
INTERNAL TIME
TRAINS
INFORMATION
12
13
BAGS, SIR?
NO, THANKS. I'M IN NO HURRY! I'LL WALK!
'KAY
BUT... WHICH WAY IS NORTH ??
LOOG OUT!
MOVE, MISTER !!

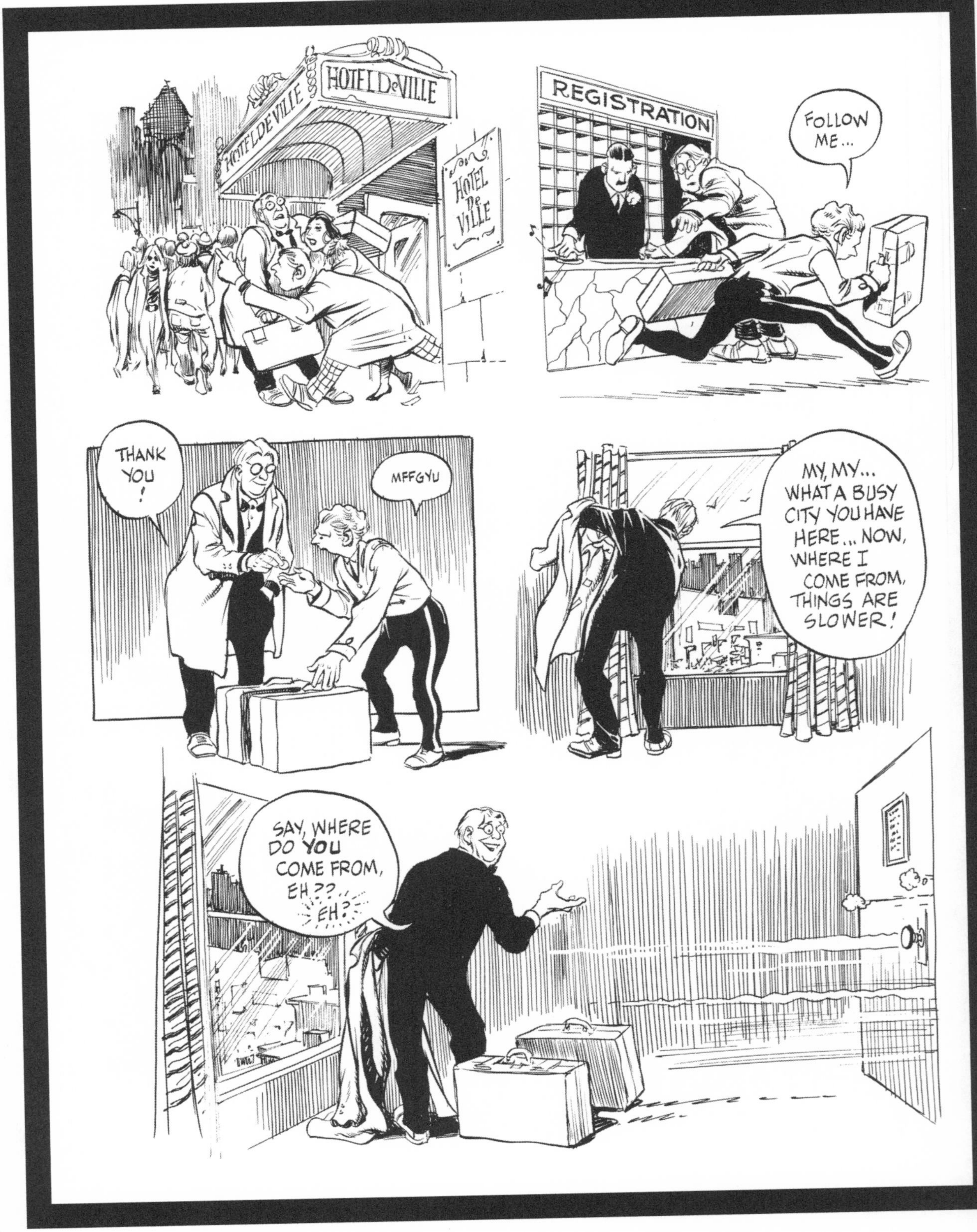
HOTEL DeVILLE
HOTEL DeVILLE
HOTEL De VILLE
REGISTRATION
FOLLOW ME...
THANK YOU!
MFFGYU
MY, MY... WHAT A BUSY CITY YOU HAVE HERE... NOW, WHERE I COME FROM, THINGS ARE SLOWER!
SAY, WHERE DO YOU COME FROM, EH??...
EH?

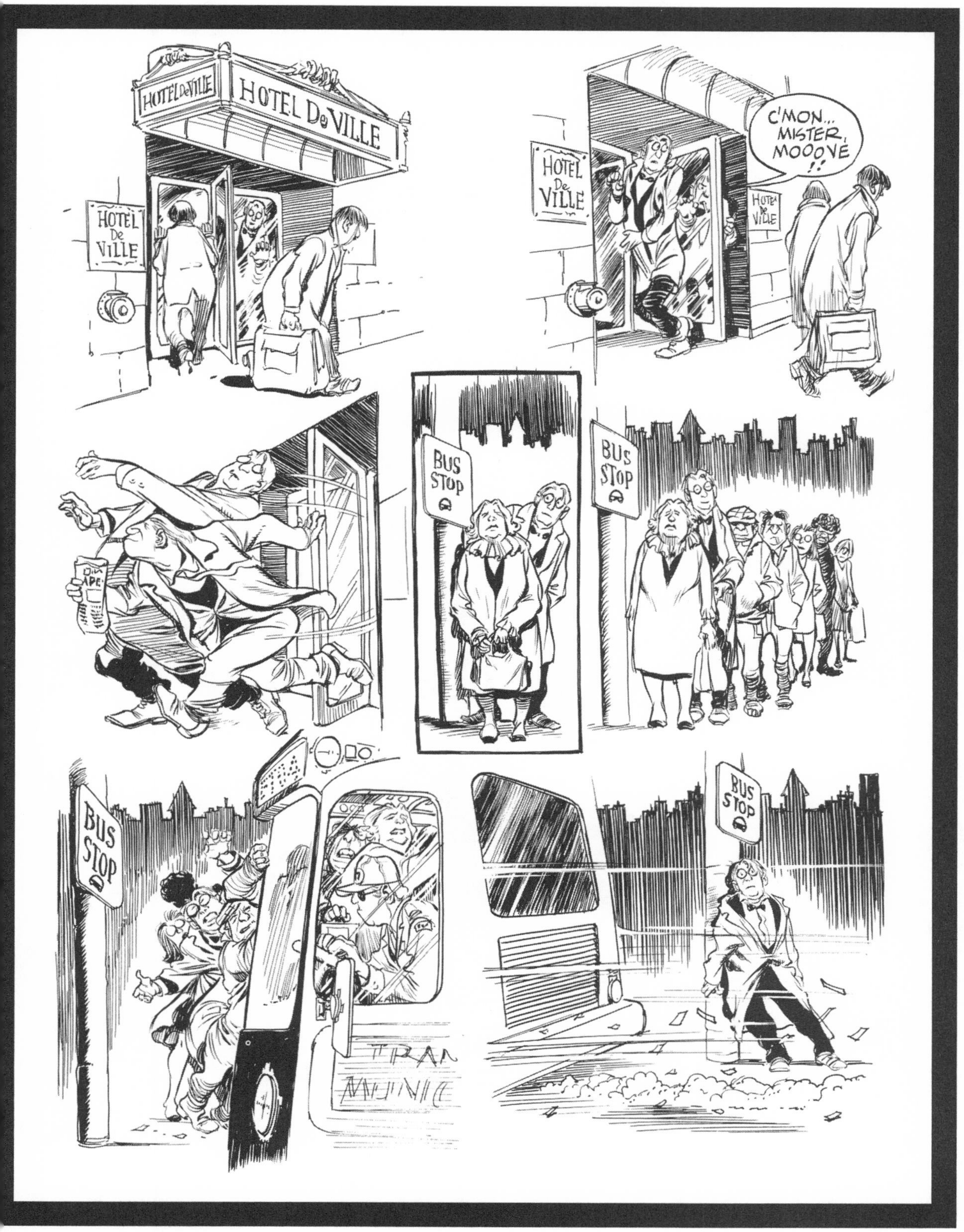
HOTEL DeVILLE
HOTEL DeVILLE
HOTEL De VILLE
HOTEL De VILLE
HOTEL De VILLE
C'MON... MISTER, MOOOVE !!
BUS STOP
BUS STOP
BUS STOP
BUS STOP

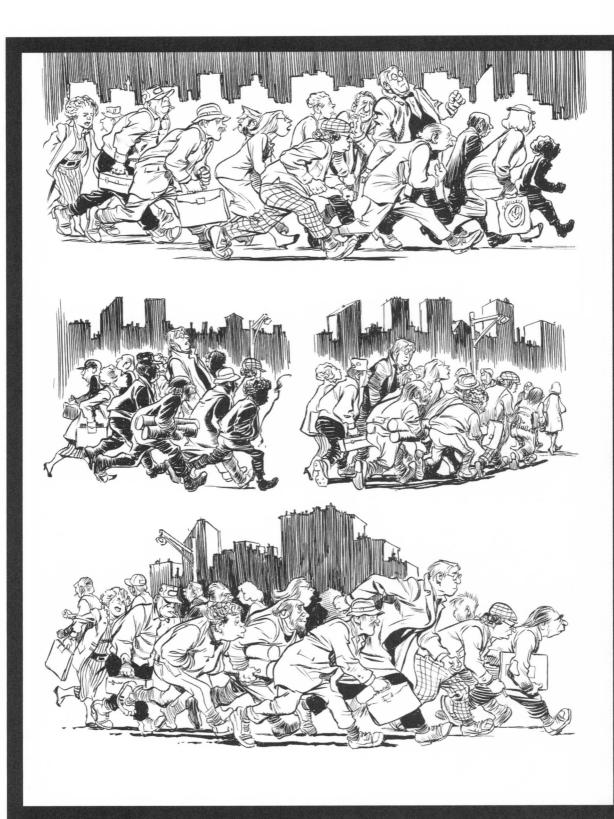

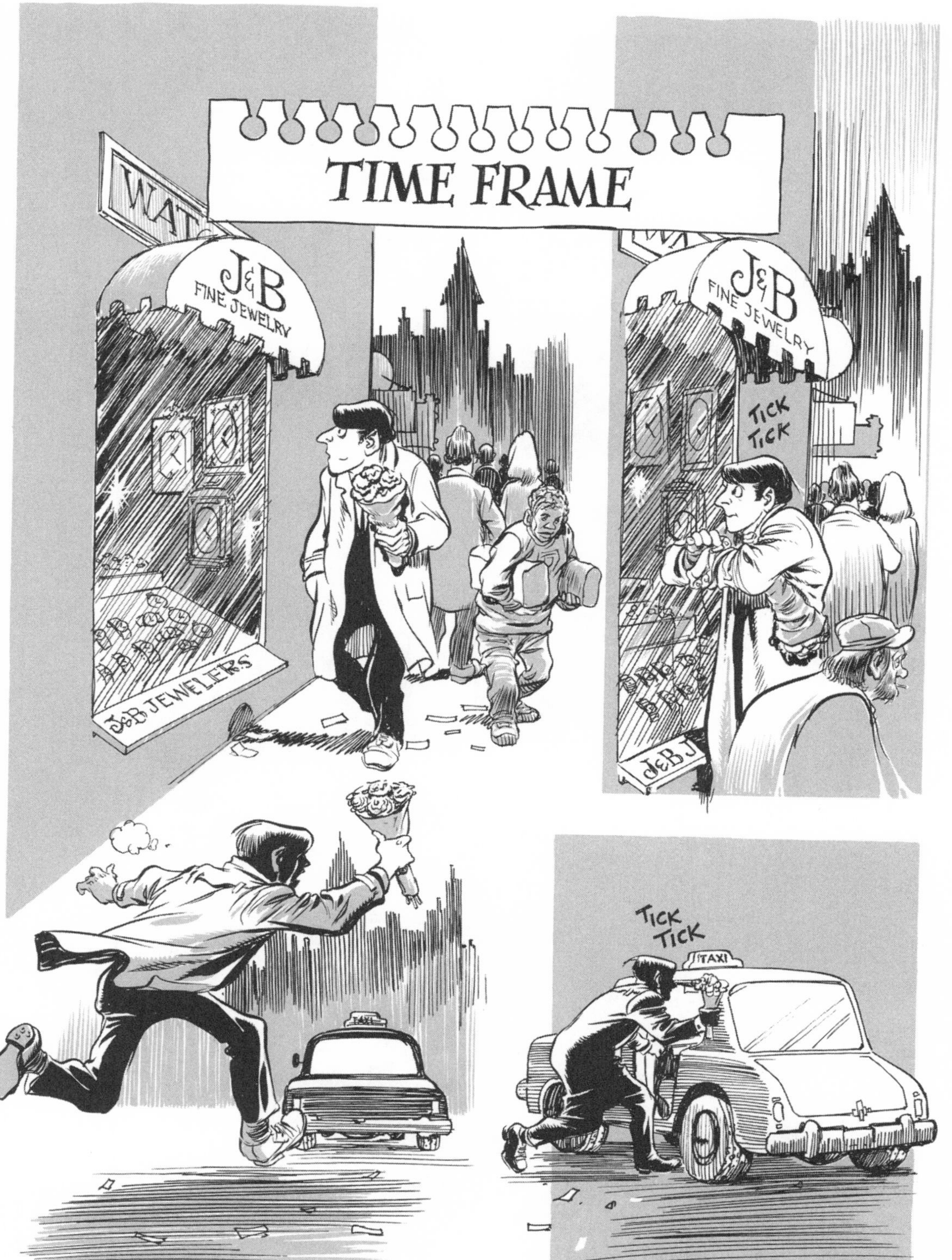
TIME FRAME
J&B FINE JEWELRY
J&B JEWELERS
J&B FINE JEWELRY
TICK TICK
TICK TICK
TAXI

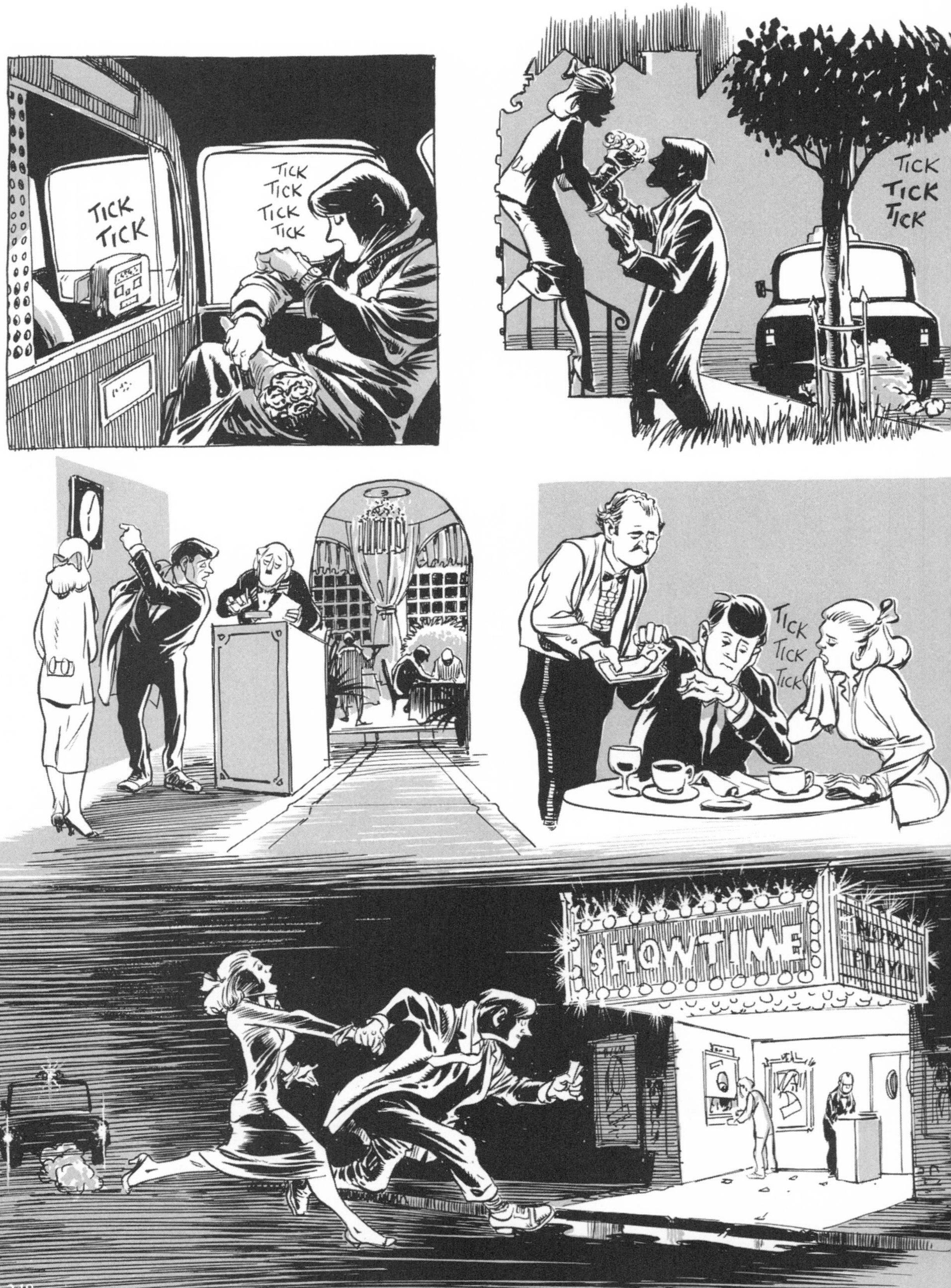
TICK TICK
TICK TICK TICK TICK
TICK TICK TICK
TICK TICK TICK
SHOWTIME

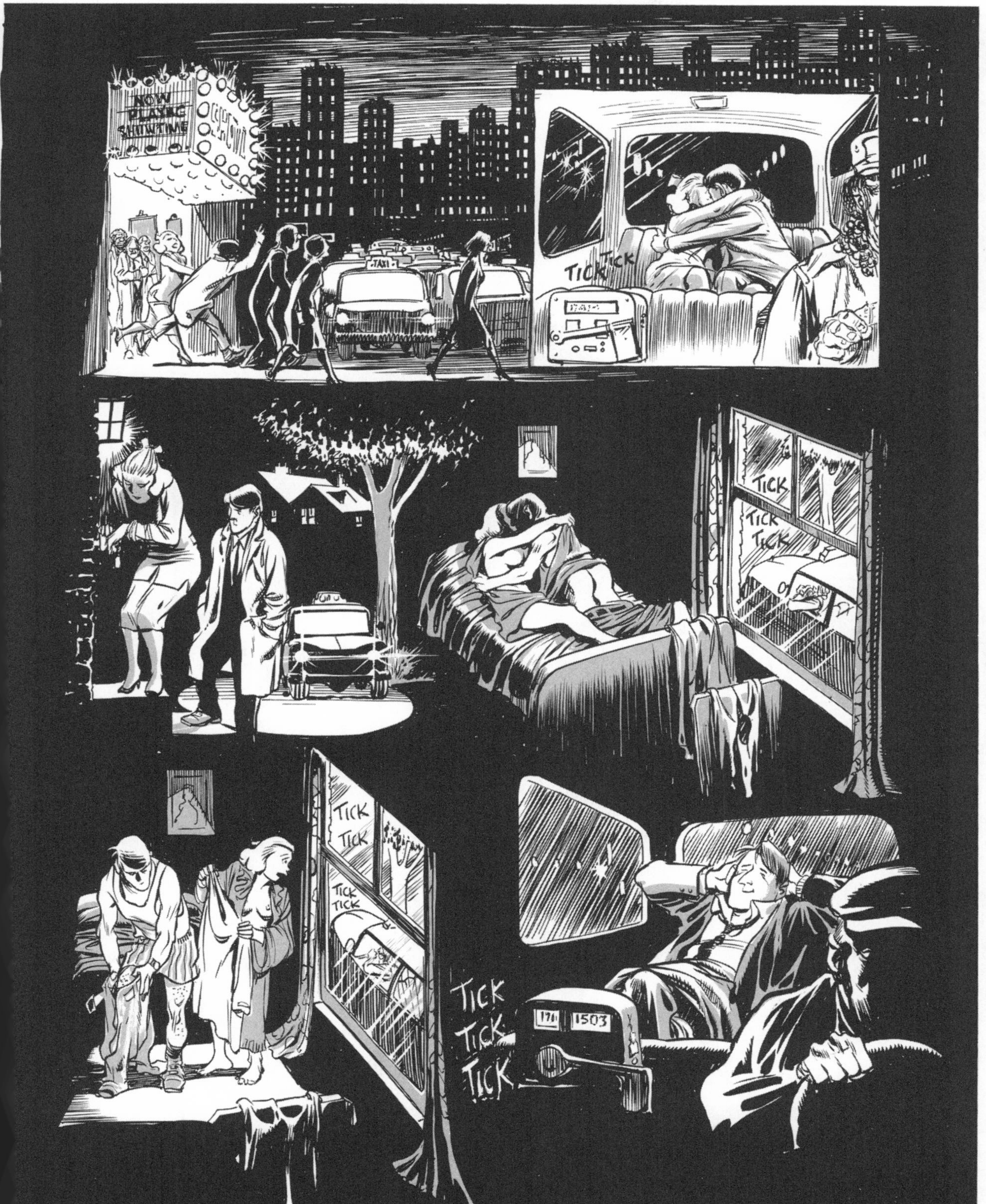
NOW PLAYING SHOWTIME
TAXI
TICK TICK
TICK
TICK
TICK
TICK
TICK
TICK TICK
TICK
TICK
TICK
1503

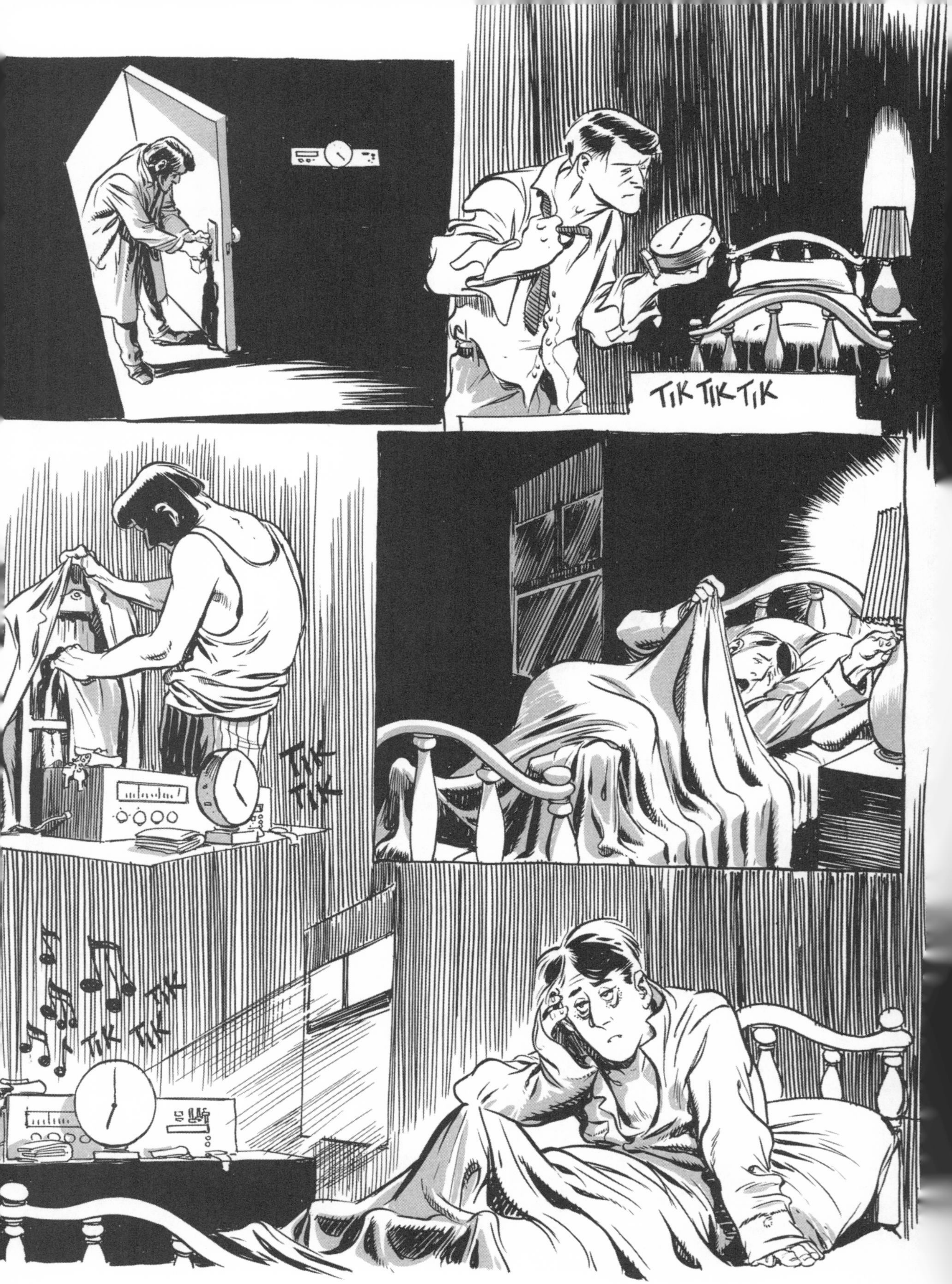
TIK TIK TIK
TIK
TIK
TIK TIK TIK

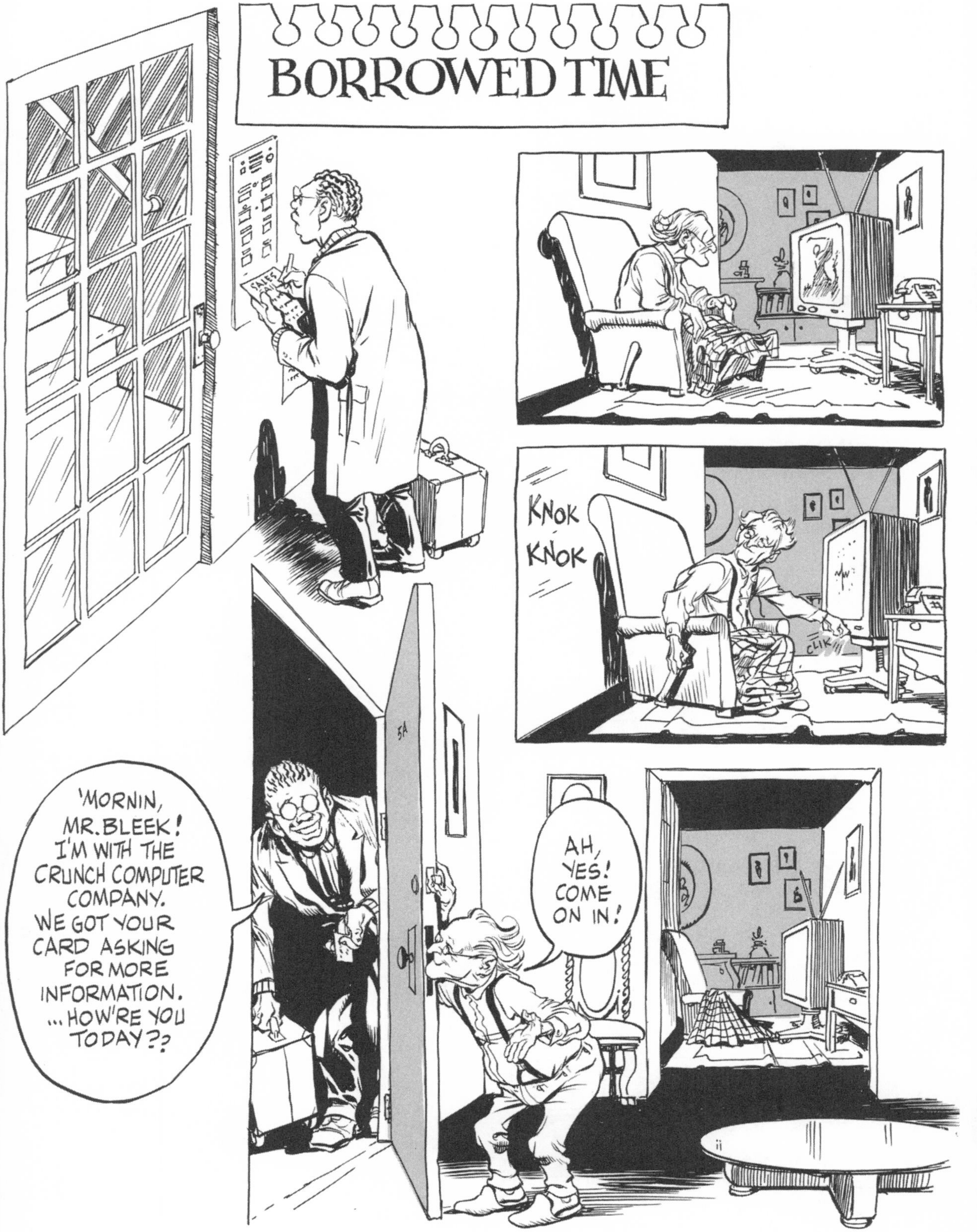
BORROWED TIME
KNOK KNOK
CLIK
'MORNIN, MR. BLEEK! I'M WITH THE CRUNCH COMPUTER COMPANY. WE GOT YOUR CARD ASKING FOR MORE INFORMATION. ...HOW'RE YOU TODAY??
AH, YES! COME ON IN!

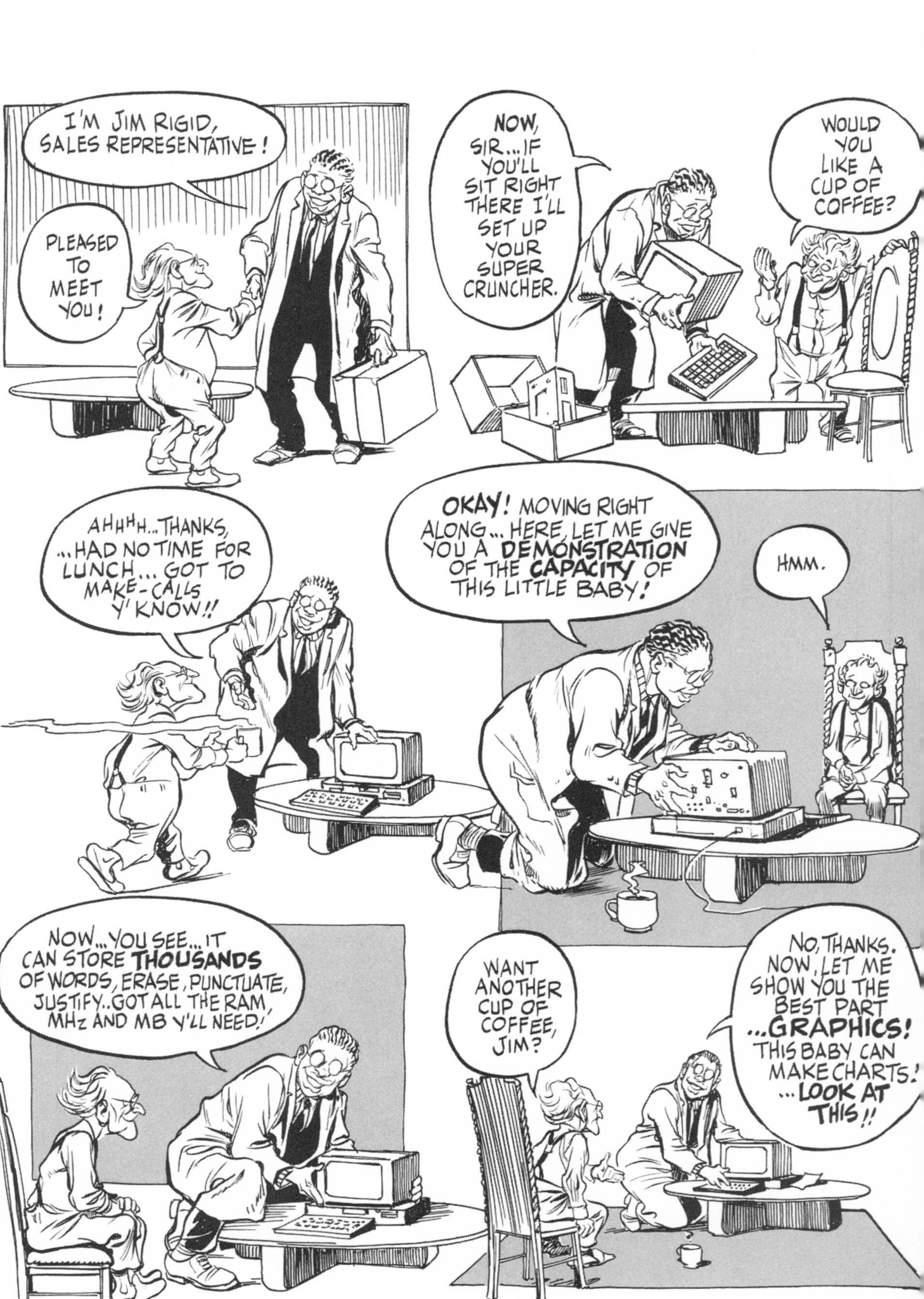
I'M JIM RIGID, SALES REPRESENTATIVE!
PLEASED TO MEET YOU!
NOW, SIR... IF YOU'LL SIT RIGHT THERE I'LL SET UP YOUR SUPER CRUNCHER.
WOULD YOU LIKE A CUP OF COFFEE?
AHHHH... THANKS, ...HAD NO TIME FOR LUNCH... GOT TO MAKE-CALLS Y' KNOW!!
OKAY! MOVING RIGHT ALONG... HERE, LET ME GIVE YOU A DEMONSTRATION OF THE CAPACITY OF THIS LITTLE BABY!
HMM.
NOW... YOU SEE... IT CAN STORE THOUSANDS OF WORDS, ERASE, PUNCTUATE, JUSTIFY.. GOT ALL THE RAM, MHz AND MB Y'LL NEED!
WANT ANOTHER CUP OF COFFEE, JIM?
NO, THANKS. NOW, LET ME SHOW YOU THE BEST PART ...GRAPHICS! THIS BABY CAN MAKE CHARTS! ...LOOK AT THIS!!

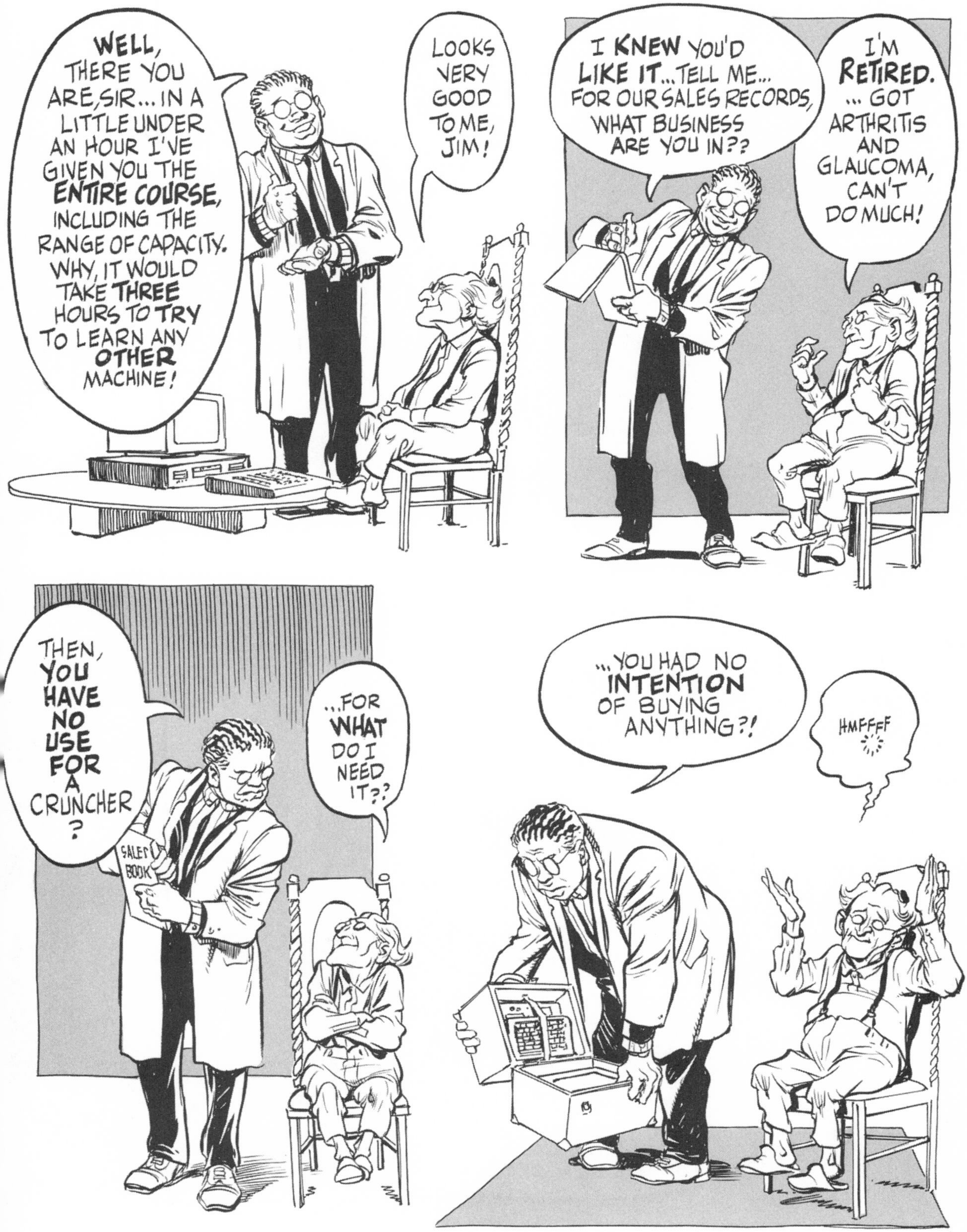
WELL, THERE YOU ARE, SIR... IN A LITTLE UNDER AN HOUR I'VE GIVEN YOU THE ENTIRE COURSE, INCLUDING THE RANGE OF CAPACITY. WHY, IT WOULD TAKE THREE HOURS TO TRY TO LEARN ANY OTHER MACHINE!
LOOKS VERY GOOD TO ME, JIM!
I KNEW YOU'D LIKE IT... TELL ME... FOR OUR SALES RECORDS, WHAT BUSINESS ARE YOU IN??
I'M RETIRED. ... GOT ARTHRITIS AND GLAUCOMA, CAN'T DO MUCH!
THEN, YOU HAVE NO USE FOR A CRUNCHER?
...FOR WHAT DO I NEED IT??
SALES BOOK
...YOU HAD NO INTENTION OF BUYING ANYTHING?!
HMFFFF

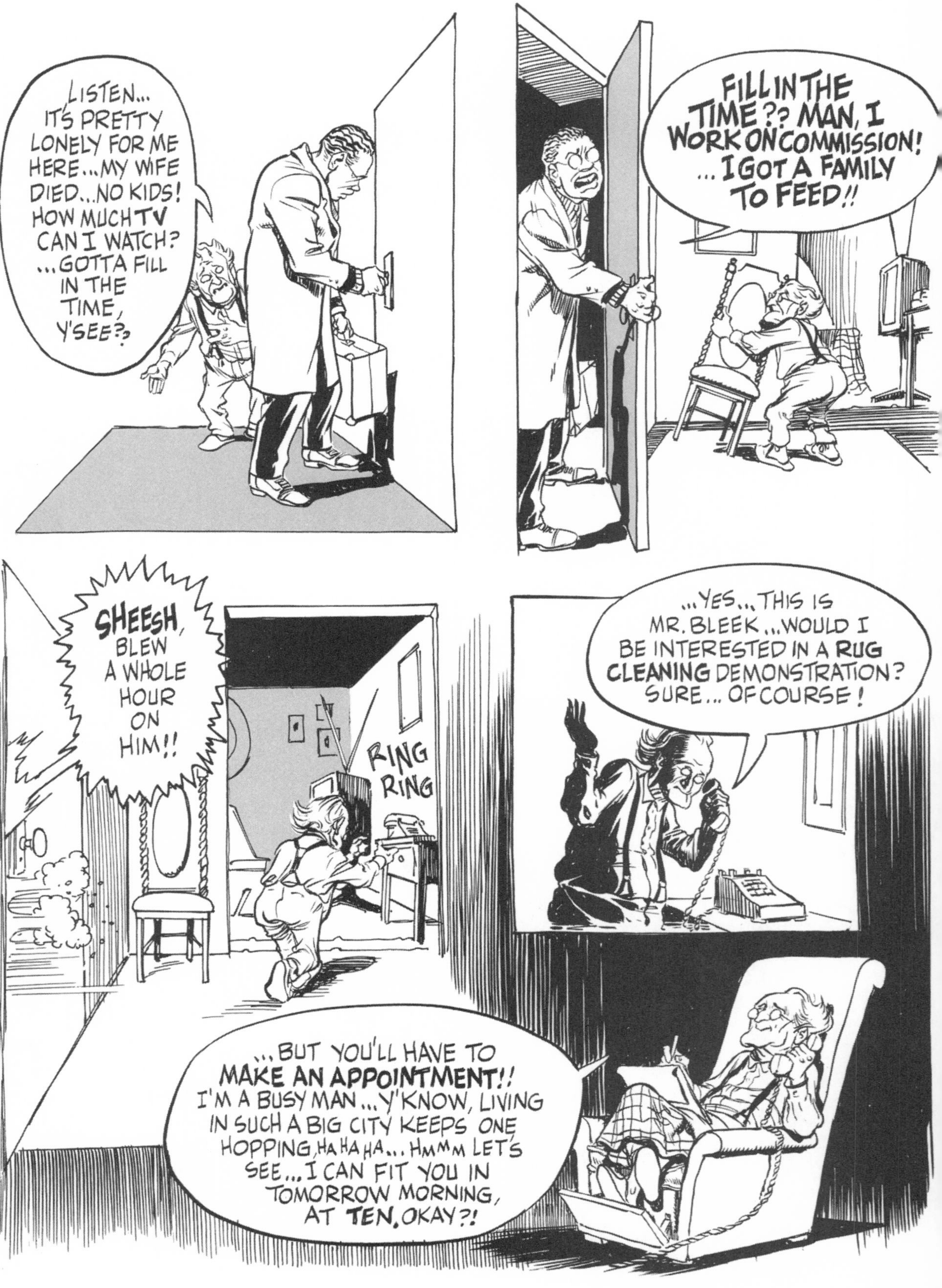
LISTEN... IT'S PRETTY LONELY FOR ME HERE... MY WIFE DIED... NO KIDS! HOW MUCH TV CAN I WATCH? ...GOTTA FILL IN THE TIME, Y'SEE?>
FILL IN THE TIME?? MAN, I WORK ON COMMISSION! ...I GOT A FAMILY TO FEED!!
SHEESH, BLEW A WHOLE HOUR ON HIM!!
RING RING
...YES... THIS IS MR. BLEEK... WOULD I BE INTERESTED IN A RUG CLEANING DEMONSTRATION? SURE... OF COURSE!
...BUT YOU'LL HAVE TO MAKE AN APPOINTMENT!! I'M A BUSY MAN... Y'KNOW, LIVING IN SUCH A BIG CITY KEEPS ONE HOPPING, HA HA HA... HMMM LET'S SEE... I CAN FIT YOU IN TOMORROW MORNING, AT TEN, OKAY?!

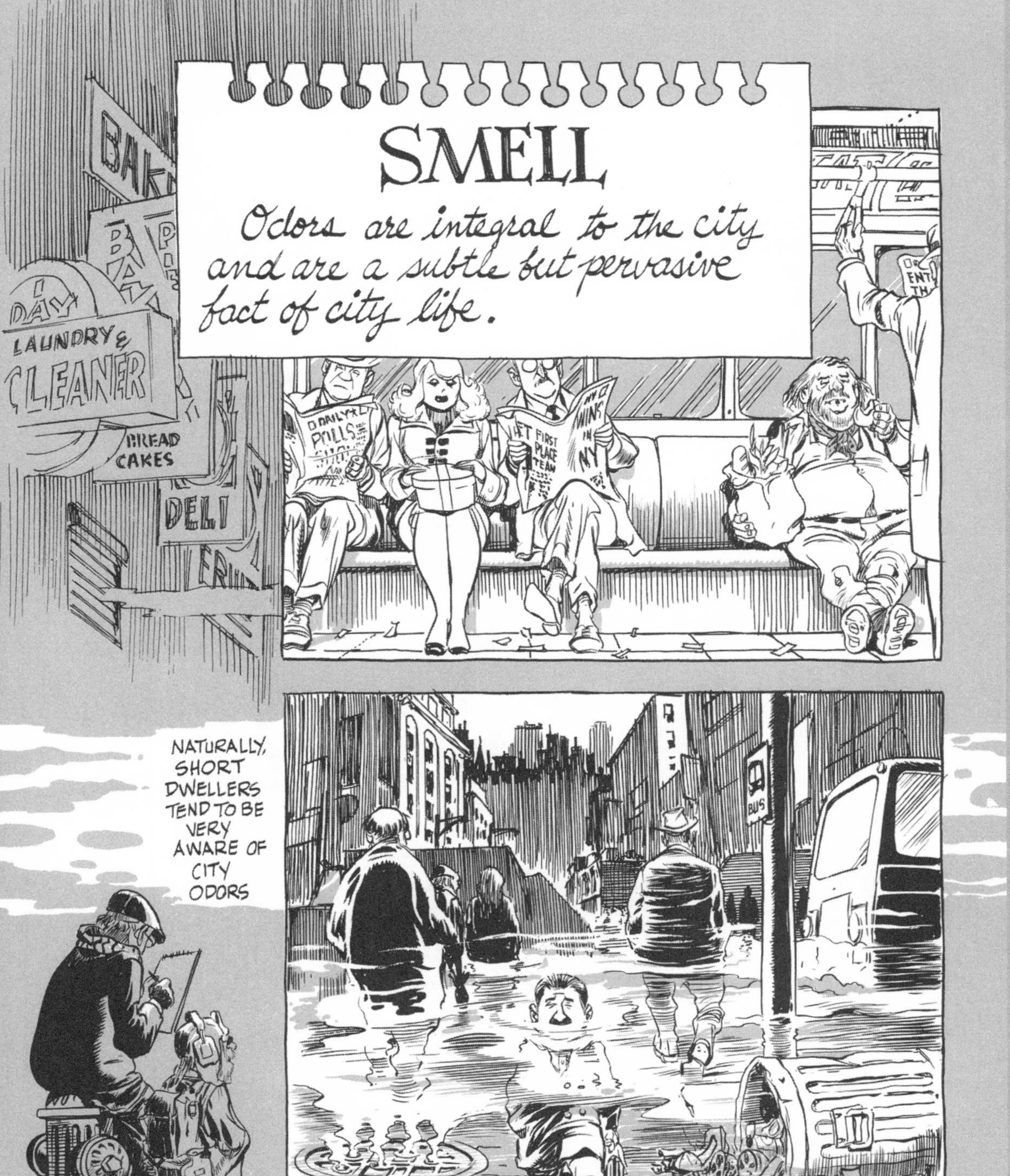
SMELL
Odors are integral to the city and are a subtle but pervasive fact of city life.
1 DAY LAUNDRY & CLEANER
BREAD CAKES
DELI
DAILY POLLS
FIRST PLACE TEAM
MINS IN NY
NATURALLY, SHORT DWELLERS TEND TO BE VERY AWARE OF CITY ODORS
BUS

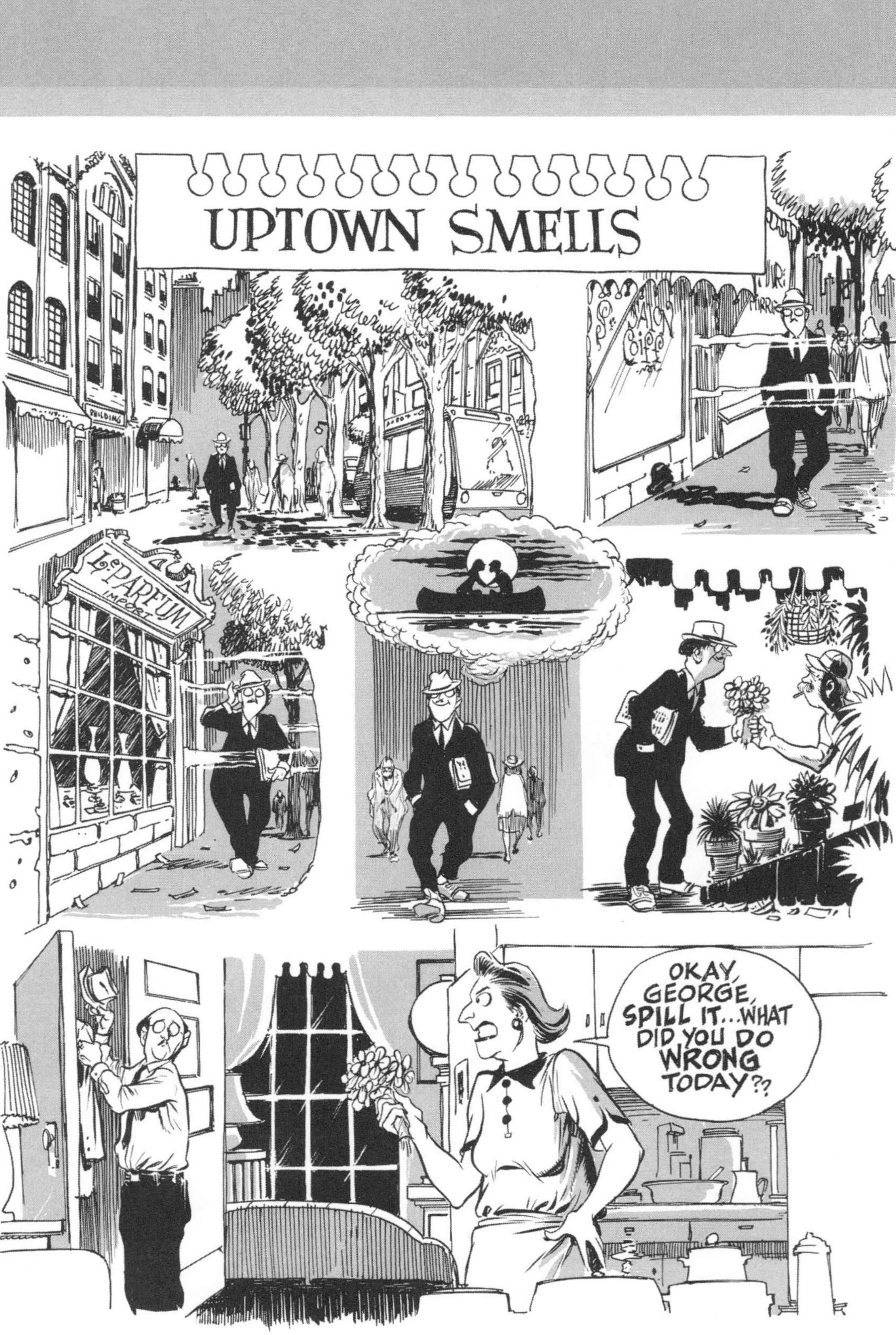
UPTOWN SMELLS
BUILDING
LE PARFUM IMPORT
OKAY, GEORGE, SPILL IT...WHAT DID YOU DO WRONG TODAY??

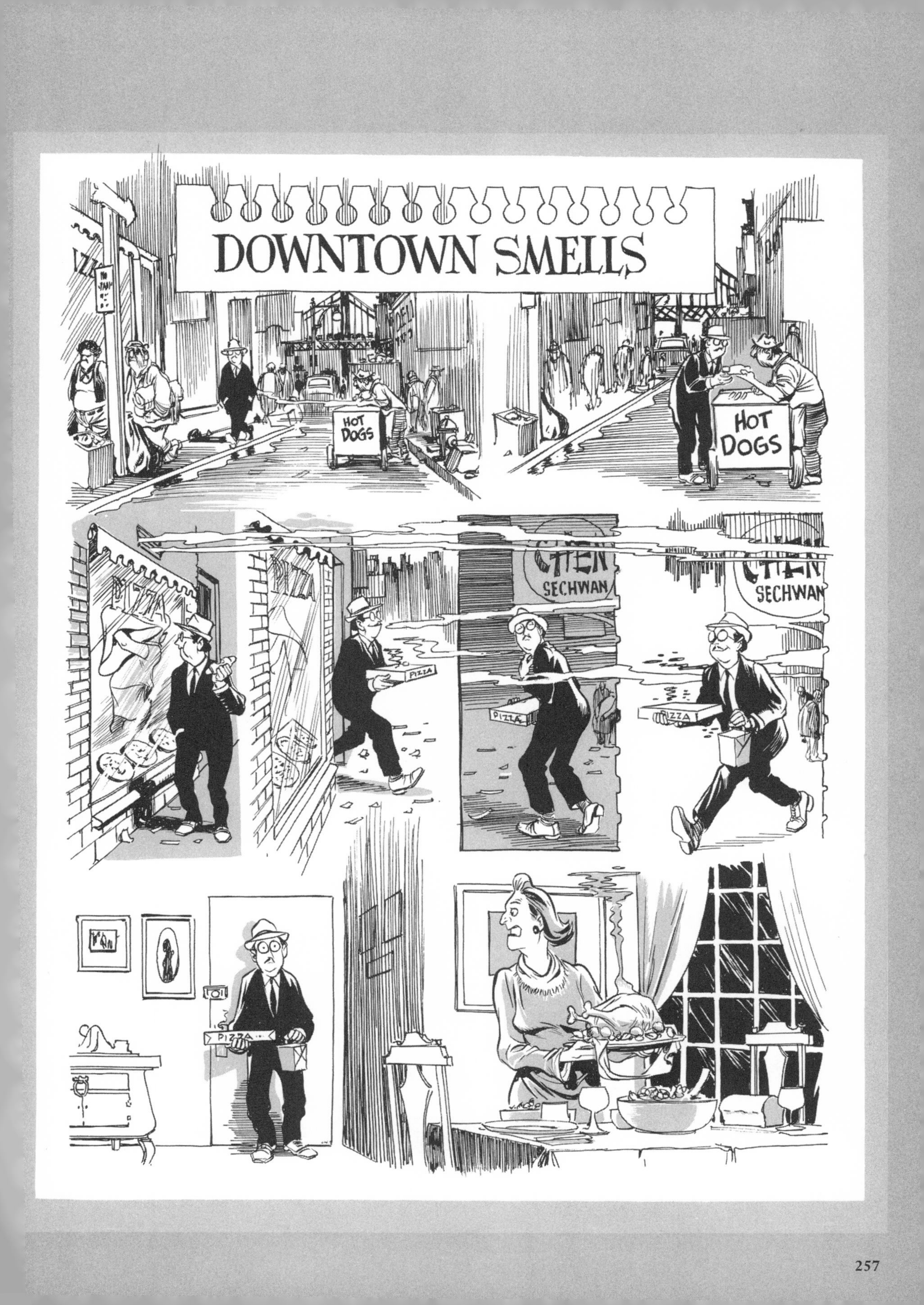
DOWNTOWN SMELLS
HOT DOGS
HOT DOGS
PIZZA
PIZZA
CHEN
SECHWAN
CHEN
SECHWAN
PIZZA
PIZZA
PIZZA
PIZZA

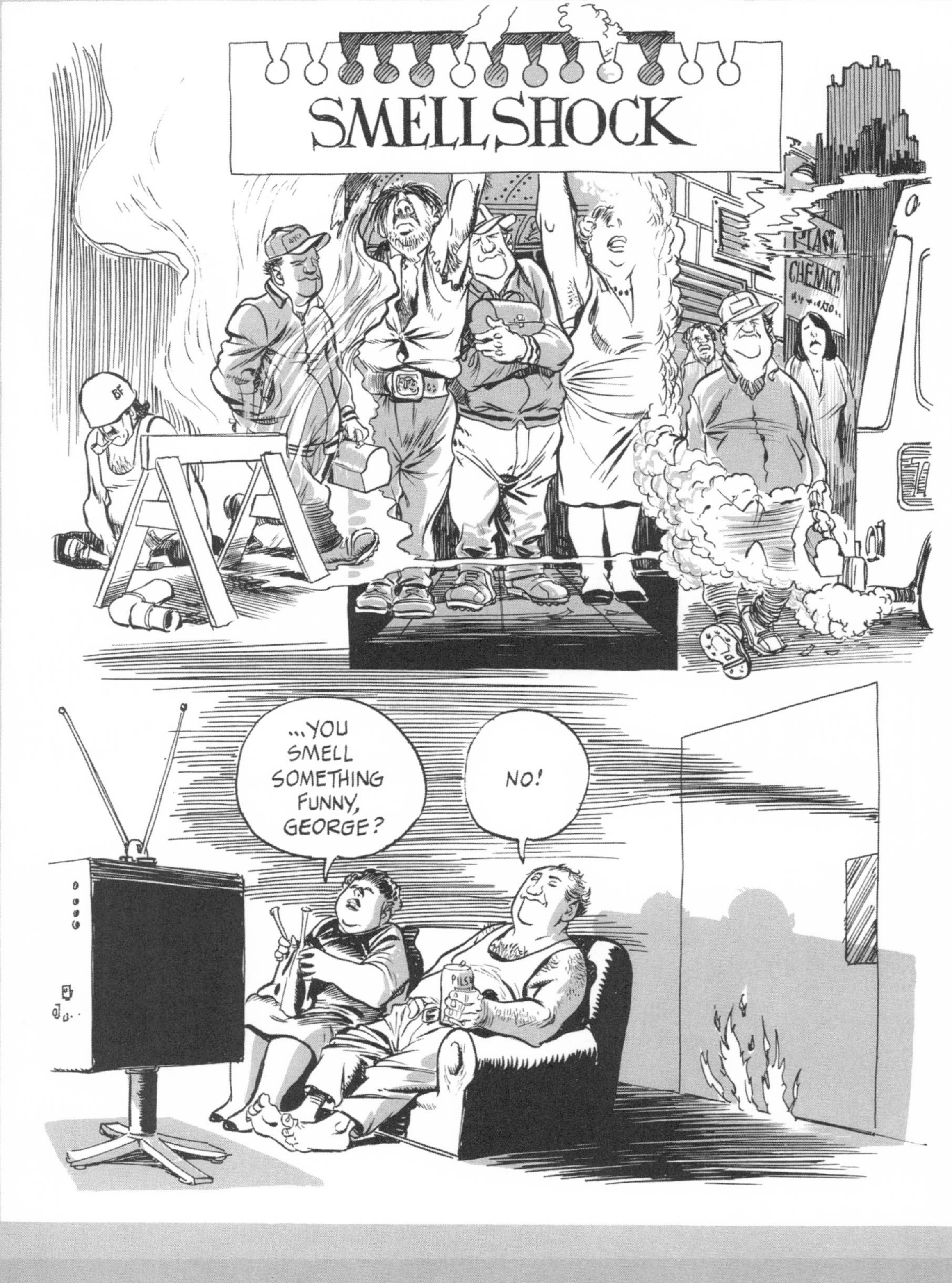
SMELLSHOCK
...YOU SMELL SOMETHING FUNNY, GEORGE?
NO!

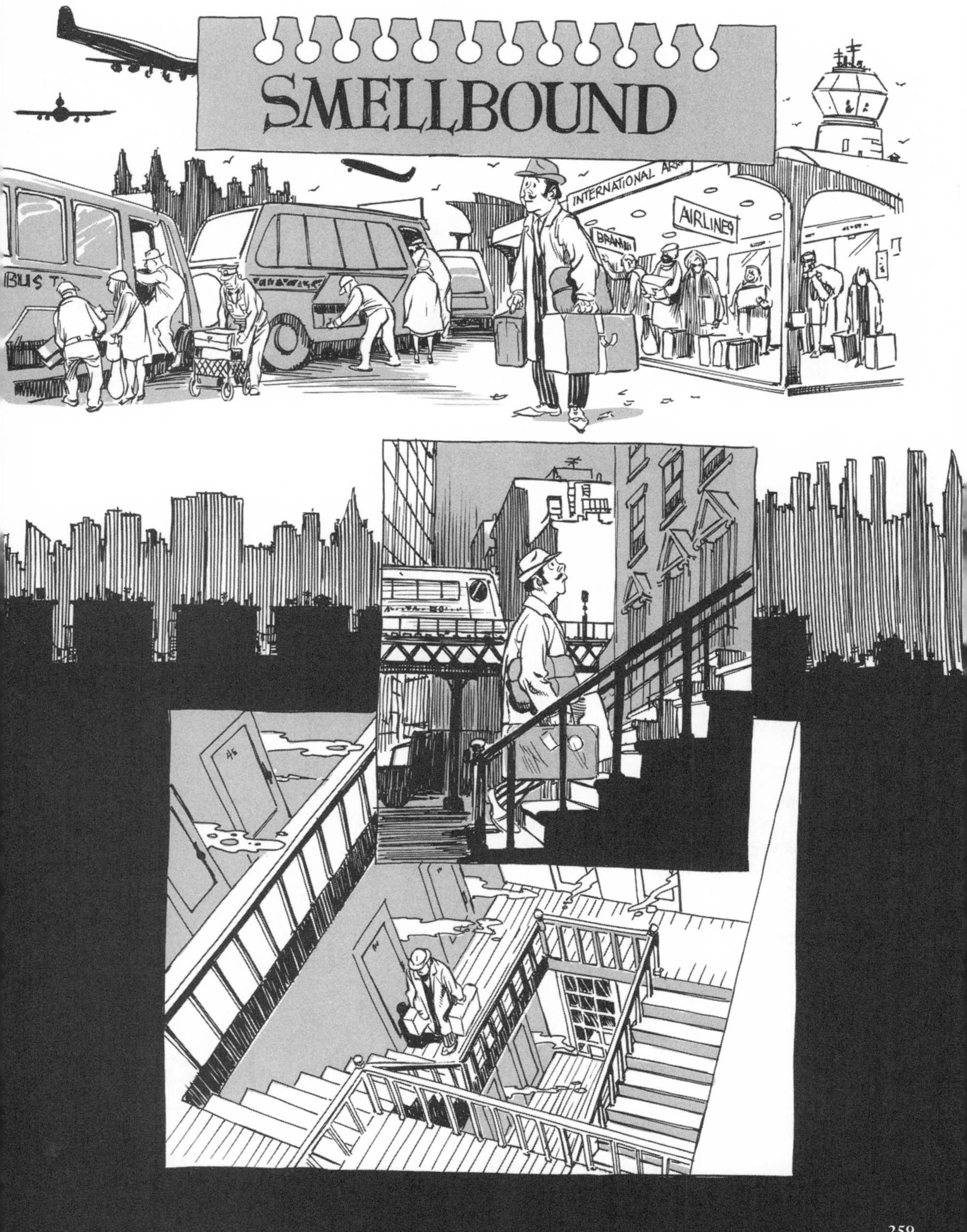
SMELLBOUND
INTERNATIONAL
AIRLINES

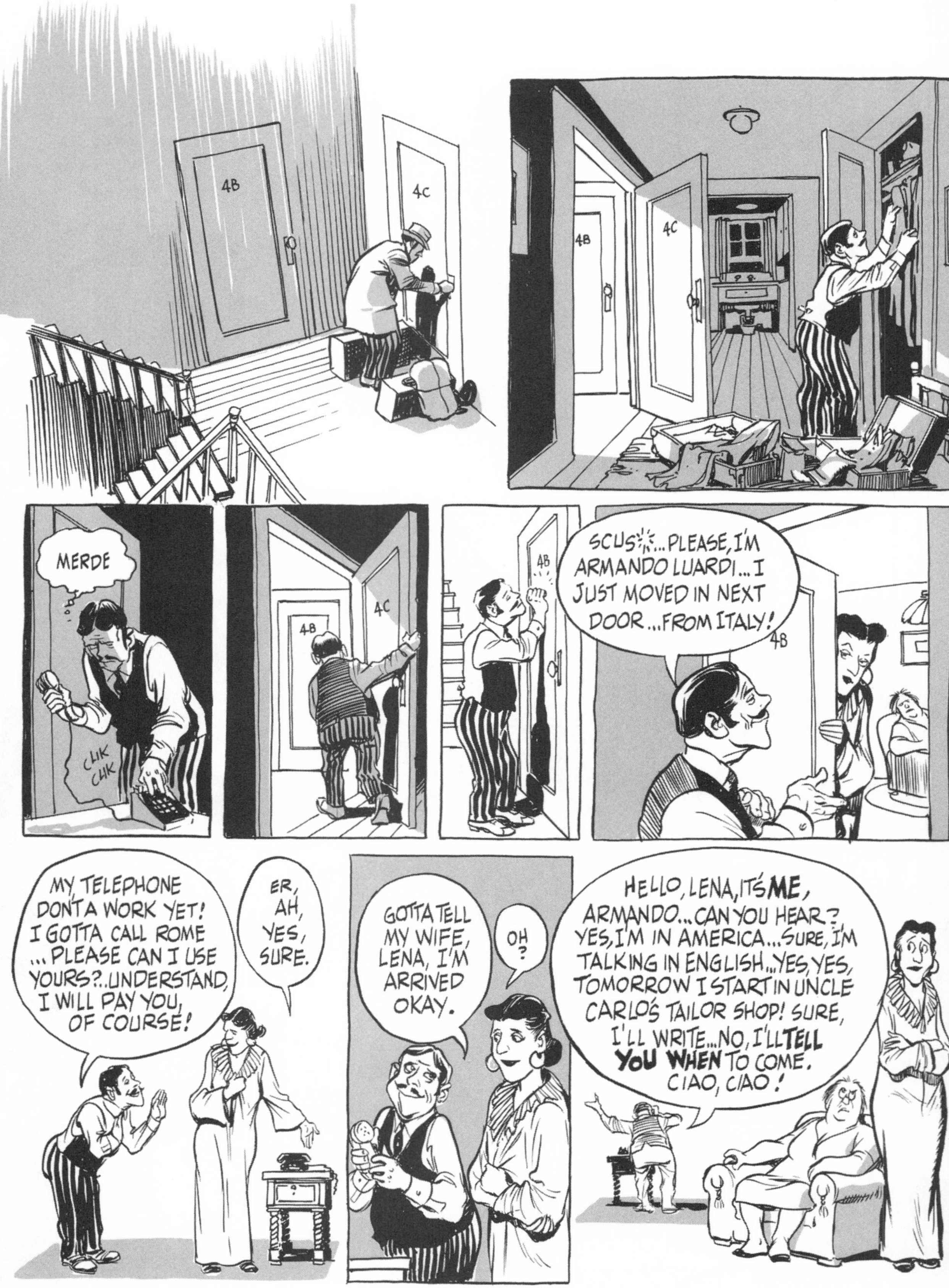
4B
4C
MERDE
CHIK CHIK
SCUS'...PLEASE, I'M ARMANDO LUARDI...I JUST MOVED IN NEXT DOOR...FROM ITALY!
MY TELEPHONE DON'T A WORK YET! I GOTTA CALL ROME ...PLEASE CAN I USE YOURS?..UNDERSTAND, I WILL PAY YOU, OF COURSE!
ER, AH, YES, SURE.
GOTTA TELL MY WIFE, LENA, I'M ARRIVED OKAY.
OH?
HELLO, LENA, IT'S ME, ARMANDO...CAN YOU HEAR? YES, I'M IN AMERICA...SURE, I'M TALKING IN ENGLISH...YES, YES, TOMORROW I START IN UNCLE CARLO'S TAILOR SHOP! SURE, I'LL WRITE...NO, I'LL TELL YOU WHEN TO COME. CIAO, CIAO!

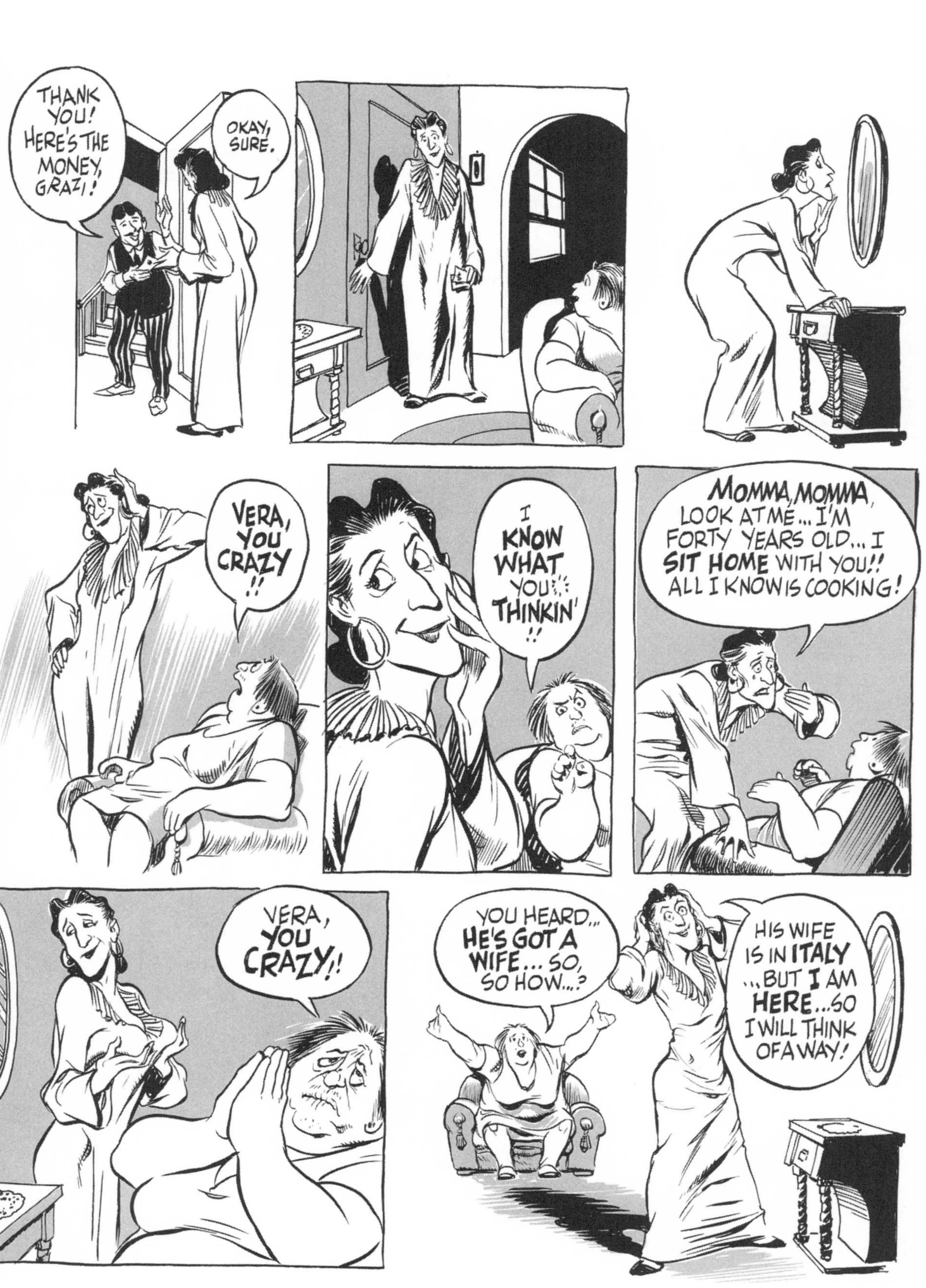
THANK YOU! HERE'S THE MONEY, GRAZI!
OKAY, SURE.
VERA, YOU CRAZY!!
I KNOW WHAT YOU THINKIN'!!
MOMMA, MOMMA, LOOK AT ME... I'M FORTY YEARS OLD... I SIT HOME WITH YOU!! ALL I KNOW IS COOKING!
VERA, YOU CRAZY!!
YOU HEARD... HE'S GOT A WIFE... SO, SO HOW...?
HIS WIFE IS IN ITALY ...BUT I AM HERE...SO I WILL THINK OF A WAY!

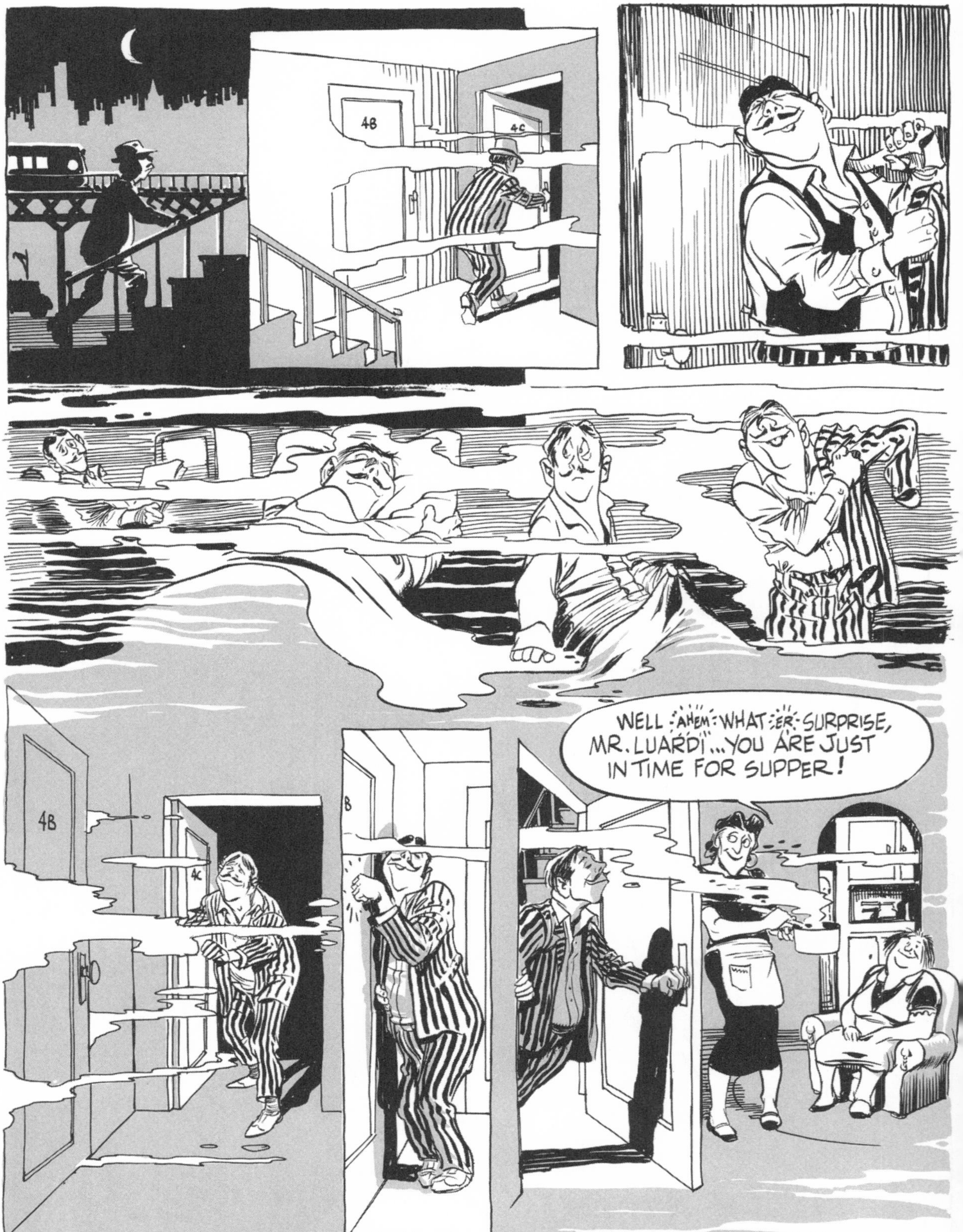
4B
4C
WELL AHEM WHAT ER SURPRISE, MR. LUARDI... YOU ARE JUST IN TIME FOR SUPPER!
4B
4C

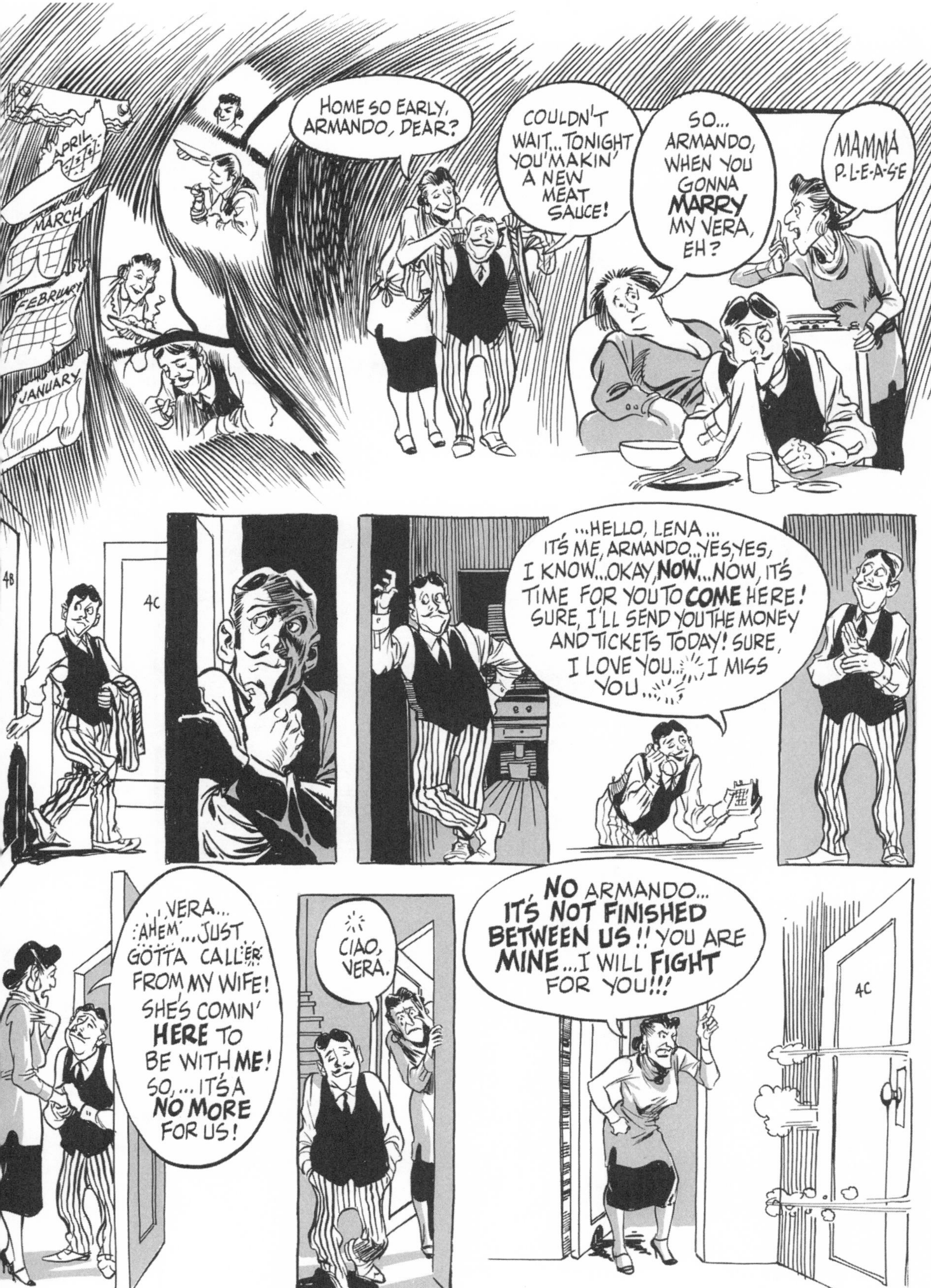
APRIL
MARCH
FEBRUARY
JANUARY
HOME SO EARLY, ARMANDO, DEAR?
COULDN'T WAIT... TONIGHT YOU'MAKIN' A NEW MEAT SAUCE!
SO... ARMANDO, WHEN YOU GONNA MARRY MY VERA, EH?
MAMMA P-L-E-A-SE
4B
4C
...HELLO, LENA... IT'S ME, ARMANDO...YES,YES, I KNOW...OKAY, NOW...NOW, IT'S TIME FOR YOU TO COME HERE! SURE, I'LL SEND YOU THE MONEY AND TICKETS TODAY! SURE, I LOVE YOU... I MISS YOU...
...VERA... AHEM...JUST GOTTA CALL'ER FROM MY WIFE! SHE'S COMIN' HERE TO BE WITH ME! SO,... IT'S A NO MORE FOR US!
CIAO, VERA.
NO ARMANDO... IT'S NOT FINISHED BETWEEN US!! YOU ARE MINE...I WILL FIGHT FOR YOU!!!
4C

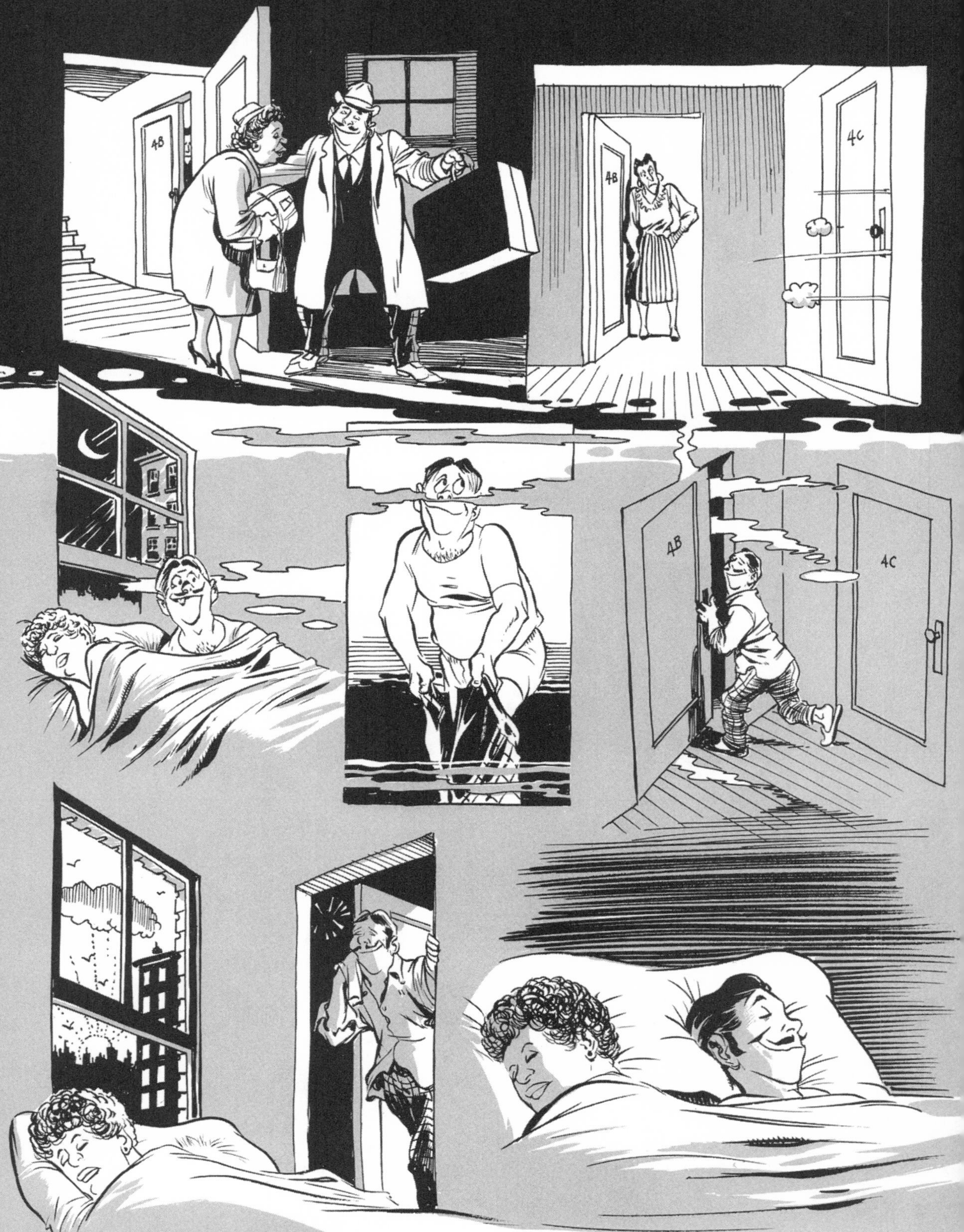
4B
4B
4C
4B
4C

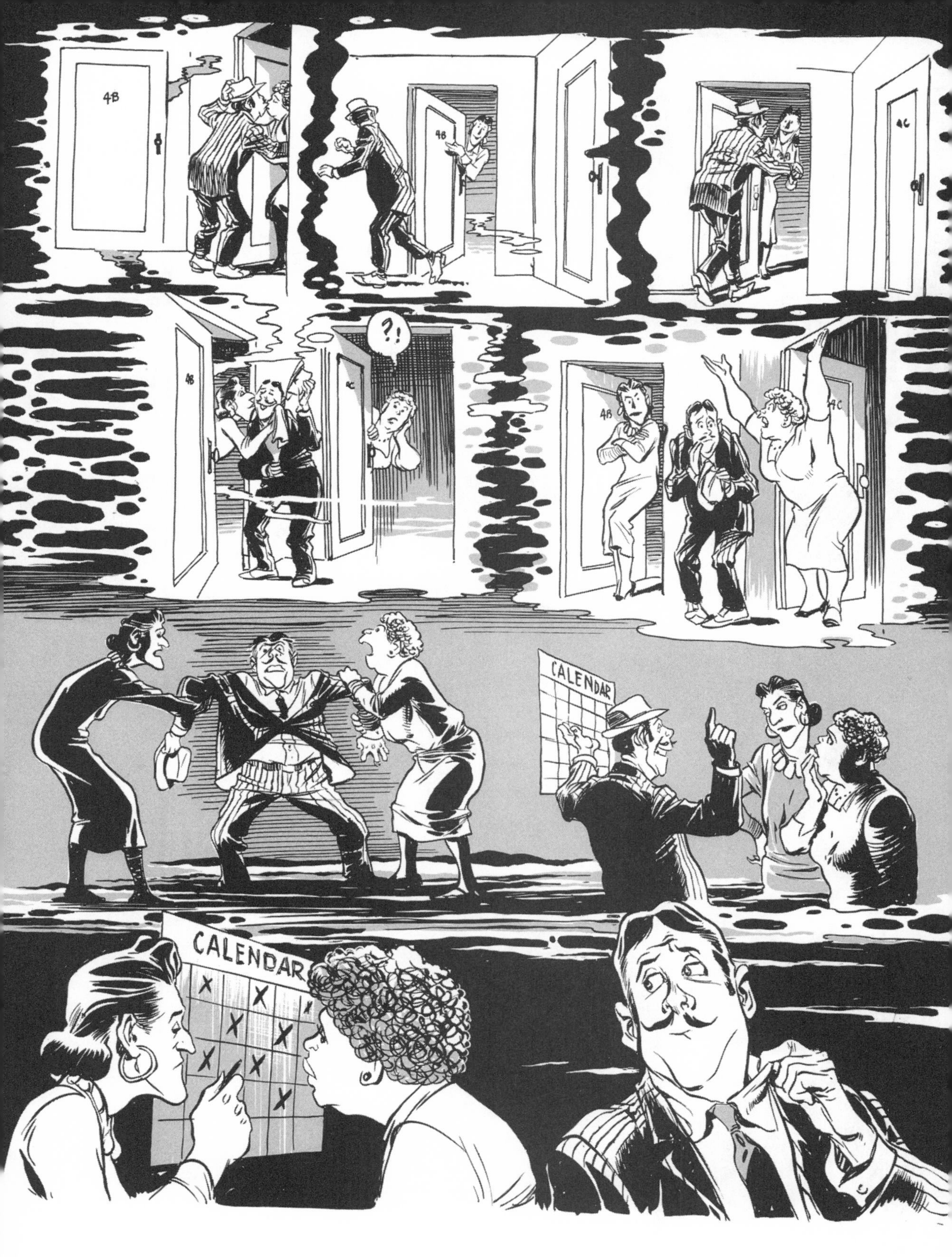
4B
4B
4C
4B
4C
?!
4B
4C
CALENDAR
CALENDAR

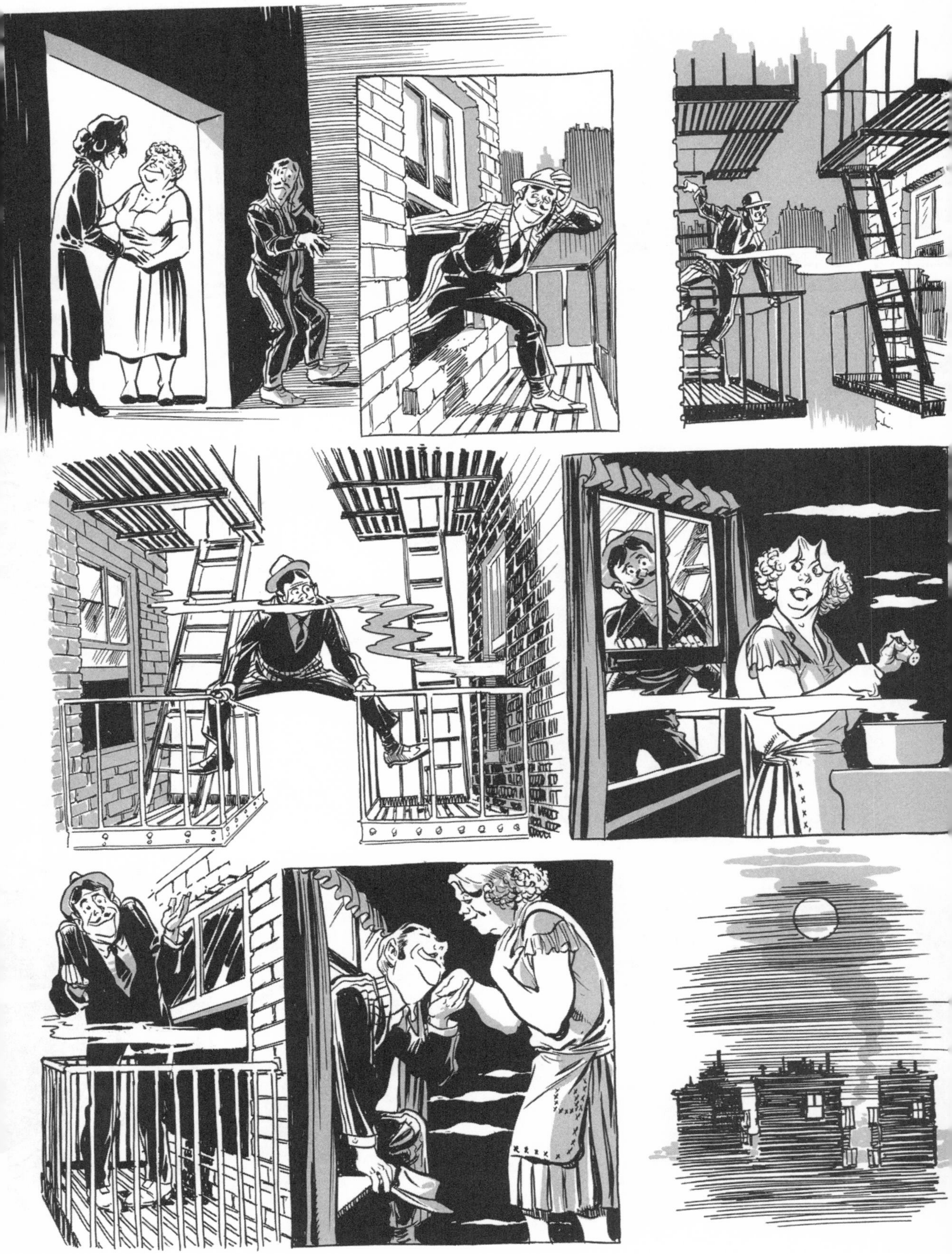

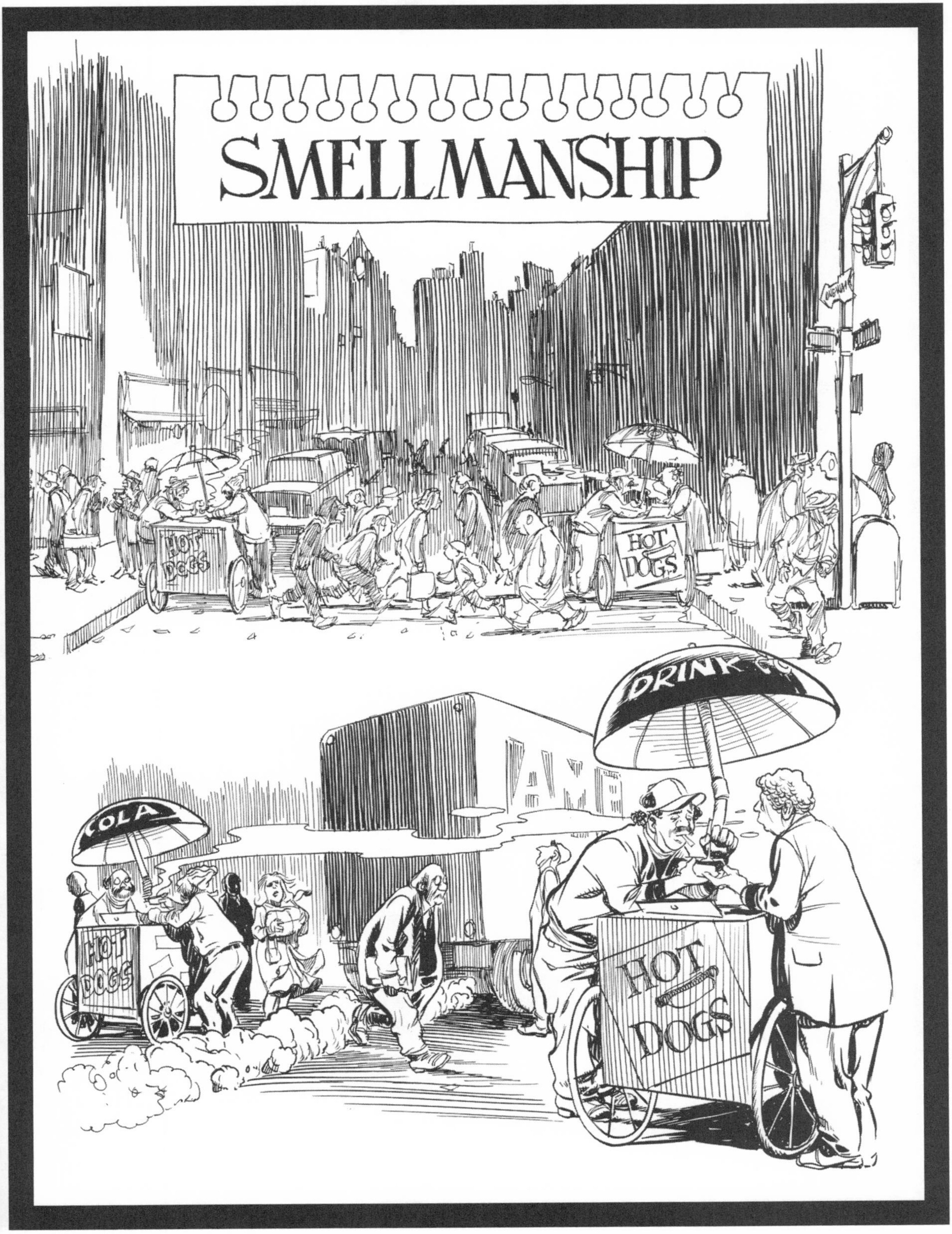
SMELLMANSHIP
HOT DOGS
HOT DOGS
DRINK
COLA
HOT DOGS
HOT DOGS

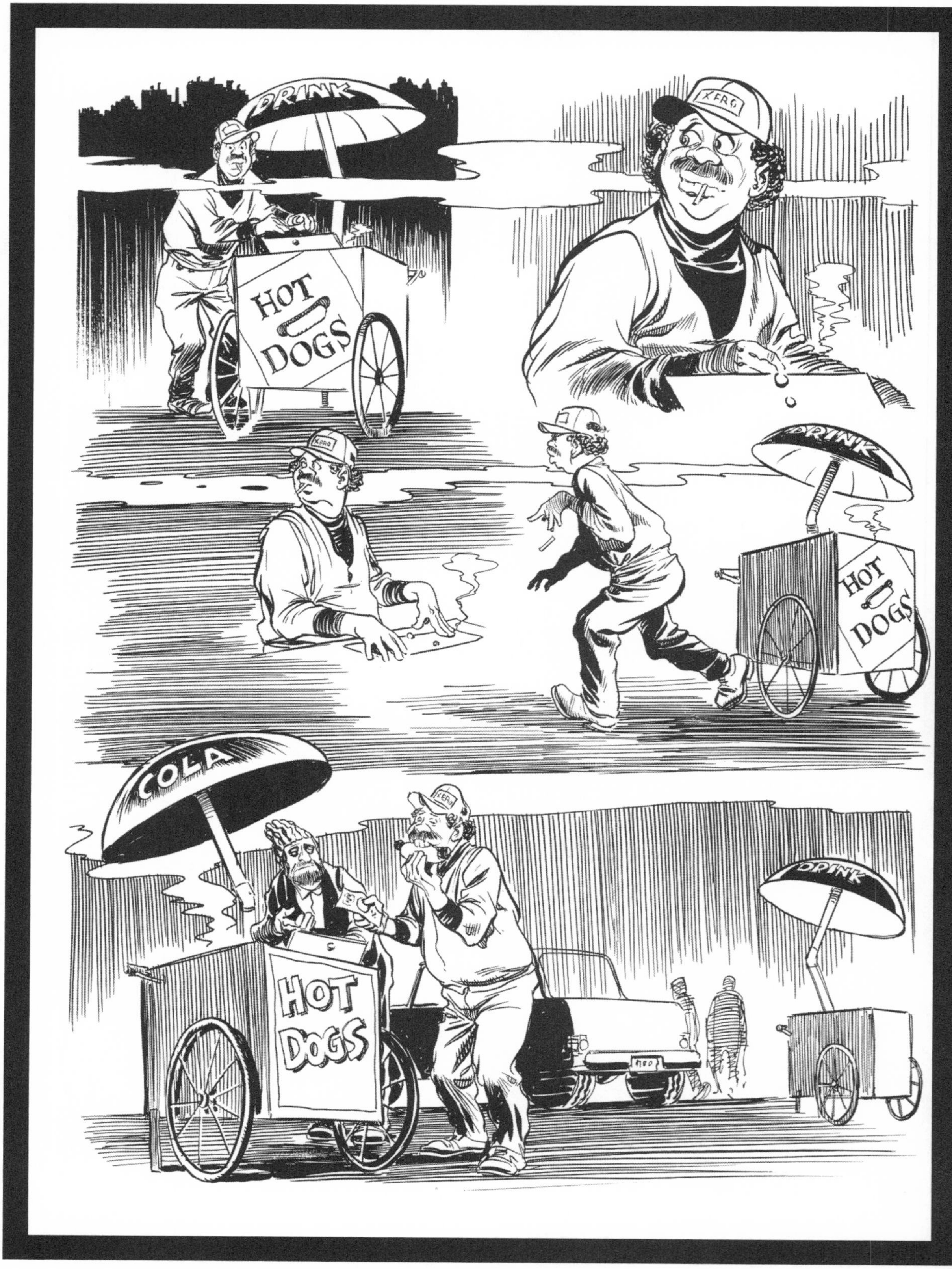
DRINK
HOT DOGS
XFRG
DRINK
HOT DOGS
COLA
HOT DOGS
DRINK

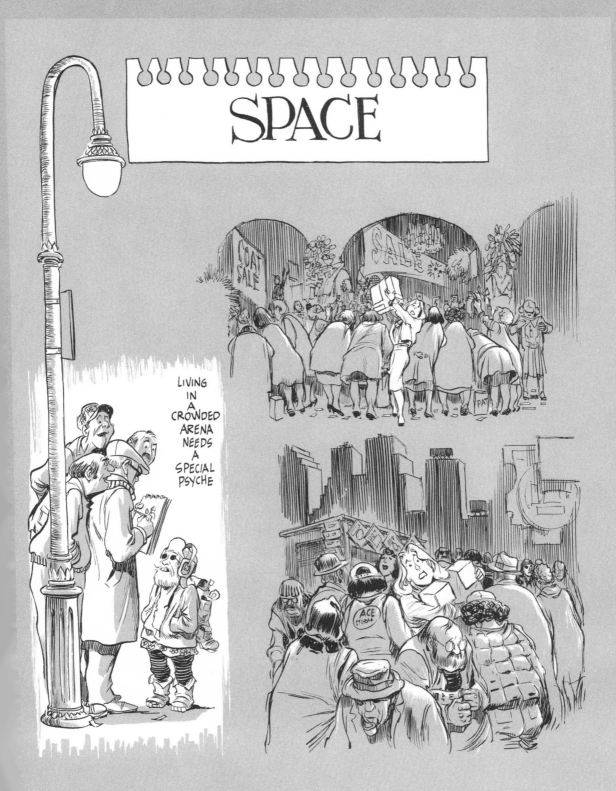

SPACE

LIVING
IN
A
CROWDED
ARENA
NEEDS
A
SPECIAL
PSYCHE

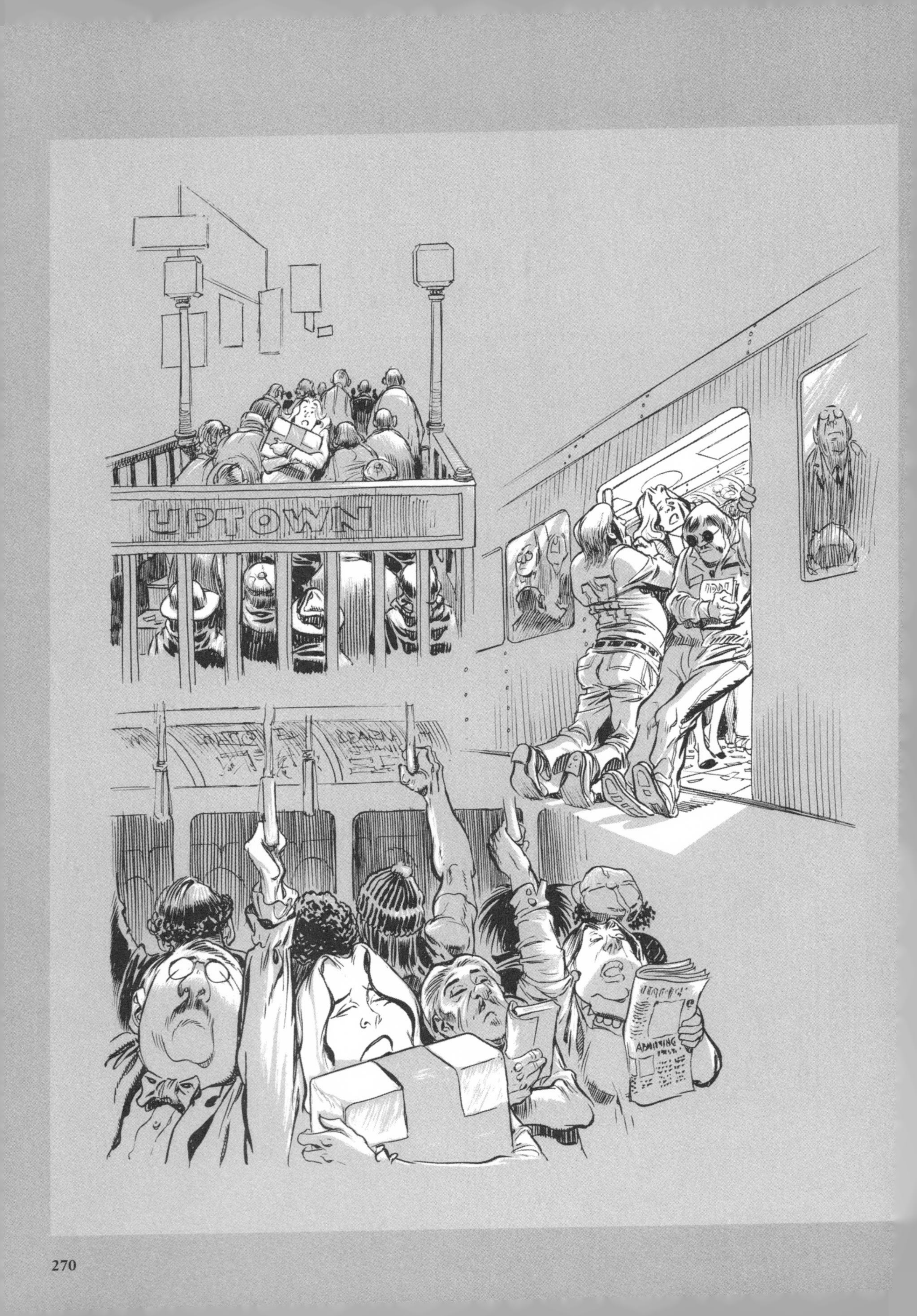
UPTOWN

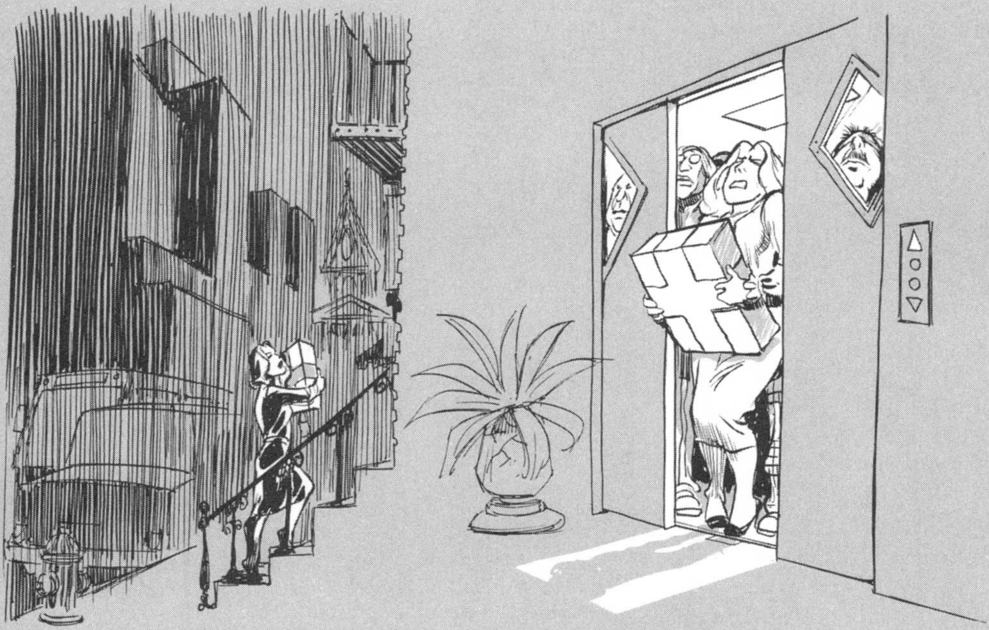

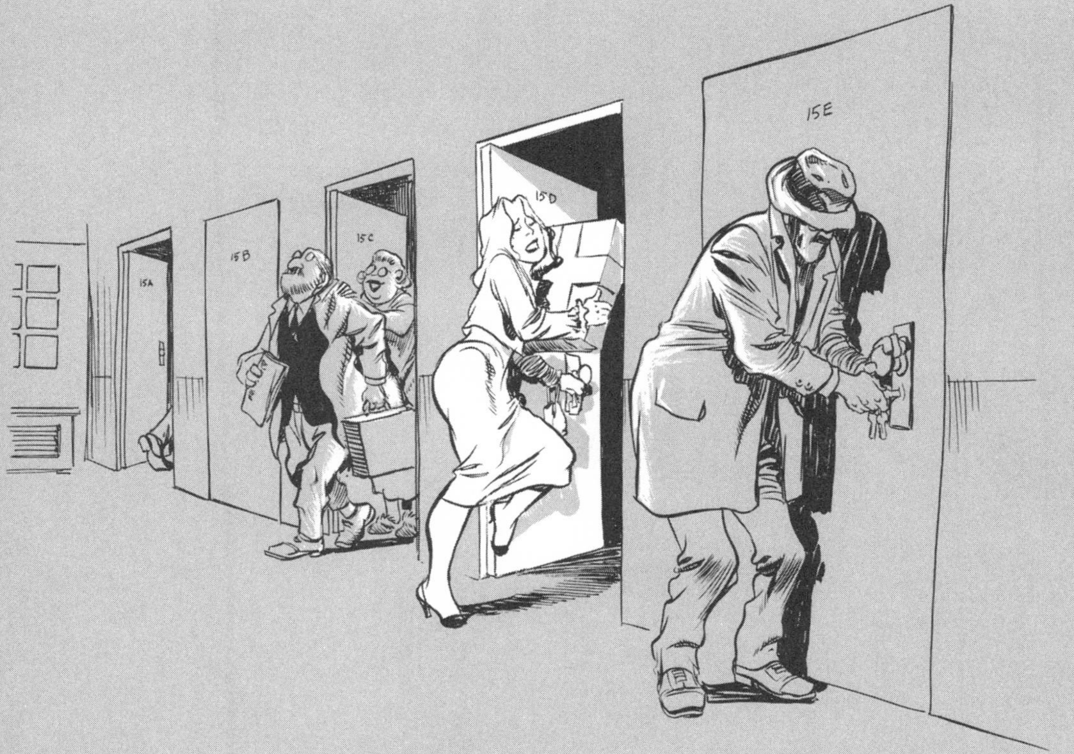
15A
15B
15C
15D
15E

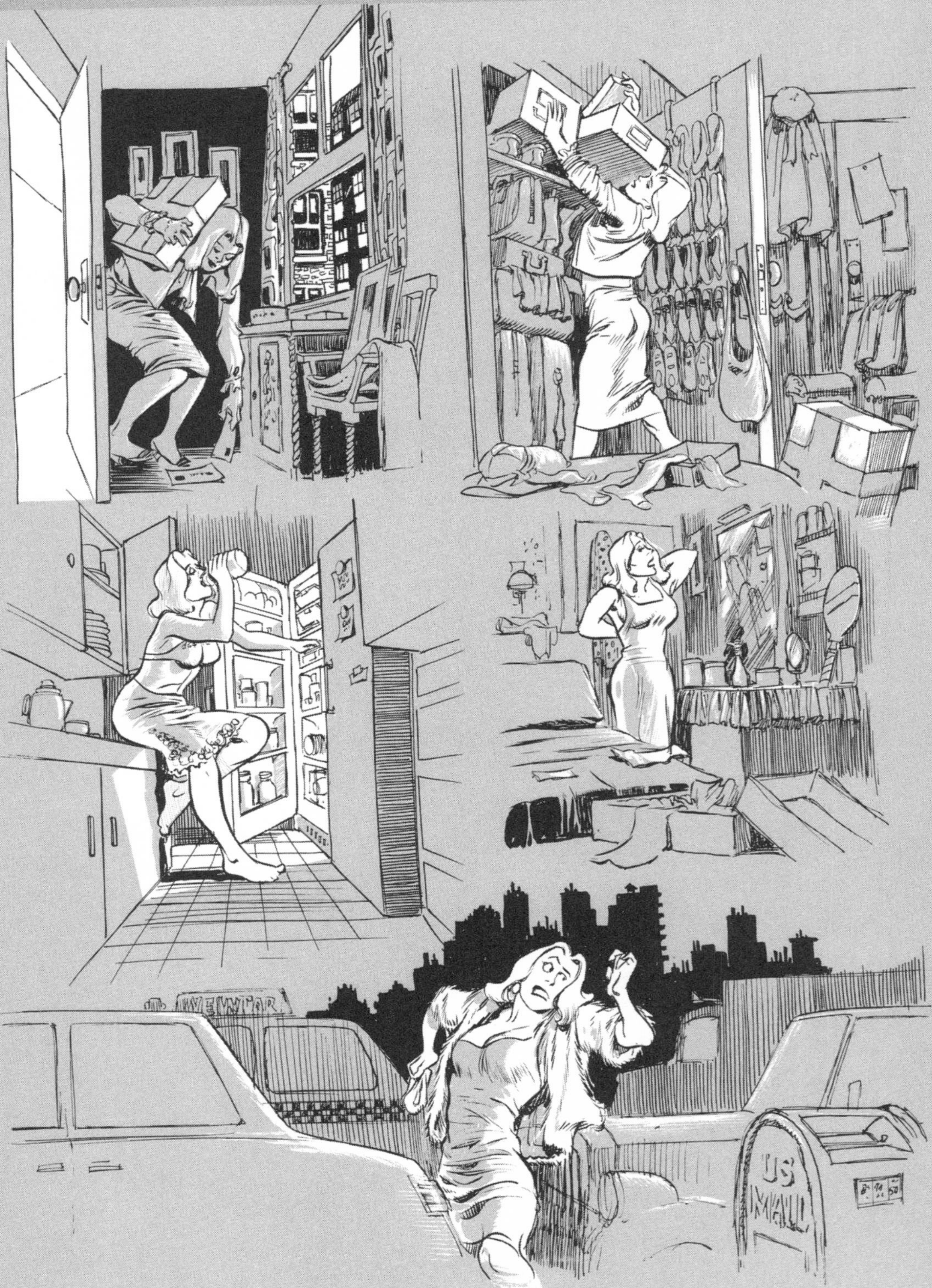
US
MAIL

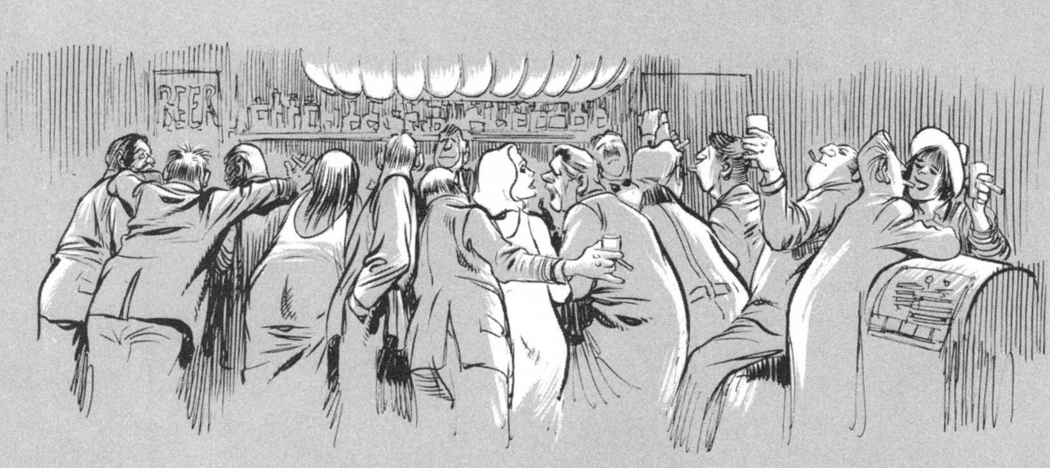
BEER

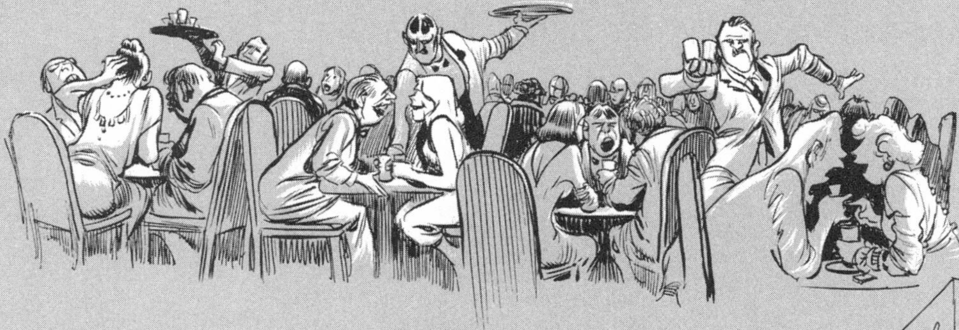

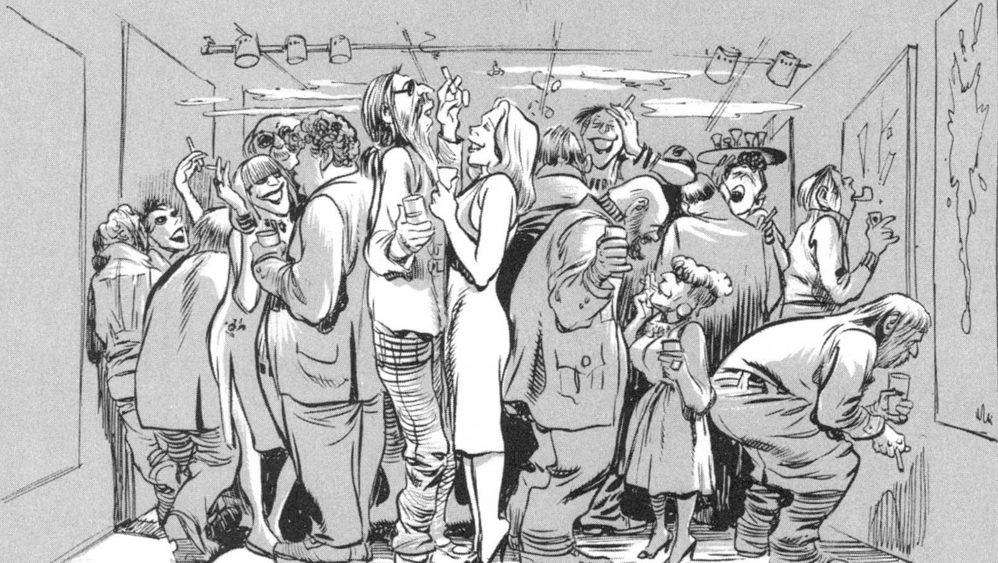

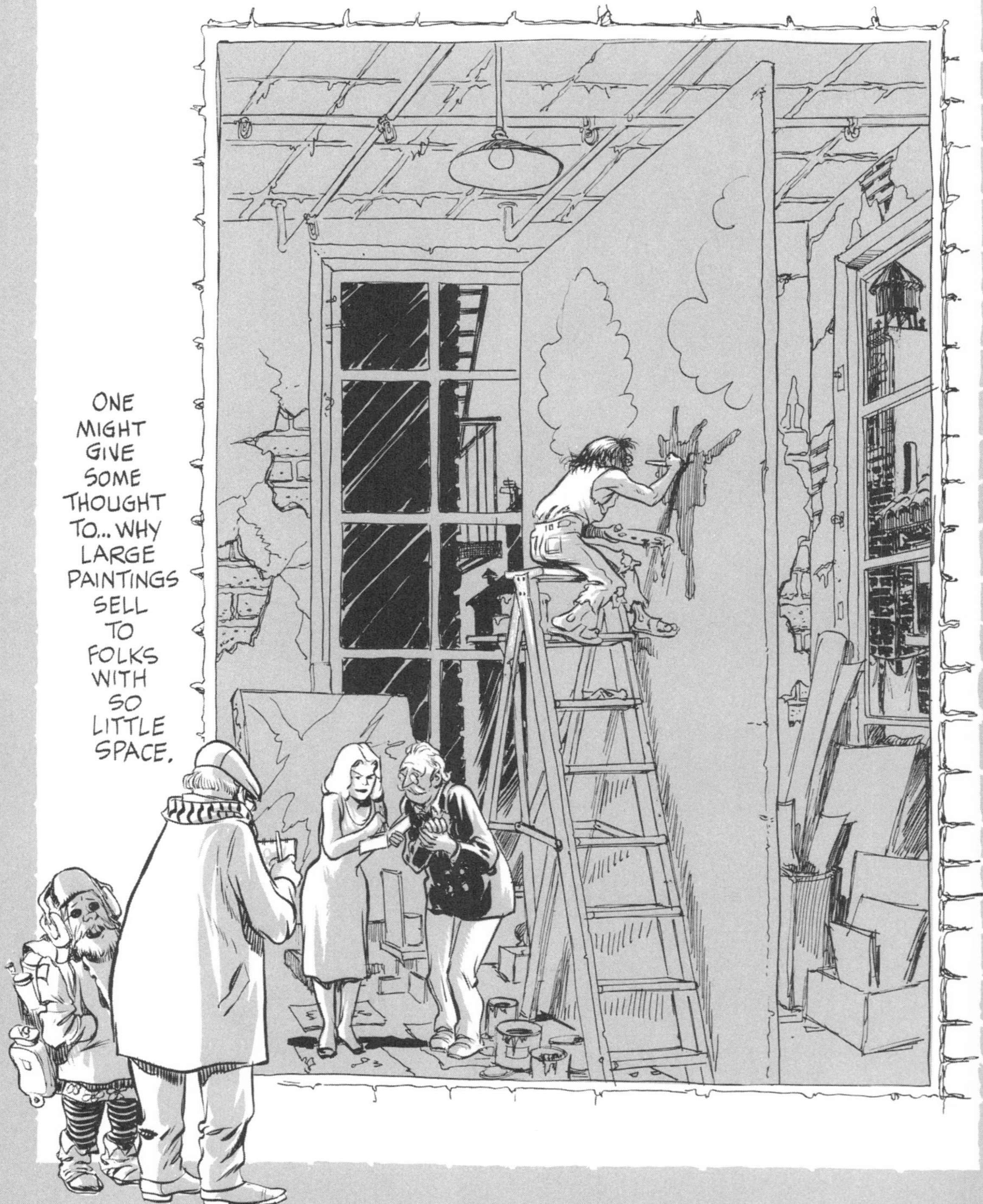
ONE MIGHT GIVE SOME THOUGHT TO... WHY LARGE PAINTINGS SELL TO FOLKS WITH SO LITTLE SPACE.

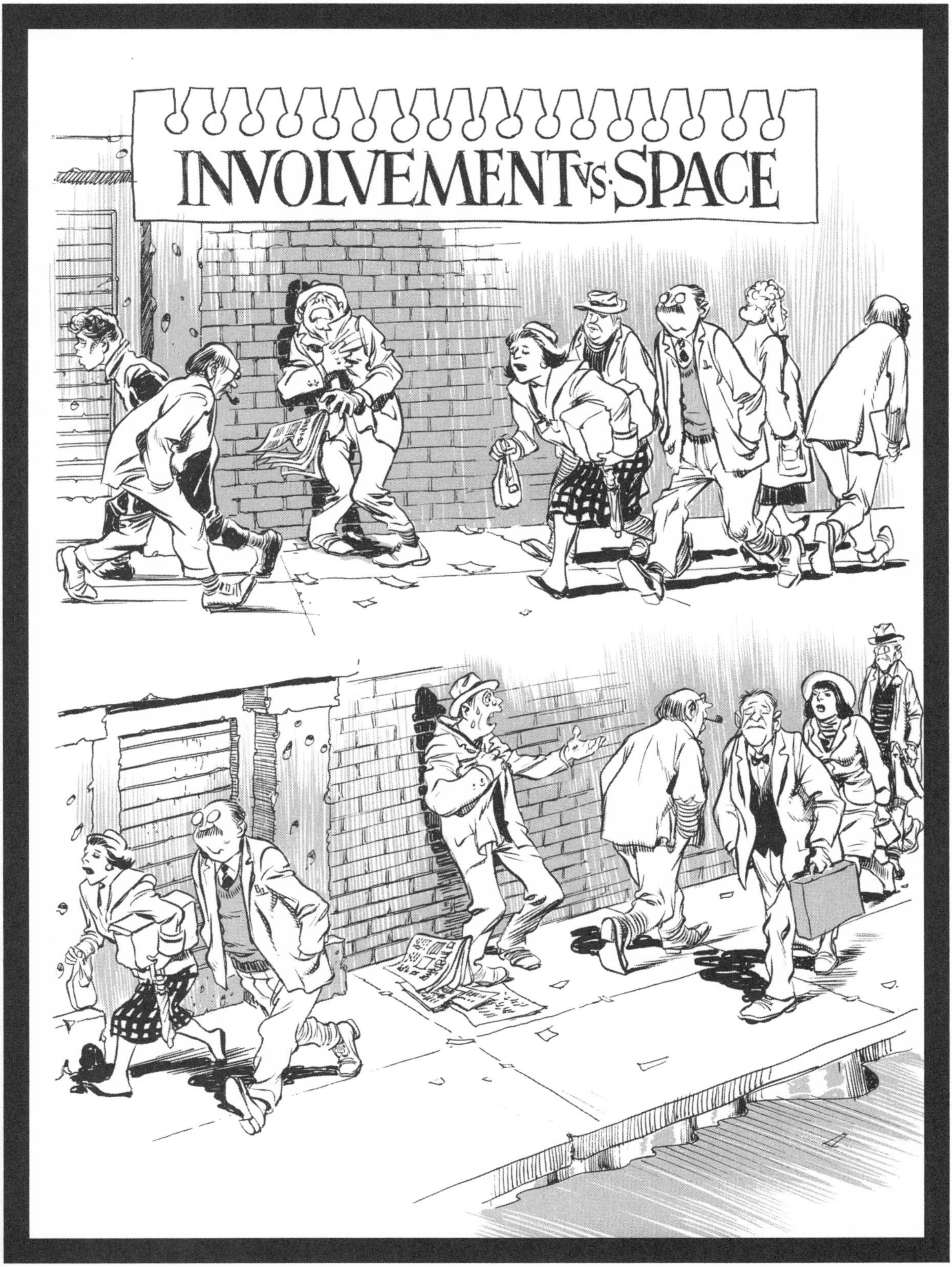
INVOLVEMENT VS. SPACE

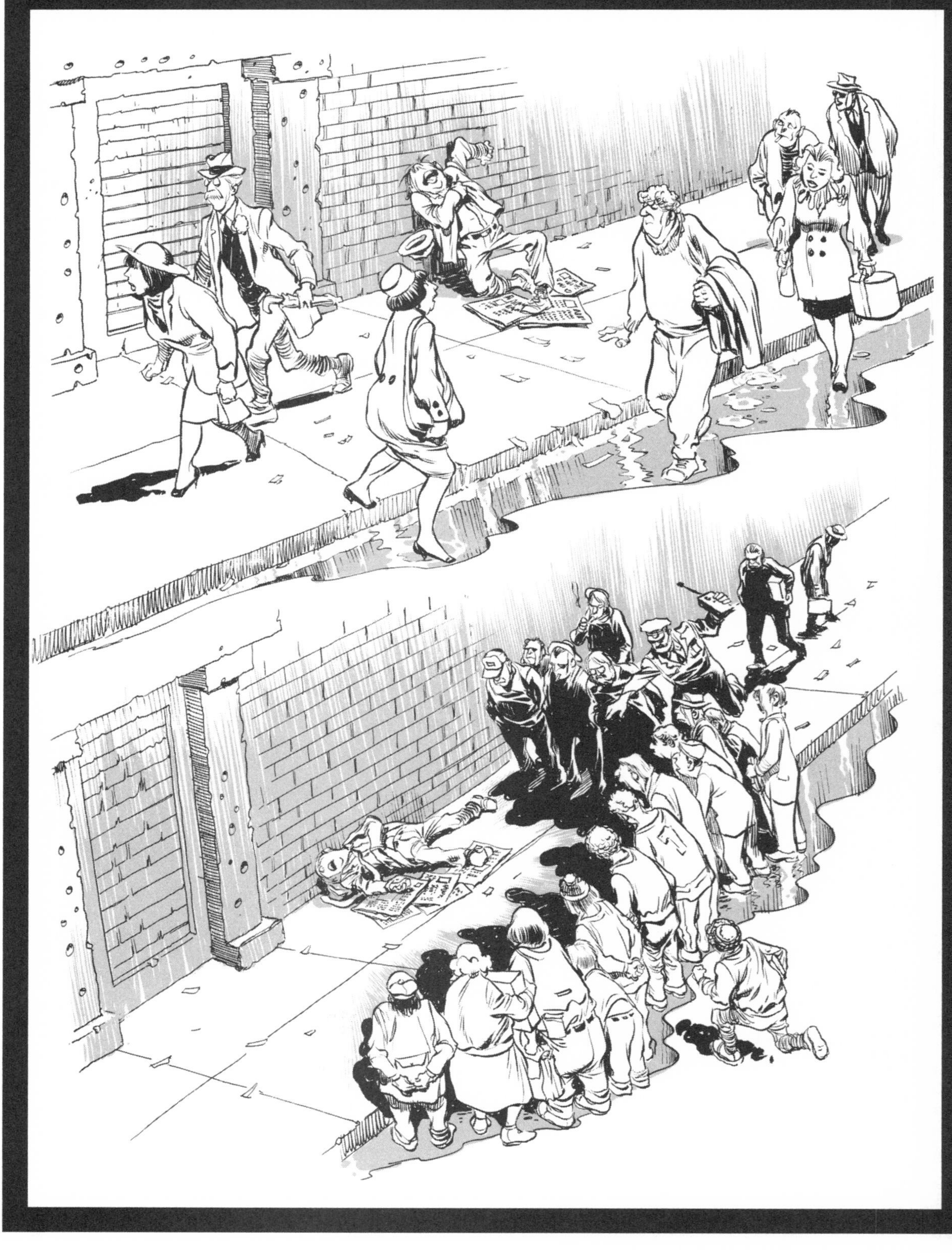

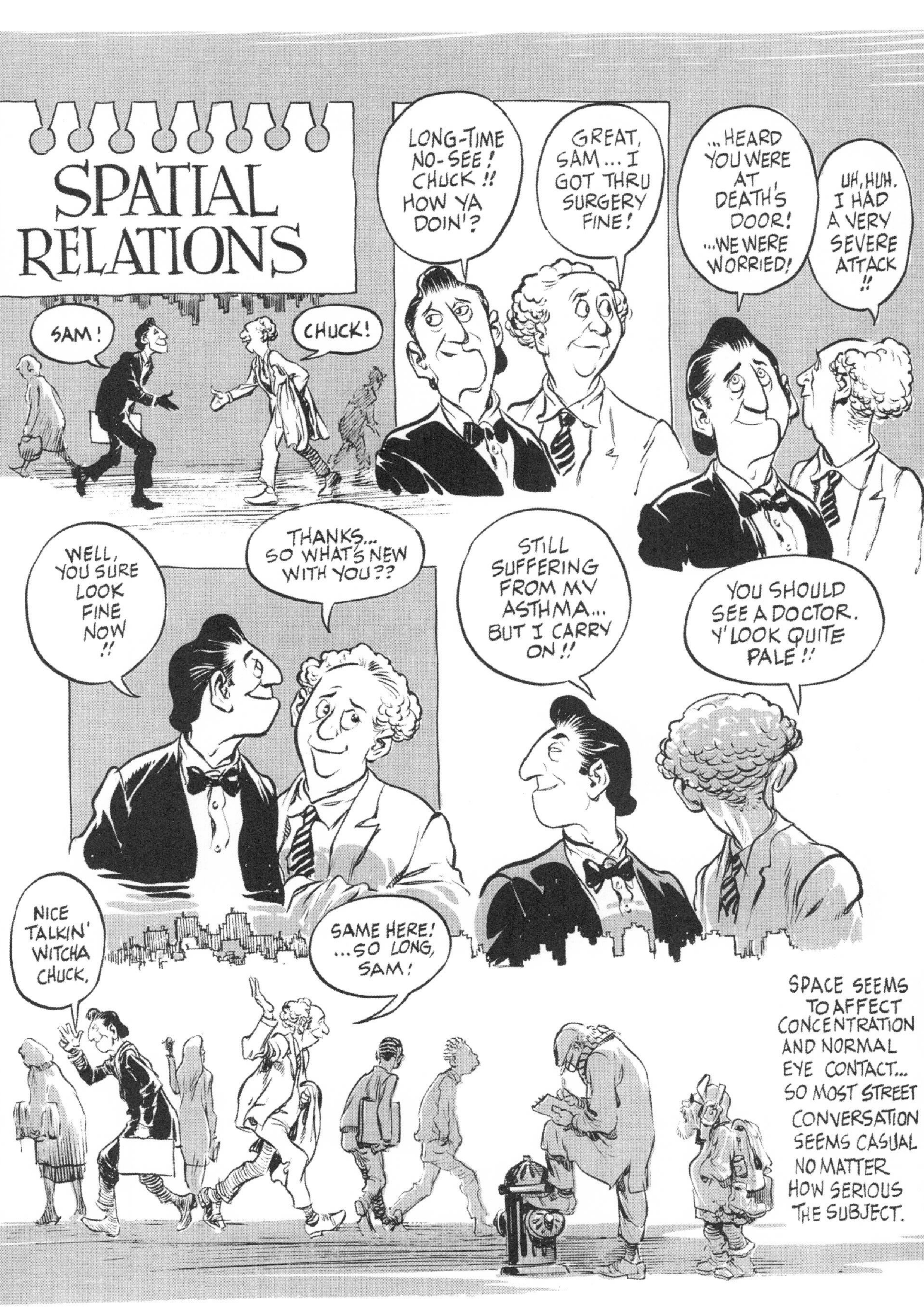
SPATIAL RELATIONS
SAM!
CHUCK!
LONG-TIME NO-SEE! CHUCK!! HOW YA DOIN'?
GREAT, SAM... I GOT THRU SURGERY FINE!
...HEARD YOU WERE AT DEATH'S DOOR! ...WE WERE WORRIED!
UH, HUH. I HAD A VERY SEVERE ATTACK!!
WELL, YOU SURE LOOK FINE NOW!!
THANKS... SO WHAT'S NEW WITH YOU??
STILL SUFFERING FROM MY ASTHMA... BUT I CARRY ON!!
YOU SHOULD SEE A DOCTOR. Y'LOOK QUITE PALE!!
NICE TALKIN' WITCHA CHUCK.
SAME HERE! ...SO LONG, SAM!
SPACE SEEMS TO AFFECT CONCENTRATION AND NORMAL EYE CONTACT... SO MOST STREET CONVERSATION SEEMS CASUAL NO MATTER HOW SERIOUS THE SUBJECT.

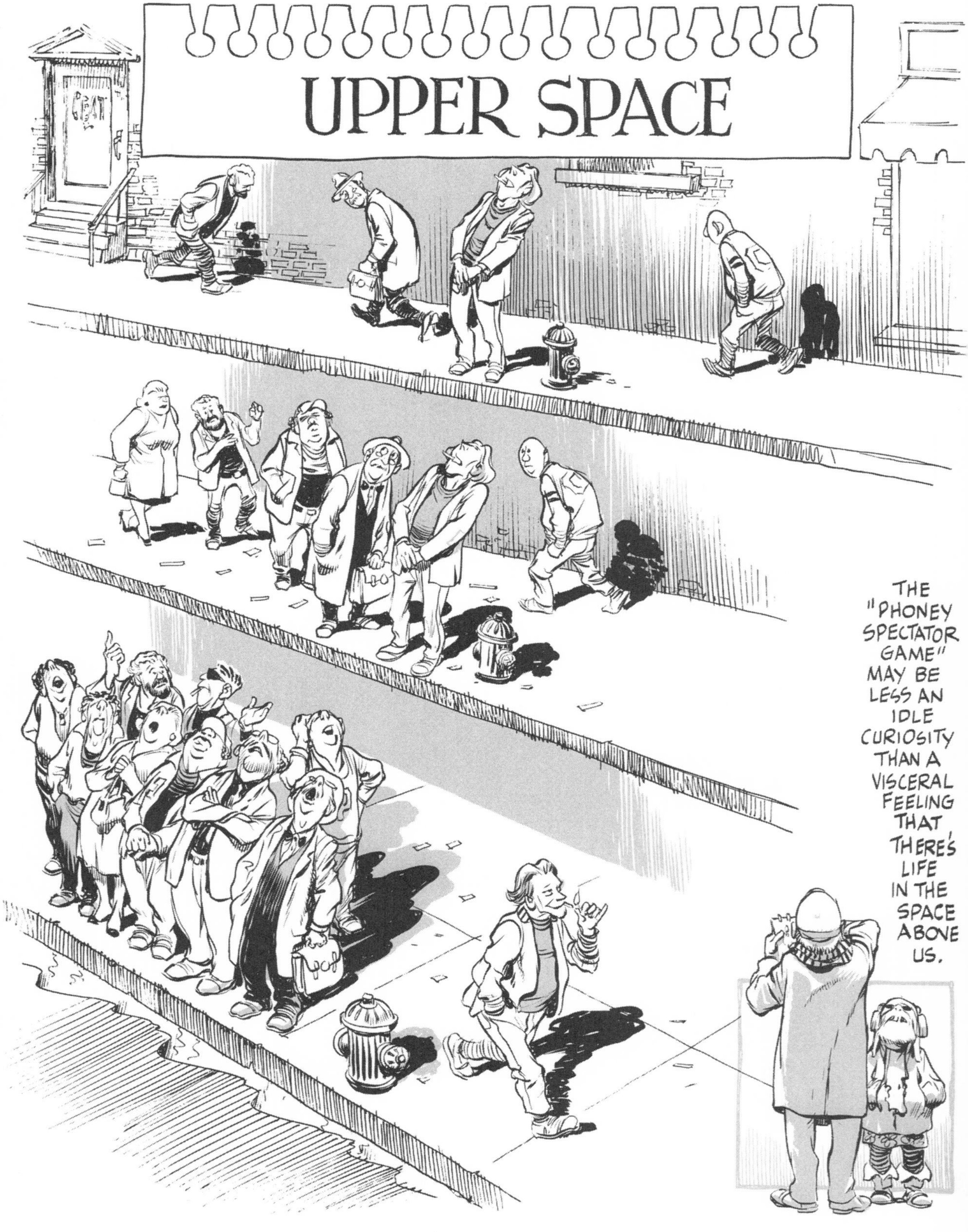
UPPER SPACE
THE "PHONEY SPECTATOR GAME" MAY BE LESS AN IDLE CURIOSITY THAN A VISCERAL FEELING THAT THERE'S LIFE IN THE SPACE ABOVE US.

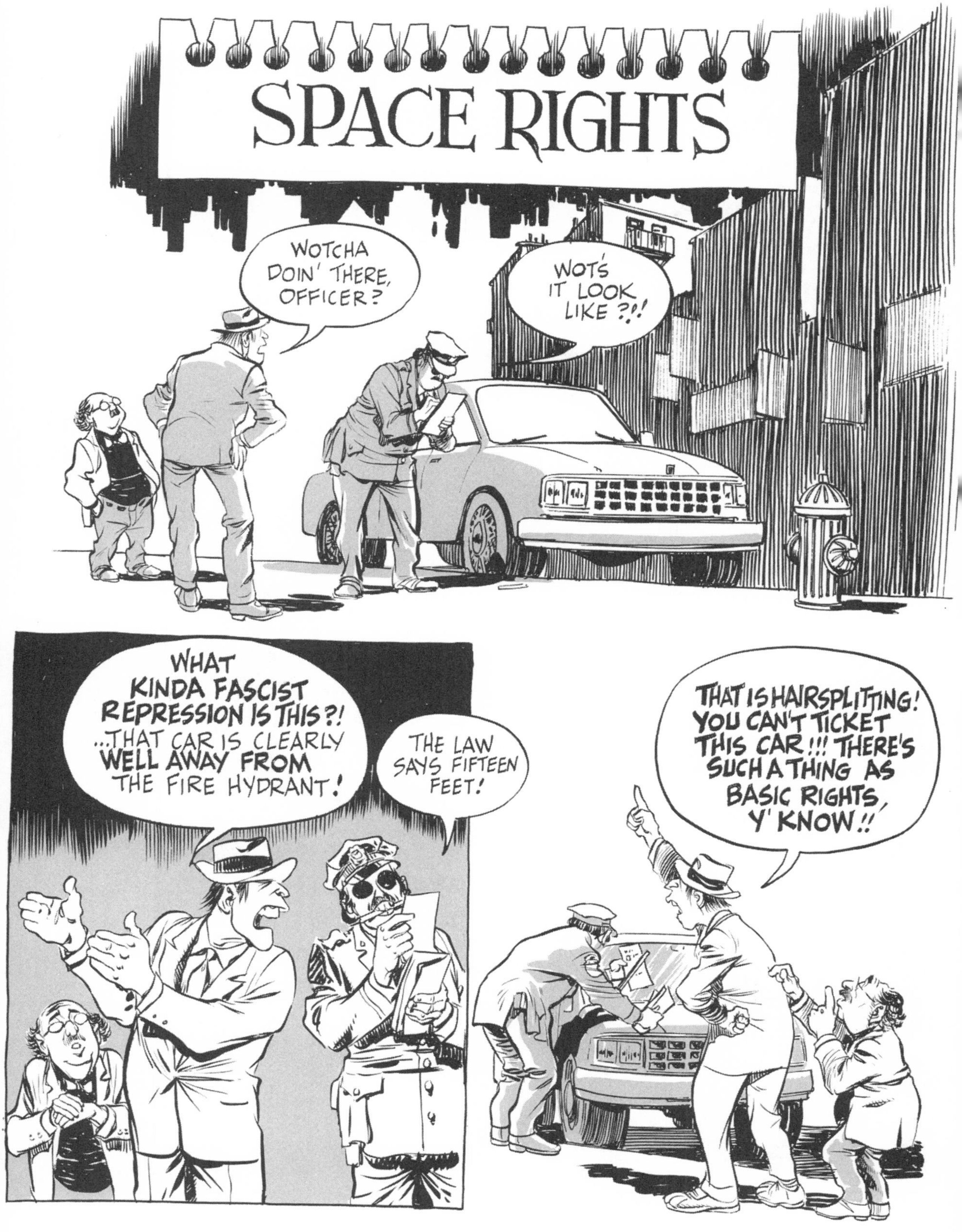
SPACE RIGHTS
WOTCHA DOIN' THERE, OFFICER?
WOT'S IT LOOK LIKE?!!
WHAT KINDA FASCIST REPRESSION IS THIS?! ...THAT CAR IS CLEARLY WELL AWAY FROM THE FIRE HYDRANT!
THE LAW SAYS FIFTEEN FEET!
THAT IS HAIRSPLITTING! YOU CAN'T TICKET THIS CAR!!! THERE'S SUCH A THING AS BASIC RIGHTS, Y' KNOW!!

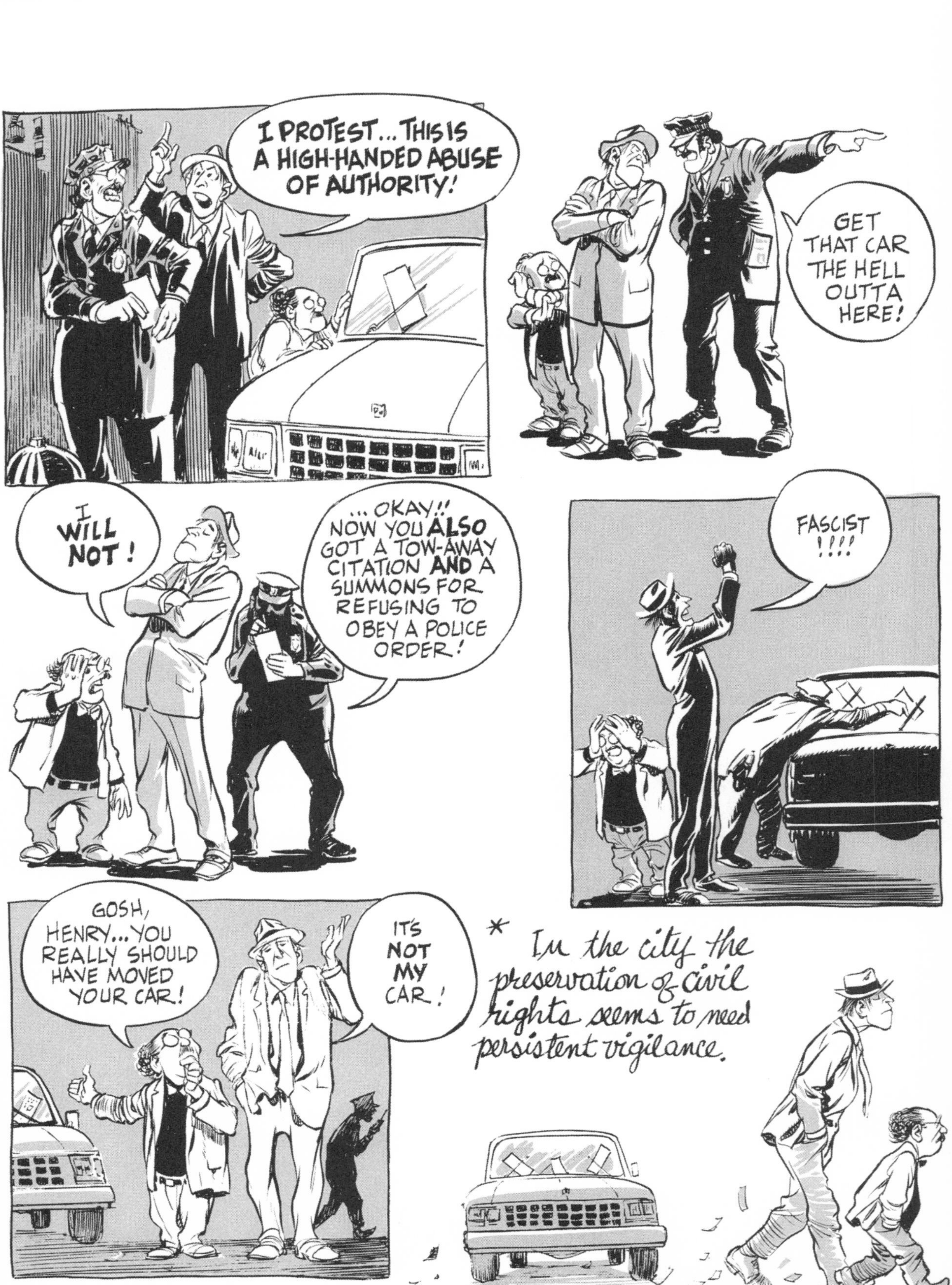
I PROTEST... THIS IS A HIGH-HANDED ABUSE OF AUTHORITY!
GET THAT CAR THE HELL OUTTA HERE!
I WILL NOT!
...OKAY!! NOW YOU ALSO GOT A TOW-AWAY CITATION AND A SUMMONS FOR REFUSING TO OBEY A POLICE ORDER!
FASCIST !!!!
GOSH, HENRY... YOU REALLY SHOULD HAVE MOVED YOUR CAR!
IT'S NOT MY CAR!
* In the city the preservation of civil rights seems to need persistent vigilance.

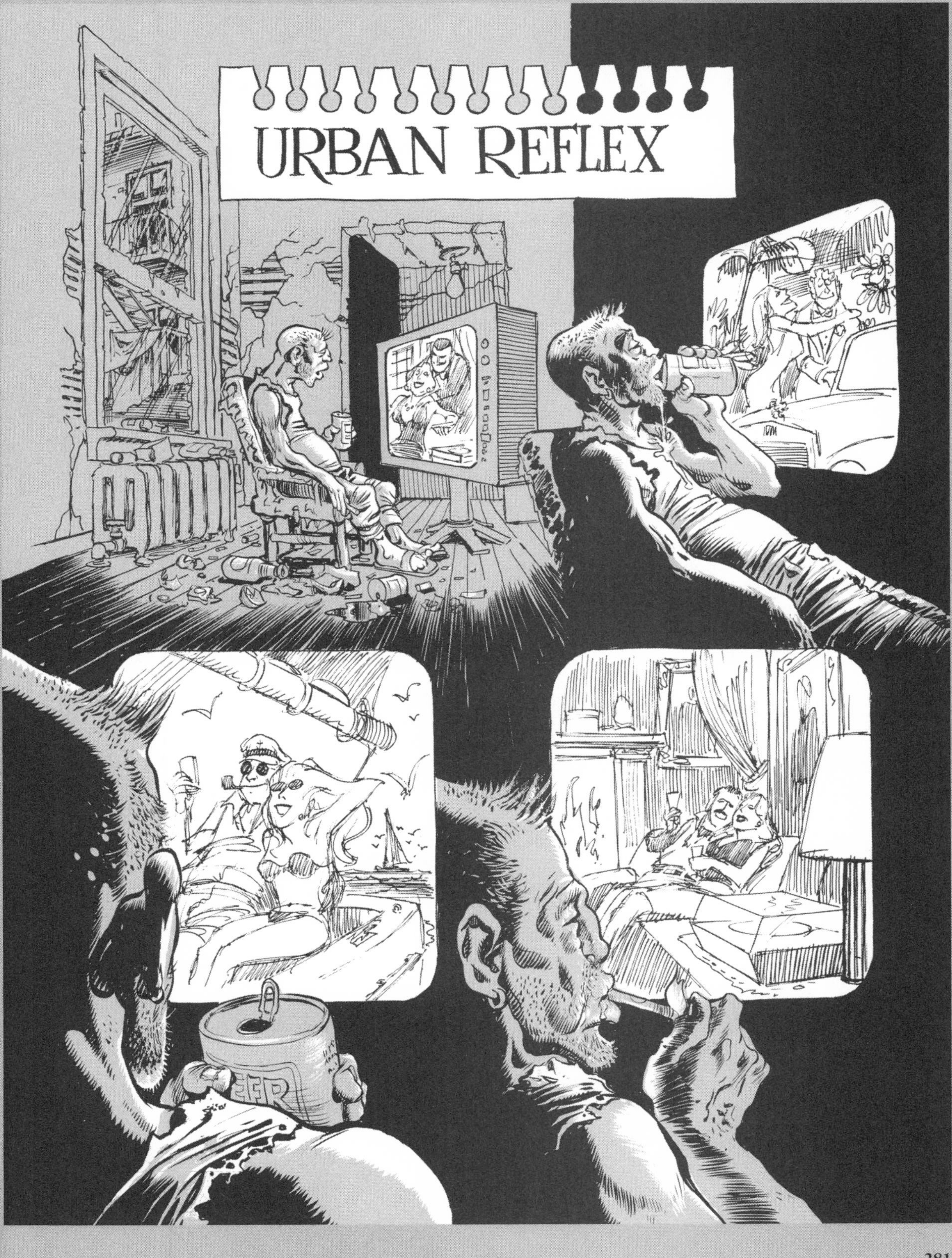
URBAN REFLEX

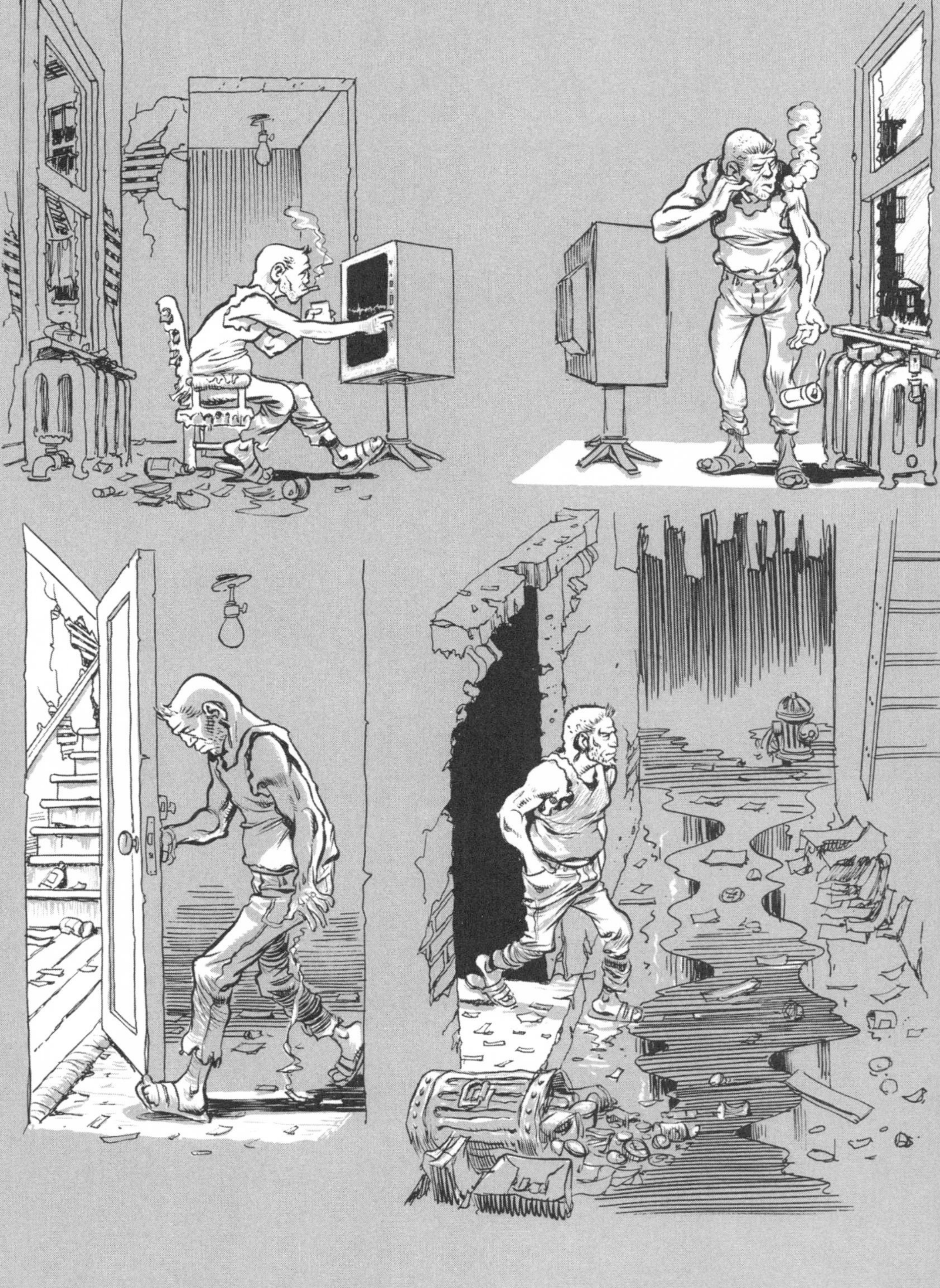

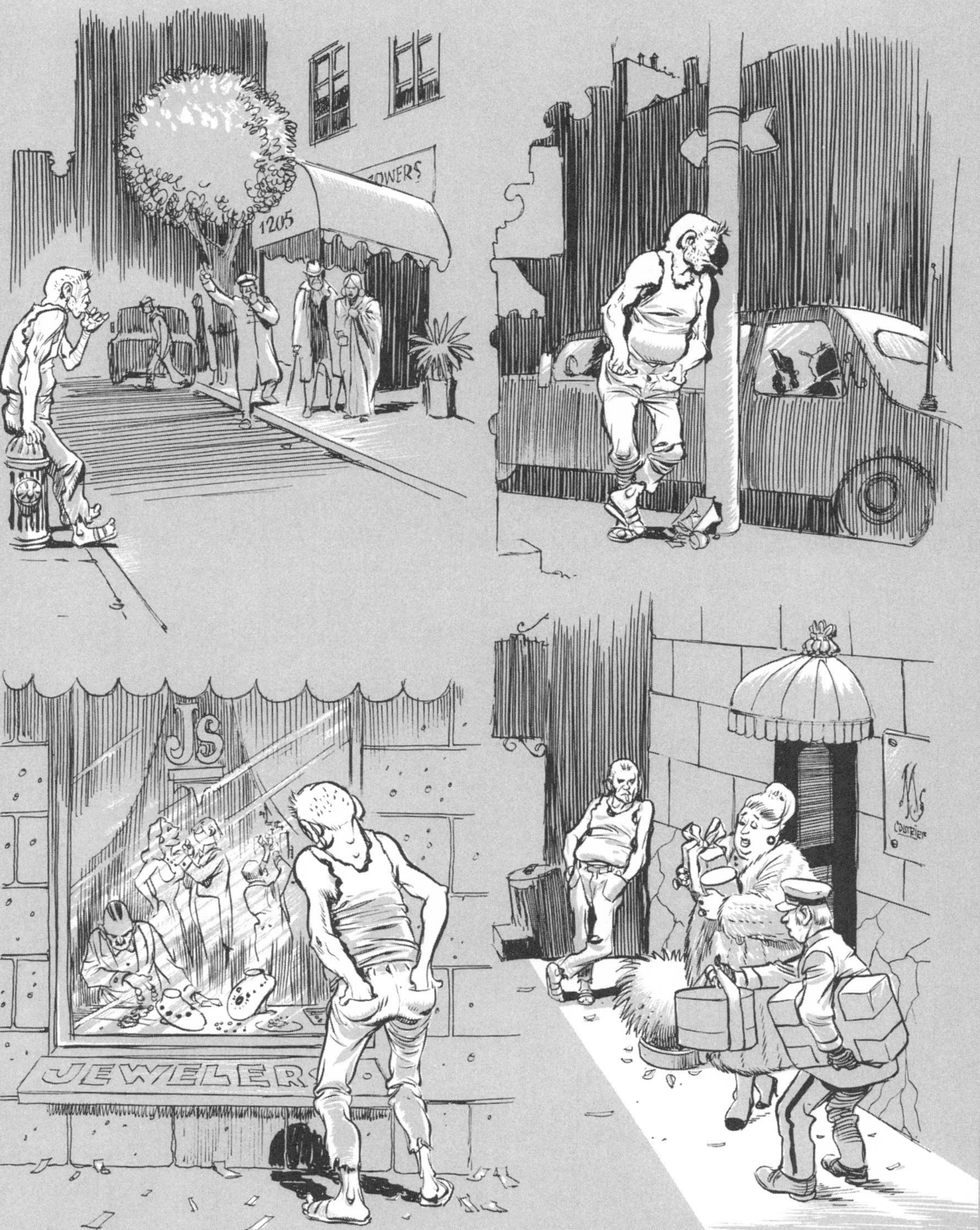
1205
JS
JEWELER

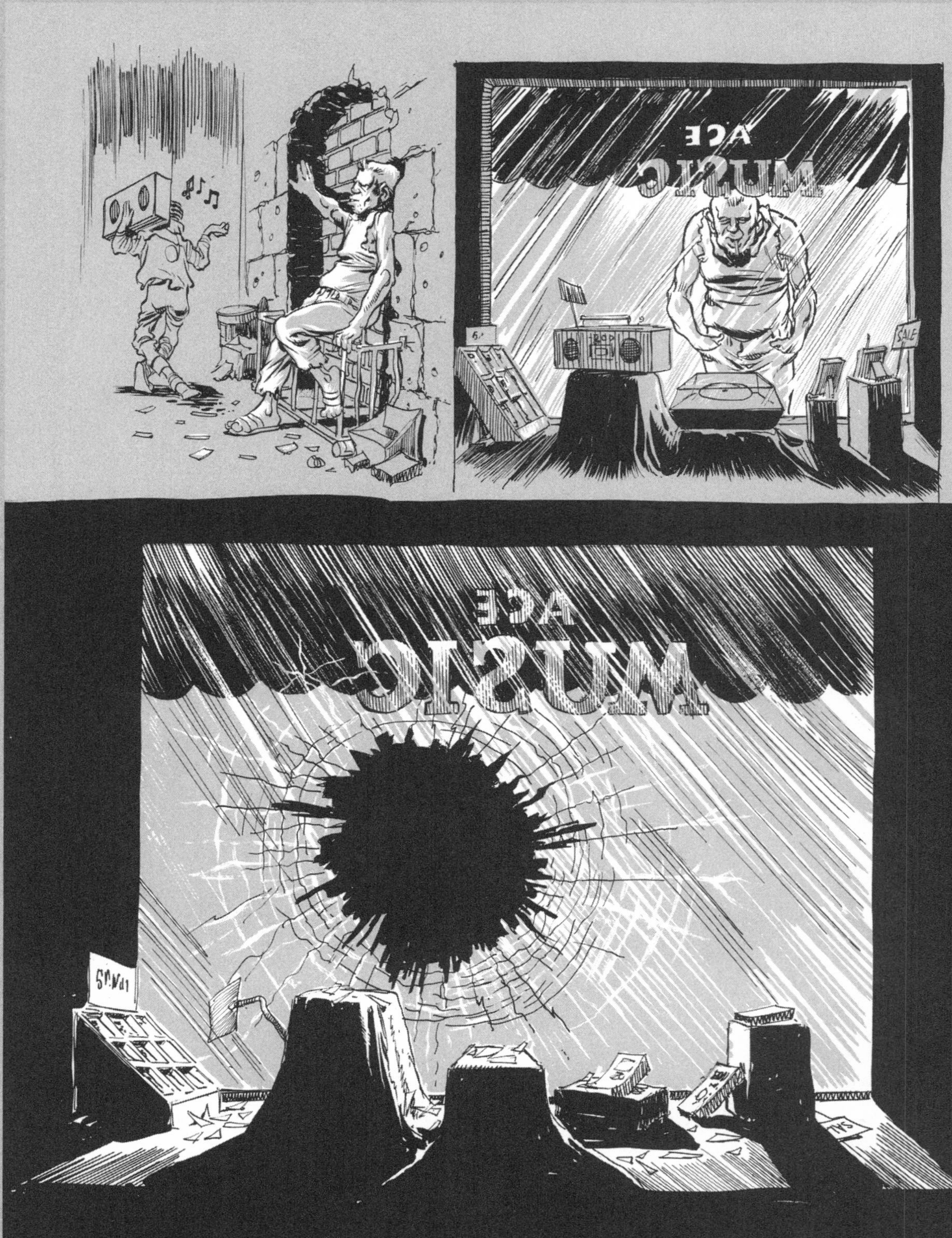
ACE
MUSIC
SALE
ACE
MUSIC

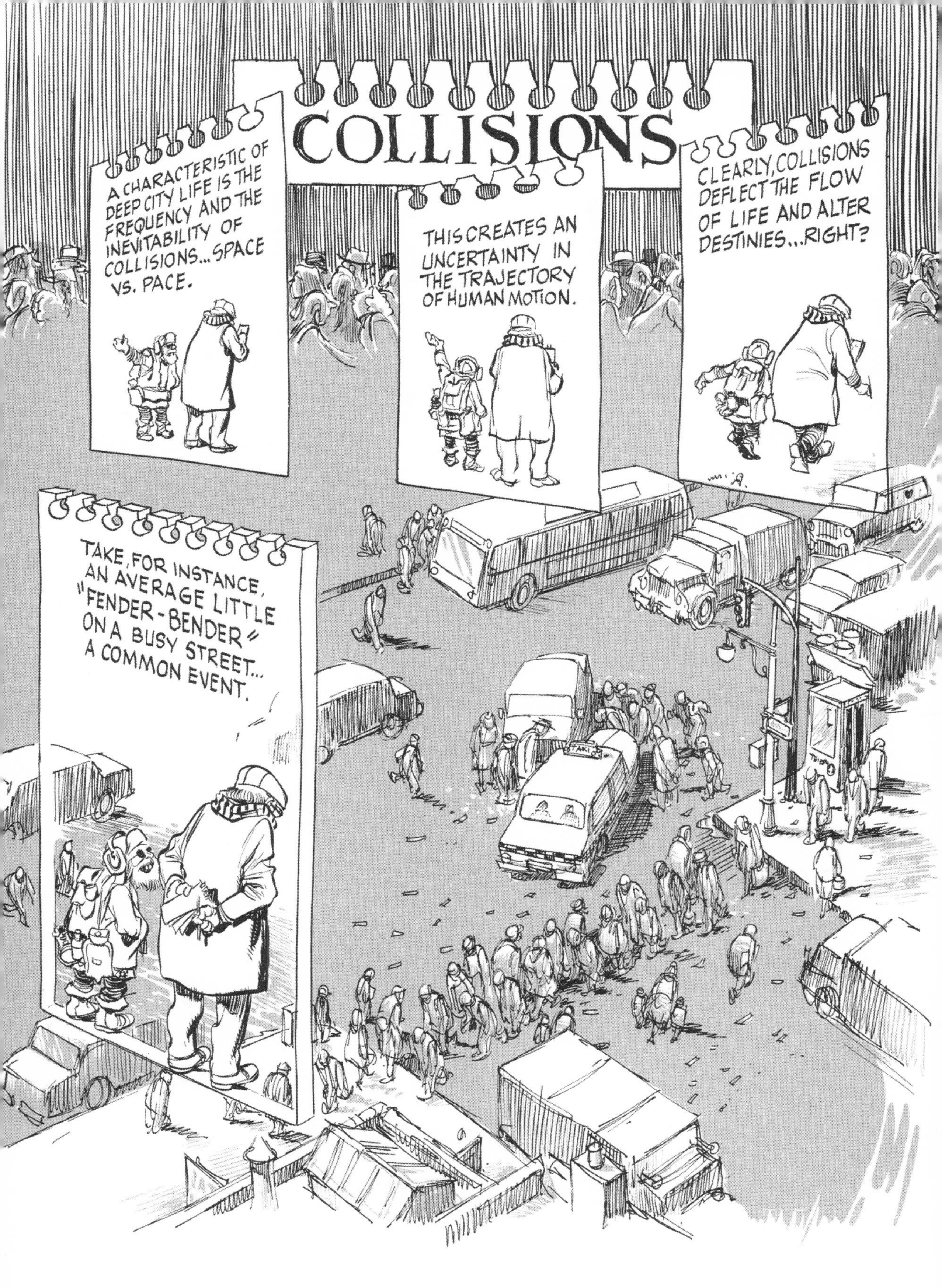
COLLISIONS
A CHARACTERISTIC OF DEEP CITY LIFE IS THE FREQUENCY AND THE INEVITABILITY OF COLLISIONS... SPACE VS. PACE.
THIS CREATES AN UNCERTAINTY IN THE TRAJECTORY OF HUMAN MOTION.
CLEARLY, COLLISIONS DEFLECT THE FLOW OF LIFE AND ALTER DESTINIES... RIGHT?
TAKE, FOR INSTANCE, AN AVERAGE LITTLE "FENDER-BENDER" ON A BUSY STREET... A COMMON EVENT.
TAXI

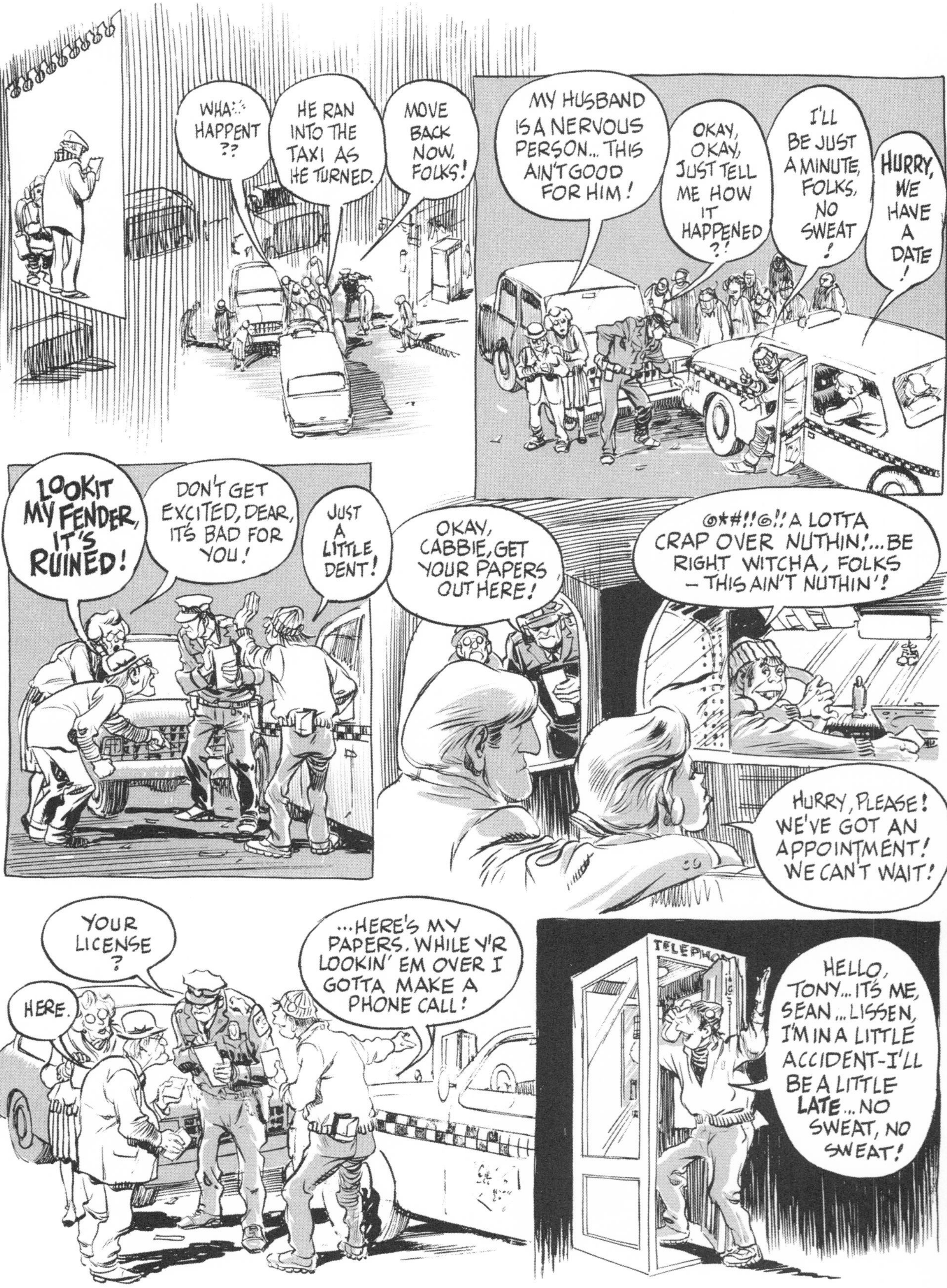
WHA: HAPPENT ??
HE RAN INTO THE TAXI AS HE TURNED.
MOVE BACK NOW, FOLKS!
MY HUSBAND IS A NERVOUS PERSON... THIS AIN'T GOOD FOR HIM!
OKAY, OKAY, JUST TELL ME HOW IT HAPPENED ?!
I'LL BE JUST A MINUTE, FOLKS, NO SWEAT!
HURRY, WE HAVE A DATE!
LOOKIT MY FENDER, IT'S RUINED!
DON'T GET EXCITED, DEAR, IT'S BAD FOR YOU!
JUST A LITTLE DENT!
OKAY, CABBIE, GET YOUR PAPERS OUT HERE!
@*#!!@!! A LOTTA CRAP OVER NUTHIN'!... BE RIGHT WITCHA, FOLKS – THIS AIN'T NUTHIN'!
HURRY, PLEASE! WE'VE GOT AN APPOINTMENT! WE CAN'T WAIT!
YOUR LICENSE ?
HERE.
...HERE'S MY PAPERS. WHILE Y'R LOOKIN' EM OVER I GOTTA MAKE A PHONE CALL!
TELEPHO
HELLO, TONY... IT'S ME, SEAN... LISSEN, I'M IN A LITTLE ACCIDENT-I'LL BE A LITTLE LATE... NO SWEAT, NO SWEAT!

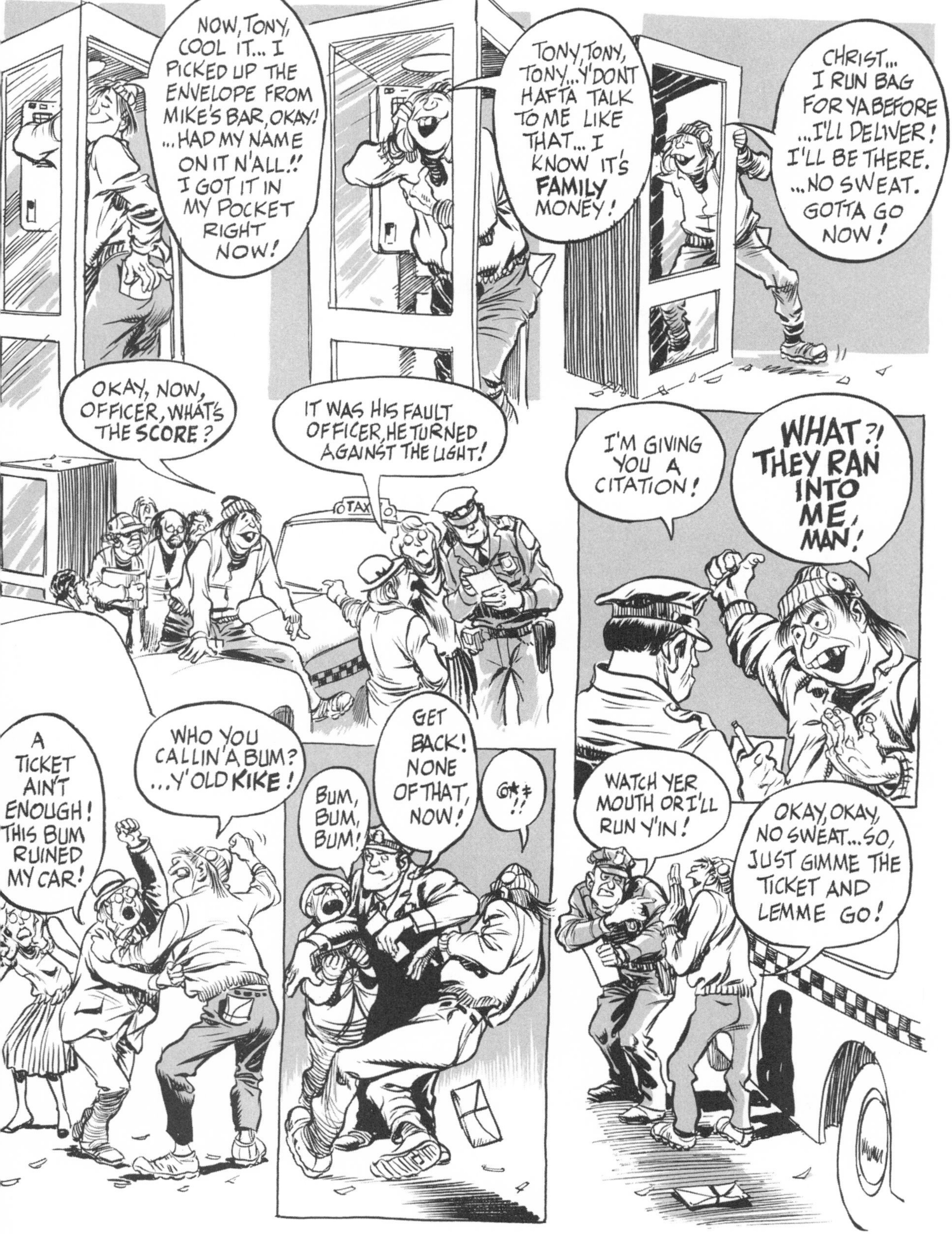

NOW, TONY, COOL IT... I PICKED UP THE ENVELOPE FROM MIKE'S BAR, OKAY! ...HAD MY NAME ON IT N'ALL.!! I GOT IT IN MY POCKET RIGHT NOW!
TONY, TONY, TONY...Y'DON'T HAFTA TALK TO ME LIKE THAT... I KNOW IT'S FAMILY MONEY!
CHRIST... I RUN BAG FOR YA BEFORE ...I'LL DELIVER! I'LL BE THERE. ...NO SWEAT. GOTTA GO NOW!
OKAY, NOW, OFFICER, WHAT'S THE SCORE?
IT WAS HIS FAULT OFFICER, HE TURNED AGAINST THE LIGHT!
TAXI
I'M GIVING YOU A CITATION!
WHAT?! THEY RAN INTO ME, MAN!
A TICKET AIN'T ENOUGH! THIS BUM RUINED MY CAR!
WHO YOU CALLIN' A BUM? ...Y'OLD KIKE!
BUM, BUM, BUM!
GET BACK! NONE OF THAT, NOW!
@*‡ !!
WATCH YER MOUTH OR I'LL RUN Y'IN!
OKAY, OKAY, NO SWEAT... SO, JUST GIMME THE TICKET AND LEMME GO!

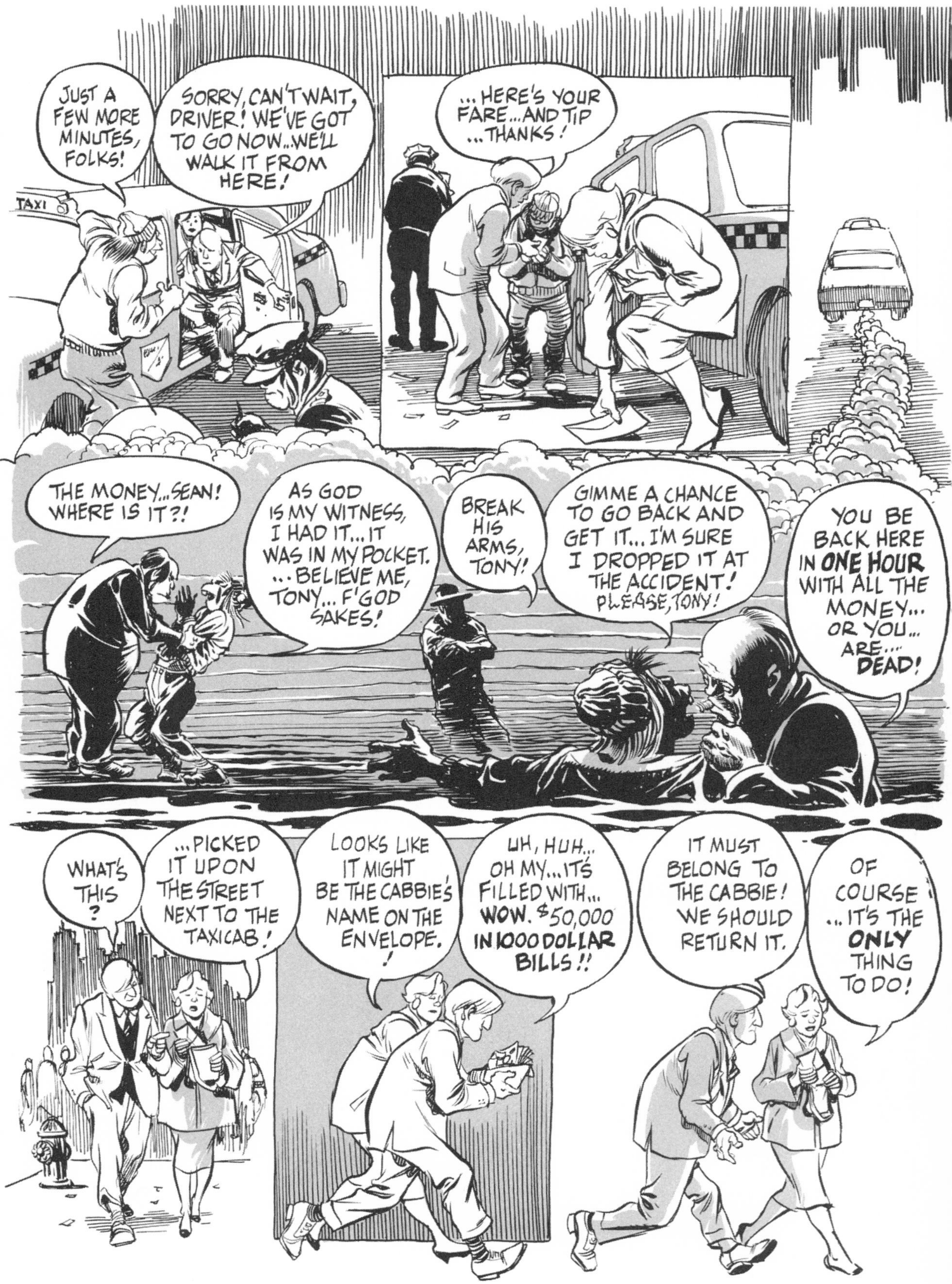
JUST A FEW MORE MINUTES, FOLKS!
SORRY, CAN'T WAIT, DRIVER! WE'VE GOT TO GO NOW...WE'LL WALK IT FROM HERE!
TAXI
...HERE'S YOUR FARE...AND TIP ...THANKS!
THE MONEY...SEAN! WHERE IS IT?!
AS GOD IS MY WITNESS, I HAD IT...IT WAS IN MY POCKET. ...BELIEVE ME, TONY... F'GOD SAKES!
BREAK HIS ARMS, TONY!
GIMME A CHANCE TO GO BACK AND GET IT... I'M SURE I DROPPED IT AT THE ACCIDENT! PLEASE, TONY!
YOU BE BACK HERE IN ONE HOUR WITH ALL THE MONEY... OR YOU... ARE.... DEAD!
WHAT'S THIS?
...PICKED IT UP ON THE STREET NEXT TO THE TAXICAB!
LOOKS LIKE IT MIGHT BE THE CABBIE'S NAME ON THE ENVELOPE.!
UH, HUH... OH MY...IT'S FILLED WITH... WOW. $50,000 IN 1000 DOLLAR BILLS!!
IT MUST BELONG TO THE CABBIE! WE SHOULD RETURN IT.
OF COURSE ...IT'S THE ONLY THING TO DO!

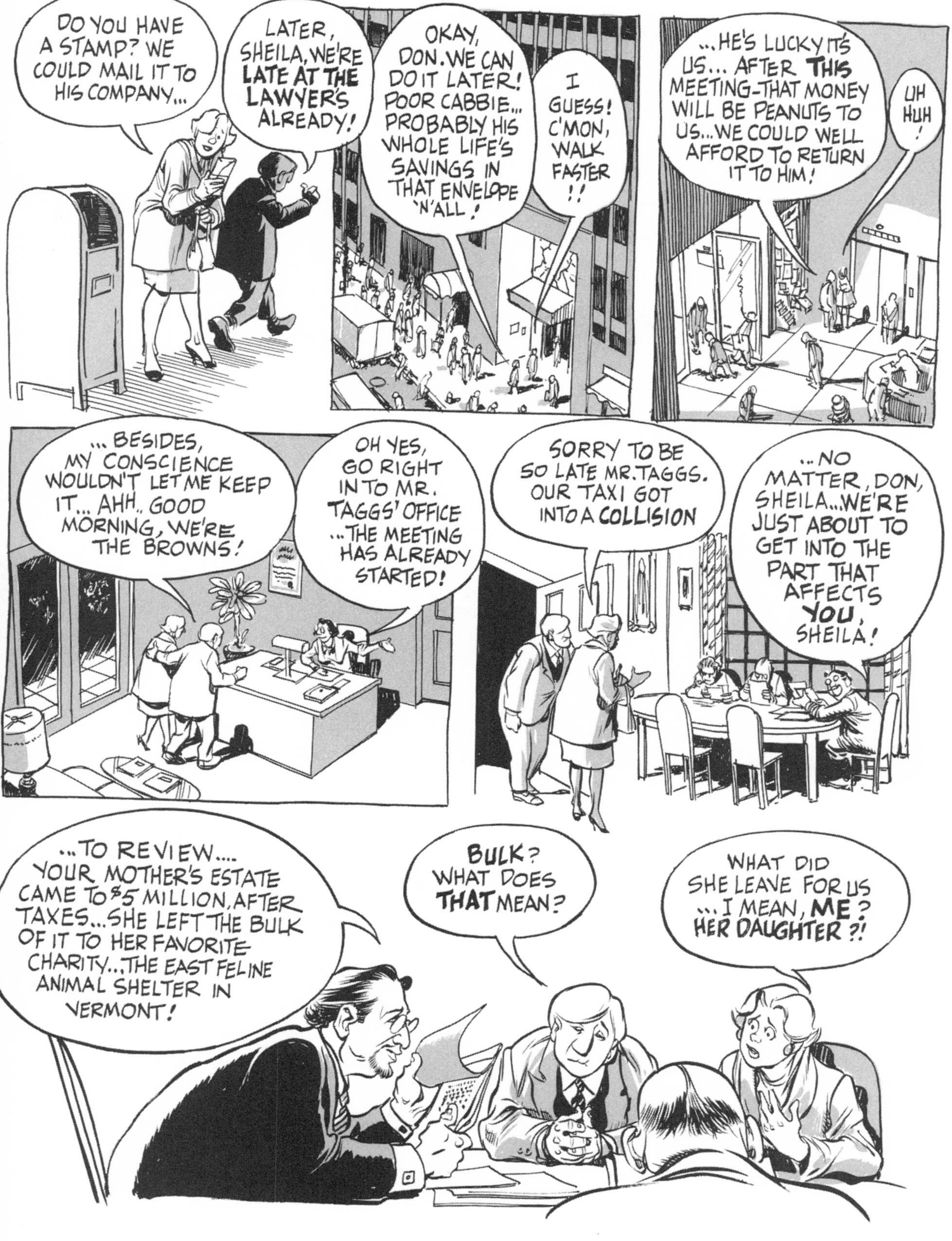
DO YOU HAVE A STAMP? WE COULD MAIL IT TO HIS COMPANY...
LATER, SHEILA, WE'RE LATE AT THE LAWYER'S ALREADY!
OKAY, DON. WE CAN DO IT LATER! POOR CABBIE... PROBABLY HIS WHOLE LIFE'S SAVINGS IN THAT ENVELOPE 'N'ALL!
I GUESS! C'MON, WALK FASTER!!
...HE'S LUCKY IT'S US... AFTER THIS MEETING-THAT MONEY WILL BE PEANUTS TO US...WE COULD WELL AFFORD TO RETURN IT TO HIM!
UH HUH!
...BESIDES, MY CONSCIENCE WOULDN'T LET ME KEEP IT... AHH.. GOOD MORNING, WE'RE THE BROWNS!
OH YES, GO RIGHT IN TO MR. TAGGS' OFFICE ...THE MEETING HAS ALREADY STARTED!
SORRY TO BE SO LATE MR. TAGGS. OUR TAXI GOT INTO A COLLISION
..NO MATTER, DON, SHEILA...WE'RE JUST ABOUT TO GET INTO THE PART THAT AFFECTS YOU, SHEILA!
...TO REVIEW.... YOUR MOTHER'S ESTATE CAME TO $5 MILLION, AFTER TAXES...SHE LEFT THE BULK OF IT TO HER FAVORITE CHARITY...THE EAST FELINE ANIMAL SHELTER IN VERMONT!
BULK? WHAT DOES THAT MEAN?
WHAT DID SHE LEAVE FOR US ...I MEAN, ME? HER DAUGHTER?!

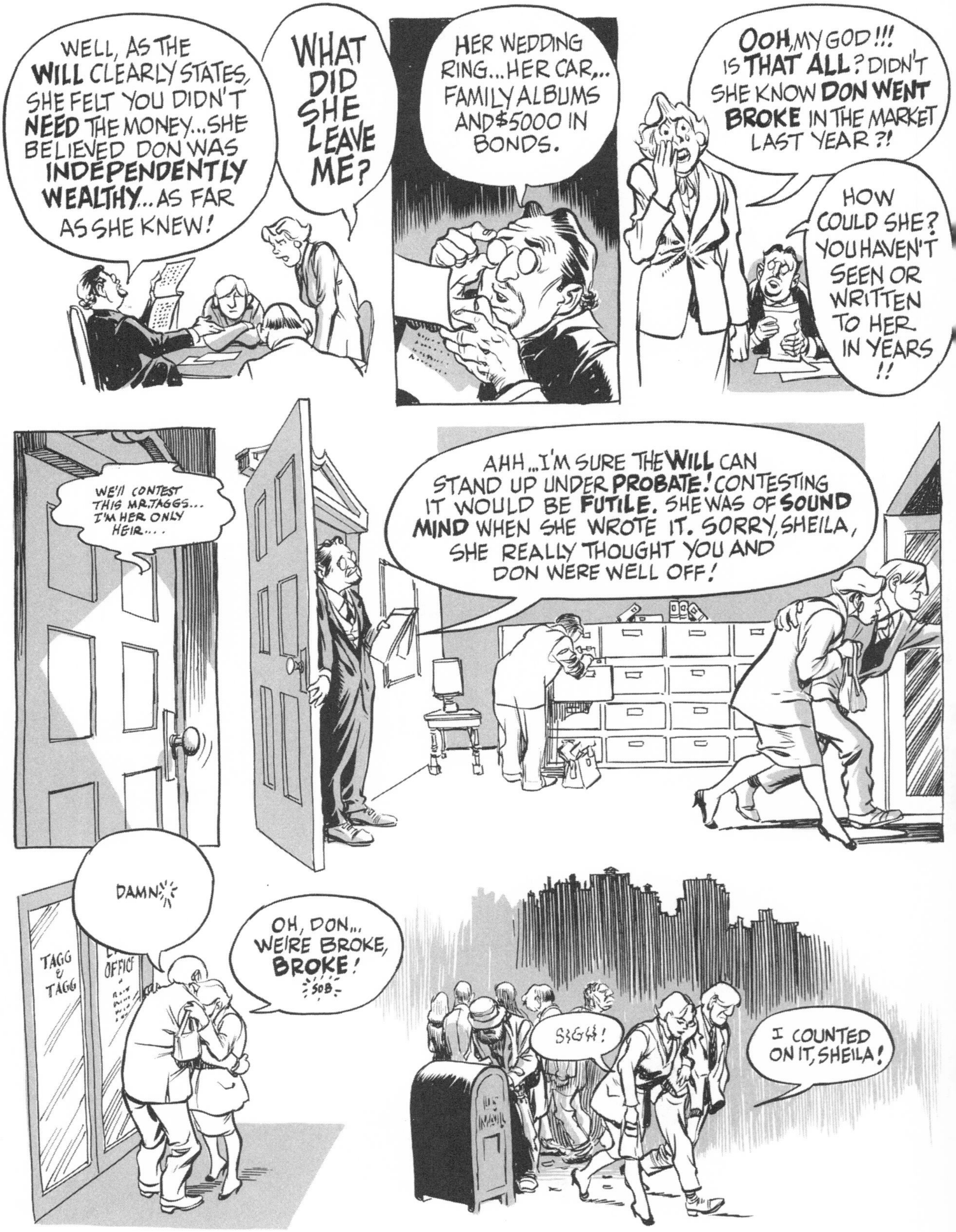

WELL, AS THE WILL CLEARLY STATES, SHE FELT YOU DIDN'T NEED THE MONEY...SHE BELIEVED DON WAS INDEPENDENTLY WEALTHY...AS FAR AS SHE KNEW!
WHAT DID SHE LEAVE ME?
HER WEDDING RING...HER CAR,... FAMILY ALBUMS AND $5000 IN BONDS.
OOH, MY GOD!!! IS THAT ALL? DIDN'T SHE KNOW DON WENT BROKE IN THE MARKET LAST YEAR?!
HOW COULD SHE? YOU HAVEN'T SEEN OR WRITTEN TO HER IN YEARS!!
WE'LL CONTEST THIS MR. TAGGS... I'M HER ONLY HEIR...
AHH...I'M SURE THE WILL CAN STAND UP UNDER PROBATE! CONTESTING IT WOULD BE FUTILE. SHE WAS OF SOUND MIND WHEN SHE WROTE IT. SORRY, SHEILA, SHE REALLY THOUGHT YOU AND DON WERE WELL OFF!
DAMN
TAGG & TAGG
OH, DON... WE'RE BROKE, BROKE!
SOB
I COUNTED ON IT, SHEILA!

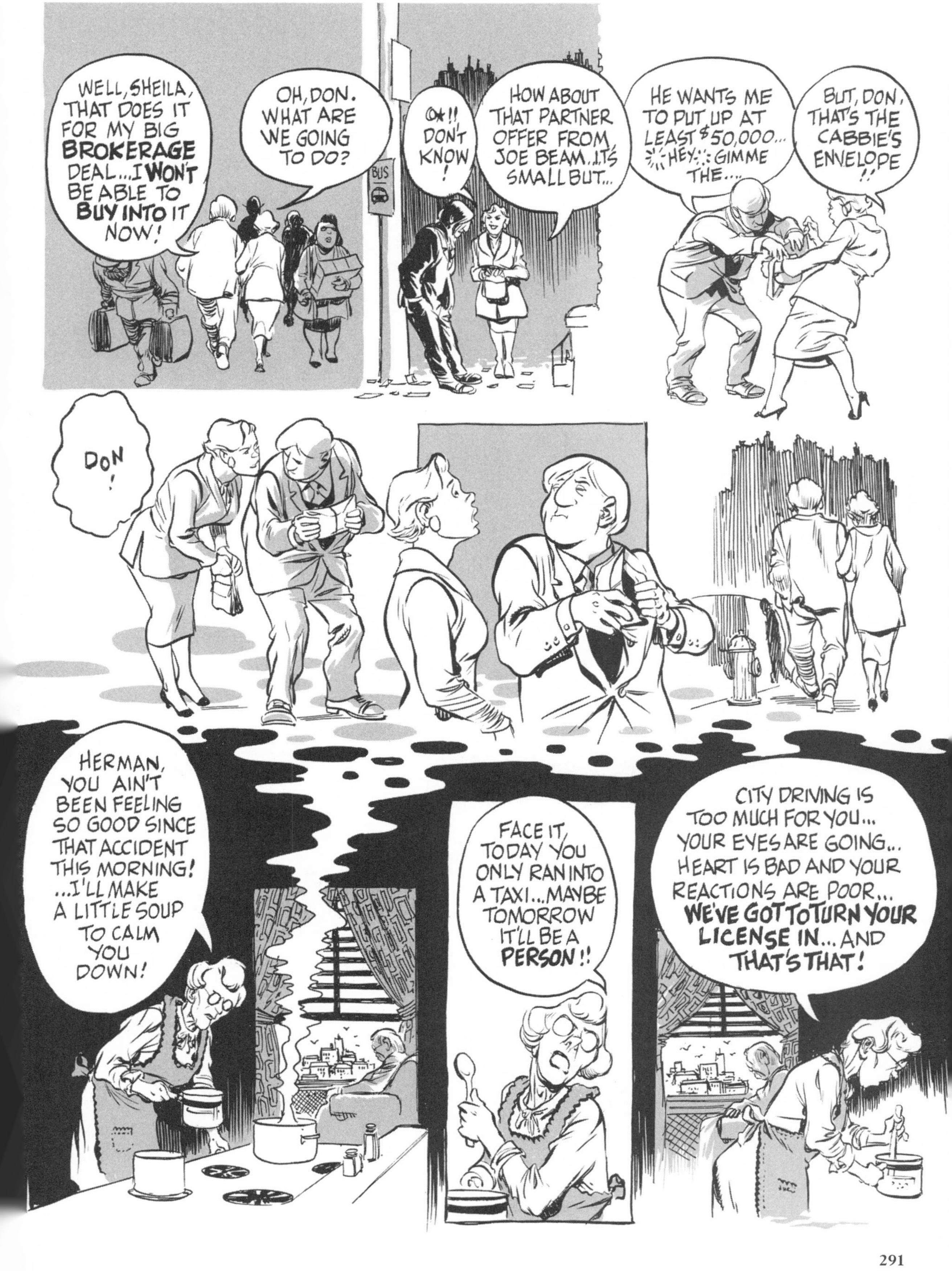
WELL, SHEILA, THAT DOES IT FOR MY BIG BROKERAGE DEAL... I WON'T BE ABLE TO BUY INTO IT NOW!
OH, DON. WHAT ARE WE GOING TO DO?
@*!! DON'T KNOW!
HOW ABOUT THAT PARTNER OFFER FROM JOE BEAM.. IT'S SMALL BUT...
BUS
HE WANTS ME TO PUT UP AT LEAST $50,000... HEY: GIMME THE....
BUT, DON, THAT'S THE CABBIE'S ENVELOPE!!
DON!
HERMAN, YOU AIN'T BEEN FEELING SO GOOD SINCE THAT ACCIDENT THIS MORNING! ...I'LL MAKE A LITTLE SOUP TO CALM YOU DOWN!
FACE IT, TODAY YOU ONLY RAN INTO A TAXI... MAYBE TOMORROW IT'LL BE A PERSON!!
CITY DRIVING IS TOO MUCH FOR YOU... YOUR EYES ARE GOING... HEART IS BAD AND YOUR REACTIONS ARE POOR... WE'VE GOT TO TURN YOUR LICENSE IN... AND THAT'S THAT!

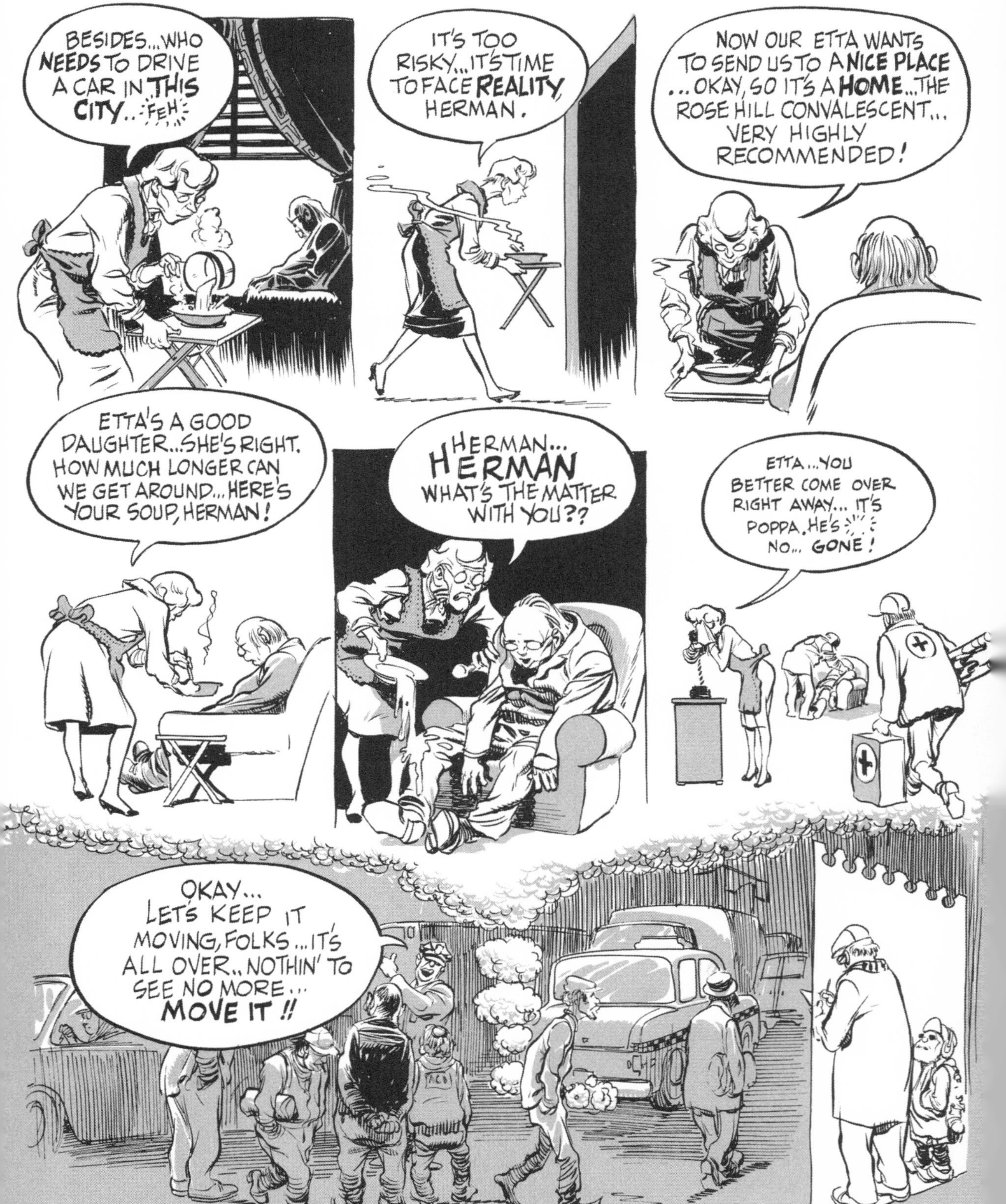
BESIDES... WHO NEEDS TO DRIVE A CAR IN THIS CITY.. FEH
IT'S TOO RISKY... IT'S TIME TO FACE REALITY, HERMAN.
NOW OUR ETTA WANTS TO SEND US TO A NICE PLACE ... OKAY, SO IT'S A HOME... THE ROSE HILL CONVALESCENT... VERY HIGHLY RECOMMENDED!
ETTA'S A GOOD DAUGHTER... SHE'S RIGHT. HOW MUCH LONGER CAN WE GET AROUND... HERE'S YOUR SOUP, HERMAN!
HERMAN... HERMAN WHAT'S THE MATTER WITH YOU??
ETTA... YOU BETTER COME OVER RIGHT AWAY... IT'S POPPA. HE'S NO... GONE!
OKAY... LET'S KEEP IT MOVING, FOLKS... IT'S ALL OVER.. NOTHIN' TO SEE NO MORE... MOVE IT!!

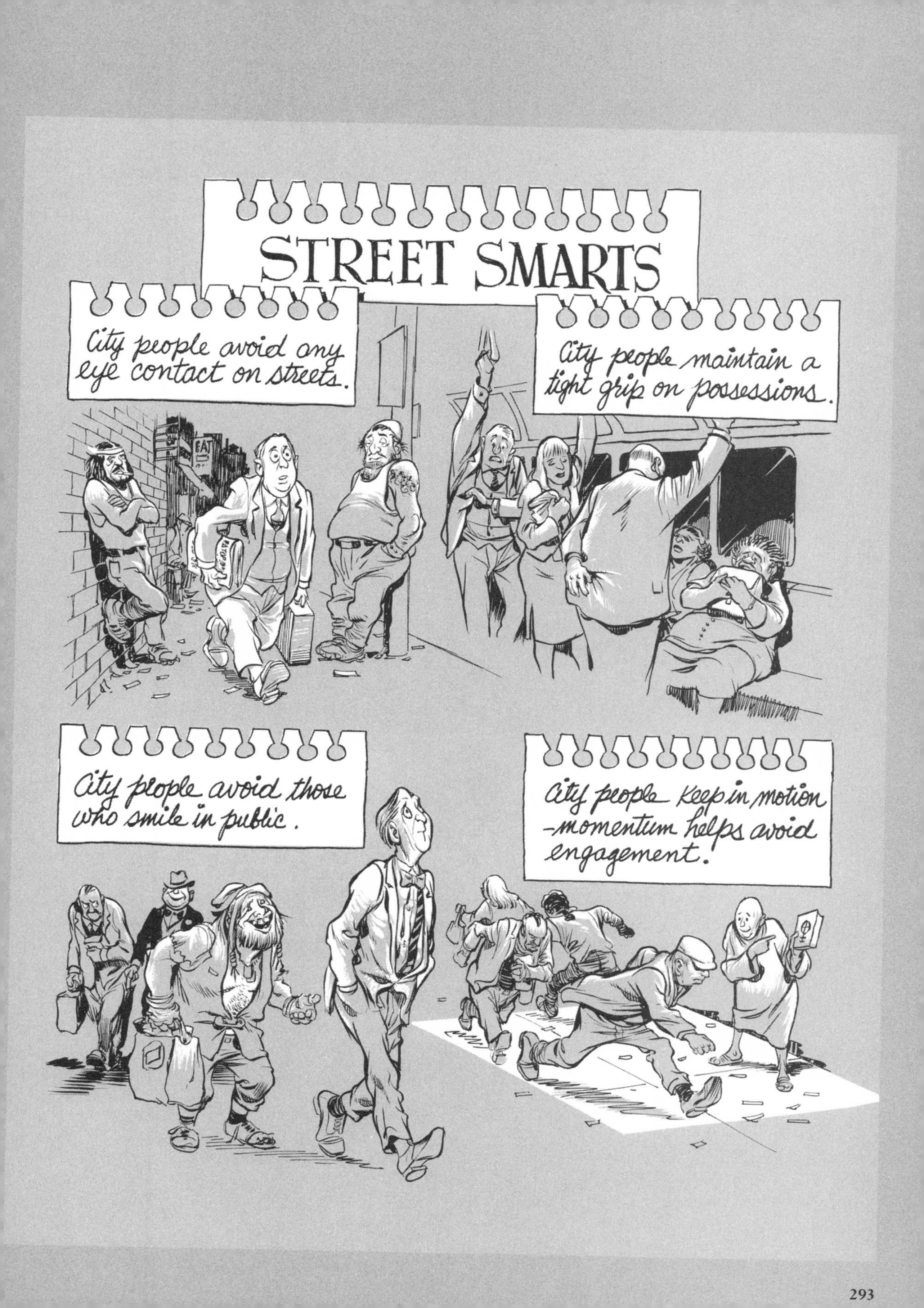
STREET SMARTS
City people avoid any eye contact on streets.
City people maintain a tight grip on possessions.
City people avoid those who smile in public.
City people keep in motion -momentum helps avoid engagement.

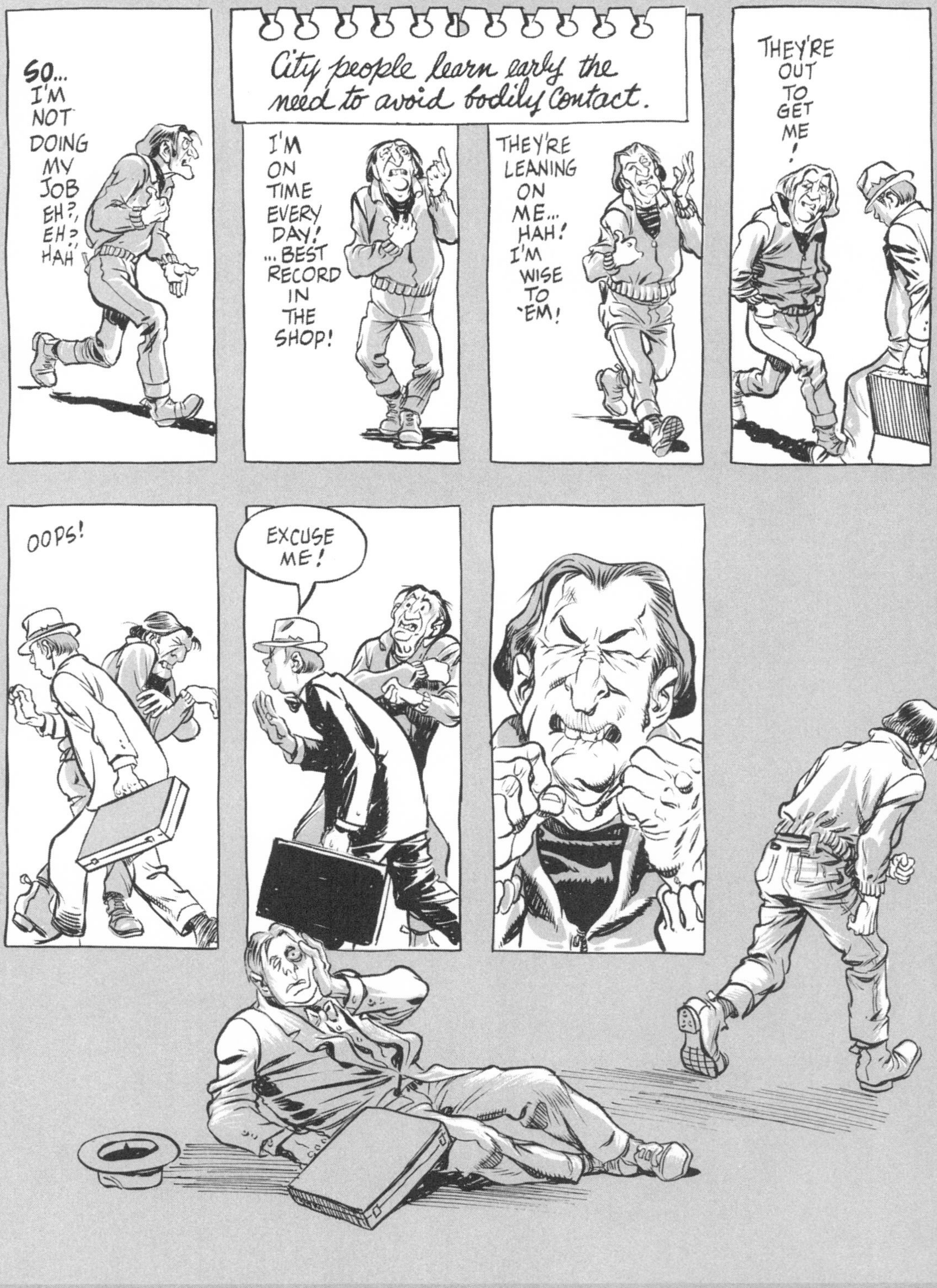
SO... I'M NOT DOING MY JOB EH?, EH? HAH!
City people learn early the need to avoid bodily contact.
I'M ON TIME EVERY DAY! ...BEST RECORD IN THE SHOP!
THEY'RE LEANING ON ME... HAH! I'M WISE TO 'EM!
THEY'RE OUT TO GET ME!
OOPS!
EXCUSE ME!

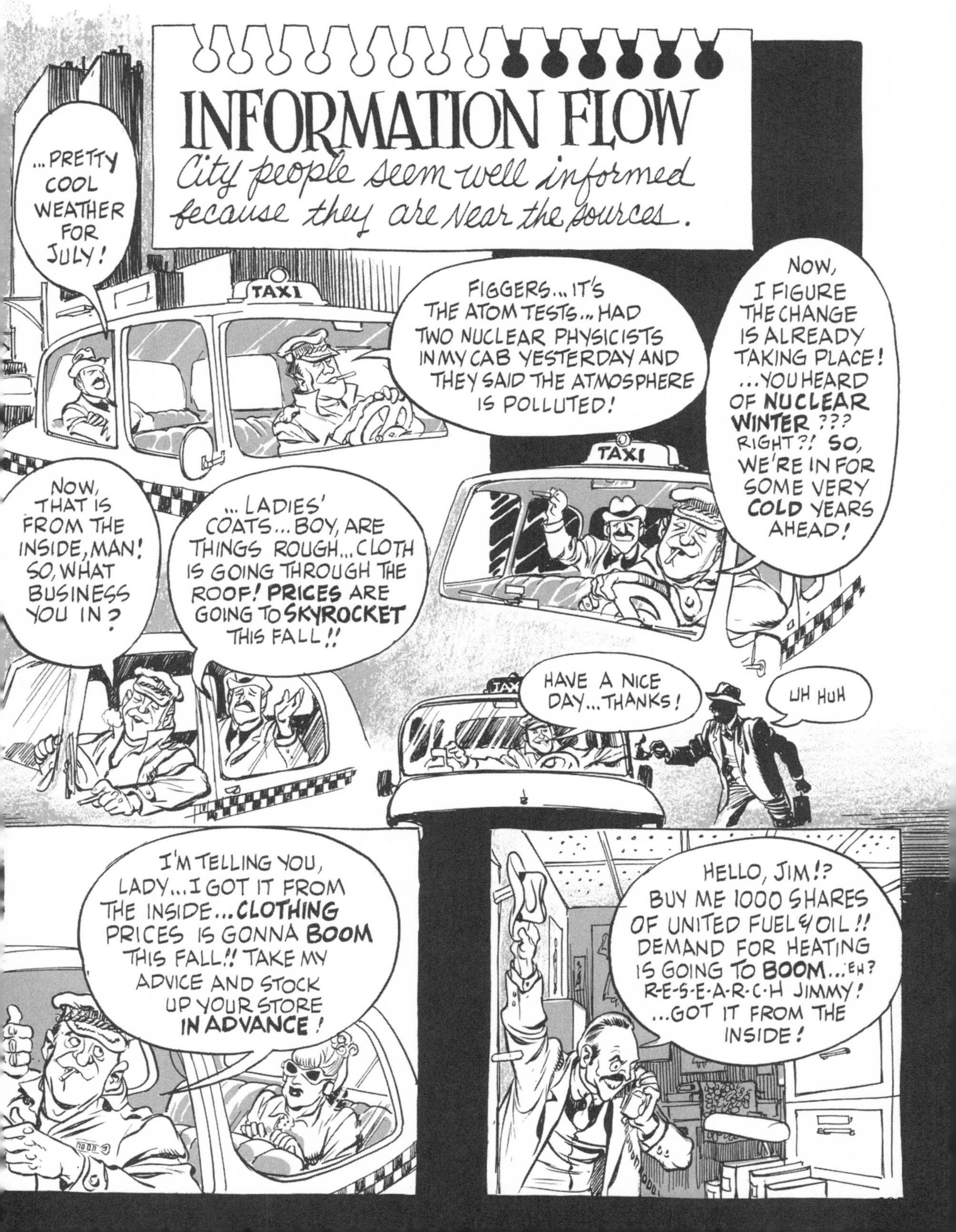
INFORMATION FLOW
City people seem well informed because they are near the sources.
...PRETTY COOL WEATHER FOR JULY!
FIGGERS... IT'S THE ATOM TESTS... HAD TWO NUCLEAR PHYSICISTS IN MY CAB YESTERDAY AND THEY SAID THE ATMOSPHERE IS POLLUTED!
NOW, I FIGURE THE CHANGE IS ALREADY TAKING PLACE! ...YOU HEARD OF NUCLEAR WINTER ??? RIGHT?! SO, WE'RE IN FOR SOME VERY COLD YEARS AHEAD!
TAXI
NOW, THAT IS FROM THE INSIDE, MAN! SO, WHAT BUSINESS YOU IN?
...LADIES' COATS... BOY, ARE THINGS ROUGH... CLOTH IS GOING THROUGH THE ROOF! PRICES ARE GOING TO SKYROCKET THIS FALL!!
HAVE A NICE DAY... THANKS!
UH HUH
I'M TELLING YOU, LADY... I GOT IT FROM THE INSIDE... CLOTHING PRICES IS GONNA BOOM THIS FALL!! TAKE MY ADVICE AND STOCK UP YOUR STORE IN ADVANCE!
HELLO, JIM!? BUY ME 1000 SHARES OF UNITED FUEL & OIL!! DEMAND FOR HEATING IS GOING TO BOOM...! EH? R-E-S-E-A-R-C-H JIMMY! ...GOT IT FROM THE INSIDE!

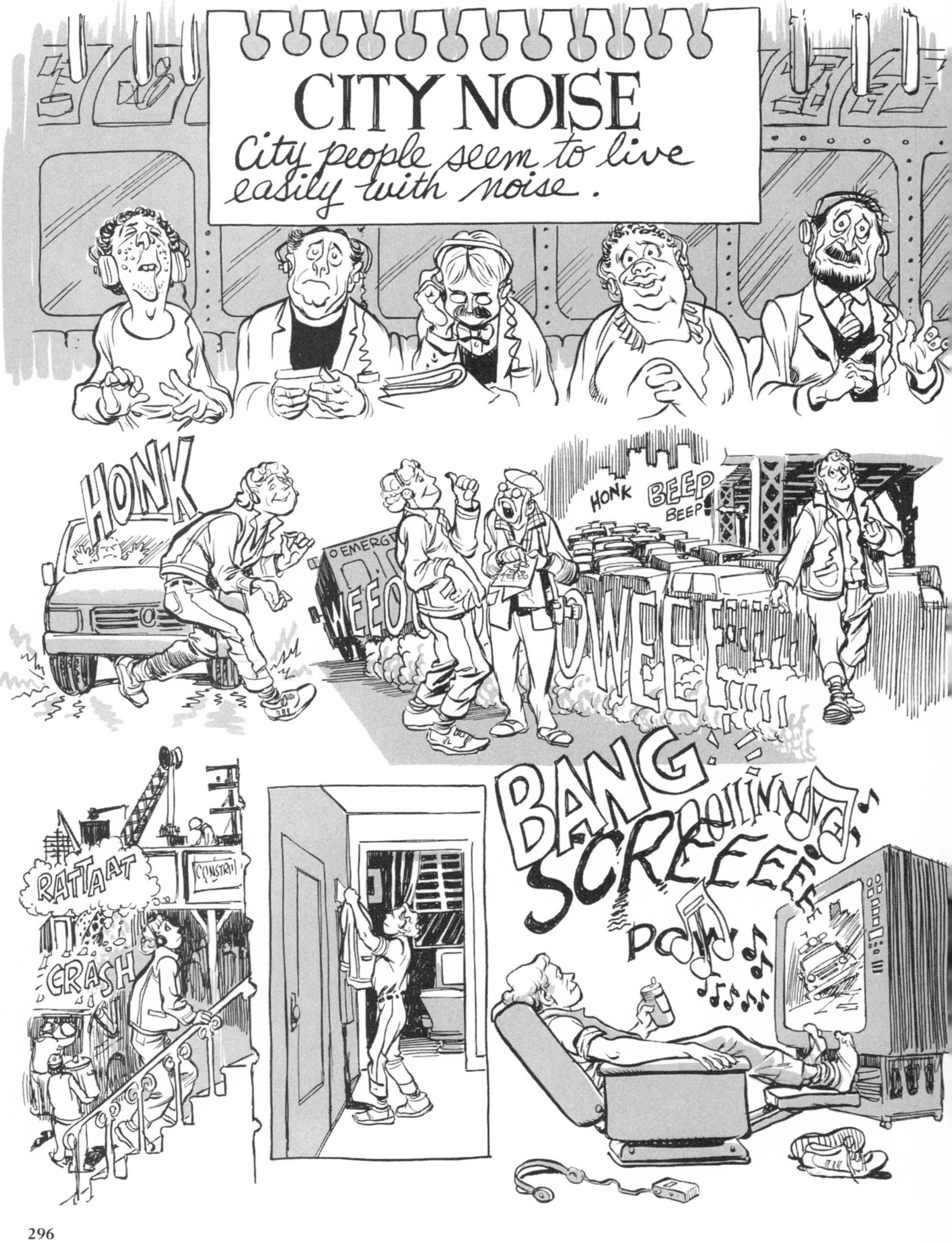
CITY NOISE
City people seem to live easily with noise.
HONK
HONK
BEEP
BEEP
BANG
SCREEEEEE
RATTAAT
CRASH

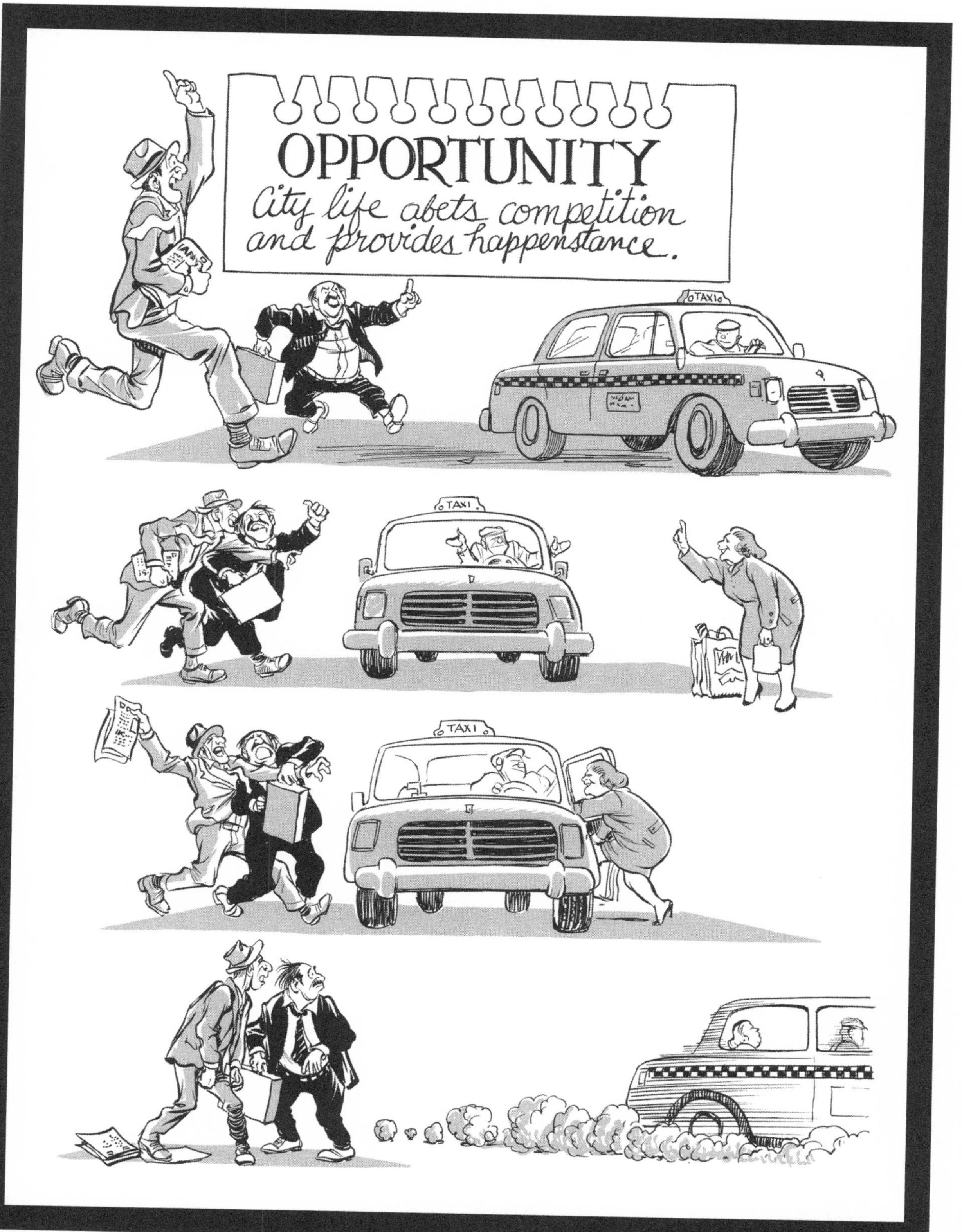
OPPORTUNITY
City life abets competition and provides happenstance.
TAXI
TAXI
TAXI

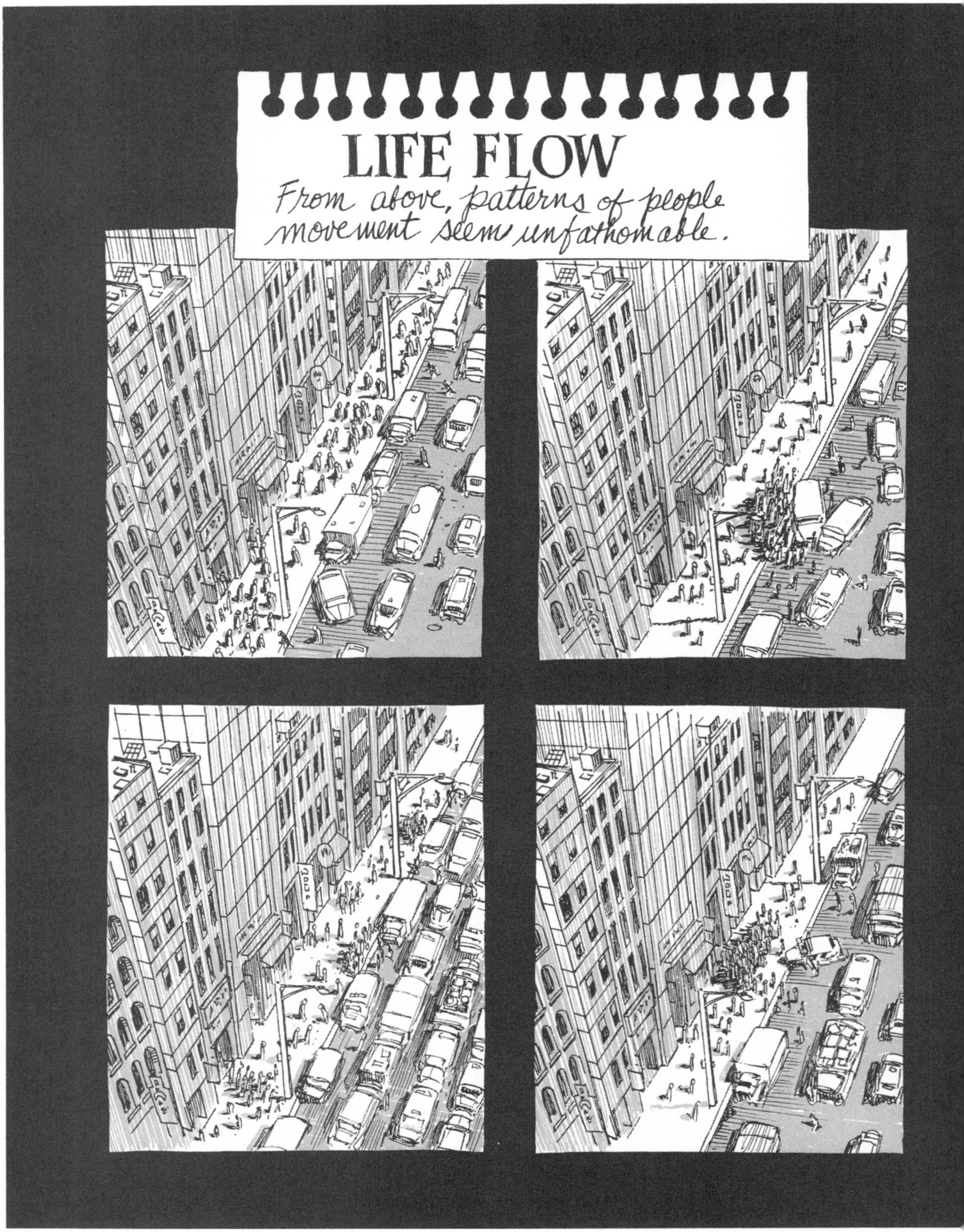
LIFE FLOW
From above, patterns of people movement seem unfathomable.

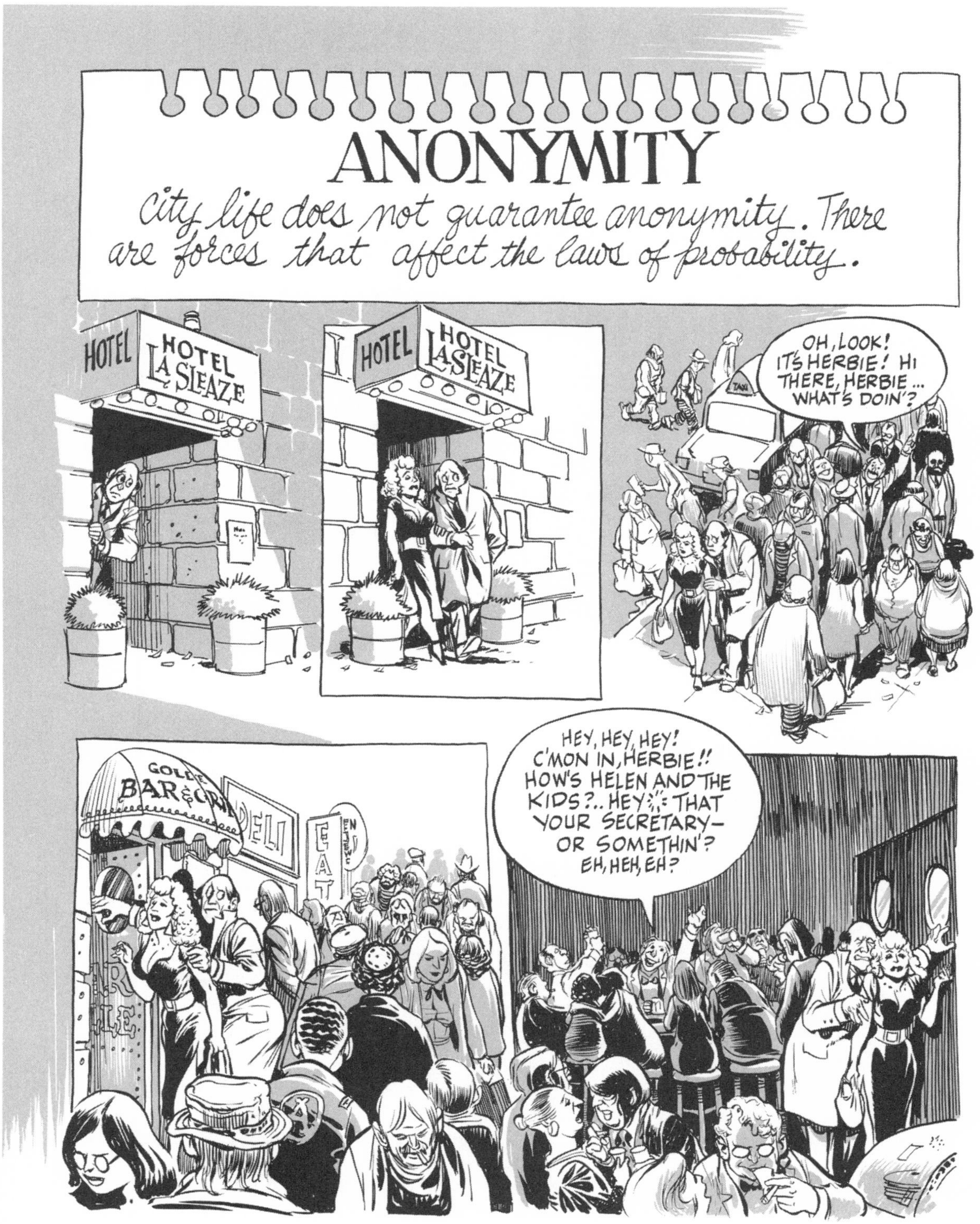

ANONYMITY
City life does not guarantee anonymity. There are forces that affect the laws of probability.
HOTEL
HOTEL LA SLEAZE
OH, LOOK! IT'S HERBIE! HI THERE, HERBIE... WHAT'S DOIN'?
EAT
HEY, HEY, HEY! C'MON IN, HERBIE!! HOW'S HELEN AND THE KIDS?.. HEY! THAT YOUR SECRETARY— OR SOMETHIN'? EH, HEH, EH?

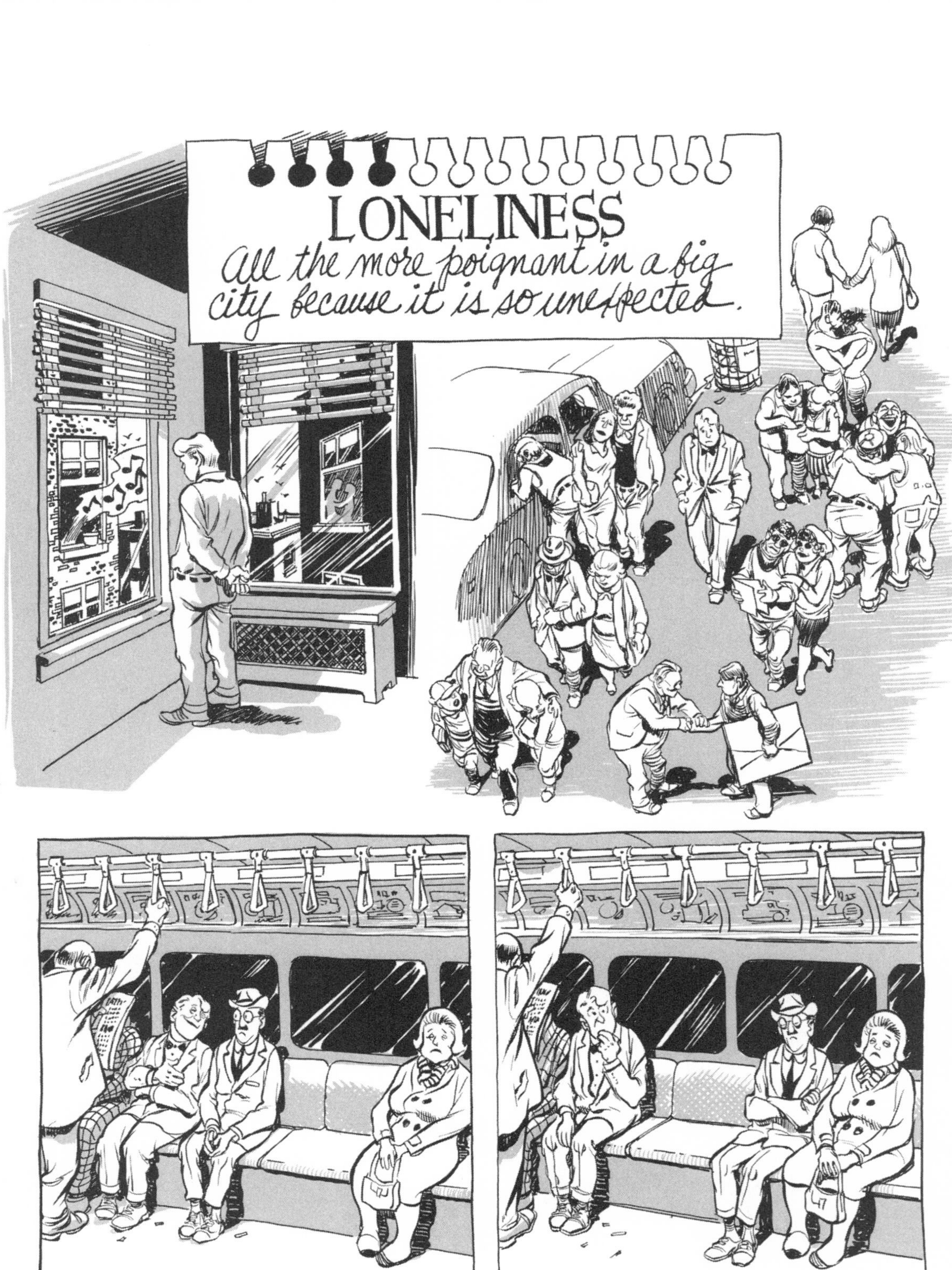
LONELINESS
All the more poignant in a big city because it is so unexpected.

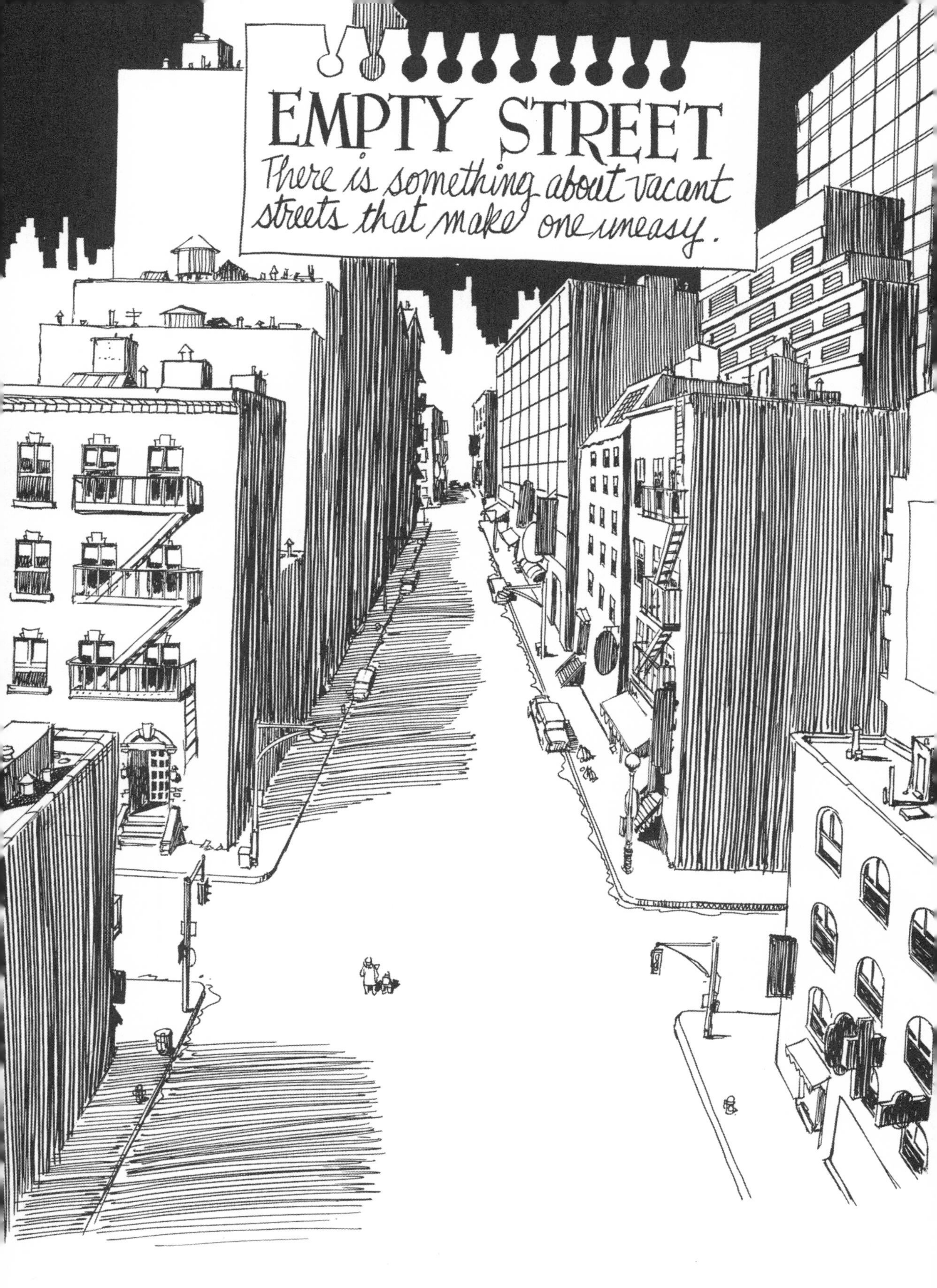
EMPTY STREET
There is something about vacant streets that make one uneasy.

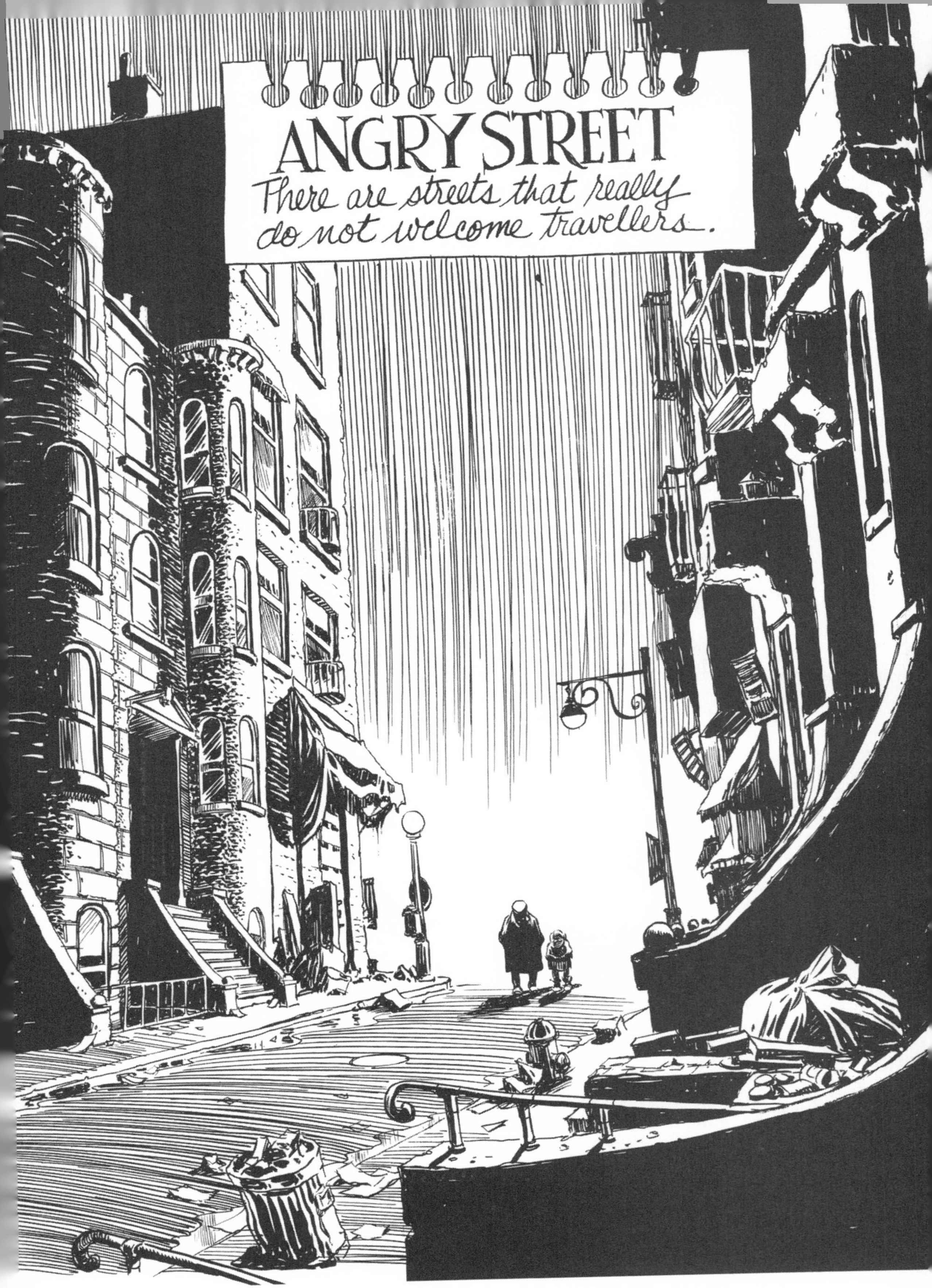
ANGRY STREET
There are streets that really do not welcome travellers.

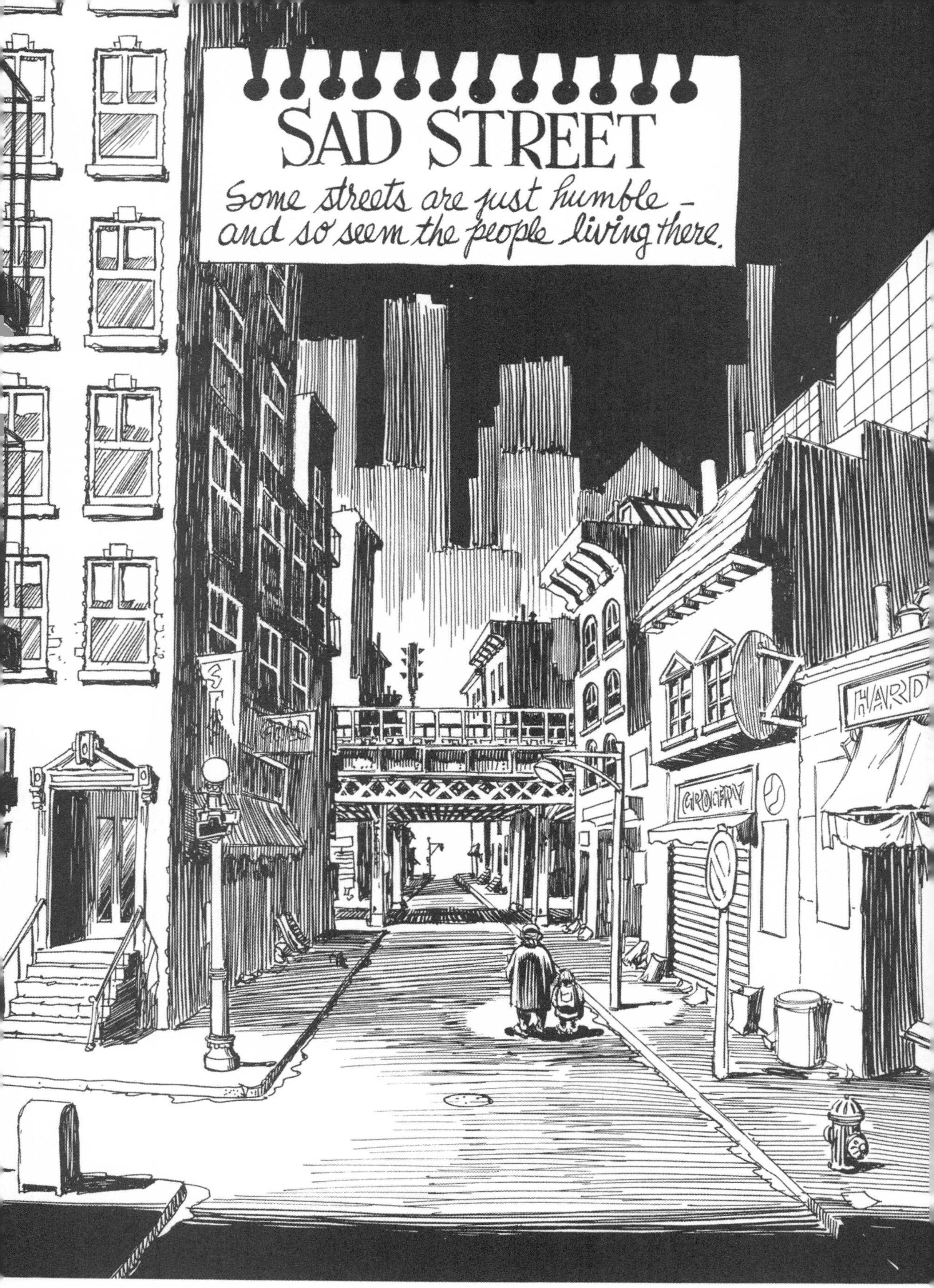
SAD STREET
Some streets are just humble - and so seem the people living there.
HARD

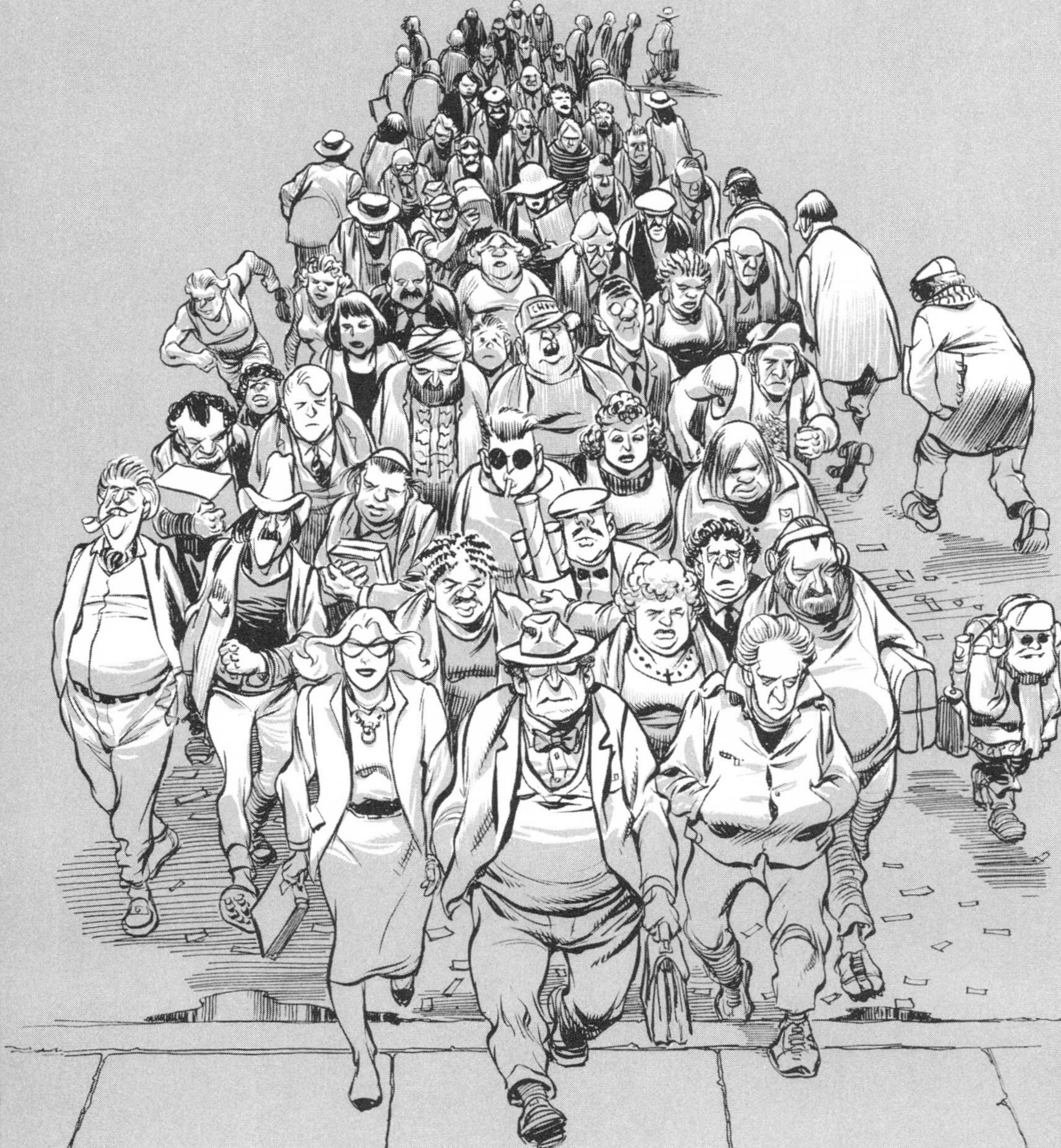

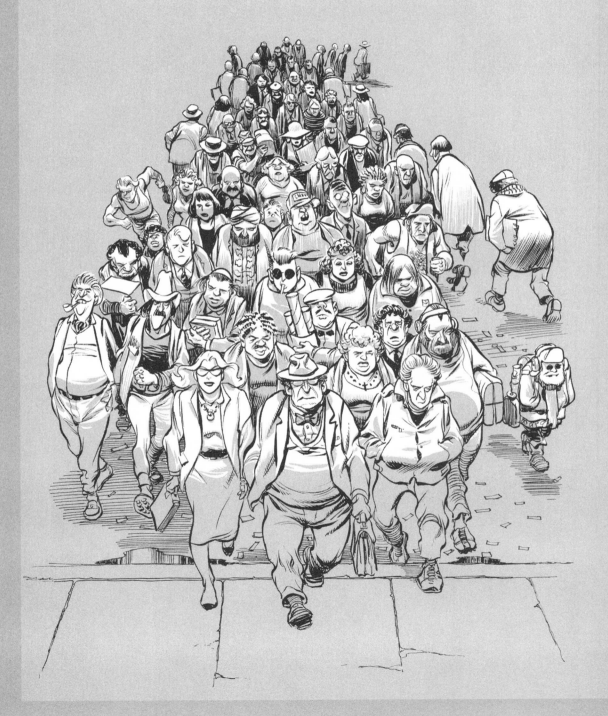

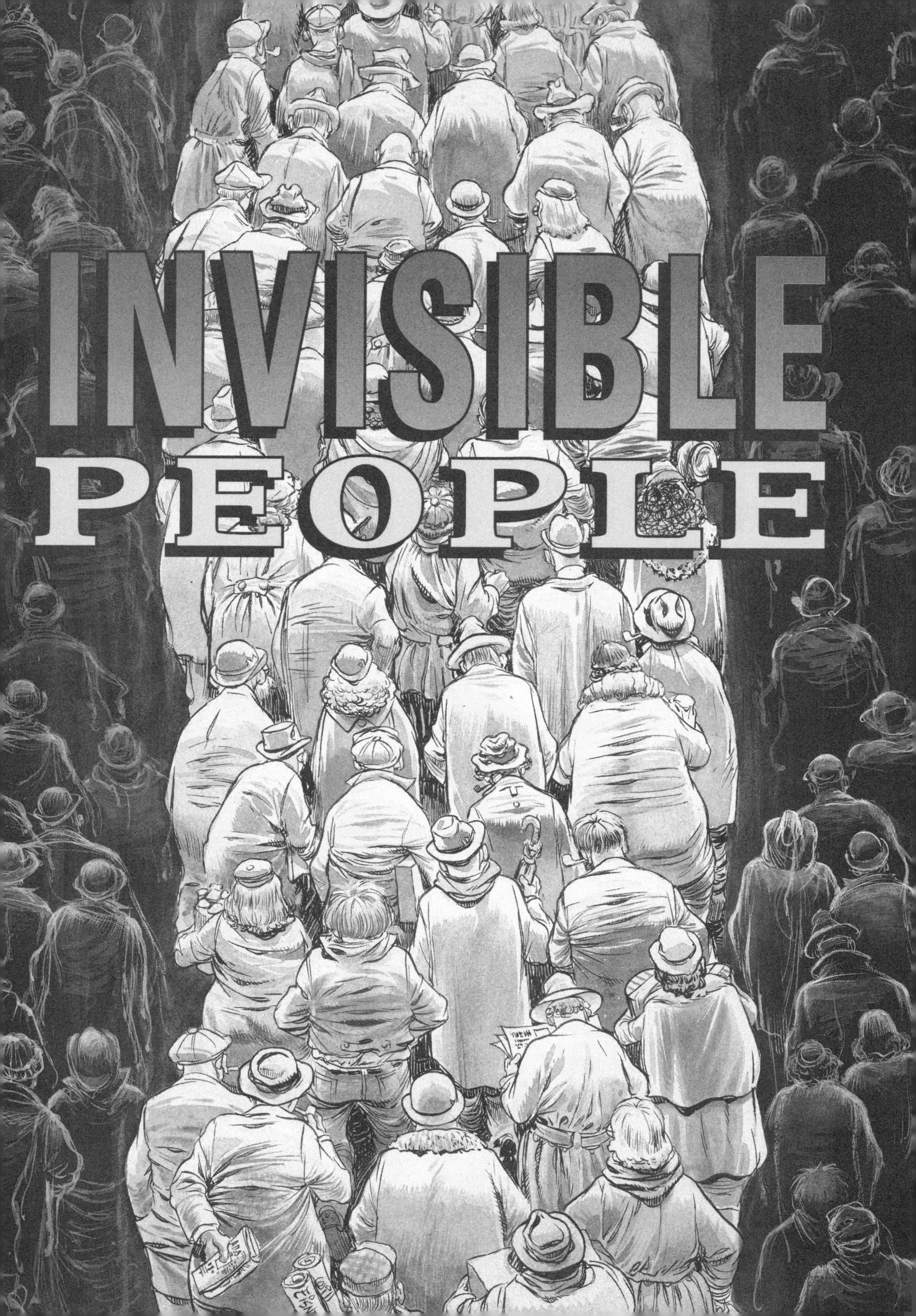

INVISIBLE
PEOPLE

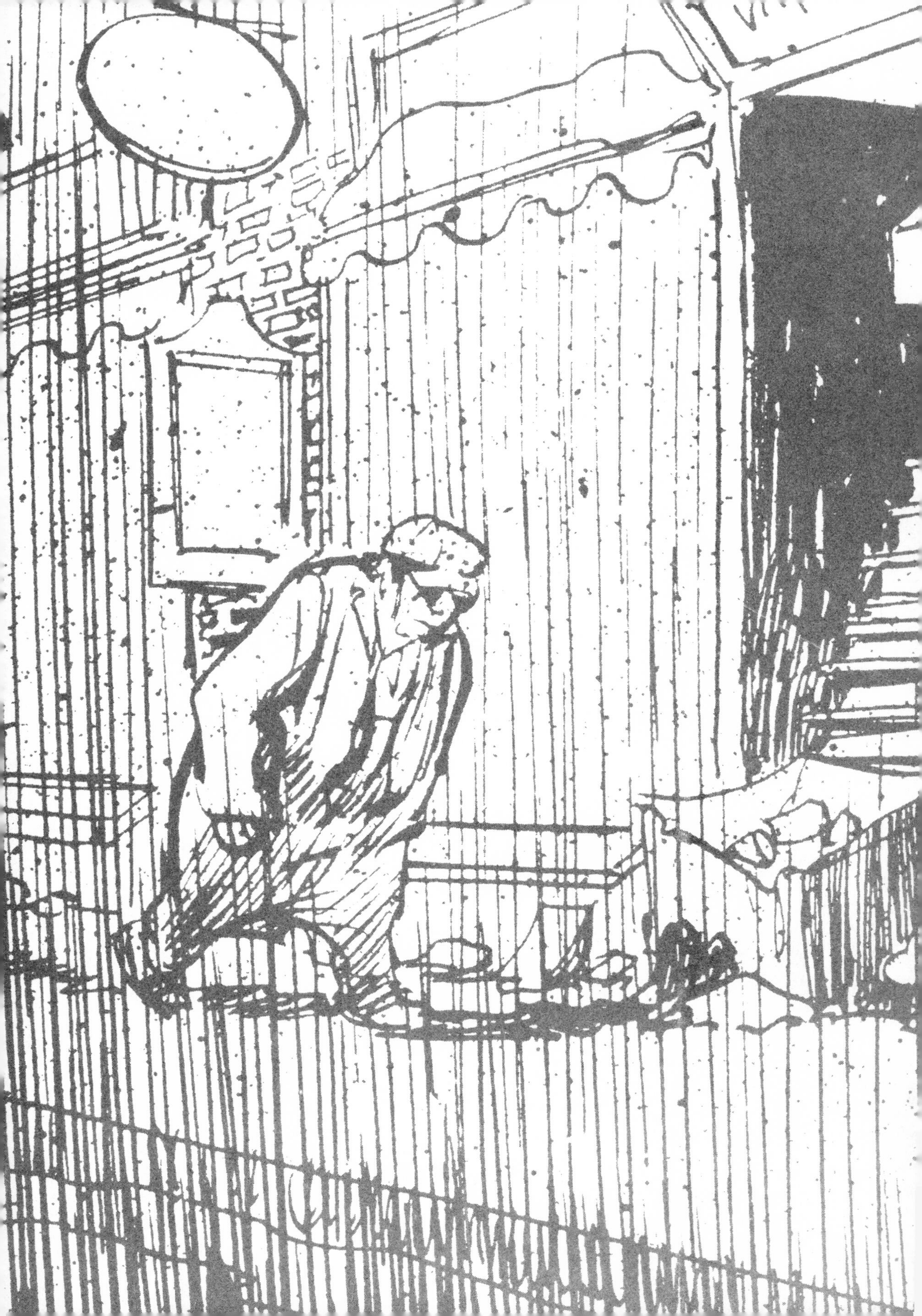

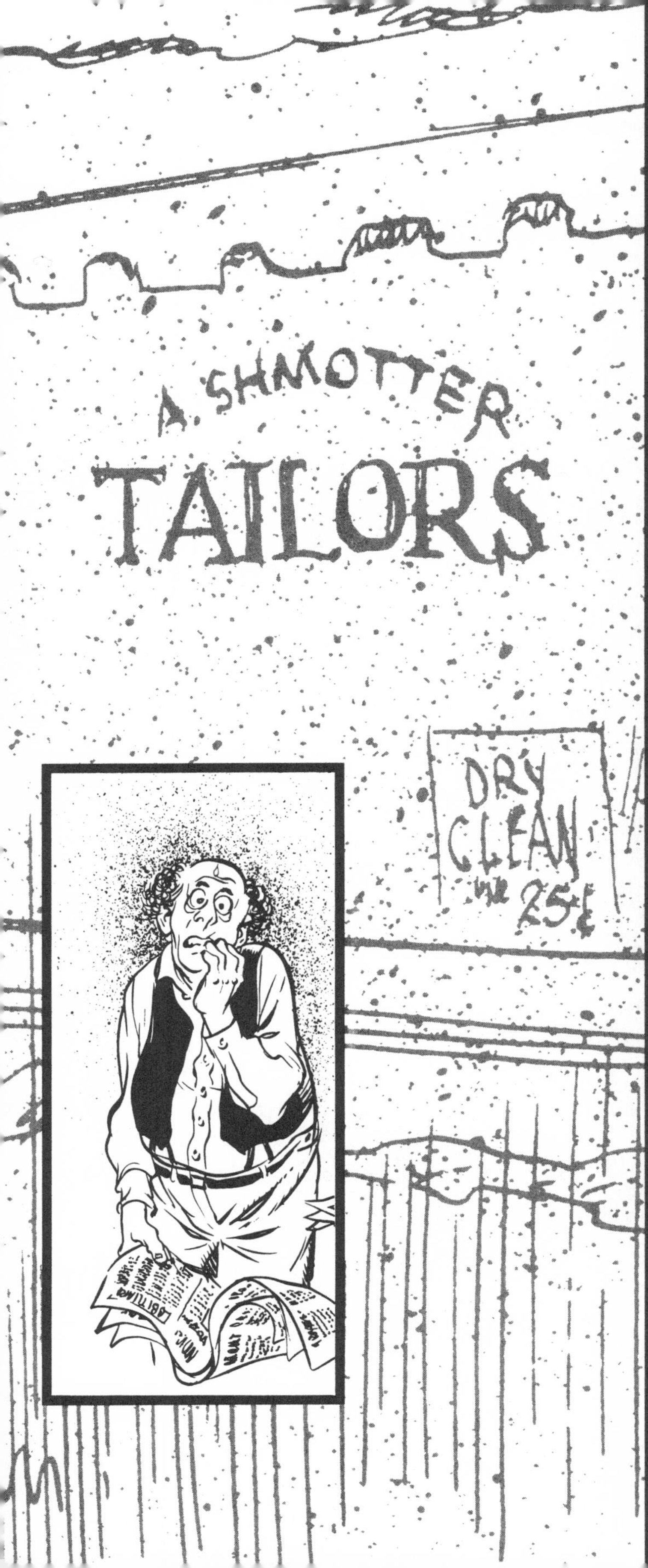
A. SHMOTTER
TAILORS
DRY CLEAN
25¢

Introduction to "Sanctum"

FROM THE EARLIEST days of my youth on the streets of the city I have been bemused by the anonymity of the people around me. The indifference of people to each other in crowded places seemed contradictory to the commonly accepted idea that cities were created for safety.

Indeed, the more time I spent on the streets the more I became aware of how unnoticed were the people who streamed past me. I grew up accepting this as a normal phenomenon of metropolitan life. Only years later did I realize how pervasive was this brutal reality and how people often accept, even welcome, invisibility as a way to deal with urban danger.

Pincus, the protagonist in "Sanctum," is a composite of someone who passed me a hundred times almost unnoticed.

I set his story during the grey 1930s because it was a time when life seemed simpler and the dynamics of city living easier to define.

The passage of years and the growth of modern social machinery has done little to change things. Today, more than ever, invisible people populate our cities.

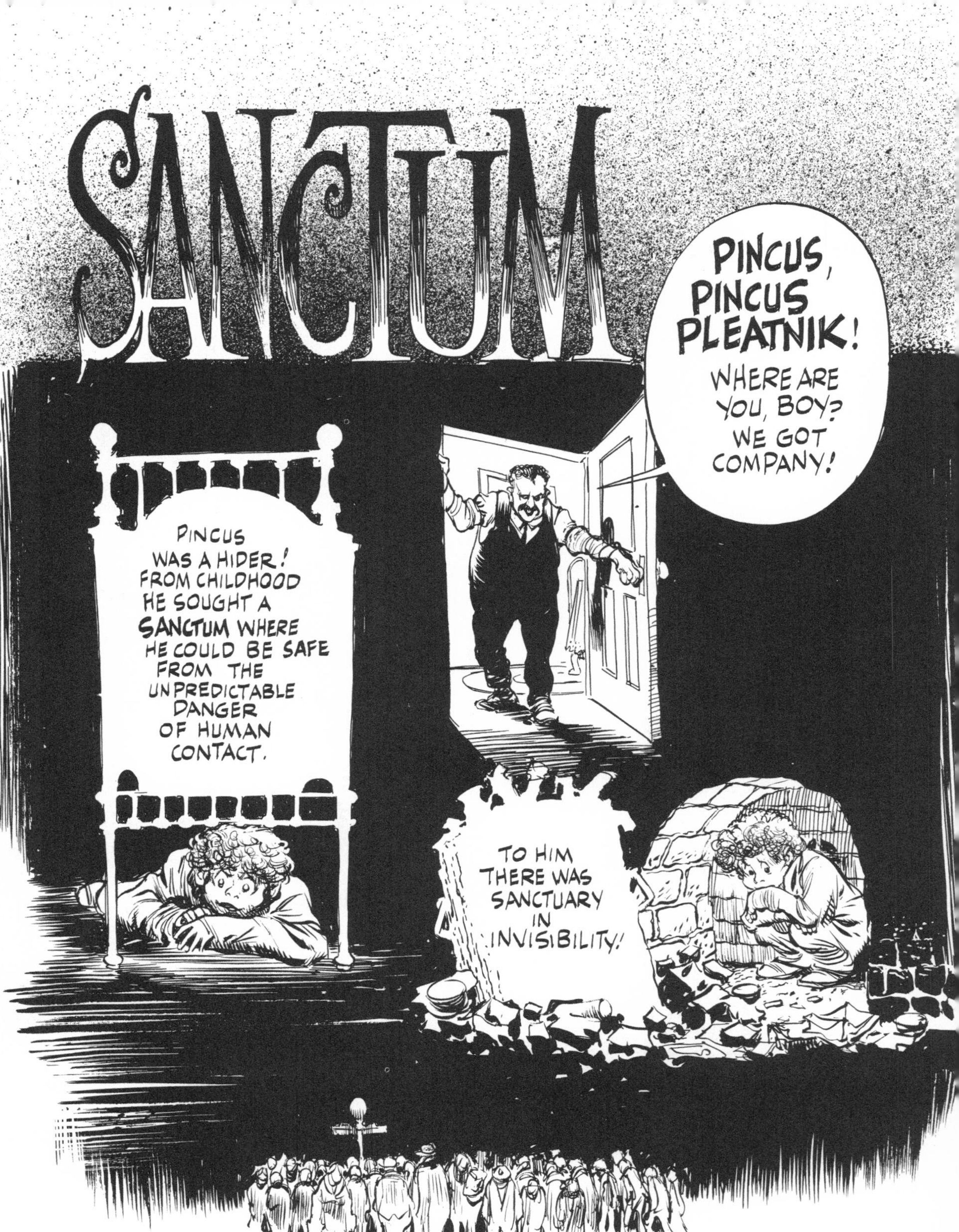

INSTINCTIVELY HE UNDERSTOOD THAT BEING UNNOTICED IS A MAJOR SKILL IN THE ART OF URBAN SURVIVAL...

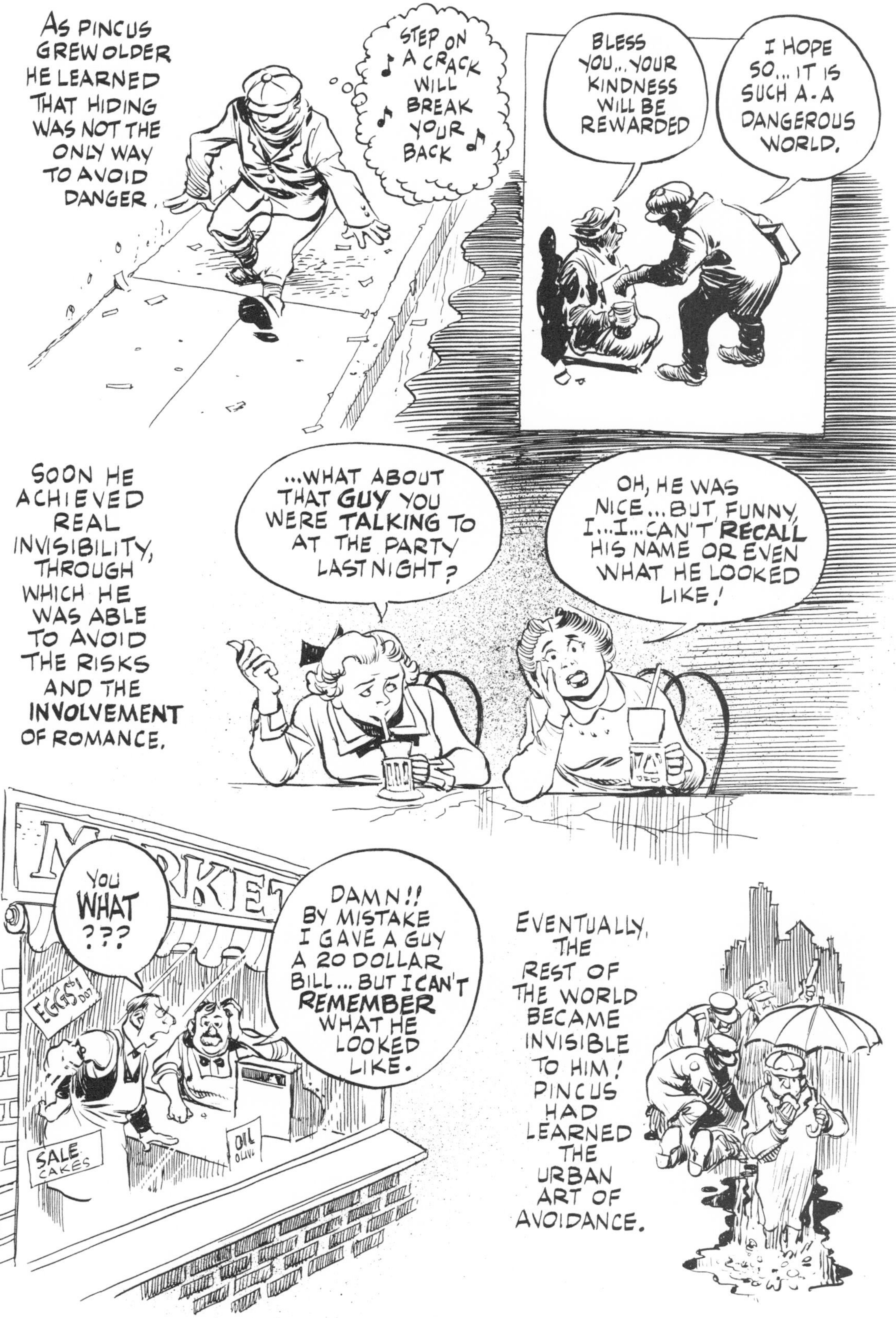
AS PINCUS GREW OLDER HE LEARNED THAT HIDING WAS NOT THE ONLY WAY TO AVOID DANGER.
STEP ON A CRACK WILL BREAK YOUR BACK
BLESS YOU... YOUR KINDNESS WILL BE REWARDED
I HOPE SO... IT IS SUCH A-A DANGEROUS WORLD.
SOON HE ACHIEVED REAL INVISIBILITY, THROUGH WHICH HE WAS ABLE TO AVOID THE RISKS AND THE INVOLVEMENT OF ROMANCE.
...WHAT ABOUT THAT GUY YOU WERE TALKING TO AT THE PARTY LAST NIGHT?
OH, HE WAS NICE... BUT FUNNY, I...I...CAN'T RECALL HIS NAME OR EVEN WHAT HE LOOKED LIKE!
MARKET
YOU WHAT ???
DAMN!! BY MISTAKE I GAVE A GUY A 20 DOLLAR BILL... BUT I CAN'T REMEMBER WHAT HE LOOKED LIKE.
EGGS
SALE CAKES
OIL
EVENTUALLY, THE REST OF THE WORLD BECAME INVISIBLE TO HIM! PINCUS HAD LEARNED THE URBAN ART OF AVOIDANCE.

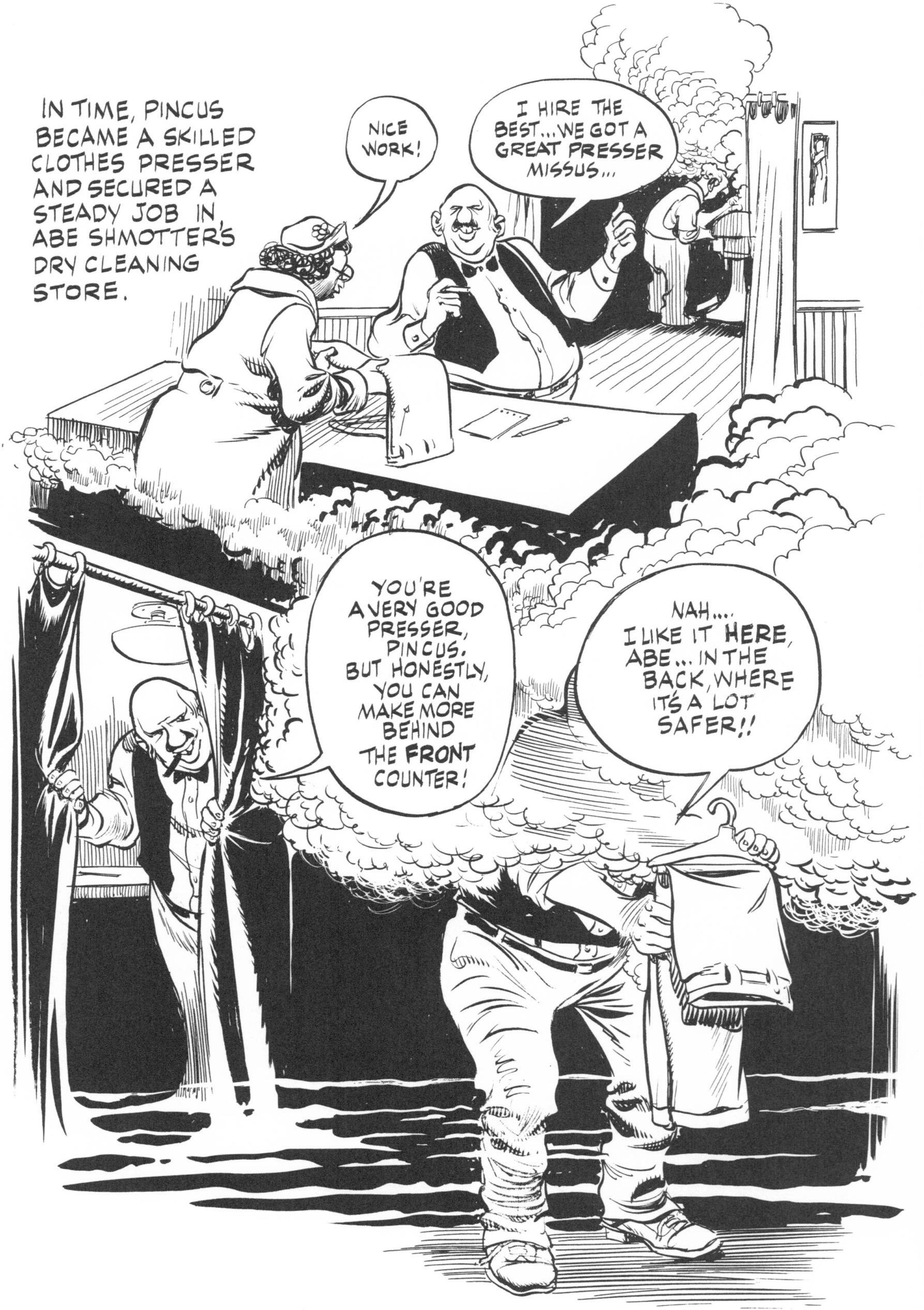
IN TIME, PINCUS BECAME A SKILLED CLOTHES PRESSER AND SECURED A STEADY JOB IN ABE SHMOTTER'S DRY CLEANING STORE.
NICE WORK!
I HIRE THE BEST... WE GOT A GREAT PRESSER MISSUS...
YOU'RE A VERY GOOD PRESSER, PINCUS. BUT HONESTLY, YOU CAN MAKE MORE BEHIND THE FRONT COUNTER!
NAH.... I LIKE IT HERE, ABE... IN THE BACK, WHERE IT'S A LOT SAFER!!

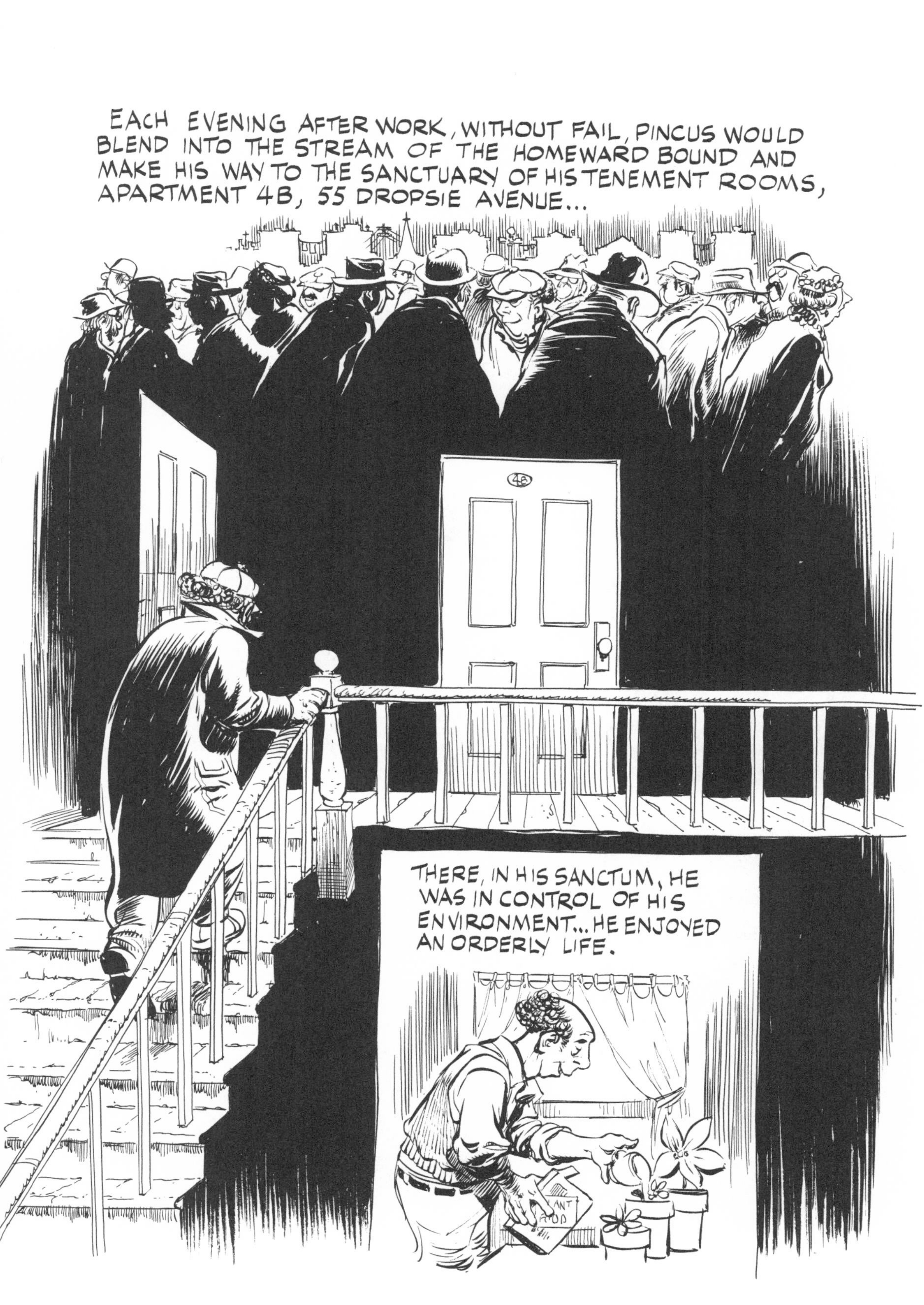
EACH EVENING AFTER WORK, WITHOUT FAIL, PINCUS WOULD BLEND INTO THE STREAM OF THE HOMEWARD BOUND AND MAKE HIS WAY TO THE SANCTUARY OF HIS TENEMENT ROOMS, APARTMENT 4B, 55 DROPSIE AVENUE...
THERE, IN HIS SANCTUM, HE WAS IN CONTROL OF HIS ENVIRONMENT... HE ENJOYED AN ORDERLY LIFE.

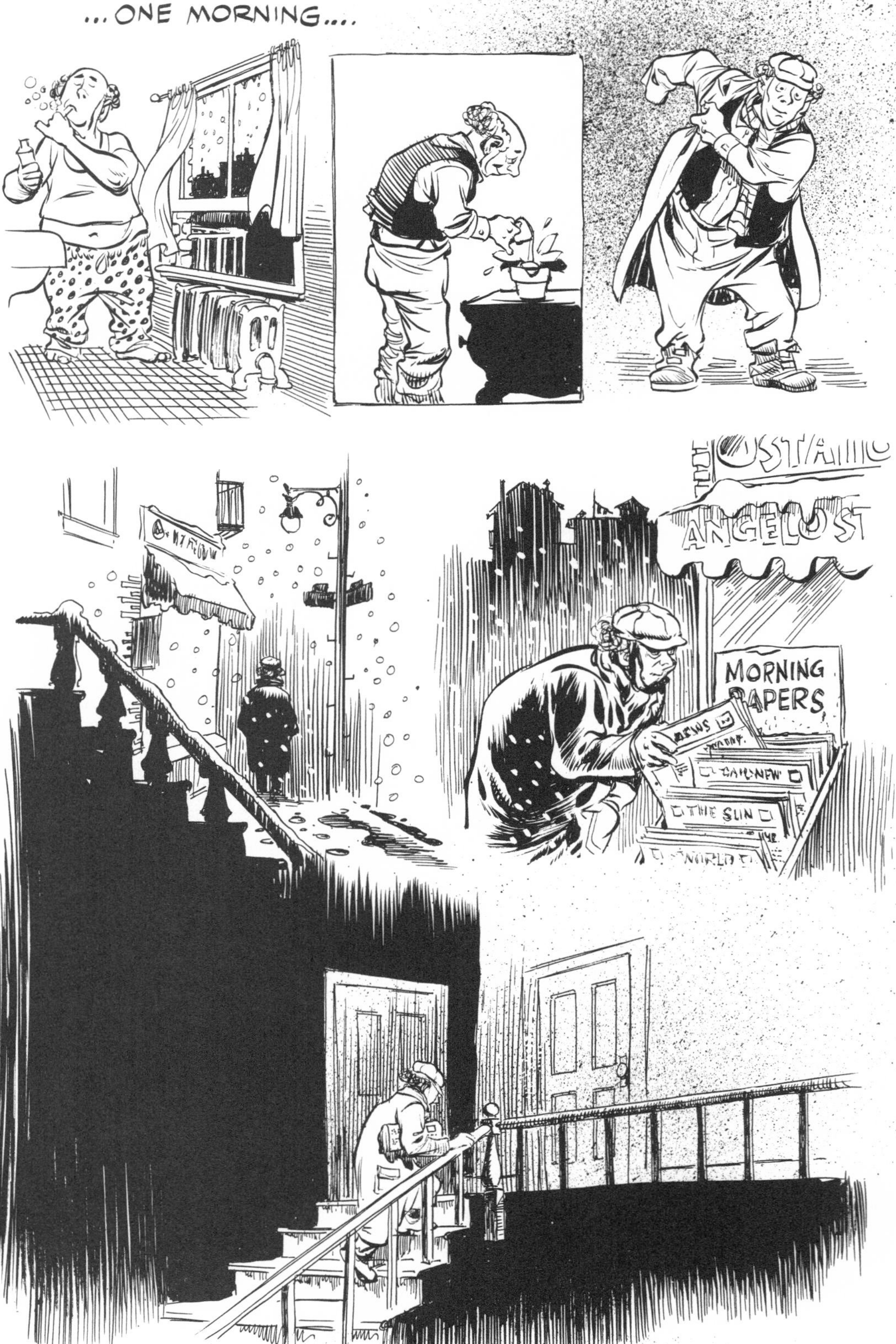
...ONE MORNING....
MORNING PAPERS
THE SUN

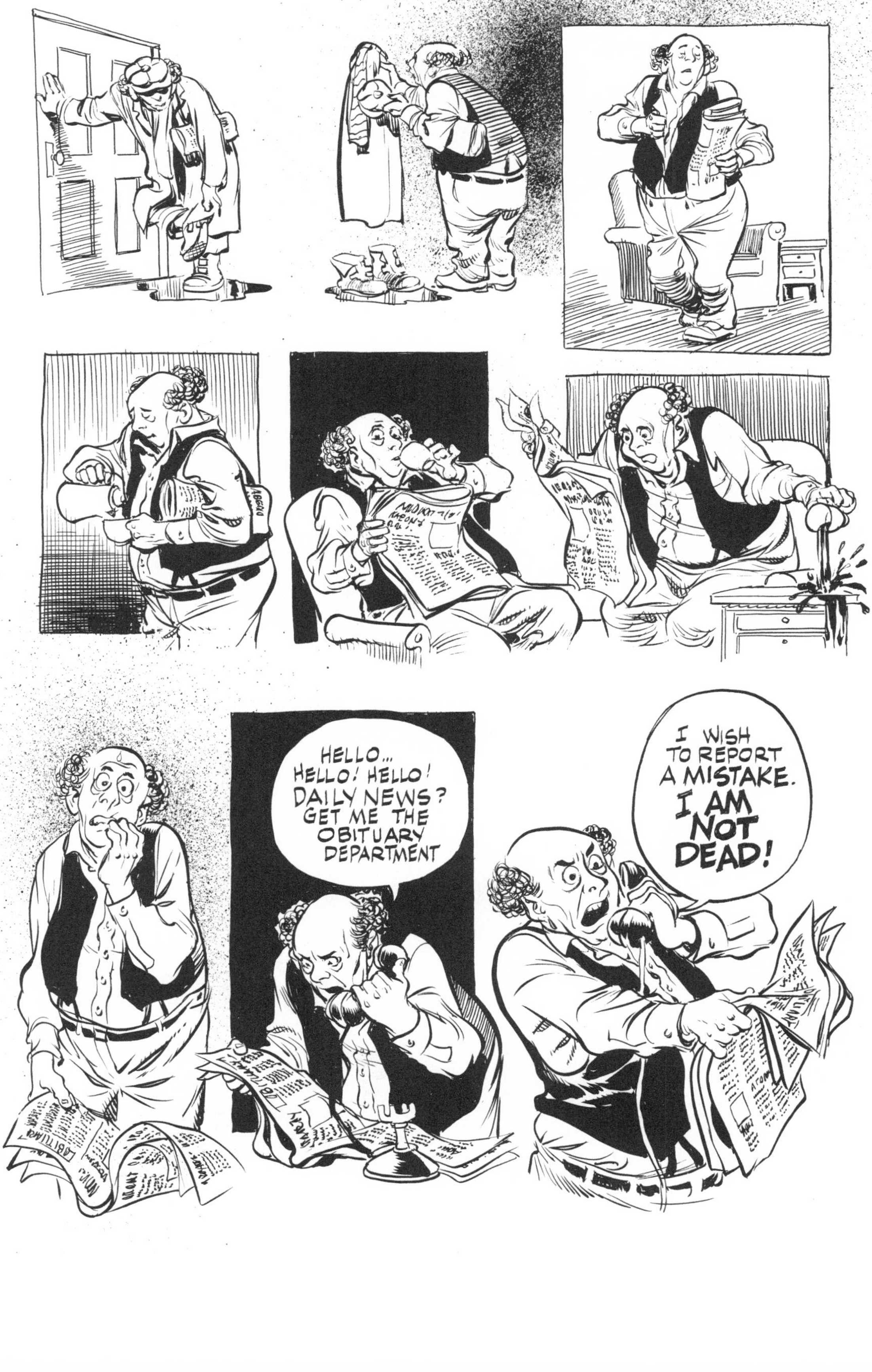
HELLO... HELLO! HELLO! DAILY NEWS? GET ME THE OBITUARY DEPARTMENT
I WISH TO REPORT A MISTAKE. I AM NOT DEAD!

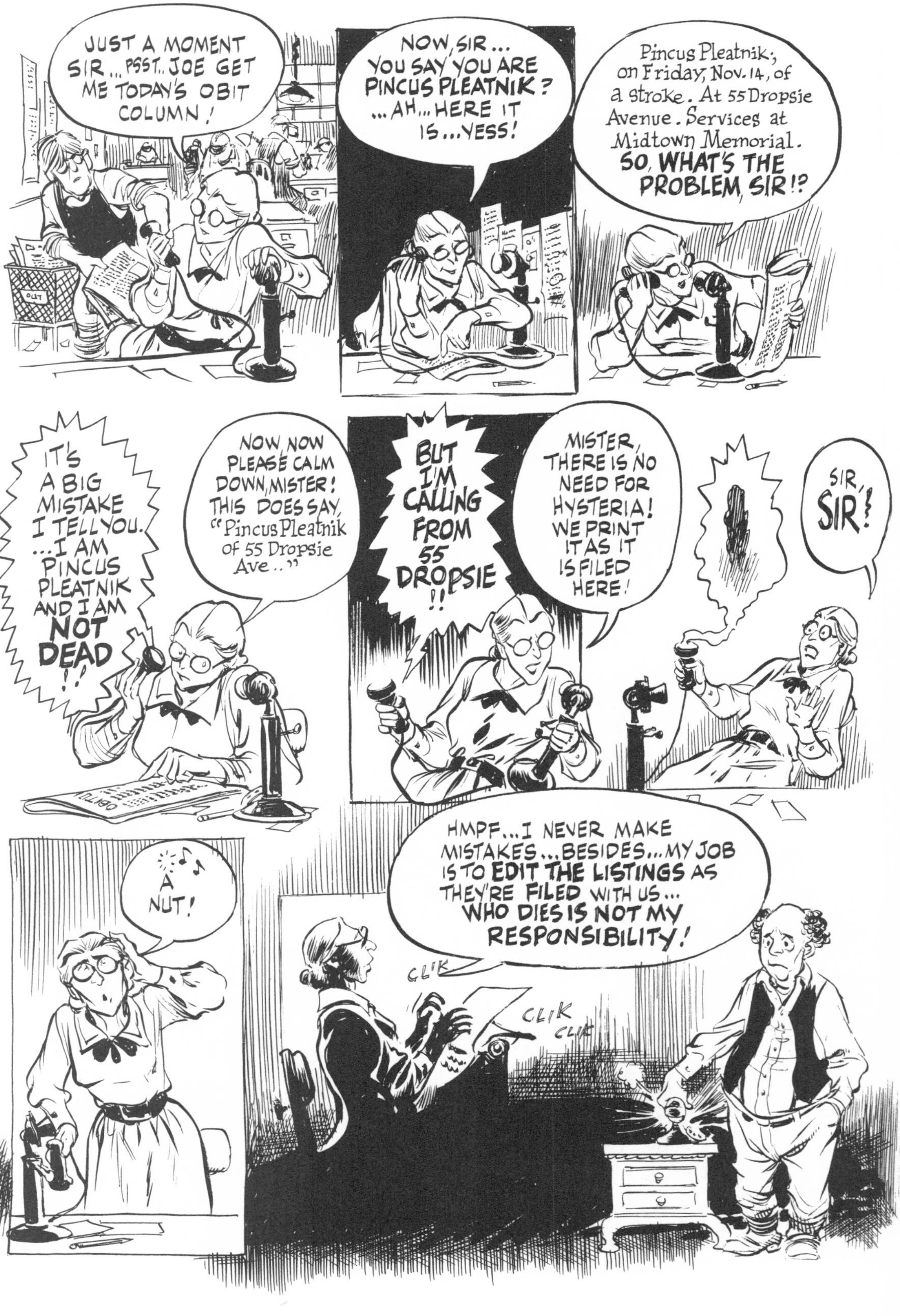
JUST A MOMENT SIR... PSST.. JOE GET ME TODAY'S OBIT COLUMN!
NOW, SIR... YOU SAY YOU ARE PINCUS PLEATNIK? ...AH... HERE IT IS...YESS!
Pincus Pleatnik:, on Friday, Nov. 14, of a stroke. At 55 Dropsie Avenue. Services at Midtown Memorial. SO, WHAT'S THE PROBLEM, SIR!?
IT'S A BIG MISTAKE I TELL YOU. ...I AM PINCUS PLEATNIK AND I AM NOT DEAD!!
NOW, NOW PLEASE CALM DOWN, MISTER! THIS DOES SAY, "Pincus Pleatnik of 55 Dropsie Ave.."
BUT I'M CALLING FROM 55 DROPSIE!!
MISTER, THERE IS NO NEED FOR HYSTERIA! WE PRINT IT AS IT IS FILED HERE!
SIR, SIR!
A NUT!
HMPF... I NEVER MAKE MISTAKES... BESIDES... MY JOB IS TO EDIT THE LISTINGS AS THEY'RE FILED WITH US... WHO DIES IS NOT MY RESPONSIBILITY!
CLIK
CLIK
CLIK

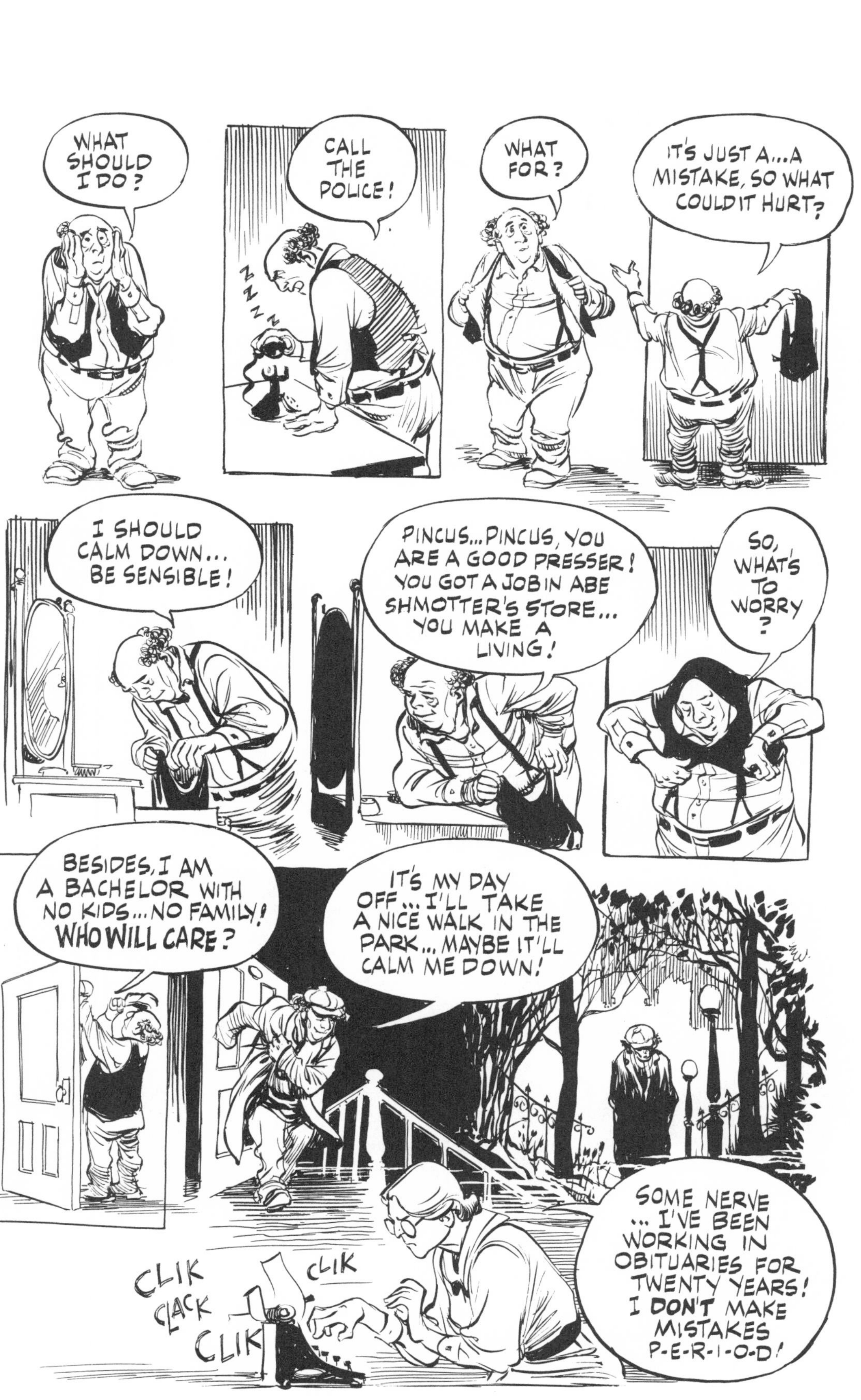
WHAT SHOULD I DO?
CALL THE POLICE!
WHAT FOR?
IT'S JUST A...A MISTAKE, SO WHAT COULD IT HURT?
I SHOULD CALM DOWN... BE SENSIBLE!
PINCUS...PINCUS, YOU ARE A GOOD PRESSER! YOU GOT A JOB IN ABE SHMOTTER'S STORE... YOU MAKE A LIVING!
SO, WHAT'S TO WORRY?
BESIDES, I AM A BACHELOR WITH NO KIDS...NO FAMILY! WHO WILL CARE?
IT'S MY DAY OFF... I'LL TAKE A NICE WALK IN THE PARK... MAYBE IT'LL CALM ME DOWN!
CLIK
CLACK
CLIK
CLIK
SOME NERVE ... I'VE BEEN WORKING IN OBITUARIES FOR TWENTY YEARS! I DON'T MAKE MISTAKES P-E-R-I-O-D!

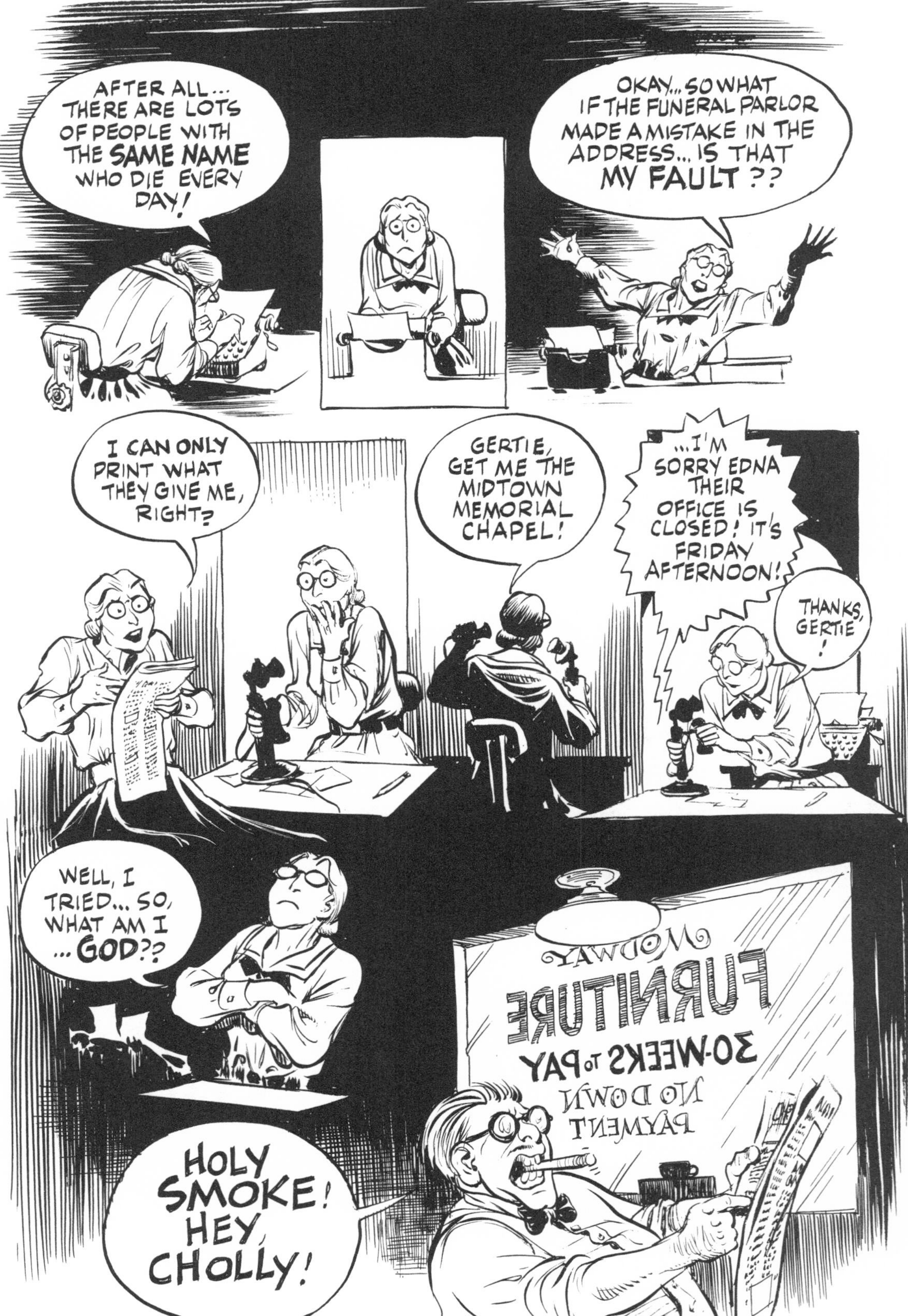
AFTER ALL... THERE ARE LOTS OF PEOPLE WITH THE SAME NAME WHO DIE EVERY DAY!
OKAY... SO WHAT IF THE FUNERAL PARLOR MADE A MISTAKE IN THE ADDRESS... IS THAT MY FAULT??
I CAN ONLY PRINT WHAT THEY GIVE ME, RIGHT?
GERTIE, GET ME THE MIDTOWN MEMORIAL CHAPEL!
...I'M SORRY EDNA THEIR OFFICE IS CLOSED! IT'S FRIDAY AFTERNOON!
THANKS, GERTIE!
WELL, I TRIED... SO, WHAT AM I ...GOD??
HOLY SMOKE! HEY, CHOLLY!

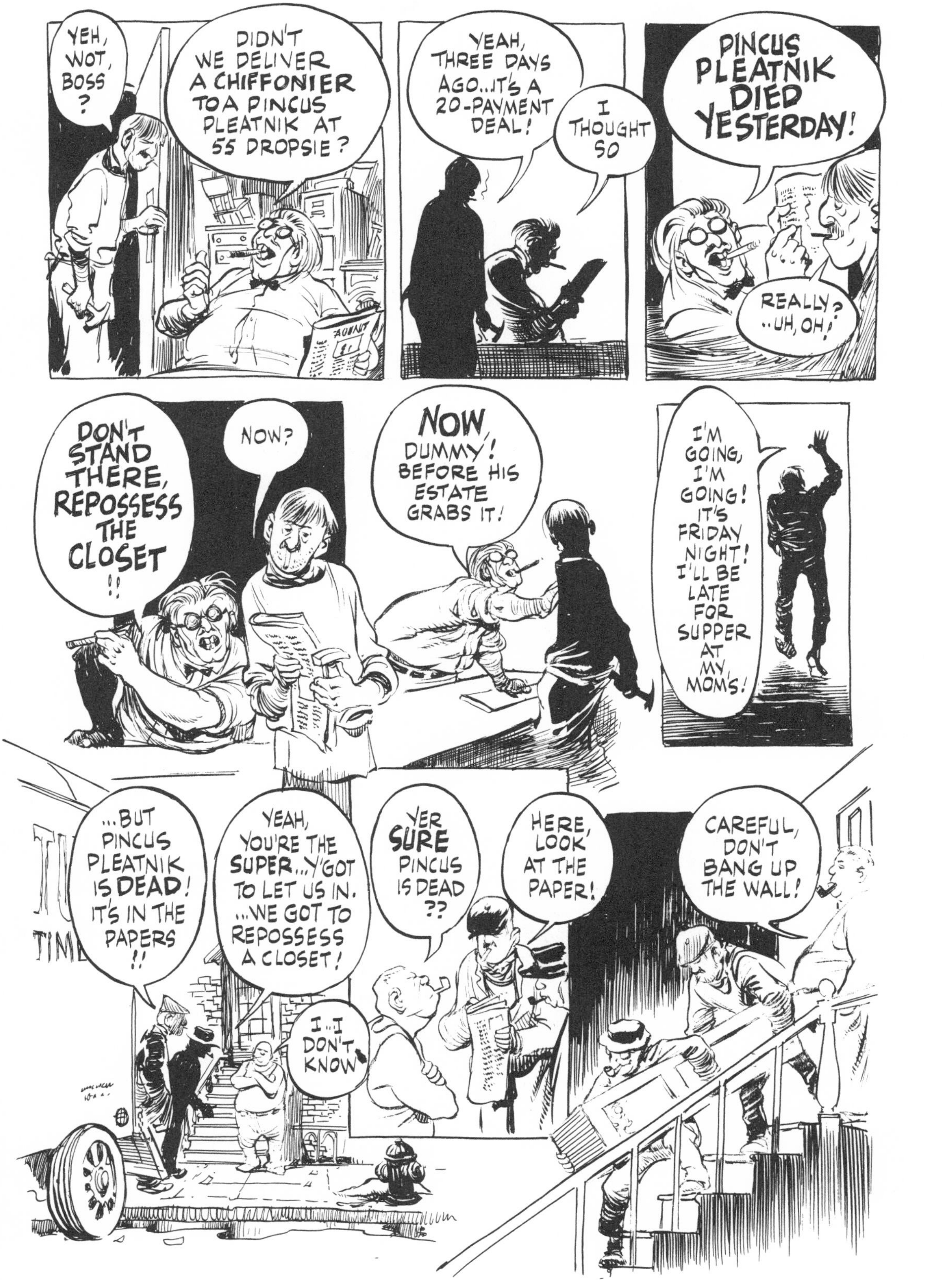
YEH, WOT, BOSS ?
DIDN'T WE DELIVER A CHIFFONIER TO A PINCUS PLEATNIK AT 55 DROPSIE ?
YEAH, THREE DAYS AGO...IT'S A 20-PAYMENT DEAL!
I THOUGHT SO
PINCUS PLEATNIK DIED YESTERDAY!
REALLY? ..UH, OH!
DON'T STAND THERE, REPOSSESS THE CLOSET !!
NOW?
NOW, DUMMY! BEFORE HIS ESTATE GRABS IT!
I'M GOING, I'M GOING! IT'S FRIDAY NIGHT! I'LL BE LATE FOR SUPPER AT MY MOM'S!
...BUT PINCUS PLEATNIK IS DEAD! IT'S IN THE PAPERS !!
YEAH, YOU'RE THE SUPER...Y'GOT TO LET US IN. ...WE GOT TO REPOSSESS A CLOSET!
I..I DON'T KNOW
YER SURE PINCUS IS DEAD ??
HERE, LOOK AT THE PAPER!
CAREFUL, DON'T BANG UP THE WALL!

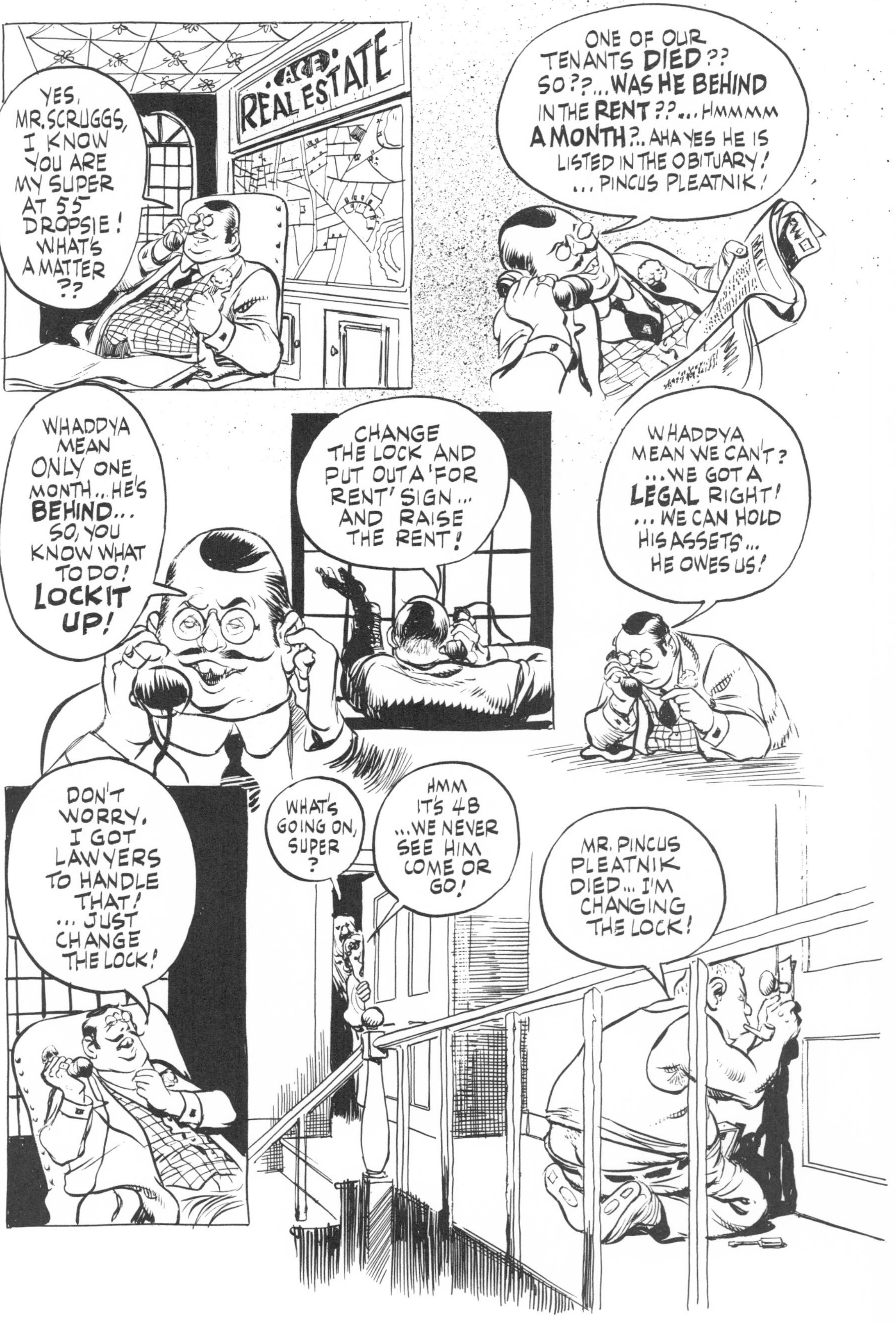
REAL ESTATE
YES, MR. SCRUGGS, I KNOW YOU ARE MY SUPER AT 55 DROPSIE! WHAT'S A MATTER ??
ONE OF OUR TENANTS DIED?? SO??... WAS HE BEHIND IN THE RENT??... HMMMM A MONTH?.. AHA YES HE IS LISTED IN THE OBITUARY! ... PINCUS PLEATNIK!
WHADDYA MEAN ONLY ONE MONTH... HE'S BEHIND... SO, YOU KNOW WHAT TO DO! LOCK IT UP!
CHANGE THE LOCK AND PUT OUT A 'FOR RENT' SIGN... AND RAISE THE RENT!
WHADDYA MEAN WE CAN'T? ... WE GOT A LEGAL RIGHT! ... WE CAN HOLD HIS ASSETS... HE OWES US!
DON'T WORRY. I GOT LAWYERS TO HANDLE THAT! ... JUST CHANGE THE LOCK!
WHAT'S GOING ON, SUPER ?
HMM IT'S 4B ...WE NEVER SEE HIM COME OR GO!
MR. PINCUS PLEATNIK DIED... I'M CHANGING THE LOCK!

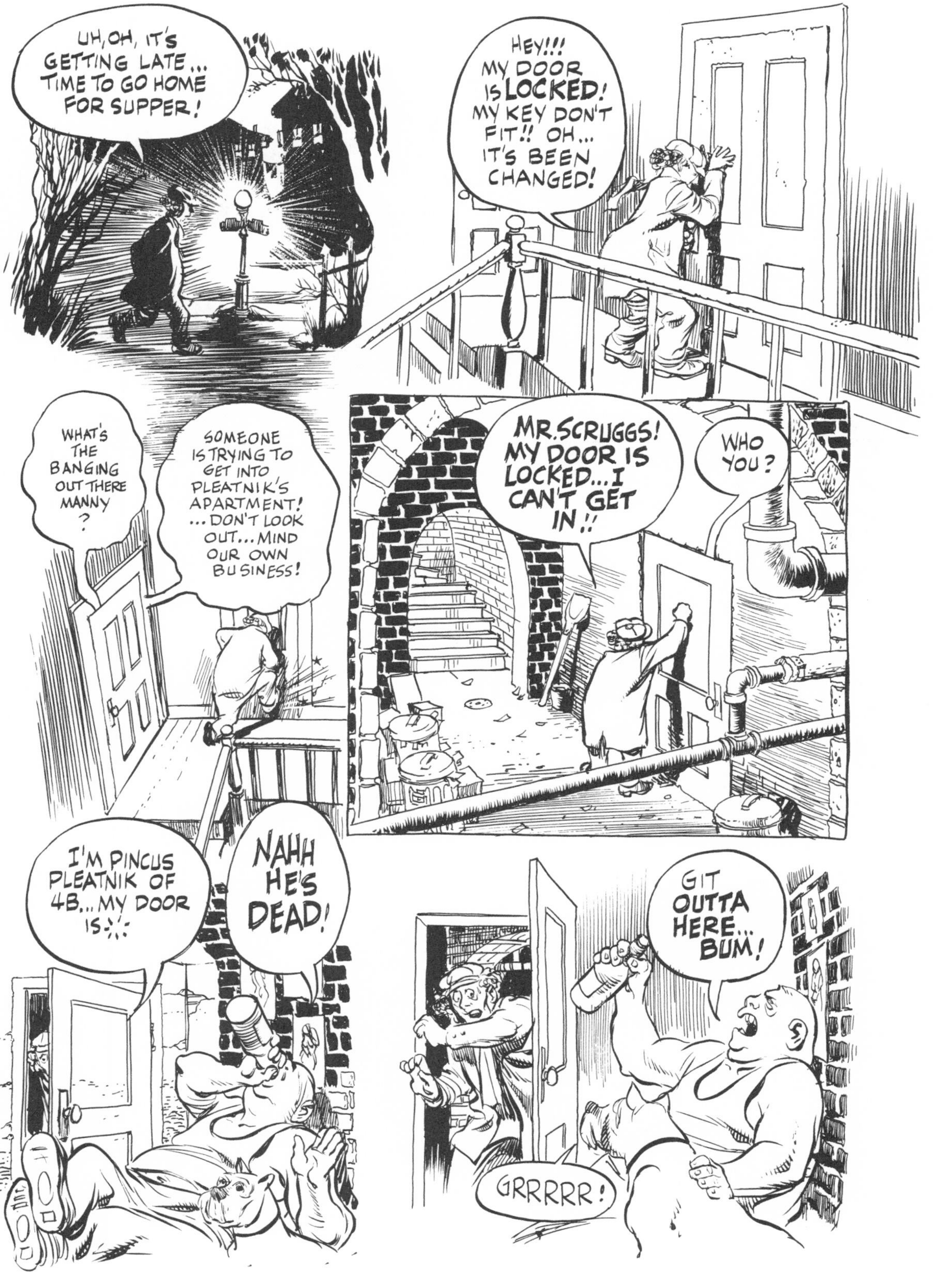
UH, OH, IT'S GETTING LATE... TIME TO GO HOME FOR SUPPER!
HEY!!! MY DOOR IS LOCKED! MY KEY DON'T FIT!! OH... IT'S BEEN CHANGED!
WHAT'S THE BANGING OUT THERE MANNY ?
SOMEONE IS TRYING TO GET INTO PLEATNIK'S APARTMENT! ...DON'T LOOK OUT...MIND OUR OWN BUSINESS!
MR. SCRUGGS! MY DOOR IS LOCKED...I CAN'T GET IN!!
WHO YOU?
I'M PINCUS PLEATNIK OF 4B...MY DOOR IS...
NAHH HE'S DEAD!
GIT OUTTA HERE... BUM!
GRRRRR!

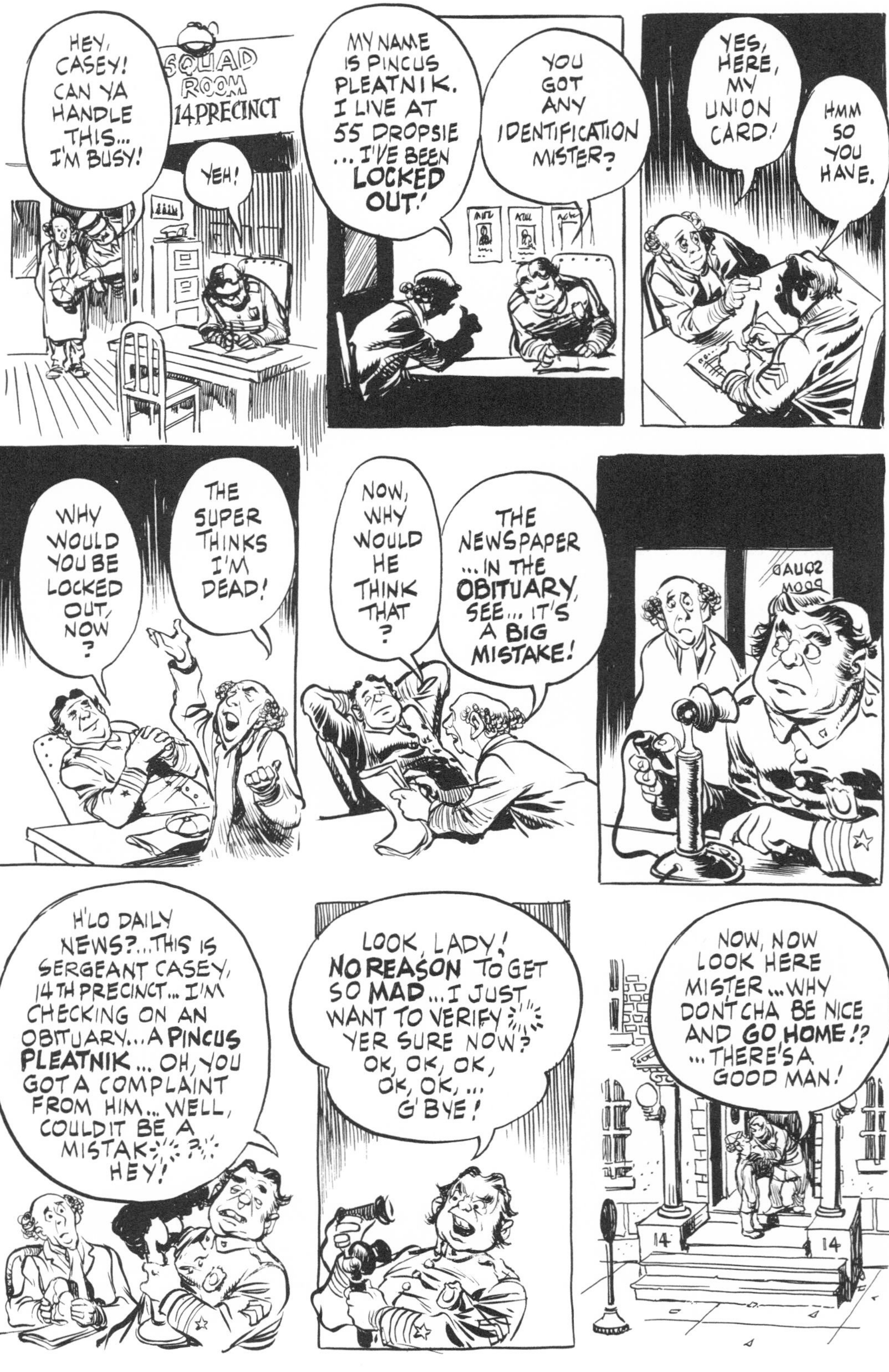

HEY, CASEY! CAN YA HANDLE THIS... I'M BUSY!
SQUAD ROOM 14 PRECINCT
YEH!
MY NAME IS PINCUS PLEATNIK. I LIVE AT 55 DROPSIE ...I'VE BEEN LOCKED OUT!
YOU GOT ANY IDENTIFICATION MISTER?
YES, HERE, MY UNION CARD!
HMM SO YOU HAVE.
WHY WOULD YOU BE LOCKED OUT, NOW?
THE SUPER THINKS I'M DEAD!
NOW, WHY WOULD HE THINK THAT?
THE NEWSPAPER ...IN THE OBITUARY, SEE... IT'S A BIG MISTAKE!
H'LO DAILY NEWS?...THIS IS SERGEANT CASEY, 14TH PRECINCT... I'M CHECKING ON AN OBITUARY...A PINCUS PLEATNIK... OH, YOU GOT A COMPLAINT FROM HIM... WELL, COULD IT BE A MISTAK-?! HEY!
LOOK, LADY! NO REASON TO GET SO MAD... I JUST WANT TO VERIFY YER SURE NOW? OK, OK, OK, OK, OK, ... G'BYE!
NOW, NOW LOOK HERE MISTER ...WHY DON'TCHA BE NICE AND GO HOME!? ...THERE'S A GOOD MAN!
14
14

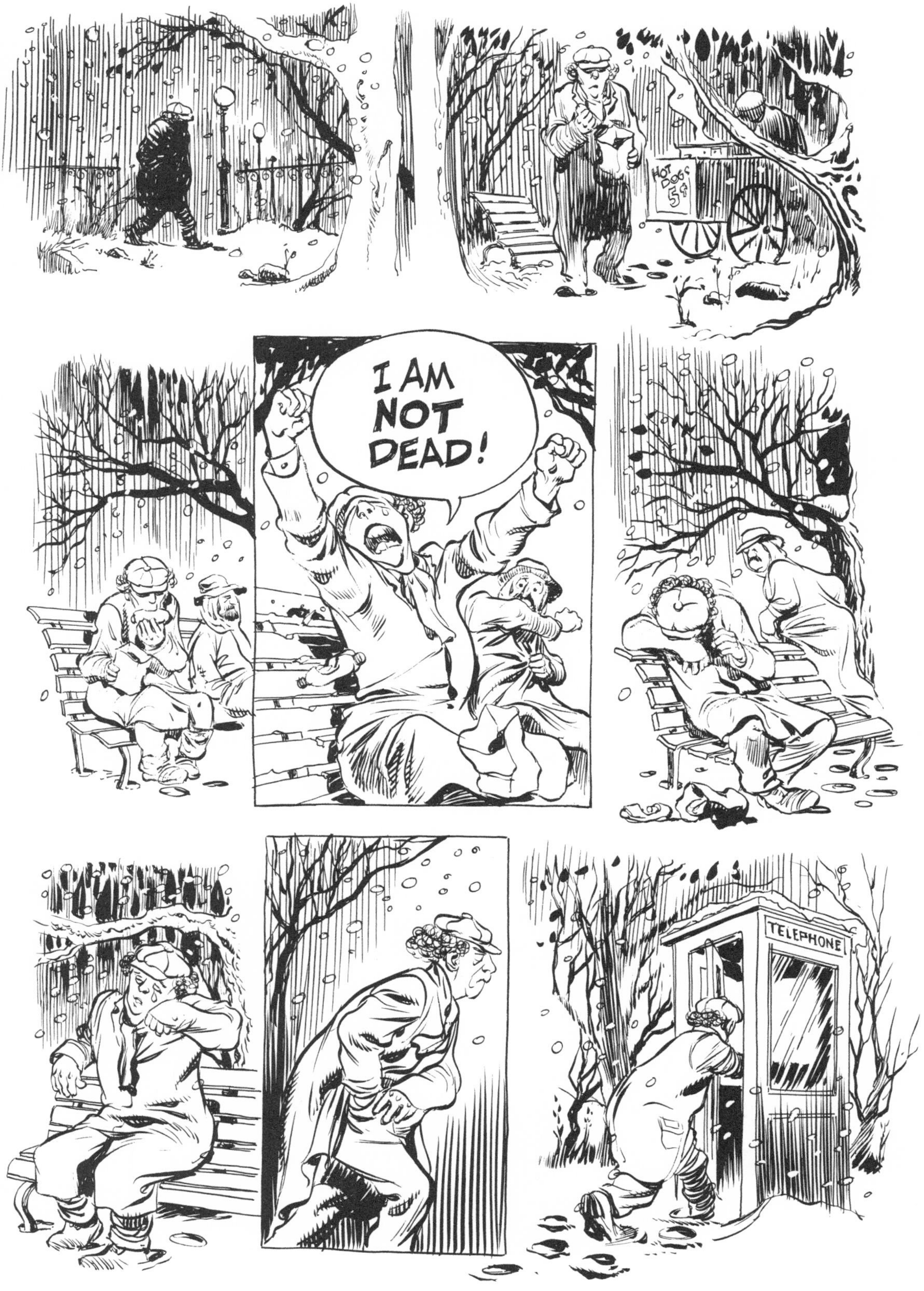
HOT DOGS 5¢
I AM NOT DEAD!
TELEPHONE

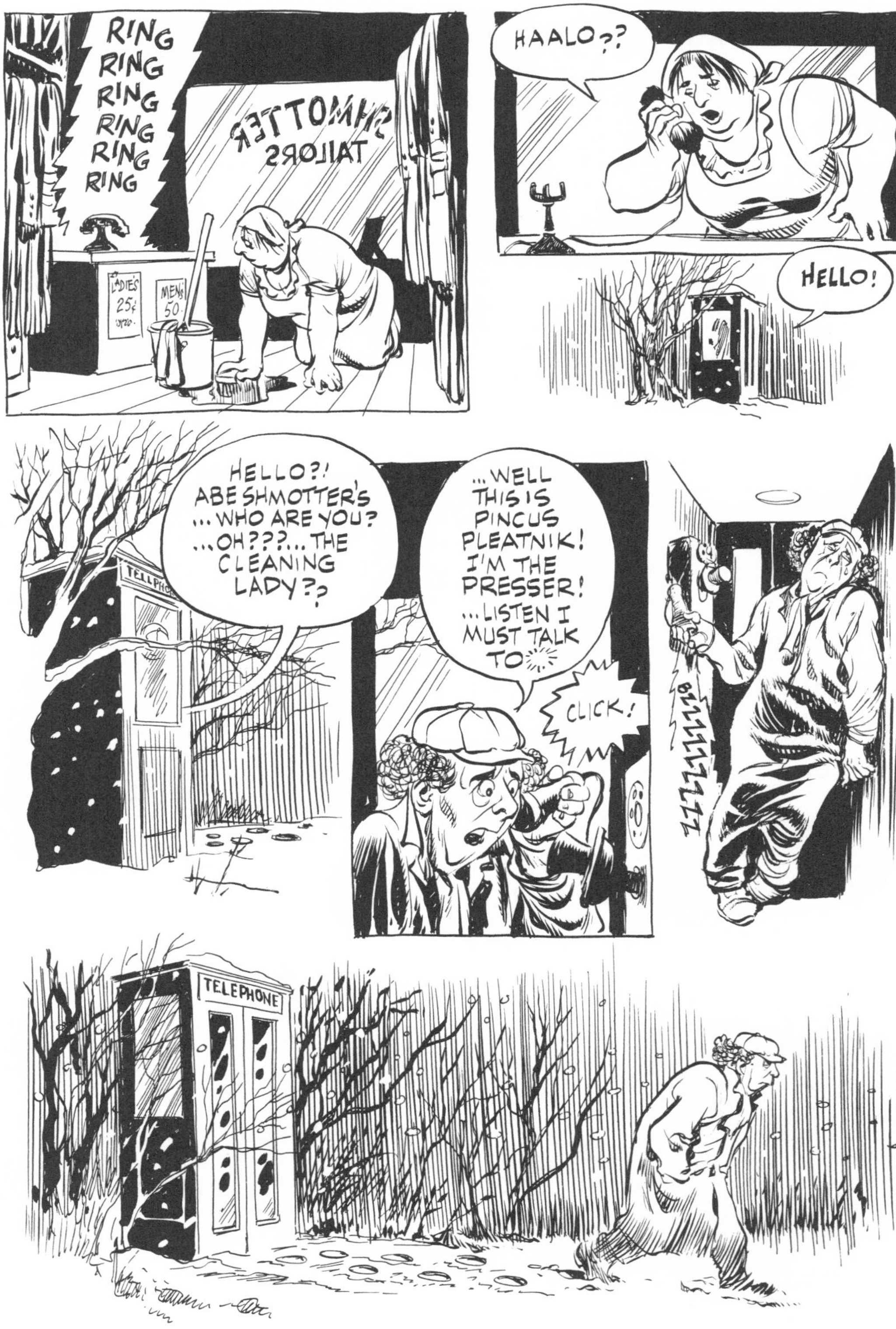
RING
RING
RING
RING
RING
RING
SHMOTTER
TAILORS
LADIES 25¢
MENS 50
HAALO??
HELLO!
HELLO?! ABE SHMOTTER's ...WHO ARE YOU? ...OH???... THE CLEANING LADY??
...WELL THIS IS PINCUS PLEATNIK! I'M THE PRESSER! ...LISTEN I MUST TALK TO
CLICK!
TELEPHONE

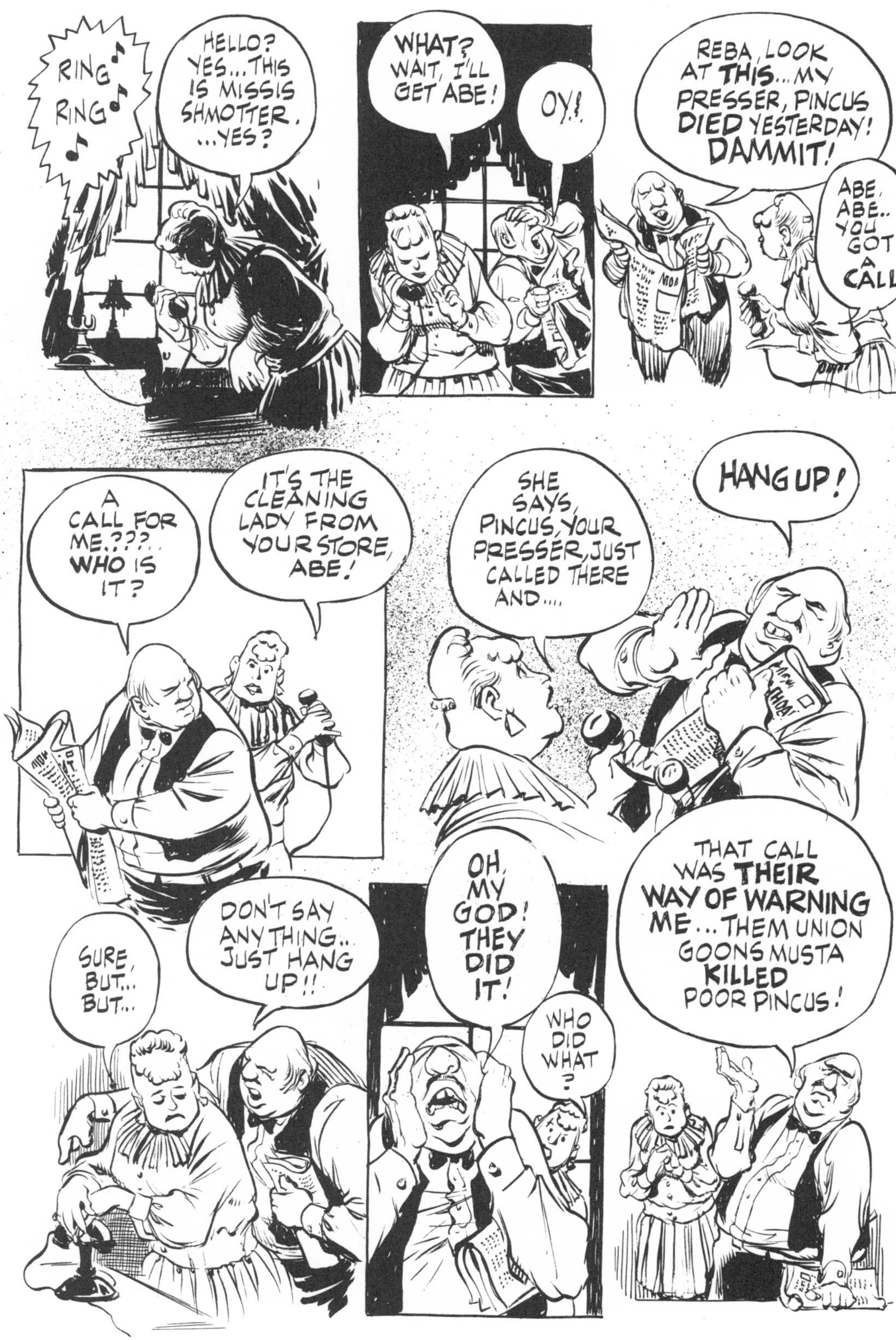
RING RING
HELLO? YES... THIS IS MISSIS SHMOTTER. ...YES?
WHAT? WAIT, I'LL GET ABE!
OY!!
REBA, LOOK AT THIS... MY PRESSER, PINCUS DIED YESTERDAY! DAMMIT!
ABE, ABE.. YOU GOT A CALL
A CALL FOR ME.???.. WHO IS IT?
IT'S THE CLEANING LADY FROM YOUR STORE, ABE!
SHE SAYS, PINCUS, YOUR PRESSER, JUST CALLED THERE AND....
HANG UP!
SURE, BUT... BUT...
DON'T SAY ANYTHING.. JUST HANG UP!!
OH, MY GOD! THEY DID IT!
WHO DID WHAT?
THAT CALL WAS THEIR WAY OF WARNING ME... THEM UNION GOONS MUSTA KILLED POOR PINCUS!

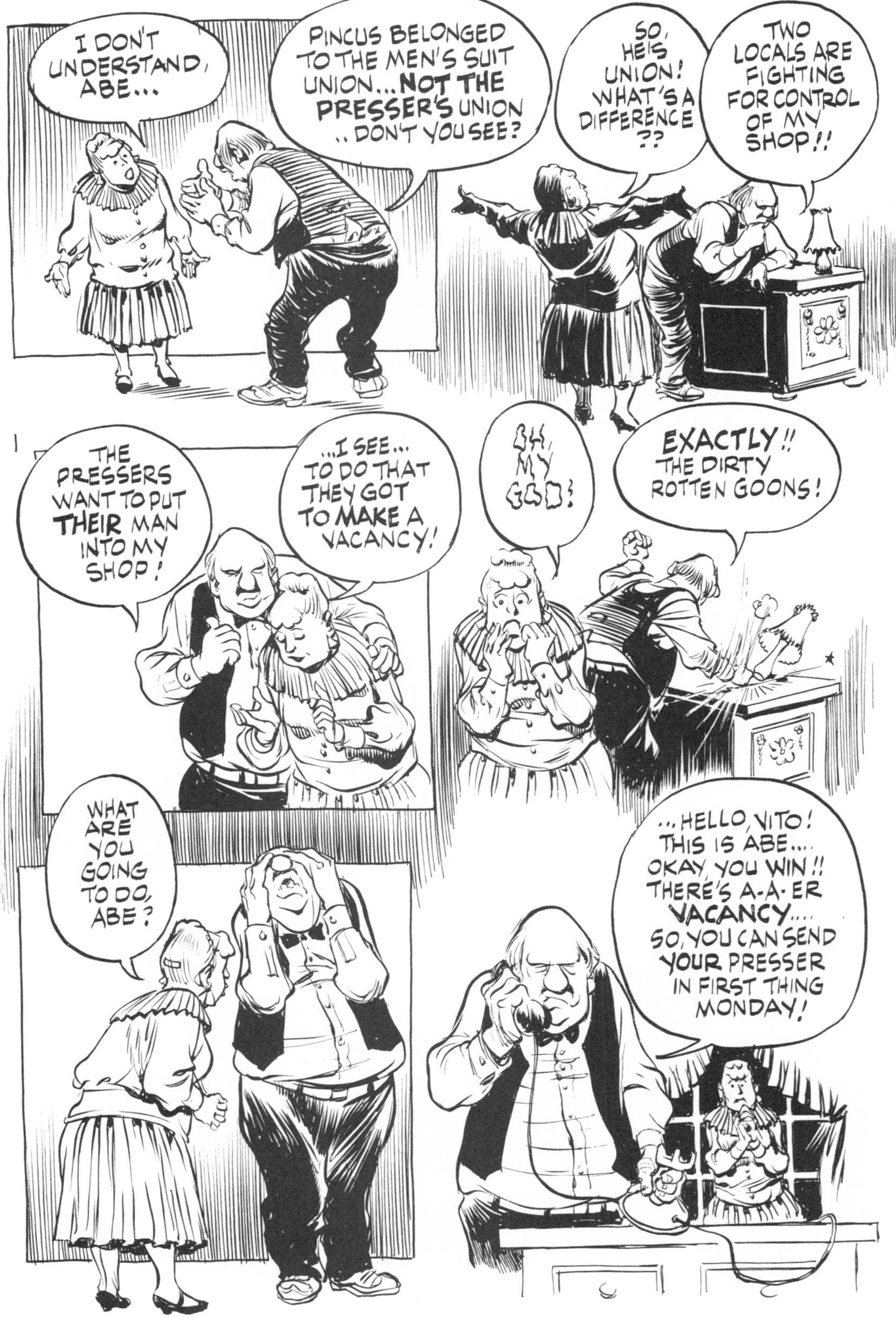
I DON'T UNDERSTAND, ABE...
PINCUS BELONGED TO THE MEN'S SUIT UNION... NOT THE PRESSER'S UNION .. DON'T YOU SEE?
SO, HE'S UNION! WHAT'S A DIFFERENCE ??
TWO LOCALS ARE FIGHTING FOR CONTROL OF MY SHOP!!
THE PRESSERS WANT TO PUT THEIR MAN INTO MY SHOP!
...I SEE... TO DO THAT THEY GOT TO MAKE A VACANCY!
OH, MY GOD!
EXACTLY!! THE DIRTY ROTTEN GOONS!
WHAT ARE YOU GOING TO DO, ABE?
...HELLO, VITO! THIS IS ABE... OKAY, YOU WIN!! THERE'S A-A-ER VACANCY.... SO, YOU CAN SEND YOUR PRESSER IN FIRST THING MONDAY!

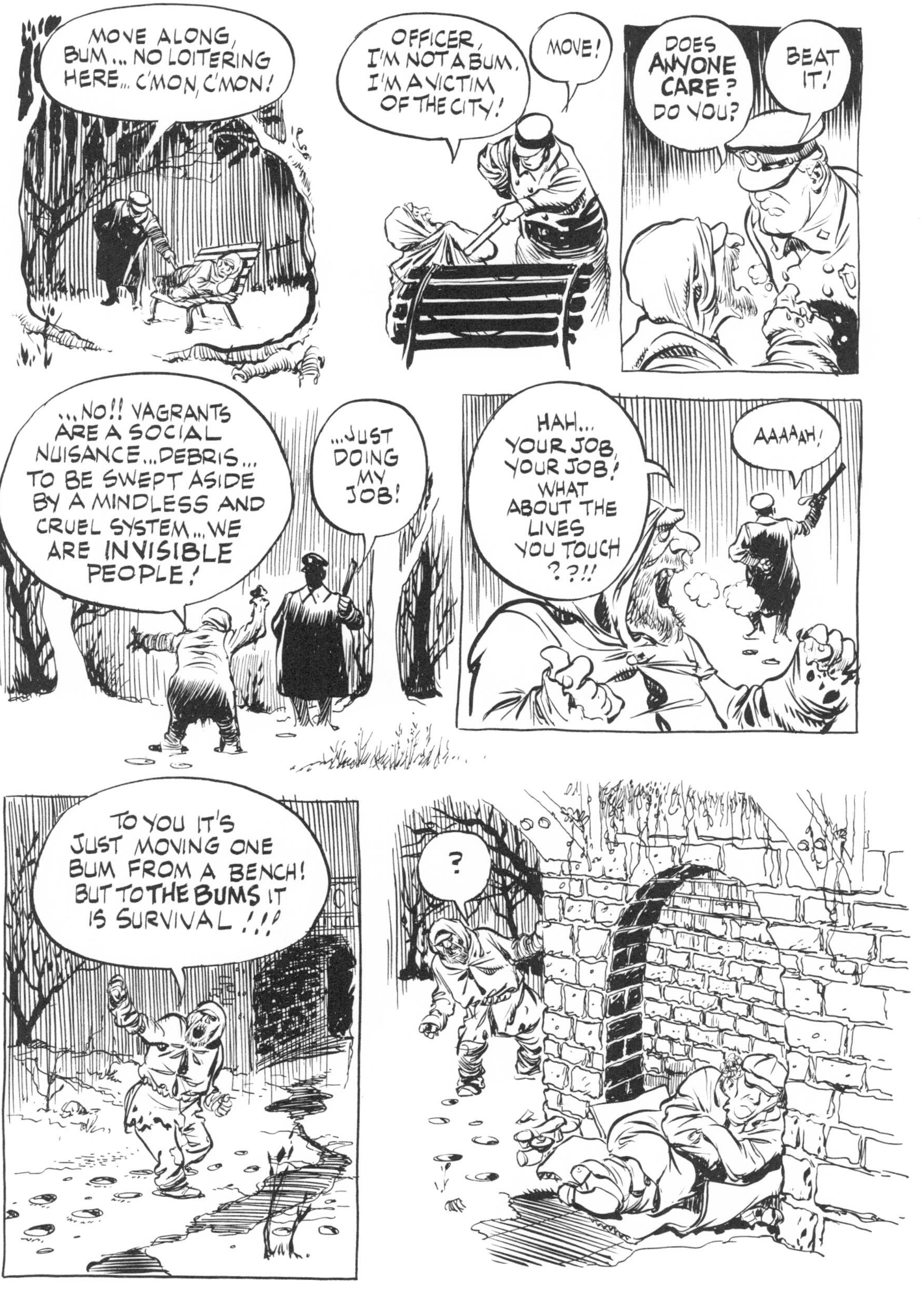

MOVE ALONG, BUM... NO LOITERING HERE... C'MON, C'MON!
OFFICER, I'M NOT A BUM, I'M A VICTIM OF THE CITY!
MOVE!
DOES ANYONE CARE? DO YOU?
BEAT IT!
...NO!! VAGRANTS ARE A SOCIAL NUISANCE...DEBRIS... TO BE SWEPT ASIDE BY A MINDLESS AND CRUEL SYSTEM... WE ARE INVISIBLE PEOPLE!
...JUST DOING MY JOB!
HAH... YOUR JOB, YOUR JOB! WHAT ABOUT THE LIVES YOU TOUCH ??!!
AAAAAH!
TO YOU IT'S JUST MOVING ONE BUM FROM A BENCH! BUT TO THE BUMS IT IS SURVIVAL!!!
?

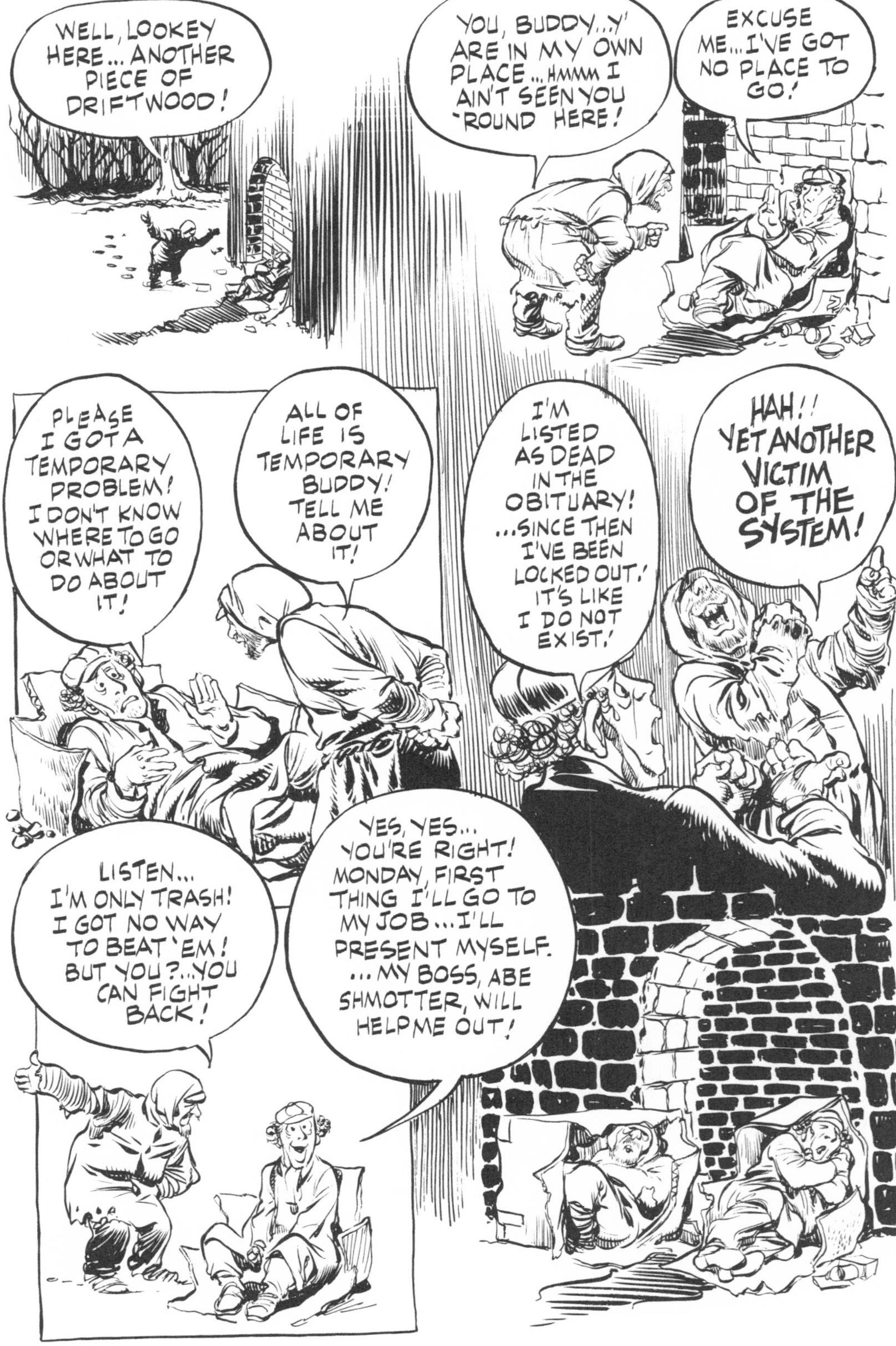
WELL, LOOKEY HERE... ANOTHER PIECE OF DRIFTWOOD!
YOU, BUDDY..Y' ARE IN MY OWN PLACE... HMMM I AIN'T SEEN YOU 'ROUND HERE!
EXCUSE ME...I'VE GOT NO PLACE TO GO!
PLEASE I GOT A TEMPORARY PROBLEM! I DON'T KNOW WHERE TO GO OR WHAT TO DO ABOUT IT!
ALL OF LIFE IS TEMPORARY BUDDY! TELL ME ABOUT IT!
I'M LISTED AS DEAD IN THE OBITUARY! ...SINCE THEN I'VE BEEN LOCKED OUT! IT'S LIKE I DO NOT EXIST!
HAH!! YET ANOTHER VICTIM OF THE SYSTEM!
LISTEN... I'M ONLY TRASH! I GOT NO WAY TO BEAT 'EM! BUT YOU?...YOU CAN FIGHT BACK!
YES, YES... YOU'RE RIGHT! MONDAY, FIRST THING I'LL GO TO MY JOB...I'LL PRESENT MYSELF. ...MY BOSS, ABE SHMOTTER, WILL HELP ME OUT!

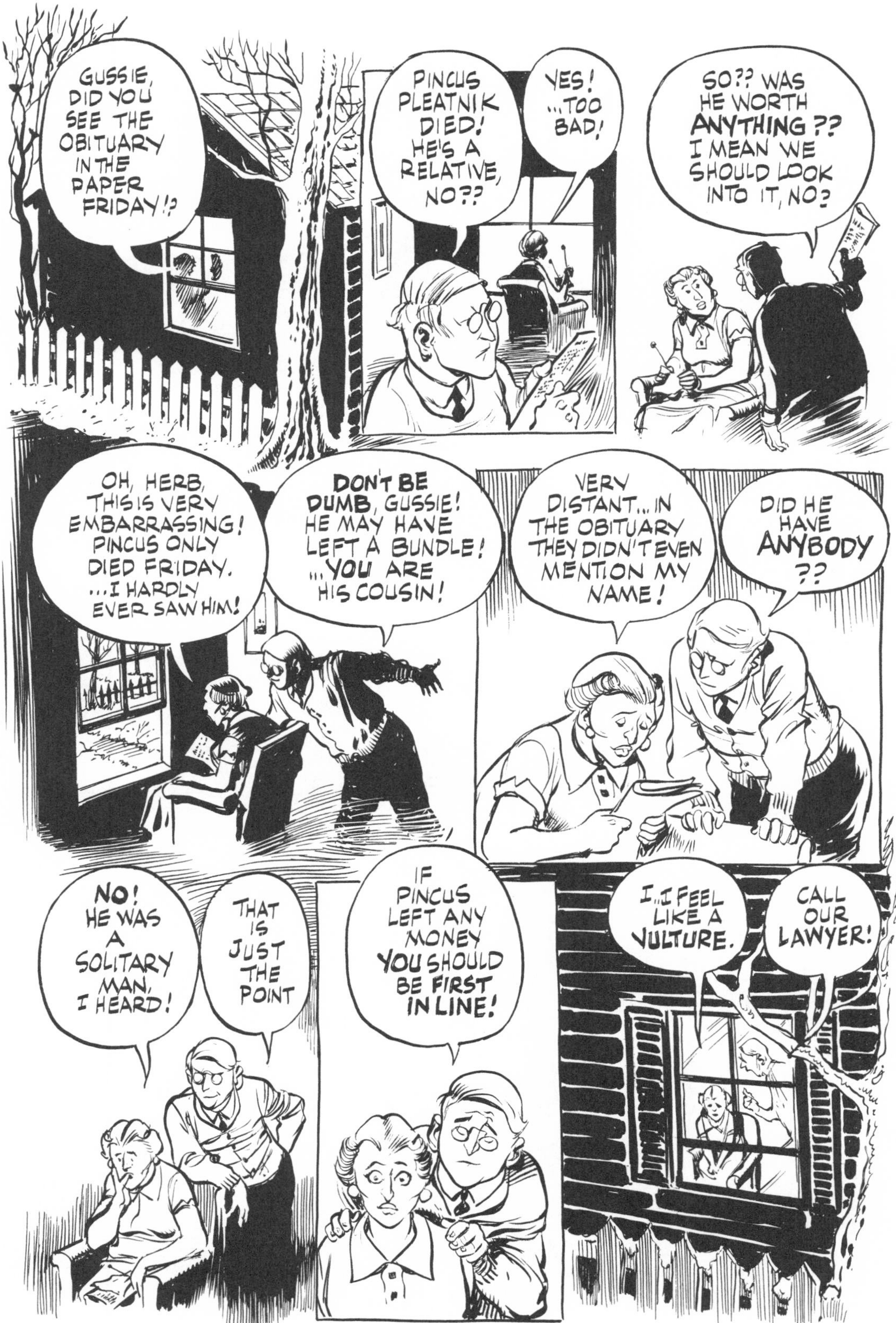
GUSSIE, DID YOU SEE THE OBITUARY IN THE PAPER FRIDAY!?
PINCUS PLEATNIK DIED! HE'S A RELATIVE, NO??
YES! ...TOO BAD!
SO?? WAS HE WORTH ANYTHING?? I MEAN WE SHOULD LOOK INTO IT, NO?
OH, HERB, THIS IS VERY EMBARRASSING! PINCUS ONLY DIED FRIDAY. ...I HARDLY EVER SAW HIM!
DON'T BE DUMB, GUSSIE! HE MAY HAVE LEFT A BUNDLE! ...YOU ARE HIS COUSIN!
VERY DISTANT... IN THE OBITUARY THEY DIDN'T EVEN MENTION MY NAME!
DID HE HAVE ANYBODY??
NO! HE WAS A SOLITARY MAN, I HEARD!
THAT IS JUST THE POINT
IF PINCUS LEFT ANY MONEY YOU SHOULD BE FIRST IN LINE!
I..I FEEL LIKE A VULTURE.
CALL OUR LAWYER!

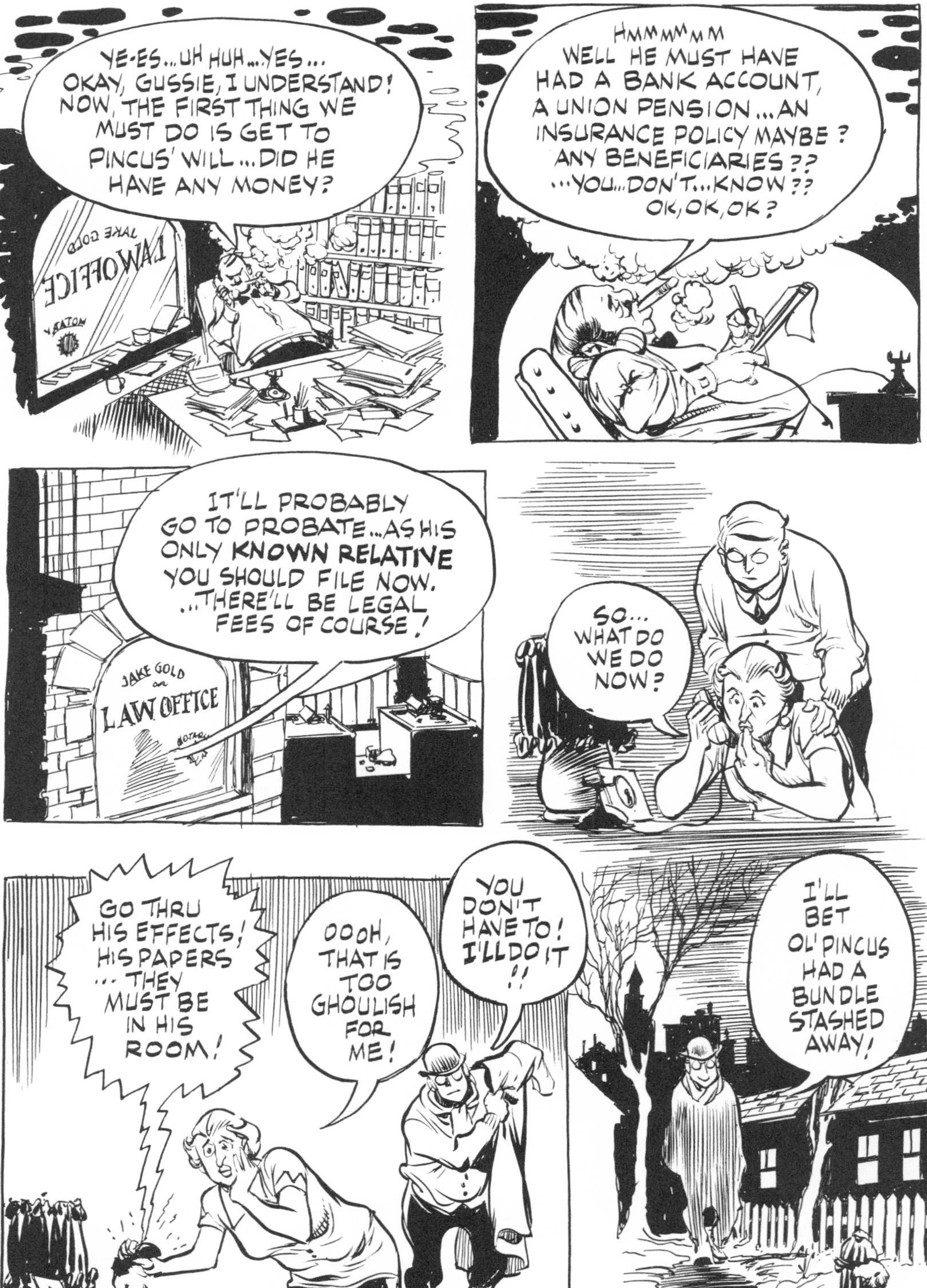

YE-ES...UH HUH...YES... OKAY, GUSSIE, I UNDERSTAND! NOW, THE FIRST THING WE MUST DO IS GET TO PINCUS' WILL...DID HE HAVE ANY MONEY?
JAKE GOLD LAW OFFICE
HMMMMMM WELL HE MUST HAVE HAD A BANK ACCOUNT, A UNION PENSION...AN INSURANCE POLICY MAYBE? ANY BENEFICIARIES?? ...YOU...DON'T...KNOW?? OK, OK, OK?
IT'LL PROBABLY GO TO PROBATE...AS HIS ONLY **KNOWN RELATIVE** YOU SHOULD FILE NOW. ...THERE'LL BE LEGAL FEES OF COURSE!
JAKE GOLD
LAW OFFICE
SO... WHAT DO WE DO NOW?
GO THRU HIS EFFECTS! HIS PAPERS ...THEY MUST BE IN HIS ROOM!
OOOH, THAT IS TOO GHOULISH FOR ME!
YOU DON'T HAVE TO! **I'LL** DO IT !!
I'LL BET OL' PINCUS HAD A BUNDLE STASHED AWAY!

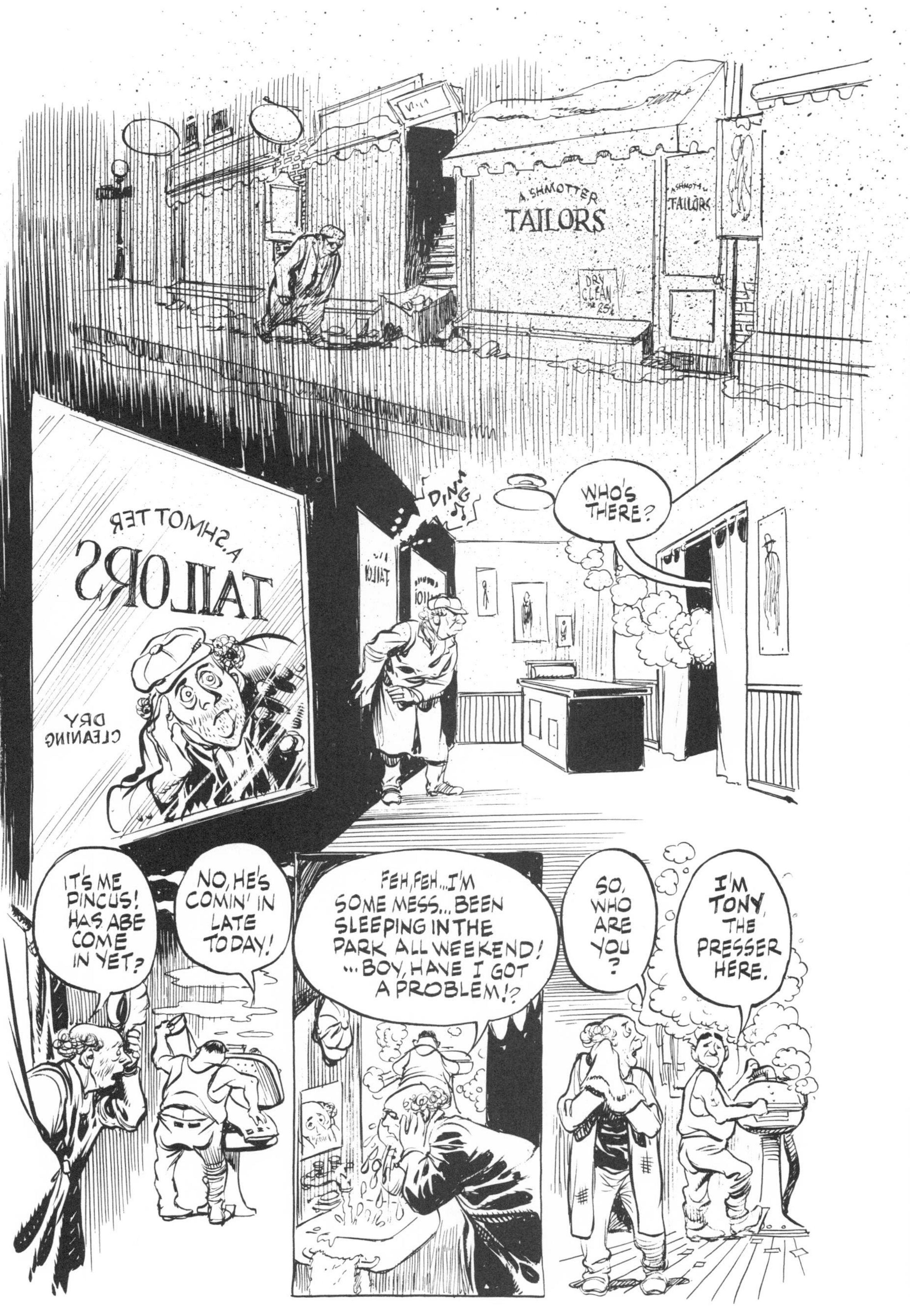
A. SHMOTTER
TAILORS
DRY CLEAN
DING
WHO'S THERE?
IT'S ME PINCUS! HAS ABE COME IN YET?
NO, HE'S COMIN' IN LATE TODAY!
FEH, FEH... I'M SOME MESS... BEEN SLEEPING IN THE PARK ALL WEEKEND! ... BOY, HAVE I GOT A PROBLEM!?
SO, WHO ARE YOU?
I'M TONY, THE PRESSER HERE.

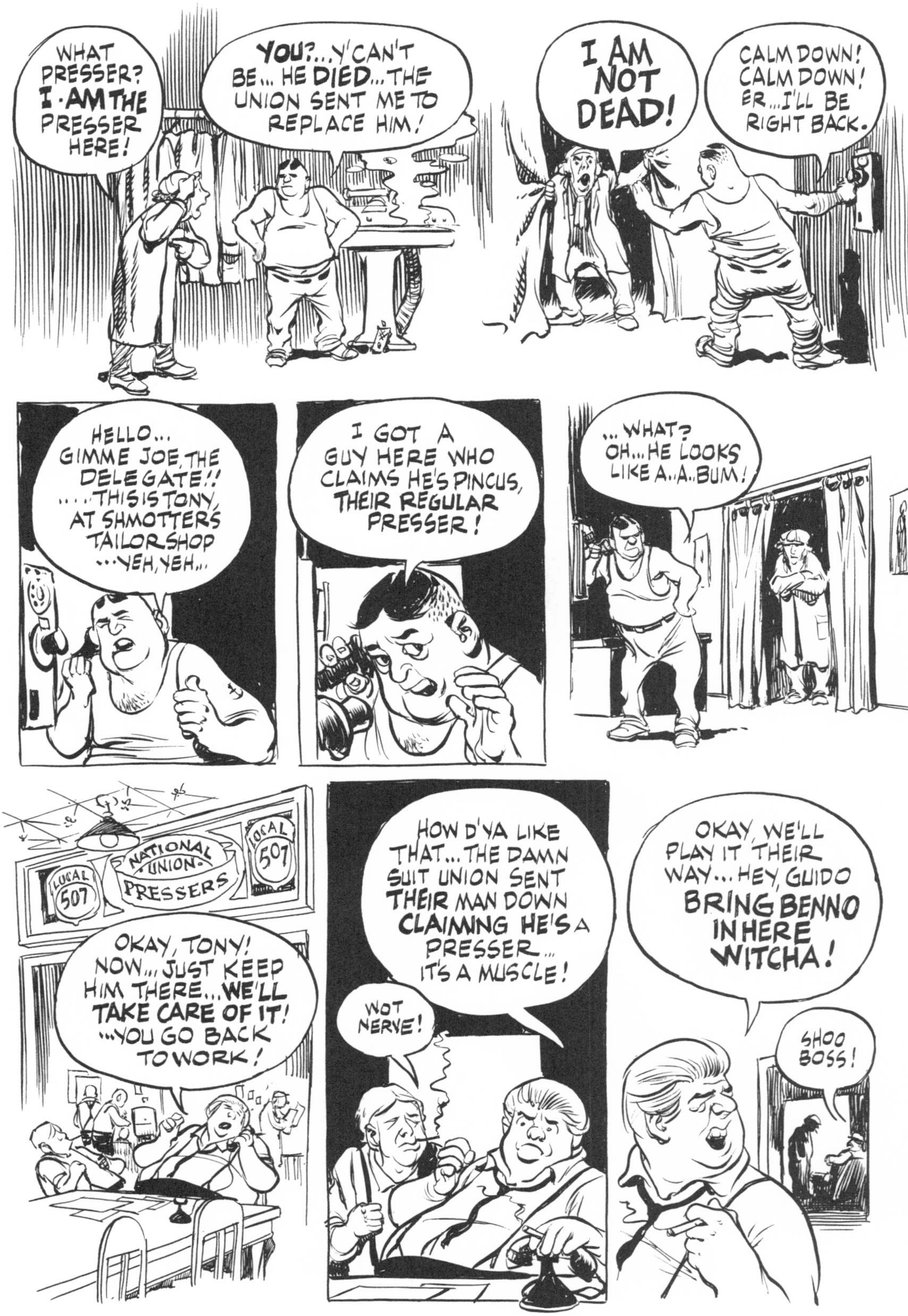
WHAT PRESSER? I-AM THE PRESSER HERE!
YOU?... Y'CAN'T BE... HE DIED... THE UNION SENT ME TO REPLACE HIM!
I AM NOT DEAD!
CALM DOWN! CALM DOWN! ER... I'LL BE RIGHT BACK.
HELLO... GIMME JOE, THE DELEGATE!! .... THIS IS TONY, AT SHMOTTER'S TAILORSHOP ... YEH, YEH...
I GOT A GUY HERE WHO CLAIMS HE'S PINCUS, THEIR REGULAR PRESSER!
... WHAT? OH... HE LOOKS LIKE A.. A.. BUM!
NATIONAL UNION PRESSERS
LOCAL 507
LOCAL 507
OKAY, TONY! NOW... JUST KEEP HIM THERE... WE'LL TAKE CARE OF IT! ...YOU GO BACK TO WORK!
HOW D'YA LIKE THAT... THE DAMN SUIT UNION SENT THEIR MAN DOWN CLAIMING HE'S A PRESSER... IT'S A MUSCLE!
WOT NERVE!
OKAY, WE'LL PLAY IT THEIR WAY... HEY, GUIDO BRING BENNO IN HERE WITCHA!
SHOO BOSS!

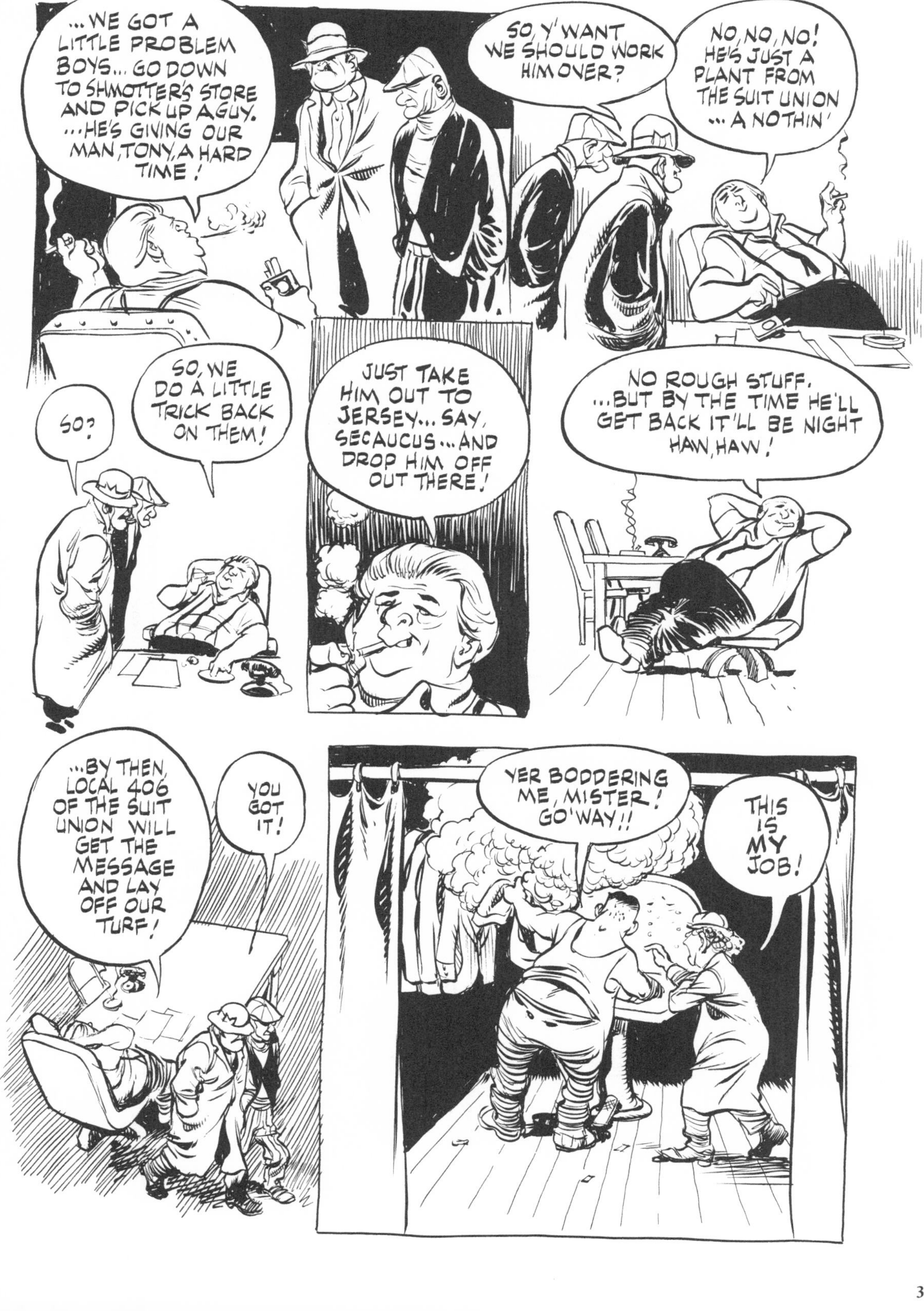
...WE GOT A LITTLE PROBLEM BOYS... GO DOWN TO SHMOTTER'S STORE AND PICK UP A GUY. ...HE'S GIVING OUR MAN, TONY, A HARD TIME!
SO, Y' WANT WE SHOULD WORK HIM OVER?
NO, NO, NO! HE'S JUST A PLANT FROM THE SUIT UNION ...A NOTHIN'
SO?
SO, WE DO A LITTLE TRICK BACK ON THEM!
JUST TAKE HIM OUT TO JERSEY... SAY, SECAUCUS... AND DROP HIM OFF OUT THERE!
NO ROUGH STUFF. ...BUT BY THE TIME HE'LL GET BACK IT'LL BE NIGHT HAW, HAW!
...BY THEN, LOCAL 406 OF THE SUIT UNION WILL GET THE MESSAGE AND LAY OFF OUR TURF!
YOU GOT IT!
YER BODDERING ME, MISTER! GO'WAY!!
THIS IS MY JOB!

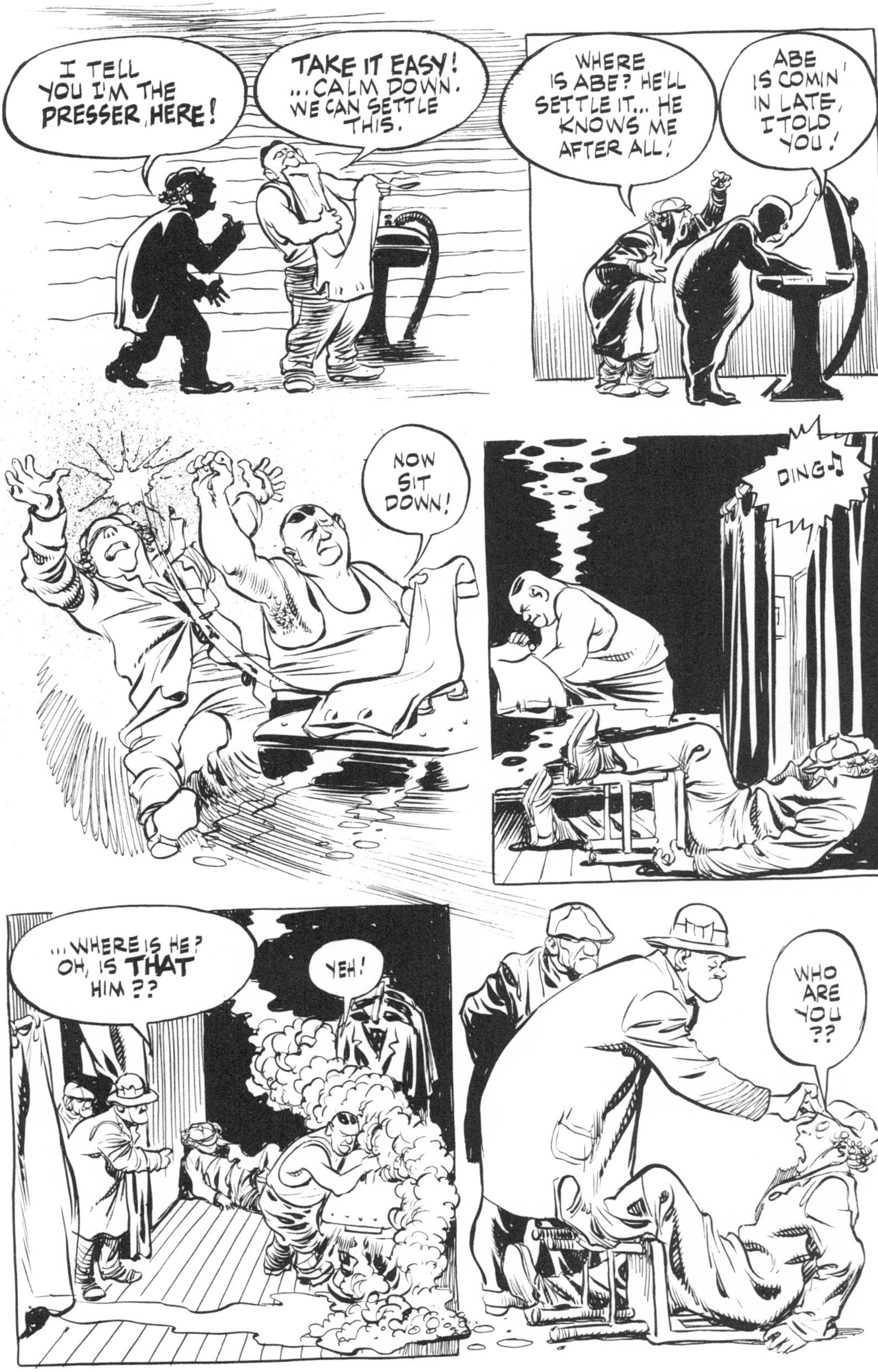
I TELL YOU I'M THE PRESSER, HERE!
TAKE IT EASY! ...CALM DOWN. WE CAN SETTLE THIS.
WHERE IS ABE? HE'LL SETTLE IT... HE KNOWS ME AFTER ALL!
ABE IS COMIN' IN LATE, I TOLD YOU!
NOW SIT DOWN!
DING♫
...WHERE IS HE? OH, IS THAT HIM??
YEH!
WHO ARE YOU??

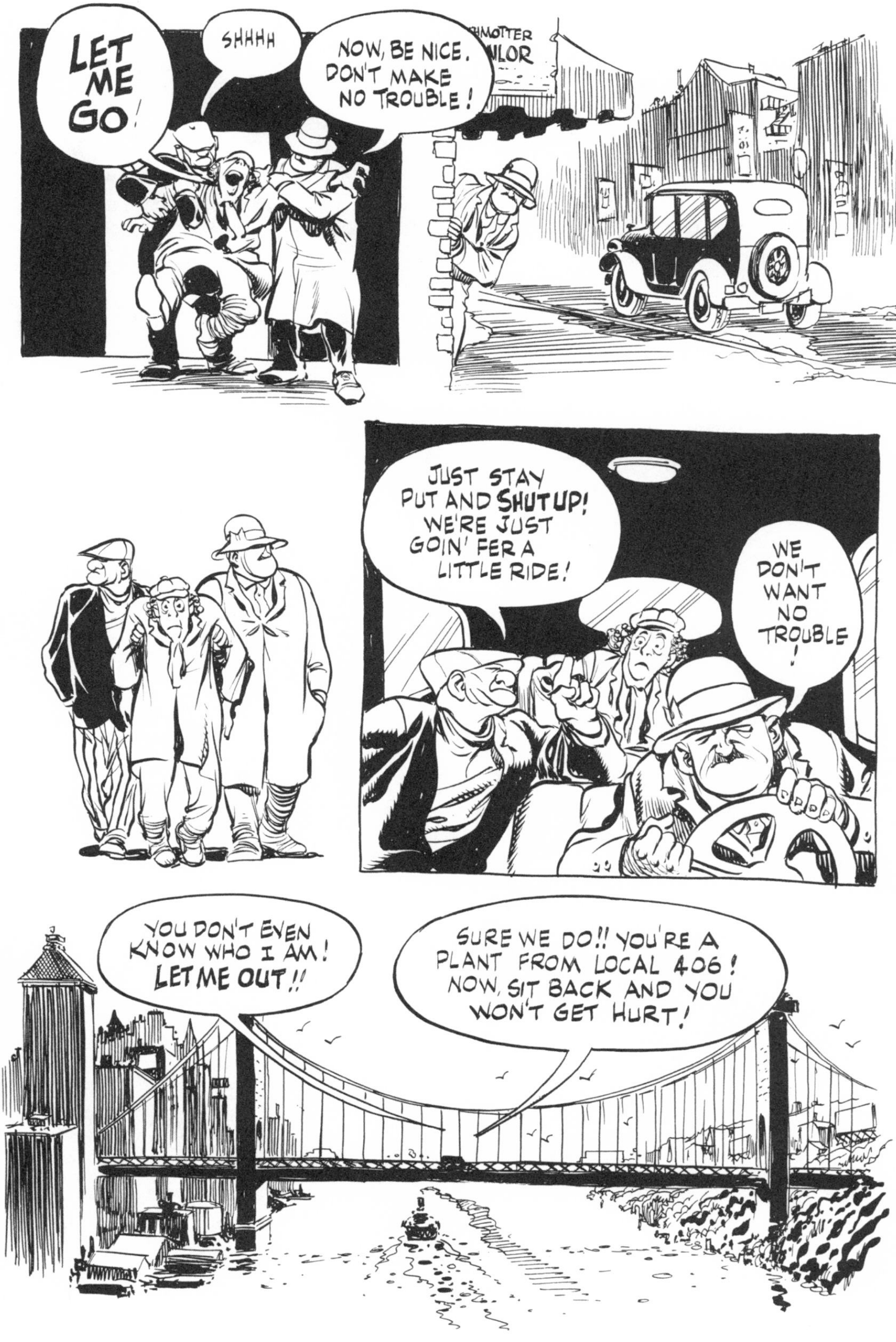
LET ME GO!
SHHHH
NOW, BE NICE. DON'T MAKE NO TROUBLE!
SCHMOTTER
NLOR
JUST STAY PUT AND SHUT UP! WE'RE JUST GOIN' FER A LITTLE RIDE!
WE DON'T WANT NO TROUBLE!
YOU DON'T EVEN KNOW WHO I AM! LET ME OUT!!
SURE WE DO!! YOU'RE A PLANT FROM LOCAL 406! NOW, SIT BACK AND YOU WON'T GET HURT!

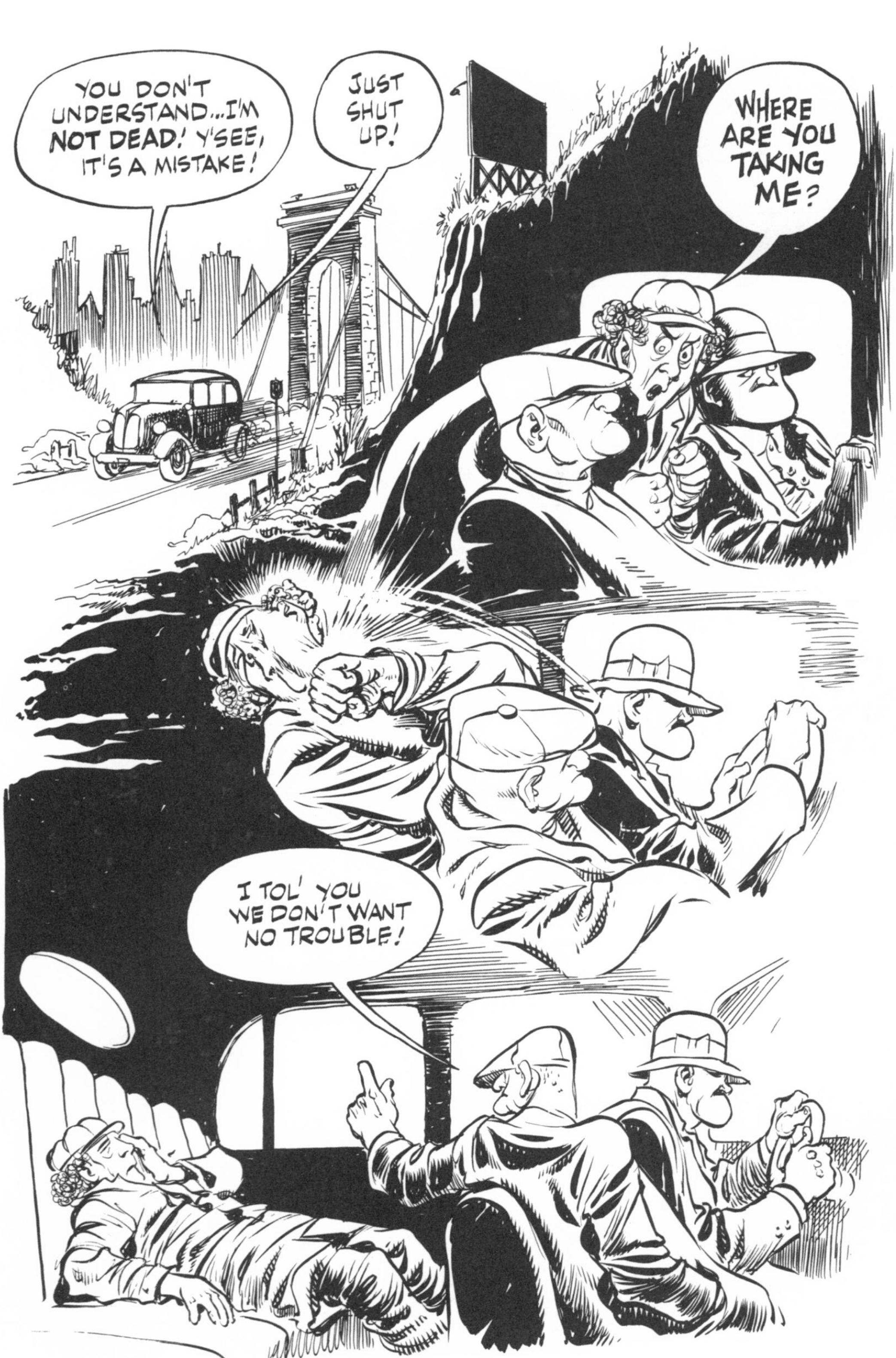
YOU DON'T UNDERSTAND...I'M NOT DEAD! Y'SEE, IT'S A MISTAKE!
JUST SHUT UP!
WHERE ARE YOU TAKING ME?
I TOL' YOU WE DON'T WANT NO TROUBLE!

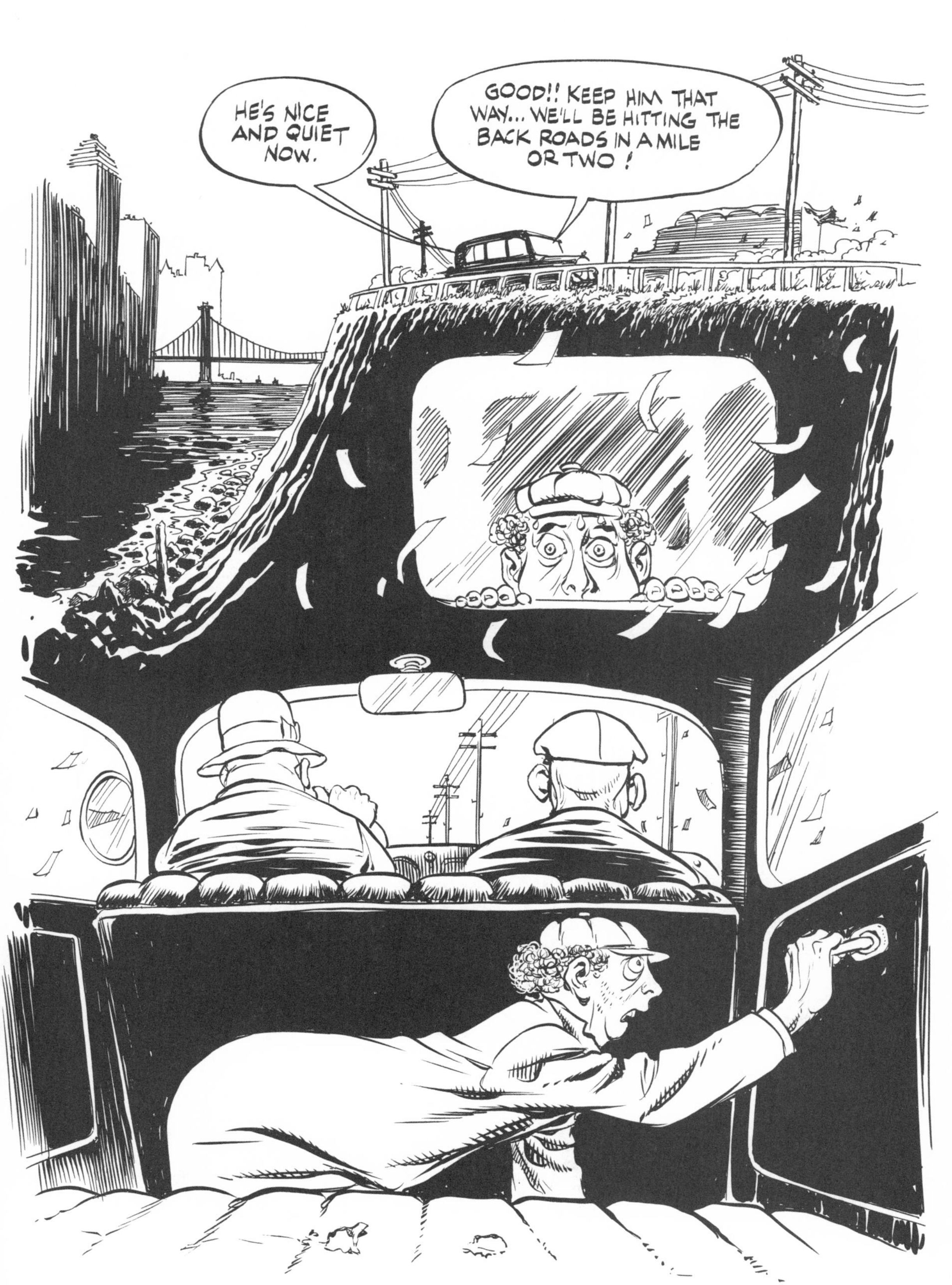
HE'S NICE AND QUIET NOW.
GOOD!! KEEP HIM THAT WAY... WE'LL BE HITTING THE BACK ROADS IN A MILE OR TWO!

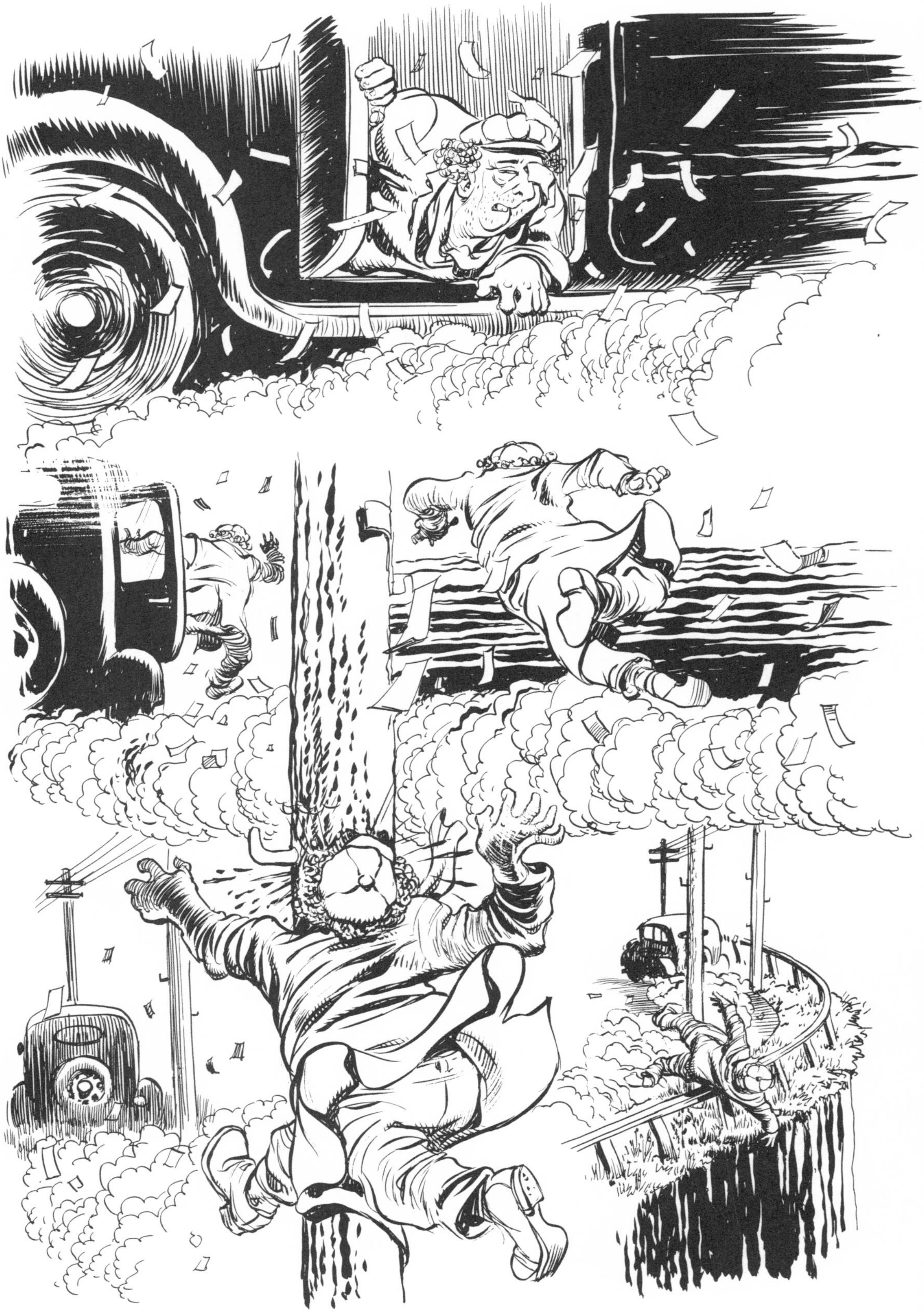

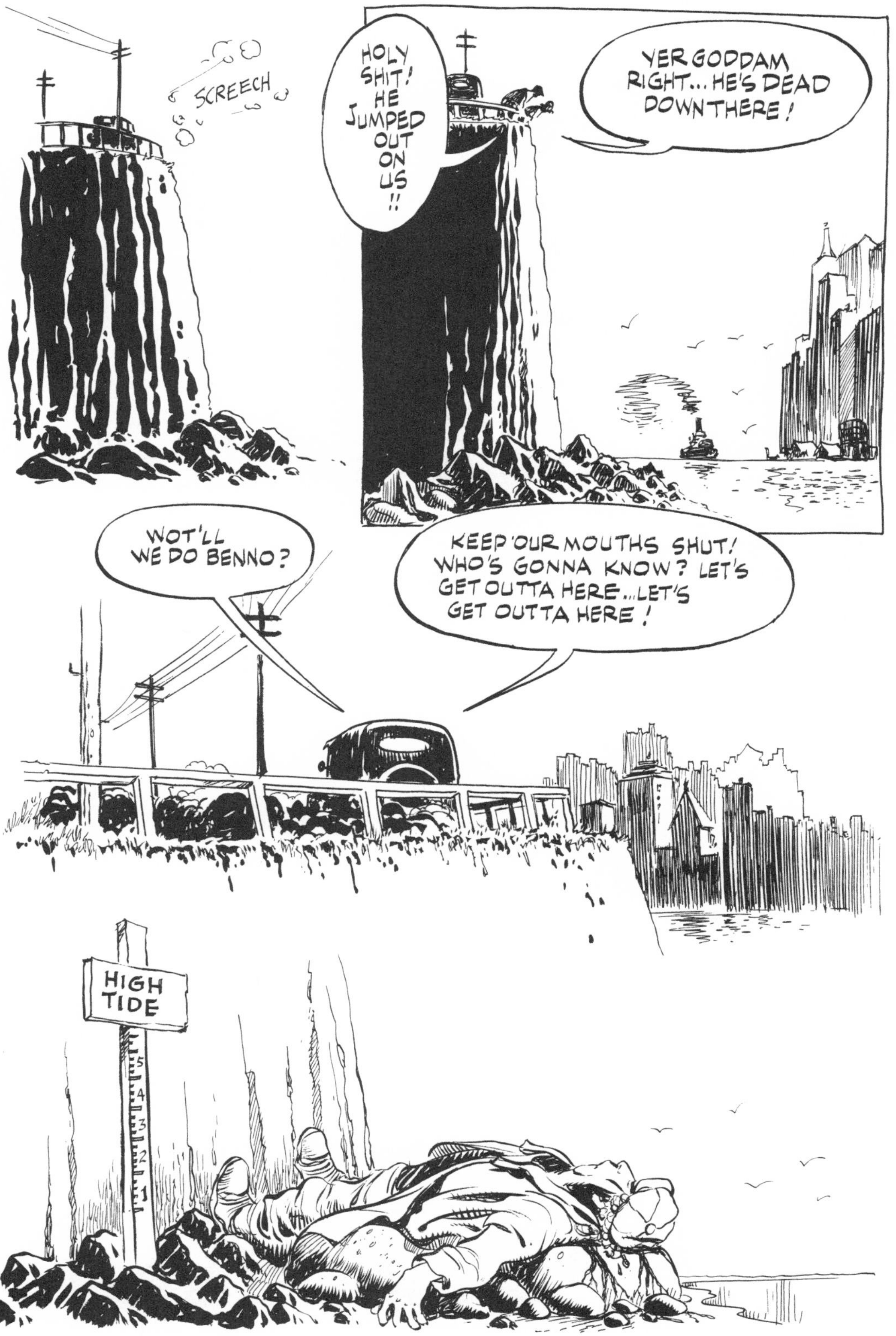
SCREECH
HOLY SHIT! HE JUMPED OUT ON US!!
YER GODDAM RIGHT... HE'S DEAD DOWN THERE!
WOT'LL WE DO BENNO?
KEEP OUR MOUTHS SHUT! WHO'S GONNA KNOW? LET'S GET OUTTA HERE...LET'S GET OUTTA HERE!
HIGH TIDE

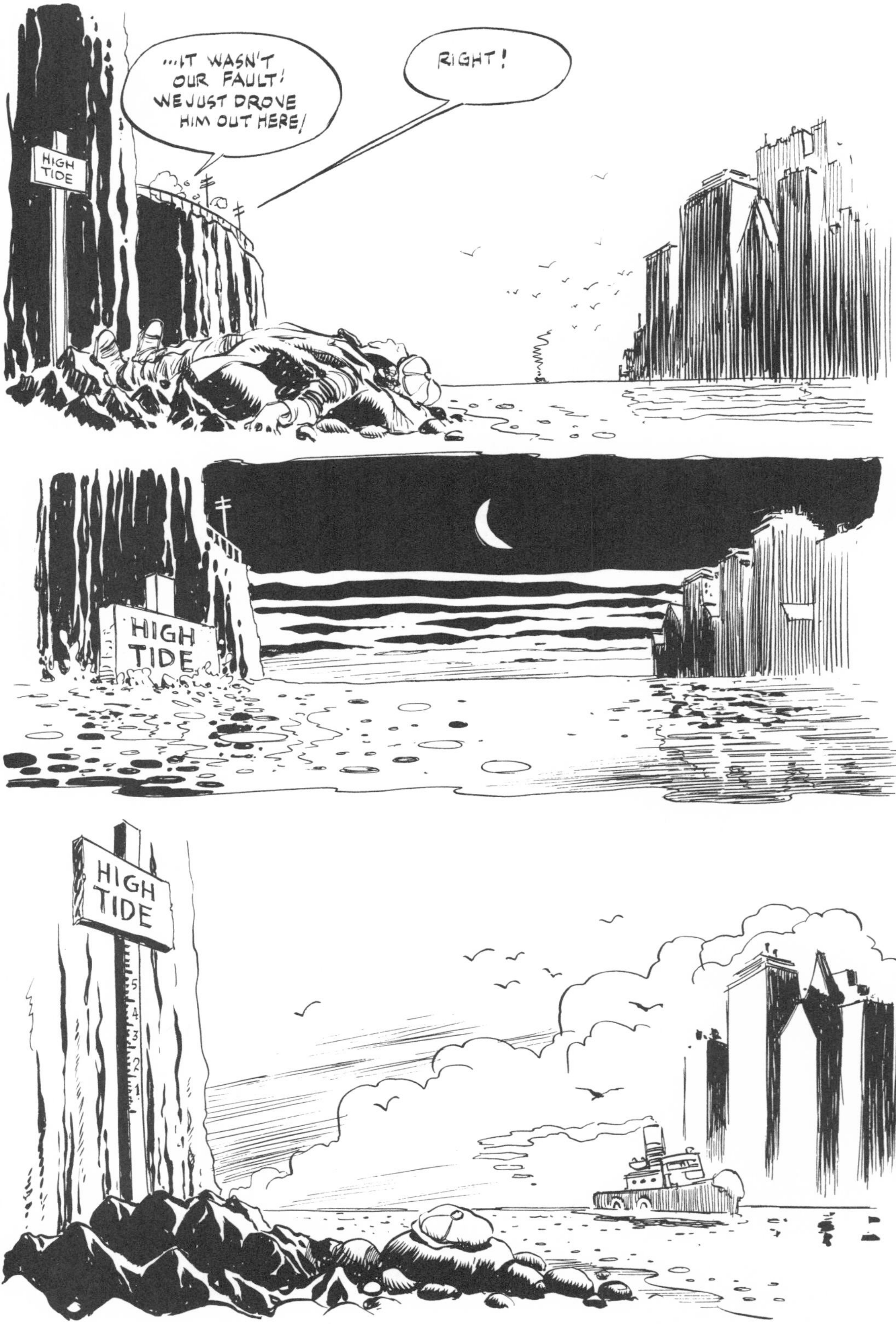
...IT WASN'T OUR FAULT! WE JUST DROVE HIM OUT HERE!
RIGHT!
HIGH TIDE
HIGH TIDE
HIGH TIDE

POSTMORTEM

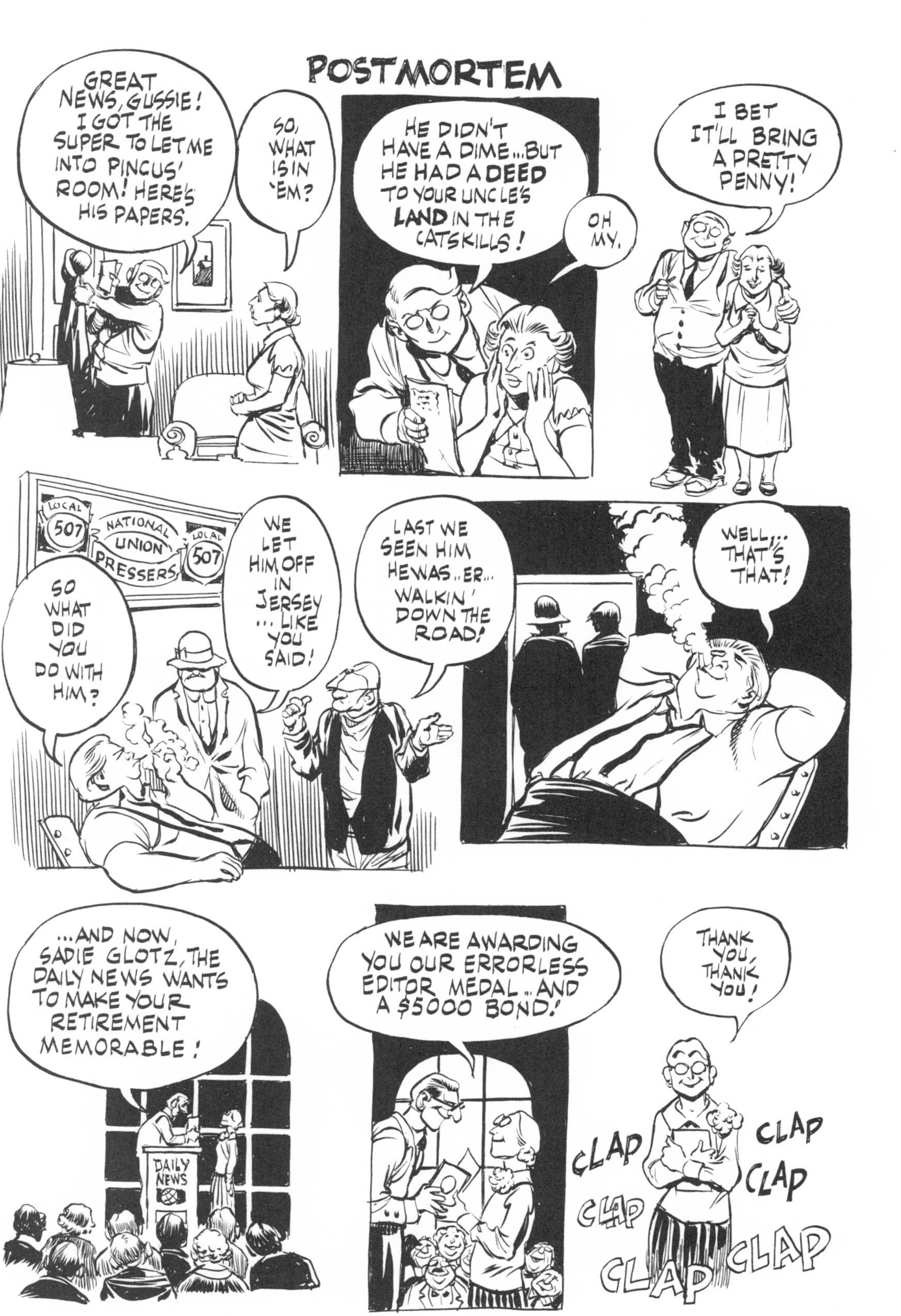
GREAT NEWS, GUSSIE! I GOT THE SUPER TO LET ME INTO PINCUS' ROOM! HERE'S HIS PAPERS.
SO, WHAT IS IN 'EM?
HE DIDN'T HAVE A DIME...BUT HE HAD A DEED TO YOUR UNCLE'S LAND IN THE CATSKILLS!
OH MY.
I BET IT'LL BRING A PRETTY PENNY!
LOCAL 507
NATIONAL UNION PRESSERS
LOCAL 507
SO WHAT DID YOU DO WITH HIM?
WE LET HIM OFF IN JERSEY ... LIKE YOU SAID!
LAST WE SEEN HIM HE WAS..ER... WALKIN' DOWN THE ROAD!
WELL... THAT'S THAT!
...AND NOW, SADIE GLOTZ, THE DAILY NEWS WANTS TO MAKE YOUR RETIREMENT MEMORABLE!
DAILY NEWS
WE ARE AWARDING YOU OUR ERRORLESS EDITOR MEDAL...AND A $5000 BOND!
THANK YOU, THANK YOU!
CLAP CLAP CLAP CLAP CLAP CLAP

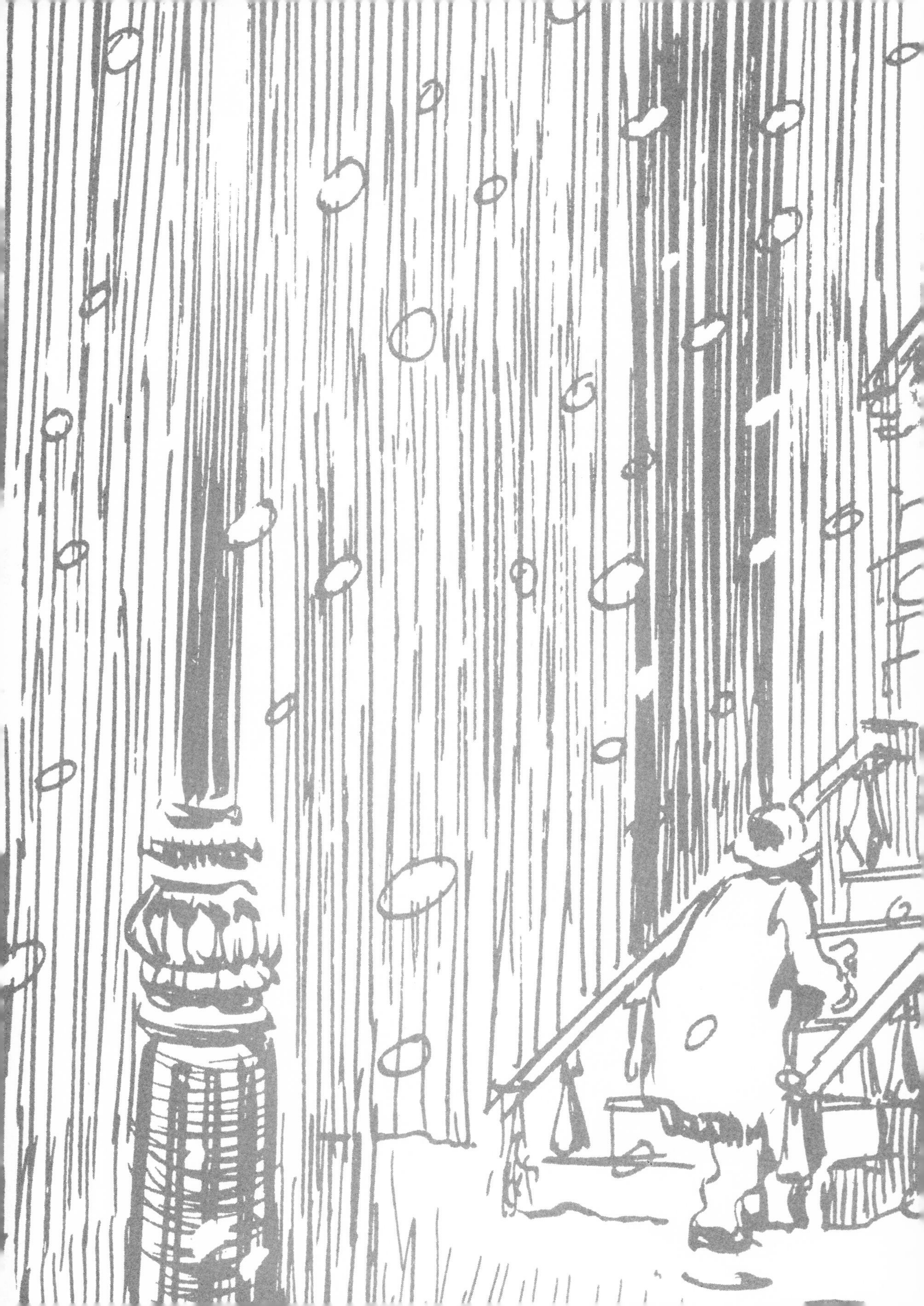

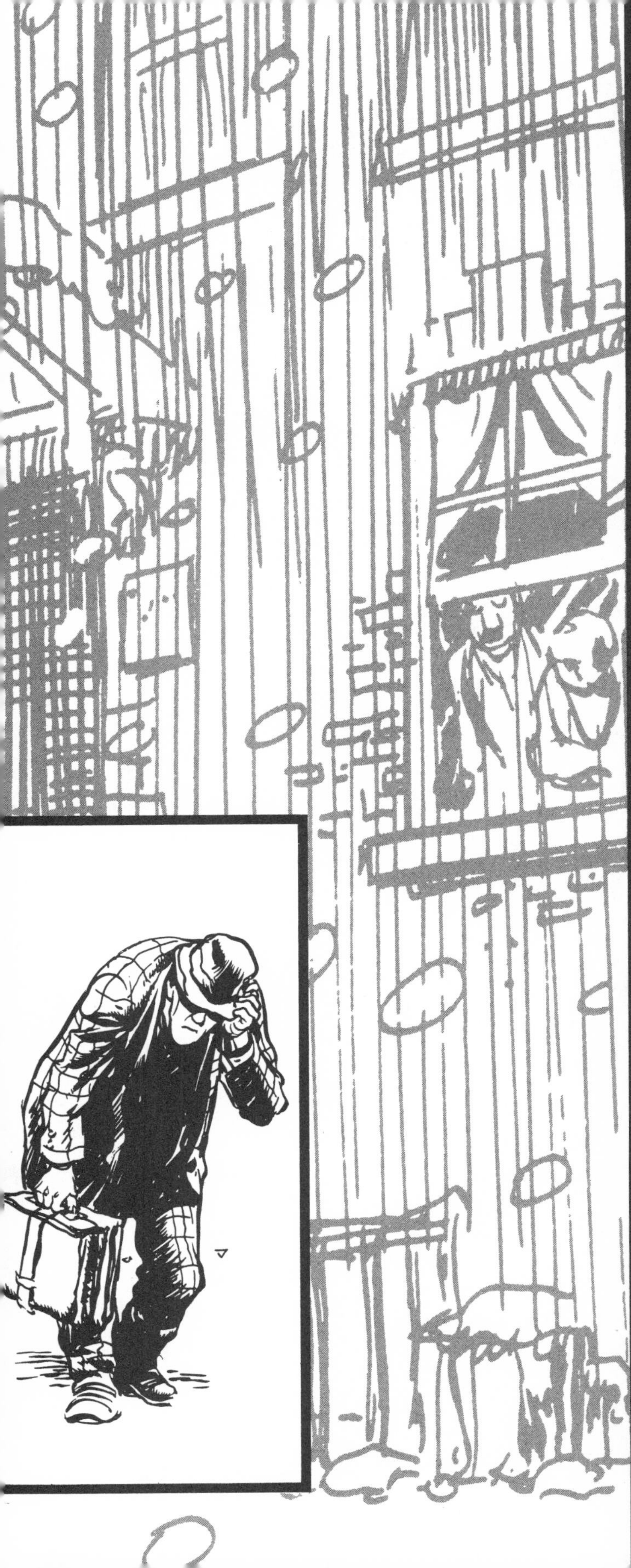

Introduction to "The Power"

WHILE NOT ALTOGETHER singular to city life, this story does reflect a facet of it. In a densely populated environment where the rhythm of living is kinetic and citizens survive by circumvention, there is little time or even inclination to dwell on the story of a single life.

The pity of it is that deep-city dwellers carefully sidestep the human debris they see in the doorways and crannies around them. Perhaps it has something to do with a fear or touching the agony of a person descending into invisibility, or maybe there simply is no time to spare in the rush to infinity.

Whatever, these dynamics reduce to nothingness the people we pass on the street.

Morris's story is one of symbolism. I see his tragedy as common to the subliminal sense of omnipotence that fuels human survival. The journey into invisilibity begins when that sense falters.

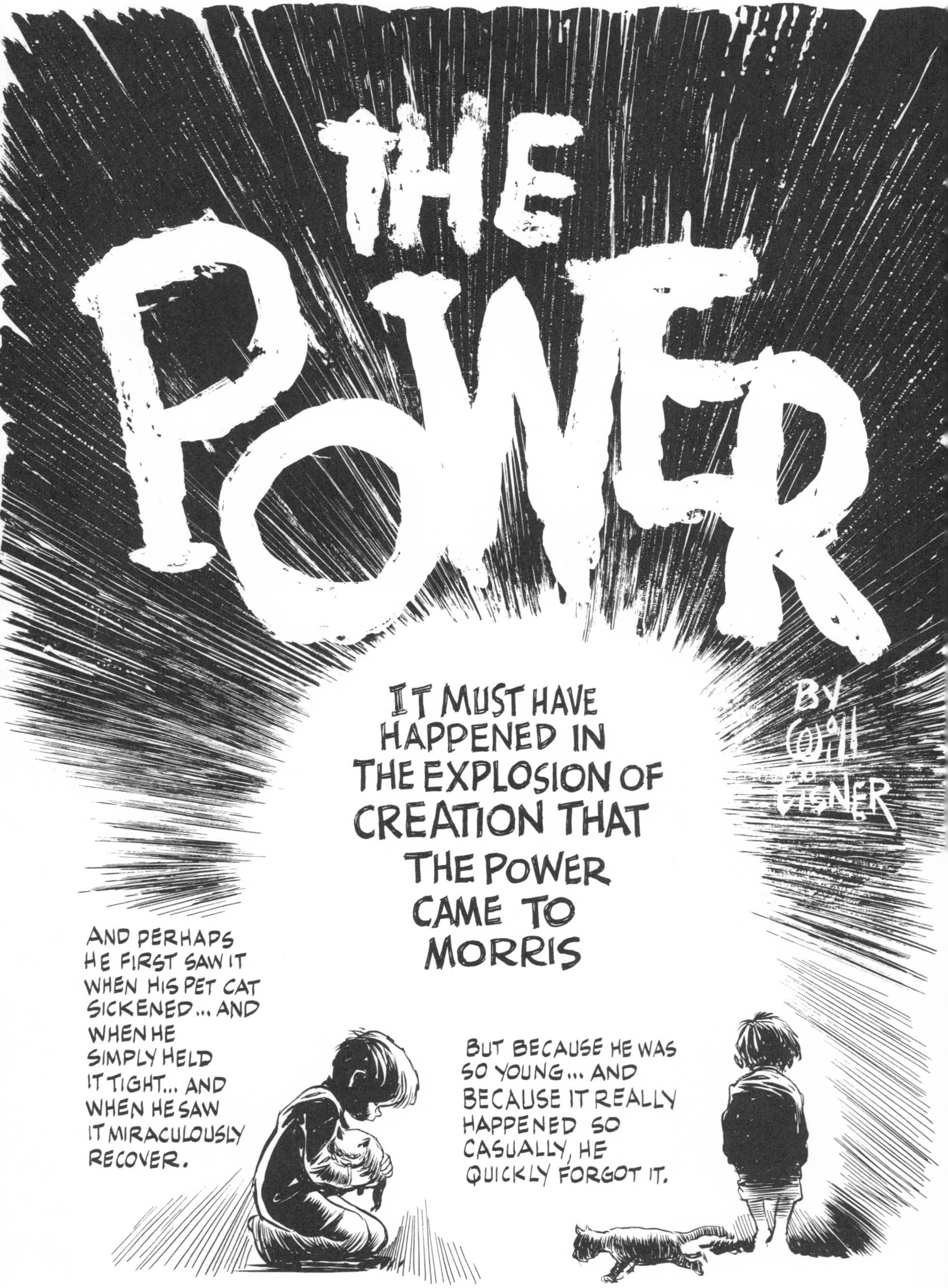
THE POWER
IT MUST HAVE HAPPENED IN THE EXPLOSION OF CREATION THAT THE POWER CAME TO MORRIS
BY Will Eisner
AND PERHAPS HE FIRST SAW IT WHEN HIS PET CAT SICKENED... AND WHEN HE SIMPLY HELD IT TIGHT... AND WHEN HE SAW IT MIRACULOUSLY RECOVER.
BUT BECAUSE HE WAS SO YOUNG... AND BECAUSE IT REALLY HAPPENED SO CASUALLY, HE QUICKLY FORGOT IT.

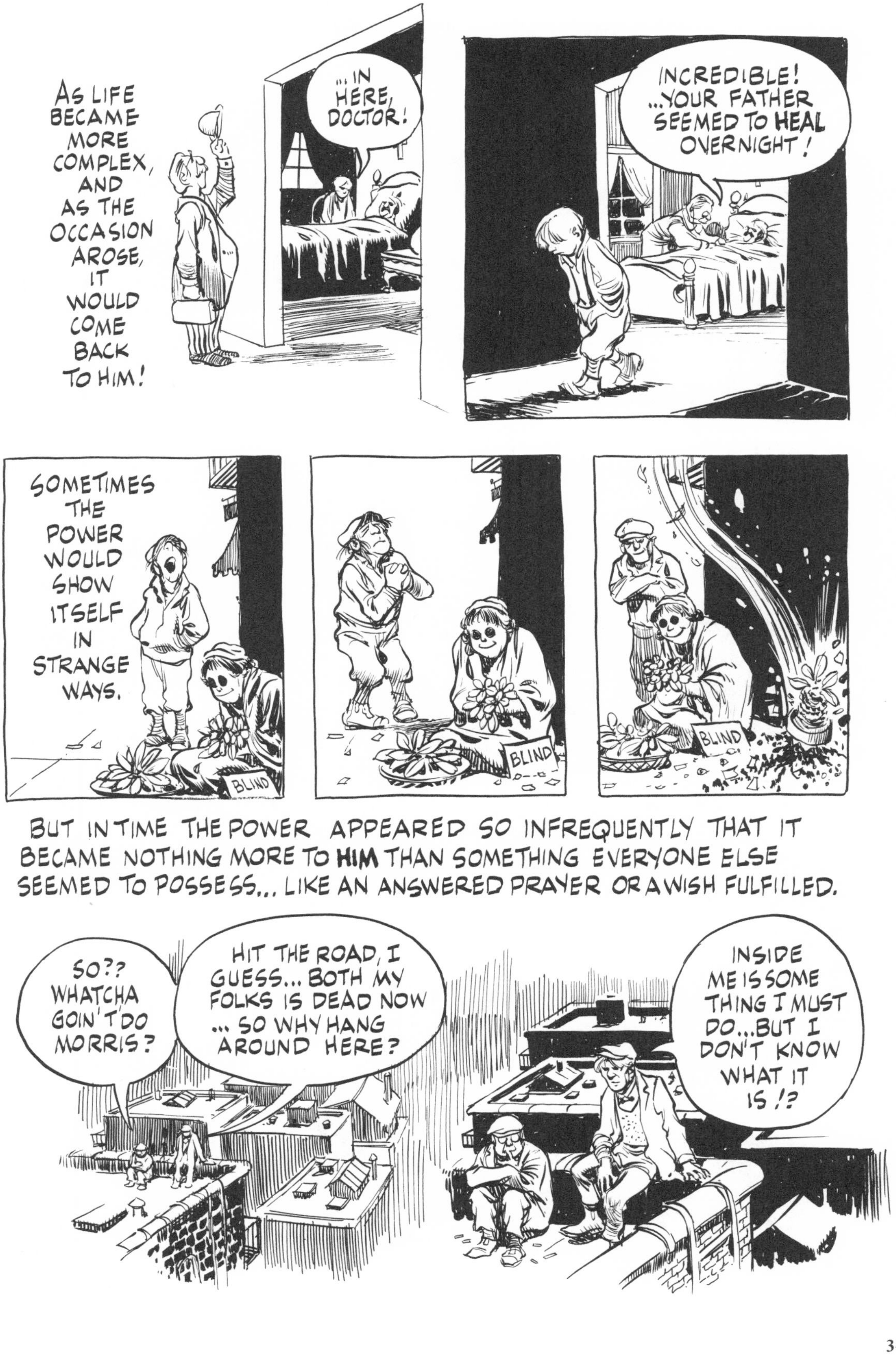
As life became more complex, and as the occasion arose, it would come back to him!
... in here, Doctor!
Incredible! ...Your father seemed to **heal** overnight!
Sometimes the power would show itself in strange ways.
BLIND
BLIND
BLIND
But in time the power appeared so infrequently that it became nothing more to **him** than something everyone else seemed to possess... like an answered prayer or a wish fulfilled.
So?? Whatcha goin't'do Morris?
Hit the road, I guess... both my folks is dead now ... so why hang around here?
Inside me is some thing I must do... but I don't know what it is!?

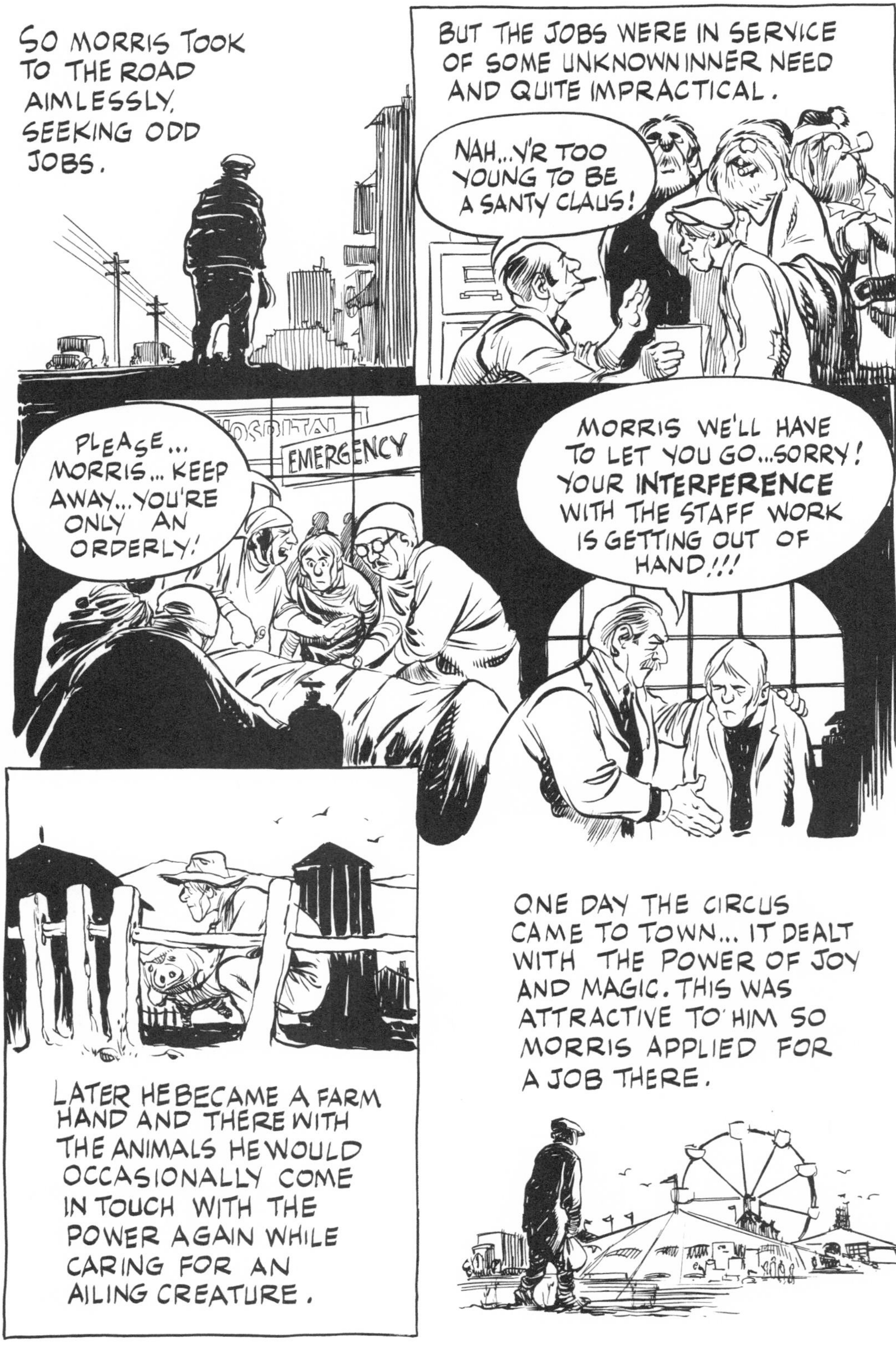

SO MORRIS TOOK TO THE ROAD AIMLESSLY, SEEKING ODD JOBS.
BUT THE JOBS WERE IN SERVICE OF SOME UNKNOWN INNER NEED AND QUITE IMPRACTICAL.
NAH...Y'R TOO YOUNG TO BE A SANTY CLAUS!
HOSPITAL
EMERGENCY
PLEASE... MORRIS... KEEP AWAY...YOU'RE ONLY AN ORDERLY!
MORRIS WE'LL HAVE TO LET YOU GO...SORRY! YOUR INTERFERENCE WITH THE STAFF WORK IS GETTING OUT OF HAND!!!
LATER HE BECAME A FARM HAND AND THERE WITH THE ANIMALS HE WOULD OCCASIONALLY COME IN TOUCH WITH THE POWER AGAIN WHILE CARING FOR AN AILING CREATURE.
ONE DAY THE CIRCUS CAME TO TOWN... IT DEALT WITH THE POWER OF JOY AND MAGIC. THIS WAS ATTRACTIVE TO HIM SO MORRIS APPLIED FOR A JOB THERE.

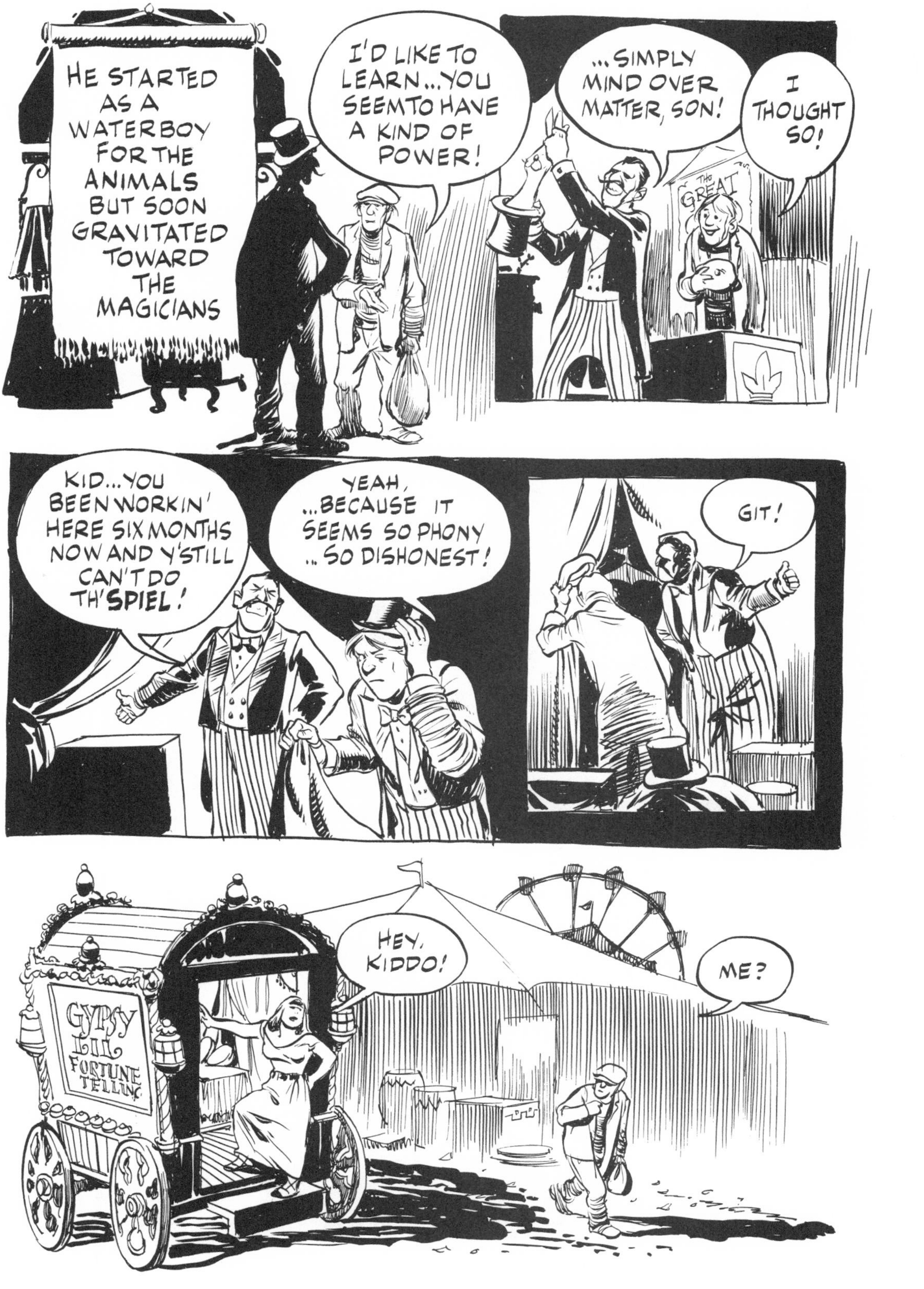
HE STARTED AS A WATERBOY FOR THE ANIMALS BUT SOON GRAVITATED TOWARD THE MAGICIANS
I'D LIKE TO LEARN...YOU SEEM TO HAVE A KIND OF POWER!
...SIMPLY MIND OVER MATTER, SON!
I THOUGHT SO!
THE GREAT
KID...YOU BEEN WORKIN' HERE SIX MONTHS NOW AND Y'STILL CAN'T DO TH' SPIEL!
YEAH, ...BECAUSE IT SEEMS SO PHONY ... SO DISHONEST!
GIT!
HEY, KIDDO!
ME?
GYPSY LIL FORTUNE TELLING

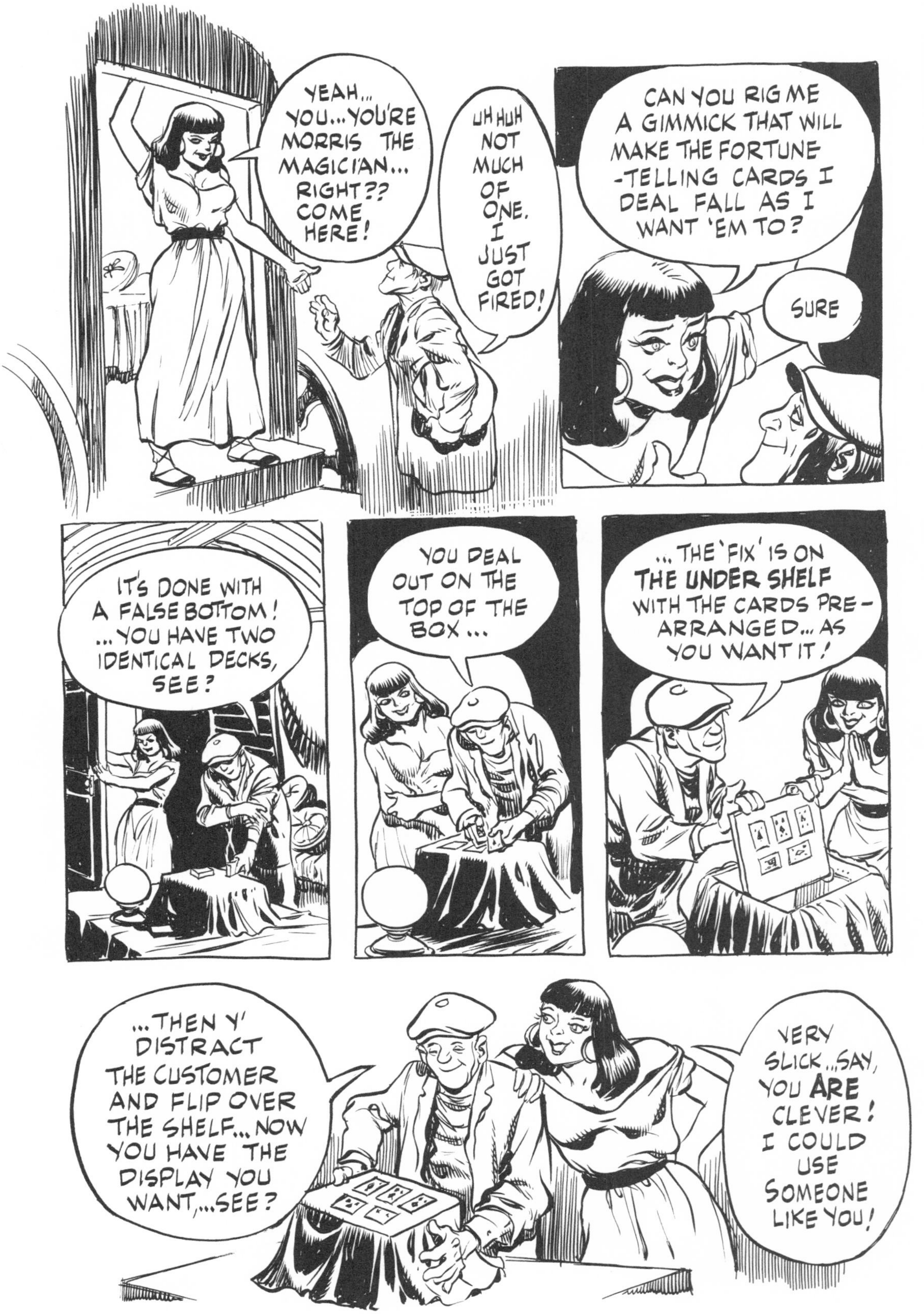
YEAH... YOU...YOU'RE MORRIS THE MAGICIAN... RIGHT?? COME HERE!
UH HUH NOT MUCH OF ONE. I JUST GOT FIRED!
CAN YOU RIG ME A GIMMICK THAT WILL MAKE THE FORTUNE-TELLING CARDS I DEAL FALL AS I WANT 'EM TO?
SURE
IT'S DONE WITH A FALSE BOTTOM! ...YOU HAVE TWO IDENTICAL DECKS, SEE?
YOU DEAL OUT ON THE TOP OF THE BOX...
...THE 'FIX' IS ON **THE UNDER SHELF** WITH THE CARDS PRE-ARRANGED... AS YOU WANT IT!
...THEN Y' DISTRACT THE CUSTOMER AND FLIP OVER THE SHELF... NOW YOU HAVE THE DISPLAY YOU WANT,...SEE?
VERY SLICK...SAY, YOU **ARE** CLEVER! I COULD USE SOMEONE LIKE YOU!

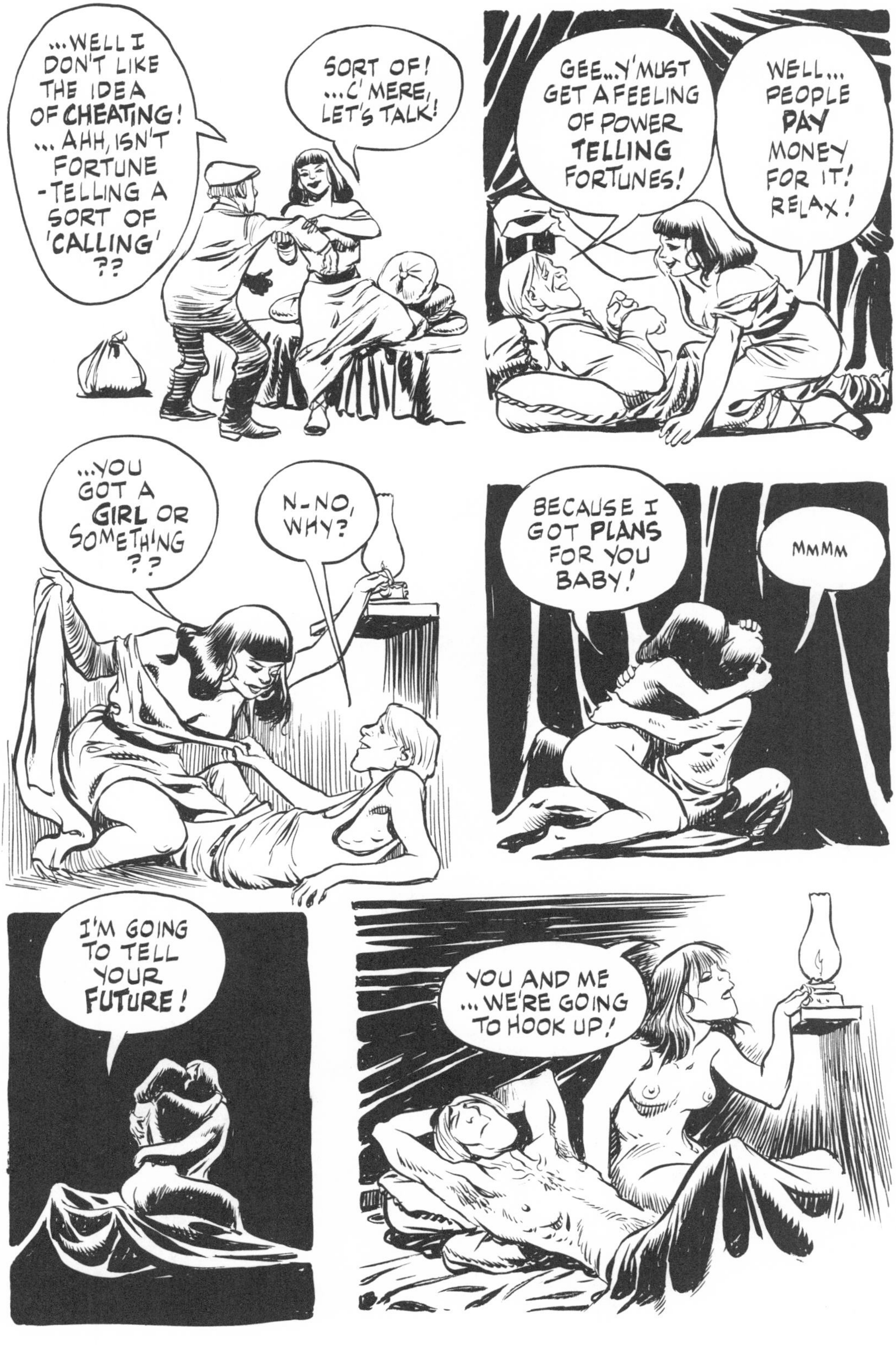
...WELL I DON'T LIKE THE IDEA OF CHEATING! ...AHH, ISN'T FORTUNE -TELLING A SORT OF 'CALLING' ??
SORT OF! ...C'MERE, LET'S TALK!
GEE...Y'MUST GET A FEELING OF POWER TELLING FORTUNES!
WELL... PEOPLE PAY MONEY FOR IT! RELAX!
...YOU GOT A GIRL OR SOMETHING ??
N-NO, WHY?
BECAUSE I GOT PLANS FOR YOU BABY!
MMMM
I'M GOING TO TELL YOUR FUTURE!
YOU AND ME ...WE'RE GOING TO HOOK UP!

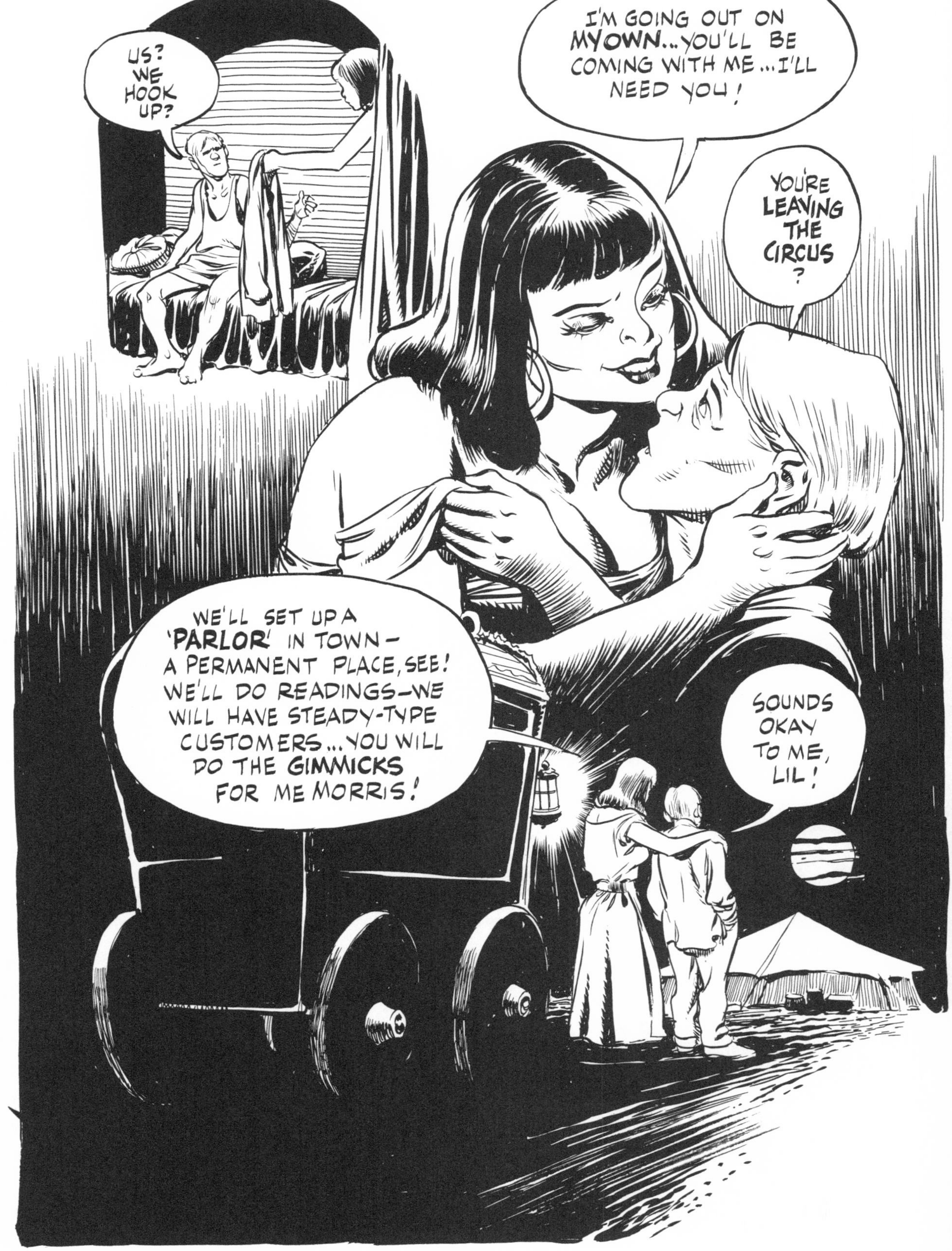
US? WE HOOK UP?
I'M GOING OUT ON MY OWN... YOU'LL BE COMING WITH ME... I'LL NEED YOU!
YOU'RE LEAVING THE CIRCUS ?
WE'LL SET UP A 'PARLOR' IN TOWN — A PERMANENT PLACE, SEE! WE'LL DO READINGS — WE WILL HAVE STEADY-TYPE CUSTOMERS... YOU WILL DO THE GIMMICKS FOR ME MORRIS!
SOUNDS OKAY TO ME, LIL!

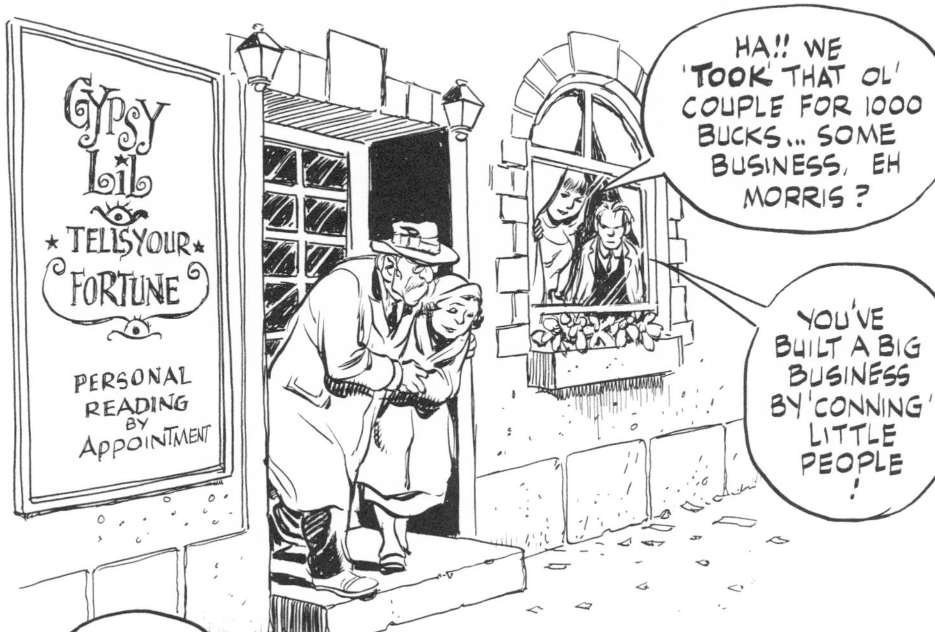
GYPSY LIL
TELLS YOUR FORTUNE
PERSONAL READING BY APPOINTMENT
HA!! WE 'TOOK' THAT OL' COUPLE FOR 1000 BUCKS... SOME BUSINESS, EH MORRIS?
YOU'VE BUILT A BIG BUSINESS BY 'CONNING' LITTLE PEOPLE!

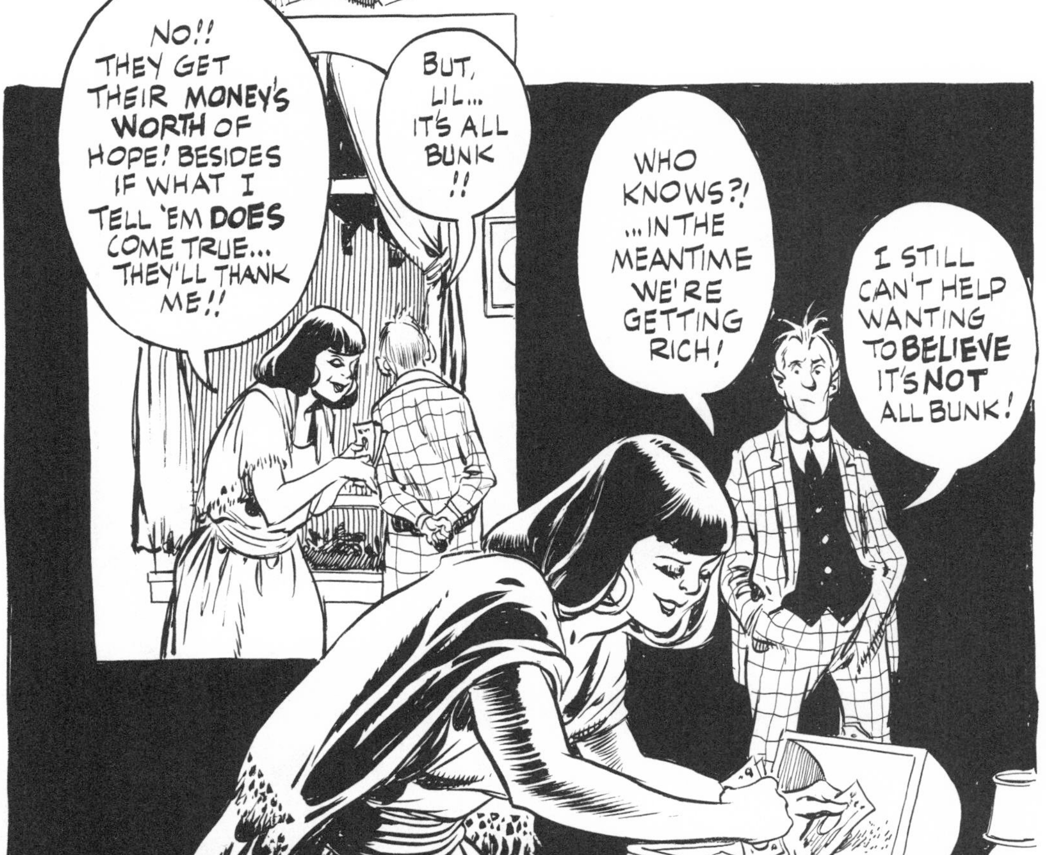
NO!! THEY GET THEIR MONEY'S WORTH OF HOPE! BESIDES IF WHAT I TELL 'EM DOES COME TRUE... THEY'LL THANK ME!!
BUT, LIL... IT'S ALL BUNK!!
WHO KNOWS?! ...IN THE MEANTIME WE'RE GETTING RICH!
I STILL CAN'T HELP WANTING TO BELIEVE IT'S NOT ALL BUNK!

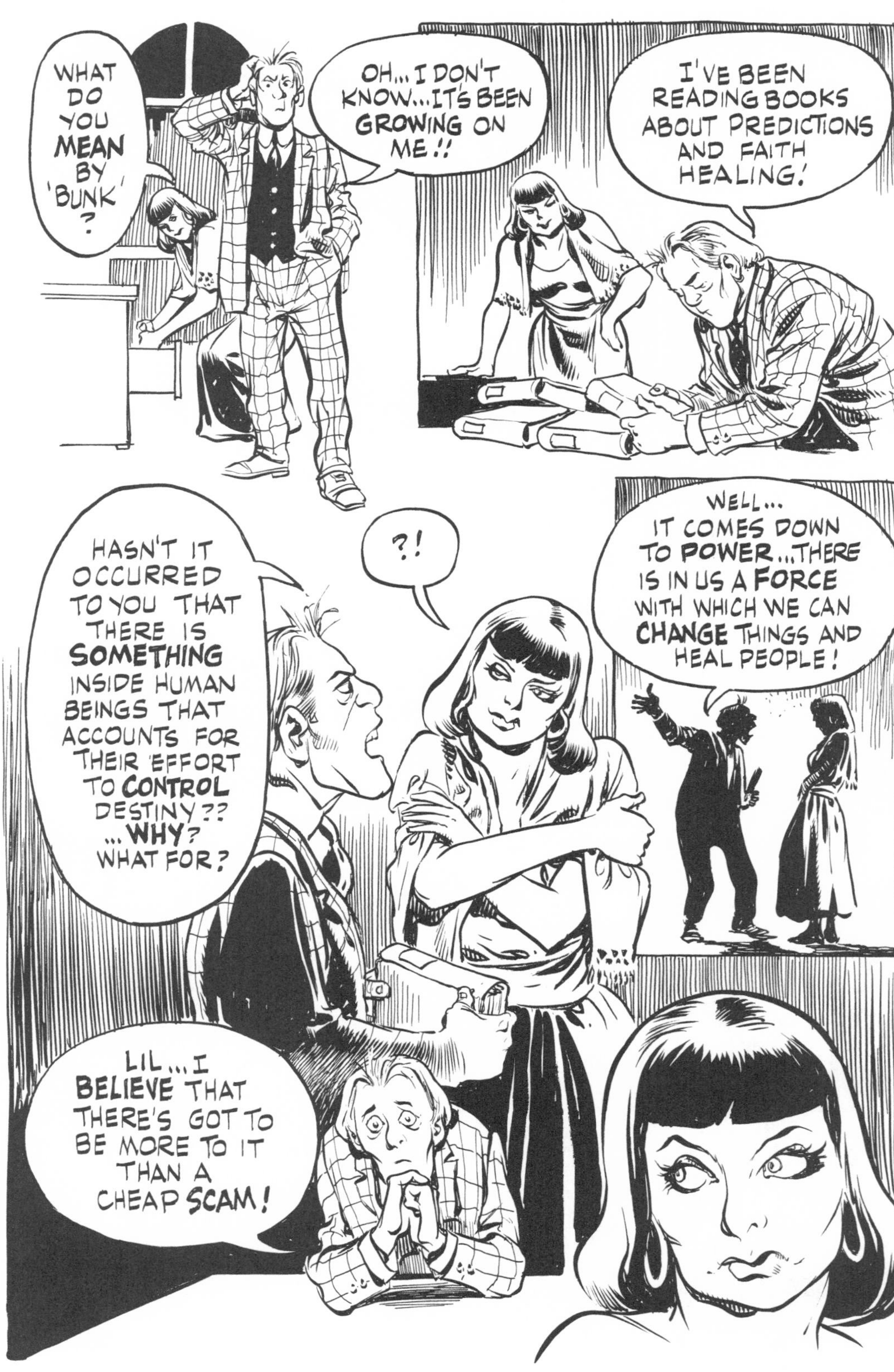
WHAT DO YOU MEAN BY 'BUNK'?
OH... I DON'T KNOW... IT'S BEEN GROWING ON ME!!
I'VE BEEN READING BOOKS ABOUT PREDICTIONS AND FAITH HEALING!
HASN'T IT OCCURRED TO YOU THAT THERE IS SOMETHING INSIDE HUMAN BEINGS THAT ACCOUNTS FOR THEIR EFFORT TO CONTROL DESTINY?? ...WHY? WHAT FOR?
?!
WELL... IT COMES DOWN TO POWER... THERE IS IN US A FORCE WITH WHICH WE CAN CHANGE THINGS AND HEAL PEOPLE!
LIL... I BELIEVE THAT THERE'S GOT TO BE MORE TO IT THAN A CHEAP SCAM!

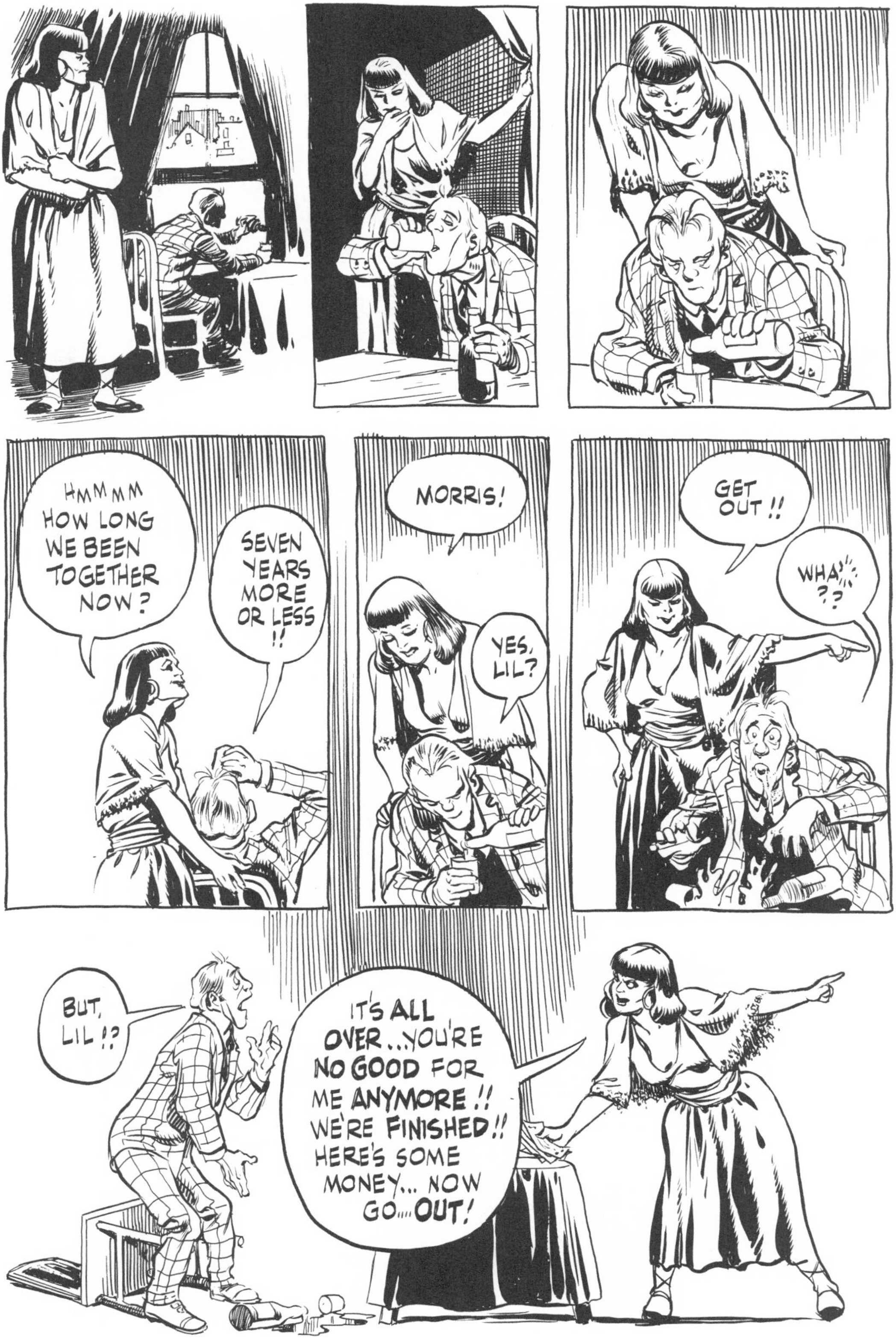
HMMMM HOW LONG WE BEEN TOGETHER NOW?
SEVEN YEARS MORE OR LESS !!
MORRIS!
YES, LIL?
GET OUT !!
WHA'... ??
BUT, LIL !?
IT'S ALL OVER... YOU'RE NO GOOD FOR ME ANYMORE !! WE'RE FINISHED !! HERE'S SOME MONEY... NOW GO.... OUT!

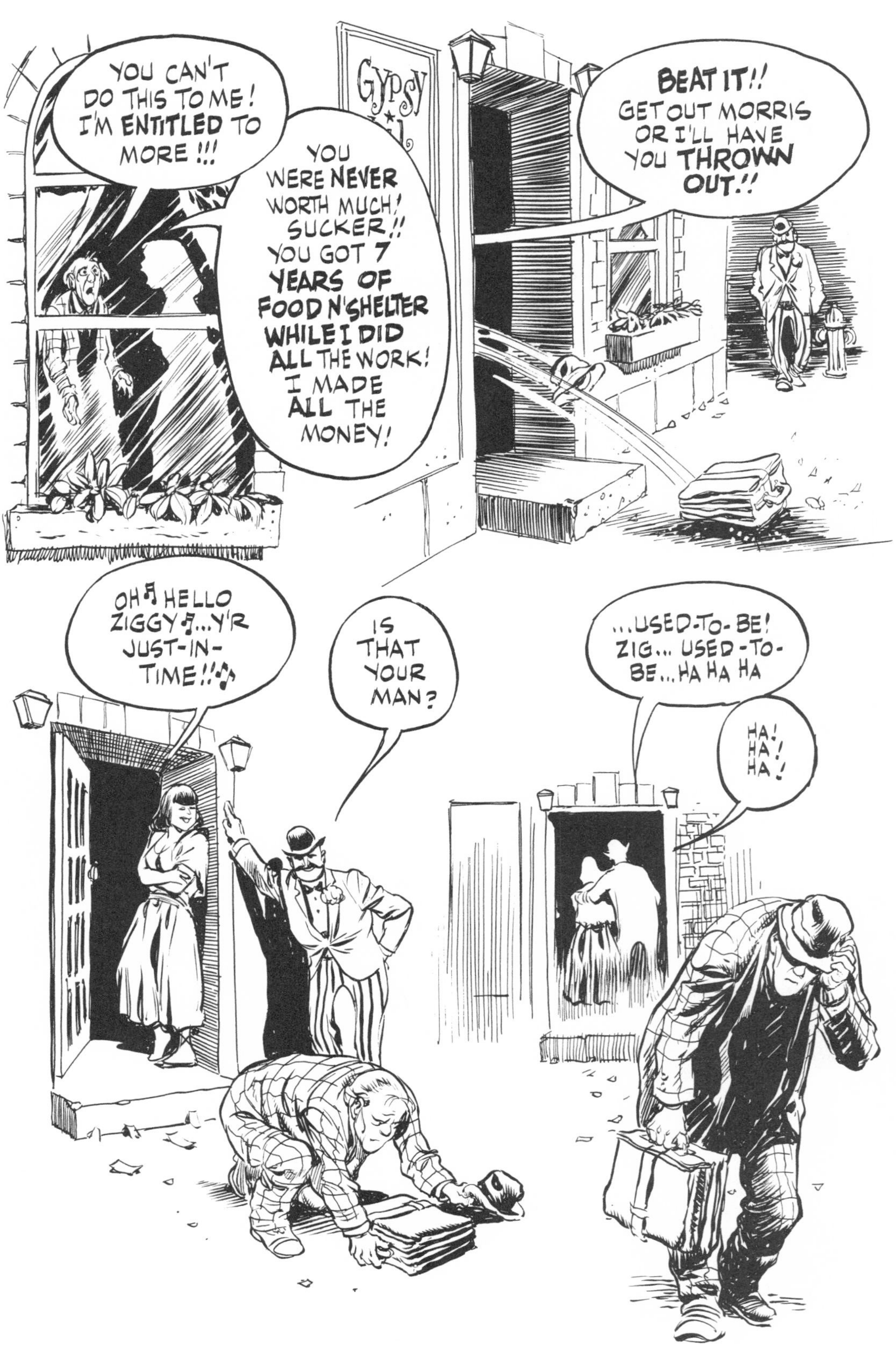
Gypsy
YOU CAN'T DO THIS TO ME! I'M ENTITLED TO MORE!!!
YOU WERE NEVER WORTH MUCH! SUCKER!! YOU GOT 7 YEARS OF FOOD N'SHELTER WHILE I DID ALL THE WORK! I MADE ALL THE MONEY!
BEAT IT!! GET OUT MORRIS OR I'LL HAVE YOU THROWN OUT!!
OH HELLO ZIGGY...Y'R JUST-IN-TIME!!
IS THAT YOUR MAN?
...USED-TO-BE! ZIG... USED-TO-BE...HA HA HA
HA! HA! HA!

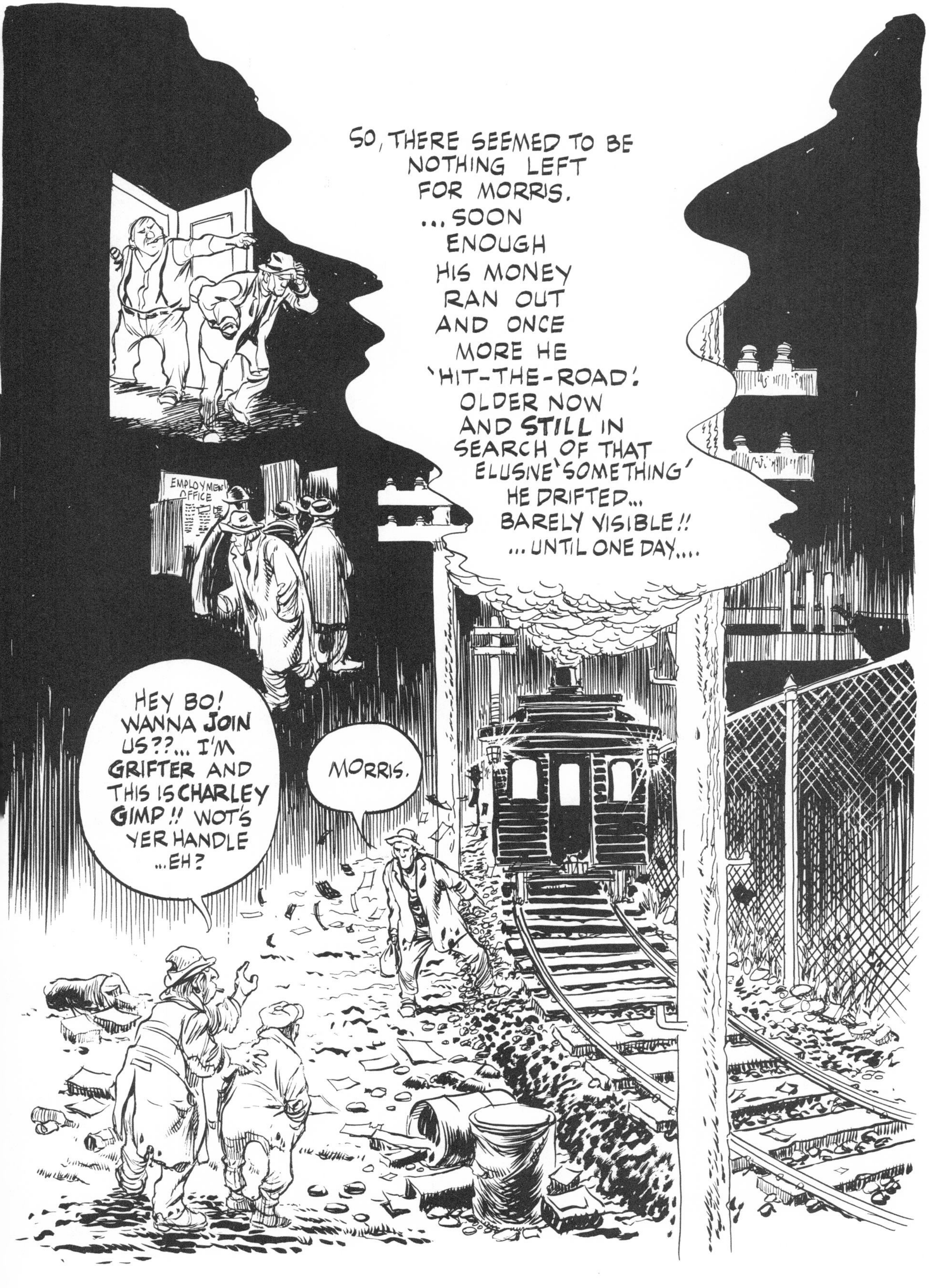

SO, THERE SEEMED TO BE NOTHING LEFT FOR MORRIS.
...SOON ENOUGH HIS MONEY RAN OUT AND ONCE MORE HE 'HIT-THE-ROAD'. OLDER NOW AND STILL IN SEARCH OF THAT ELUSIVE 'SOMETHING' HE DRIFTED... BARELY VISIBLE!! ...UNTIL ONE DAY....
EMPLOYMENT OFFICE
HEY BO! WANNA JOIN US??... I'M GRIFTER AND THIS IS CHARLEY GIMP!! WOT'S YER HANDLE ...EH?
MORRIS.

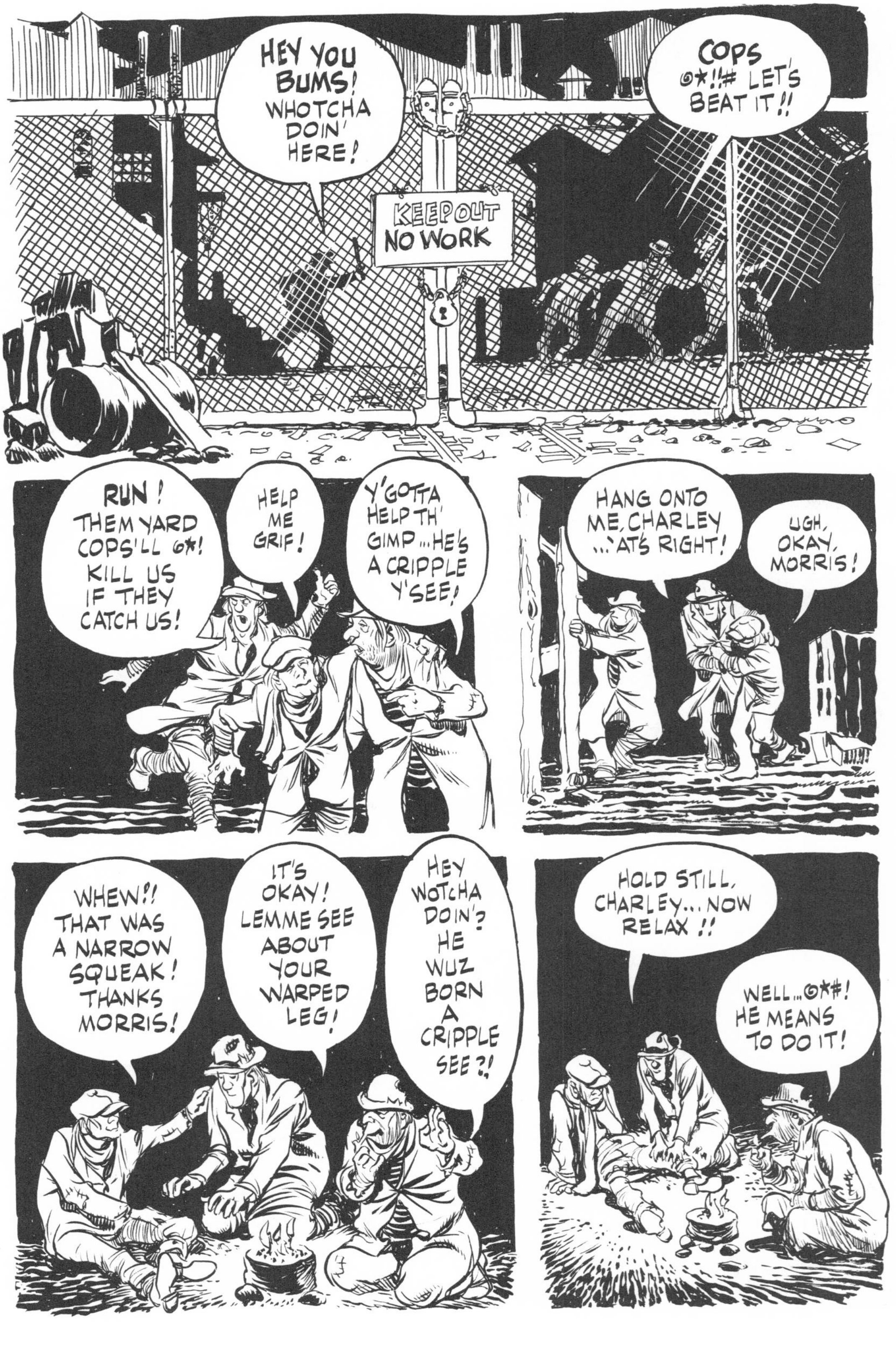
HEY YOU BUMS! WHOTCHA DOIN' HERE!
KEEP OUT NO WORK
COPS ©*!!# LET'S BEAT IT!!
RUN! THEM YARD COPS'LL ©*! KILL US IF THEY CATCH US!
HELP ME GRIF!
Y'GOTTA HELP TH' GIMP...HE'S A CRIPPLE Y'SEE!
HANG ONTO ME, CHARLEY ...'AT'S RIGHT!
UGH, OKAY, MORRIS!
WHEW?! THAT WAS A NARROW SQUEAK! THANKS MORRIS!
IT'S OKAY! LEMME SEE ABOUT YOUR WARPED LEG!
HEY WOTCHA DOIN'? HE WUZ BORN A CRIPPLE SEE?!
HOLD STILL, CHARLEY... NOW RELAX!!
WELL...©*#! HE MEANS TO DO IT!

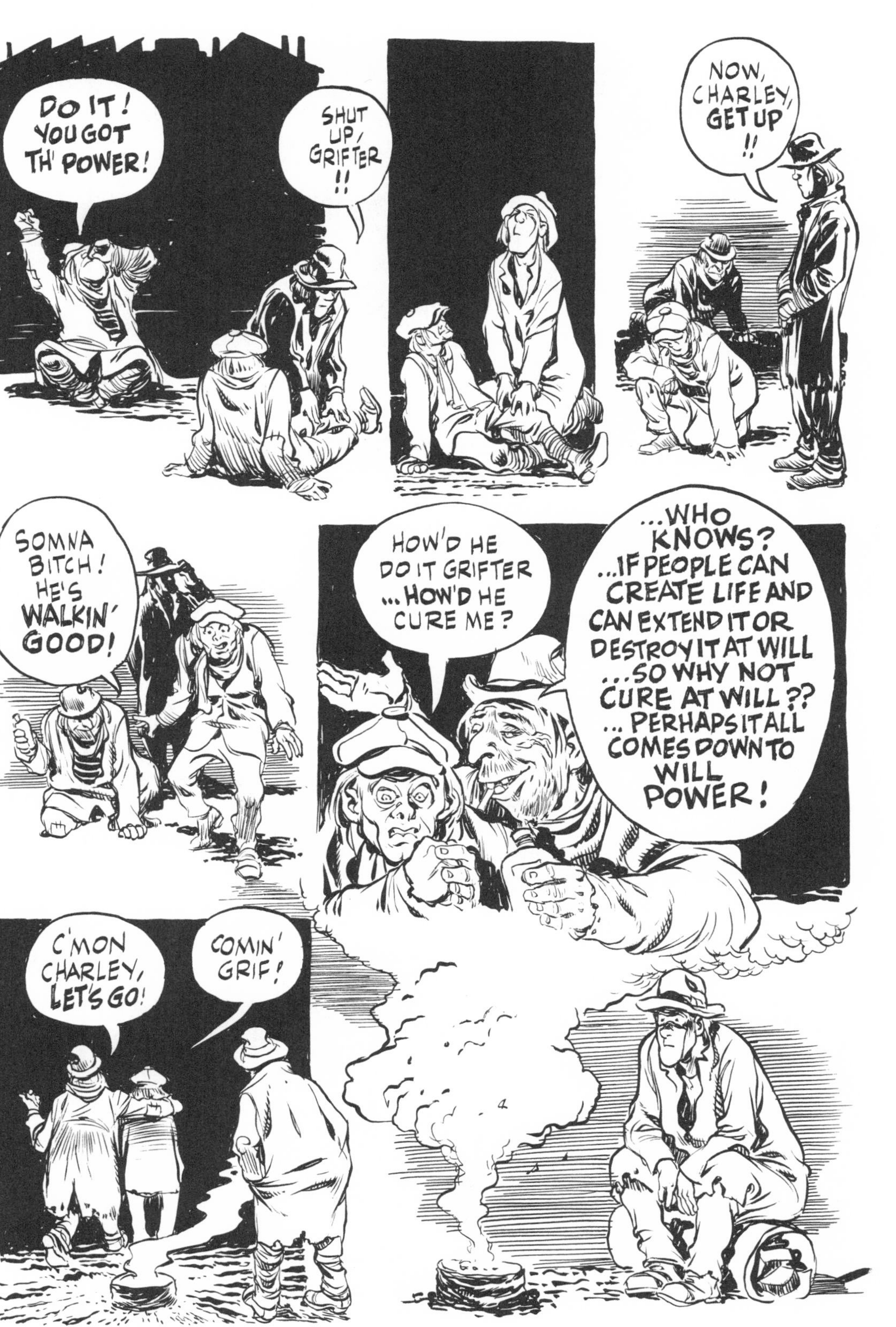
DO IT! YOU GOT TH' POWER!
SHUT UP, GRIFTER !!
NOW, CHARLEY, GET UP !!
SOMNA BITCH! HE'S WALKIN' GOOD!
HOW'D HE DO IT GRIFTER ...HOW'D HE CURE ME?
...WHO KNOWS? ...IF PEOPLE CAN CREATE LIFE AND CAN EXTEND IT OR DESTROY IT AT WILL ...SO WHY NOT CURE AT WILL?? ...PERHAPS IT ALL COMES DOWN TO WILL POWER!
C'MON CHARLEY, LET'S GO!
COMIN' GRIF!

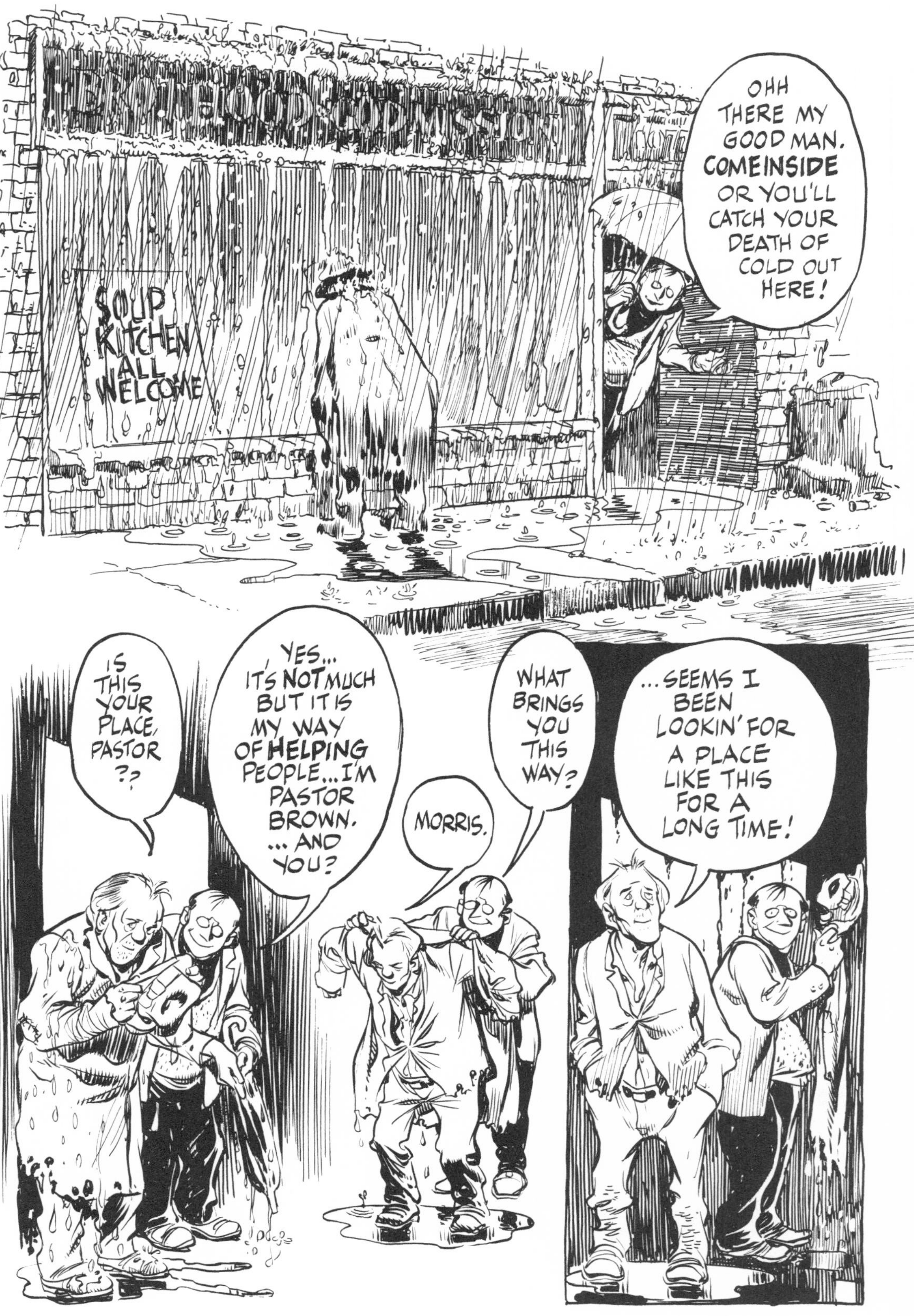
SOUP KITCHEN ALL WELCOME
OHH THERE MY GOOD MAN. COMEINSIDE OR YOU'LL CATCH YOUR DEATH OF COLD OUT HERE!
IS THIS YOUR PLACE, PASTOR ??
YES... IT'S NOT MUCH BUT IT IS MY WAY OF HELPING PEOPLE... I'M PASTOR BROWN. ...AND YOU?
MORRIS.
WHAT BRINGS YOU THIS WAY?
...SEEMS I BEEN LOOKIN' FOR A PLACE LIKE THIS FOR A LONG TIME!

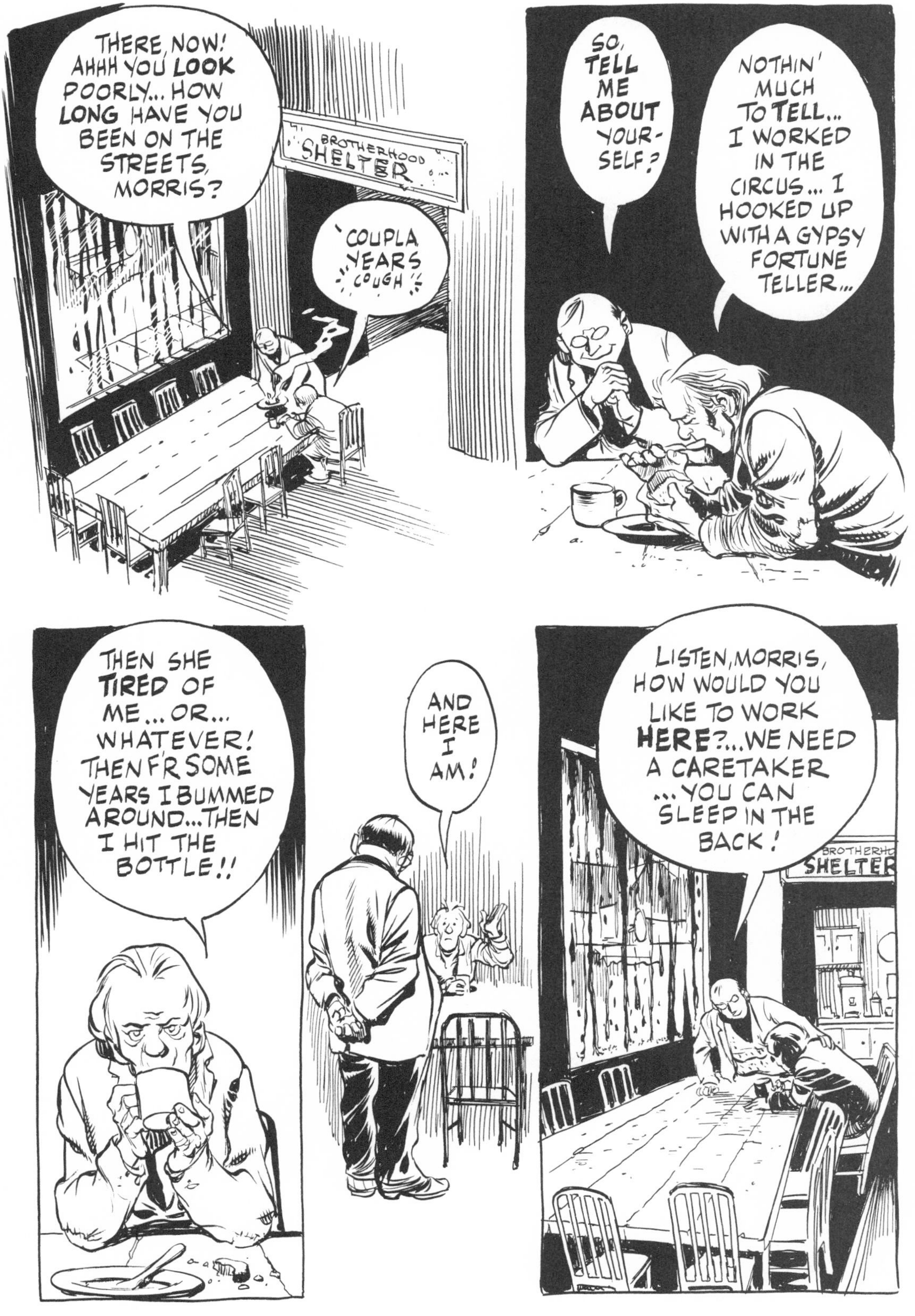
THERE, NOW! AHHH YOU LOOK POORLY... HOW LONG HAVE YOU BEEN ON THE STREETS, MORRIS?
BROTHERHOOD SHELTER
`COUPLA YEARS COUGH
SO, TELL ME ABOUT YOUR-SELF?
NOTHIN' MUCH TO TELL... I WORKED IN THE CIRCUS... I HOOKED UP WITH A GYPSY FORTUNE TELLER...
THEN SHE TIRED OF ME... OR... WHATEVER! THEN F'R SOME YEARS I BUMMED AROUND... THEN I HIT THE BOTTLE!!
AND HERE I AM!
LISTEN, MORRIS, HOW WOULD YOU LIKE TO WORK HERE?... WE NEED A CARETAKER ... YOU CAN SLEEP IN THE BACK!
SHELTER

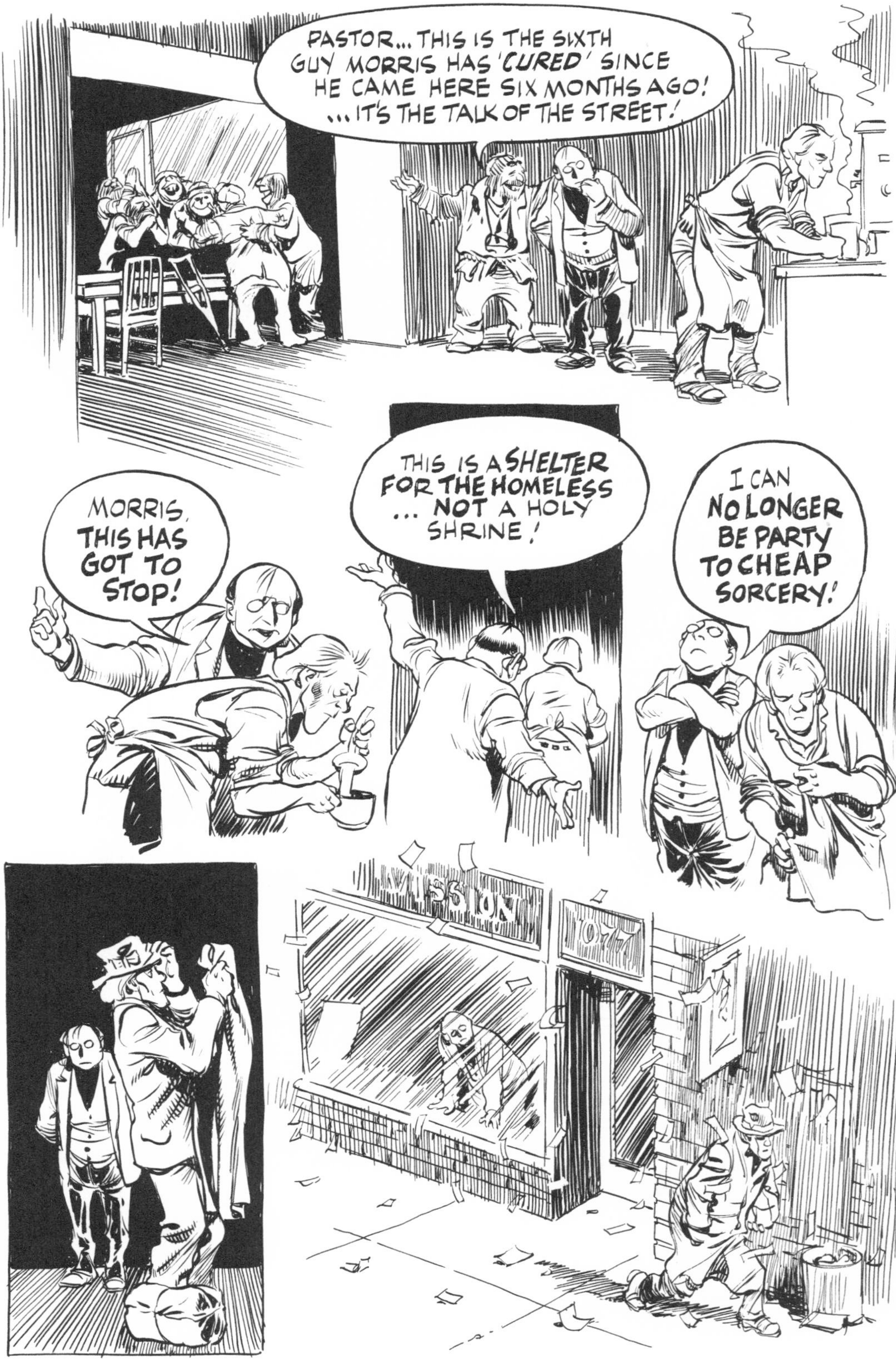
PASTOR... THIS IS THE SIXTH GUY MORRIS HAS 'CURED' SINCE HE CAME HERE SIX MONTHS AGO! ... IT'S THE TALK OF THE STREET!
MORRIS, THIS HAS GOT TO STOP!
THIS IS A SHELTER FOR THE HOMELESS ... NOT A HOLY SHRINE!
I CAN NO LONGER BE PARTY TO CHEAP SORCERY!
MISSION
1077

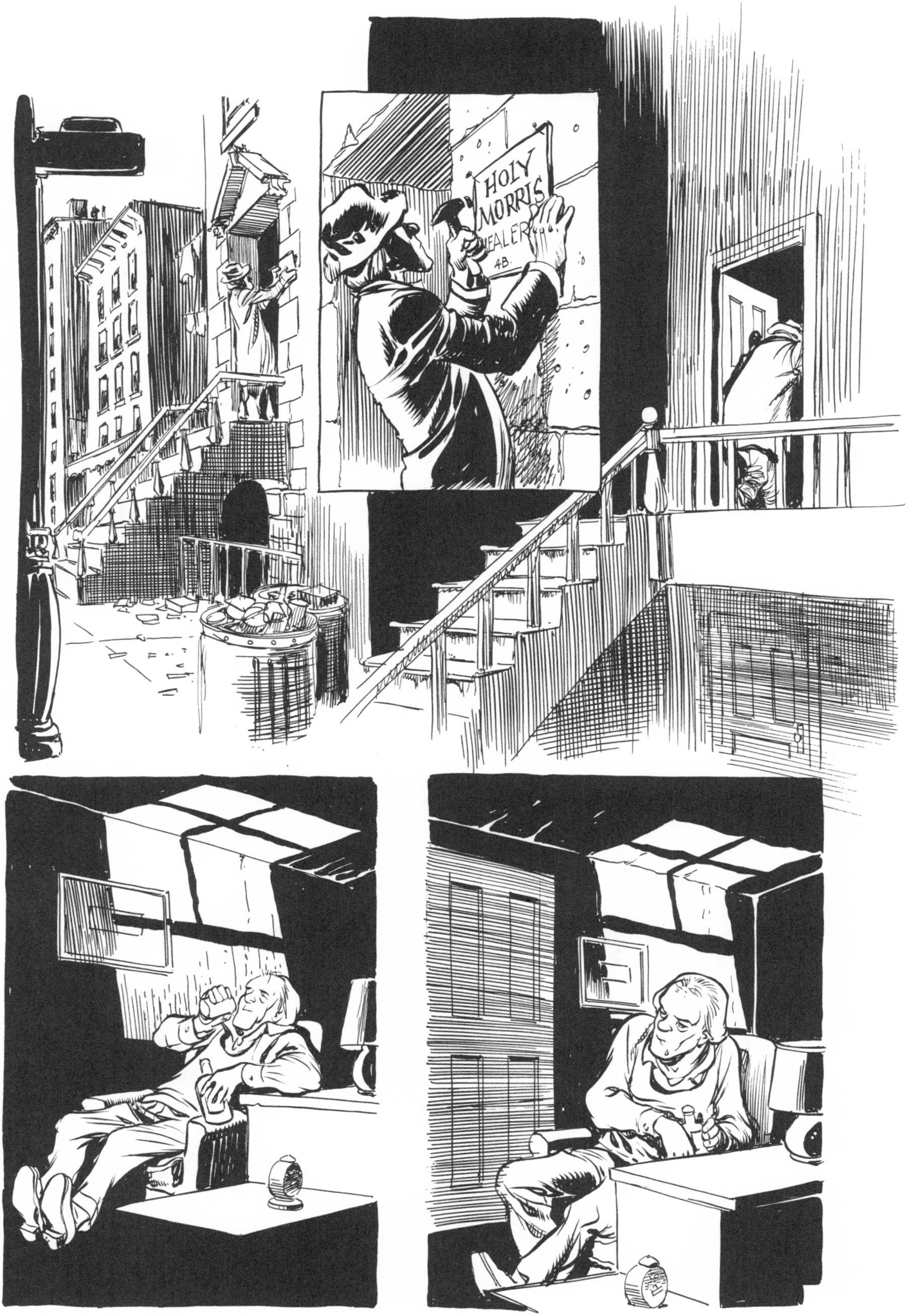
HOLY
MORRIS
4B.

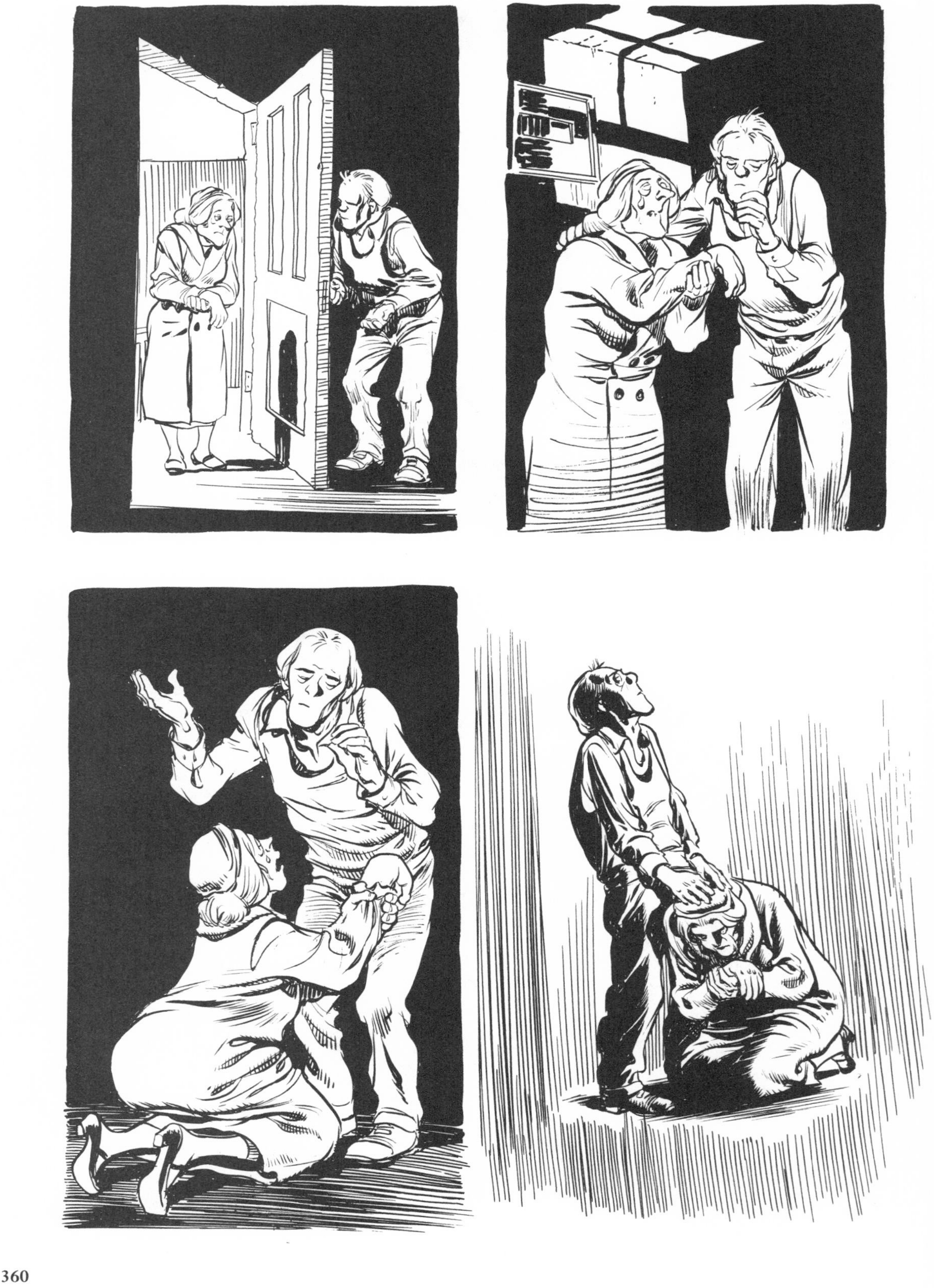

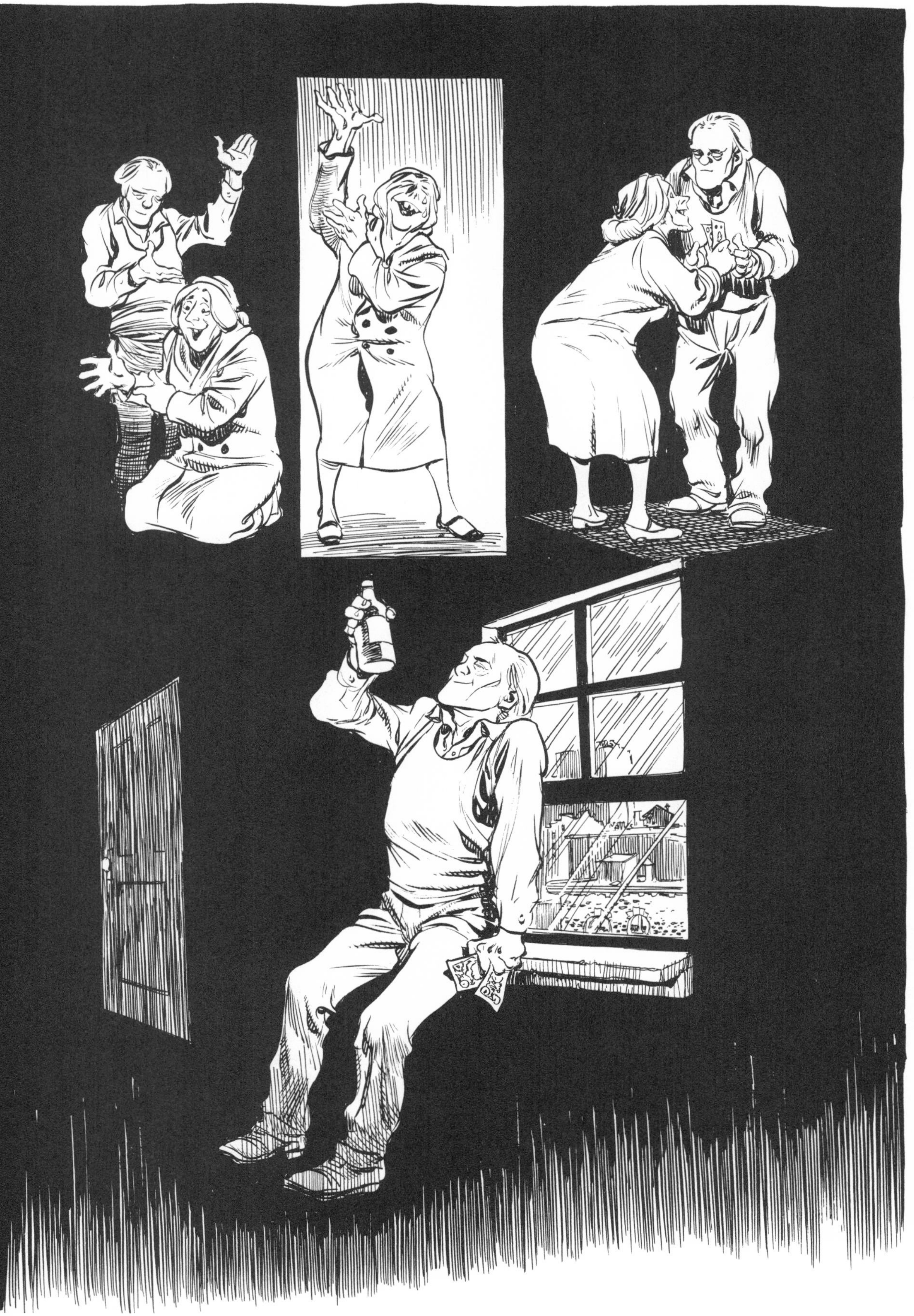

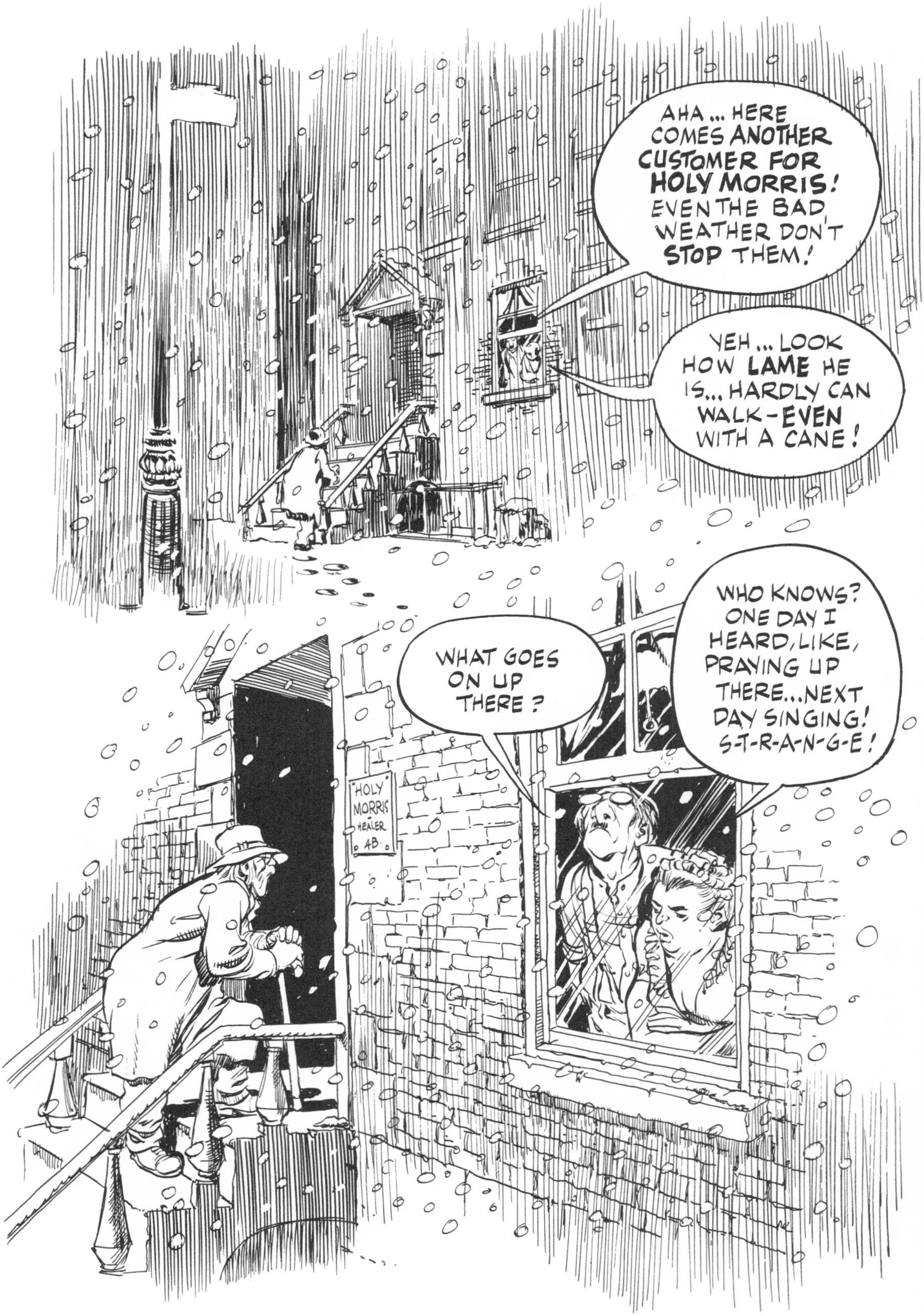
AHA ... HERE COMES ANOTHER CUSTOMER FOR HOLY MORRIS! EVEN THE BAD WEATHER DON'T STOP THEM!
YEH ... LOOK HOW LAME HE IS... HARDLY CAN WALK-EVEN WITH A CANE!
HOLY MORRIS HEALER 4B
WHAT GOES ON UP THERE?
WHO KNOWS? ONE DAY I HEARD, LIKE, PRAYING UP THERE...NEXT DAY SINGING! S-T-R-A-N-G-E!

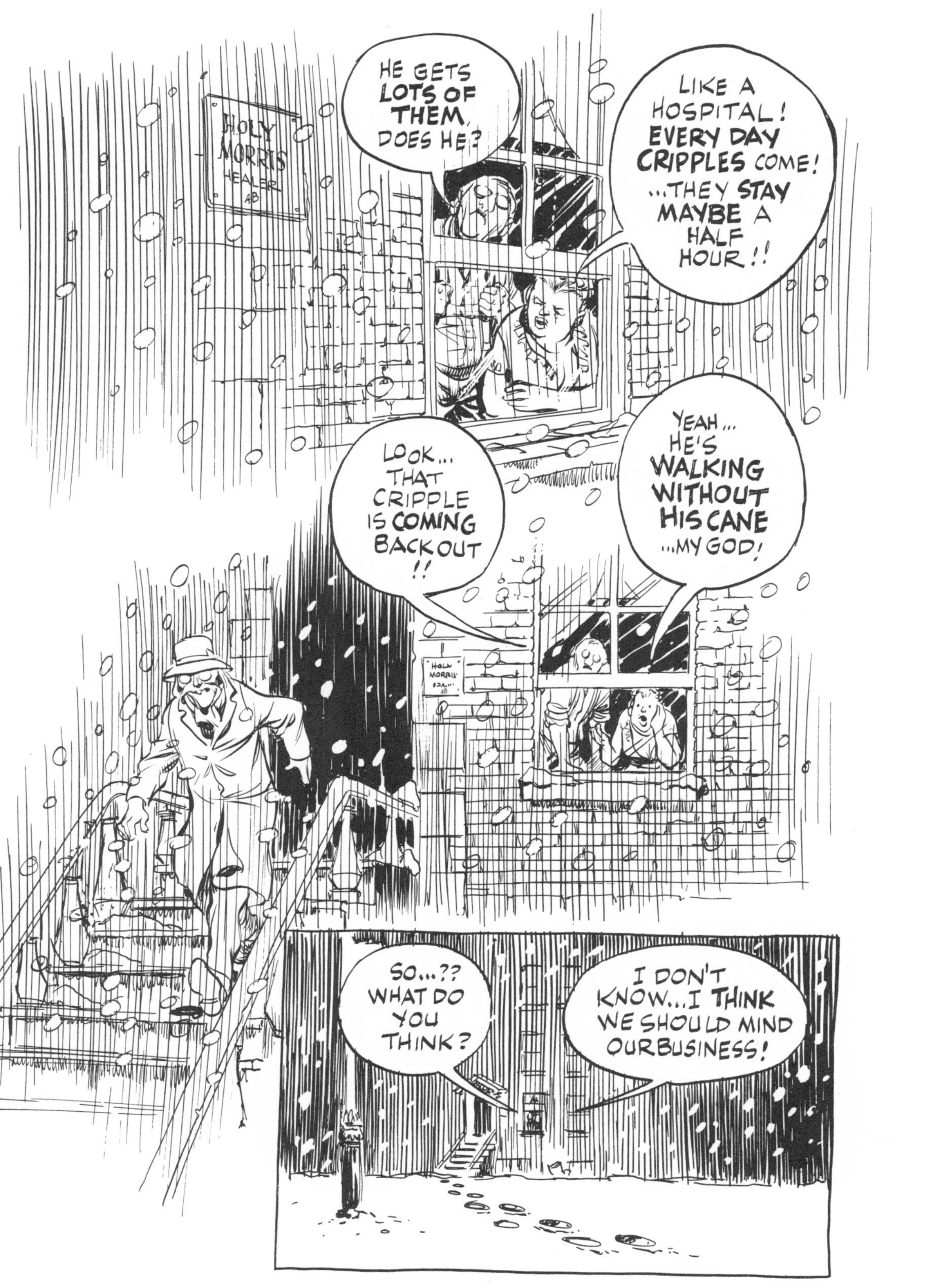
HOLY MORRIS HEALER
HE GETS LOTS OF THEM, DOES HE?
LIKE A HOSPITAL! EVERY DAY CRIPPLES COME! ...THEY STAY MAYBE A HALF HOUR!!
LOOK... THAT CRIPPLE IS COMING BACK OUT!!
YEAH... HE'S WALKING WITHOUT HIS CANE ...MY GOD!
SO...?? WHAT DO YOU THINK?
I DON'T KNOW...I THINK WE SHOULD MIND OUR BUSINESS!

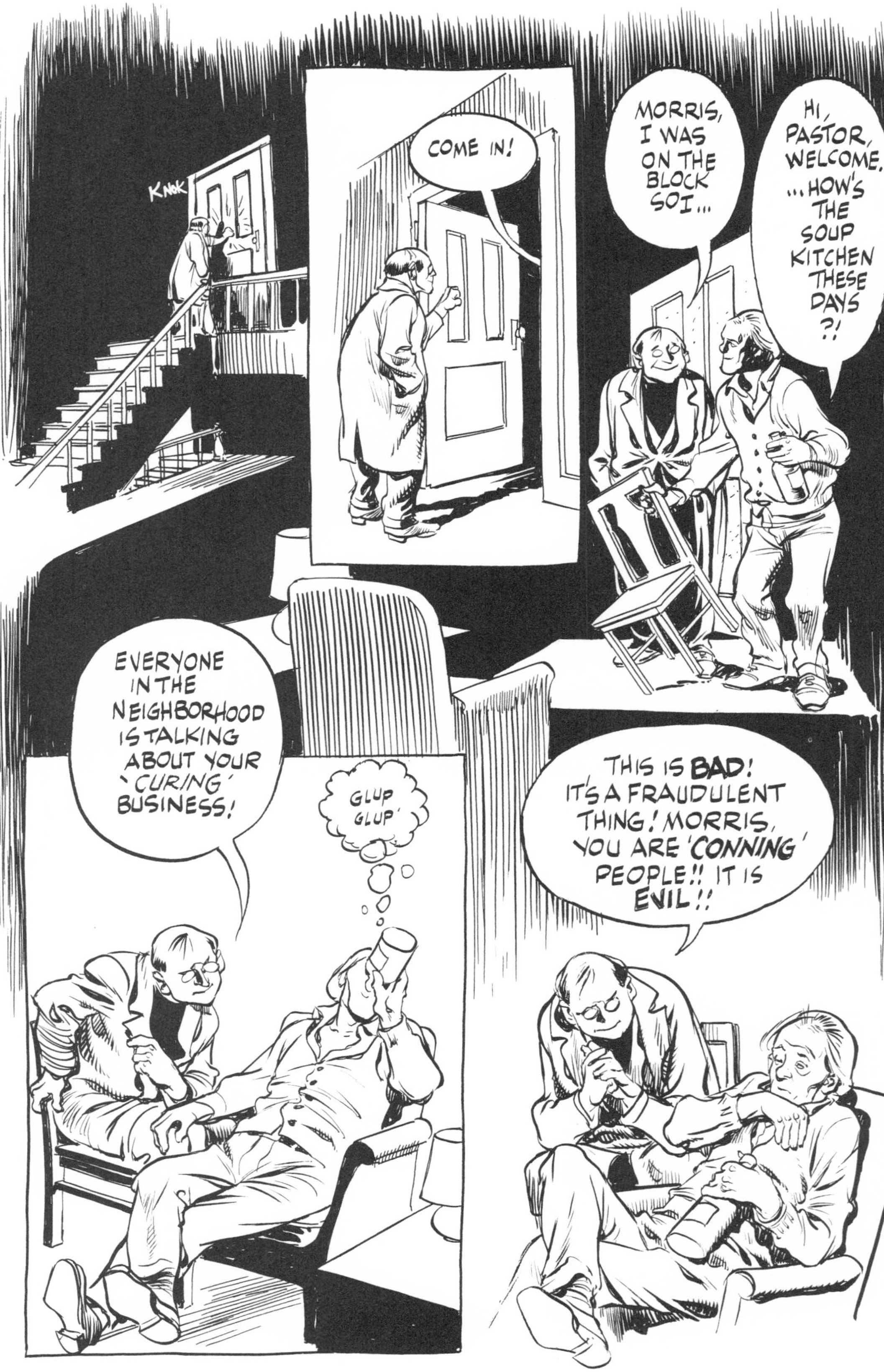
KNOK
COME IN!
MORRIS, I WAS ON THE BLOCK SO I...
HI, PASTOR, WELCOME. ...HOW'S THE SOUP KITCHEN THESE DAYS?!
EVERYONE IN THE NEIGHBORHOOD IS TALKING ABOUT YOUR 'CURING' BUSINESS!
GLUP GLUP
THIS IS BAD! IT'S A FRAUDULENT THING! MORRIS, YOU ARE 'CONNING' PEOPLE!! IT IS EVIL!!

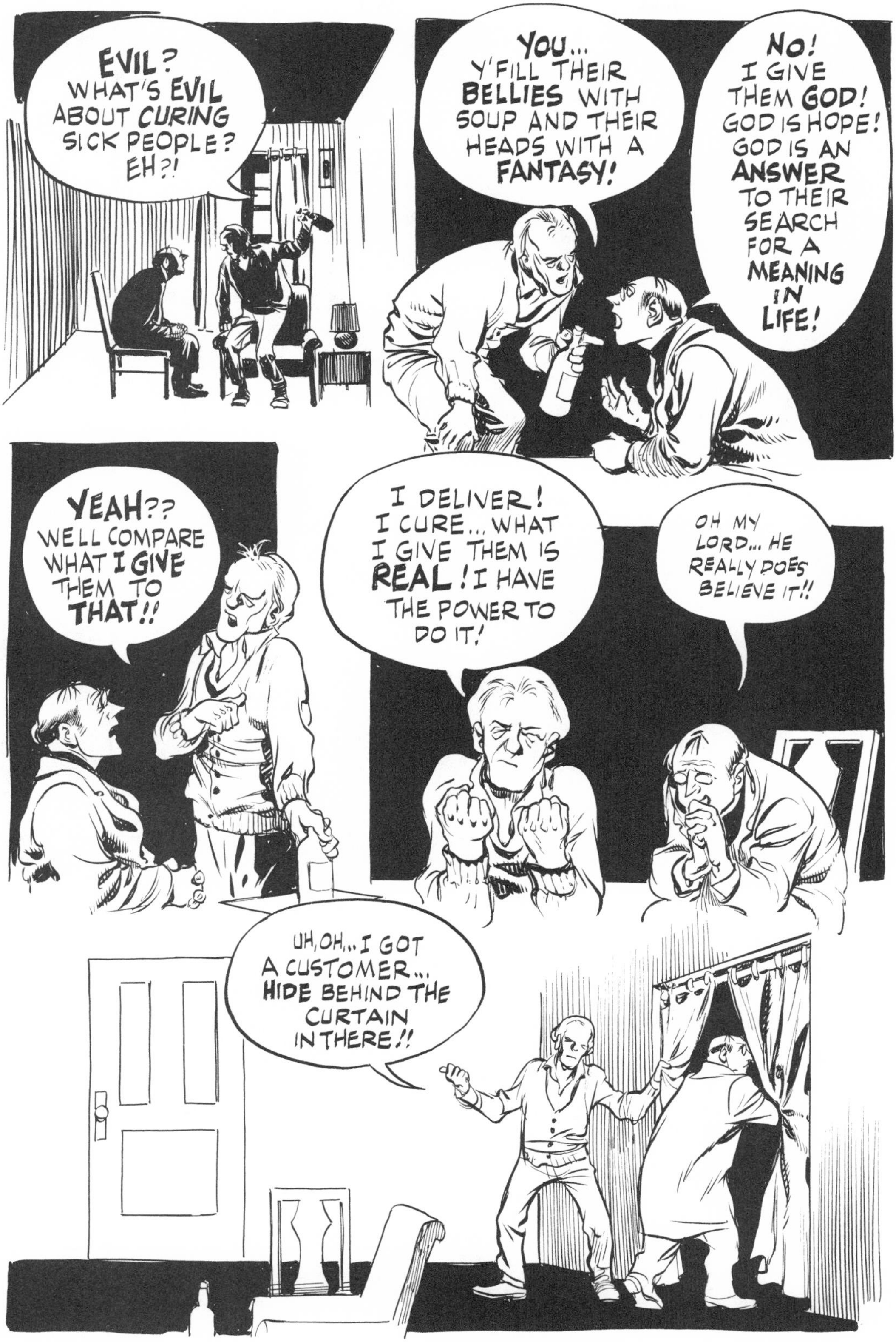
EVIL? WHAT'S EVIL ABOUT CURING SICK PEOPLE? EH?!
YOU... Y'FILL THEIR BELLIES WITH SOUP AND THEIR HEADS WITH A FANTASY!
NO! I GIVE THEM GOD! GOD IS HOPE! GOD IS AN ANSWER TO THEIR SEARCH FOR A MEANING IN LIFE!
YEAH?? WELL COMPARE WHAT I GIVE THEM TO THAT!!
I DELIVER! I CURE... WHAT I GIVE THEM IS REAL! I HAVE THE POWER TO DO IT!
OH MY LORD... HE REALLY DOES BELIEVE IT!!
UH, OH... I GOT A CUSTOMER... HIDE BEHIND THE CURTAIN IN THERE!!

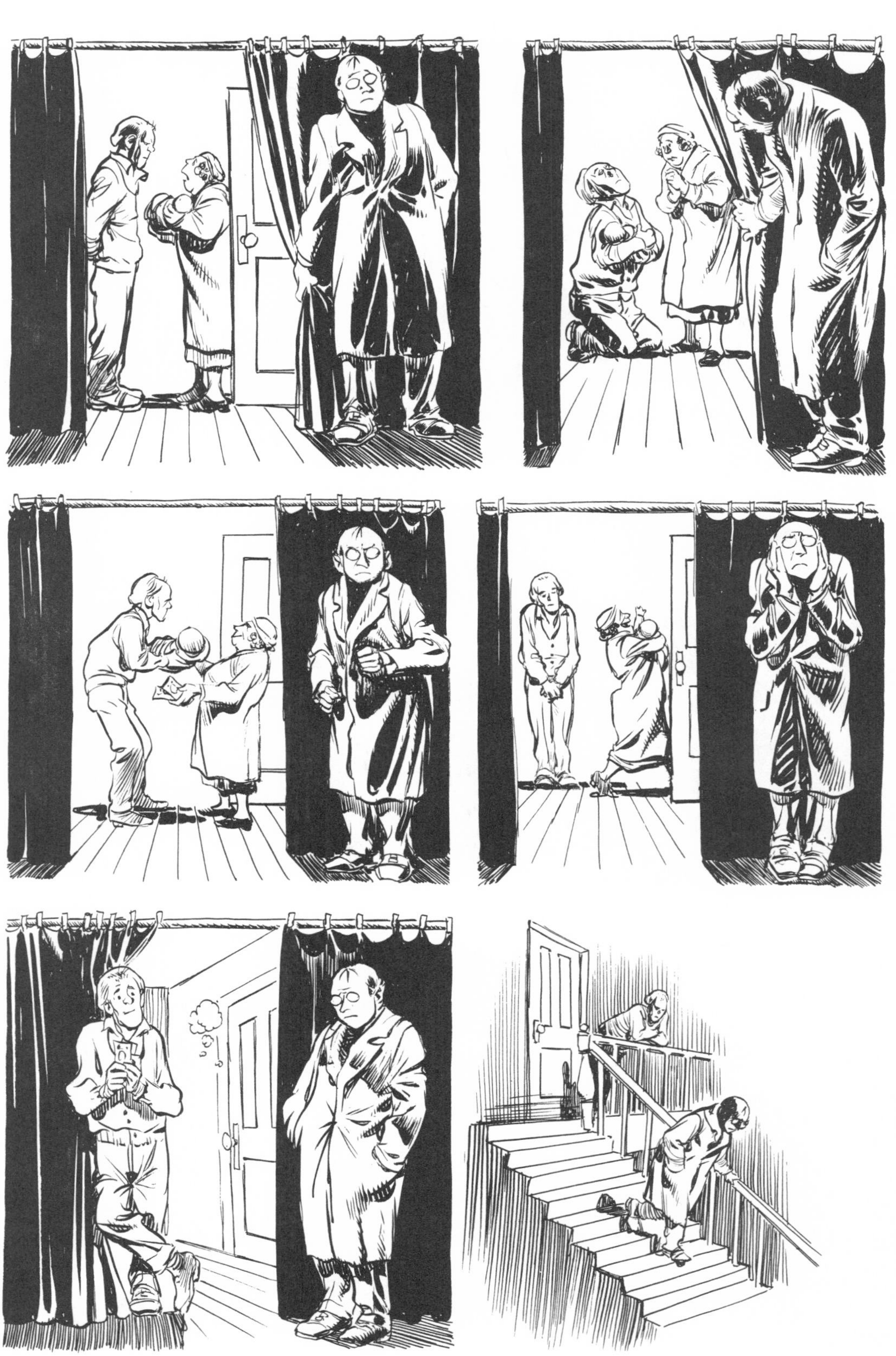

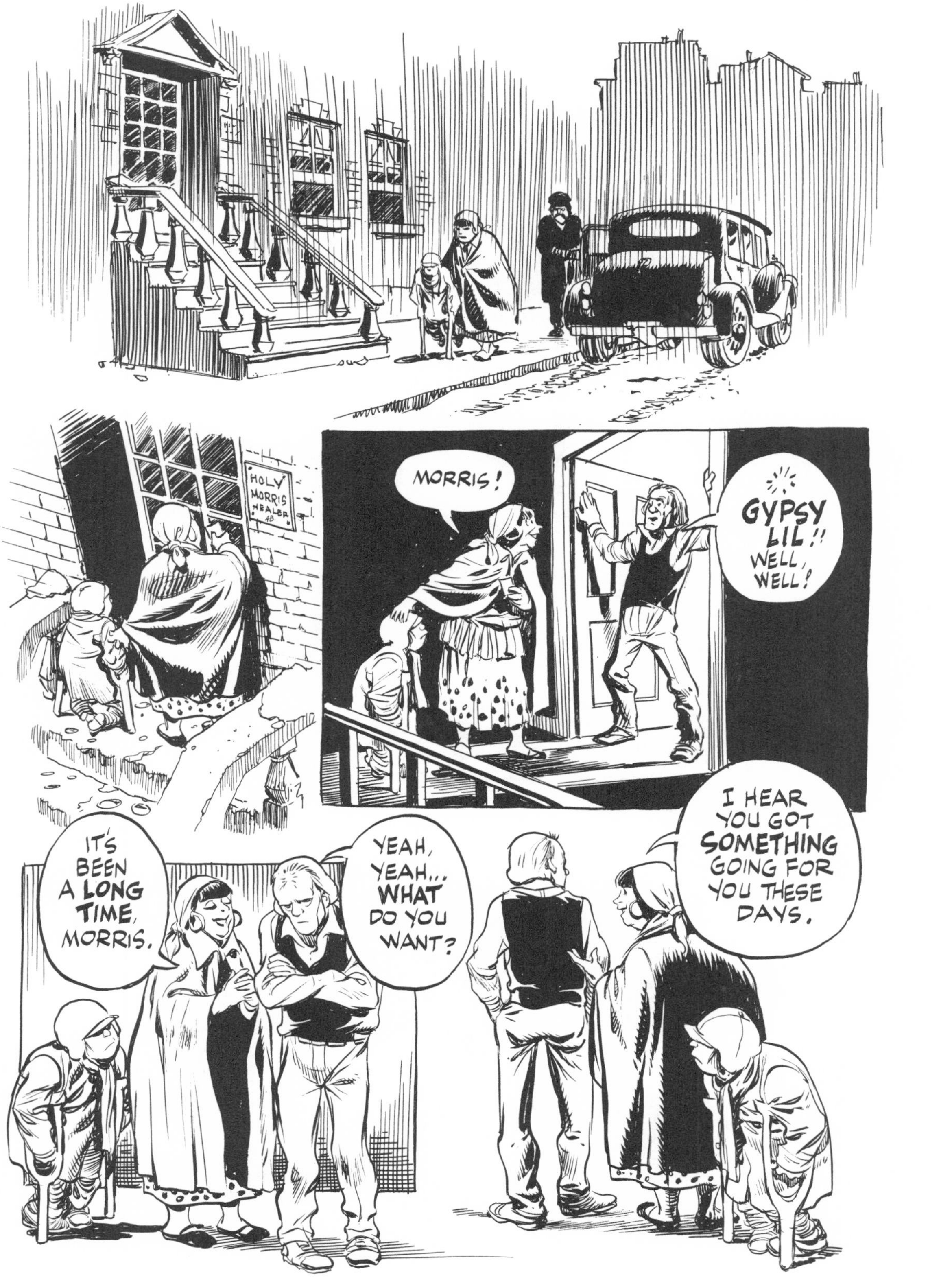
HOLY MORRIS HEALER
MORRIS!
GYPSY LIL!! WELL, WELL!
IT'S BEEN A LONG TIME, MORRIS.
YEAH, YEAH... WHAT DO YOU WANT?
I HEAR YOU GOT SOMETHING GOING FOR YOU THESE DAYS.

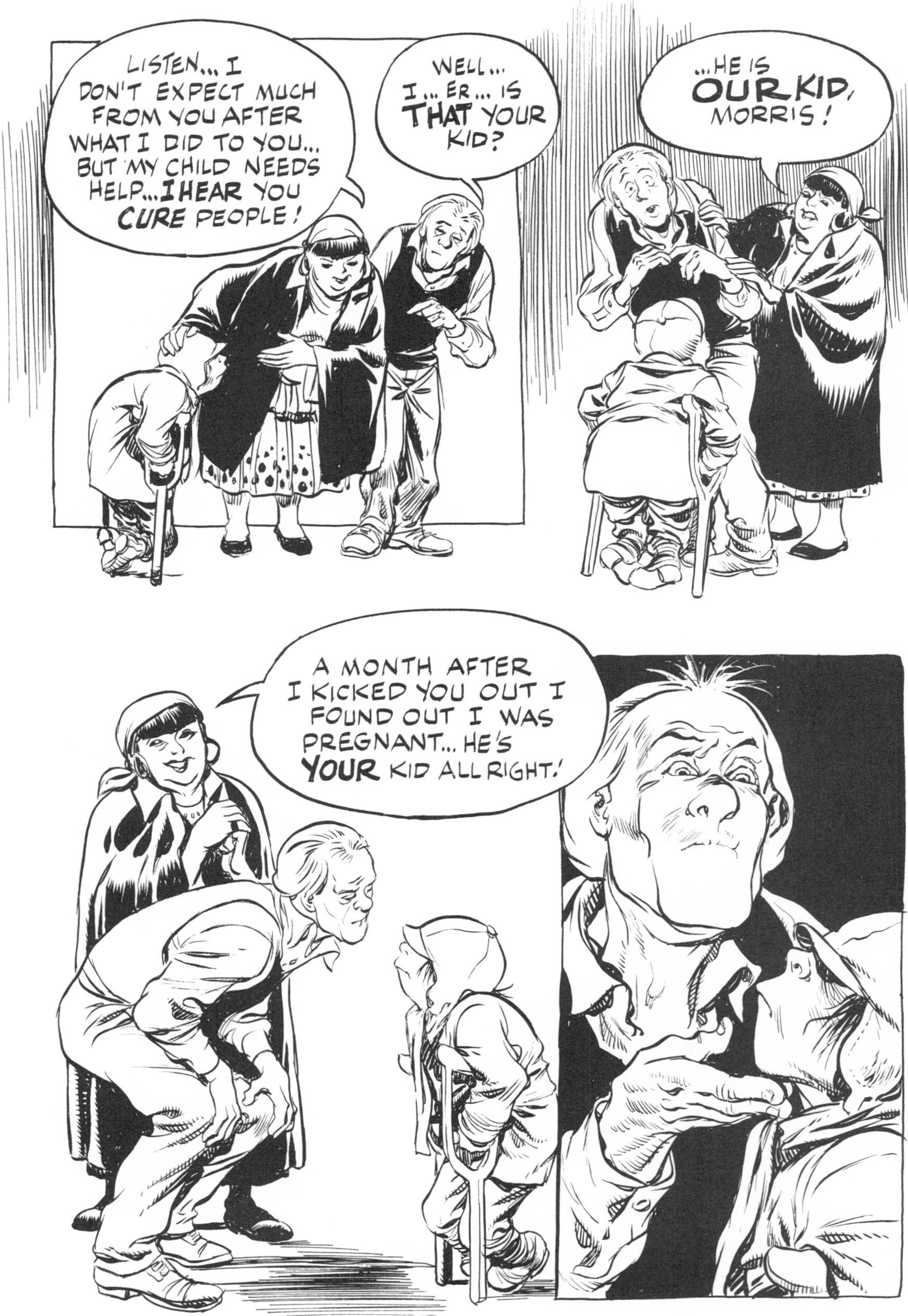
LISTEN... I DON'T EXPECT MUCH FROM YOU AFTER WHAT I DID TO YOU... BUT MY CHILD NEEDS HELP... I HEAR YOU CURE PEOPLE!
WELL... I... ER... IS THAT YOUR KID?
...HE IS OUR KID, MORRIS!
A MONTH AFTER I KICKED YOU OUT I FOUND OUT I WAS PREGNANT... HE'S YOUR KID ALL RIGHT!

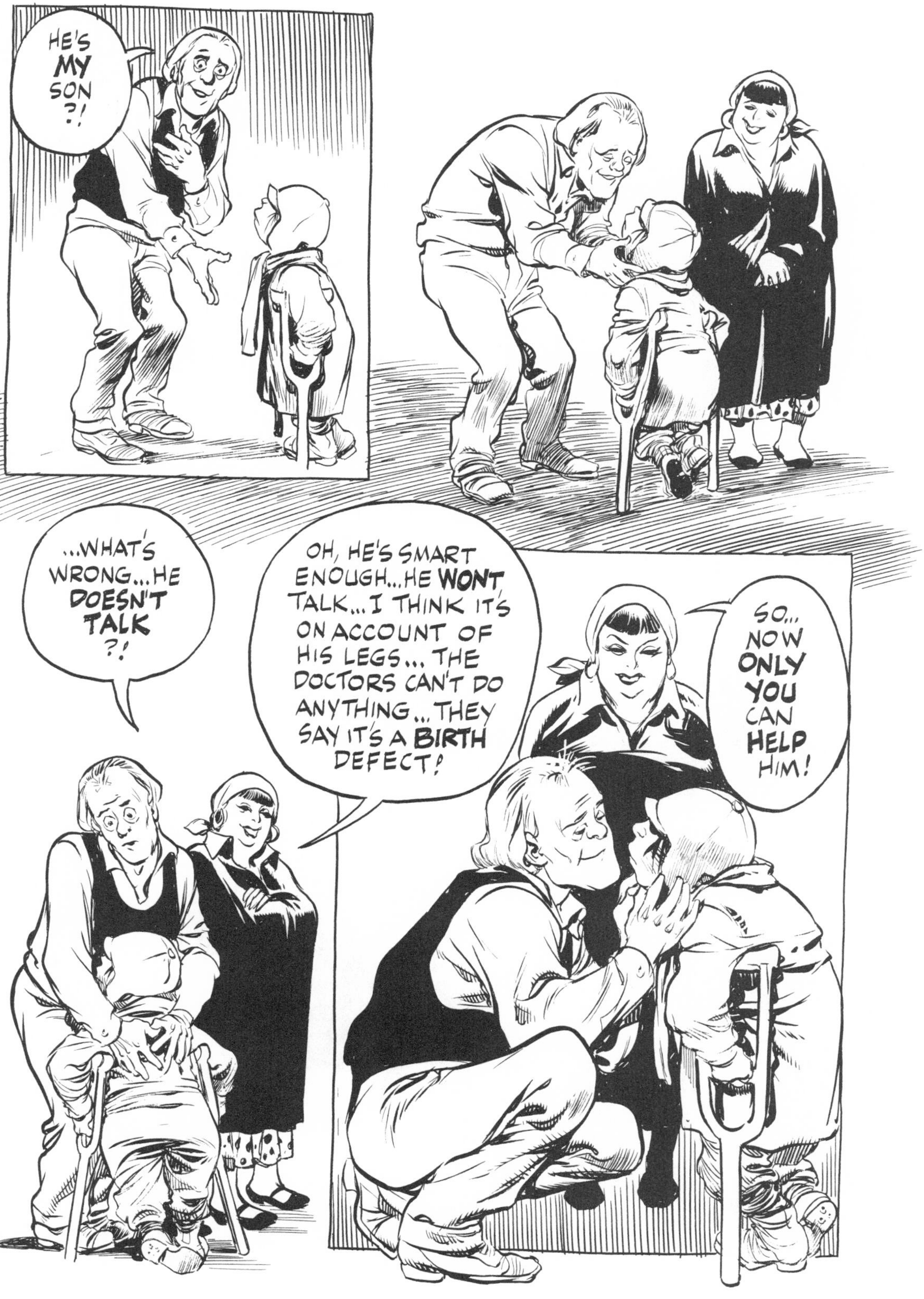
HE'S MY SON ?!
...WHAT'S WRONG...HE DOESN'T TALK ?!
OH, HE'S SMART ENOUGH...HE WON'T TALK...I THINK IT'S ON ACCOUNT OF HIS LEGS... THE DOCTORS CAN'T DO ANYTHING...THEY SAY IT'S A BIRTH DEFECT!
SO... NOW ONLY YOU CAN HELP HIM!

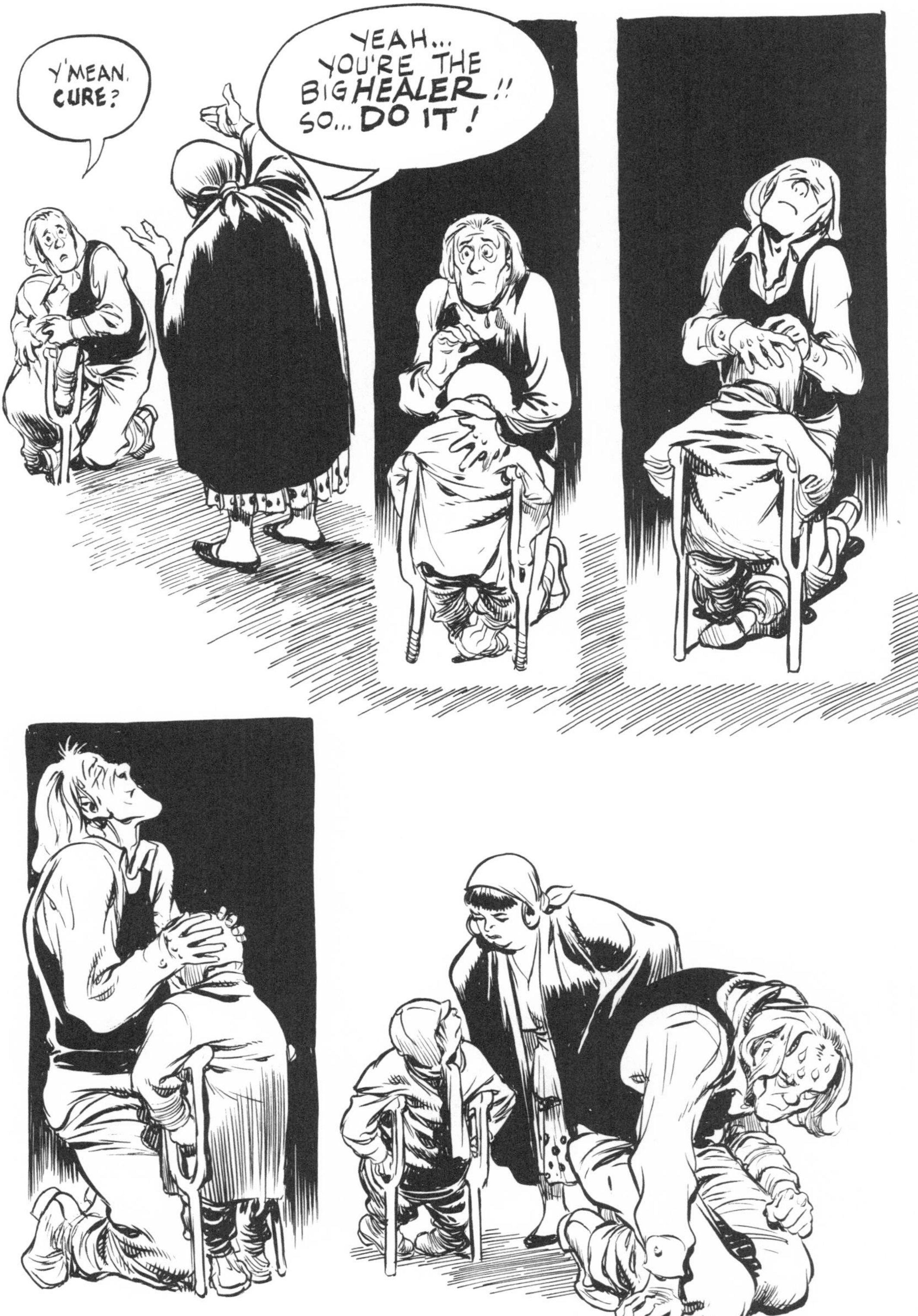
Y'MEAN, CURE?
YEAH... YOU'RE THE BIG HEALER!! SO... DO IT!

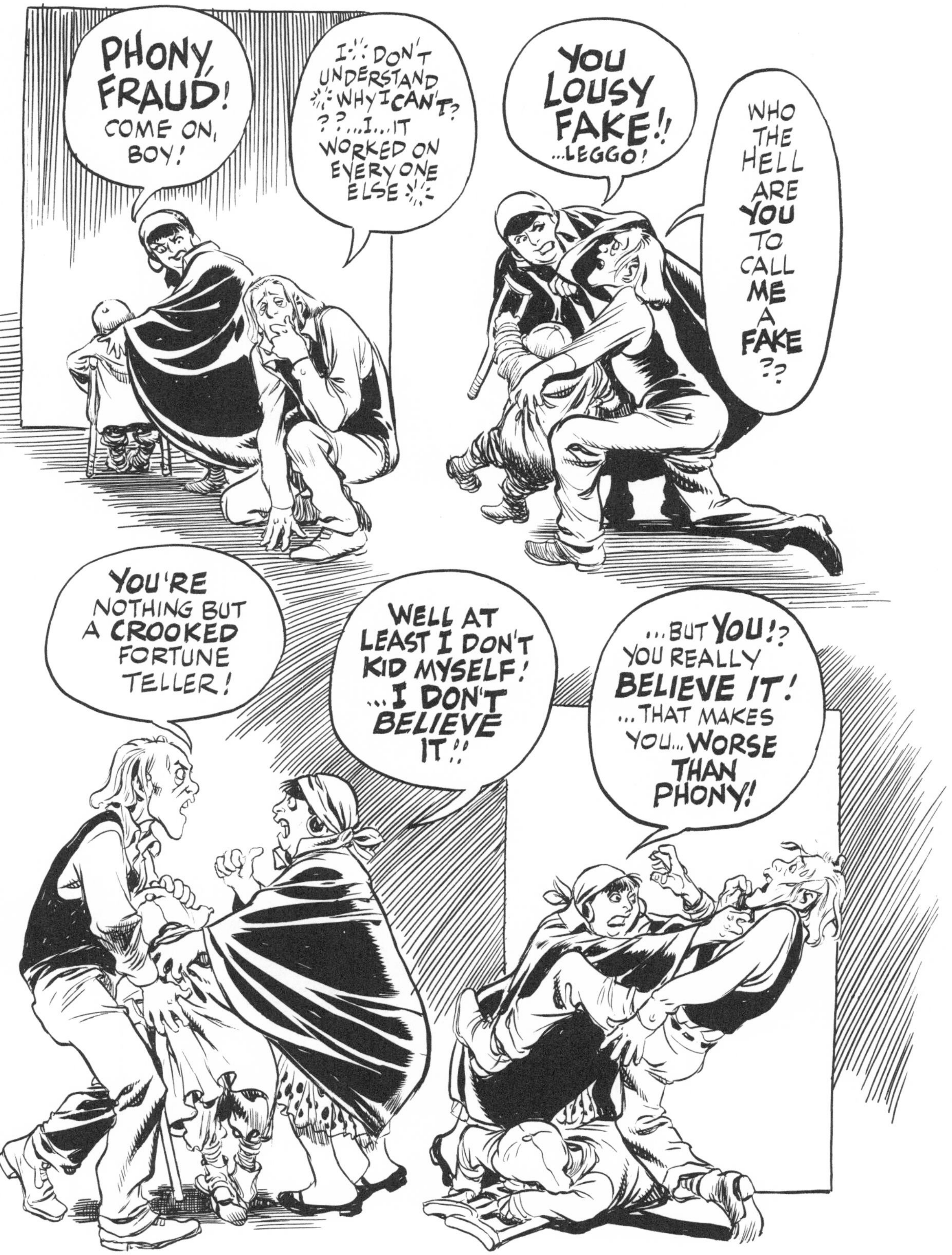
PHONY, FRAUD! COME ON, BOY!
I-:: DON'T UNDERSTAND WHY I CAN'T?? ?...I...IT WORKED ON EVERYONE ELSE
YOU LOUSY FAKE!! ...LEGGO!
WHO THE HELL ARE YOU TO CALL ME A FAKE??
YOU'RE NOTHING BUT A CROOKED FORTUNE TELLER!
WELL AT LEAST I DON'T KID MYSELF! ...I DON'T BELIEVE IT!!
...BUT YOU!? YOU REALLY BELIEVE IT! ...THAT MAKES YOU...WORSE THAN PHONY!

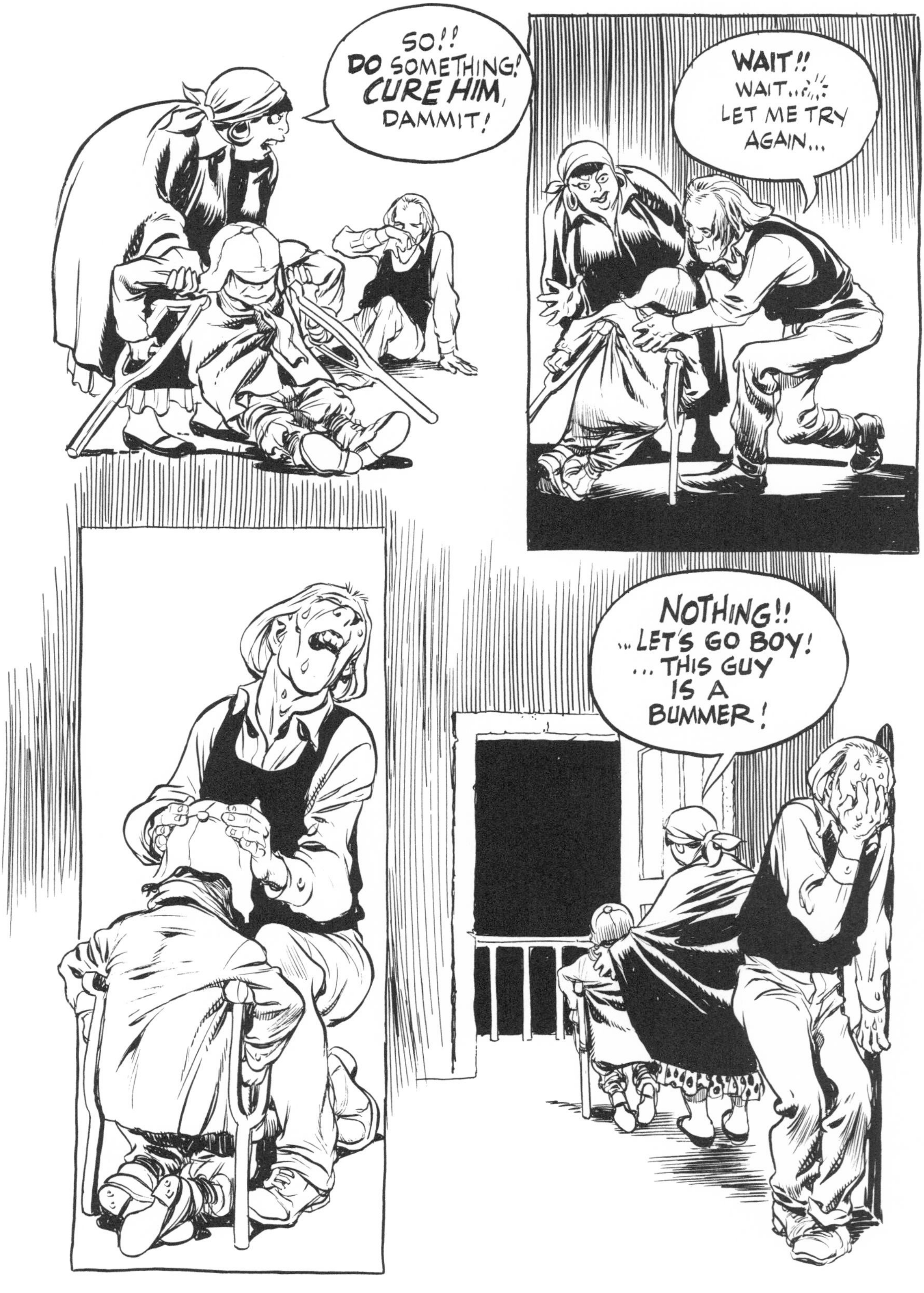
SO!! DO SOMETHING! CURE HIM, DAMMIT!
WAIT!! WAIT... LET ME TRY AGAIN...
NOTHING!! ...LET'S GO BOY! ...THIS GUY IS A BUMMER!

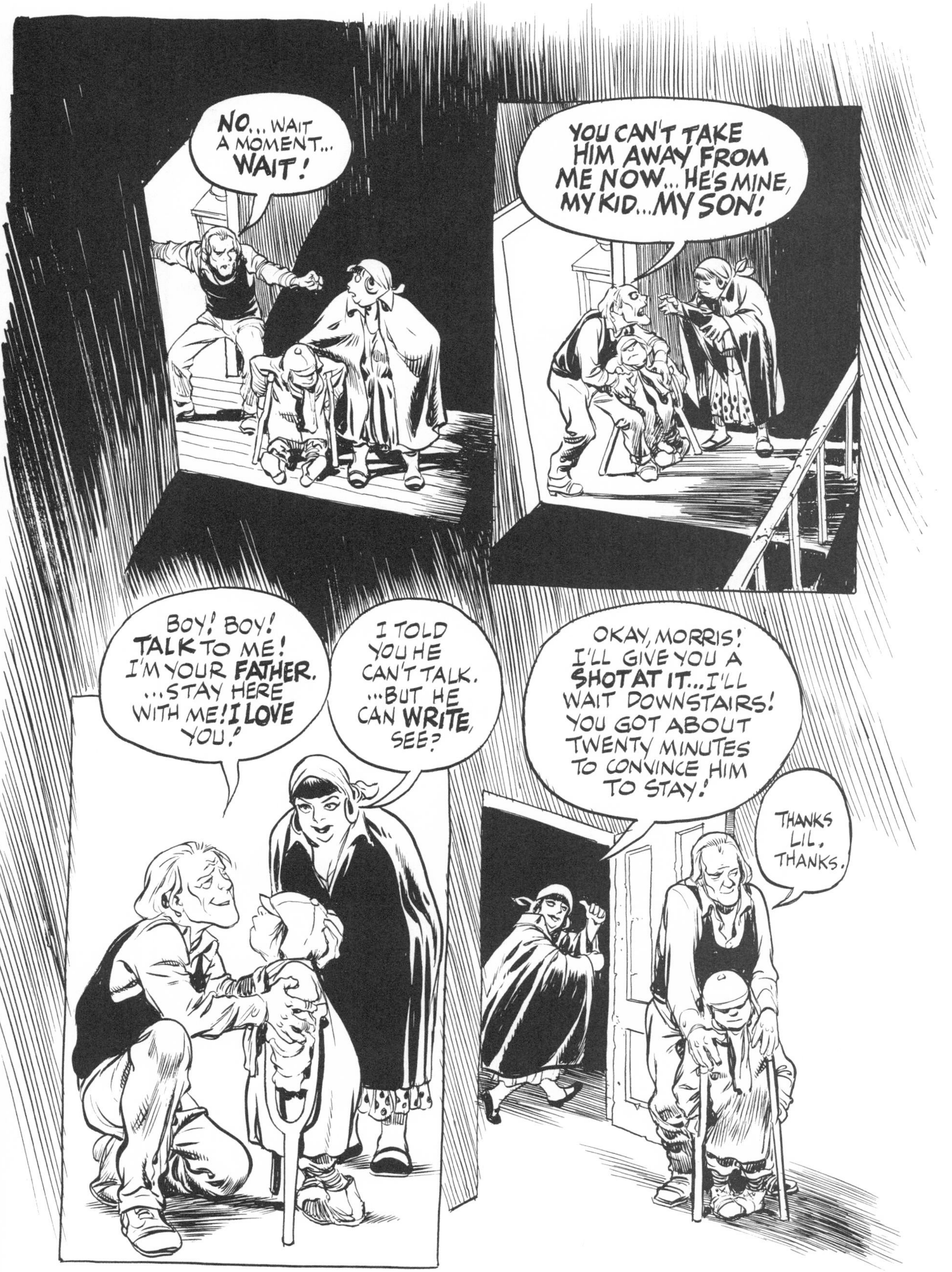
NO... WAIT A MOMENT... WAIT!
YOU CAN'T TAKE HIM AWAY FROM ME NOW... HE'S MINE, MY KID... MY SON!
BOY! BOY! TALK TO ME! I'M YOUR FATHER. ...STAY HERE WITH ME! I LOVE YOU!
I TOLD YOU HE CAN'T TALK. ...BUT HE CAN WRITE, SEE?
OKAY, MORRIS! I'LL GIVE YOU A SHOT AT IT... I'LL WAIT DOWNSTAIRS! YOU GOT ABOUT TWENTY MINUTES TO CONVINCE HIM TO STAY!
THANKS LIL. THANKS.

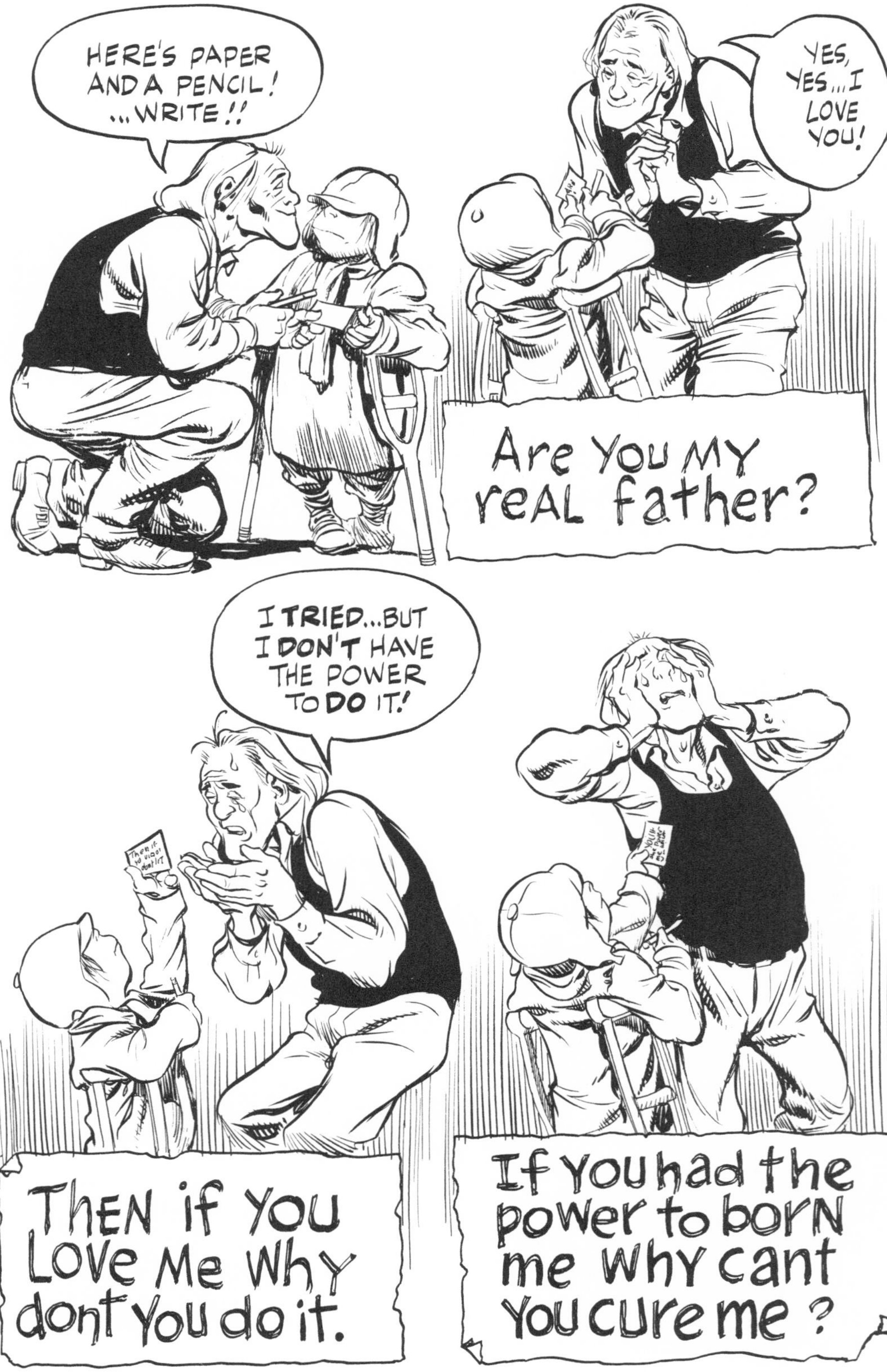
HERE'S PAPER AND A PENCIL! ...WRITE!!
YES, YES...I LOVE YOU!
Are You MY real father?
I TRIED...BUT I DON'T HAVE THE POWER TO DO IT!
Then if You Love Me Why dont You do it.
If You had the power to born me Why cant You cure me ?

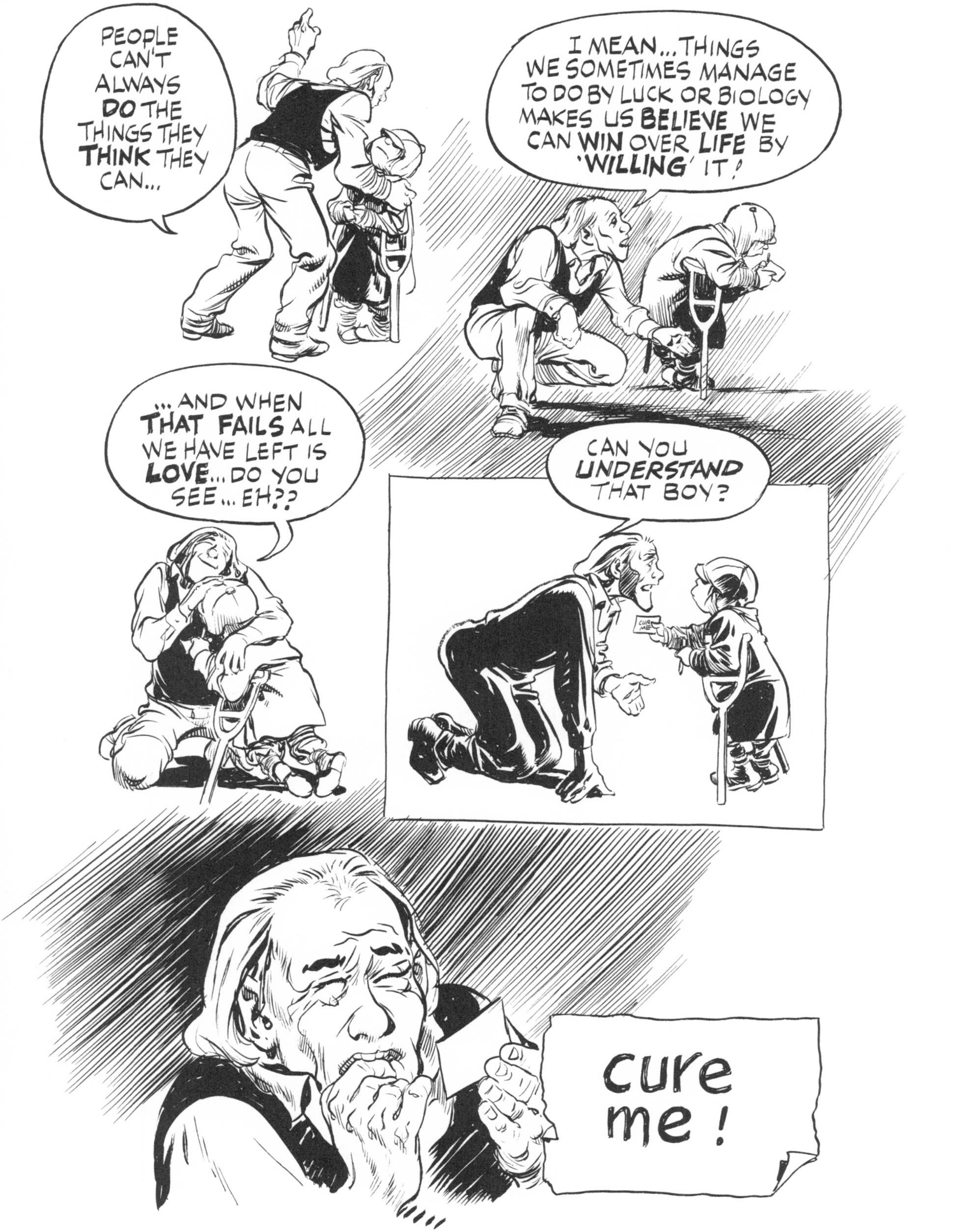
PEOPLE CAN'T ALWAYS DO THE THINGS THEY THINK THEY CAN...
I MEAN... THINGS WE SOMETIMES MANAGE TO DO BY LUCK OR BIOLOGY MAKES US BELIEVE WE CAN WIN OVER LIFE BY 'WILLING' IT!
...AND WHEN THAT FAILS ALL WE HAVE LEFT IS LOVE... DO YOU SEE... EH??
CAN YOU UNDERSTAND THAT BOY?
cure me!

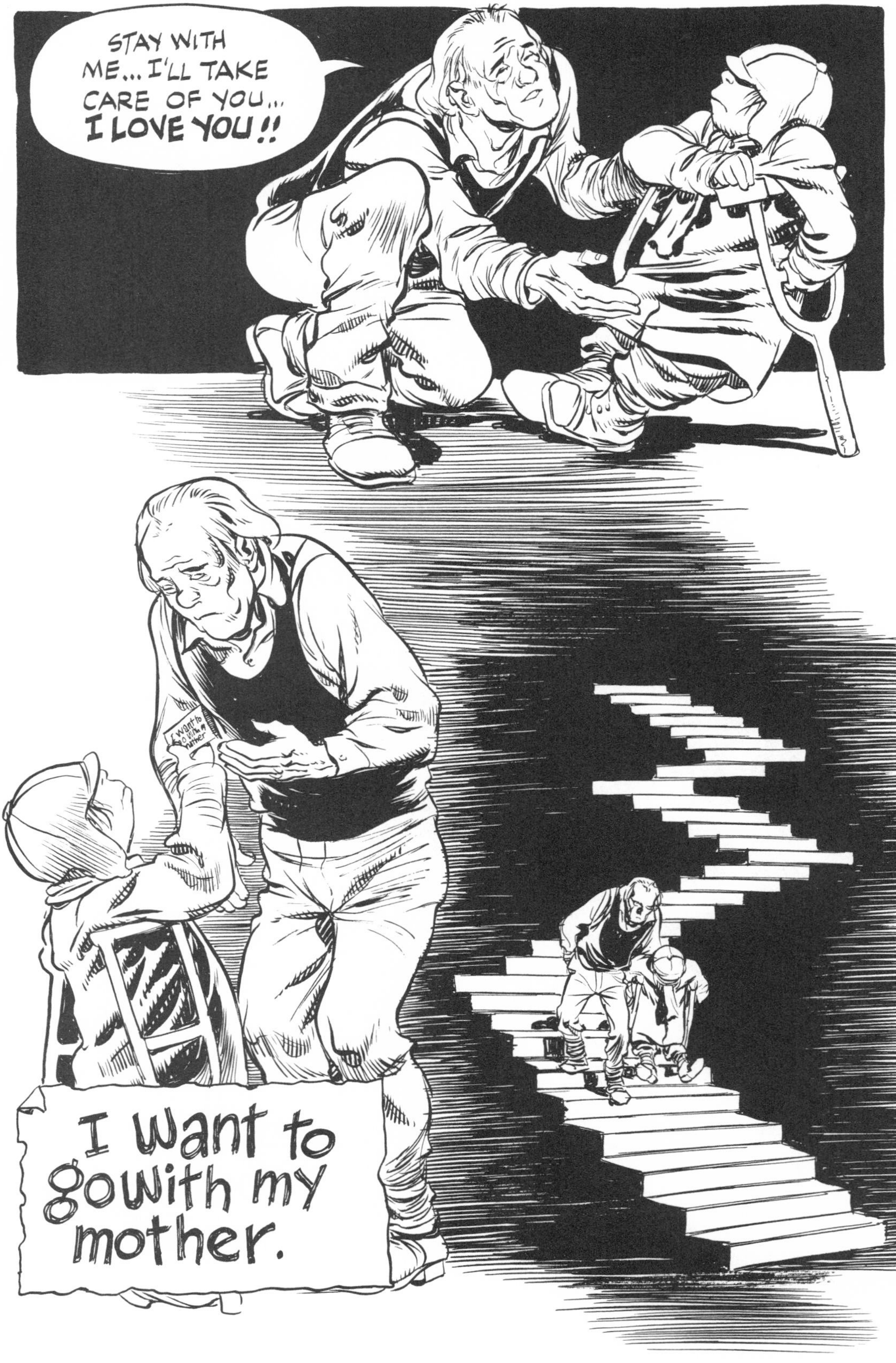
STAY WITH ME... I'LL TAKE CARE OF YOU... I LOVE YOU!!
I want to go with my mother.

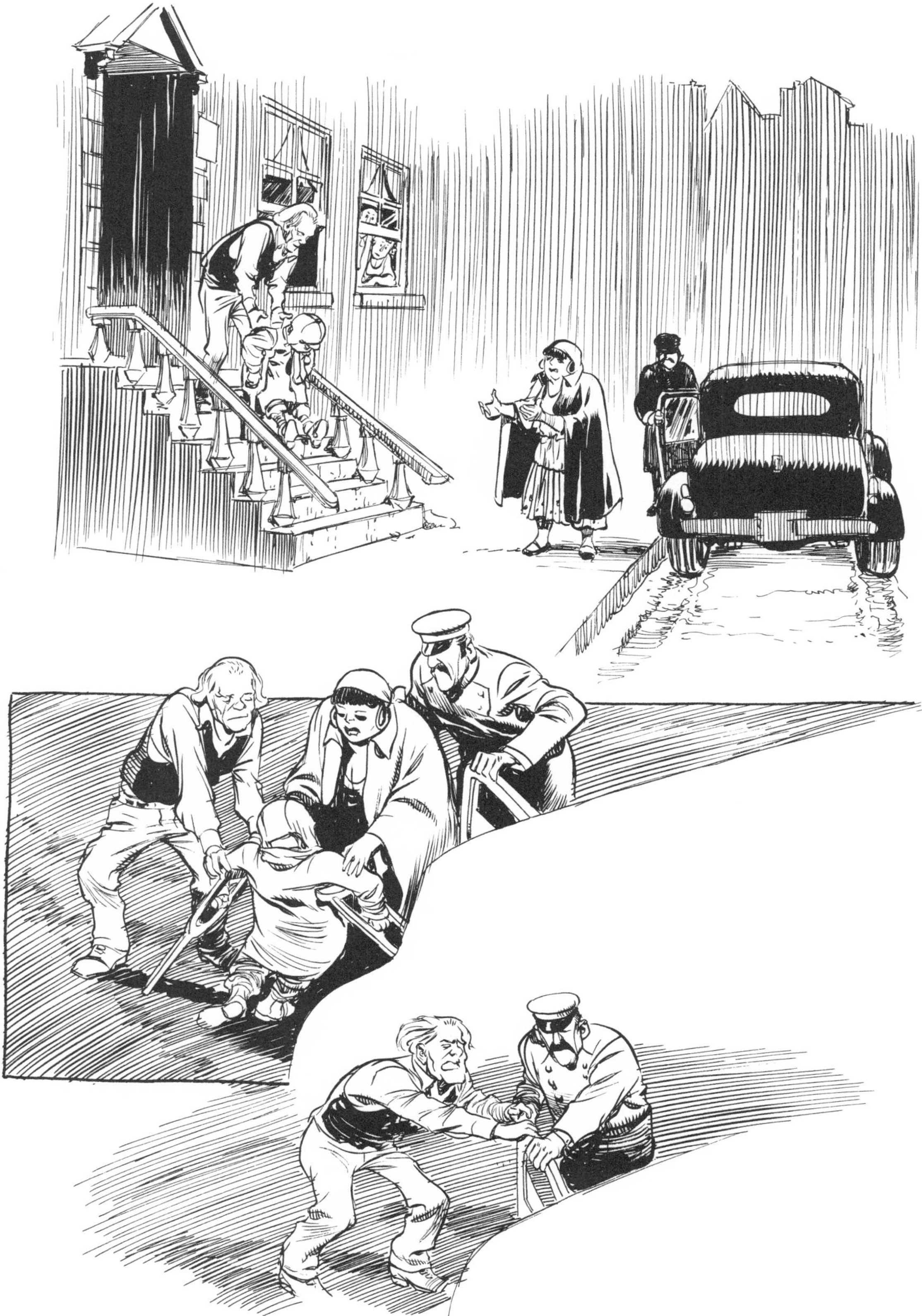

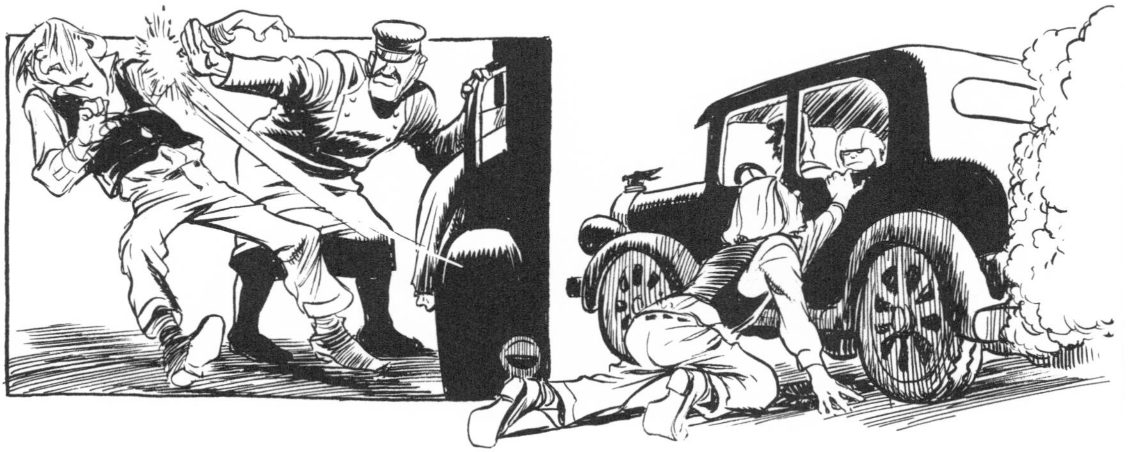

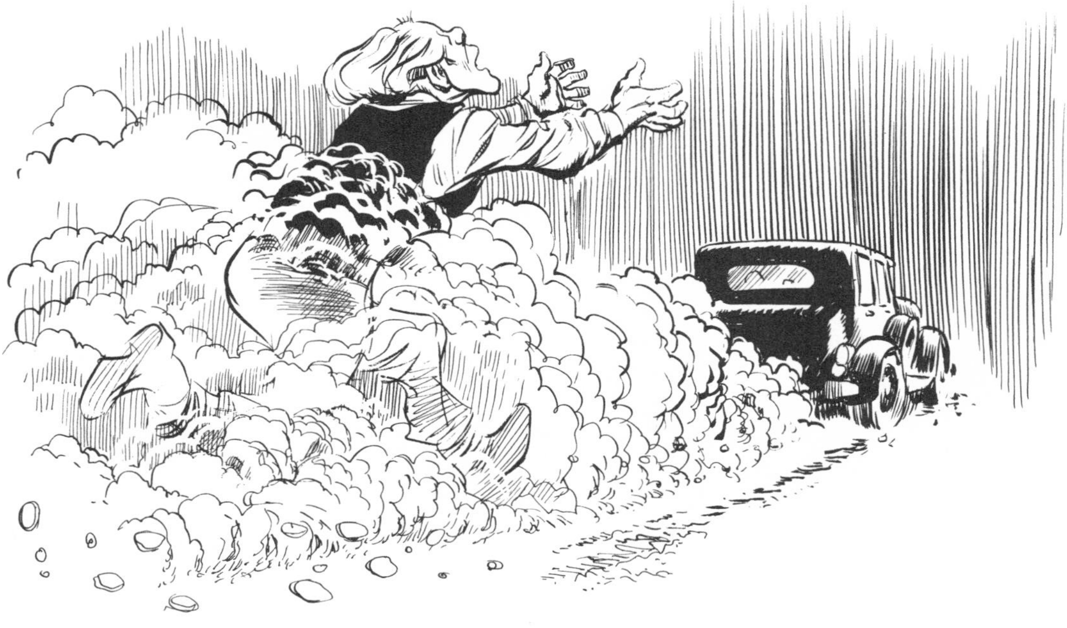

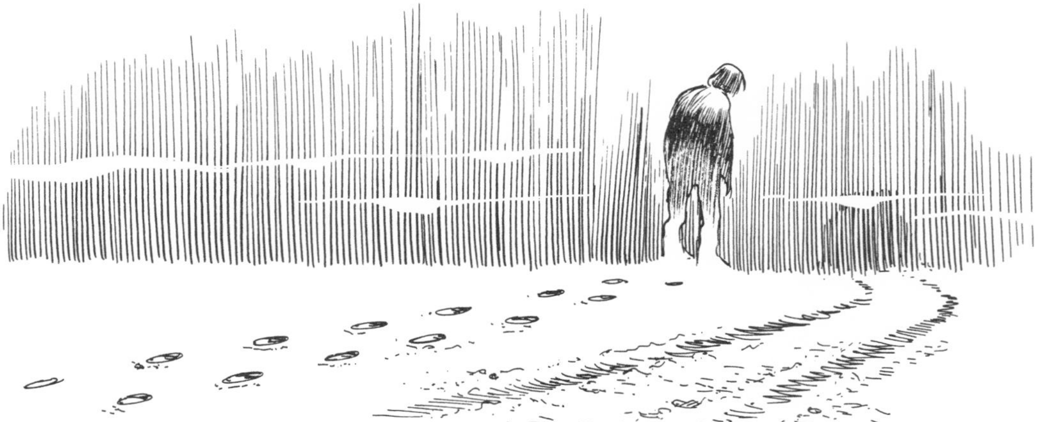

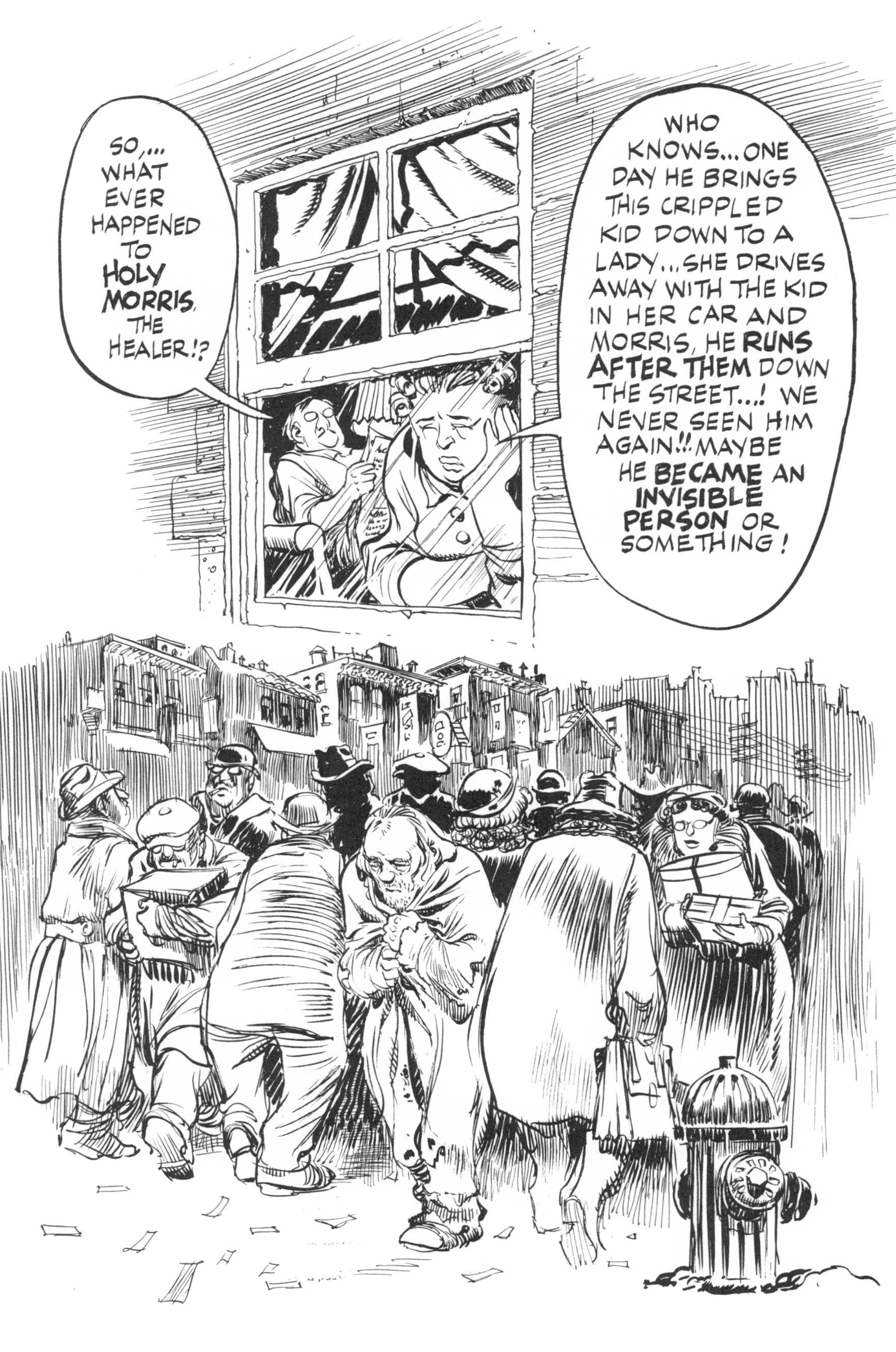

SO,... WHAT EVER HAPPENED TO **HOLY MORRIS**, THE HEALER!?
WHO KNOWS... ONE DAY HE BRINGS THIS CRIPPLED KID DOWN TO A LADY... SHE DRIVES AWAY WITH THE KID IN HER CAR AND MORRIS, HE **RUNS AFTER THEM** DOWN THE STREET...! WE NEVER SEEN HIM AGAIN!! MAYBE HE **BECAME** AN **INVISIBLE PERSON** OR SOMETHING!

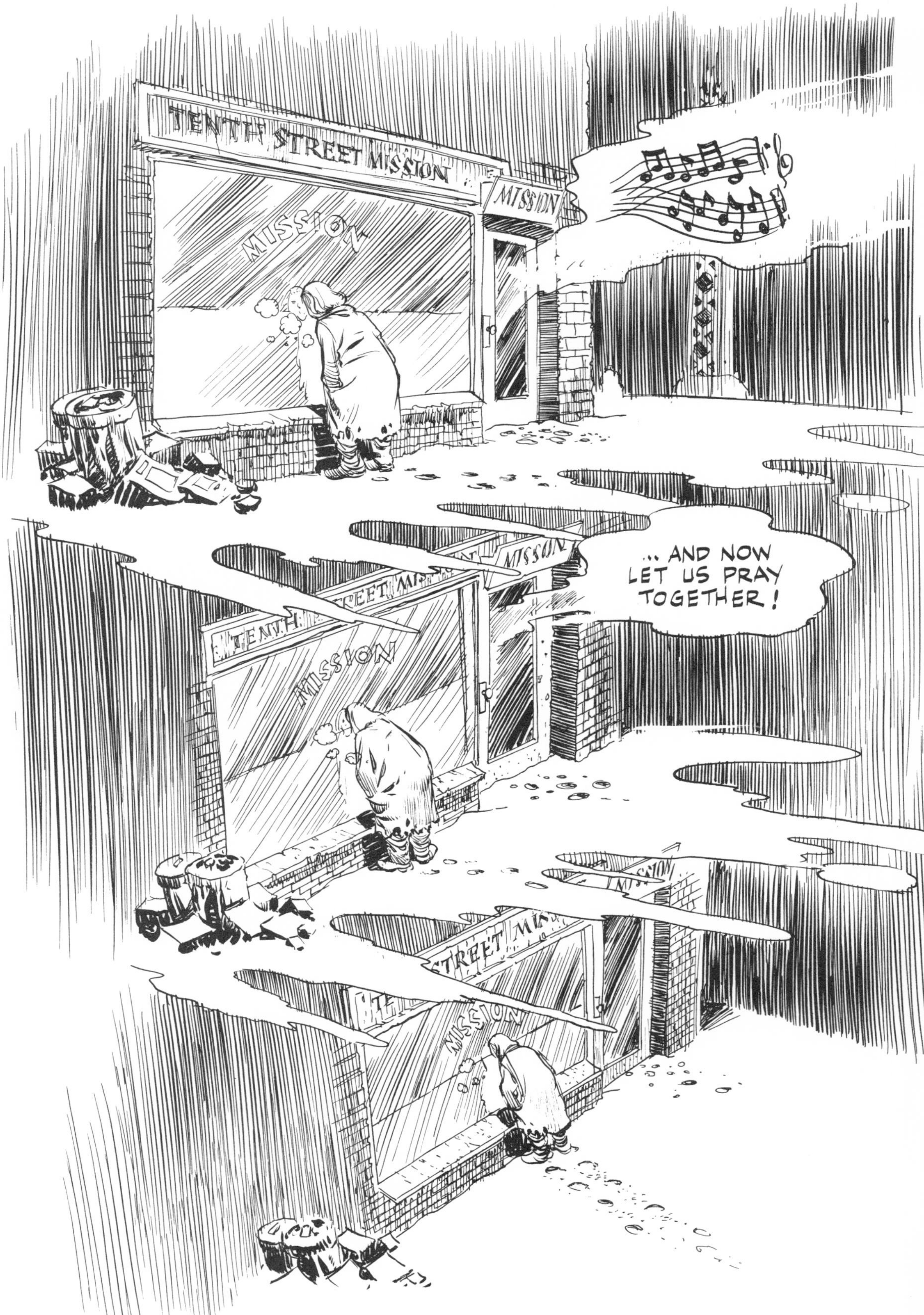
TENTH STREET MISSION
MISSION
MISSION
... AND NOW LET US PRAY TOGETHER!

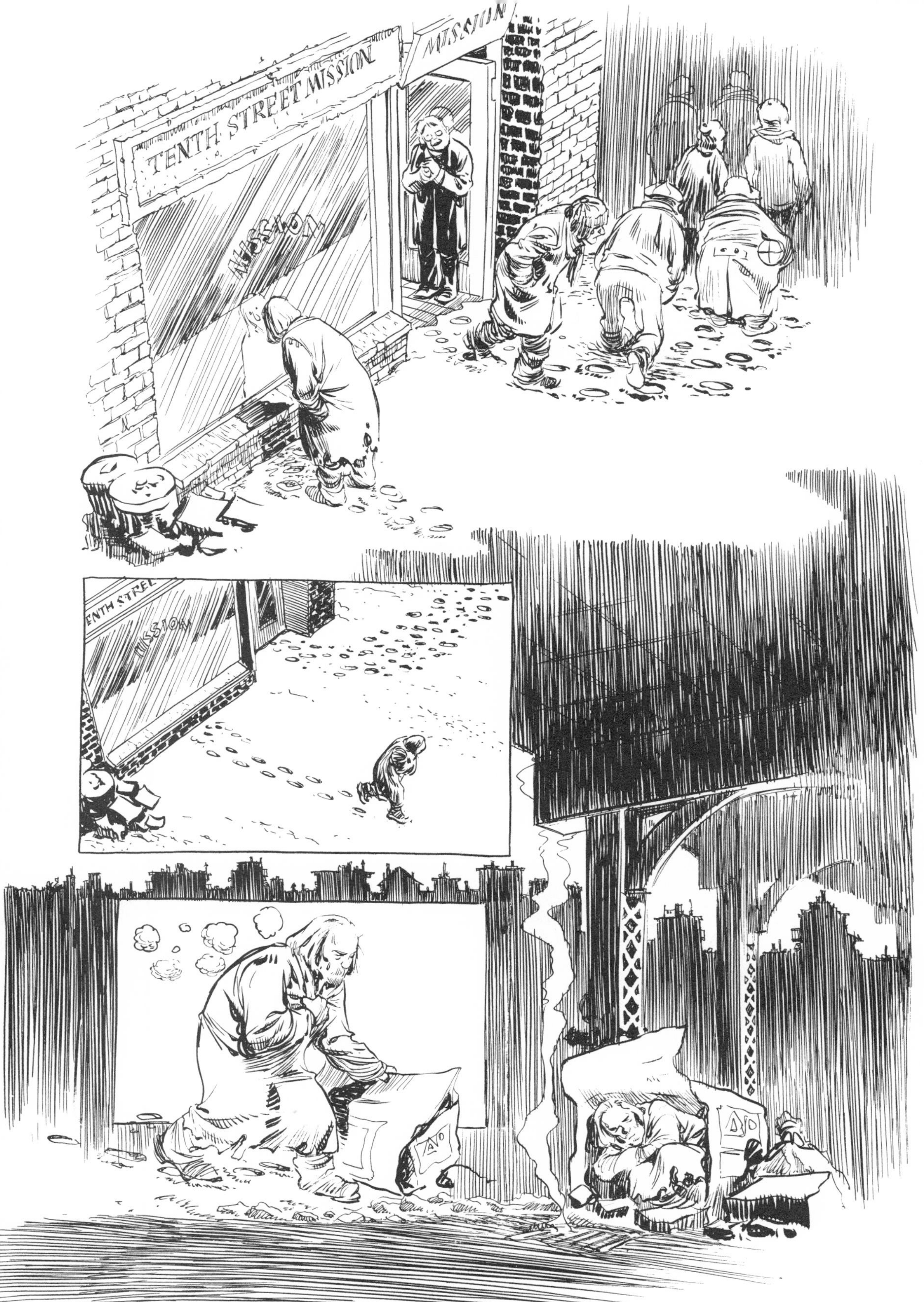

TENTH STREET MISSION
MISSION
MISSION
TENTH STRE
MISSION

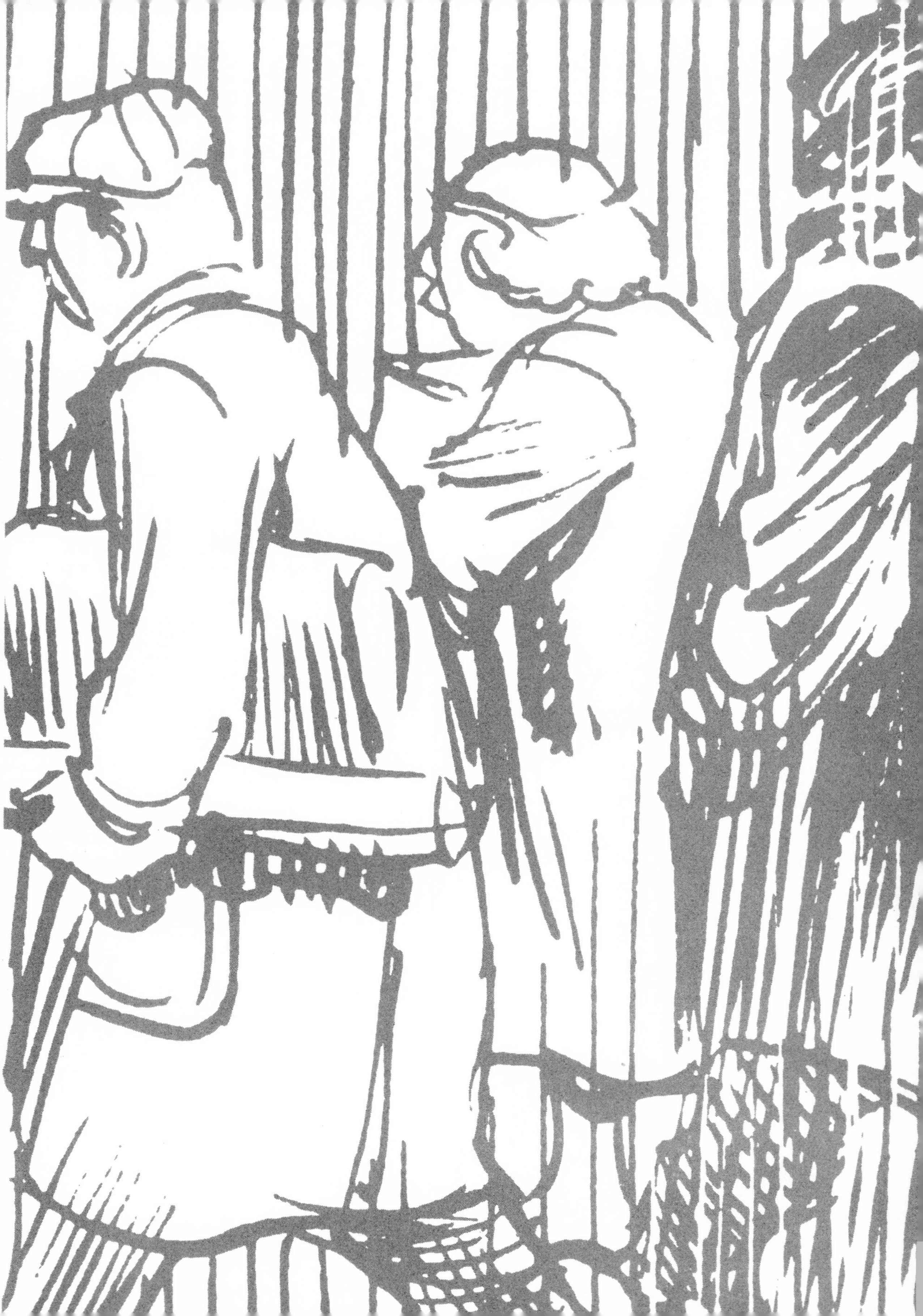

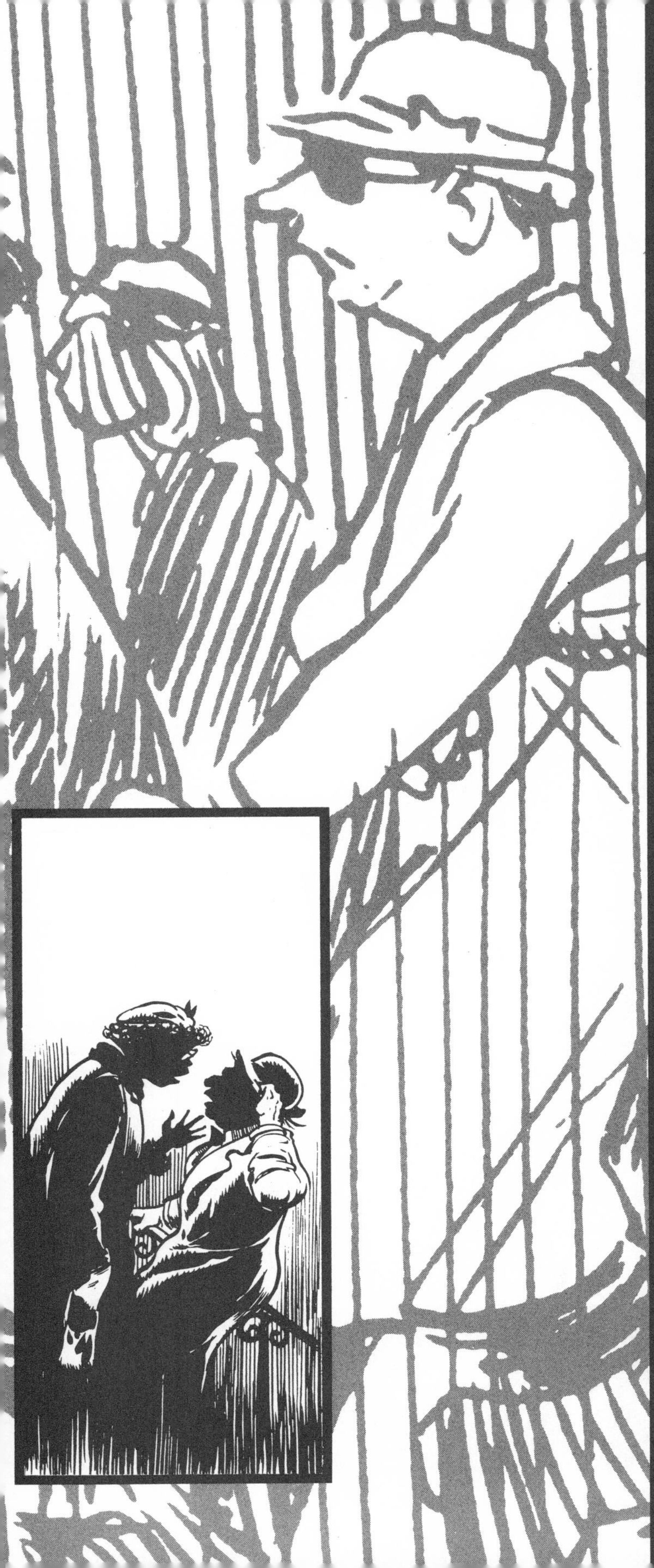

Introduction to "Mortal Combat"

INVISIBILITY is a rite of refuge in which urban citizens who fall or are thrown out of orbit find shelter.

To simply exist in a cocoon of grief or to be set adrift by irreplaceable loss, emotional disaster, unremitting pain or loneliness requires the protection of invisibility. It is a way to survive *in vitro*.

In the city this is easy; the individuals comprising the seamless mass of humanity flowing by are invisible to each other. The surrounding world is no more than a painted backdrop.

In relating the story of Herman, who became the unwilling prize in a clash of wills, I hoped to evoke the helplessness of a person caught in an intersection of the traffic of life.

Herman's dilemma is one of the dangers of group living.

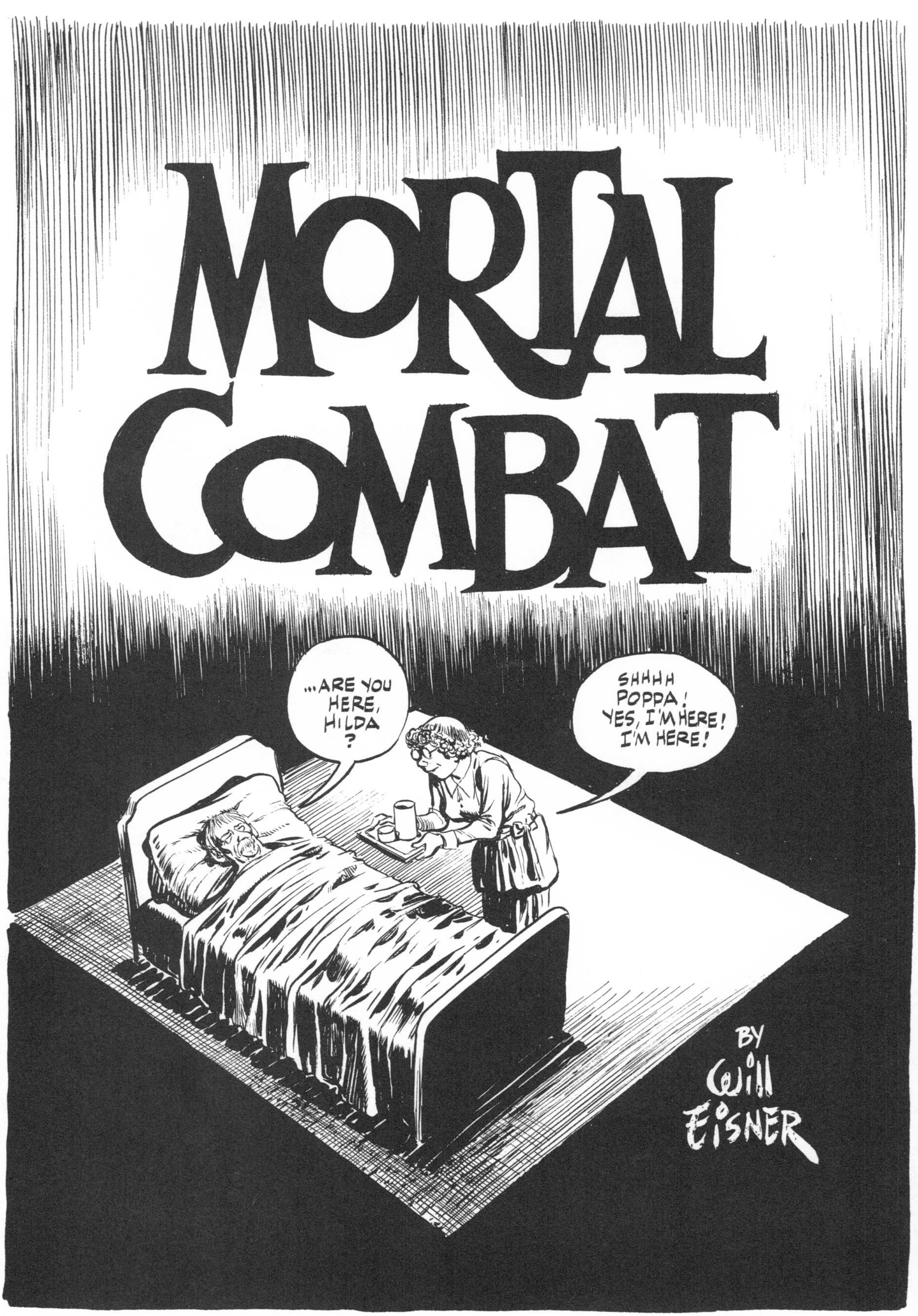
MORTAL COMBAT
...ARE YOU HERE, HILDA ?
SHHHH POPPA! YES, I'M HERE! I'M HERE!
BY Will Eisner

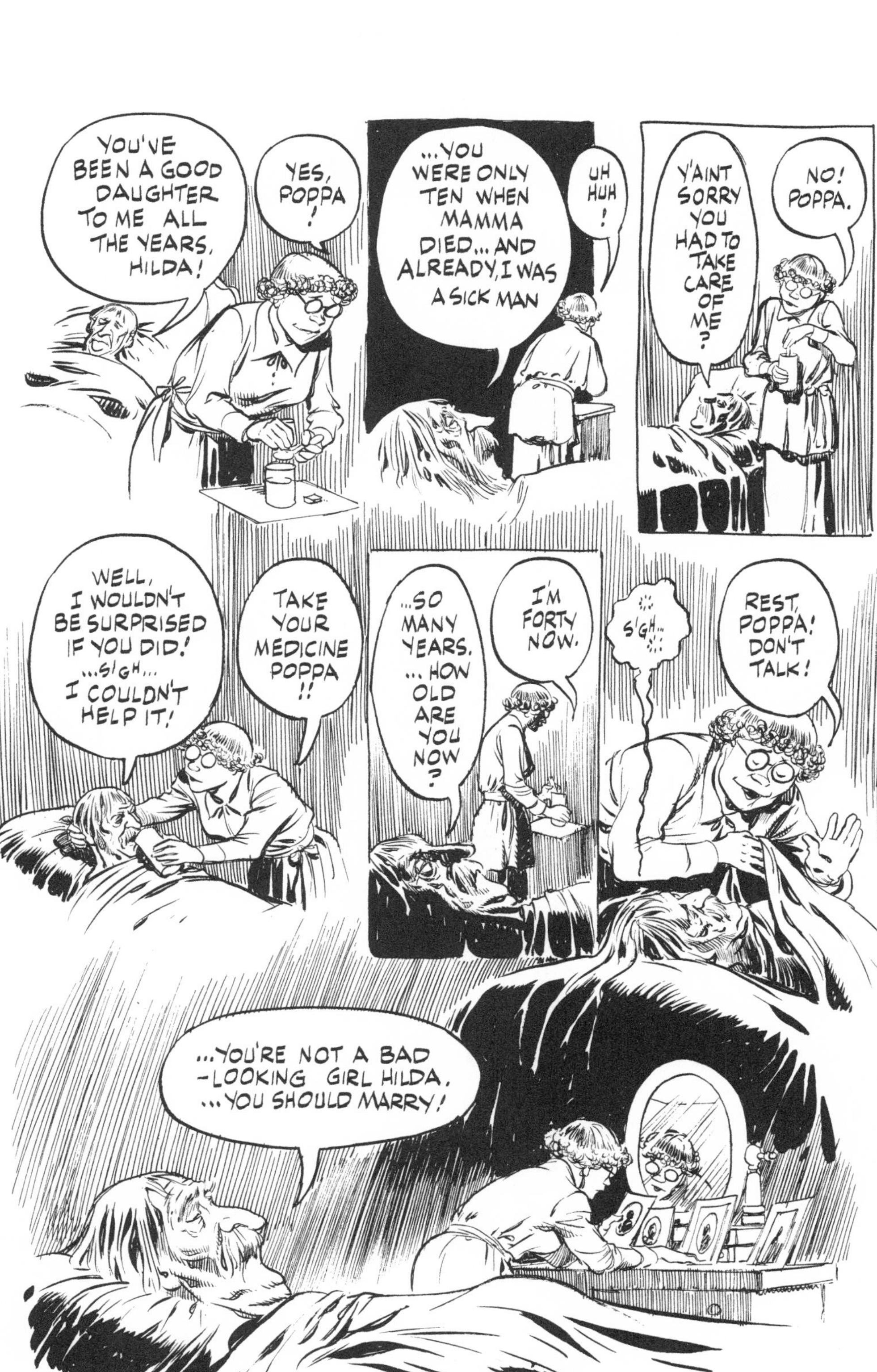
YOU'VE BEEN A GOOD DAUGHTER TO ME ALL THE YEARS, HILDA!
YES, POPPA!
...YOU WERE ONLY TEN WHEN MAMMA DIED... AND ALREADY, I WAS A SICK MAN
UH HUH!
Y'AINT SORRY YOU HAD TO TAKE CARE OF ME?
NO! POPPA.
WELL, I WOULDN'T BE SURPRISED IF YOU DID! ...SIGH... I COULDN'T HELP IT!
TAKE YOUR MEDICINE POPPA!!
...SO MANY YEARS. ...HOW OLD ARE YOU NOW?
I'M FORTY NOW.
SIGH...
REST, POPPA! DON'T TALK!
...YOU'RE NOT A BAD-LOOKING GIRL HILDA. ...YOU SHOULD MARRY!

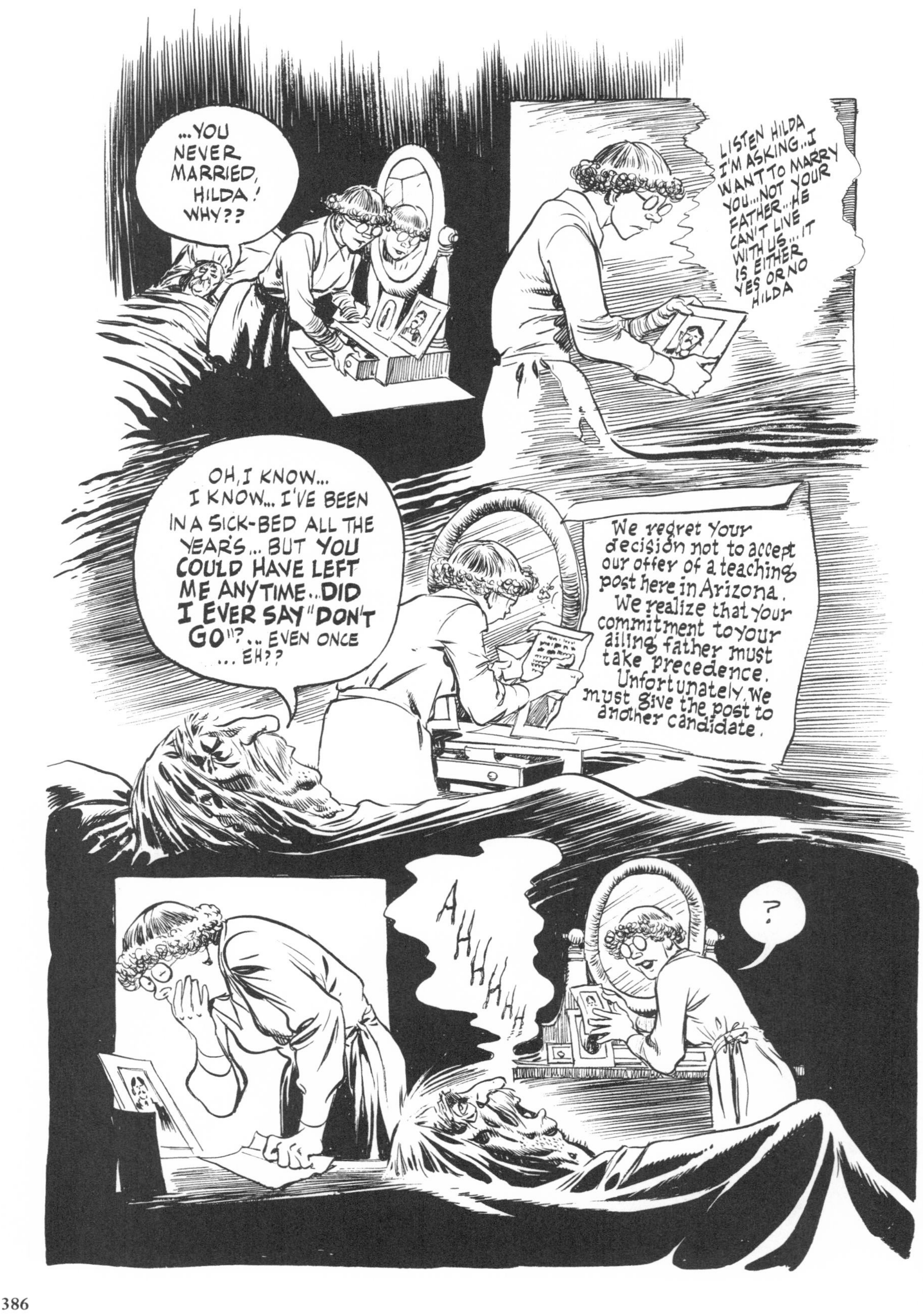
...YOU NEVER MARRIED, HILDA! WHY??
LISTEN HILDA I'M ASKING.. I WANT TO MARRY YOU...NOT YOUR FATHER...HE CAN'T LIVE WITH US...IT IS EITHER YES OR NO HILDA
OH, I KNOW... I KNOW... I'VE BEEN IN A SICK-BED ALL THE YEARS... BUT YOU COULD HAVE LEFT ME ANYTIME...DID I EVER SAY "DON'T GO"?.. EVEN ONCE ... EH??
We regret your decision not to accept our offer of a teaching post here in Arizona. We realize that your commitment to your ailing father must take precedence. Unfortunately, we must give the post to another candidate.
AHHHHHH
?

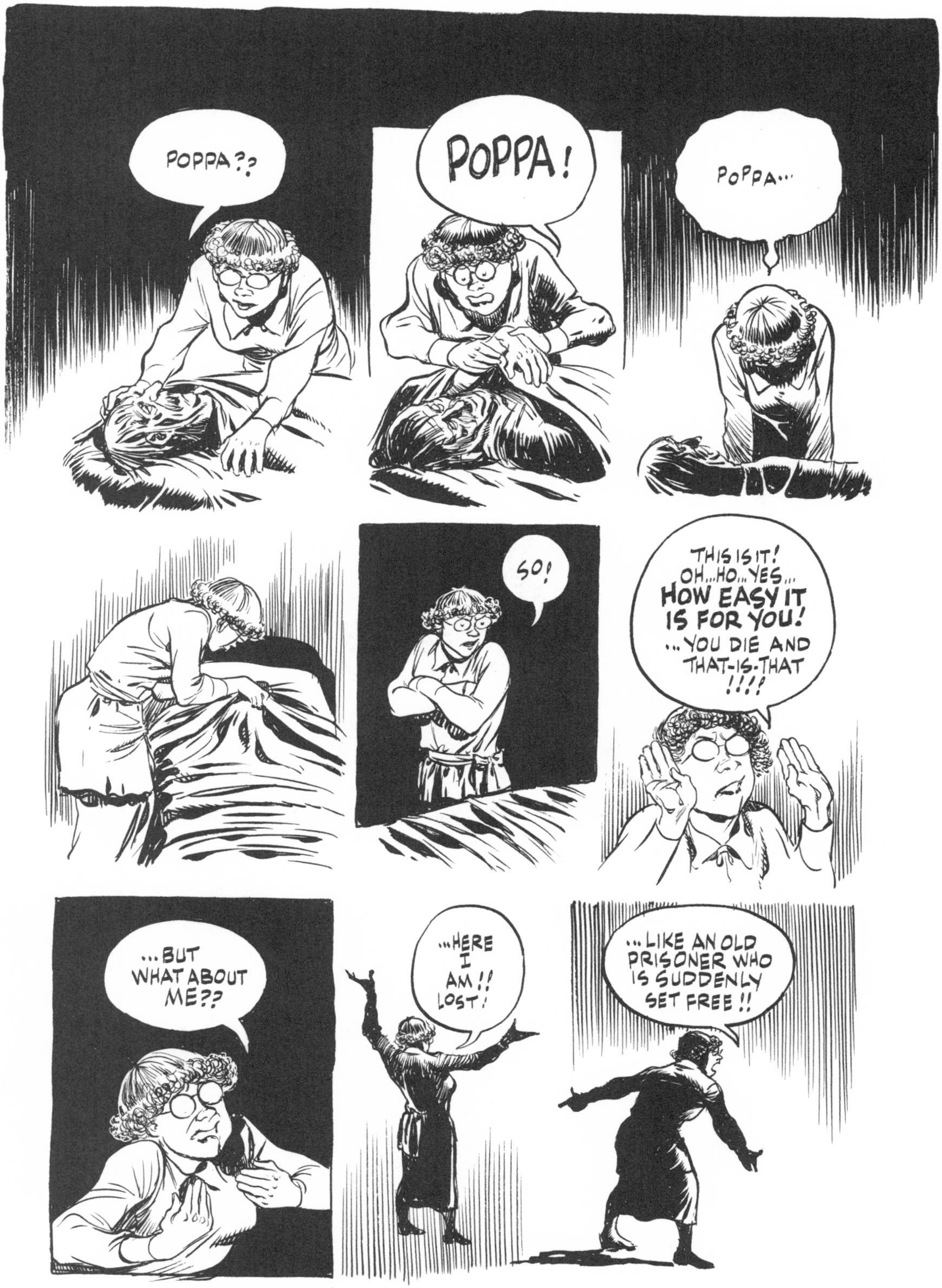
POPPA??
POPPA!
POPPA...
SO!
THIS IS IT! OH...HO...YES... HOW EASY IT IS FOR YOU! ...YOU DIE AND THAT-IS-THAT !!!!
...BUT WHAT ABOUT ME??
...HERE I AM!! LOST!
...LIKE AN OLD PRISONER WHO IS SUDDENLY SET FREE!!

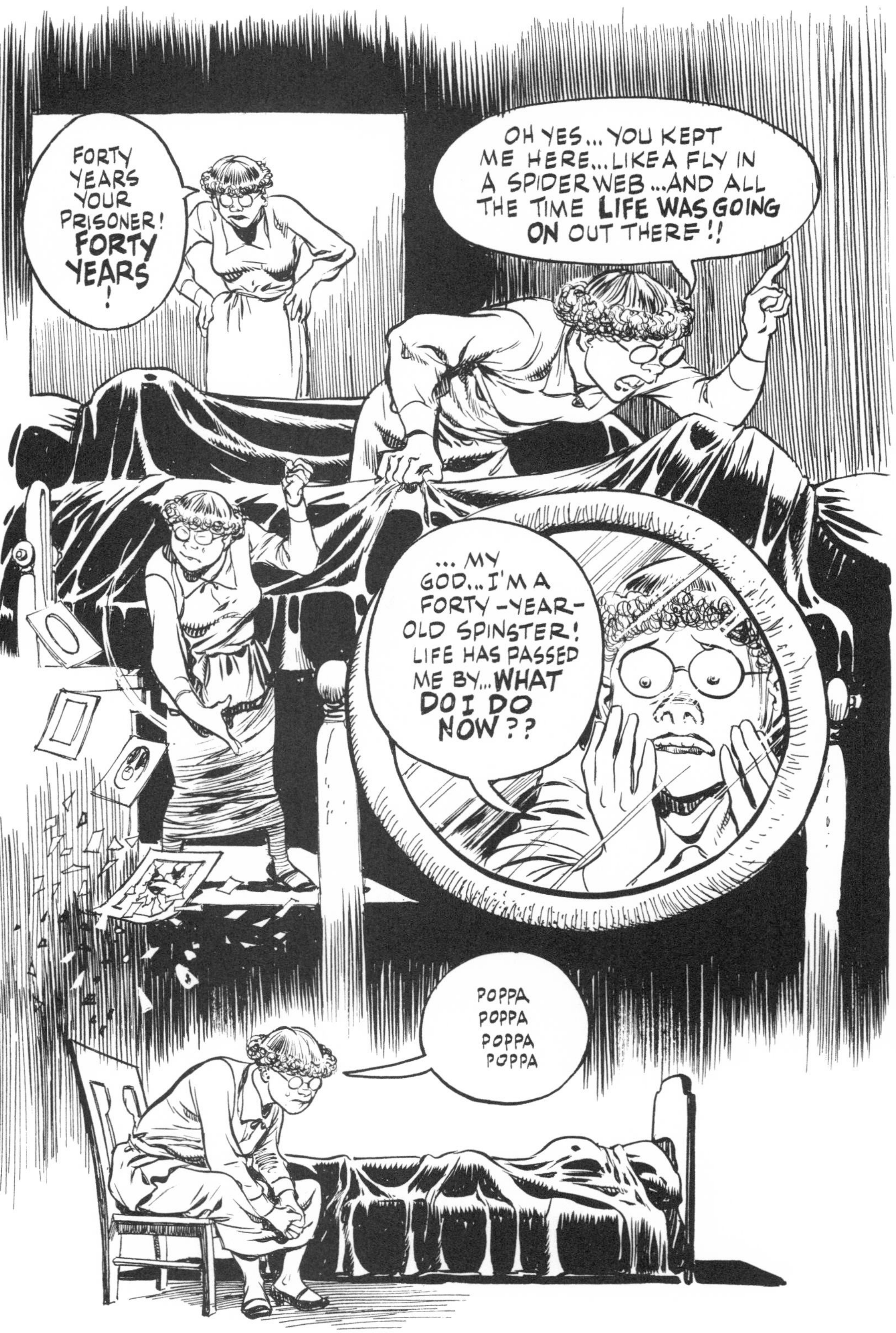
FORTY YEARS YOUR PRISONER! FORTY YEARS!
OH YES... YOU KEPT ME HERE... LIKE A FLY IN A SPIDER WEB... AND ALL THE TIME LIFE WAS GOING ON OUT THERE!!
... MY GOD... I'M A FORTY-YEAR-OLD SPINSTER! LIFE HAS PASSED ME BY... WHAT DO I DO NOW??
POPPA POPPA POPPA POPPA

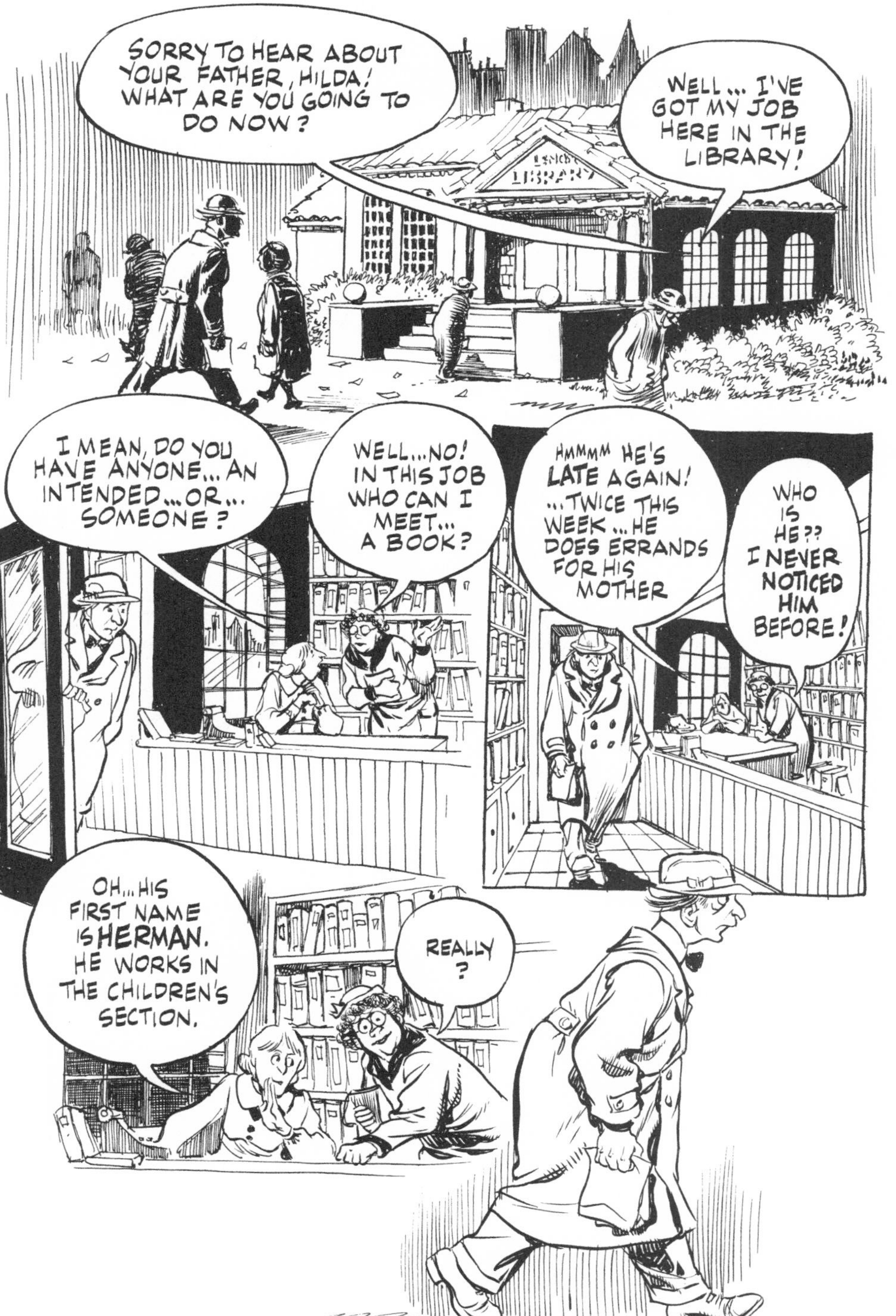
SORRY TO HEAR ABOUT YOUR FATHER, HILDA! WHAT ARE YOU GOING TO DO NOW?
WELL ... I'VE GOT MY JOB HERE IN THE LIBRARY!
LIBRARY
I MEAN, DO YOU HAVE ANYONE... AN INTENDED...OR... SOMEONE?
WELL...NO! IN THIS JOB WHO CAN I MEET... A BOOK?
HMMMM HE'S LATE AGAIN! ...TWICE THIS WEEK...HE DOES ERRANDS FOR HIS MOTHER
WHO IS HE?? I NEVER NOTICED HIM BEFORE!
OH...HIS FIRST NAME IS HERMAN. HE WORKS IN THE CHILDREN'S SECTION.
REALLY?

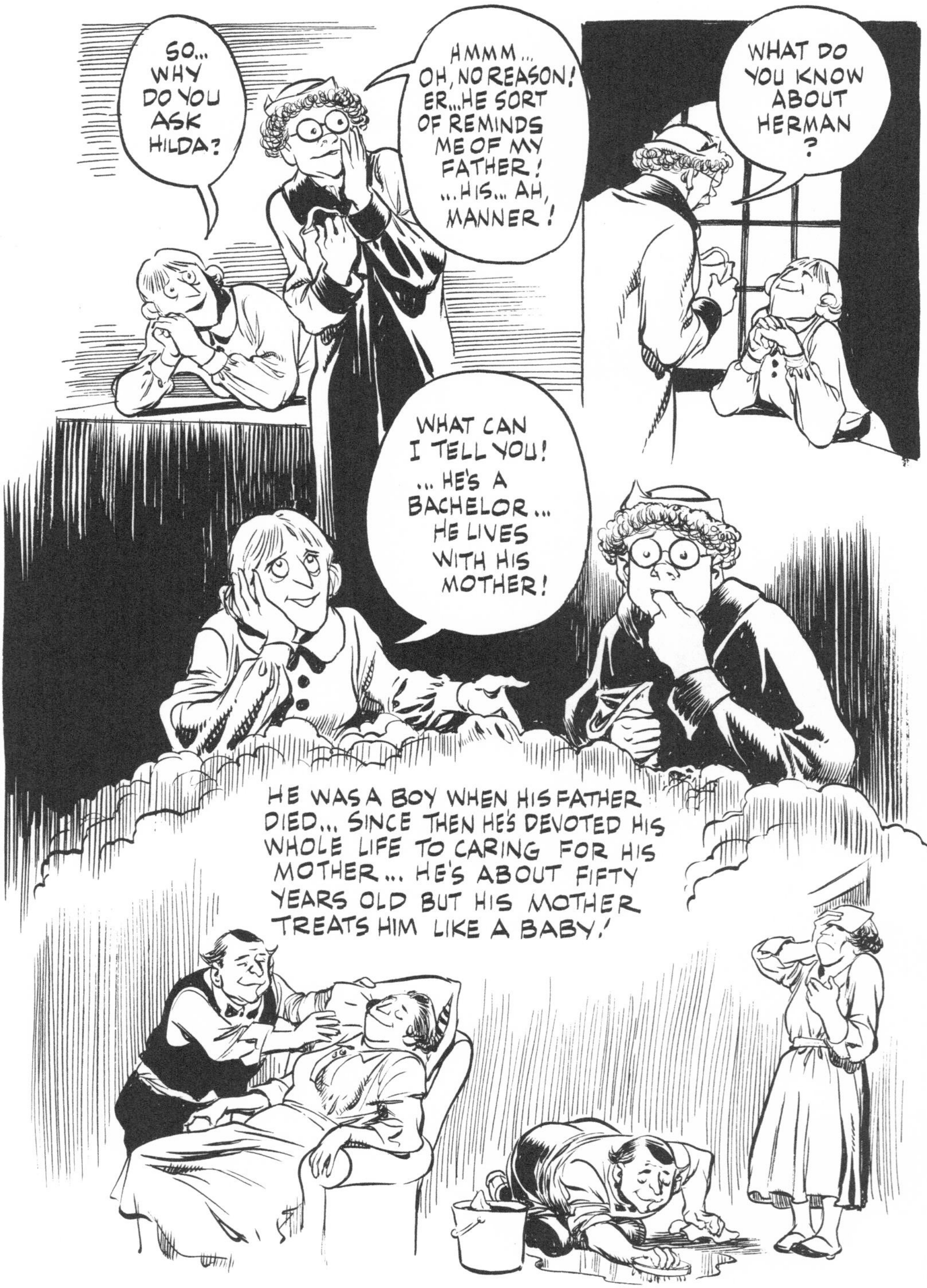
SO... WHY DO YOU ASK HILDA?
HMMM... OH, NO REASON! ER... HE SORT OF REMINDS ME OF MY FATHER! ...HIS... AH, MANNER!
WHAT DO YOU KNOW ABOUT HERMAN?
WHAT CAN I TELL YOU! ... HE'S A BACHELOR... HE LIVES WITH HIS MOTHER!
HE WAS A BOY WHEN HIS FATHER DIED... SINCE THEN HE'S DEVOTED HIS WHOLE LIFE TO CARING FOR HIS MOTHER... HE'S ABOUT FIFTY YEARS OLD BUT HIS MOTHER TREATS HIM LIKE A BABY!

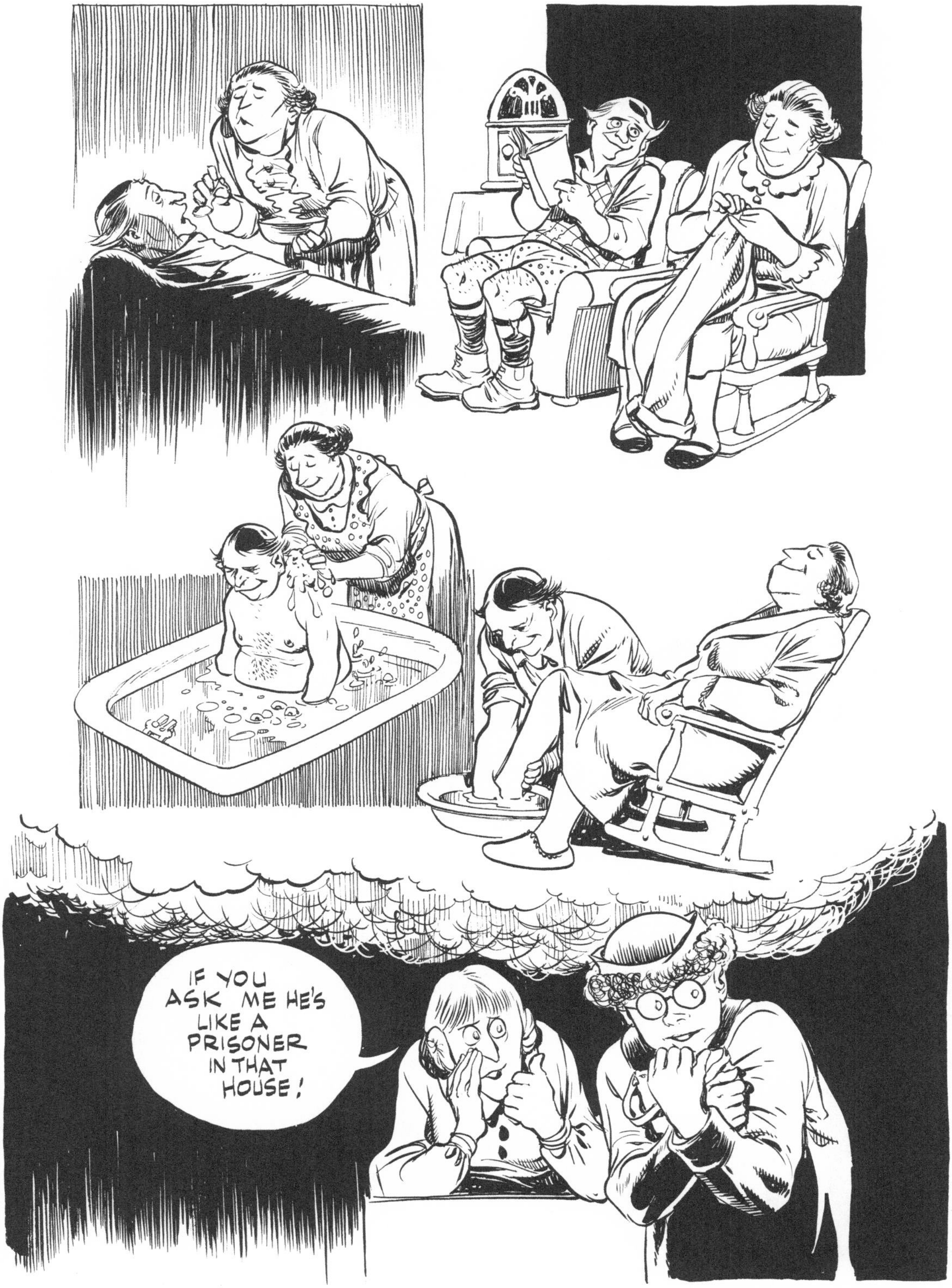
IF YOU ASK ME HE'S LIKE A PRISONER IN THAT HOUSE!

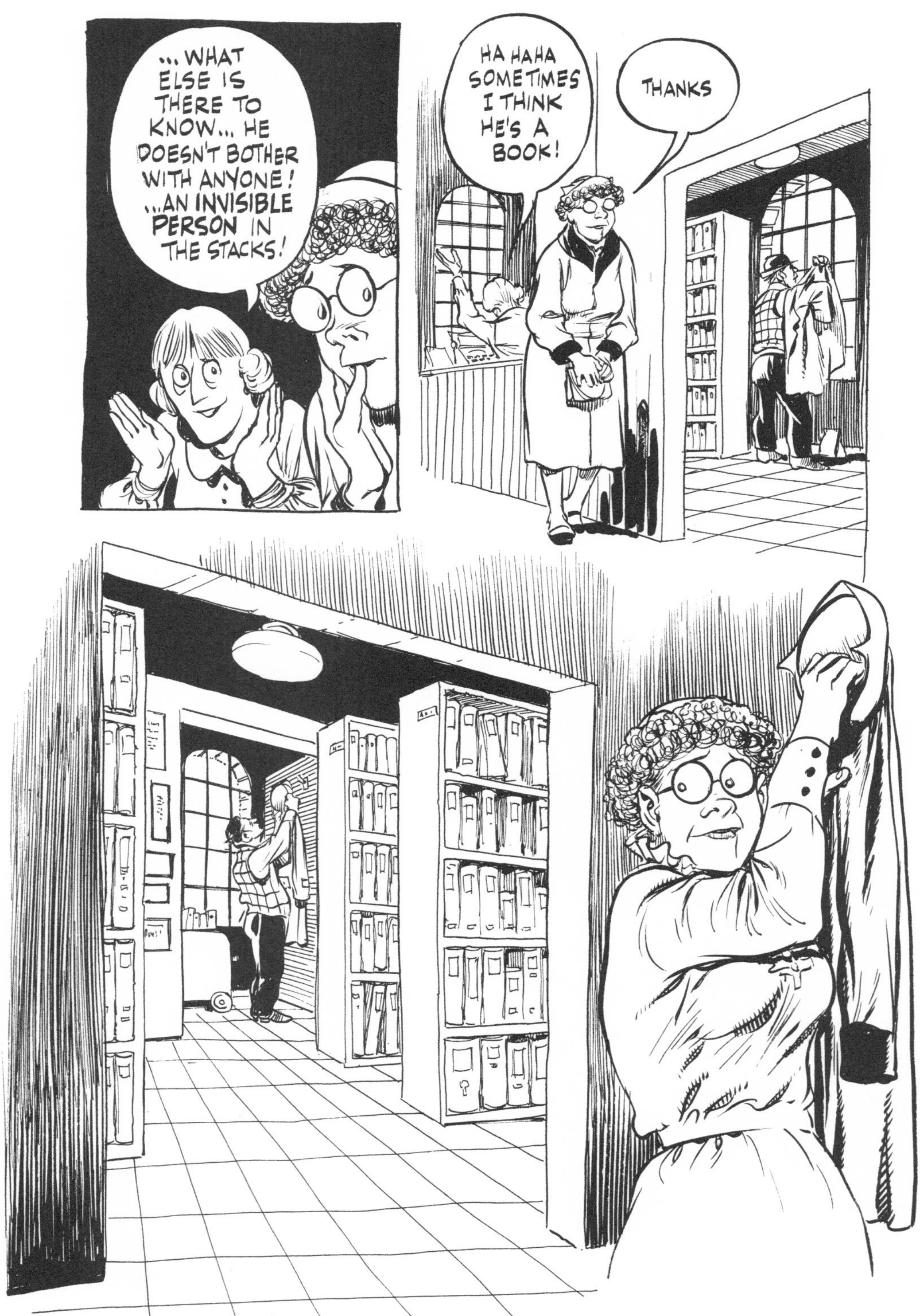
...WHAT ELSE IS THERE TO KNOW... HE DOESN'T BOTHER WITH ANYONE! ...AN INVISIBLE PERSON IN THE STACKS!
HA HAHA SOMETIMES I THINK HE'S A BOOK!
THANKS

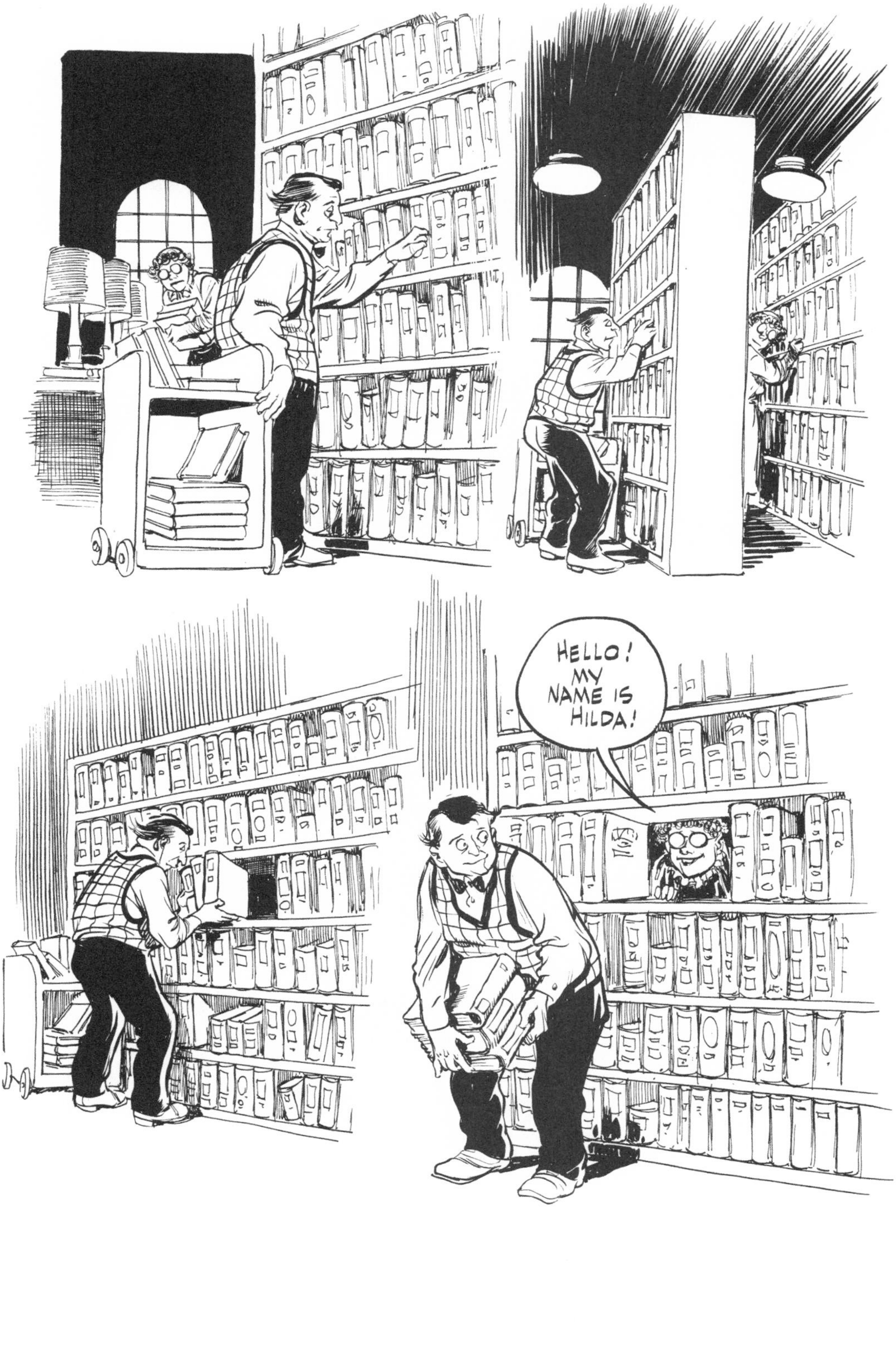
HELLO! MY NAME IS HILDA!

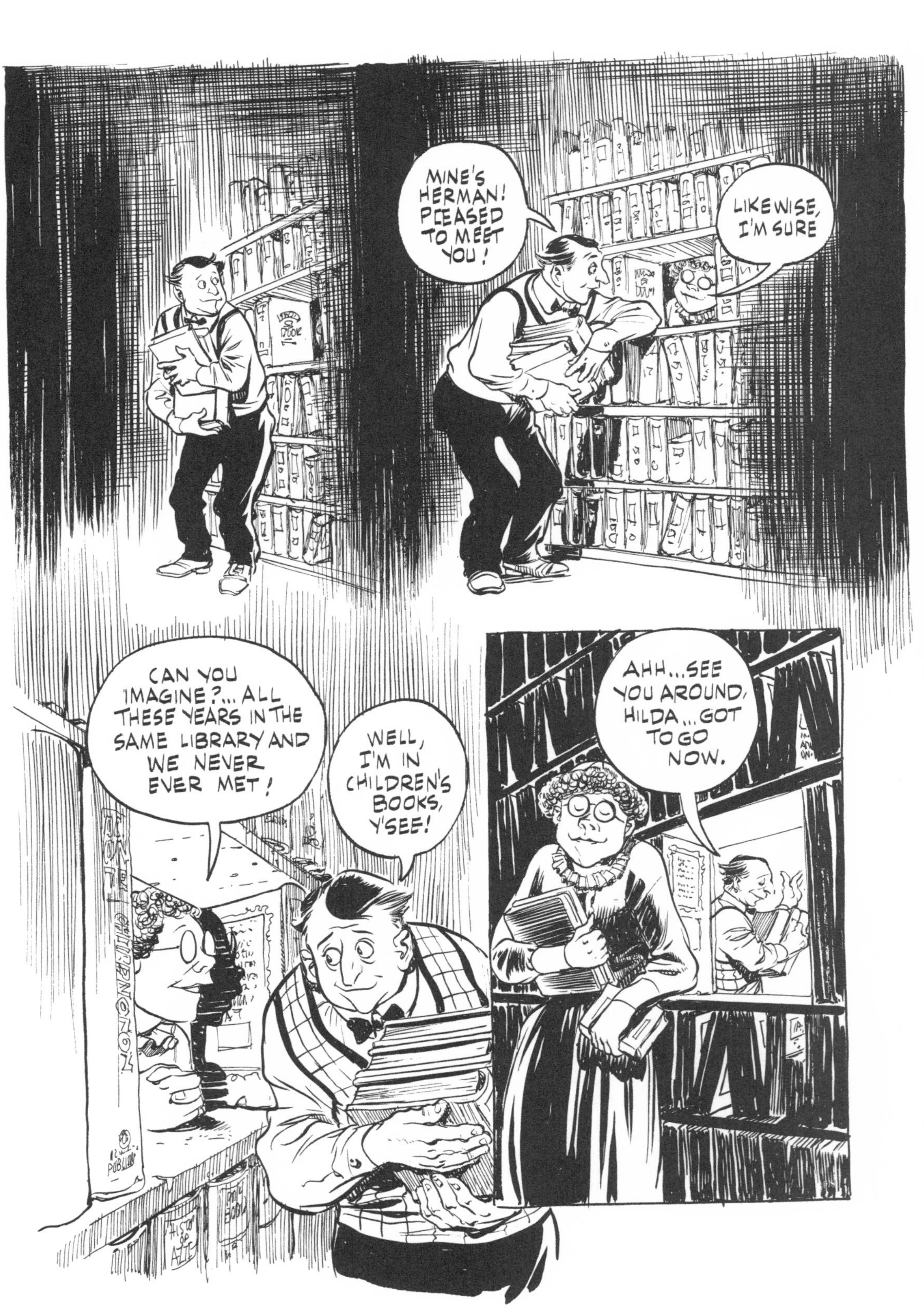
MINE'S HERMAN! PLEASED TO MEET YOU!
LIKEWISE, I'M SURE
CAN YOU IMAGINE?... ALL THESE YEARS IN THE SAME LIBRARY AND WE NEVER EVER MET!
WELL, I'M IN CHILDREN'S BOOKS, Y'SEE!
AHH... SEE YOU AROUND, HILDA... GOT TO GO NOW.

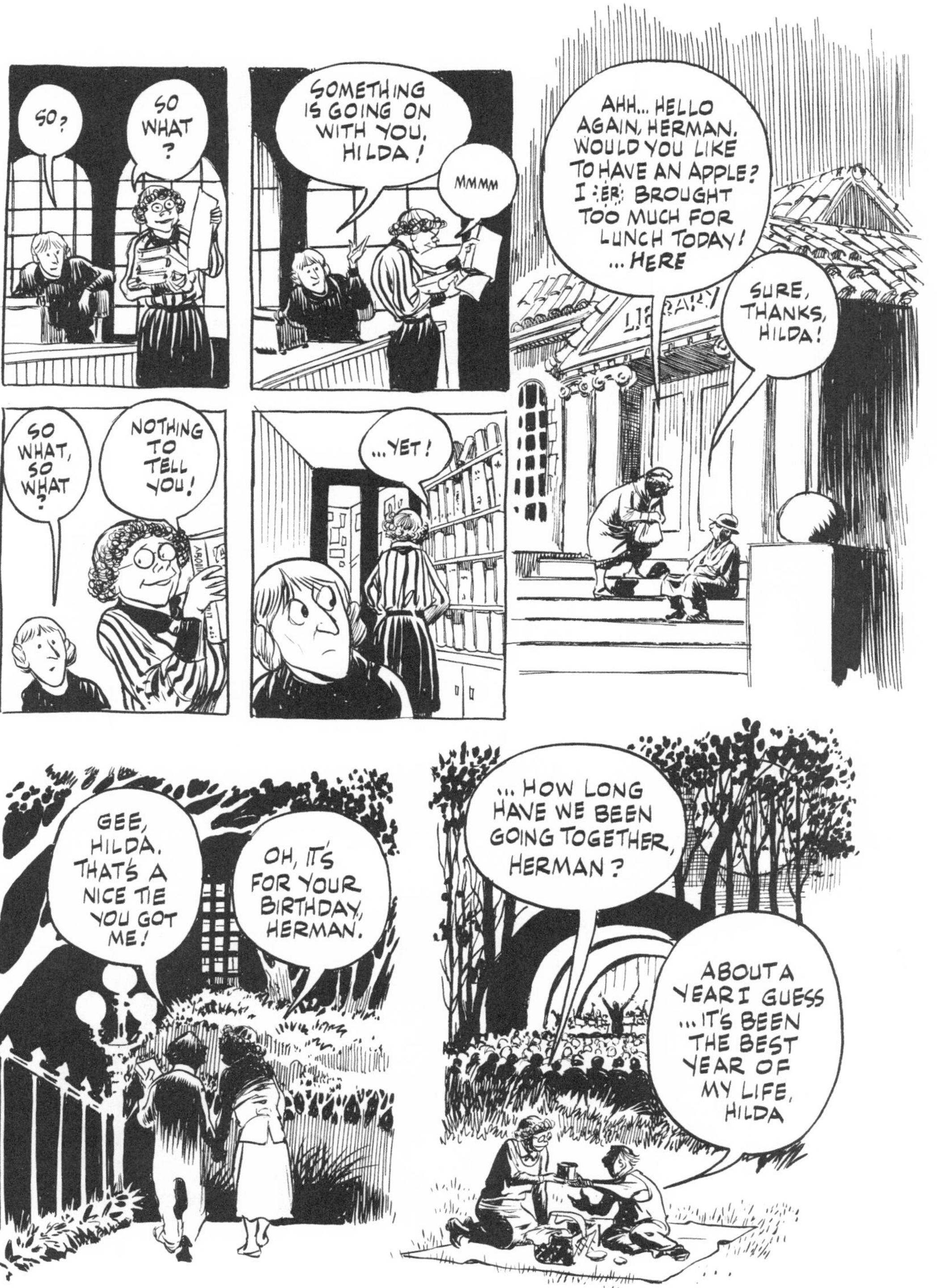
SO?
SO WHAT ?
SOMETHING IS GOING ON WITH YOU, HILDA!
MMMM
SO WHAT, SO WHAT ?
NOTHING TO TELL YOU!
...YET!
AHH... HELLO AGAIN, HERMAN. WOULD YOU LIKE TO HAVE AN APPLE? I :ER: BROUGHT TOO MUCH FOR LUNCH TODAY! ...HERE
SURE, THANKS, HILDA!
GEE, HILDA. THAT'S A NICE TIE YOU GOT ME!
OH, IT'S FOR YOUR BIRTHDAY, HERMAN.
... HOW LONG HAVE WE BEEN GOING TOGETHER, HERMAN?
ABOUT A YEAR I GUESS ...IT'S BEEN THE BEST YEAR OF MY LIFE, HILDA

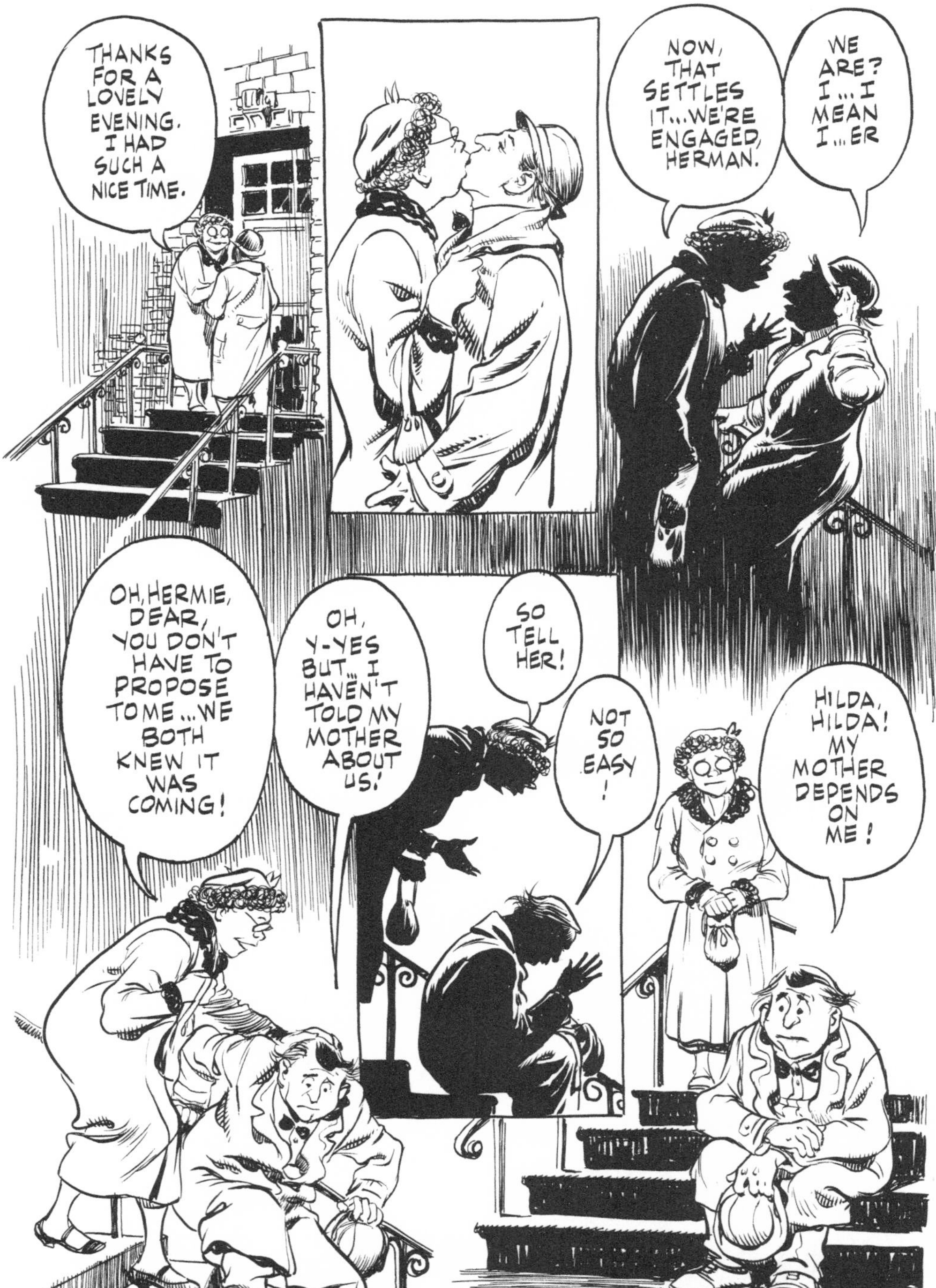
THANKS FOR A LOVELY EVENING. I HAD SUCH A NICE TIME.
NOW, THAT SETTLES IT...WE'RE ENGAGED, HERMAN.
WE ARE? I...I MEAN I...ER
OH, HERMIE, DEAR, YOU DON'T HAVE TO PROPOSE TO ME...WE BOTH KNEW IT WAS COMING!
OH, Y-YES BUT... I HAVEN'T TOLD MY MOTHER ABOUT US!
SO TELL HER!
NOT SO EASY!
HILDA, HILDA! MY MOTHER DEPENDS ON ME!

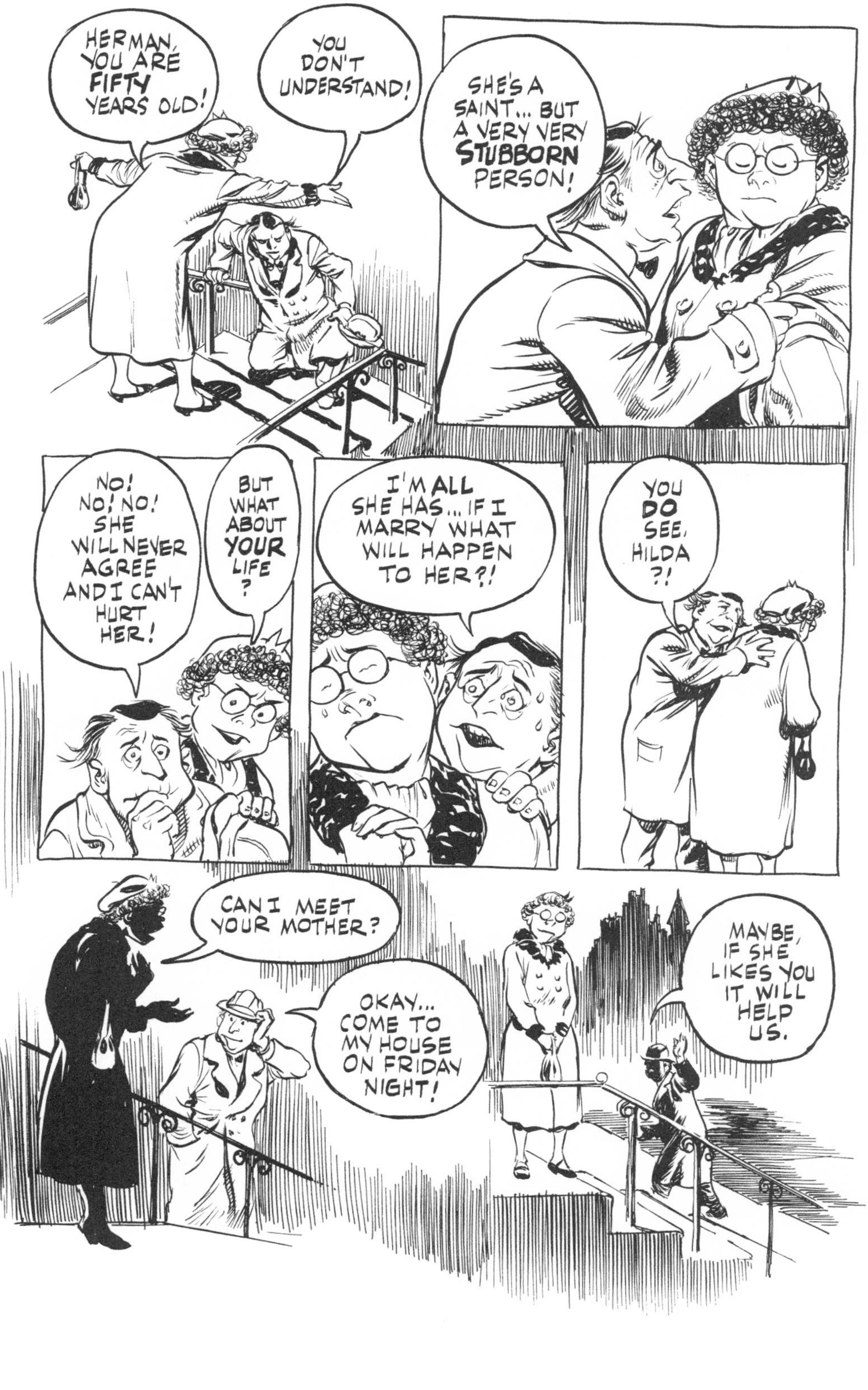
HERMAN, YOU ARE FIFTY YEARS OLD!
YOU DON'T UNDERSTAND!
SHE'S A SAINT... BUT A VERY VERY STUBBORN PERSON!
NO! NO! NO! SHE WILL NEVER AGREE AND I CAN'T HURT HER!
BUT WHAT ABOUT YOUR LIFE?
I'M ALL SHE HAS... IF I MARRY WHAT WILL HAPPEN TO HER?!
YOU DO SEE, HILDA?!
CAN I MEET YOUR MOTHER?
OKAY... COME TO MY HOUSE ON FRIDAY NIGHT!
MAYBE, IF SHE LIKES YOU IT WILL HELP US.

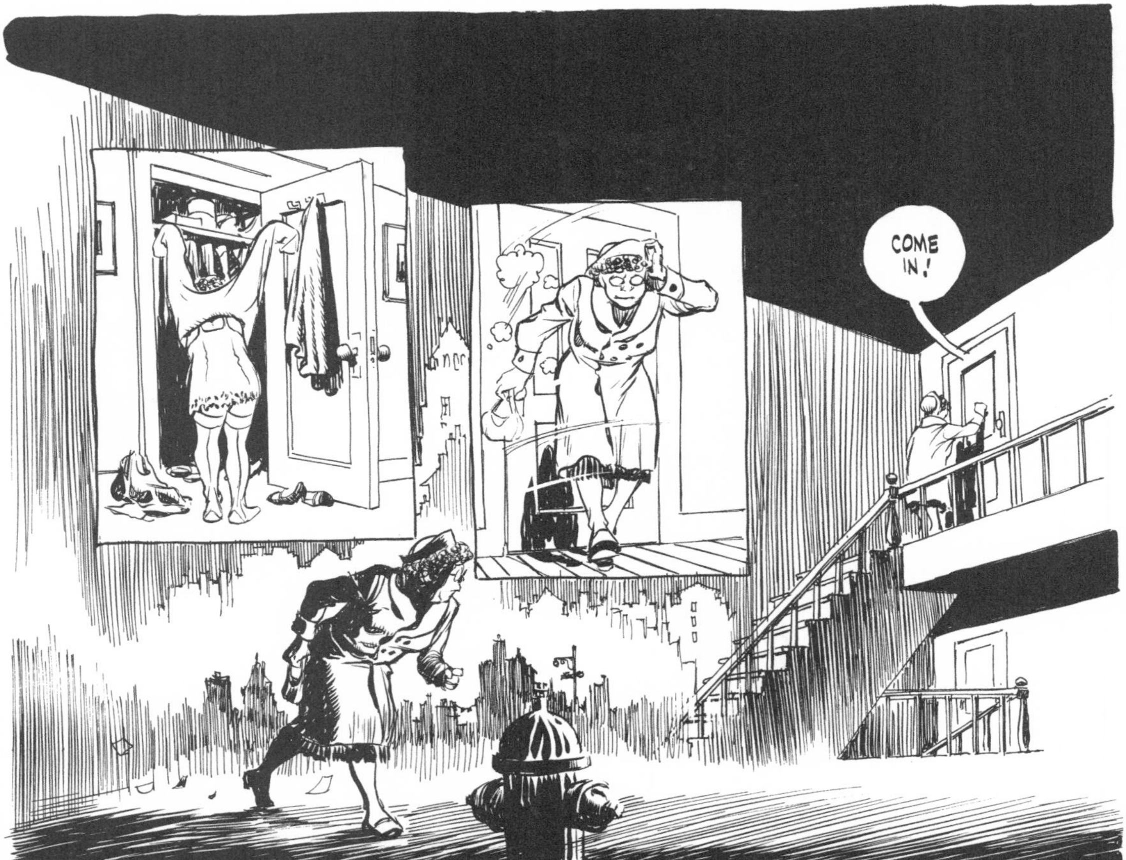
COME IN!

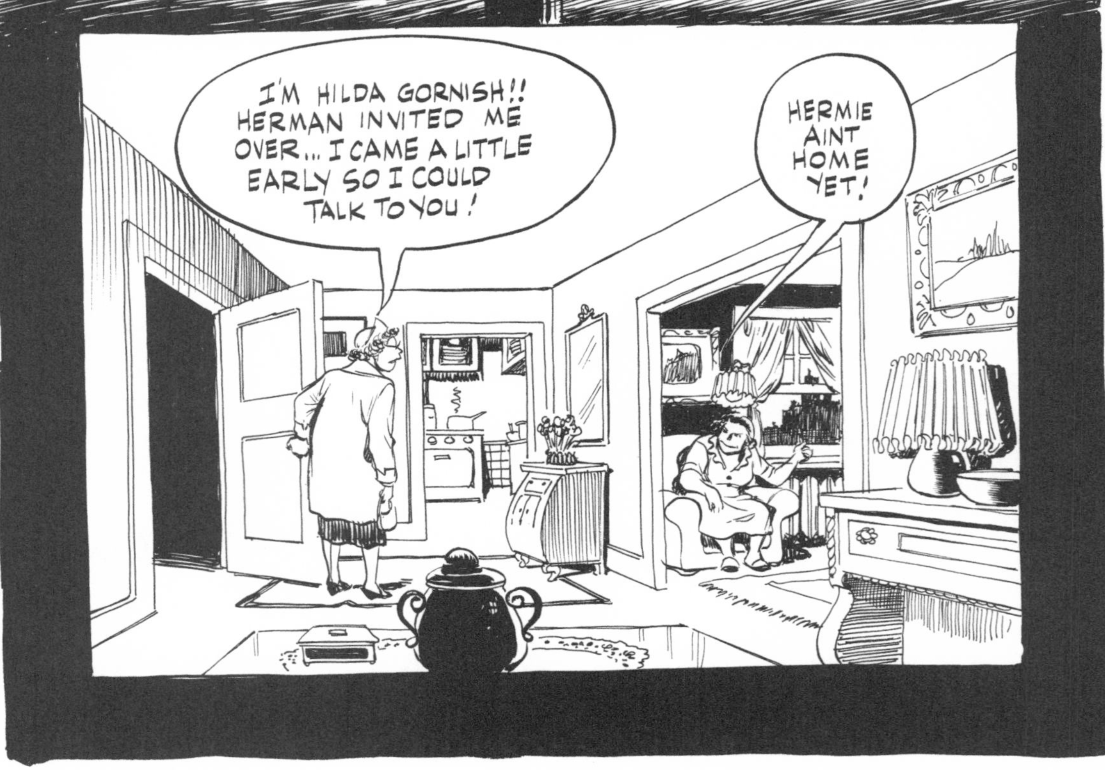
I'M HILDA GORNISH!! HERMAN INVITED ME OVER... I CAME A LITTLE EARLY SO I COULD TALK TO YOU!
HERMIE AINT HOME YET!

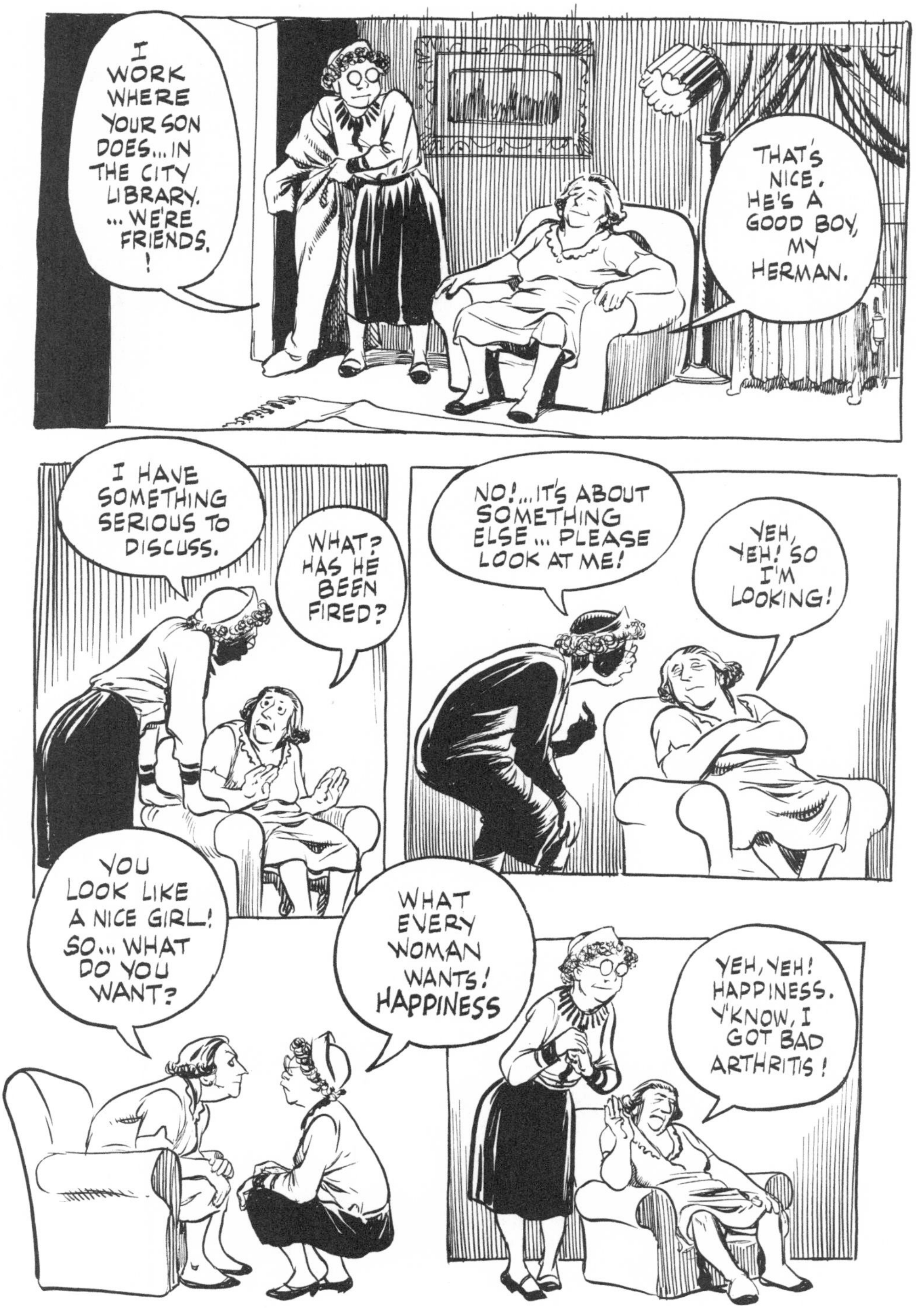
I WORK WHERE YOUR SON DOES... IN THE CITY LIBRARY. ...WE'RE FRIENDS. !
THAT'S NICE. HE'S A GOOD BOY, MY HERMAN.
I HAVE SOMETHING SERIOUS TO DISCUSS.
WHAT? HAS HE BEEN FIRED?
NO!...IT'S ABOUT SOMETHING ELSE ... PLEASE LOOK AT ME!
YEH, YEH! SO I'M LOOKING!
YOU LOOK LIKE A NICE GIRL! SO... WHAT DO YOU WANT?
WHAT EVERY WOMAN WANTS! HAPPINESS
YEH, YEH! HAPPINESS. Y'KNOW, I GOT BAD ARTHRITIS!

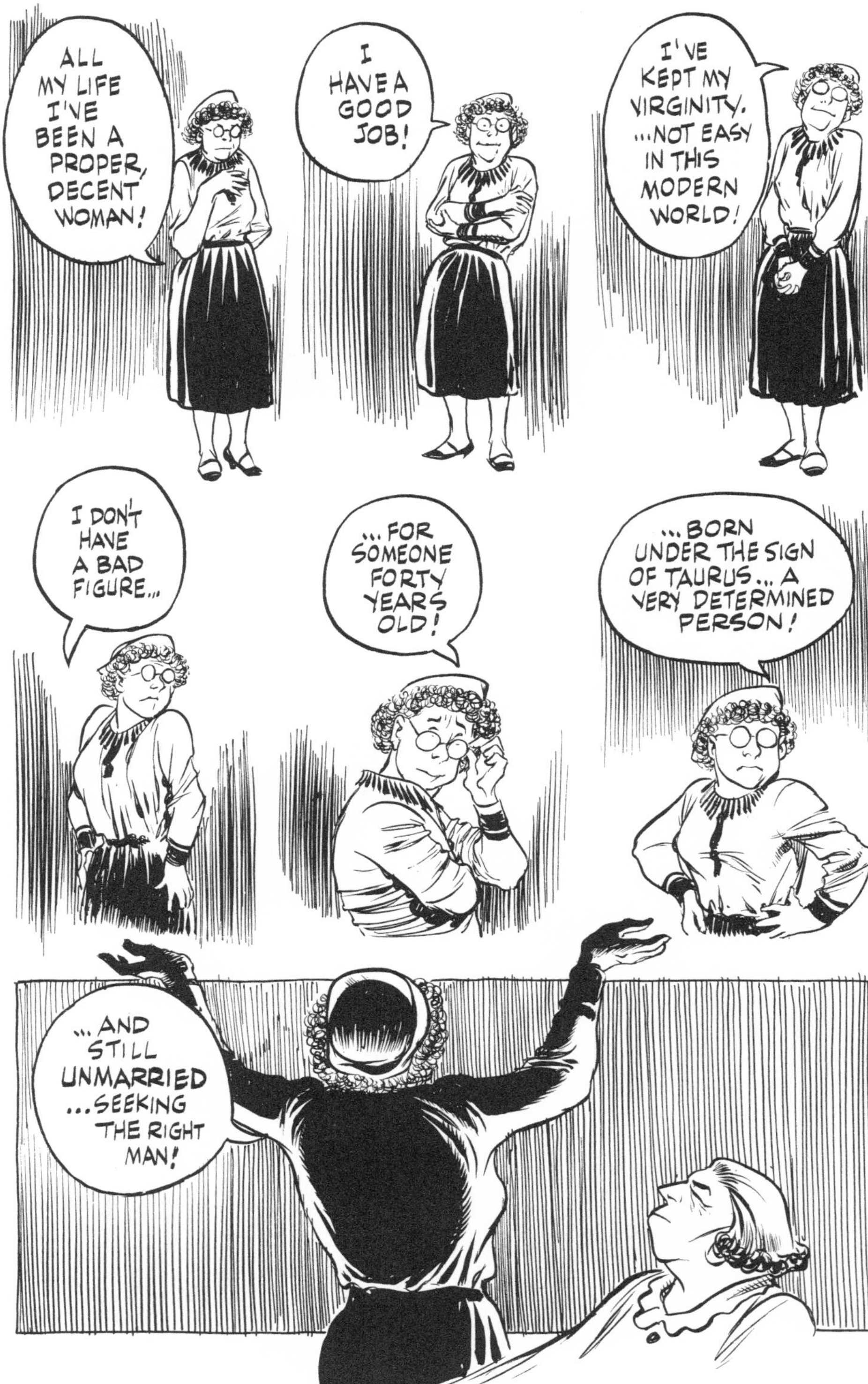
ALL MY LIFE I'VE BEEN A PROPER, DECENT WOMAN!
I HAVE A GOOD JOB!
I'VE KEPT MY VIRGINITY. ...NOT EASY IN THIS MODERN WORLD!
I DON'T HAVE A BAD FIGURE...
...FOR SOMEONE FORTY YEARS OLD!
...BORN UNDER THE SIGN OF TAURUS... A VERY DETERMINED PERSON!
...AND STILL UNMARRIED ...SEEKING THE RIGHT MAN!

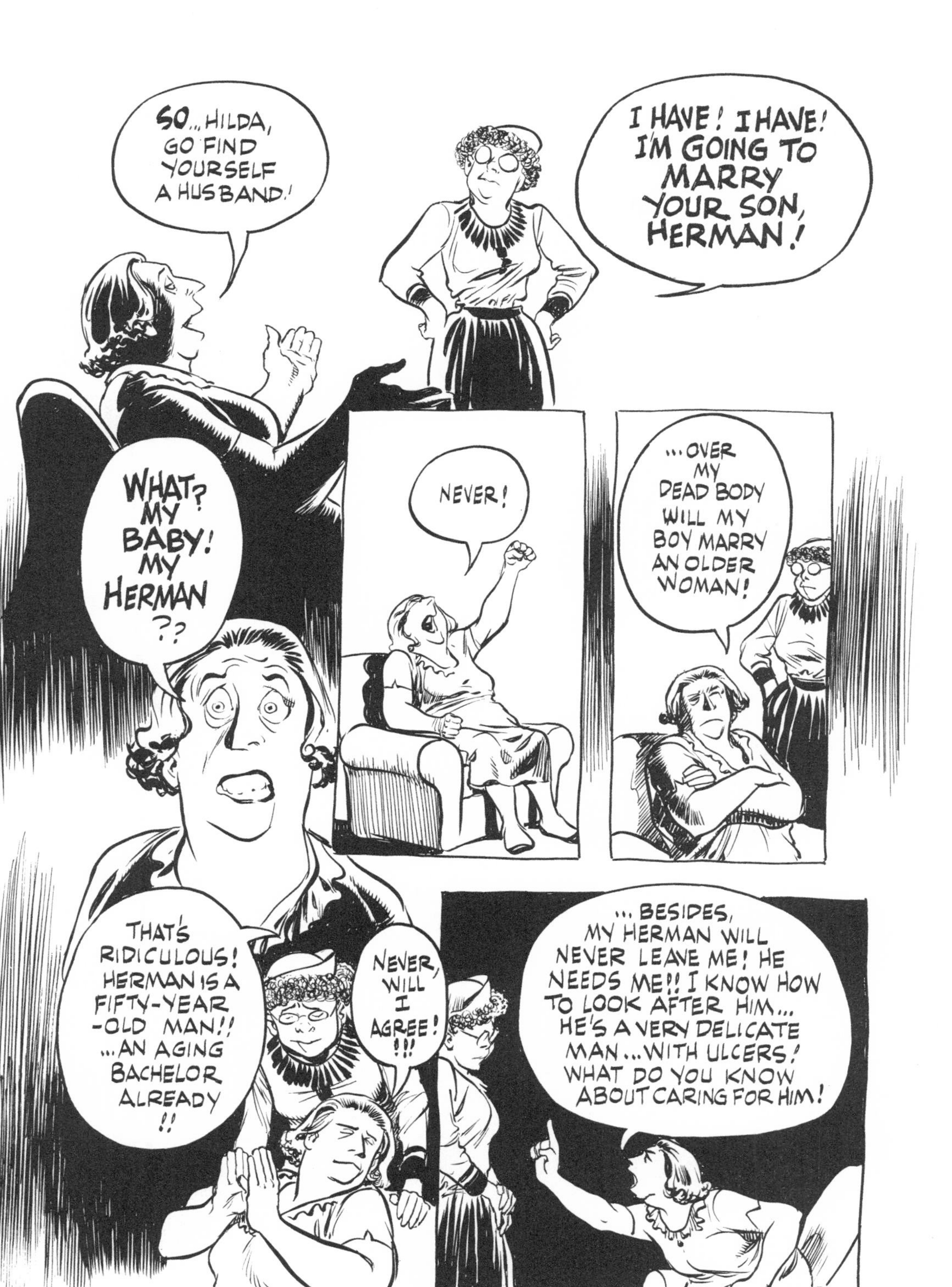
SO... HILDA, GO FIND YOURSELF A HUSBAND!
I HAVE! I HAVE! I'M GOING TO MARRY YOUR SON, HERMAN!
WHAT? MY BABY! MY HERMAN ??
NEVER!
...OVER MY DEAD BODY WILL MY BOY MARRY AN OLDER WOMAN!
THAT'S RIDICULOUS! HERMAN IS A FIFTY-YEAR-OLD MAN!! ...AN AGING BACHELOR ALREADY !!
NEVER, WILL I AGREE! !!!
... BESIDES, MY HERMAN WILL NEVER LEAVE ME! HE NEEDS ME!! I KNOW HOW TO LOOK AFTER HIM... HE'S A VERY DELICATE MAN... WITH ULCERS! WHAT DO YOU KNOW ABOUT CARING FOR HIM!

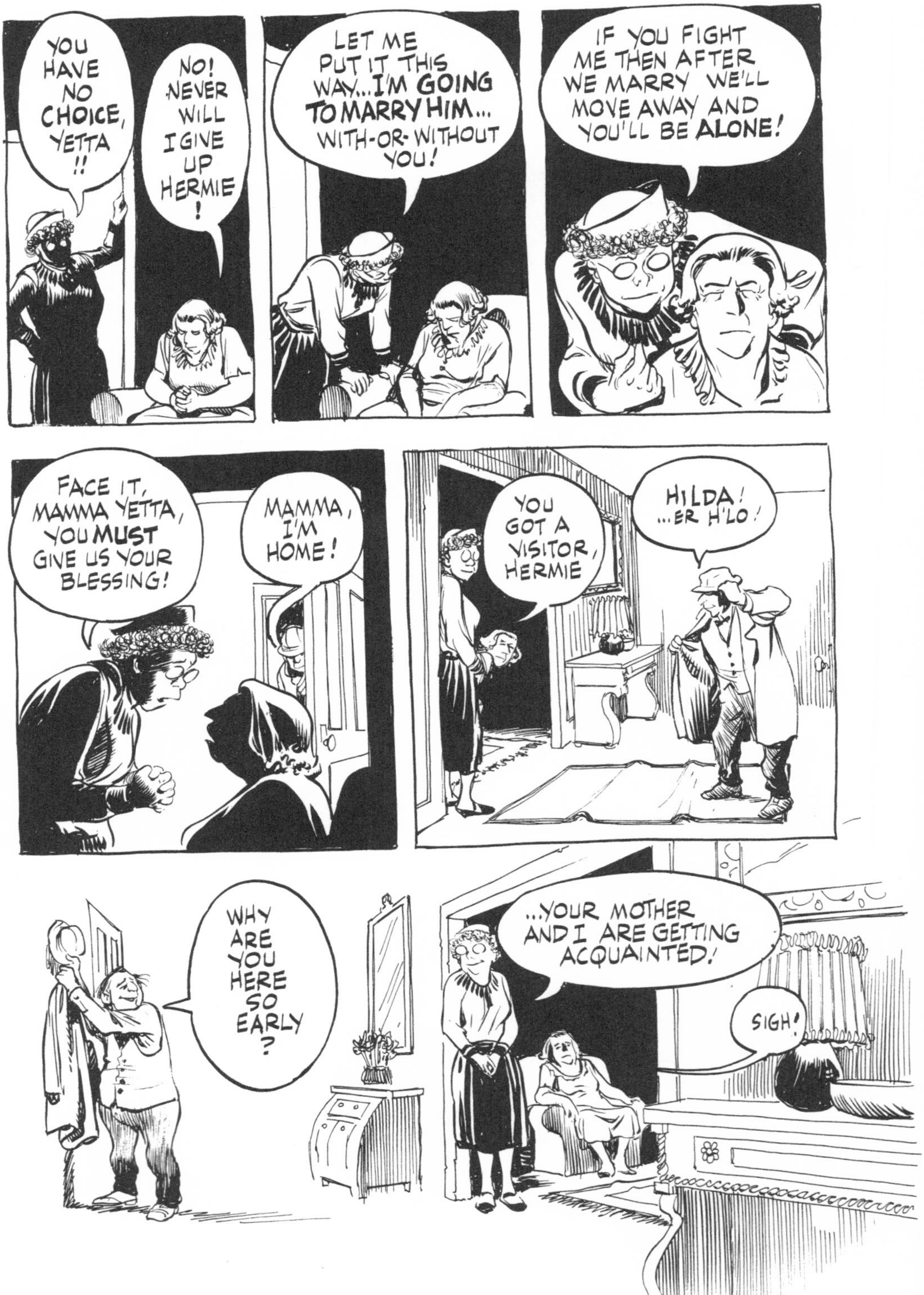

YOU HAVE NO CHOICE, YETTA !!
NO! NEVER WILL I GIVE UP HERMIE !
LET ME PUT IT THIS WAY... I'M GOING TO MARRY HIM... WITH-OR-WITHOUT YOU!
IF YOU FIGHT ME THEN AFTER WE MARRY WE'LL MOVE AWAY AND YOU'LL BE ALONE!
FACE IT, MAMMA YETTA, YOU MUST GIVE US YOUR BLESSING!
MAMMA, I'M HOME!
YOU GOT A VISITOR, HERMIE
HILDA! ...ER H'LO!
WHY ARE YOU HERE SO EARLY ?
...YOUR MOTHER AND I ARE GETTING ACQUAINTED!
SIGH!

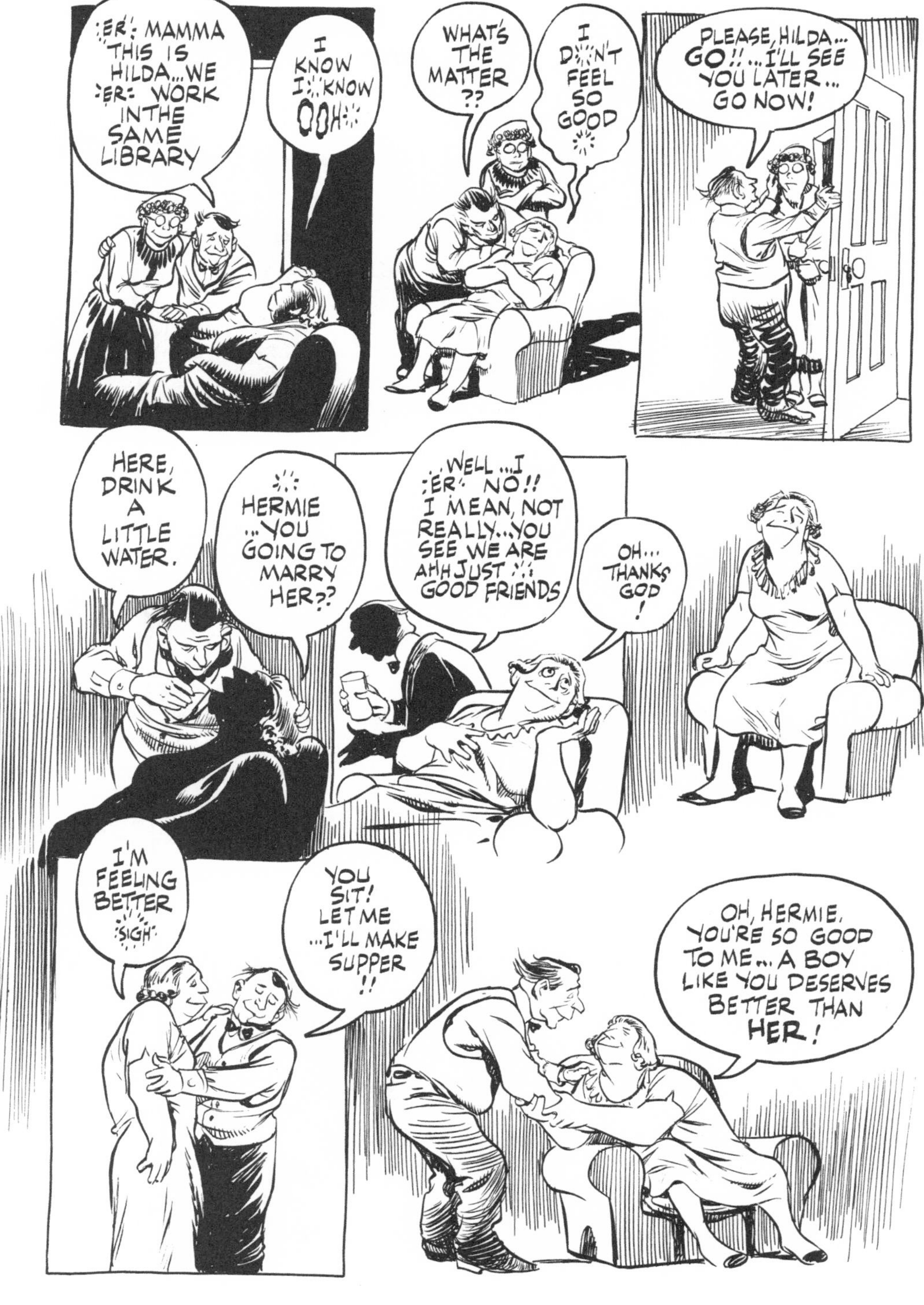

:ER: MAMMA THIS IS HILDA...WE :ER: WORK IN THE SAME LIBRARY
I KNOW I KNOW OOH
WHAT'S THE MATTER ??
I DON'T FEEL SO GOOD
PLEASE, HILDA... GO!! ...I'LL SEE YOU LATER... GO NOW!
HERE, DRINK A LITTLE WATER.
HERMIE ...YOU GOING TO MARRY HER??
WELL...I :ER: NO!! I MEAN, NOT REALLY...YOU SEE WE ARE AHH JUST GOOD FRIENDS
OH... THANKS GOD!
I'M FEELING BETTER SIGH
YOU SIT! LET ME ...I'LL MAKE SUPPER !!
OH, HERMIE, YOU'RE SO GOOD TO ME... A BOY LIKE YOU DESERVES BETTER THAN HER!

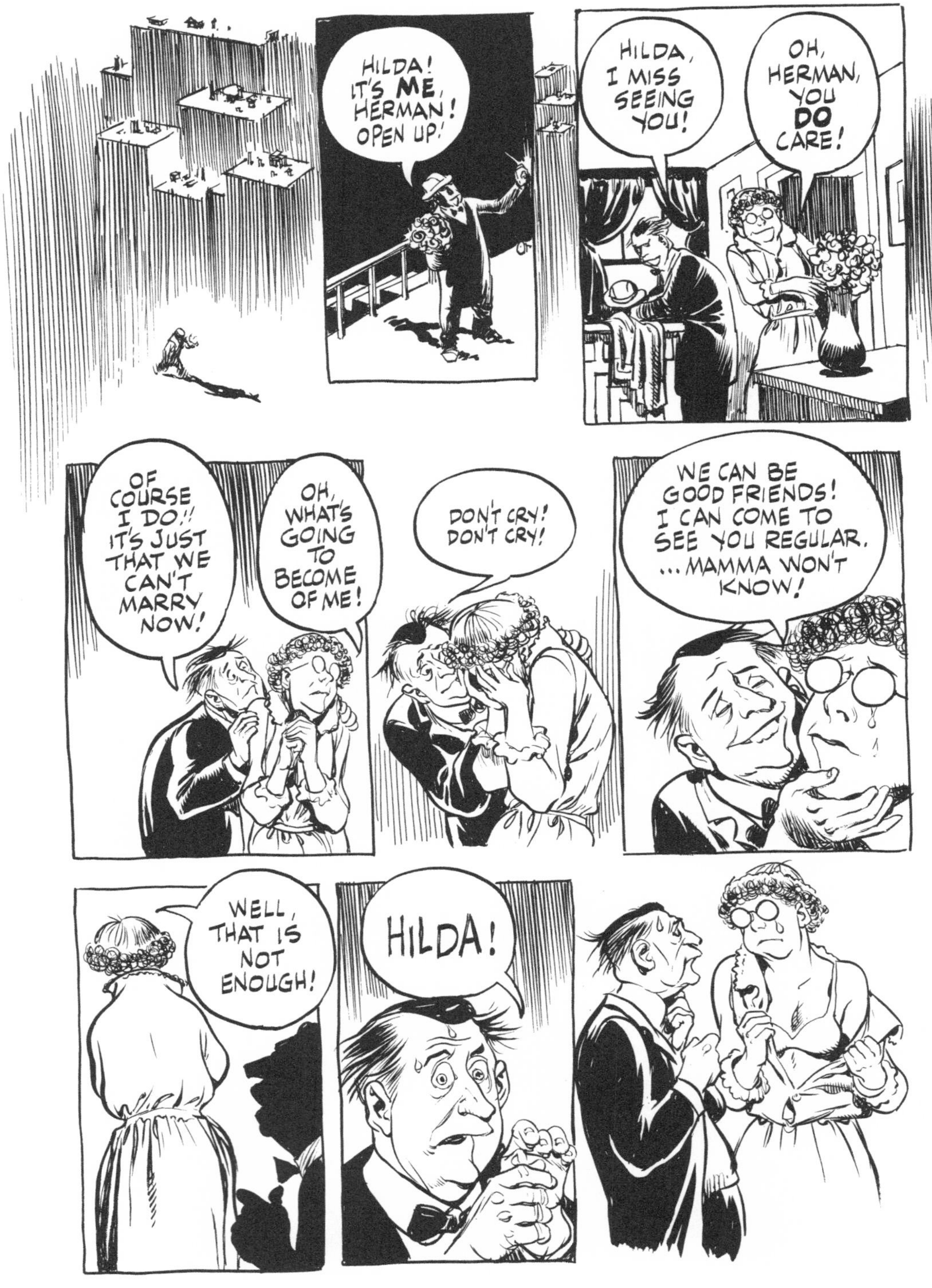
HILDA! IT'S **ME**, HERMAN! OPEN UP!
HILDA, I MISS SEEING YOU!
OH, HERMAN, YOU **DO** CARE!
OF COURSE I DO!! IT'S JUST THAT WE CAN'T MARRY NOW!
OH, WHAT'S GOING TO BECOME OF ME!
DON'T CRY! DON'T CRY!
WE CAN BE GOOD FRIENDS! I CAN COME TO SEE YOU REGULAR. ...MAMMA WON'T KNOW!
WELL, THAT IS NOT ENOUGH!
HILDA!

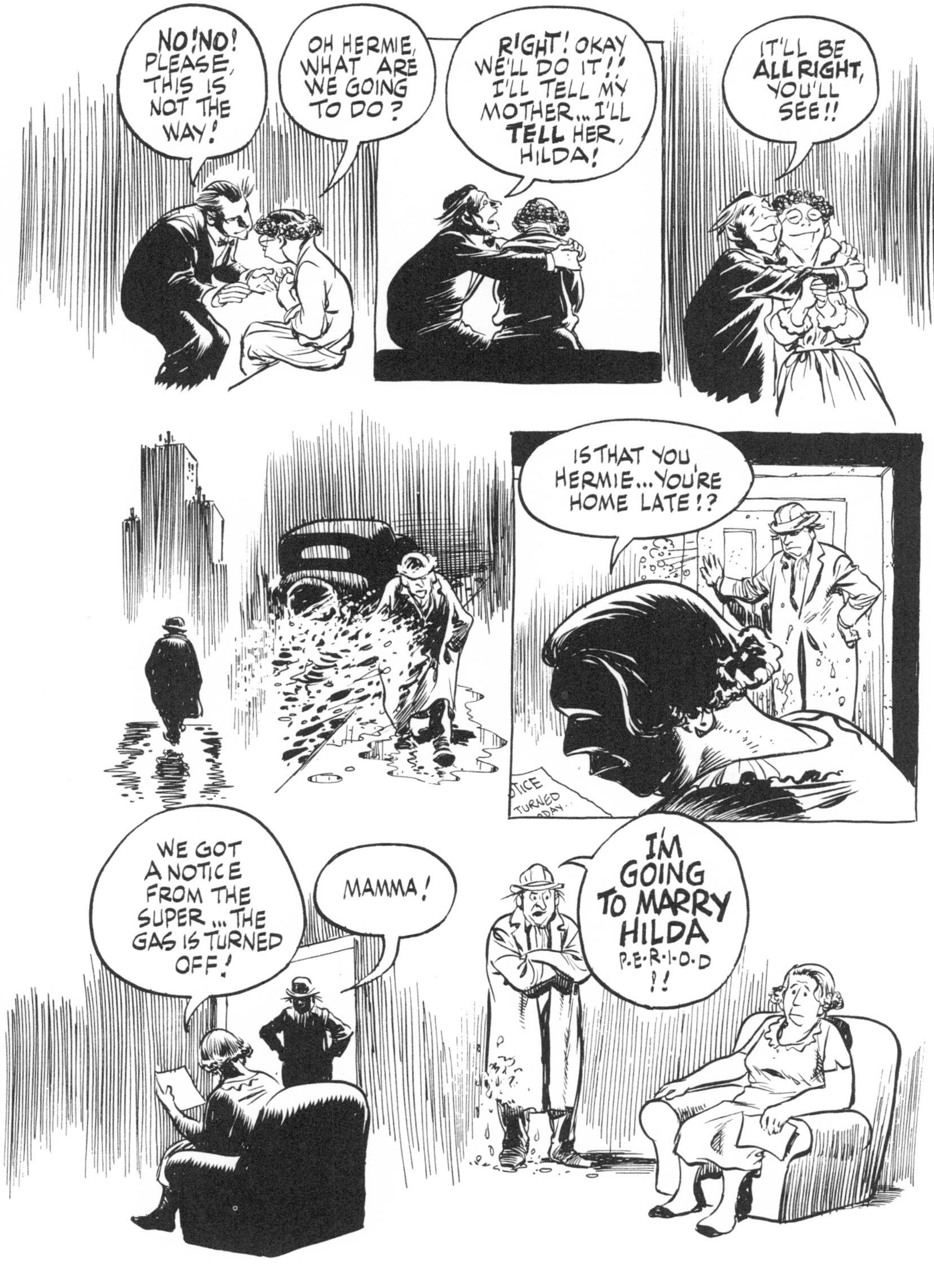

NO! NO! PLEASE, THIS IS NOT THE WAY!
OH HERMIE, WHAT ARE WE GOING TO DO?
RIGHT! OKAY WE'LL DO IT!! I'LL TELL MY MOTHER... I'LL TELL HER, HILDA!
IT'LL BE ALL RIGHT, YOU'LL SEE!!
IS THAT YOU HERMIE... YOU'RE HOME LATE!?
WE GOT A NOTICE FROM THE SUPER... THE GAS IS TURNED OFF!
MAMMA!
I'M GOING TO MARRY HILDA P-E-R-I-O-D!!

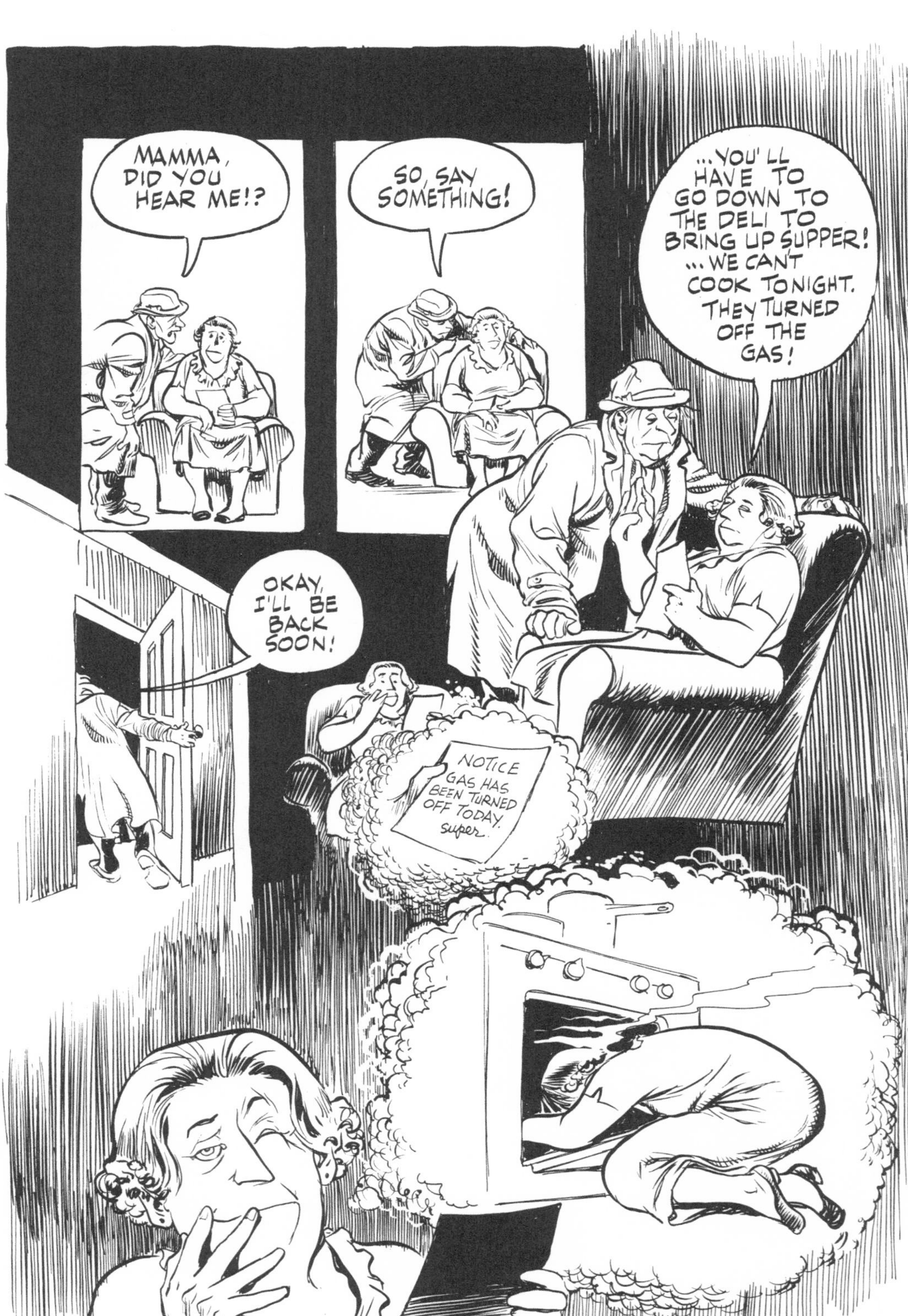
MAMMA, DID YOU HEAR ME!?
SO, SAY SOMETHING!
...YOU'LL HAVE TO GO DOWN TO THE DELI TO BRING UP SUPPER! ...WE CAN'T COOK TONIGHT. THEY TURNED OFF THE GAS!
OKAY, I'LL BE BACK SOON!
NOTICE GAS HAS BEEN TURNED OFF TODAY. super

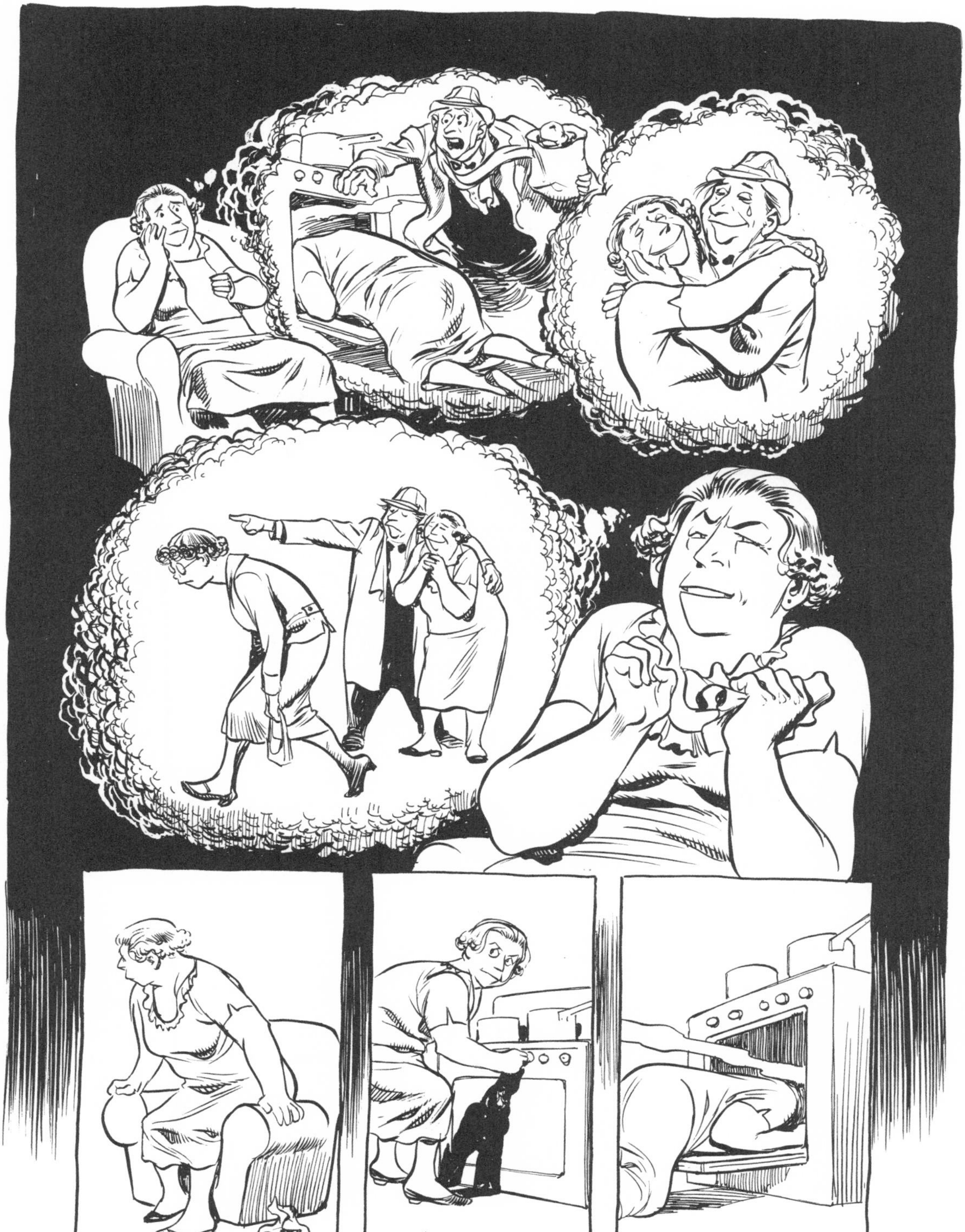

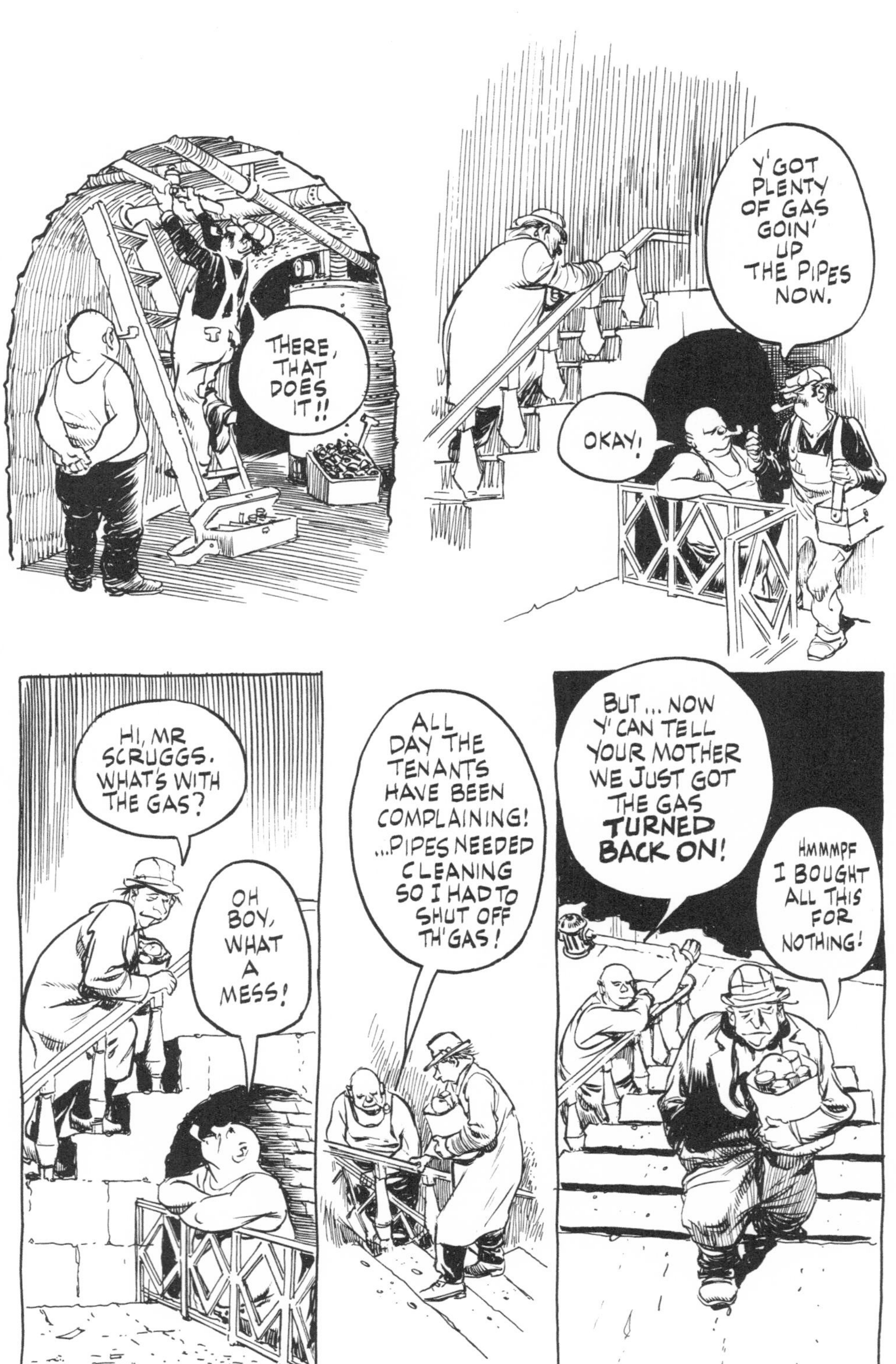
THERE, THAT DOES IT!!
Y'GOT PLENTY OF GAS GOIN' UP THE PIPES NOW.
OKAY!
HI, MR SCRUGGS. WHAT'S WITH THE GAS?
OH BOY, WHAT A MESS!
ALL DAY THE TENANTS HAVE BEEN COMPLAINING! ...PIPES NEEDED CLEANING SO I HAD TO SHUT OFF TH'GAS!
BUT... NOW Y' CAN TELL YOUR MOTHER WE JUST GOT THE GAS **TURNED BACK ON!**
HMMMPF I BOUGHT ALL THIS FOR NOTHING!

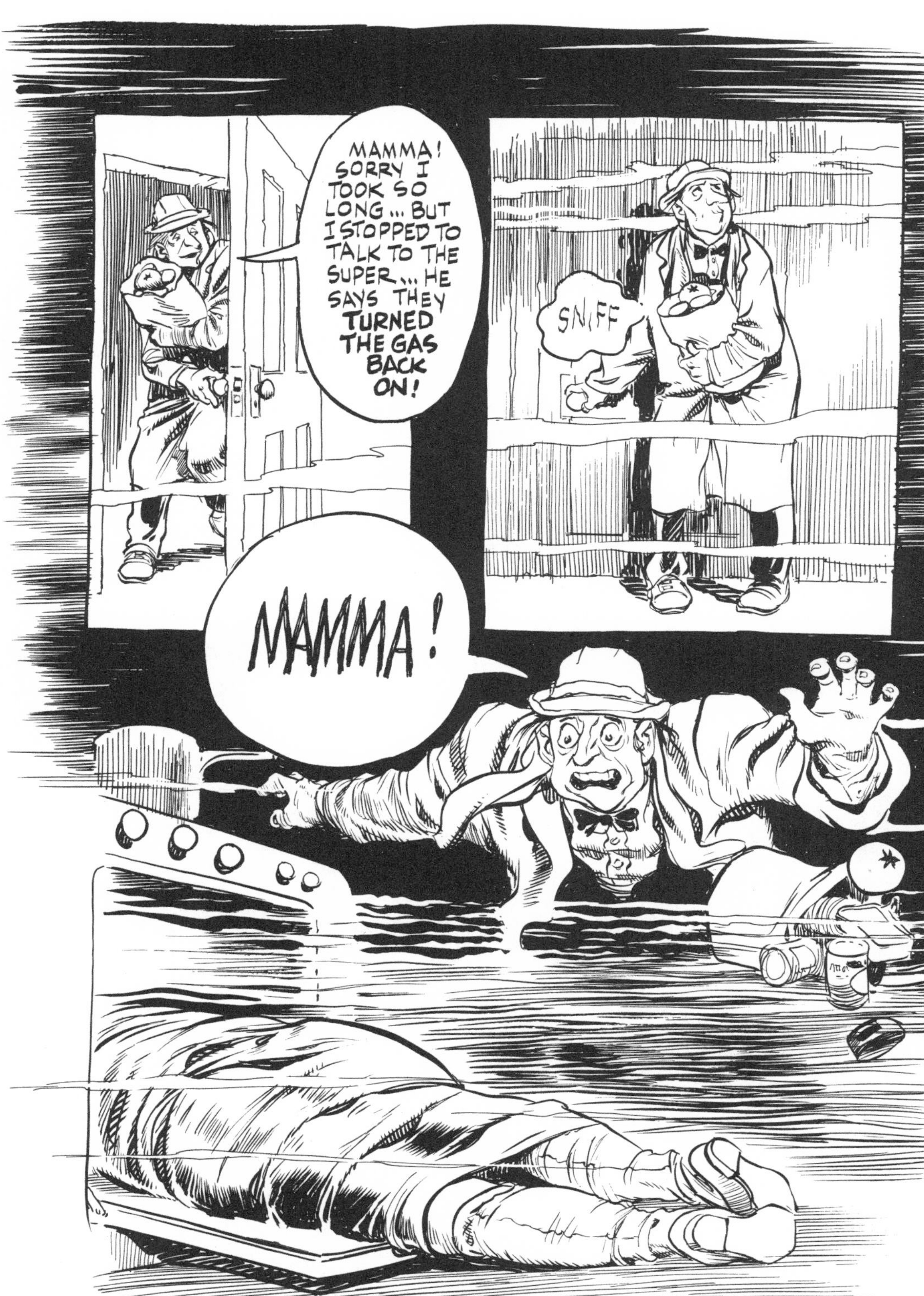

MAMMA! SORRY I TOOK SO LONG ... BUT I STOPPED TO TALK TO THE SUPER ... HE SAYS THEY TURNED THE GAS BACK ON!
SNIFF
MAMMA!

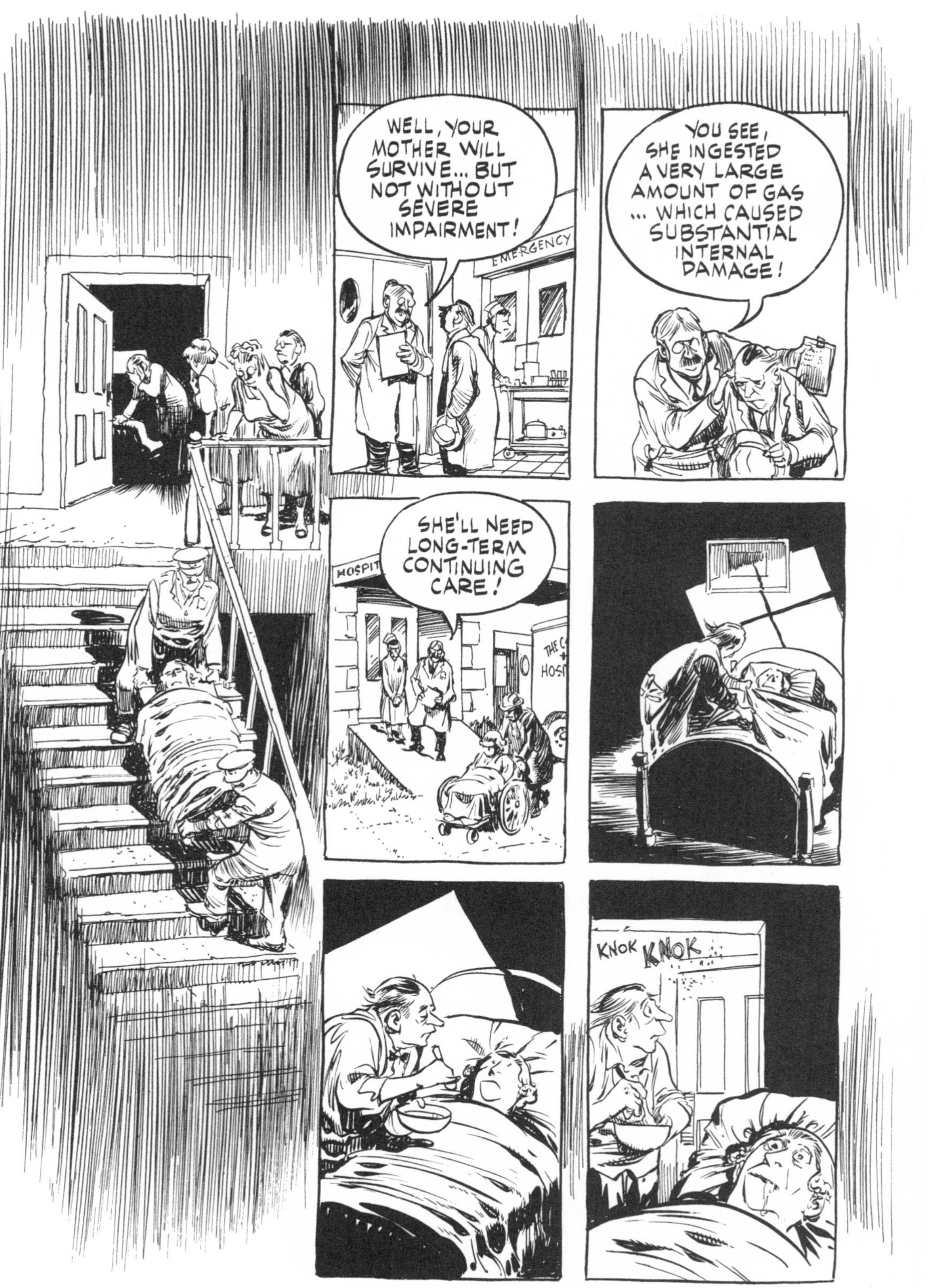
WELL, YOUR MOTHER WILL SURVIVE... BUT NOT WITHOUT SEVERE IMPAIRMENT!
EMERGENCY
YOU SEE, SHE INGESTED A VERY LARGE AMOUNT OF GAS ... WHICH CAUSED SUBSTANTIAL INTERNAL DAMAGE!
HOSPIT
SHE'LL NEED LONG-TERM CONTINUING CARE!
KNOK KNOK

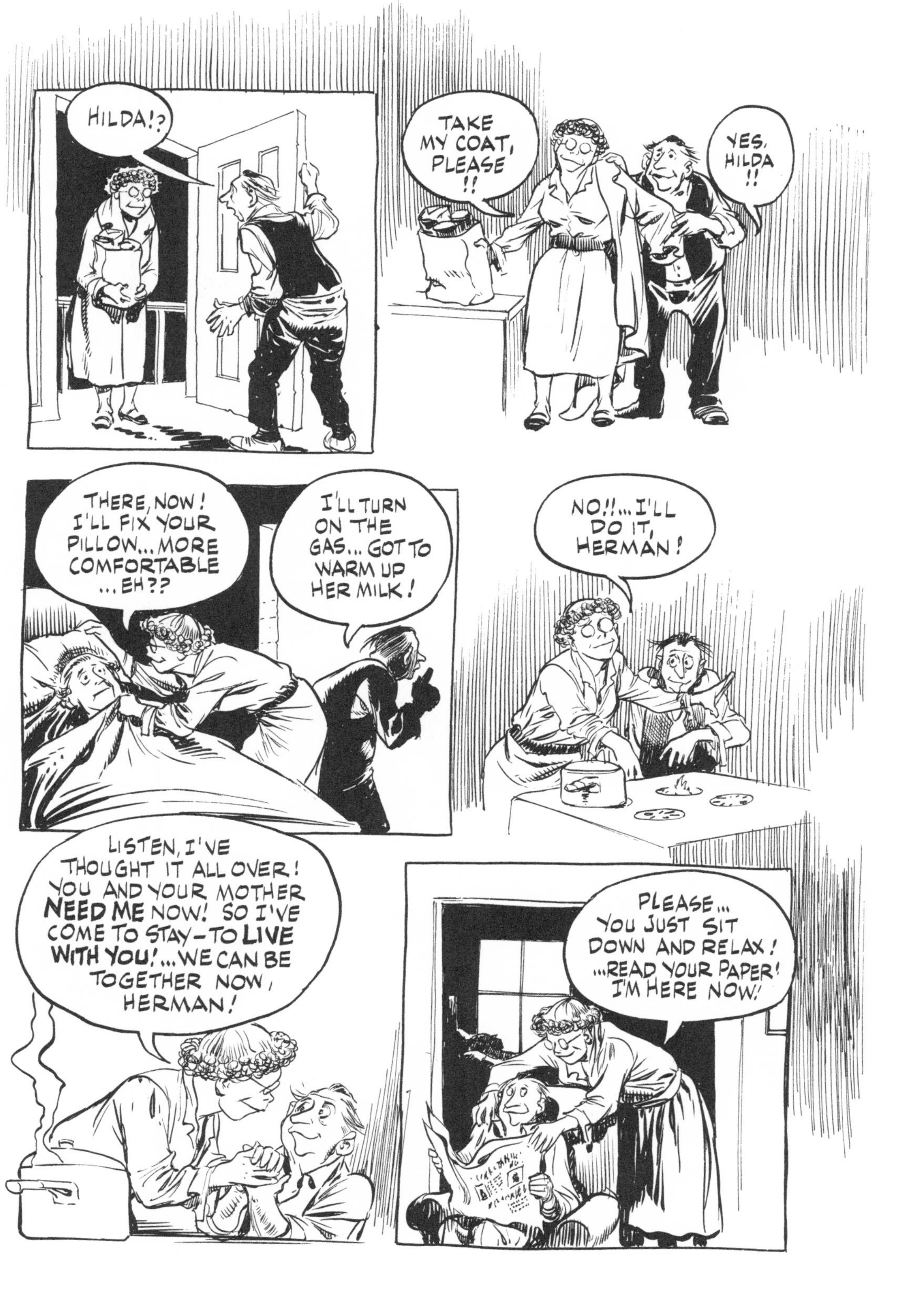
HILDA!?
TAKE MY COAT, PLEASE !!
YES, HILDA !!
THERE, NOW! I'LL FIX YOUR PILLOW... MORE COMFORTABLE ...EH??
I'LL TURN ON THE GAS... GOT TO WARM UP HER MILK!
NO!!... I'LL DO IT, HERMAN!
LISTEN, I'VE THOUGHT IT ALL OVER! YOU AND YOUR MOTHER **NEED ME** NOW! SO I'VE COME TO STAY—TO **LIVE WITH YOU!**... WE CAN BE TOGETHER NOW, HERMAN!
PLEASE... YOU JUST SIT DOWN AND RELAX! ...READ YOUR PAPER! I'M HERE NOW!

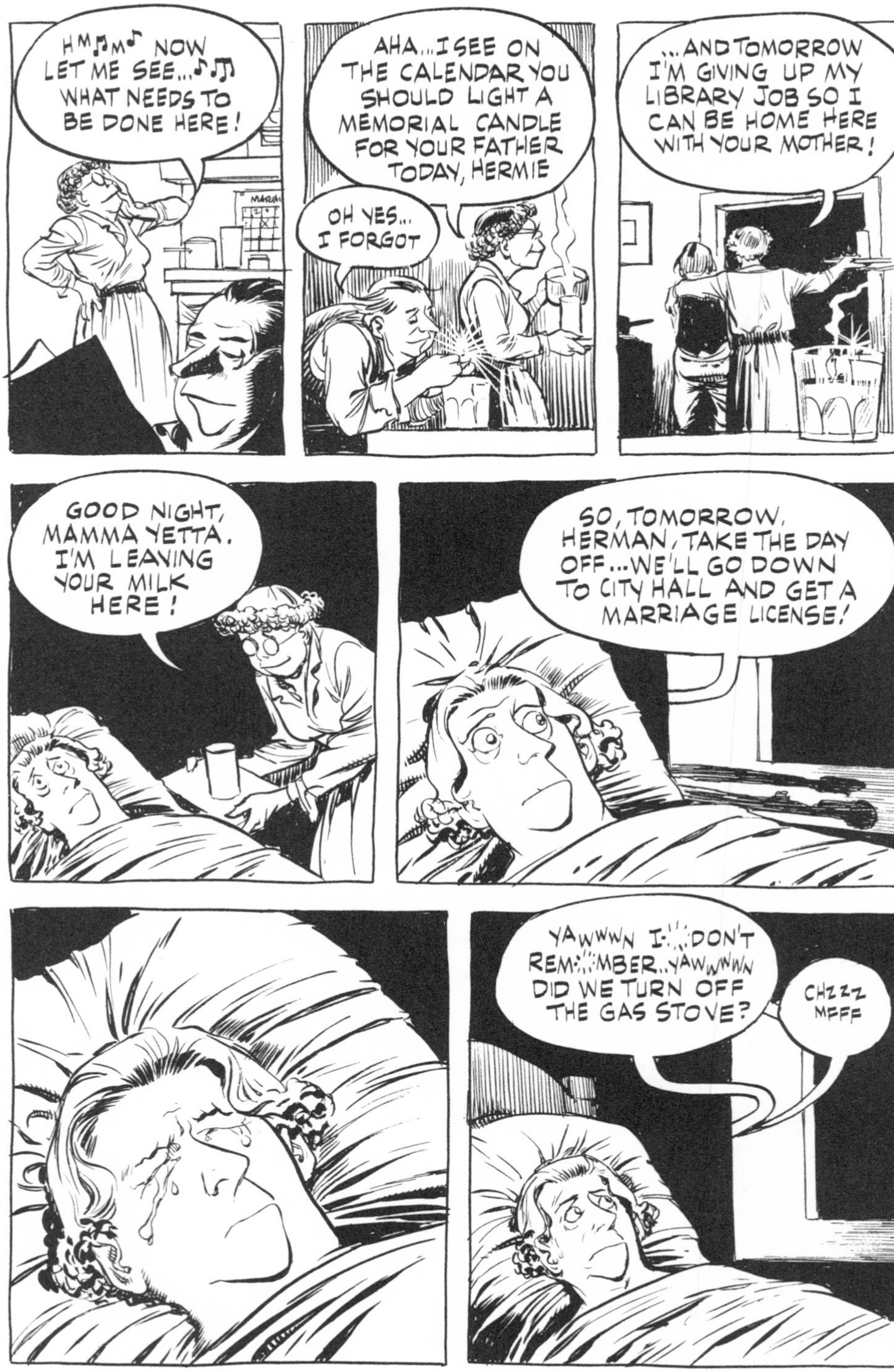
HM♫M♪ NOW LET ME SEE...♪♫ WHAT NEEDS TO BE DONE HERE!
AHA...I SEE ON THE CALENDAR YOU SHOULD LIGHT A MEMORIAL CANDLE FOR YOUR FATHER TODAY, HERMIE
OH YES... I FORGOT
...AND TOMORROW I'M GIVING UP MY LIBRARY JOB SO I CAN BE HOME HERE WITH YOUR MOTHER!
GOOD NIGHT, MAMMA YETTA. I'M LEAVING YOUR MILK HERE!
SO, TOMORROW, HERMAN, TAKE THE DAY OFF...WE'LL GO DOWN TO CITY HALL AND GET A MARRIAGE LICENSE!
YAWWWN I-...DON'T REM...MBER..YAWWWWN DID WE TURN OFF THE GAS STOVE?
CHZZZ MFFF

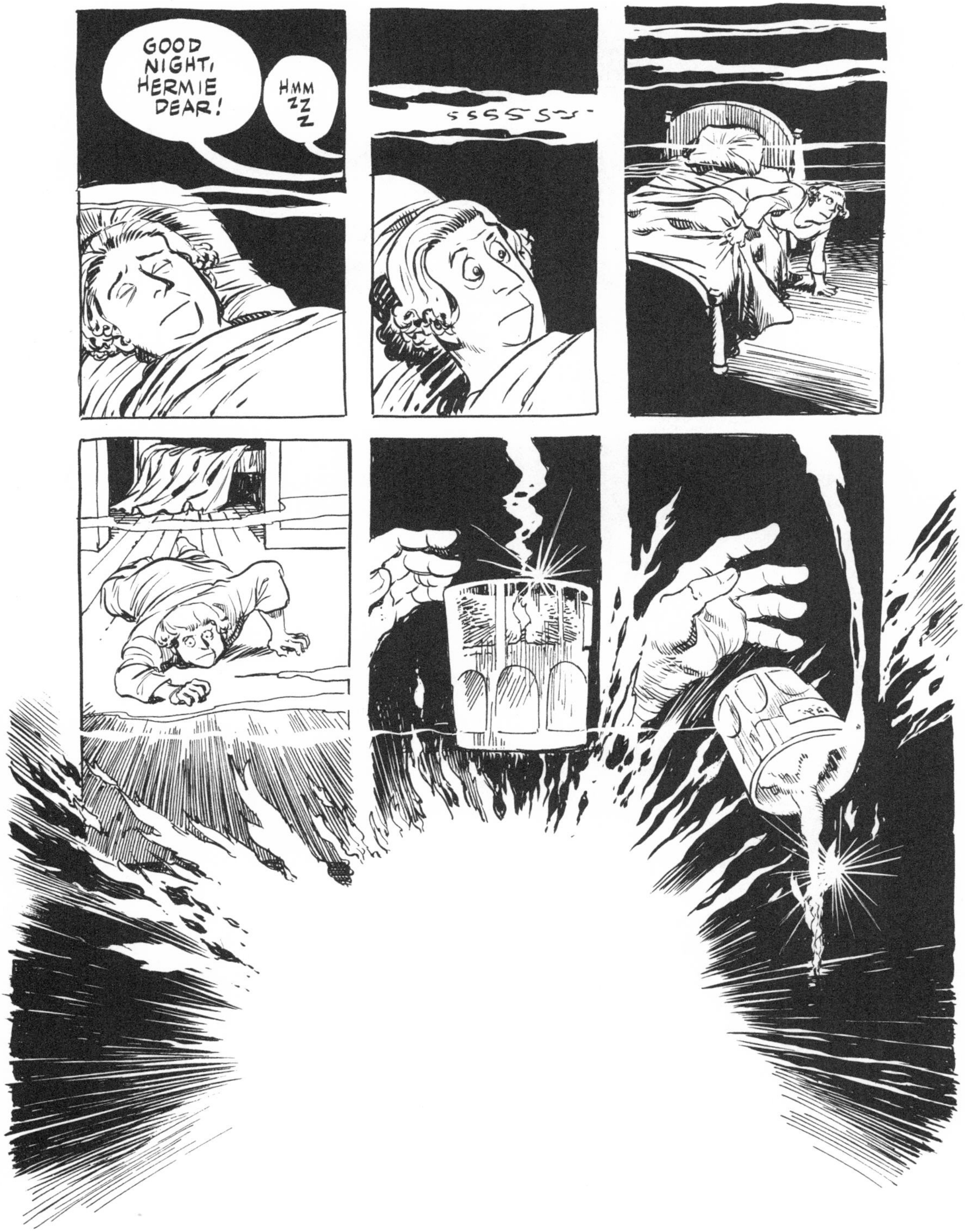
GOOD NIGHT, HERMIE DEAR!
HMM ZZ Z
SSSSS~

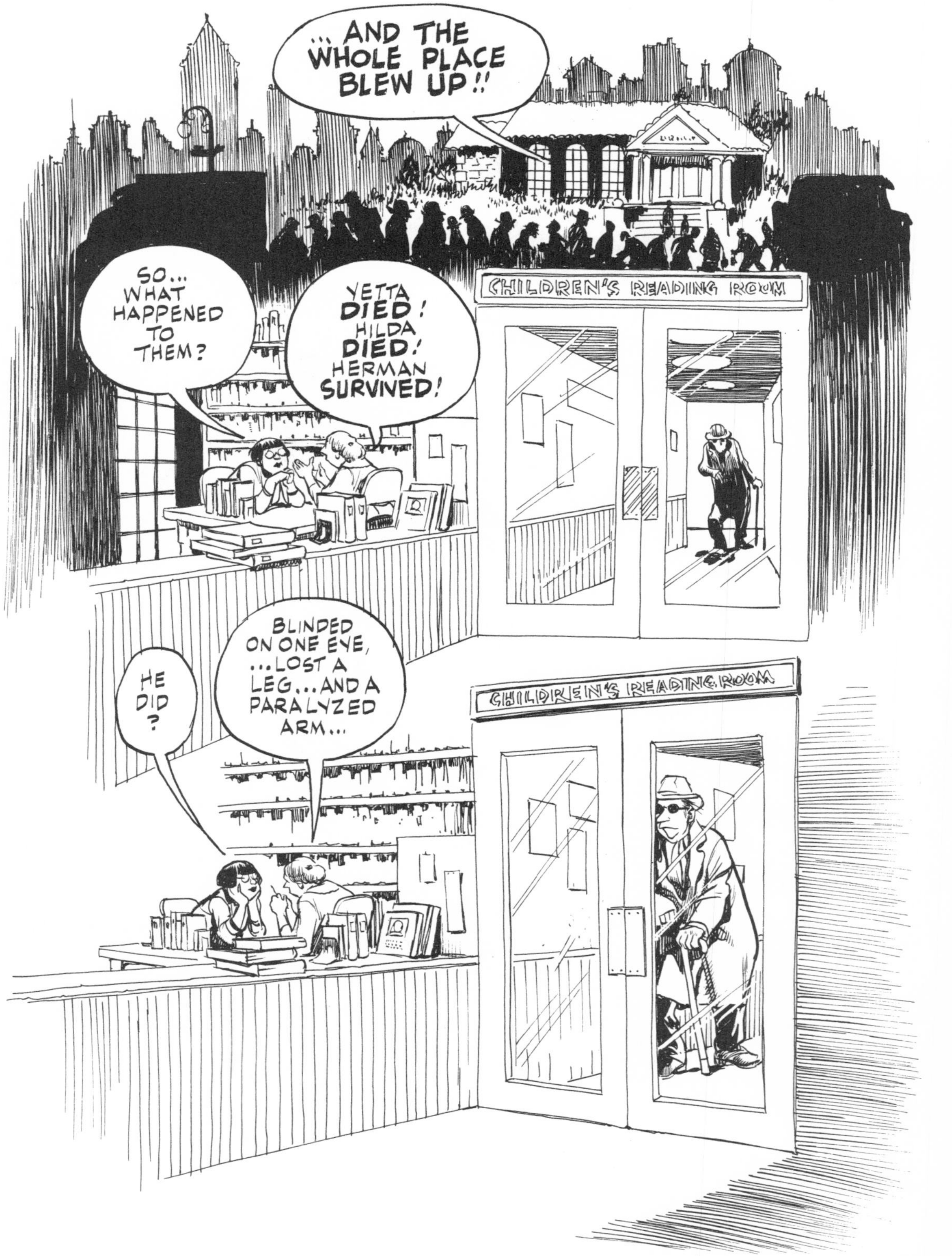
...AND THE WHOLE PLACE BLEW UP!!
SO... WHAT HAPPENED TO THEM?
YETTA DIED! HILDA DIED! HERMAN SURVIVED!
CHILDREN'S READING ROOM
HE DID?
BLINDED ON ONE EYE, ...LOST A LEG...AND A PARALYZED ARM...
CHILDREN'S READING ROOM

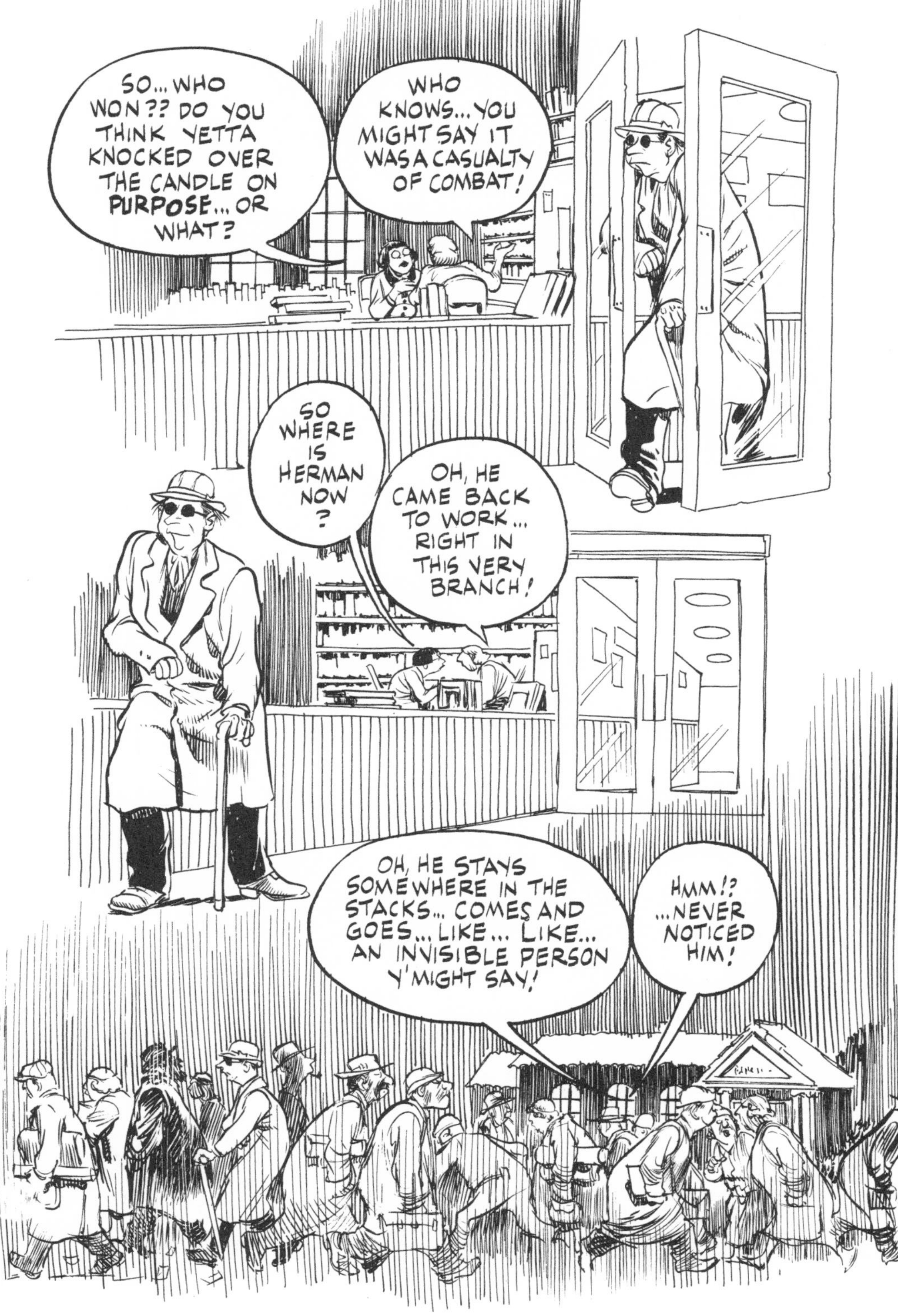
SO... WHO WON?? DO YOU THINK YETTA KNOCKED OVER THE CANDLE ON PURPOSE... OR WHAT?
WHO KNOWS... YOU MIGHT SAY IT WAS A CASUALTY OF COMBAT!
SO WHERE IS HERMAN NOW?
OH, HE CAME BACK TO WORK... RIGHT IN THIS VERY BRANCH!
OH, HE STAYS SOMEWHERE IN THE STACKS... COMES AND GOES... LIKE... LIKE... AN INVISIBLE PERSON Y'MIGHT SAY!
HMM!? ...NEVER NOTICED HIM!

Out-Takes

The following three pages were created by Will Eisner at the time he created the respective stories, but he later removed them. The Monroe Mensh page from *The Building* (1987) was replaced with page 163 of this compendium. Eisner apparently felt this first version was too abrupt in explaining Mensh's fateful sacrifice. The variant of "Empty Street" from *City People Notebook* (1989) is a night scene he perhaps thought might be too close to the dark "Angry Street" which followed. In his replacement (page 301) Eisner not only lightened the image but made himself and his homeless companion tiny to emphasize the emptiness. "Pincus" was to have been one of several full-page character illustrations in *Invisible People* (1992) an idea Eisner decided to abandon.

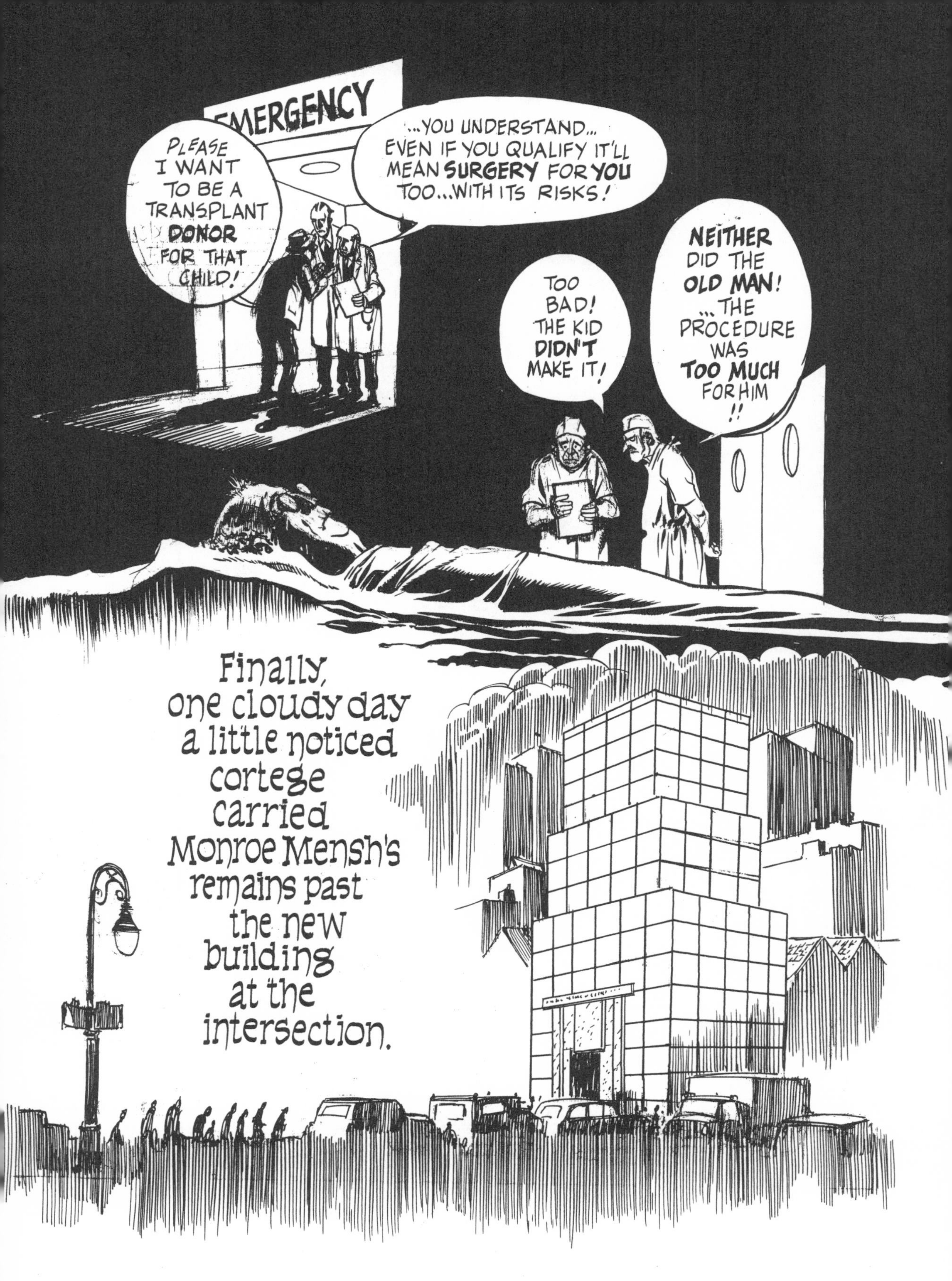
EMERGENCY
PLEASE I WANT TO BE A TRANSPLANT DONOR FOR THAT CHILD!
...YOU UNDERSTAND... EVEN IF YOU QUALIFY IT'LL MEAN SURGERY FOR YOU TOO...WITH ITS RISKS!
TOO BAD! THE KID DIDN'T MAKE IT!
NEITHER DID THE OLD MAN! ...THE PROCEDURE WAS TOO MUCH FOR HIM !!
Finally, one cloudy day a little noticed cortege carried Monroe Mensh's remains past the new building at the intersection.

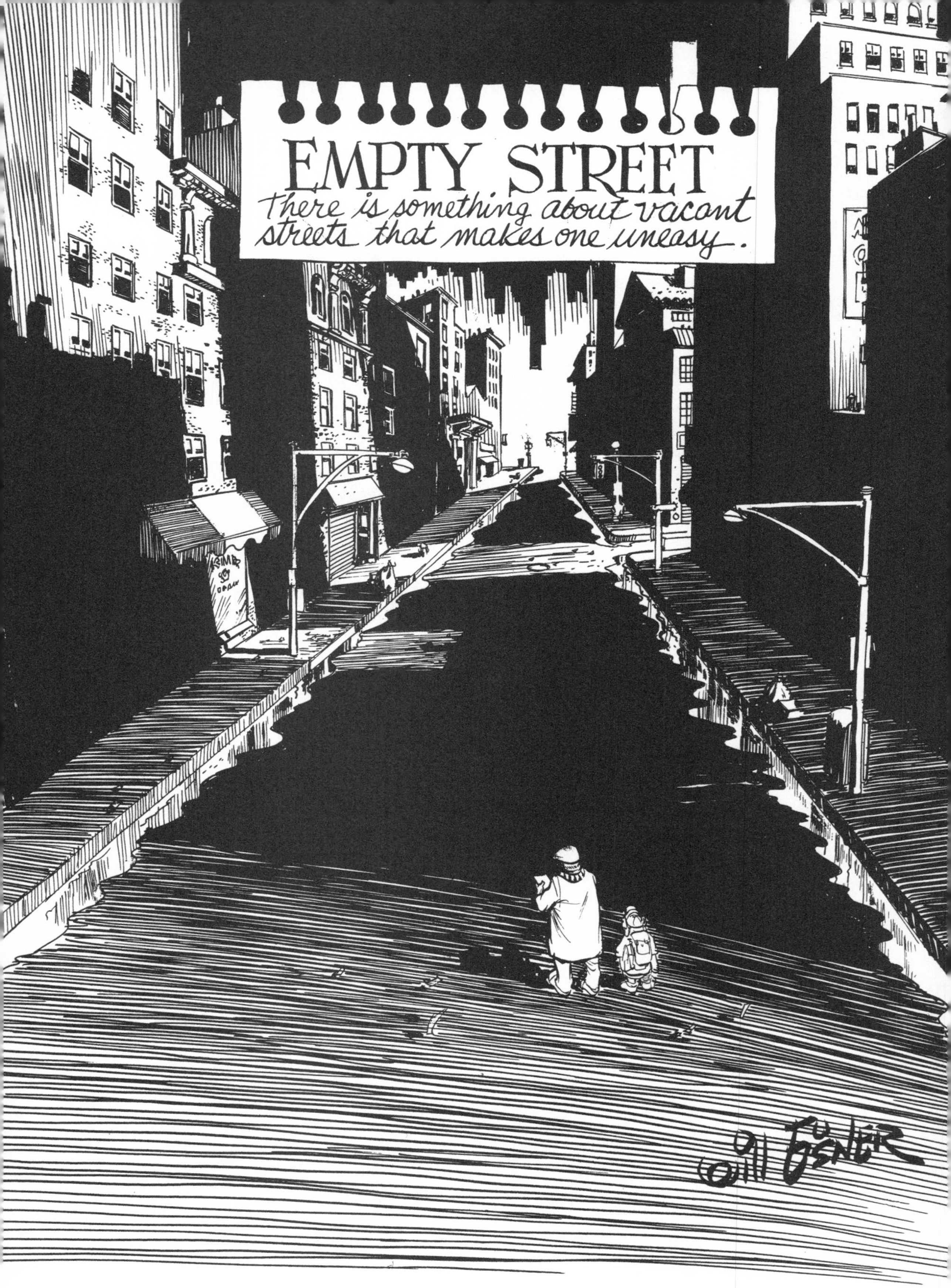
EMPTY STREET
there is something about vacant streets that makes one uneasy.
Will Eisner

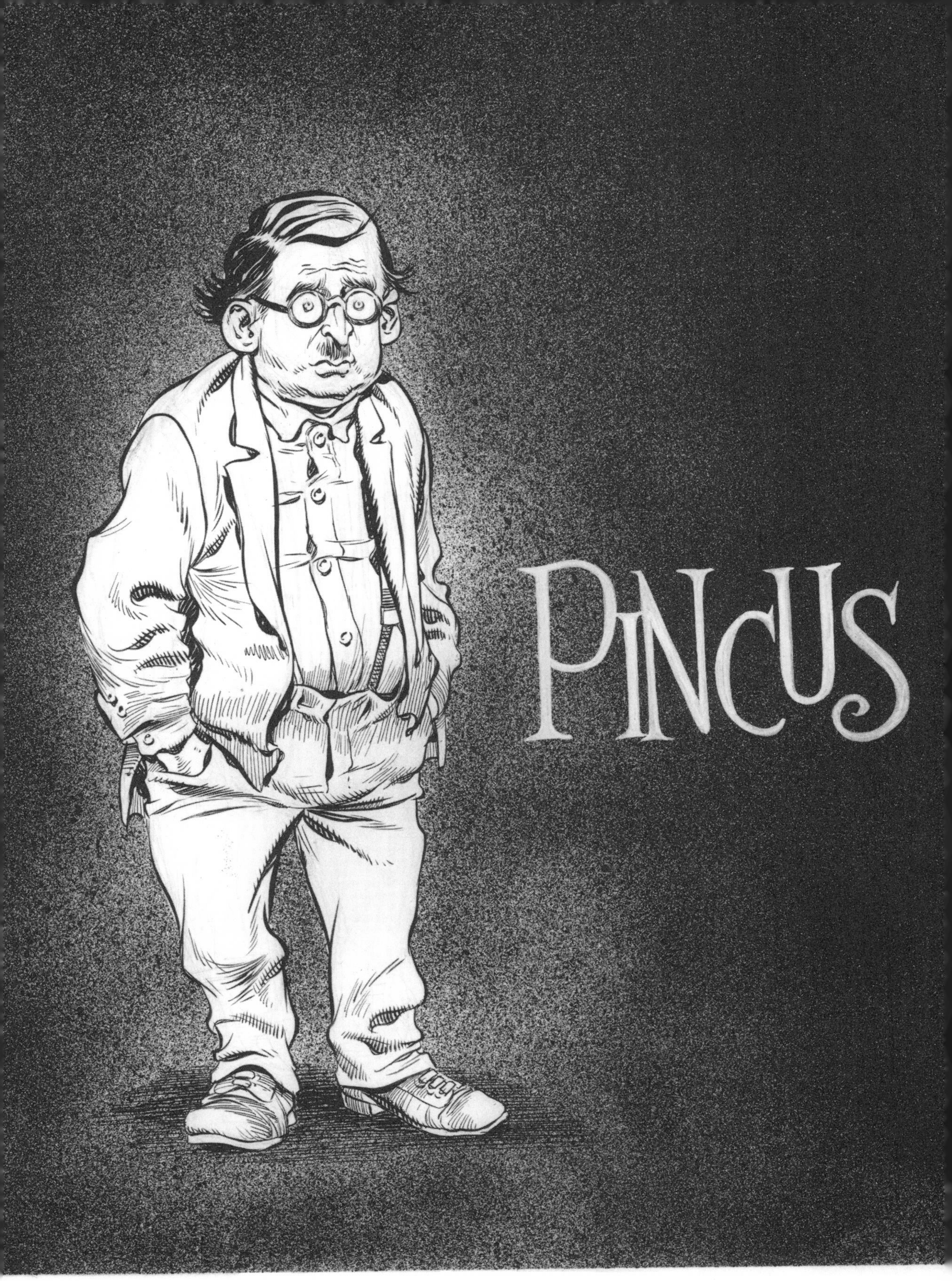
PINCUS

About the Author

Will Eisner (1917–2005) was the grand old man of comics. He was present at the birth of the comic book industry in the 1930s, creating such titles as *Blackhawk* and *Sheena, Queen of the Jungle*. He created *The Spirit* in 1940, syndicating it for twelve years as a unique and innovative sixteen-page Sunday newspaper insert, with a weekly circulation of 5 million copies. In the seven decades since, *The Spirit* has almost never been out of print. As a Pentagon-based warrant officer during World War Two, Eisner pioneered the instructional use of comics, continuing to produce them for the U.S. Army under civilian contract into the 1970s, along with educational comics for clients as diverse as General Motors and elementary school children.

In 1978 Eisner created the first successful "graphic novel," *A Contract With God*, launching a bold new literary genre. Nearly twenty celebrated graphic novels by him followed. Since 1988 the comic industry's top award for excellence has been "The Eisner." He has received numerous honors and awards worldwide, including, ironically, several Eisners and only the second Lifetime Achievememt Award bestowed by the National Foundation for Jewish Culture (2002). Michael Chabon's Pulitzer Prize–winning novel *The Amazing Adventures of Kavalier & Clay* is based in good part on Eisner.